LAND LAW

Land Law

Themes and Perspectives

Edited by
SUSAN BRIGHT
and
JOHN DEWAR

OXFORD UNIVERSITY PRESS

This book has been printed digitally and produced in a standard specification
in order to ensure its continuing availability

OXFORD
UNIVERSITY PRESS

Great Clarendon Street, Oxford OX2 6DP

Oxford University Press is a department of the University of Oxford.
It furthers the University's objective of excellence in research, scholarship,
and education by publishing worldwide in

Oxford New York

Auckland   Cape Town Dar es Salaam   Hong Kong   Karachi
Kuala Lumpur Madrid Melbourne Mexico City   Nairobi
New Delhi Shanghai Taipei Toronto
With offices in
Argentina Austria Brazil Chile Czech Republic France Greece
Guatemala Hungary Italy Japan South Korea Poland Portugal
Singapore Switzerland Thailand Turkey Ukraine Vietnam

Oxford is a registered trade mark of Oxford University Press
in the UK and in certain other countries

Published in the United States
by Oxford University Press Inc., New York

© The various Contributors 1998

ISBN   978-0-19-876455-7

Printed and bound in Great Britain by
CPI Antony Rowe, Chippenham and Eastbourne

CONTENTS

Part Four: Policy Issues in Land Law

Part Five: Doctrinal Issues in Land Law

ABBREVIATIONS

AGPS	Australian Government Publishing Service
CA	Children Act 1989
CHAR	Campaign for the Homeless and Rootless
CLS	Critical Legal Studies
DoE	Department of the Environment
ECJ	European Court of Justice
FAO	Food and Agriculture Organization (of UN)
FLA	Family Law Act 1996
IoH	Institute of Housing
LPA	Law of Property Act 1925
MAFF	Ministry of Agriculture, Fisheries and Food
MCA	Matrimonial Causes Act 1973
NACAB	National Association of Citizens' Advice Bureaux
OJ	Official Journal
PPG1	Planning Policy Guidance Note 1
RDP	Reconstruction and Development Programme
SHAC	Shelter Housing Aid Centre
TOLATA	Trusts of Land and Appointment of Trustees Act 1996

TABLE OF CASES

TABLE OF LEGISLATION

Legislation has been arranged by country. European Community material is at the end of the Table.

SWITZERLAND

UNITED KINGDOM

RULES OF THE SUPREME COURT

STATUTORY INSTRUMENTS

UNITED STATES OF AMERICA

EUROPEAN COMMUNITY
Treaties, Conventions, Legislation (alphabetical order)

NOTES ON CONTRIBUTORS

GREGORY ALEXANDER is Professor of Law at the Cornell University Law School, Ithaca, New York, where he teaches property, legal history, and trusts and estates. He has just completed a book on the history of legal discourse about property from the American Revolution to the present, and has published widely on theoretical aspects of property law.

STUART ANDERSON is Professor of Law at the University of Otago, New Zealand, having previously held appointments at the University of Oxford and the London School of Economics and Political Science. He has research and teaching interests in property law, modern legal history, and public law.

GRAHAM BATTERSBY is Edward Bramley Professor of Law in the University of Sheffield. The author of many articles mainly on land law and trusts, he edited the last edition of *Williams on Title* and wrote the title 'Sale of Land' in the 4th edition of *Halsbury's Laws of England*.

PETER BIRKS QC, FBA is Regius Professor of Civil Law in the University of Oxford and a Fellow of All Souls College. His principal research interests are Restitution and Roman Law.

ANNE BOTTOMLEY teaches at the University of Kent, Canterbury, England. She is on the editorial board of Feminist Legal Studies and, following the publication in 1995 of *Feminist Perspectives on the Foundational Subjects of Law*, is now joint series editor of a series of collections to be published by Cavendish Publishing on feminist perspectives on law. She studied at Sussex University, The London School of Economics, and Cambridge.

CHRISTOPHER BRIGHT is a Partner with Linklaters & Paines, London, specializing in European law, competition policy, and regulatory work. He studied law at the Universities of Aberystwyth, Dalhousie, and Oxford. He has published widely in the areas of competition law, utilities regulation, and European law.

SUSAN BRIGHT teaches at St Hilda's College, Oxford. She has previously taught at Essex University and practised as a solicitor doing commercial property work in London. Her main research interest is in real property law and she is the co-author of *Landlord and Tenant Law: The Nature of Tenancies* (1995).

MICHAEL CARDWELL is Senior Lecturer in the Department of Law at the University of Leeds. His publications have been in the field of agricultural law, with particular emphasis on Common Agricultural Policy quotas.

DAVID CLARKE is Professor of Law and Head of the Department of Law at the University of Bristol. He is the author, co-author, or contributor to a number of books on aspects of property or landlord and tenant law and maintains an active interest in practice as consultant solicitor to the firm of Osborne Clarke.

DAVID COWAN is a Lecturer in the Department of Law at the University of Bristol, and author of *Homelessness: The (In-)Appropriate Applicant* as well as many other articles on homelessness and the law.

PATRICIA CRITCHLEY is a Law Fellow at Hertford College, Oxford, with special interests in land law, trusts, and family property. Her doctoral thesis is on the subject of property law formalities.

JOHN DEWAR is Professor of Law at Griffith University in Brisbane, Australia. He has taught at the Universities of Lancaster, Warwick, and Oxford. He is the author of *Law and the Family* (2nd edn., 1992) and has published in the areas of family law, land law, and trusts.

SHAUNNAGH DORSETT is Lecturer in Law at Griffith University in Brisbane, Australia. She has a Masters from the University of Calgary and is currently working on a Ph.D. at the University of New South Wales in comparative native title issues. She has published in the areas of land law, indigenous peoples and the law, and legal history. Her current research considers the interaction of native title and property law.

JULIA FIONDA is Lecturer in Law at King's College, London. She has published articles and books in the fields of homelessness and the law, and criminal justice.

JOSHUA GETZLER is Fellow in Law at St Hugh's College, Oxford, and Lecturer in the Oxford Law Faculty. After studying history and law at the Australian National University in the 1980s, he wrote a dissertation at Oxford on the history of property law. He is now working on the history and economics of trust law.

KEVIN GRAY is Professor of Law in the University of Cambridge and a Fellow of Trinity College. He has written widely on comparative law, property law and theory, human rights, family and social welfare law, housing law, and the law of the environment.

SUSAN FRANCIS GRAY is Senior Lecturer in Law in the University of Greenwich. Formerly a solicitor in private practice, she has spent many years as a Registrar in HM Land Registry.

KATE GREEN teaches law at the University of East London. She is particularly interested in land law and legal theory, especially in the area of feminist legal theory, and is known not only for her textbooks in land law but also for her work in exploring land law through different theoretical perspectives.

CHARLES HARPUM is Law Commissioner for England and Wales and is a Fellow of Downing College, Cambridge. He has written widely on property law and is presently completing the sixth edition of Megarry and Wade's *Law of Real Property*.

DENZIL MILLICHAP specializes in environmental law at Linklaters & Paines. His main work is the practitioners' text, *The Effective Enforcement of Planning Controls*, which developed from nationwide empirical work which he conducted on the topic at University College, London. He writes and lectures on a range of planning topics and has acted in an editorial capacity on three loose-leaf publications.

ALAIN POTTAGE lectures in law at the London School of Economics.

MICHAEL ROBERTSON is Senior Lecturer in Law at Griffith University in Brisbane, Australia. He was formerly Professor of Law at the University of Natal in South Africa. He has practised as both an Attorney and an Advocate in South Africa, and has studied at Natal, Warwick, and Griffith universities. He has published various books and articles on human rights law, property law, and legal service delivery.

LISA WHITEHOUSE is Lecturer in Law at the University of Hull, with special interests in property, equity, and company law. Her doctoral thesis examines the law of mortgages, with particular reference to the repossession process.

INTRODUCTION

Susan Bright and John Dewar

Land Law has a poor reputation amongst undergraduates. Its study is often approached with something between dread and resignation. It has not witnessed the flourishing of critical, theoretical, historical, contextual, or doctrinal treatment enjoyed by some of its more glamorous companions in the core undergraduate syllabus. There are some writers who have made notable efforts to bring the subject closer to the mainstream of intellectual debate in and around law as a discipline, and most of them are represented here; but these are exceptional cases, and we suspect that teaching practices have changed little in the recent past.

Against this background, this book sets out with three purposes in mind. The first is to provide undergraduates studying the subject for the first time with material that sets the subject in a wider context. By doing so, we believe that Land Law will be revealed to be more dynamic, and controversial, than its unglamorous reputation might suggest, as well as being of crucial relevance to our social, political, and economic life. In putting this collection together, we have tried to ensure that there is a chapter relevant to most topics covered in a conventional Land Law syllabus. In other words, it is a book to be used alongside a traditional text, to be returned to throughout a course of study, rather than read at the outset and then discarded.

The second is to include material that points the way towards a reformed teaching practice. Many of the chapters offer more or less explicit critiques of the way the subject is taught, of what is included and excluded. Recurrent themes include, for example, the way in which the conventional Land Law syllabus tends to emphasize private law at the expense of public law, and uncritically emphasizes the rights of the individual owner without regard to the responsibilities of ownership and to the wider community interests in land. Chapters in this book make the case for including, for example, housing law, planning law, European law, and agricultural law as part of our understanding of what Land Law is about. More generally, we have gathered material that presents Land Law as exemplifying debates about the wider ramifications of property in society. By providing material on these topics, we hope to provide a platform for those teachers, who wish to do so, to recast their thinking about the boundaries of their discipline.

The third purpose concerns those who write and think about the subject. Although this collection reflects current trends in Land Law scholarship, so that many of the authors will be familiar names, it is also intended to generate a critical mass of new thinking and writing about Land Law, a new tradition of Land Law scholarship. For that reason, some of our contributors will not be familiar names, but are young scholars seeking to take the subject in new, and diverse, directions. However, as will be evident from a reading of the contents page, the new 'tradition' we have in mind is an extremely diverse one, and embraces feminist, critical, historical, philosophical, political, policy-oriented, and doctrinal treatments.

In seeking to weave substantive coverage of the conventional syllabus with respect for a wide range of intellectual approaches to the subject, and to fulfil our ambition of suggesting new ways of teaching and researching it, we have elected to arrange the chapters around a series of five themes. Each of the five parts of the book reflect one of those themes.

In Part One, 'The Idea of Property in Land', Kevin Gray and Susan Francis Gray, and Gregory Alexander, offer different theoretical perspectives on what is meant by 'property' in land. Kevin Gray and Susan Francis Gray suggest that the 'intractable nature of some of Land Law's structural dilemmas' can be explained as stemming from English Land Law's oscillation between three models of property in land: what they call property as a fact (which gives primacy to sustained and factual possession of land), property as a right (which emphasizes abstract rights divorced from the factual matrix), and property as a responsibility. The first model is evident in the law of adverse possession, a body of law which Kate Green discusses in Part Three. The model of property as responsibility considers property in land not so much as a bundle of rights vested in one individual—as in traditional conceptualizations of ownership—but instead as a disaggregated set of 'individuated elements of land-based utility' whose exercise is heavily regulated by the state and which collectively amount to a concept of property as restraint and 'commonality of obligation'. This concept of property in land resurfaces at various points in other chapters in the book, most notably in Parts Three and Four. Millichap, for instance, argues that planning law should recapture the concern for the community evident in earlier planning cases. Alexander also proposes alternative models of liberal ownership which again accommodate norms that support the wider interests of the community. The Grays suggest that no one of the three models of property which they put forward predominates, nor do they exist in opposition to each other: instead, they set up a creative tension which contributes to the richness of Land Law.

Gregory Alexander considers the contribution of US Critical Legal Studies (CLS) to Land Law scholarship. CLS writers have challenged the 'Blackstonian' conception of property ownership in land—that is, the idea that there is an identifiable, single, absolute owner of land. This conception—also discussed by Susan Bright in her chapter—has had a profound influence on the way issues concerning land have been framed in legal debate, yet it is both descriptively inaccurate (in that it is often difficult to identify a single individual as clearly the sole and absolute owner of land) and means that, in practice, the multiple community interests in the way land is used or distributed are left out of account.

Alexander explores some of the contradictions in liberal conceptions of land ownership, especially the tension between the principles of freedom of disposition and free alienability. He outlines the CLS response to arguments against compulsory standard terms (e.g., of habitability in leases) and to the argument that private ownership is more efficient than alternative forms of ownership; and he details critical perspectives based on gender and race (each of which are echoed, in different jurisdictions, in the later chapters by Anne Bottomley, Shaunnagh Dorsett, and Michael Robertson).

He then turns to what he calls 'reconstructive theories' concerning land ownership, each of which represents an attempt to develop a third way between 'state socialism and *laissez-faire* capitalism', and which hold out the hope of 'realizing progressive goals'. He discusses three such theories: the 'social-relations model', 'social-republican property', and 'civic property'. Each theory represents a modification of the Blackstonian conception of private property, by recognizing the existence of legitimate community interests in the formulation of the rights of property and their enforcement. The third of these theories, civic property (a close cousin of the Grays' conception of property as responsibility), emphasizes the social obligations attached to land ownership and stresses the role played by property ownership in collective life, both nationally and internationally. It foreshadows the themes picked up in Part Three concerning the role of Land Law in vindicating rights of citizenship (for example, in the process of reconciliation in South Africa) and in Part Four concerning land use and the internationalization of Land Law.

It is often said that Land Law carries the heavy imprint of history: but what counts as 'history' for these purposes is often limited to an account of the emergence of the doctrine of tenures. Part Two, 'Land Law in History', suggests that the range of historical materials relevant to understanding Land Law can be expanded. Joshua Getzler, for example, explores the Roman law ideas of property in land, and suggests that many of those ideas have left a deep impression on modern English Land Law, mainly in consequence of their influence on the great English jurists and systematizers of English law, such as Bracton and Blackstone. The rustic and urban praedial servitudes found in Roman law, for example, closely resemble the easements and covenants found in common law systems. Although some Roman conceptions, such as allodial titles, did not find their way into English law, they have profoundly influenced civil law thinking about ownership and title; and, as other contributors suggest (including the Grays and the Brights), English land lawyers, in an era of European integration, cannot ignore that civilian tradition.

For English land lawyers, the Law of Property legislation of 1925 looms large. It is frequently appealed to as embodying certain 'polices' that assist in resolving modern disputes over land. And yet, although the legislation resulted in a Land Law unique in the common law world, it yielded no formal code of Land Law concepts; nor, as Stuart Anderson's chapter suggests, can it be seen as embodying any distinctive set of policies. Instead, he suggests a number of different ways in which the story of the 1925 legislation can be told, drawing variously on the political debates around landed wealth and the practices of settlement in the late nineteenth century, the struggle for professional control of the market for land transfer, and the biographical history of the individuals who were responsible for the final text. To these different histories can be added the history of the subsequent reception of the legislation by textbook writers and judges. In the light of this, Anderson suggests, it cannot be said that the drafters clearly intended one particular operation for a section over another; and that appeals to history do not remove the responsibility to address what the role of the legislation should be today.

When land lawyers think of title to land, they are likely to think in terms of the bureaucratic systems of title registration that have so successfully taken root in most common law-derived jurisdictions (albeit in different forms), and which have almost entirely replaced older lawyer-dominated methods of providing evidence of ownership. Students are sometimes encouraged to assume (perhaps under the influence of one of Anderson's narratives) that title registration is a purely adjectival or procedural body of law, severable from consideration of the underlying substantive structure. Yet, as Alain Pottage suggests in his chapter, when viewed in a historical perspective, there is a close relationship between the practices or techniques of evidencing ownership and the expectations that arise from ownership itself. Viewed in this way, the introduction of land registration, which created new possibilities in what could be recorded and guaranteed, not only made evidence of title autonomous from events 'on the ground' but also permitted the development of a wider range of complex rights of ownership. And yet, as Pottage shows, the success of land registration depends in large part on the security of the expectations it generates, and on the willingness of owners (or their lawyers) to trust the system to produce the results it promised.

The 1925 legislation is by no means the only legislation with which students of Land Law are concerned. Indeed, there has in recent years been a steady flow of important statutory reforms in the areas of conveyancing, trusts of land, land registration, and landlord and tenant. The source of most of this legislative activity has been the Law Commission, which has maintained a strong commitment to the reform of conveyancing and real property law since its creation in 1965. In his chapter, Charles Harpum assesses the Law Commission's contribution to law reform in recent years and offers an account of the genesis of some recent legislation, such as the Law of Property (Miscellaneous Provisions) Act 1989 and the Trusts of Land and Appointment of Trustees Act 1996.

Part Three, 'Land Law and Citizenship', is premised on the view that land plays an important part in fulfilling many of the basic human needs essential to existence, and that the law plays a significant part in controlling access to that resource, and thus the life chances of the population. It explores the ways in which the rules governing the ownership or acquisition of land contribute to understandings of citizenship, through the inclusion or exclusion of certain social groups from the enjoyment of land. The writers in this section approach this theme from a number of perspectives, some with more explicitly articulated conceptions of citizenship than others. Some of the contributions suggest that, if the assumptions mentioned above are accepted, we should reconsider the boundaries of the subject as traditionally conceived, especially by exploring the connections between the public and private spheres implied by the link between property and citizenship.

One much criticized area of doctrine has been the law relating to the acquisition of equitable interests in land under informal trusts, an area of law that has often been said to discriminate against women by favouring financial over non-financial contributions to property acquisition, and by insisting on clear evidence of agreements over property ownership. Anne Bottomley re-visits this body of law in the light of recent judicial and academic developments. She finds cause to praise the work of Mr Justice (now Lord Justice) Waite in his attempts to temper what she calls the potential 'relationship blindness' of the principles set out in *Lloyd's Bank* v. *Rosset*.[1] Bottomley suggests that Waite LJ's willingness, evident in cases such as *Hammond* v. *Mitchell*[2] and *Midland Bank* v. *Cooke*,[3] to look for evidence of the necessary 'common intention' in the background evidence detailing the parties' 'sexual-domestic' relationship, is a significant advance in judicial treatment of these cases, which have often proceeded as if the parties are strangers to each other and have set accordingly high standards for proof of agreements concerning ownership.

This leads her to examine Simon Gardner's recent, and eloquently expressed, call that the law in this area be more sensitive to the nature of the parties' relationship, and in particular that some conceptual vehicle be found that is capable of recognizing the reality of 'trust and collaboration' that is often present in these cases.[4] Although attracted to this, Bottomley is troubled, as a feminist, by Gardner's strategy of relying on marriage, or

---

[1] [1991] 1 AC 107. [2] [1991] 1 WLR 1127. [3] [1995] 4 All ER 564.
[4] Gardner, 'Rethinking Family Property' (1993) 109 LQR 263.

marriage-like relationships, as presumptive evidence of the necessary trust and collaboration: although it recognizes the relationship as an important factor in shaping the outcome of disputes, it also has the potential to ignore imbalances of power *between* the individuals in that relationship. She goes on to argue that 'intention' does, after all, form a sound basis for doctrine in this area, provided that judges are sensitive, in ways exemplified by Waite LJ, to the other 'intended meanings' in the background facts of each case. Women, she concludes, wish 'to be seen as citizens rather than continually portrayed as wives'.

The law on adverse possession is often treated as a quaint, perhaps anachronistic, illustration of the maxim that 'possession is nine-tenths of the law'. Kate Green shows, in her 'archaeological' reading of the case law on adverse possession, that there is more to it than this, and that there are underlying similarities between the way in which the law defines a successful adverse possessor and the way in which citizenship itself is defined in law. She argues that the case law on adverse possession reveals an attachment to a mythic archetype, the 'ideal English land owner', 'a self-interested and rational individual who makes a permanent mark on the landscape'; and that there is a similarity between this character and that of 'the citizen'. In both contexts, of land ownership and of citizenship, this archetype serves to exclude those who do not conform: the transient, the irrational, and those who are not wholly self-interested. One reason for this, she suggests, is that modern conceptions of property ownership and citizenship were forged at much the same time, in the early phase of capitalist growth.

In their chapters, Dave Cowan and Julia Fionda (on homelessness), and Lisa Whitehouse (on mortgage repossessions), approach the question of Land Law and citizenship in a slightly different way. Although access to housing is perhaps one of the most basic human rights, and (in the view of some) one of the cornerstones of citizenship, they argue that English law recognizes no right to housing as such, but instead confers access to housing primarily on those who can afford to pay for it at market rates: a citizenry (for these purposes) of consumers. For the rest, there is limited, poor-quality, statutory provision, allocated mainly on the basis of official judgements about whether the applicant falls into the category of deserving or undeserving.

Dave Cowan and Julia Fionda begin their chapter on homelessness with a critique of Land Law as an academic discipline. They argue that, as commonly taught, Land Law courses pay no attention to the 'public' aspects of the subject such as homelessness, or to those aspects dealing with access to land. This is in spite of the fact that many of the topics covered in conventional Land Law courses, such as mortgage repossession, can themselves be triggers for homelessness. Instead, the subject focuses on what they call the rights of the included, the consumer-citizens, rather than the rights of the excluded. They argue that the boundaries of Land Law should be expanded to embrace the law on homelessness, in keeping with an expanded notion of citizenship and its implications for access to land. Their chapter goes on to provide an introduction to the study of homelessness and statutory responses to it, and then surveys some empirical evidence of how the law works in practice.

In her study of mortgage repossessions, Lisa Whitehouse suggests that these proceedings have to be seen against a background of a government policy of encouraging individuals to satisfy their housing needs through the market—that is, through owner-occupation. This is a form of tenure that usually involves raising the purchase price by mortgage finance. In a mortgage relationship, the individual is viewed in law as a consumer: a rational, satisfaction-maximizing individual exercising choices in the light of perfect market information. She suggests that, although this may be consistent with an image of the citizen as consumer promoted by the Conservative administration of the 1980s and early 1990s (as exemplified, for example, by 'the Citizens' Charter'), and with a housing policy that sought to reduce the role of the state in housing provision, it fails to recognize the uniquely important commodity, housing, which is effectively the subject matter of the transaction. Her study of county court mortgage repossession proceedings suggests that, if rights to housing and due process (which, in her view, are implied by citizenship) are to be taken seriously, reform of the relevant law and procedures is required.

In a stable social democracy such as the United Kingdom, where debates over basic questions such as the distribution of land ownership (as opposed to access to, or use of, land) seem to have been largely laid to rest, it is perhaps easy to forget that the question of who gets to own land at all is an essentially political one. Yet in other jurisdictions, especially those coming to terms with a colonial legacy of dispossession of Indigenous peoples, the issue of how land rights should be allocated is still very much at the centre of political and legal debate. Two such jurisdictions, Australia and South Africa, are discussed here. Although there are important differences between them, both cases illustrate the connection between recognition of the land rights of previously dispossessed groups, on the one hand, and attempts at political reconciliation and social reconstruction, on the other.

In both cases, an important question is how successful these attempts are likely to be. In her chapter on native title in Australia, Shaunnagh Dorsett suggests that the landmark decision of the High Court of Australia in *Mabo* v. *Queensland*,[5] in which it was held that Indigenous claims to land survived colonisation of the Australian continent and are recognized by the common

---

[5] *Mabo* v. *State of Queensland (No. 2)* (1992) 175 CLR 1.

law, has had limited practical effect on the rights of Indigenous Australians. As she points out, five years on from *Mabo*, there have been no other successful claims in the courts to native title in Australia. She attributes this in part to the inability of Australian law (the relevant history of which she outlines) to recognize the distinctive nature of native title claims. In short, she suggests, these claims fail because they do not conform to the Western stereotypes of property right. She argues that new understandings of property are necessary if modern Australian law is to avoid repeating or perpetuating the pattern of dispossession of Indigenous peoples.

Unlike Australia, South Africa is in the early stages of its transition to democracy. As Michael Robertson's chapter illustrates, a key element of that transition is a substantial programme of land reform. That programme has three components: restitution of land to those from whom it was taken under the apartheid regime by virtue of racially discriminatory legislation; the redistribution of land to ensure a wider distribution of landownership, especially amongst the poor; and tenure reform. Drawing on the history of land reform in South America, Robertson suggests that South Africa is pursuing a distinctive policy which, as Robertson terms it, emphasizes the 'social purpose' of land. This is a policy of land reform that emphasizes the community's obligation to the user of land, and which sees land reform as an instrument of welfare provision and of economic policy. Thus, the provision of land is seen as a way of fighting poverty, of providing sources of food and shelter, and the means of economically productive activity. This resurrects an essentially liberal view of property as the individual's guarantee of dignity and autonomy, thereby marking a clear distinction from the issues raised in the Australian context. Although it is still too early to say whether this reform programme will meet its ambitious objectives, Robertson's chapter, like those in Part One, offers a reminder of the persistence and potential of liberal notions of property rights in land, as well as their potential contradictions.

Part Four is entitled 'Policy Issues in Land Law'. This part of the book takes particular aspects of social, commercial, and economic life on which Land Law impacts and examines whether the traditional doctrinal methodology of Land Law provides a satisfactory response to the problems they raise. John Dewar's chapter explores the complexities of the law relating to the family home. He argues that, although English law remains nominally committed to the principle of separation of property (that is, that marriage or marriage-like cohabitation have no formal impact on the property rights of family members), so that the family home is officially invisible to English law, there are nevertheless many ways in which that principle is honoured more in the breach than the observance. He suggests that, first, the laws of real property, conveyancing, and trusts have become so modified when it comes to the family home (or 'familialized') that there now exists a body of law that has no application outside that context, and that the law in this area bears the imprint of some clear judicial policies of what he calls 'give and take'; and, secondly, that there is a growing number of statutory provisions dealing exclusively with the family home, to such an extent that it is now possible to say that there is a nascent, albeit jumbled, statutory regime governing the family home *as such*. He goes on to explore the various failed attempts to reform this area of the law, and to suggest a framework for thinking about the legal issues raised by it.

Christopher and Susan Bright explore some of the implications of the European Union for domestic Land Law. The idea that European law has any relevance to Land Law may come as a surprise to some, but, as the Brights demonstrate, its actual and potential impact is considerable. After assessing the Union's competence to act in matters concerning land (which includes consideration of the nascent 'takings' jurisprudence developing in European law), they go on to consider the potential impact of Treaty provisions, such as the four freedoms and Articles 85 and 86. They show how EU law is concerned with questions concerning allocation of land ownership, the freedom of leaseholders to impose ties in leases, and the ability of owners of 'essential facilities' to deny access to potential competitors. They also look at the ways in which the EU is already actively intervening in matters relating to land—including environmental policy, consumer protection, and agriculture—and consider the further possibilities of harmonization of European real-property laws, including that of creating a 'euro-title' to land, by analogy, for example, with the concept of the Community trademark.

A set of problems that has so far eluded a satisfactory solution in English law has been those arising from communal living, or multiple occupation of the same building. In some jurisdictions, these have been overcome through condominium or strata title legislation. David Clarke examines the problems flowing from English law's reliance on the lease as the means of handling horizontal, rather than vertical, divisions of property. He looks in detail at the English long leasehold, commonly used for flats, and at the piecemeal legislative reforms protecting the leaseholder that have been introduced in England and Wales, which, he suggests, fall a long way short of any comprehensive code. He explores some of the solutions arrived at in other jurisdictions, notably Scotland, Hong Kong, and New Zealand, and at strata title legislation in Australia; and concludes by considering the proposals in England and Wales for a new concept of commonhold.

In his chapter, Michael Cardwell explores some of the legal aspects of the agricultural use of land. This is a surprisingly neglected subject, particularly in view of the large proportion of the surface area of England and Wales devoted to agriculture. His chapter shows how legal regulation of agricultural land is a central concern to all governments. Promotion of particular modes of tenure and tenure control can be used to influence the issue of who farms (new entrants or established farmers), the standards of husbandry, long-term efficiency, and environmental standards. He discusses the recently enacted Agricultural Tenancies Act 1995 and its likely effect. He then considers legal controls on food production (such as quotas) imposed by the European Union, and the encouragement of non-agricultural uses of land (through subsidy rules and tenancy laws), both of which affect levels of food production and can be used to promote sustainable and environmentally sound uses of land. His chapter demonstrates the complex interrelation of Land Law, the statutory regulation of tenancies, planning, and environmental law, European agricultural law and policy, and the law of international trade.

Millichap's chapter looks at the history of state controls on land use, and suggests that there may be aspects of that history that are relevant to current planning law and policy. He begins by discussing how the Victorian corpus of private law concepts paid little attention to the social impacts of development, and thereby created the conditions of overcrowding, ill health, and social tension in urban areas that were to lead to intervention by the state. He describes how early legislation on sanitation provoked a hostile reaction from the courts and how they rediscovered 'natural justice' principles in order to protect private property. The battle between judiciary and legislature over intervention in property ownership continued therafter: it was not until the 1920s that at least one member of the senior judiciary expressed principled support for intervening in the landowner's right to develop his land.

Millichap thus draws attention to a landmark Court of Appeal decision[6]— a case since forgotten even by specialists in planning law. This, he argues, established the principle that the planning system had created 'community rights' in property. Even so, the traditional concepts of property law continued to exert a pull. In 1995 the House of Lords, taking a historical perspective on the development of the planning code, accepted that the courts should not interfere with policy-based attempts to promote the interests of communities. This chapter thus examines the interweaving of legislation, case law, and policy throughout the history of planning control. It suggests that the current rationale for planning ('public interest') should be replaced by the (forgotten) principle of 'community rights'—first set out in 1920. Such a principle would encourage the perspective of the lawyer (and the planner) to shift from that of the individual landholder to a concern for the community (whether at the neighbourhood, town, city, or even global level).

Doctrinal analysis, or what is sometimes called the 'black letter' or expository approach to legal scholarship, is the oldest tradition of all those in

---

[6] *Re Ellis and the Ruislip–Northwood Urban Council* [1920] 1 KB 343.

evidence in this book. Its primary subject matter is the raw material of the law, cases and legislation; and its objectives are, in general, to draw out the internal coherence (or incoherence) or logical consistencies (or inconsistencies) of that corpus of material. It proceeds largely by its own lights, with its own methodologies, which are close to those of the judge or barrister, rather than drawing explicitly on other disciplines, to generate its insights. It has proved to be a rich and productive tradition of Land Law scholarship (indeed, all the other contributions to this collection exemplify its techniques, more or less); and, as the contributions to Part Five, 'Doctrinal Issues in Land Law' suggest, it continues to be such.

Part 5 opens with a valuable point of entry to understanding some of the intricacies of Land Law. Peter Birks suggests that there are five 'keys' to a proper conceptual understanding of the subject: those of time, space, reality, duality, and formality. He suggests that, once students understand that Land Law deals with slices of time in respect of finite space, by means of a limited range of 'real' as opposed to personal rights, that these rights must be formally created and evidenced, and that there are a number of 'dualities' (such as that of law and equity), they will be a long way towards a proper understanding of the subject. Birks illustrates each 'key' by reference to examples, and suggests that what threads them together is 'facilitation'—that is, the role played by law in helping people achieve their objectives.

The remaining chapters in this part deal with two of Birks's keys: formality and reality. Graham Battersby and Patricia Critchley approach the question of formality in different ways. Battersby surveys the different legal doctrines that provide exceptions to, or qualify, requirements of formality in land transactions. He draws a primary distinction between those doctrines that legitimate the originally unlawful (such as adverse possession and prescription) and those which give effect to informal arrangements affecting land (such as implied trusts and estoppel). As Battersby points out, these rules are further overlaid with another set of formal requirements arising out of the system of land registration (although requirements of registration are themselves subject to well-known exceptions, such as overriding interests). In each case, he examines the rationales for the doctrines and, although he concludes that they are justified, he suggests that there are areas in which reform is urgently needed.

Patricia Critchley is concerned more directly with the rules imposing requirements of formality, rather than with the exceptions to those rules. She is concerned to investigate why those rules exist and what purposes they serve. She analyses the idea of legal formality itself and then proceeds to outline the benefits and detriments of formality requirements. She suggests that her analytical framework is of use in making judgments about the application of formality rules in a particular case, and that attention to the policies underlying those rules may provide a clear way through some substantive debates.

Susan Bright's chapter is concerned with what Birks calls 'reality': that is, the rules dictating which interests can or cannot exist as 'real' or proprietary rights. In the first part of her chapter she explores what it means to be the 'owner' of an estate in land, drawing on different conceptual approaches to 'ownership'. The tendency to emphasize the distinctiveness of the common law system of ownership of estates (the property as a right notion identified by the Grays), as a point of contrast to the civilian notions of dominium (discussed by Getzler), can lead scholars to be dismissive of ownership as a concept of value to English land lawyers. Susan Bright suggests that to think of 'estate ownership' as a form of ownership of land can help to explain the line drawn by land lawyers between owning an estate and owning a lesser interest in the land. She suggests that ownership is best encapsulated by viewing it as holding an 'open-ended' set of use rights and privileges over land in the manner recently proposed by Professor Harris in his book, *Property and Justice*.[7]

The second part of her chapter discusses interests in land, such as easements and covenants, rights which do not confer these 'open-ended' user rights and privileges. On the whole, these rights have been neglected by theorists and she seeks to identify common features of these interests, as well as the reasons for excluding other rights relating to land, such as licences, and, perhaps controversially, estoppel claims, from the category of proprietary interests. She puts forward the view that, in order to be accepted as a property right, the right must be unique (not substitutable), capable of practical enforcement, identifiable, and non-'personality dependent'.

In her conclusion, Susan Bright suggests that the notion of estates in the 1925 legislation has proven remarkably durable as a method of landholding, notwithstanding the vast and rapid social and economic upheaval since.

What this volume seeks to illustrate, however, is that to confine a discussion of Land Law to a detailed exposition of the scheme set out by this legislation, of estates, and interests, and modes of third-party protection, is a narrow and limiting picture of what Land Law is really about. Analysis of who can and who cannot own land, of the way in which Land Law reinforces particular images of citizenship and responds to the needs of particular groups and economic interests, provides a much richer tapestry to work with. Land Law can be used to tell a story about society, about its values, about the included and the excluded, of whether land is to provide a means of exclusion and control, or a resource to be harnessed and nurtured and shared. It is hoped that this collection will help you to read that story.

[7] Harris, *Property and Justice* (Oxford: Oxford University Press, 1996).

PART ONE
THE IDEA OF PROPERTY IN LAND

1

THE IDEA OF PROPERTY IN LAND

Kevin Gray and Susan Francis Gray

It is just over a century since, in a paper still regarded as seminal, Oliver Wendell Holmes observed that the trouble with law was not that there had been too much theory but rather that there had not been enough.[1] We must, therefore, begin with some conceptualization about property.

A BRIEF INTRODUCTION TO THE JURISPRUDENCE OF PROPERTY

Few concepts are quite so fragile, so elusive and so often misused as the idea of property. Most everyday references to property are unreflective, naïve and relatively meaningless. Frequently the lay person (and even the lawyer) falls into the trap of supposing the term 'property' to connote the *thing* which is the object of 'ownership'. But the beginning of truth about property is the realization that property is not a *thing* but rather a *relationship* which one has with a thing. It is infinitely more accurate, therefore, to say that one has property *in* a thing than to declare that the thing is one's property.[2]

To claim 'property' in a resource is, in effect, to assert a strategically important degree of control over that resource; and to conflate or confuse this relationship of control with the actual thing controlled may often prove to be an analytical error of some substance. 'Property' is, rather, the word used to describe particular concentrations of power *over* things and resources. The term 'property' is simply an abbreviated reference to a quantum of socially permissible power exercised in respect of a socially valued resource. Used in this way, the word 'property' reflects its semantically correct root by identifying the condition of a particular resource as being

---

[1] 'The Path of the Law', 10 Harv. L. Rev. 457 at 476 (1896–7). See now 110 Harv. L. Rev. 989 (1996–7).

[2] 'In legal usage property is not the land or thing, but is *in* the land or thing' (*Dorman* v. *Rodgers* (1982) 148 CLR 365, *per* Murphy J at 372). See also Bentham, *An Introduction to the Principles of Morals and Legislation*, ed. Harrison (Oxford: Oxford University Press, 1948), 337, n. 1 (ch. XVI, sect. 26).

'proper' to a particular person.[3] In this deeper sense, as we shall see later, the language of 'property' may have more in common with 'propriety' than with entitlement; and the notion of a 'property right' may ultimately have more to do with perceptions of 'rightness' than with any understanding of enforceable exclusory title.

It may be noted, furthermore, that the power relationship implicit in property is not absolute but relative: there may well be gradations of 'property' in a resource. The amount of 'property' which a specified person may claim in any resource is capable of calibration—along some sort of sliding scale—from a maximum value to a minimum value. Of course, where this value tends towards zero it will become a misuse of language to say that this person has any 'property' at all in the resource in question. Apart from such cases, however, it remains feasible—and indeed important—to measure the quantum of 'property' which someone has in a particular resource at a particular time. Far from being a monolithic notion of standard content and invariable intensity, 'property' thus turns out to have an almost infinitely gradable quality. And it follows, moreover, that to have 'property' in a resource may often be entirely consistent with the acquisition or retention by others of 'property' in the same resource. It is, in fact, the complex interrelation of these myriad gradations of 'property' which comprises the stuff of modern land law.

But let us explore some of these ideas in a less abstract context.

GRADATIONS OF PROPERTY

When, as an invited guest, you attend a dinner party in our home in Eden Street, you would no more think of asserting that you have 'property' in our home than you would think of claiming any entitlement to walk away with our knives and forks or with our pictures and books. You are clearly no trespasser, for we requested the pleasure of your company. Provided that you do not abuse our invitation by sliding drunkenly down the bannisters,[4] you continue to enjoy the jural immunity which attaches to the recipient of a bare licence or permission to enter upon another's land. At the end of the evening we will bid you goodbye at our door and, in Celtic (though not Anglo-Saxon) custom, one of us will stand watching respectfully until you disappear from sight. But it would strain accepted understandings of

---

[3] The sense conveyed here is similar to that in which a 'proper thing' meant, in archaic usage, 'one's own thing' (see Gray, *Elements of Land Law* (1st edn., London: Butterworths, 1987); 8).

[4] See *The Carlgarth* [1927] P 93, *per* Scrutton LJ at 110 ('When you invite a person into your house to use the staircase, you do not invite him to slide down the bannisters').

both lay and legal language to suggest that, even for the brief span of our dinner party, you had any property in our land.[5]

This isolated vignette speaks volumes about the indefinable quality of property in land and the complex psycho-spatial assumptions which underpin perceptions of ownership. Throughout this entire social encounter your relationship with 'our' land could never have been described as 'proprietary' in nature—not even if, towards the end of the evening, you pottered around the kitchen helping to make the coffee or plundered the cupboards in a desperate search for another bottle of wine. Your land-based rights were, at all times, essentially personal, moral, and social. You were entitled to the cordiality of welcome and mutuality of respect properly given to any duly invited guest. Your legal rights were measurable in negative terms only: your liability in trespass was suspended so long as you did not overstep the ambit of the licence granted by our invitation. But property in the land never ceased to be ours; indeed it was by virtue of the prerogative of property that we retained the right to dictate the terms on which access might be had to our land by a stranger. We admitted you to our home; by means of some implicit fiat we constrained your conduct whilst present there; and we finally saw you off the land at the conclusion of the licensed period of entry. Here—albeit heavily suffused by the courtesies of social intercourse—are found the indicia of the classical conception of property—the power to control access, to prioritize competing modes of user and, ultimately, to exclude the stranger.

This apparently straightforward analysis of property in land is, of course, capable of permutation through several hypothetical changes of circumstance. Suppose that, instead of inviting you to dinner in our home, we installed you as a lodger in one of the attic bedrooms. In return for a weekly rent, you now enjoy the use of this room together with a share of the kitchen and bathroom facilities in the house. Or suppose, alternatively, that we converted a complete floor of our house into a self-contained flat which we let to you for a period of two years. Or even imagine that during our dinner party we agreed to sell you the entire house[6] and have since transferred the registered title to you. On which of these various hypotheses could you now credibly claim to have 'property' in the land? In at least some of these instances the identification of property in the land will have

---

[5] This must be so notwithstanding the extremely broad definition of the word 'land' as inclusive of buildings and parts of buildings attached to the physical solum (see Law of Property Act 1925, ss. 62(1), (2), 205(1)(ix); Land Registration Act 1925, s. 3(viii)). See also *Elitestone Ltd* v. *Morris* [1997] 1 WLR 687 at 691G–H.

[6] For a bizarre instance, arising in Australia, of a house purchase allegedly agreed at a dinner party, see *Lezabar Pty. Ltd.* v. *Hogan* (1989) 4 BPR 9498. See, however, Law of Property (Miscellaneous Provisions) Act 1989, s. 2(1).

become suddenly more difficult—partly because the issues postulated may not be principally, or even necessarily, legal in nature.

Just as perplexing, although perhaps in a different way, may be the question whether you could claim any 'property' in our land in Eden Street if you were our next-door neighbour and we permitted you a right of way across our back garden or promised you that we would use our own premises for residential purposes only. Yet, as will appear later, the standard interpretation of such events in English law would indicate that at least some of the property in our land has thereby been passed to you.

AMBIVALENT CONCEPTUAL MODELS OF PROPERTY

The task of the present chapter is to outline the various ways in which English law—and perhaps, more generally, common law jurisprudence— handles the idea of property in land. It will be argued that our dominant models of property in land fluctuate inconsistently between three rather different perspectives. It will be suggested that this doctrinal uncertainty—this deep structural indeterminacy—explains the intractable nature of some of land law's classic dilemmas, whilst simultaneously impeding constructive responses to the more immediately pressing challenges of twenty-first century land law. The common law world has never really resolved whether property in land is to be understood in terms of empirical facts, artificially defined rights, or duty-laden allocations of social utility. Although these three perspectives sometimes interact and overlap, it remains ultimately unclear whether the substance of property resides in the raw data of human conduct or in essentially positive claims of abstract entitlement or in the socially directed control of land use. In short, the idea of property in land oscillates ambivalently between the behavioural, the conceptual, and the obligational, between competing models of property as a *fact*, property as a *right*, and property as a *responsibility*.

Property as a Fact

Much of the genius of the common law derives from a rough-and-ready grasp of the empirical realities of life. According to this perspective, the identification of property in land is an earthily pragmatic affair. There is a deeply anti-intellectual streak in the common law tradition which cares little for grand or abstract theories of ownership,[7] preferring to fasten instead upon the raw organic facts of human behaviour. This perspective is preoccupied with what happens on the ground rather than with what emerges

[7] See *Commissioner for Railways et al.* v. *Valuer-General* [1974] AC 328, *per* Lord Wilberforce at 351H–352A.

from the heaven of concepts. Accordingly, the crude empiricism of this outlook leaves the recognition of property to rest upon essentially intuitive perceptions of the degree to which a claimant successfully asserts *de facto* possessory control over land.[8] On this view property in land is more about fact than about right; it derives ultimately not from 'words upon parchment'[9] but from the elemental primacy of sustained possession.[10] Property in land is thus measurable with reference to essentially behavioural data; it expresses a visceral insight into the current balance of human power relationships in respect of land. And it is, indeed, the psycho-social nature of this understanding of property which serves to discriminate between many of the hypothetical variants of the property question posed earlier in this chapter.

Concealed within this behavioural notion of property is, inevitably, some primal perception of the *propriety* of one's nexus with land.[11] To have 'property' in land is not merely to allege some casual physical affinity with a particular piece of land, but rather to stake out some sort of claim to the legitimacy of one's personal space in this land. It is to assert that the land is 'proper' to one; that one has some significant self-constituting, self-realizing, self-identifying connection with the land; that the land is, in some measure, an embodiment of one's personality and autonomy. To claim 'property' in land is to arrogate at least a limited form of sovereignty over the land and to allege that one has some emotion- or investment-backed security in it. To have 'property' in land connotes, ultimately, a deeply instinctive self-affirming sense of belonging and control; and it is precisely this sense of possessory control which identifies the two proprietary estates acknowledged today in English law,[12] the fee simple absolute (or freehold estate) and the term of years absolute (or leasehold estate).

---

[8] 'Possession' has been described as 'a conclusion of law defining the nature and status of a particular relationship of control by a person over land' (*Mabo* v. *Queensland (No. 2)* (1992) 175 CLR 1, *per* Toohey J at 207).

[9] Blackstone could see 'no foundation in nature or in natural law, why a set of words upon parchment should convey the dominion of land . . .' (*Commentaries on the Laws of England* (4 vols., 1st edn., Oxford: Oxford University Press, 1765–9; rep. Chicago: University of Chicago Press, 1979), ii. 2).

[10] 'In some deep sense the sustained exercise of exclusory power is perhaps all there really is to the grand claim of proprietary ownership. Behind all the brave philosophical and political rhetoric of conventional property talk there lurks only the unattractive rumble of state-sanctioned *force majeure*' (Gray, 'Property in Common Law Systems', in van Maanen and van der Walt (eds., *Property Law on the Threshold of the 21st Century* (Antwerp: MAKLU, 1996), 265).

[11] Once again even the etymological links between such terms as 'property', 'proper', 'appropriate', and 'propriety' serve to underscore the value-laden complexity of the inter-relating nuances of property talk.

[12] See Law of Property Act 1925, s. 1(1).

Such inner awareness of property in land is, of course, essentially pre-legal in character. But no matter how elusive and inexpressible the nature of the psychological link, its absence is recognizably familiar. The obverse of property in land is found in the lurking unease experienced by the trespasser and in the diffidently self-conscious demeanour evinced by those who do not feel quite 'at home' in a stranger's territory. In some degree the obverse of property is disempowerment, disorientation, and alienation—the uncomfortable realization that one's presence on land is either improper or crucially dependent on the sufferance of another.[13] The student who tiptoes across the landing for the two baths per week permitted by his landlady cannot credibly claim to have any property in his landlady's house. Equally, for reasons soon to be reinforced, the lodger who takes up occupancy of our attic bedroom in Eden Street—as distinct from the person who receives a lease of a self-contained flat in the same house—can claim no proprietary estate in the land.[14]

So potent is this behavioural connotation of property relationships that, even today, common law courts frequently resort to curiously unlegalistic language in identifying the existence of the estates of the fee simple and the term of years. It is no accident that the legal notion of property in land is still articulated in terms which are strikingly crude and unsophisticated. Thus, for instance, the property enjoyed by the leaseholder, and *a fortiori* by the freeholder, is often said to be characterized by the freedom each has to 'call the place his own'.[15] As Coke CJ famously observed long ago in *Semayne's Case*,[16] 'the house of every one is to him as his castle and fortress'. Much more recently, in seeking to capture the essence of the leasehold estate, Lord Denning MR could frame the issue only as a deeply intuitive empirical inquiry—that is, whether the relevant occupier had a 'stake' in the premises, as distinct from a mere 'permission for himself personally to occupy'.[17] It is by virtue of such stakeholding—by virtue of some gut sense

[13] See Williams, 'Spirit-Murdering the Messenger: The Discourse of Fingerpointing as the Law's Response to Racism', 42 U. Miami L. Rev. 127 at 129 (1987).

[14] It is in precisely the same sense that a guest cannot claim to have 'property' in a hotel room. The hotel guest may enjoy a temporarily exclusive use of his room but does not have overall territorial control (see *Bradley* v. *Baylis* (1881) 8 QBD 195, *per* Jessel MR at 216).

[15] *Street* v. *Mountford* [1985] AC 809, *per* Lord Templeman at 818A. By contrast, 'a licensee lacking exclusive possession can in no sense call the land his own' (ibid., *per* Lord Templeman at 816C).

[16] (1604) 5 Co. Rep. 91a at 91b, 77 ER 194 at 195.

[17] *Marchant* v. *Charters* [1977] 1 WLR 1181 at 1185G. Here the Court of Appeal held that the occupier of the disputed 'attractive bachelor service apartment' was merely a lodger and not a tenant, a finding later endorsed by the House of Lords in *Street* v. *Mountford* [1985] AC 809 at 824G–825C. Similar outcomes have emerged in cases involving long-term hotel residents (*Appah* v. *Parncliffe Investments Ltd.* [1964] 1 WLR 1064 at 1071; *Luganda* v. *Service Hotels Ltd.* [1969] 2 Ch. 209 at 217D) and residents in an old people's home (*Abbeyfield (Harpenden) Society Ltd.* v. *Woods* [1968] 1 WLR 374 at 376F–H).

of belonging—that the leaseholder or tenant can properly be described as 'able to exercise the rights of an owner of land, which is in the real sense his land albeit temporarily and subject to certain restrictions.'[18]

Throughout the history of English land law the operative concept has been *possession* rather than *ownership*: the common lawyer's overwhelming concern has been with the externally verifiable modalities of possessory control.[19] Indeed, the property of estate ownership is ultimately a derivative of 'exclusive possession',[20] a phrase used in English law to denote not merely an exclusive factual presence upon land but also some inner assumption as to the power relationships generated by such presence. Correspondingly, the absence of estate ownership is epitomized in the 'property deficit' inherent, for instance, in the status of the mere 'lodger'. The lodger, unlike the tenant, is subject to the supervisory authority of the owner, who at all times 'retains his character of master of the house, and . . . retains the general control and dominion over the whole house'.[21] In the modern context, declared Lord Templeman in *Street v Mountford*,[22] a residential occupier can claim no proprietary estate in the land if he is provided with attendance or services which require the owner or his servants to 'exercise unrestricted access to and use of the premises.' In such circumstances it is the owner who 'retains possession' precisely in order to supply the attendance or services.[23]

In terms of this empirical perspective, the critical determinant of property in land is the mode of behaviour consciously adopted by the claimant occupier. The occupier is, in some elusive sense, the master of his own

[18] *Street* v. *Mountford* [1985] AC 809, *per* Lord Templeman at 816B.

[19] This feature of the common law tradition is just as evident outside the English jurisdiction. In *R* v. *Toohey; ex p. Meneling Station Pty. Ltd.* (1982) 158 CLR 327 at 342–3, the High Court of Australia declared a statutory grazing licence to constitute a mere personal right and no proprietary 'estate or interest' in land, emphasizing the extraordinary fragility of the licence in question. In so far as it was liable to summary cancellation and conferred no right on the licensee to effect improvements on the land without permission, the licence failed to resonate with the plenitude of possessory control which characterizes the notion of property in land. See also *Koowarta* v. *Bjelke-Petersen* (1982) 153 CLR 168 at 184 ('property' held not to include 'a right to mere possession under a licence to occupy').

[20] 'Exclusive possession de jure or de facto, now or in the future, is the bedrock of English land law' (*Hunter* v. *Canary Wharf Ltd.* [1997] 2 WLR 684, *per* Lord Hoffmann at 706B). See also Windeyer J's classic reference to exclusive possession as 'the proper touchstone' of a lease or tenancy (*Radaich* v. *Smith* (1959) 101 CLR 209 at 223).

[21] *Thompson* v. *Ward* (1871) LR 6 CP 327, *per* Bovill CJ at 361. Other early legal definitions of the term 'lodger' similarly emphasize the idea that lodgers 'submit themselves to [the owner's] control' (*Ancketill* v. *Baylis* (1882) 10 QBD 577 at 586). See also *Bradley* v. *Baylis* (1881) 8 QBD 195 at 219. Significantly, in *Street* v. *Mountford* [1985] AC 809 at 817H–818D, the House of Lords invoked this wealth of nineteenth century 'lodger' jurisprudence to illuminate the essence of leasehold tenure.

[22] [1985] AC 809 at 818A.

[23] *Antoniades* v. *Villiers* [1990] 1 AC 417, *per* Lord Templeman at 459F–G.

destiny: he is accredited with the quantum of property which corresponds most closely to the quality of his own behaviour. Estate ownership is thus self-determining and self-righting. Both the freehold and the leasehold estates are marked out by a distinctive degree of overall territorial control[24] and by a general immunity from uncontracted supervisory regulation.[25] Both estates imply extensive rights of quiet and exclusive enjoyment,[26] and the *de facto* assertion of such rights by an occupier tends to confirm the presence of a proprietary estate in this person.[27]

It is on this basis that 'exclusive and unrestricted use of a piece of land' generally connotes a claim to either a freehold[28] or a leasehold[29] estate rather than any claim of mere easement.[30] In *Copeland v. Greenhalf*,[31] for example, the wheelwright who littered an extensive strip of another's land with motor vehicles and junk metal was presumed to be asserting an ownership in fee simple, since his was 'virtually a claim to possession of the servient tenement, if necessary to the exclusion of the owner.'[32] Likewise,

[24] The right to exclude strangers is a 'fundamental element of the property right' (*Kaiser Aetna v. United States*, 444 US 164, *per* Rehnquist J at 179–80 (1979)) and 'traditionally . . . one of the most treasured strands in an owner's bundle of property rights' (*Loretto v. Teleprompter Manhattan CATV Corp.*, 458 US 419, *per* Marshall J at 435 (1982)). See also *Entick v. Carrington* (1765) 19 Howell's State Trials 1029 at 1066; *Gerhardy v. Brown* (1985) 159 CLR 70 at 150.

[25] Thus, in *Westminster CC v. Clarke* [1992] 2 AC 288 at 301H–302A, the House of Lords denied that a tenancy might be claimed by an occupant of a room in a council-run hostel for homeless persons. The council's detailed control over and intimate surveillance of all activities on the premises was held to be inconsistent with the assertion of any proprietary estate. See also *Guppys (Bridport) Ltd. v. Brookling* (1984) 269 EG 846 at 850.

[26] Thus, for instance, the leaseholder may 'keep out strangers and keep out the landlord unless the landlord is exercising limited rights reserved to him by the tenancy agreement to enter and view and repair' (*Street v. Mountford* [1985] AC 809, *per* Lord Templeman at 816C).

[27] Even an express documentary denial or qualification of a particular occupier's exclusive possession may, paradoxically, indicate this degree of possessory control to have been an intrinsic (and possibly irreducible) attribute of the occupancy in question (see *Goldsworthy Mining Ltd. v. Federal Commissioner of Taxation* (1973) 128 CLR 199, *per* Mason J at 213; *Wik Peoples v. Queensland* (1996) 187 CLR 1, *per* Brennan CJ at 73, *per* Toohey J at 117).

[28] *Reilly v. Booth* (1890) 44 Ch. D. 12, *per* Lopes LJ at 26. See also *Metropolitan Railway Co. v. Fowler* [1892] 1 QB 165 at 175. The conveyance of rights of exclusive user even over a defined quantum of air space constitutes a freehold grant rather than any easement (see *Bursill Enterprises Pty. Ltd. v. Berger Bros. Trading Co. Pty. Ltd.* (1971) 124 CLR 73 at 91; *Tileska v. Bevelon* (1989) 4 BPR 9601 at 9606).

[29] See *Wik Peoples v. Queensland* (1996) 187 CLR 1, *per* Toohey J at 116 ('the point is not so much that a "lease" confers exclusive possession; it is that the conferring of exclusive possession is an indication that the arrangement in question is a lease').

[30] In proper cases the courts may reclassify a right as an easement irrespective of the precise label accorded by grantor and grantee (see *Riley v. Penttila* [1974] VR 547 at 560).

[31] [1952] Ch. 488 at 498.

[32] See also *Ward v. Kirkland* [1967] Ch. 194 at 223E; *Grigsby v. Melville* [1972] 1 WLR 1355, [1974] 1 WLR 80; *Harada v. Registrar of Titles* [1981] VR 743 at 753.

a water company's installation of a sewer in privately owned land invests the company as a freeholder with 'the absolute property in the sewer (the whole of the space occupied by the sewer)'.[33] Indeed, the distinction between fee simple and easement has been said to turn on whether a disputed grant of user rights so derogates from the totality of the grantor's rights that the grantee is left 'free to act as if [he] were the owner of the freehold.'[34] Accordingly user of a right of way merely as a means of non-exclusive passage and re-passage over another's land may qualify as a valid easement, but not the much more extensive claim to utilize the way as a parking lot.[35]

The constitutive effect of empirical fact is also evident in other contexts. In delineating, for example, the borderline between the lease and the licence, courts are now accustomed to direct their attention towards the 'factual matrix and genesis'[36] of any written occupancy agreement.[37] Attention must be paid 'to the facts and surrounding circumstances and to what people do as well as to what people say'.[38] In seeking out 'the substance and reality of the transaction',[39] the courts effectively ensure that 'where the language of licence contradicts the reality of lease, the facts must prevail.'[40] The courts are, therefore, empowered to overturn any superficial label which falsely describes the parties' legal relationship,[41] and any contractual terms which are blatantly or cynically inconsistent with the reasonably practical circumstances of an agreed occupancy are liable to be discarded as 'pro non scripto'.[42]

---

[33] *Taylor* v. *North West Water* (1995) 70 P & CR 94 at 107.

[34] *Mercantile General Life Reassurance Co. of Australia Ltd.* v. *Permanent Trustee Australia Ltd.* (1989) NSW Conv. R. 55–441, *per* Powell J at 58, 211.

[35] See *Keefer* v. *Arillotta* (1977) 72 DLR (3d) 182 at 189. In some circumstances the right to park a car may be validly created as an easement so long as the rights claimed do not amount to an arrogation of exclusive beneficial user of the entire servient tenement, thereby depriving the servient owner of 'any reasonable use of his land, whether for parking or anything else' (*London & Blenheim Estates Ltd.* v. *Ladbroke Retail Parks Ltd.* [1992] 1 WLR 1278 at 1288C).

[36] *Crancour Ltd.* v. *Da Silvaesa* (1986) 52 P & CR 204, *per* Purchas LJ at 229.

[37] The parties' conduct subsequent to the date of their agreement is highly relevant as to 'whether the documents were or were not genuine documents giving effect to the parties' true intentions' (*Antoniades* v. *Villiers* [1990] 1 AC 417, *per* Lord Oliver of Aylmerton at 469C, *per* Lord Jauncey of Tullichettle at 475F).

[38] *Antoniades* v. *Villiers* [1990] 1 AC 417, *per* Lord Templeman at 463H–464A.

[39] Ibid., *per* Lord Ackner at 466C.

[40] Ibid., *per* Lord Templeman at 463C. Any element of 'pretence' detected in this process is severable from the agreement as 'obviously inconsistent with the realities of the situation' (*Hadjiloucas* v. *Crean* [1988] 1 WLR 1006, *per* Mustill LJ at 1023H–1024A).

[41] 'A cat does not become a dog because the parties have agreed to call it a dog' (*Antoniades* v. *Villiers* [1990] 1 AC 417, *per* Bingham LJ at 444B). See also *Street* v. *Mountford* [1985] AC 809, *per* Lord Templeman at 819E–F.

[42] *Antoniades* v. *Villiers* [1990] 1 AC 417, *per* Lord Jauncey of Tullichettle at 477A.

The primarily factual orientation of this perspective has been borne out in a number of cases where the courts have castigated as mere 'pretence'[43] a range of unrealistic or improbable terms aimed at disabling any proprietary claim on the part of the occupier. Accordingly effect is denied, for instance, to bizarre contractual terms, never enforced in practice, which require a 'licensee' to vacate his rented room every day between 10.30 a.m. and midday[44] or to allow a 'licensor' at any time to use impossibly cramped premises in common with a young cohabiting couple 'and such other licensees or invitees as the licensor may permit from time to time to use the said rooms'.[45] In such circumstances the superficial denial of the occupiers' overall territorial control is amply falsified by the actual behaviour of the parties.[46]

Nowhere is the self-defining quality of property as an empirical fact more clearly demonstrated than in the law of adverse possession of land. Here, irrespective of the state of the proprietorship register or concurrent paper ownership, the fact of uncontested long possession eventually confers an impregnable title upon the actual occupier.[47] English law presumes that any person in possession of land has a fee simple estate in the land[48] unless and until the contrary is shown.[49] Possession of land, even if tortiously acquired,[50] immediately generates a 'property' in the land which, if unchallenged for the duration of the legally stipulated limitation period,[51] conclusively bars all prior rights of recovery.[52] Title to land being essentially relative, the law of adverse possession accordingly endorses an uncompen-

---

[43] See *Antoniades* v. *Villiers* [1990] 1 AC 417, *per* Lord Templeman at 462H.

[44] *Aslan* v. *Murphy (No. 1)* [1990] 1 WLR 766 at 772H–773A. See also *Crancour Ltd.* v. *Da Silvaesa* (1986) 52 P & CR 204 at 215, 224.

[45] *Antoniades* v. *Villiers* [1990] 1 AC 417 at 463E.

[46] As Lord Jauncey of Tullichettle observed in *Antoniades* v. *Villiers* [1990] 1 AC 417 at 476D–E, the 'common user' clause, read literally, would have permitted an unlimited number of strangers to share the flat with the young couple 'even to the extent of sharing the joys of the double bed'.

[47] *Buckinghamshire CC* v. *Moran* [1990] Ch. 623, *per* Nourse LJ at 644B–C.

[48] *Peaceable d. Uncle* v. *Watson* (1811) 4 Taunt. 16 at 17, 128 ER 232.

[49] 'Possession is good against all the world except the person who can shew a good title' (*Asher* v. *Whitlock* (1865) LR 1 QB 1, *per* Cockburn CJ at 5).

[50] 'Every fee simple is not legitimum' (Coke, *The First Part of the Institutes of the Laws of England (Co. Litt.)* (11th edn., London, 1719), 2a). See also *Leach* v. *Jay* (1878) 9 Ch. D. 42 at 45; *Newington* v. *Windeyer* (1985) 3 NSWLR 555 at 563E; *Buckinghamshire CC* v. *Moran* [1990] Ch. 623 at 644D; *Mabo* v. *Queensland (No. 2)* (1992) 175 CLR 1 at 209.

[51] The normal limitation period is statutorily fixed as twelve years (Limitation Act 1980, s. 15(1)).

[52] See *Mabo* v. *Queensland (No. 2)* (1992) 175 CLR 1, *per* Toohey J at 211. Long possession thus matures a wrong into a right (see *Buckinghamshire CC* v. *Moran* [1990] Ch. 623, *per* Nourse LJ at 644C–D), but, even before the squatter's title finally becomes unchallengeable, he acquires ancillary rights to defend his possession against strangers and to sell or devise his possessory fee simple interest (see *Asher* v. *Whitlock* (1865) LR 1 QB 1 at 6–7; *Newington* v. *Windeyer* (1985) 3 NSWLR 555 at 563F).

sated shift of economic value to the squatter or interloper 'in the interests of peace'.[53] Such a compromise operates to ensure that property in land conforms to the lived boundaries rather than the reverse; and in this way the long possession rule incorporates a controlled trade-off between documentary title and pragmatic fact which serves to avert endless and costly controversy.

Even in this context, however, the possessory control which activates the Limitation Act bears a significantly qualified meaning: the concept of 'possession' is an amalgam of externally verifiable physical and mental phenomena. 'Possession' can be attributed to the squatter (and time can run in his favour) only if he has both factual possession (a *factum possessionis*) and the requisite intention to possess (*animus possidendi*).[54] The *factum* of possession depends upon a showing that the claimant has asserted a 'complete and exclusive physical control'[55] over the land in question; and such evidence of *factum* must always be coupled with proof in the claimant of 'an intention for the time being to possess the land to the exclusion of all other persons, including the owner with the paper title'.[56]

In this connection a survey of the physical facts relating to land can be heavily definitive of title. Should a squatter apply to register his title on the basis of adverse possession,[57] it is the practice of the Land Registry to instruct a surveyor to inspect the land in question. The surveyor records the exact position on site of physical boundary features such as fences and hedges; he estimates the age of these features; he reports on the way in which access to the land is obtained and controlled and on the person who appears to be in actual occupation; and he describes the use being made of the land by the squatter. The duration of the squatter's occupation, its exclusivity, and the acts of user relied upon are thus subjected to empirical verification; and prior to inspection of the land the squatter will have been required to establish by statutory declaration the facts on which his claim is based and his intention in taking control of and making use of the land.

[53] *Minister of State for the Army* v. *Dalziel* (1944) 68 CLR 261, *per* Latham CJ at 276. It is perhaps worth noting that the areas of land involved in contemporary claims of long possession are rarely large tracts of uncharted wilderness but more commonly comprise a tiny slice of realty abstracted by mistake—usually through inaccurate fencing—from the tenement of a neighbour.

[54] *Powell* v. *McFarlane* (1977) 38 P & CR 452, *per* Slade J at 470; *Buckinghamshire CC* v. *Moran* [1990] Ch. 623, *per* Slade LJ at 636B–C.

[55] Ibid., *per* Slade LJ at 641B. Although the intensity of this control must vary with different kinds of terrain, it must be shown that 'the alleged possessor has been dealing with the land in question as an occupying owner might have been expected to deal with it and that no-one else has done so' (*Powell* v. *McFarlane* (1977) 38 P & CR 452 at 471).

[56] *Buckinghamshire CC* v. *Moran* [1990] Ch. 623, *per* Slade LJ at 643E. See also *Powell* v. *McFarlane* (1977) 38 P & CR 452 at 471–2.

[57] Land Registration Act 1925, s. 75(2).

In a rather different context, further confirmation of the ultimately undeniable quality of empirically constituted property emerges from contemporary experience relating to native land rights in Australia. Here controversy
has centred on the current legal status of the customary rights of aboriginal
peoples to roam and forage over traditional tracts of country. These rights,
although scarcely expressible in terms of the common law doctrine of
estates and interests in land, had been enjoyed for countless centuries prior
to the arrival of European settlers. The Aboriginal's intimate nexus with his
land has often been characterized in terms of a 'spiritual, cultural and social
identity'[58] with the terrain, finding its highest fulfilment in the performance
of a duty to 'look after country'. Aboriginal ownership, said Brennan J in
R. v. Toohey; ex p. Meneling Station Pty. Ltd.,[59] is 'primarily a spiritual affair
rather than a bundle of rights'. Until relatively recently, however, courts
tended firmly to deny the proprietary quality of the Aboriginal's usufructu-
ary relationship with his traditional lands,[60] taking the view that all native
title had been extinguished in any event by the assumption of Crown
sovereignty over lands then considered as unowned or *terra nullius*.

In *Mabo v. Queensland (No. 2)* the High Court of Australia was finally
forced to recognize the impossibility of declaring that, after tens of thousands of years of occupancy, the Aboriginal peoples of Australia were mere
'trespassers on the land on which they and their ancestors had lived'[61] and
had been converted by European colonization into 'intruders in their own
homes and mendicants for a place to live'.[62] It is now acknowledged that
native or traditional land rights survived the Crown's acquisition of sovereign or radical title[63] and may not necessarily have been extinguished even
by subsequent Crown grants of leasehold titles to incoming settlers.[64]
Brennan J (later Chief Justice of Australia) declined to believe that the
indigenous inhabitants of a settled colony lost all 'proprietary interest' in the
land which they continued to occupy[65] or could 'lawfully have been driven into the sea at any time after annexation'.[66] For Brennan J, 'a community which asserts and asserts effectively that none but its members has any
right to occupy or use the land has an interest in the land that must be pro-

---

[58] *Gerhardy v. Brown* (1985) 159 CLR 70, *per* Brennan J at 136.

[59] (1982) 158 CLR 327 at 358.

[60] See *Milirrpum v. Nabalco Pty. Ltd.* (1971) 17 FLR 141 at 269–71, where Blackburn J
expressly dismissed evidence that the aboriginal claimants 'think and speak of the land as
being theirs' as merely connoting that they 'think and speak of the land as being in a very
close relationship to them'. For Blackburn J, it was 'easier . . . to say that the clan belongs to
the land than that the land belongs to the clan'.

[61] (1992) 175 CLR 1, *per* Toohey J at 184.   [62] Ibid., *per* Brennan J at 29.

[63] A similar view has been taken by the Supreme Court of Canada in *R v. Côté* (1996)
138 DLR (4th) 385.

[64] *Wik Peoples v. Queensland* (1996) 187 CLR 1.

[65] *Mabo v. Queensland (No. 2)* (1992) 175 CLR 1 at 40.   [66] (1992) 175 CLR 1 at 66.

prietary in nature: there is no other proprietor . . . The ownership of land within a territory in the exclusive occupation of a people must be vested in that people.'[67] Accordingly Brennan J accepted—and it is now widely agreed to be clear law[68]—that the customary land claims of Aboriginals comprise a 'proprietary community title' which represents 'a burden on the Crown's radical title' even after the assumption of Crown sovereignty over the territory in question.[69]

Property as a Right

The foregoing analysis of the law of real property has concentrated on property in land as a perception of socially constituted fact. A rather different—and not entirely consistent—focus is provided by the competing assessment of property in land as comprising various assortments of artificially defined jural right.[70] On this view, the law of real property becomes distanced from the physical reality of land and enters a world of conceptual—indeed some would say virtually mathematical—abstraction.[71] In sharp contrast to the crudely empirical foundations of property as a fact, the vision of property as a right rests upon a complex calculus of carefully calibrated 'estates' and 'interests' in land, all underpinned by the political theory implicit in the doctrine of tenure.[72] All property relationships with land are, accordingly, analysed at one remove—through the intermediacy of an estate or interest in land. No citizen can claim that he or she owns the physical *solum*, merely that he or she owns some unitary jural right in or over that *solum*. One has 'property' in an abstract right rather than 'property' in a physical thing.

There is indeed much in English land law to support the characterization of property as composite bundles of incorporeal right. Here, however, an important distinction must be drawn between the Crown's ultimate or

---

[67] Ibid., at 51.   [68] See *Wik Peoples* v. *Queensland* (1996) 187 CLR 1 at 214.

[69] See now Native Title Act 1993. For a similar approach in Canada, see *R.* v. *Van der Peet* (1996) 137 DLR (4th) 289, *per* McLachlin J at 382.

[70] 'Property, in relation to land, is a bundle of rights exercisable with respect to the land' (*Minister of State for the Army* v. *Dalziel* (1944) 68 CLR 261, *per* Rich J at 285).

[71] The intellectual constructs of land law move 'in a world of pure ideas from which everything physical or material is entirely excluded' (see Lawson, *The Rational Strength of the English Law* (London: Oxford University Press, 1951), 79).

[72] At one level the distinction between property as a fact and property as a right can seem merely a difference of emphasis; as indicated earlier, these two perceptions of proprietary essence are subtly interrelated. For instance, in the law of adverse possession, property, established as a fact, is deemed to generate property as a right. In other contexts (such as those involving an express grant of rights), it is the right which ordinarily generates the fact. The threshold question is, however, whether property is conceived *primarily* in predetermined categories of abstract right or as the raw emanation of socially constituted fact. Which is the more potent proprietary trigger—artificially defined grant or essentially undeniable fact?

'radical' title to all land and the proprietary estates or interests which may be parcelled out amongst the subjects of the Crown. The Crown's 'radical' title has been described as 'a postulate of the doctrine of tenure and a concomitant of sovereignty'.[73] This radical title is simply a brute emanation of the sovereign power acquired through physical conquest.[74] It denotes the political authority of the Crown both to grant interests in the land to be held of the Crown and also to prescribe the residue of unalienated land as the sovereign's beneficial demesne. The Crown's radical title is, in truth, no proprietary title at all,[75] but merely an expression of the *Realpolitik* which served historically to hold together the theory of tenure.[76] Under the tenurial system of tiered or hierarchical landholding, all land in England (save unalienated Crown land) was held, in relationships of reciprocal obligation,[77] either mediately or immediately of the Crown. It remains the case even today that no subject can own lands allodially[78]—that is, outside the tenurial scheme of things—although all tenures have now been commuted to a uniform 'socage tenure' directly from the Crown.[79]

It was left to the doctrine of estates to quantify the grades of abstract entitlement which might be enjoyed by any particular tenant (or landholder)

---

[73] *Mabo* v. *Queensland (No. 2)* (1992) 175 CLR 1, *per* Brennan J at 48.

[74] 'Radical title links international and constitutional law notions with those which support the private law of proprietary rights and interests in land' (*Wik Peoples* v. *Queensland* (1996) 187 CLR 1, *per* Gummow J at 186). For reference to the 'uncannily parallel' notions of state sovereignty and private property, see Gray, 'Property in Thin Air', [1991] CLJ 252 at 304; 'The Ambivalence of Property', in Prins (ed.), *Threats without Enemies* (London: Earthscan Publications, 1993), 169.

[75] It is significant, for instance, that the ancient Crown lands still cannot be registered as freehold titles under the Land Registration Act 1925—'a major, but unremarked, lacuna in the system of land registration in England and Wales' (*Scmlla Properties Ltd.* v. *Gesso Properties (BVI) Ltd.* [1995] BCC 793 at 798). The Crown cannot hold land of itself; and the Land Registry is empowered to register title only to 'estates' in 'land', the latter term statutorily requiring the existence of 'tenure' (see Land Registration Act 1925, ss. 2(1), 3(viii)).

[76] There is a danger that the location of radical title in the Crown may prompt the inaccurate suggestion that 'ownership' of all land reposes in the Crown or that the Crown is the only true 'owner' of land in England and Wales. This extrapolation from radical title to a concept of Crown 'ownership' is almost certainly a modern innovation, dating (significantly) only from the era of imperial expansion in the seventeenth and eighteenth centuries (*Wik Peoples* v. *Queensland* (1996) 187 CLR 1, *per* Gummow J at 186–7). See also Simpson, *A History of the Land Law* (2nd edn., Oxford: Oxford University Press, 1986; repr. 1996), 47–8.

[77] 'In an understanding of these relationships . . . "proprietary language is out of place" ' (see *Wik Peoples* v. *Queensland* (1996) 187 CLR 1, *per* Gummow J at 186, quoting Milsom, *The Legal Framework of English Feudalism* (Cambridge: Cambridge University Press, 1976), 39).

[78] *Minister of State for the Army* v. *Dalziel* (1944) 68 CLR 261, *per* Latham CJ at 277.

[79] See Law of Property Act 1922, s. 128, Sch. 12, para. 1. All tenants in fee simple are today presumed to hold directly of the Crown as 'tenants in chief'. In consequence, where a fee simple is terminated by disclaimer, it is generally safe to assume that the escheat will be to the Crown rather than to some mesne (or intermediate) lord (see *Scmlla Properties Ltd.* v. *Gesso Properties (BVI) Ltd.* [1995] BCC 793 at 799).

within the tenurial framework. This doctrine spelt out a rich taxonomy of 'estates' in the land, each estate representing an artificial proprietary construct interposed between the tenant and the physical object of his tenure. Each tenant owned (and still owns) not land but an *estate* in land.[80] The precise nature of the estate was graded by its temporal duration and by the possible attachment of variegated conditions precedent or subsequent. Each common law estate—whether the fee simple, the fee tail, or the life estate—comprised a time-related segment of the bundle of rights and powers exercisable over land; and the doctrine of estates effectively provided diverse ways in which three-dimensional realty might be carved up in a fourth dimension of time.[81]

In the form of the common law estates, English land law thus comprised, from the earliest times, a field of highly manipulable abstract constructs which conferred enormous flexibility in the management of wealth. Of these proprietary rights in land, the amplest was, of course, the fee simple, an estate of potentially unlimited duration which still confers 'the widest powers of enjoyment in respect of all the advantages to be derived from the land itself and from anything found on it'.[82] Even in relation to this estate, however, it is significant that the effect of disclaimer[83] or other escheat is to terminate the freehold and to return the relevant land to the Crown.[84] Thus the implosion of the largest common law estate simply revests the land within the allodium of the Crown,[85] in rather the same way in which a lease for years falls in for the lessor on the expiration of the term granted.

In general it can be said that the substitution of the abstract estate in land (in place of land itself) as the object of proprietary rights has had the

---

[80] *Minister of State for the Army* v. *Dalziel* (1944) 68 CLR 261, *per* Latham CJ at 277. 'The "estate" which a subject held in land as tenant was itself property which was the subject of "ownership" both in law and in equity' (*Mabo* v. *Queensland (No. 2)* (1992) 175 CLR 1, *per* Deane and Gaudron JJ at 80).

[81] As was argued so elegantly in *Walsingham's Case* (1573) 2 Plowd. 547 at 555, 75 ER 805 at 816–17, 'the land itself is one thing, and the estate in the land is another thing, for an estate in the land is a time in the land, or land for a time, and there are diversities of estates, which are no more than diversities of time . . .'.

[82] *Wik Peoples* v. *Queensland* (1996) 187 CLR 1, *per* Gummow J at 176. In so far as real property represents a 'bundle of rights' exercisable with respect to the land, 'the tenant of an unencumbered estate in fee simple has the largest possible bundle' (see *Minister of State for the Army* v. *Dalziel* (1944) 68 CLR 261, *per* Rich J at 285).

[83] Disclaimer occurs with increasing frequency pursuant to Insolvency Act 1986, s. 178(2), which empowers a company liquidator to disclaim 'onerous property' (see *Scmlla Properties Ltd.* v. *Gesso Properties (BVI) Ltd.* [1995] BCC 793 at 805).

[84] See also *Re David James & Co. Ltd.* [1991] 1 NZLR 219 at 223–4; *Rural Banking and Finance Corpn. of New Zealand Ltd.* v. *Official Assignee* [1991] 2 NZLR 351 at 356.

[85] The freehold title 'goes back to the Crown on the principle that all freehold estate originally came from the Crown, and that where there is no one entitled to the freehold estate by law it reverts to the Crown' (*Re Mercer and Moore* (1880) 14 Ch. D. 287, *per* Jessel MR at 295).

profoundest influence on English law. Historically this conceptual leger-demain has facilitated almost endless disaggregations of title through grants of series of differentially graded estates in land. Thus each successive inter-est could enjoy an immediate jural reality as of the date of grant, each being freely commerciable (i.e. mortgageable) long before the estate in question vested in possession. Indeed, the ingenious compromise of the doctrine of estates often seemed to provide a functional, and theoretically acceptable, form of substituted ownership in respect of the all-important resource of land.[86]

Today the taxonomy of the common law estates is still largely preserved in the property legislation of 1925, although with necessary modifications and additions.[87] The fee simple absolute in possession remains as the pri-mary estate in English law and is now joined as a legal estate by the term of years absolute.[88] Admittedly the fragmentation of title through the grant of successive estates and interests has become—for reasons both fiscal and social—rather less common, but the old estates of the common law survive albeit more often in equitable than in legal form.[89] In conjunction with this group of abstract proprietary constructs the 1925 Act confirms the existence of a range of other interests and charges (such as easements, mortgages, rights of entry, estate contracts, and interests under trust) which are vari-ously capable of being held either at law or in equity or indiscriminately.[90] Thus the 1925 legislation seeks to maintain consistently the dogma that landownership and use are mediated by the distribution, not of land as such, but of intangible jural entitlements interposed between persons and land. The perspective embraced by the statutory schema is of property as a right, precisely on the footing that the only property one can have is *in* a right.

Yet English land law remains inevitably a curious blend of the concep-tual and the pragmatic, the cerebral and the material. Certainly, the con-ceptual purity of systematically ordered estates and interests provides an intellectual base for the rational manipulation of axiomatic truths and for the multiple applications of propositional dogma so familiar to the student. But even the austere regime of the 1925 property legislation contains its

---

[86] See Kirby J's recent reference to the fee simple as the 'local equivalent of full owner-ship' (*Wik Peoples* v. *Queensland* (1996) 187 CLR 1 at 250). See also *Mabo* v. *Queensland (No. 2)* (1992) 175 CLR 1, *per* Deane and Gaudron JJ at 80).

[87] Indeed the scheme of title registration contained in the Land Registration Act 1925 is actually premised on the intellectual construct of the estate (see Land Registration Act 1925, s. 2(1)).

[88] Law of Property Act 1925, s. 1(1).

[89] See Law of Property Act 1925, ss. 1(3), (8), 7(1). Being relegated to equitable status only, the life estate, the fee tail, and all fee simple estates other than the absolute and condi-tional are capable of creation—if at all—only under a statutorily regulated 'trust of land' (Trusts of Land and Appointment of Trustees Act 1996, s. 2(1)).

[90] Law of Property Act 1925, s. 1(2), (3).

share of mongrelized ideas, convenient adaptations, and internal contradictions. English land law reveals, for instance, an intermittent tendency to conflate property as fact with property as right, as evidenced by the way in which statutory definitions of 'land' are expressly fashioned to include 'an easement, right, privilege, or benefit in, over, or derived from land'.[91] This reification of intangible entitlement—a frequent feature of the common law mind-set—brings about the result that appurtenant easements become notionally affixed to their dominant tenement rather as fixtures become annexed to realty,[92] their benefit passing with any subsequent conveyance or transfer of the relevant land.[93]

Similar fusions of the abstract and the material appear elsewhere. A landlord's reversionary estate is deemed to constitute a notional dominant tenement sufficient to permit the enforcement of restrictive covenants against a subtenant,[94] even though the term 'dominant tenement' is understood in most other contexts to connote a quite specific plot of physical land. Again, the doctrine of 'lost modern grant', which presumes the prescriptive acquisition of an easement following continuous user as of right for a period of twenty years, embodies a glaring juxtaposition of empirically founded and right-based notions of property in land. Here the sheer fact of long user provides the basis for a 'convenient and workable fiction'[95] that some incorporeal right of easement was once the subject of a formal grant which has since been misplaced and lost.[96]

Irrespective of this kind of inconsistency, it is clear that other, perhaps far-reaching, consequences follow where the property perspective focuses on artificial jural abstractions rather than on physically verifiable phenomena. In the absence of more empirical forms of identification, a premium is immediately placed on the maintenance of strict definitional boundaries around the various intellectual constructs which form part of the overall scheme. Thus the intangible character of property entitlements dramatically intensifies the need for rigorous conceptual clarity, a feature which tends in turn to reinforce the apparent absoluteness of the abstract rights concerned. 'Property' must have a clear-cut or crystalline quality which admits of no doubt either as to its presence or, just as important, as to its absence or infringement. The rights to which 'property' relates must have a hard-edged definitional integrity conducive to the intellectual orderliness of the

---

[91] Law of Property Act 1925, s. 205(1)(ix); Land Registration Act 1925, s. 3(viii).

[92] Law of Property Act 1925, s. 187(1).

[93] Law of Property Act 1925, s. 62(1). See also Land Registration Rules 1925, r. 251.

[94] *Hall* v. *Ewin* (1888) 37 Ch. D. 74 at 79; *Teape* v. *Douse* (1905) 92 LT 319 at 320; *Wik Peoples* v. *Queensland* (1996) 187 CLR 1 at 94.

[95] *Simmons* v. *Dobson* [1991] 1 WLR 720, *per* Fox LJ at 723B.

[96] See *Bryant* v. *Foot* (1867) LR 2 QB 161 at 181; *Dalton* v. *Angus & Co.* (1881) 6 App. Cas. 740 at 811–12.

regime as a whole. 'Property' must come in neat, discrete, pre-packaged conceptual compartments, immune from capricious tampering or even well-intentioned amplification.[97]

This preoccupation with definitional rigour is a consistent theme of English property law. In *National Provincial Bank Ltd.* v. *Ainsworth*,[98] in one of the most indicative passages of legal prose contained in the law reports, Lord Wilberforce famously declared that, before a right or interest can be admitted into the 'category of property, or of a right affecting property', it must be 'definable, identifiable by third parties, capable in its nature of assumption by third parties, and have some degree of permanence or stability'. A striking demonstration of this concern with discrete definition occurred in the relatively recent reaffirmation of the 'certainty of term' requirement in the law of leases. In *Prudential Assurance Co. Ltd.* v. *London Residuary Body*[99] the House of Lords declined to overrule a 500-year-old principle that the maximum duration of a term of years must be ascertainable at the commencement of the lease. Although the decision was in many ways reached against its better judgment,[100] the House nevertheless endorsed the historic view that the conceptual parameters of asset entitlement must be definable with certainty *ab initio*.[101] Open-endedness of definition would otherwise destroy the intrinsic orderliness of the common-law estates by confusing the term of years with the one perpetual estate recognized by the common law, the estate in fee simple.

A similar concern with definitional boundaries is evident in the law of servitudes. English law has traditionally been concerned to draw stringent limits around the species of right which may properly be asserted as easements and negative covenants. The result has been the general imposition of rigorous requirements that incorporeal rights properly classifiable as servitudes should relate to ascertainable dominant and servient tenements and should confer a demonstrable element of 'accommodation', 'protection', or 'benefit' upon the alleged dominant tenement.[102] Moreover,

---

[97] 'It is not in the power of a vendor to create any rights not connected with the use or enjoyment of the land, and annex them to it: nor can the owner of land render it subject to a new species of burthen, so as to bind it in the hands of an assignee. "Incidents of a novel kind cannot be devised, and attached to property, at the fancy or caprice of any owner" ' (*Ackroyd* v. *Smith* (1850) 10 CB 164 at 188, 138 ER 68, *per* Cresswell J at 77–8, quoting *Keppell* v. *Bailey* (1834) 2 My. & K 517 at 535, 39 ER 1042 at 1049).

[98] [1965] AC 1175 at 1247G–1248A.

[99] [1992] 2 AC 386 at 394E–H, confirming *Lace* v. *Chantler* [1944] KB 368.

[100] [1992] 2 AC 386, *per* Lord Griffiths at 396B, *per* Lord Browne-Wilkinson at 396G–397A, *per* Lord Mustill at 397B.

[101] Otherwise 'the court does not know what to enforce' (*Ashburn Anstalt* v. *Arnold* [1989] Ch. 1, *per* Fox LJ at 12E).

[102] See Gray, *Elements of Land Law* (2nd edn., London: Butterworths, 1993), 1065–9, 1143–7.

considerations of marketability, justiciability, and enforceability have alike combined to force the categoric exclusion of any user rights which are loose, over broad, or ill defined.[103] This definitional vigilance has been particularly apparent, for example, in relation to the law of easements. No right may be asserted as an easement if it is 'too vague and too indefinite'.[104] Thus there can be no easement in respect of a prospect or view.[105] Likewise there can be no claim of easement in relation to the uninterrupted access of light or air except through defined apertures in a building.[106] No easement can protect the unimpeded and general flow of air across one's neighbour's land for the purpose of preventing chimneys from smoking.[107] There is no easement of indefinite privacy;[108] nor does English law recognize as an easement any claim to wander at will over another's land.[109]

In conventional theory such tight definitional constrictions have served to distinguish and delimit the kinds of right which, unlike mere licences and contracts, have the capacity to affect later purchasers of land. The imposition of severely limiting criteria has thus been rationalized as necessary to prevent the proliferation of undesirable long-term burdens or 'clogs upon title' which would have sterilized land by rendering it unmarketable. Nowadays, however, it is far from clear that the restrictive definition of servitudes has any particularly beneficial effect: the admission of broader categories of utility and prohibition within the definition of allowable servitudes might well enhance the enjoyment of land in a crowded environment, promoting rather than inhibiting the character of a locality and its consequent attractiveness on the open market.

In reality the argument for conceptual discreteness in the law of servitudes tends to conceal, just as effectively today as it did over a century ago, that the crucial issue at stake is often the permissible boundary of entrepreneurial initiative in the exploitation and development of land resources. In rejecting any easement of wind access for a windmill in 1861, Erle CJ observed that such a claim would 'operate as a prohibition to a most

---

[103] See e.g. *Webb* v. *Bird* (1861) 10 CB (NS) 268, *per* Erle CJ at 282, 142 ER 455 at 460 ('I am at a loss to conceive what would be an interruption of such a right as is claimed here').

[104] *Harris* v. *De Pinna* (1886) 33 Ch. D. 238, *per* Chitty J at 250. See also *Copeland* v. *Greenhalf* [1952] Ch. 488 at 498 (where Upjohn J could find no authority in support of the idea that 'a right of this wide and undefined nature can be the proper subject-matter of an easement').

[105] *William Aldred's Case* (1610) 9 Co. Rep. 57b at 58b, 77 ER 816 at 821; *Hunter* v. *Canary Wharf Ltd.* [1997] 2 WLR 684 at 702B, 711B–H, 727F–G.

[106] See *Harris* v. *De Pinna* (1886) 33 Ch. D. 238 at 250–1, 262; *Allen* v. *Greenwood* [1980] Ch. 119 at 129C.

[107] *Bryant* v. *Lefever* (1879) 4 CPD 172 at 178, 180.

[108] *Browne* v. *Flower* [1911] 1 Ch. 219 at 225.

[109] *Re Ellenborough Park* [1956] Ch. 131 at 176, 180–4. See also *Attorney-General* v. *Antrobus* [1905] 2 Ch. 188 at 208.

formidable extent to the owners of the adjoining lands—especially in the neghbourhood [sic] of a growing town'.[110] Uncannily similar language was used in 1997 when, in *Hunter v. Canary Wharf Ltd.*,[111] the House of Lords held unactionable the extensive interference with television reception brought about by the recently constructed Canary Wharf Tower. Starting from the premiss of a 'rule of common law which, absent easements, entitles an owner of land to build what he likes on his land',[112] the House of Lords indicated that, just as in the case of disputed access to a prospect or wind and air flow, English law knows no such right as a prescriptive easement to receive a television signal.[113] The House pointed in particular to the indeterminate nature of the amenity supposedly injured,[114] the inordinate range of potentially aggrieved viewers,[115] and the supposedly intolerable restriction otherwise imposed upon the freedom of the commercial developer.[116] The correctness of the outcome may be disputed, but the *Canary Wharf* case clearly suggests that the discreteness of definition accorded to the conceptual abstractions of English land law may well have a critical interface with large issues relating to environmental protection and the quality of urban life in the twenty-first century.

On the less immediate plane of grand analysis, it remains one of the ironies of English law that the concentration on strict definition of crystalline fragments of entitlement has precluded the more general formulation of anything resembling a comprehensive or holistic theory of *dominium* in the continental sense.[117] The tabulation of discrete, but interlocking, estates and interests in land has quietly submerged any call to develop a fuller

---

[110] *Webb* v. *Bird* (1861) 10 CB (NS) 268 at 284, 142 ER 455 at 461.

[111] [1997] 2 WLR 684.

[112] [1997] 2 WLR 684, *per* Lord Hoffmann at 712F. See also *per* Lord Goff of Chieveley at 689A–B, *per* Lord Hope of Craighead at 727B–728A. Cf. Lord Cranworth's proposition in *Tapling* v. *Jones* (1865) 11 HLC 290 at 311, 11 ER 1344 at 1353, that each might 'use his own land by building on it as he thinks most to his interest'.

[113] [1997] 2 WLR 684 at 711H, 721A, 727H.

[114] 'Radio and television signals . . . may come from various directions over a wide area as they cross the developer's property. They may be of various frequencies . . . Their passage from one point to another is invisible . . .' ([1997] 2 WLR 684, *per* Lord Hope of Craighead at 727H).

[115] [1997] 2 WLR 684, *per* Lord Hoffmann at 712G.

[116] [1997] 2 WLR 684, *per* Lord Hope of Craighead at 728A ('If he were to be restricted by an easement from putting up a building which interfered with these signals, he might not be able to put up any substantial structures at all. The interference with his freedom would be substantial'). See also *Phipps* v. *Pears* [1965] 1 QB 76 at 83A.

[117] Civilian systems of property law acknowledge ownership as an absolute jural relationship between a person and a thing. Following Roman law, the great codes of continental law define property in highly abstract terms of *dominium*—the right to enjoy a thing and to dispose of it in the most absolute manner (see *Code civil*, art. 544; *Bürgerliches Gesetzbuch*, para. 903; *Burgerlijk Wetboek*, s. 5:1; Swiss Civil Code, art. 641).

theory of title. Whether this shortcoming can ultimately survive the integration of English law within the emerging common law of Europe must rank as a matter of heightening speculation. Indeed, the single most striking feature of English land law is precisely the absence, within its conceptual apparatus, of overarching notions of *ownership*. The common law knows no absolute title;[118] all title remains relative and, even in its statutory form, essentially defeasible.[119] Accordingly, the common lawyer is fundamentally unable to make abstract pronouncements as to the ownership of land, for the entire methodology of the common law militates against such definitive identification. The common law's crude proprietary technique is restricted to determinations as to which of two claimants of an estate has the better claim. In this sense the common lawyer can never say who owns, but only who does not, albeit that such a ruling tends in practice to leave the preferred claimant with a fee simple title which is at least *pro tempore* unchallengeable.

Other, less obvious but not less significant, implications have gathered around the conceptualization of property as a *right* rather than as a *fact*. During the twentieth century a preoccupation with the supposedly crystalline essence of property rights has conduced to a wholly mistaken theory as to the potential significance of property for third parties. Common lawyers, having once conceived of property in terms of artificially pre-packaged commodities of tightly defined right, found it easy to embrace the seductive fallacy which still pervades the common law understanding of property. 'Property' appeared to comprise those rights which were sufficiently hard-edged and durable to be commerciable and, no less perversely, it seemed to follow that only those rights which could be bought and sold could ever constitute 'property'. In other words, the crisp definitional quality which facilitates the commercial trading of identifiable assets began—in a wholly illusory relationship of cause and effect—to make alienability or transmissibility appear as essential qualifying characteristics or hallmarks of 'property' itself.[120]

---

[118] It is arguably only with the advent of a statutory regime of title registration—particularly on a more comprehensive basis (see Land Registration, England and Wales: The Registration of Title Order 1989 (SI 1989/1347))—that English law begins to recognize anything approaching absolute title in real property. In truth, however, registration of title under the Land Registration Act 1925 provides not so much for recordation of an intrinsically perfect form of ownership but rather for the artificial attribution of a statutorily defined 'absolute title' as a consequence of state-endorsed registration (cf. *Breskvar* v. *Wall* (1971) 126 CLR 376, *per* Barwick CJ at 385, *per* Windeyer J at 400).

[119] See Land Registration Act 1925, s. 82(1).

[120] See e.g. *Dorman* v. *Rodgers* (1982) 148 CLR 365, *per* Gibbs CJ at 367, *per* Stephen J at 369–70, *per* Aickin J at 378. It is relatively rare to find any judicial disclaimer of the proposition that transferability is an essential characteristic of property, but see *Dorman* v. *Rodgers* (1982) 148 CLR 365, *per* Murphy J at 374; *R.* v. *Toohey; ex p. Meneling Station Pty. Ltd.* (1982) 158 CLR 327, *per* Mason J at 342–3.

Nor did the fallacy stop there. In a closely associated *non sequitur*, it came to be believed that, in order to enjoy 'proprietary' as distinct from merely 'personal' quality, rights must be capable of an even more general third-party impact. Not only must rights of property be capable of conferring benefits on third parties through onward sale; their proprietary character was, in turn, reinforced by their potential to impose enforceable burdens on other strangers. Beguiled again by the heavily formative pragmatics of the nineteenth century market place, the common lawyer fell into the lazy confusion that something was 'property' if sufficiently identifiable to burden third parties and, conversely, that the only rights which could adversely affect third parties were rights sufficiently clear-cut and durable to constitute 'property'.[121] Hence emerged the convenient, but wholly mendacious, proposition that asset entitlements comprised 'property' if enforceable against strangers; and such entitlements were, of course, enforceable against strangers provided that they were 'proprietary'.

The absurd circularity of this concentration on assignability of benefit and enforceability of burden is almost too embarrassing to recount,[122] yet its influence has infiltrated even the most exalted levels of common law decision-making. In so far as proprietary character is made to depend upon some supposed quality of 'permanence' or 'stability'—to use the terms adopted by Lord Wilberforce in *National Provincial Bank Ltd.* v. *Ainsworth*[123]—the definition of 'property' becomes patently self-fulfilling. Quite often—as, for instance, with the 'deserted wife's equity' in dispute in *Ainsworth* itself—the reason for asking whether a particular right is *proprietary* is precisely in order to determine whether the right is capable of binding third parties and thereby attaining the relevantly critical qualities of 'permanence' and 'stability'. Proprietary character cannot be credibly or satisfactorily predicated in terms of tautological consequence, although this is exactly the trap induced by the common lawyer's ready disposition to see property as discrete blocks of conceptual entitlement. The initial judgment whether a particular claim is sufficiently hard-edged and durable to rank as property has tended, quite irrationally, to predetermine the question of binding impact on strangers.[124]

---

[121] See Russell LJ's reference in *National Provincial Bank Ltd.* v. *Hastings Car Mart Ltd.* [1964] Ch. 665 at 696 to 'rights in reference to land which have the quality of being capable of enduring through different ownerships of the land, according to normal conceptions of title to real property . . .'.

[122] See, however, *Colbeam Palmer Ltd.* v. *Stock Affiliates Pty. Ltd.* (1968) 122 CLR 25, *per* Windeyer J at 34. See also Gray, 'Property in Thin Air', 292–3.

[123] [1965] AC 1175 at 1247G–1248A.

[124] Exactly this preoccupation with the supposed substantive quality of the disputed right has bedevilled the chequered history of the law of contractual licences. In *Ashburn Anstalt* v. *Arnold* [1989] Ch. 1 at 24D, the Court of Appeal indicated, with heavy emphasis, that 'a contractual licence does not create a property interest'. Yet *Ashburn Anstalt* may ultimately

Lord Wilberforce's proprietary criteria of alienability and enduring impact have often served to stultify emerging, and important, developments in the law—another example coming to the fore in the contemporary recognition of traditional land rights in Australia. Once again it was, significantly, the conceptualization of property in terms of abstract right rather than empirical fact which, for two centuries, disabled the common law from recognizing the proprietary nature of Australian native title. In dealing with aboriginal land claims in *Milirrpum* v. *Nabalco Pty. Ltd.*,[125] Blackburn J had thought that 'property, in its many forms, generally implies . . . the right to alienate'. In view, however, of the Gove Land claimants' express repudiation of any right of alienation, Blackburn J found 'so little resemblance between property, as our law . . . understands that term, and the claims of the plaintiffs for their clans' that these claims could not be considered 'in the nature of proprietary interests'. As already indicated in this chapter, it was only some twenty years later, with the controversial decision of the High Court in *Mabo* v. *Queensland (No. 2)*,[126] that it finally became accepted that Australia's native peoples had not lost all 'proprietary interest' in their traditional homelands.[127] The evidence of pragmatic fact had triumphed over the jurisprudence of abstract entitlement.

During the 1980s and 1990s case law developments across the common law world have pointed to one further disadvantageous implication of the tendency to package property thinking into discretely defined units of abstract entitlement. The common law theory of estates concentrates almost exclusively on the temporal calibration of each particular estate and says little, if anything, about the precise content of the powers attached to the estate. Thus, effectively, the conceptual apparatus of property in rights has disabled any deeper scrutiny of the variable intensity of property in land. For instance, the common law tradition has generally accepted, albeit unthinkingly, that the estate owner enjoys an absolute prerogative to determine precisely who may enter or remain on his land.[128] The estate owner

mark something of a turning point, in that Fox LJ was prepared to concede (at 25H) that, in some limited circumstances, a contractual licence may bind a third party where 'the conscience of the estate owner is affected' by the relevant transaction. The critical question may thus come to relate more closely to the conscientiousness of the third party than to the intrinsic nature of the rights which it is sought to enforce against him (see also *Bahr* v. *Nicolay (No. 2)* (1988) 164 CLR 604, *per* Brennan J at 653).

[125] (1971) 17 FLR 141 at 272–3.   [126] (1992) 175 CLR 1.

[127] (1992) 175 CLR 1, *per* Brennan J at 40.

[128] See *Wood* v. *Leadbitter* (1845) 13 M & W 838 at 844–5, 153 ER 351 at 354; *Marrone* v. *Washington Jockey Club*, 227 US 633 at 636 (1912); *Madden* v. *Queens County Jockey Club, Inc.*, 72 NE 2d 697 at 698 (1947); *Heatley* v. *Tasmanian Racing and Gaming Commission* (1977) 14 ALR 519 at 538; *Lambert* v. *Roberts* [1981] 2 All ER 15 at 19d; *Colet* v. *The Queen* (1981) 119 DLR (3d) 521 at 526; *Gerhardy* v. *Brown* (1985) 159 CLR 70 at 150; *Russo* v. *Ontario Jockey Club* (1988) 46 DLR (4th) 359 at 364.

accordingly exercises an uncontrolled and virtually unchallengeable discretion to exclude any person from trespassing on that land.

While this rule of peremptory exclusion may make perfect sense within, say, the domestic curtilage, there is today growing support for the proposition that arbitrary and potentially capricious powers of exclusion can no longer comprise an inevitable incident of property in *all* kinds of land and that the unqualified assertion of such powers may in practice derogate from fundamental principles of human freedom and dignity.[129] Can it really be the case, for example, that the corporate owner of a large shopping centre can exclude someone 'simply for wearing a green hat or a paisley tie' or because he has 'blond hair, or . . . is from Pennsylvania'?[130] Is it really true that the owner of an extensive tract of uninhabited wild country may, on a whim, deny entry for reasonable and wholly harmless recreational use? The notion is slowly beginning to infiltrate the common law concept of property that the relative size or character of the territory and the social merit or virtue of competing uses impose an inevitable qualification on the workability of the trespassory concept.[131]

Many common law jurisdictions have, accordingly, seen a move away from an 'arbitrary exclusion rule' towards a 'reasonable access rule' under which the estate owner of quasi-public premises may exclude members of the public only on grounds which are objectively reasonable.[132] This shift has necessarily involved a more subtle gradation of the exclusory powers inherent in estate ownership[133] and a more careful taxonomy of the kinds of land which are appropriately included within the scope of the 'reasonable access rule'.[134] In a crowded urban environment, where recreational,

[129] See Gray, 'Equitable Property', (1994) 47(2) CLP 157 at 172–181.

[130] *Brooks* v. *Chicago Downs Association, Inc.*, 791 F. 2d 512 at 514, 518 (1986).

[131] There have been suggestions, particularly in Australia, that the scale of a landholding may impact upon the degree to which that land can properly be subjected to an estate owner's comprehensive regulatory control (see *Hackshaw* v. *Shaw* (1984) 155 CLR 614, *per* Deane J at 659; *Gerhardy* v. *Brown* (1985) 159 CLR 70, *per* Mason J at 103–4). See most recently *Wik Peoples* v. *Queensland* (1996) 187 CLR 1 at 244, 246, where Kirby J thought it 'unlikely' that there could have been any parliamentary intention to invest an estate owner with absolute exclusory power under pastoral leases covering 'huge areas as extensive as many a county in England and bigger than some nations' in 'remote and generally unvisited' terrain. In such areas, declared Kirby J (at 233), 'talk of "exclusive possession" or "exclusive occupation" has an unreal quality' (see also *per* Gaudron J at 154).

[132] See Gray, 'Property in Common Law Systems', 265–8.

[133] See e.g. the famous 'sliding scale test' formulated by the Supreme Court of New Jersey in *State* v. *Schmid*, 423 A. 2d 615 at 629–30 (1980), according to which 'as private property becomes, on a sliding scale, committed either more or less to public use and enjoyment, there is actuated, in effect, a counterbalancing between expressional and property rights.'

[134] Thus, for instance, the 'reasonable access rule' may properly apply to locations such as a shopping mall (*New Jersey Coalition Against War in the Middle East* v. *JMB Realty Corporation*, 650 A. 2d 757 (NJ 1994)), a public library (*Kreimer* v. *Bureau of Police for Town of Morristown*, 958 F. 2d 1242 (3rd Cir. 1992)), a university campus (*State* v. *Schmid*, 423

associational, and expressional space is increasingly at a premium, an unanalysed, monolithic privilege of arbitrary exclusion is no longer tenable. Although the English experience has characteristically lagged behind that of other jurisdictions,[135] modern courts are being required to mark out a spectrum of differing intensities of exclusory power, ranging from the purely private zone (where unchallengeable exclusory power is still in order) through an intermediate category of quasi-public land and extending finally towards a category of genuinely public property (where the arbitrary exclusory power is manifestly and entirely unacceptable). In the process, however, it is clear that once again the recognition of a new contemporary morality in property relationships has been impeded, rather than promoted, by a right-based analysis of property in land.

Property as a Responsibility

A third model of property in land is provided by an alternative—less widely acknowledged—perspective which views property, not in terms of an abstract estate or interest, but in terms of each of the isolable strands of utility or use power which combine variously as the constituent elements of any land interest. By a process sometimes known as 'conceptual severance',[136] this approach separates and identifies the many elements of utility which can characterize relationships with land, and then concedes the label 'property' to each individual element in turn.

A. 2d 615 (1980)), a casino (*Uston* v. *Resorts International Hotel, Inc.*, 445 A. 2d 370 (1982)), an airport concourse (*The Queen in Right of Canada* v. *Committee for the Commonwealth of Canada* (1991) 77 DLR (4th) 385), and a railway station (*Streetwatch* v. *National Railroad Passenger Corporation*, 875 F. Supp. 1055 (SDNY 1995)); but not to a domestic residence (*Robins* v. *PruneYard Shopping Centre*, 592 P. 2d 341 at 347 (1979)), a working laboratory (*Commonwealth* v. *Hood*, 452 NE 2d 188 (Mass 1983)), a hospital (*Estes* v. *Kapiolani Medical Center*, 787 P. 2d 216 (Hawaii 1990); *Attorney-General of Ontario* v. *Dieleman* (1995) 117 DLR (4th) 449 at 730–2), a nursing home (*Cape Cod Nursing Home Council* v. *Rambling Rose Rest Home*, 667 F. 2d 238 (1981)), an abortion clinic (*Darcey* v. *Pre-Term Foundation Clinic* [1983] 2 NSWLR 497; *Attorney-General of Ontario* v. *Dieleman* (1995) 117 DLR (4th) 449 at 732–6), or a nuclear installation (*Semple* v. *Mant* (1985) 39 SASR 282).

135 See *CIN Properties Ltd.* v. *Rawlins* [1995] 2 EGLR 130 at 134. Here the Court of Appeal endorsed the property-owner's exclusion *sine die* of a group of black youths from a city-centre shopping mall, even though no charge of misconduct (or other rational ground of eviction) had been made out against them. This decision was the subject of an application to the European Commission of Human Rights *sub nom Anderson and Others* v. *United Kingdom* (Application No. 33689/96). This application was eventually declared inadmissible by the Commission on 27 October 1997, largely because the UK had not ratified Protocol No. 4, Article 2 of the European Convention on Human Rights, which guarantees the right to liberty of movement.

136 The phrase originates in Radin, 'The Liberal Conception of Property: Cross Currents in the Jurisprudence of Takings', 88 Col. L. Rev. 1667 (1988).

Land may, of course, be turned to advantage in many overlapping ways; it may generate utilities of occupancy, enjoyment, consumption, investment, exploitation, exchange, endowment, aesthetic appreciation, and so on. These elements of utility all require to be held in some sort of balance, and our third model of property in land focuses on the way in which the precise balance or mix of utilities inherent in any particular landholding is subjected, through state intervention, to an overarching criterion of publicly defined responsibility.[137] It follows, moreover, that, when there is any addition to, or subtraction from, the bundle of utilities enjoyed by any person, it can be suggested that a movement or transaction of 'property' has occurred—a proposition not only of venerable authority in English law,[138] but also of huge contemporary relevance to the jurisprudence of environmental regulation and just compensation.

On the present analysis, property comprises not so much a bundle of rights as a bundle of individuated elements of land-based utility. The modern governmental role in regulating all land use is now so pervasive that these elements of utility are best seen as dispensed in various combinations by the state, subject only to occasional alteration either by private bargain or in accordance with supervening considerations of community policy. A plethora of regulatory controls, over matters ranging from urban planning to the conservation of natural resources, testifies to the constant engagement of the modern state in the constraint of land user for purposes of public amenity and welfare. Estate ownership is thus constantly stripped back to a bare residuum of socially permitted power over land resources, and the regime of property in land comprises simply a distribution—on a vast scale—of diverse patterns of state-approved usufruct, each heavily conditioned by the public interest. In effect, property in land is constituted by those publicly endorsed user forms which the state, at its discretion, allows individuals to enjoy consonantly with large strategies of public policy and social design. Property is no more than a defeasible privilege for the citizen.

Once conceived as a variable aggregation of socially permitted land uses, property in land comes to consist, not so much in a *fact* or a *right*, but rather in a state-directed *responsibility* to contribute towards the optimal exploitation of all land resources for communal benefit. Indeed, our third model of property emphatically incorporates a concept not of *right* but of *restraint*. Property no longer articulates the arrogance of entitlement, but expresses instead the commonality of obligation. Far from being an untrammelled right, property is liable to be curtailed on all sides by an interpenetrating

---

[137] It is interesting, in view of the increasing drive towards European harmonization, to note the prescription in article 14(2) of the German *Grundgesetz* that 'property imposes duties. Its use should also serve the welfare of the community'.

[138] See e.g. the effect achieved by the decision in *Tulk* v. *Moxhay* (1848) 2 Ph. 774, 41 ER 1143.

sense of civic responsibility. All property in land is held subject to—and is redefined by—a wide range of socially conditioned constraints. The estate owner may sometimes believe that he enjoys a plenitude of power to do as he wills with 'his' land, but his freedom of action is dramatically circumscribed. In consequence of either privately bargained covenant or (more usually nowadays) statutory planning control, he has little or no automatic entitlement to alter 'his' land, develop or extend it, change its use, paint it whatever colour he likes, still less to destroy it if he so chooses.[139] 'His' land is, moreover, vulnerable to compulsory purchase by the state, on less than satisfactory terms, if such unconsented transfer should ever be found to serve a higher public interest[140] or if he should fail to maintain the land to a standard deemed appropriate by some state official.[141] His proud claim of 'property' is in reality immensely fragile.

It follows, on this view, that the deep structure of property is not absolute, autonomous, and oppositional. It is, instead, delimited by a strong sense of community-directed obligation, and is rooted in a contextual network of mutual constraint and social accommodation mediated by the agencies of the state.[142] So distant is this perception from the classic liberal image of property as a self-interested claim of unfettered power that some American commentators have now begun to predict a wholesale reconstruction or reinterpretation of property in terms of 'socially derived' privileges of use.[143] 'Property' becomes not a summation of individualized power over scarce resources, but an allocative mechanism for promoting the efficient or ecologically prudent utilization of such resources. So analysed, this community-oriented approach to property in land plays a quite obviously pivotal role in the advancement of our environmental welfare.[144]

---

[139] See Town and Country Planning Act 1990, part III; Planning (Listed Buildings and Conservation Areas) Act 1990, part I, ch III.

[140] Planning and Compensation Act 1991, part III.

[141] See Environmental Protection Act 1990, s. 81(4) (in conjunction with Local Land Charges Act 1975, s. 1(1)(a)); Housing Act 1985, s. 300(3).

[142] One American scholar, Eric Freyfogle, has spoken of a 'a new property jurisprudence of human interdependence'. For Freyfogle, 'autonomous, secure property rights have largely given way to use entitlements that are interconnected and relative . . . Property use entitlements will be phrased in terms of responsibilities and accommodations rather than rights and autonomy. A property entitlement will acquire its bounds from the particular context of its use, and the entitlement holder will face the obligation to accommodate the interests of those affected by his . . . use' (Freyfogle, 'Context and Accommodation in Modern Property Law', 41 Stan. L. Rev. 1529 at 1530–1 (1988–9)).

[143] For the roots of this approach, see Caldwell, 'Rights of Ownership or Rights of Use?—The Need for a New Conceptual Basis for Land Use Policy', 15 William and Mary L. Rev. 759 at 766 (1973–4).

[144] Thus e.g. in *Tesco Stores Ltd.* v. *Secretary of State for the Environment* [1995] 1 WLR 759, the House of Lords recently indicated that the considerations properly regarded as 'material'

Implicit in this third perspective on property is also the acknowledgement that distinct quantums of 'property' in the same land can be distributed simultaneously amongst a number of persons and entities (including the state). The 'property' held by each thus comprises some significant element of land-based utility directed and coordinated towards a defined common good; and the quantum of property enjoyed by each in the same land may be subject to variation by means of either private negotiation or direct state intervention. For instance, the fee simple owner who grants a right of way to his neighbour has simply achieved a marginal shift—in his neighbour's favour—of the balance of utility which previously represented his property in the land in question. Significantly, the recipient of such an easement is recognized, within the statutory canon of estates and interests, as holding property in the servient land of either a legal or an equitable character.[145]

The forerunner of modern state-controlled land-use regulation was, of course, the privately bargained restrictive covenant,[146] and it seems clear that the law of restrictive covenants served as an early and valuable form of environmental protection in the developing urban context. When, from *Tulk* v. *Moxhay*[147] onwards, English courts began to enforce freehold restrictive covenants against purchasers, there was no doubt that both the affected freeholder and the restrictive covenantee could truthfully assert that each held some form of 'property' in the servient land, albeit graded by differing degrees of intensity. The freeholder retained 'property' in his land although burdened by some qualified power of veto vested in the covenantee; and, in so far as the covenantee enjoyed a significant control over the user of the freeholder's land, the utility thereby allocated to the covenantee also comprised a form of 'property' in the same land.

The restrictive covenantee's entitlement is now, of course, duly formalized as an equitable proprietary interest within the categories of estates and

to the outcome of a planning application to construct a supermarket would include the fact that the applicant had offered to fund communal off-site benefits (such as a new link road which would help to relieve the local traffic congestion likely to be exacerbated by the proposed development). Thus a willingness to defray the external costs imposed on the community by a proposed development of land can properly be one of the conditions on which a local planning authority may grant permission for the development.

[145] Law of Property Act 1925, s. 1(2)(a), (3).

[146] It is not without significance that private restrictive covenants often came to operate as a localized form of private legislation, preserving various kinds of residential and environmental amenity for future generations of successive owners. Indeed the modern rejuvenation of the 'building scheme' or 'scheme of development' is explicitly premised on the recognition of an intention 'to lay down what has been referred to as a local law for the estate for the common benefit of all the several purchasers of it' (see *Re Dolphin's Conveyance* [1970] Ch. 654, *per* Stamp J at 662A).

[147] (1848) 2 Ph. 774, 41 ER 1143.

interests recognized by the 1925 legislation.[148] The proprietary interest created by mutually restrictive undertakings gave each covenantee, in practice, a stake in a common strategy for the constructive coordination of their respective user preferences.[149] The regime of private ordering embodied in individually bargained restrictive covenants has now been superseded, in many respects, by the socialized obligations imposed by contemporary planning and environmental legislation.[150] On one view this development merely underscores the fact that the modern state retains an eminent domain or overriding property in all land—perhaps the most significant present-day emanation of the Crown's radical title[151]—which provides the state with a dominating stake in the determination of land-use priorities. It is equally arguable that the existence today of a substantial regime of public planning control enables all citizens, in some quite important sense, to claim a certain quantum of property in everyone else's land. Plain beyond cavil, however, is the point that property in land, whether defined empirically or abstractly, is now vulnerable to the all-invasive effect of socially derived land-use regulation.[152] Today the concept of property in land may well denote no more than a temporarily licensed form of utility or user privilege which may be extended, varied, or withdrawn at the sole discretion of the state and on terms dictated by it.

Some of the most pressing questions of twenty-first-century land law are likely to revolve around the terms on which state intervention may alter the precise composition of the bundle of utilities which, at any time, comprise a citizen's 'property' in land. Amidst intensifying concern with

---

[148] Law of Property Act 1925, s. 1(3). See also *Commonwealth of Australia* v. *State of Tasmania* (1983) 158 CLR 1, *per* Deane J at 286 ('The benefit of a restrictive covenant . . . can constitute a valuable asset. It is incorporeal but it is, nonetheless, property'). For some the proprietary status of the restrictive covenant is reinforced by the fact that the covenantee (or his successor) can commonly command a cash premium or equivalent value for release of the covenant; and the Lands Tribunal has statutory power to order the payment of compensation on discharge or modification of a restriction (Law of Property Act 1925, s. 84(1)(c)).

[149] In much the same way the law of easements has served to coordinate the simultaneous exercise of compatible modes of land use, without necessitating costly buyouts of neighbouring land in order merely to secure the optimal utilization of one's own land.

[150] See also Town and Country Planning Act 1990, s. 106 (as substituted by Planning and Compensation Act 1991, s. 12(1)), which adapts the restrictive covenant, in the guise of a 'planning obligation', as a significant instrument of planning control.

[151] Eminent domain—the public power to requisition land—has been aptly described as 'the proprietary aspect of sovereignty' (*Minister of State for the Army* v. *Dalziel* (1944) 68 CLR 261, *per* Rich J at 284).

[152] The squatter's title may, for instance, be founded on brute fact, but he takes subject to all existing restrictive covenants affecting the land (see *Re Nisbet and Potts' Contract* [1906] 1 Ch. 386 at 402–4) and his user of the land is just as clearly qualified by current planning controls.

environmental quality, the regulatory state exercises an ever-increasing surveillance over permissible modes of land use and the definition of 'property' has suddenly emerged as one of the key variables of environmental argument. Many critical problems of environmental protection make sense only if their property dimension is recognized—and indeed recognized not in terms of empirical fact or abstract entitlement, but rather in terms of individuated elements of community-responsive utility. As yet, however, English courts, somewhat in arrear of their counterparts in other areas of the common law world, have been slow to acknowledge the property component inherent in such issues.

In *R. v. Thurrock Borough Council, ex p. Blue Circle Industries*,[153] for instance, a local authority had been prepared, in return for money or money's worth, to release a tenant company from a leasehold covenant which would specifically have required the use of only high-density baled domestic refuse at a landfill site. The Court of Appeal declined to hold that the proposed relaxation of the leasehold terms would constitute a 'disposal' to the tenant of 'any interest in or over land',[154] taking the view that such a phrase covered only 'some altogether more fundamental surrender of proprietorial rights'.[155] Nourse LJ found it 'impossible' to describe a landlord's right to control the use of demised land as a 'proprietary interest in an asset' or as 'an interest in the land', since it was 'at the most, a right in relation to land' rather than 'a right over land'.[156] Far-reaching consequences followed from this failure to recognize that variation of the tenant's permitted use of land would transfer to it more of the 'property' in that land. The Court of Appeal's decision effectively allowed the tenant to degrade the disputed land with other, less wholesome, forms of waste and even precluded the local authority from obtaining, on behalf of the local community, money compensation for such spoliation.[157] The *Thurrock Borough Council* case amply demonstrates how a conventional concentration on property as a crystalline bundle of *rights* can preclude a more realistic awareness of property as comprehending a variable bundle of *utilities*.[158]

---

[153] (1994) 69 P & CR 79.   [154] Town and Country Planning Act 1990, ss. 233, 336.

[155] (1994) 69 P & CR 79, *per* Simon Brown LJ at 85.

[156] Ibid., at 85–6. This outcome is strange, not least because it conflicts with long-standing authority that a landlord, armed with a restrictive covenant against a tenant, has an equitable proprietary interest enforceable, beyond the area of privity of estate, in accordance with the doctrine of notice (*Hall* v. *Ewin* (1888) 37 Ch. D. 74 at 78–80; *Teape* v. *Douse* (1905) 92 LT 319 at 320). See also *Mander* v. *Falcke* [1891] 2 Ch. 554 at 557–8.

[157] The decision in *Thurrock* even sits uncomfortably beside the general tendency in English property law to regard commerciable rights as *ipso facto* proprietary (see above, text accompanying n. 120). The local authority had seemed alarmingly willing to barter away environmental integrity in return for money payment.

[158] For a similar approach in a different context, see *Government of Mauritius* v. *Union Flacq Sugar Estates Co. Ltd.* [1992] 1 WLR 903, *per* Lord Templeman at 911D.

Even more important implications may flow from the conceptualization of property as severable utilities rather than unitary rights. Much modern governmental activity involves, not the outright compulsory acquisition of a fee simple or leasehold interest by the state, but the imposition of substantial community-oriented restrictions upon the free enjoyment of estate ownership. Today most common law jurisdictions are, therefore, increasingly troubled by the question whether the imposition of extensive environmental regulation can ever constitute an acquisition or taking of 'property' from the citizen which requires the payment of publicly funded compensation. For instance, the alteration of a planning authority's structure plan[159] or the designation of an area as a 'conservation area'[160] or the listing of a building as having 'special architectural or historic interest'[161] can exert a serious financial impact upon the development potential of a landholding. But the critical issue does not concern the statutory competence of regulatory measures in defence of the natural or cultural heritage. It relates instead to the identification of the precise source which should bear the cost of the environmental protection which we all profess to desire. Environmental amenity constantly comes at a price which must be paid by either the general community or some subset of it.

In England the consistent trend in recent years has been to truncate the availability of public compensation for the disadvantageous economic impact of land-use regulation. The Planning and Compensation Act 1991 finally withdrew all but a few special circumstances from the scope of the compensatory mechanism.[162] Although doubtless reflective of a parsimonious governmental fiscal policy, the general denial of compensation also derives substantial strength from a developing perception that the estate owner's bundle of utilities is intrinsically delimited by certain social or community-oriented obligations of a positive nature. Supervening community concerns—particularly in the context of environmental integrity—operate *ab initio* as a latent, but ever-present, qualification upon title.

There is, nevertheless, a risk that excessive regulation may, at some point, shade into confiscation,[163] thus disproportionately concentrating the cost of community-directed restrictions on a few selected landholders[164] rather

---

[159] Town and Country Planning Act 1990, s. 32(1).

[160] Planning (Listed Buildings and Conservation Areas) Act 1990, s. 69(1).

[161] Ibid., s. 1(1).   [162] See Planning and Compensation Act 1991, s. 31.

[163] In a classic discussion of this point, Holmes J once acknowledged that, 'while property may be regulated to a certain extent, if regulation goes too far it will be recognized as a taking' (*Pennsylvania Coal Co.* v. *Mahon*, 260 US 393 at 415 (1922)). See also *Belfast Corpn.* v. *O. D. Cars Ltd.* [1960] AC 490 at 519–20, 525, where both Viscount Simonds and Lord Radcliffe conceded that the extinction or excessive limitation of particular land-users may sometimes, in substance, constitute an expropriation.

[164] The problem acquires an even sharper edge where a newly privatized commercial concern, having functioned formerly within the public sector, retains the advantage of a

than diffusing this cost amongst the benefited public at large.[165] This danger will acquire a new significance as and when the UK ratifies or otherwise gives effect to Article 1 of the First Protocol of the European Convention on Human Rights, which guarantees that 'every natural or legal person is entitled to the peaceful enjoyment of his possessions'.[166] The European Court of Human Rights has already shown itself to be peculiarly sensitive, in the regulatory context, to the uncompensated abstraction of any of the individual elements of proprietary utility. In the *Case of Sporrung and Lönnroth*,[167] the Court noted that a state-directed zoning order and prohibition on construction, whilst leaving 'intact' some of the applicants' use rights, had 'affected the very substance of ownership', rendering their 'right of property . . . precarious and defeasible'. Accordingly there had been 'an interference with the applicants' right of property' in breach of Article 1. The Court insisted that regulatory activity must strike a 'fair balance . . . between the protection of the right of property and the requirements of the general interest'.[168] Here the applicants had been caused to bear 'an individual and excessive burden which could have been rendered legitimate only if they had had the possibility . . . of claiming compensation'.[169]

---

statutory power to diminish the utility enjoyed by the private citizen in circumstances where such regulation operates disproportionately for the benefit of the equity shareholders in the privatized company. When, for instance, the Environment Agency pays a privatized water company (or 'water undertaker') for the right to operate jet skis for profit on a reservoir constructed by the company (see Water Resources Act 1991, ss. 20(2)(b), 158(1)(d)), it is the adjoining landowners who, by suffering the disutility of constant noise pollution, are compelled to contribute to the water company's profits and enhance the dividends received by its distant shareholders.

[165] See the classic proposition in US takings jurisprudence that regulatory intervention must be compensable if the withholding of compensation would amount to 'forcing some people alone to bear public burdens which, in all fairness and justice, should be borne by the public as a whole' (*Armstrong* v. *United States*, 364 US 40, *per* Black J at 49 (1960)). See also *Penn Central Transportation Co.* v. *New York City*, 438 US 104, *per* Brennan J at 124 (1978); *Newcrest Mining (WA) Ltd.* v. *Commonwealth of Australia* (1997) 147 ALR 42, *per* Kirby J at 134.

[166] Article 1 continues: 'no one shall be deprived of his possessions except in the public interest and subject to the conditions provided for by law and by the general principles of international law.'

[167] Series A No. 52, para. 60 (1982).   [168] Ibid., para. 73.

[169] Later property cases in the European Court have likewise emphasized the overriding importance of a test of 'proportionality'. In the *Case of The Holy Monasteries* v. *Greece*, Series A No. 301, paras. 70–1 (1994), the Court reiterated the need for a ' "fair balance" between the demands of the general interests of the community and the requirements of the protection of the individual's fundamental rights'. Significantly, the Court considered the statutory availability of compensation to be 'material to the assessment whether the contested measure respects the requisite fair balance and, notably, whether it does not impose a disproportionate burden on the applicants'.

Thus the question may soon again surface in England, as almost everywhere else in the common law world, whether governmental dislocation of existing use powers can ever constitute a compensable taking of 'property' in land. One extreme view now gaining substantial support in the USA is that *any* state-directed subtraction from a landholder's utilities for environmental purposes is necessarily a taking of 'property' which requires public compensation.[170] Only in this way, it is argued, can the individual citizen be enabled to withstand the rampant environmental fascism practised nowadays by his government. If the community wants environmental welfare, it must purchase it fairly, rather than merely dumping the cost randomly on certain unlucky citizen-owners of real estate.

It is doubtful whether this anti-communitarian stance is ultimately sustainable, but care is certainly required to arrive at a more subtle evaluation of the true proprietary impact of environmental regulation. The recent history of the 'regulatory taking' problem evidences the weaknesses implicit in characterizing property in land merely as one or other of the abstract unitary rights contained within the formal canon of land interests. So often the crucial issues revolve around the impairment or abstraction of merely one of the individuated strands of utility woven into the composite jural entitlement of a common law estate or interest.[171]

In *Newcrest Mining (WA) Ltd.* v. *Commonwealth of Australia*,[172] for example, a mineral company purchased mining leases in an area which was later incorporated by the Australian Federal Government within the Kakadu National Park. The mining company was now precluded, by force of federal statute, from any operations for the recovery of minerals. The question arose whether this regulatory exercise had resulted in any acquisition of 'property' by the Federal Government requiring the payment of just compensation.[173] In the Australian High Court McHugh J declined to find any such acquisition of 'property', not least on the ground that the mining company's 'property interests . . . in the land and minerals would continue as before'. The effect of the Federal Government's regulatory action was

---

[170] The Fifth Amendment to the US Constitution provides that 'no person shall be . . . deprived of . . . property, without due process of law; nor shall private property be taken for public use, without just compensation'. Accordingly recent years have witnessed the introduction in many US state legislatures of Private Property Rights Bills designed to 'help slay the regulatory monster' (see Laura Underkuffler-Freund, 'Takings and the Nature of Property', 9 Can. J. L. and Juris. 161 (1996)). The battle-cry is no longer *No taxation without representation*, but rather *No regulation without compensation*.

[171] Hence the current American preoccupation with the problem of 'partial deprivation resulting from a regulatory imposition' (*Florida Rock Industries, Inc.* v. *United States*, 18 F. 3d 1560 at 1568 (Fed. Cir. 1994)).

[172] (1997) 147 ALR 42.

[173] See the Constitution of the Commonwealth of Australia, s. 51(xxxi).

'merely to impinge on [the company's] rights to exploit those interests'.[174] The Commonwealth of Australia already owned the reversionary interests in the land and minerals and 'both as a matter of substance and form . . . obtained nothing which it did not already have'.[175]

This approach did not, however, find favour with other members of the High Court. Delivering the principal majority judgment, Gummow J considered that the Federal Government's action had the consequence 'as a legal and practical matter, of denying to [the company] the exercise of its rights under the mining tenements.' In his view there was here 'an effective sterilisation of the rights constituting the property in question',[176] thereby activating the constitutional requirement of just compensation. Kirby J likewise thought it improper to expand a national park for public benefit 'at an economic cost to the owners of valuable property interests in sections of the park whose rights are effectively confiscated to achieve that end'.[177]

Newcrest Mining may well demonstrate how proprietary subtraction is more accurately identified by reference to shifts of utility than by any analysis of formal rights. But it cannot be the case that *all* regulatory dislocations of a landholder's utility constitute compensable deprivations of 'property'. As Justice Holmes once observed, 'government could hardly go on if, to some extent, values incident to property could not be diminished without paying for every such change in the general law'.[178] In some circumstances, moreover, environmental regulation results in no net loss at all to the affected landholder, as, for example, where the diffused public benefit of the regulation secures an 'average reciprocity of advantage' to everyone concerned.[179] Indeed, Eric Freyfogle has recently pointed out that 'land-

---

[174] A similar approach emerged in *Lucas* v. *South Carolina Coastal Council* (1992) 505 US 1003. Here the US Supreme Court indicated a strong view that a supervening state prohibition of further residential construction in a fragile coastline area had the effect of depriving an aspiring property developer of '*all* economically beneficial uses in the name of the common good'. This being so, the developer could claim compensation on the basis of a 'taking' of his 'property'. Blackmun J dissented, however, on the basis that the Petitioner 'can enjoy other attributes of ownership, such as the right to exclude others . . . Petitioner can picnic, swim, camp in a tent, or live on the property in a movable trailer . . . Petitioner also retains the right to alienate the land, which would have value for neighbors and for those prepared to enjoy proximity to the ocean without a house . . .' ((1992) 505 US 1003 at 1043–4).

[175] (1997) 147 ALR 42 at 81.   [176] Ibid., at 130.   [177] Ibid., at 133.

[178] *Pennsylvania Coal Co.* v. *Mahon*, 260 US 393 at 413 (1922). See also the remark of Viscount Simonds that legislative attenuation of an owner's user rights 'can be affected without a cry being raised that Magna Carta is dethroned or a sacred principle of liberty infringed' (*Belfast Corpn.* v. *O. D. Cars Ltd.* [1960] AC 490 at 519).

[179] *Pennsylvania Coal Co.* v. *Mahon*, 260 US 393, *per* Holmes J at 415 (1922). See also *Commonwealth of Australia* v. *State of Tasmania* (1983) 158 CLR 1 at 283; *Lucas* v. *South Carolina Coastal Council* (1992) 505 US 1003 at 1017–18. 'The trial court must consider: are

use restrictions do not so much limit property rights as they . . . promote and protect them'.[180]

Accordingly the task facing the modern jurisprudence of environmental property is to discriminate between those elements of land-based utility whose impairment constitutes a true taking of 'property' (and is therefore compensable) and those other elements which a landholder may properly be expected (without compensation) to forgo in favour of the communal good. US courts have acknowledged, for instance, that some forms of regulatory intervention, whilst causing economic harm, do not interfere with 'interests that were sufficiently bound up with the reasonable expectations of the claimant to constitute "property" . . .'.[181] It is at this point, significantly, that we return full circle to a conception of 'property' as 'propriety'; and indeed a deep subtext of 'propriety' pervades the entire social and legal definition of 'property'.[182] Thus US courts have long denied that any compensable taking occurs where a restriction is imposed 'to protect the public health, safety, or morals from dangers threatened'.[183] In such cases the restriction comprises merely the 'prohibition of a noxious use' which, on any analysis, never fell within the original complement of powers incident to title. Title has never conferred any intrinsic power to inflict avoidable harm on the public interest.

In this context the crucial variable has now become the degree to which courts are prepared to hold that the proprietary utilities available to a landholder are inherently curtailed by a community-directed obligation to conserve and promote fragile features of the environment. It is precisely this identification of existing tacit constraints on user which has become the most difficult and controversial issue of modern takings law, effectively transforming the environmental debate into a major struggle about the definition of property in land.

In *Lucas v. South Carolina Coastal Council*,[184] for instance, a property

there direct compensating benefits accruing to the property, and others similarly situated, flowing from the regulatory environment? Or are the benefits, if any, generally and widely shared through the community and the society, while the costs are focused on a few?' (*Florida Rock Industries, Inc.* v. *United States*, 18 F. 3d 1560 at 1571 (Fed. Cir. 1994)).

[180] 'The principal beneficiaries of land-use controls are not the public at large, but other landowners, and the principal proponents of land-use restrictions are the neighbors who expect to benefit from them' (Freyfogle, 'The Construction of Ownership', (1996) U. Ill. L. Rev. 173 at 181).

[181] See *Penn Central Transportation Co.* v. *New York City*, 438 US 104, *per* Brennan J at 124–5 (1978).

[182] See Gray, 'Equitable Property', 207–8.

[183] The phrase was originally that of the dissenting Brandeis J in *Pennsylvania Coal Co.* v. *Mahon*, 260 US 393 at 417 (1922). See also *Mugler* v. *Kansas*, 123 US 623, *per* Harlan J at 665 (1887) ('all property . . . is held under the implied obligation that the owner's use of it shall not be injurious to the community').

[184] (1992) 505 US 1003, 120 L. Ed. 2d 798, 112 S. Ct. 2608 (1992).

speculator, intending to construct luxury beachfront homes in a notoriously unstable coastal area, was frustrated by supervening state legislation which prohibited further building operations on land purchased by him at a price of almost $1 million. The Supreme Court of South Carolina denied that there had been any compensable taking of 'property', partly on the ground that the regulatory intervention, by arresting the hazardous development of an environmentally sensitive and hurricane-torn shoreline, was designed 'to prevent serious public harm'.[185] The US Supreme Court overturned this outcome, ruling that public compensation could be denied only if the regulation merely confirmed the restrictions which 'background principles of the State's law of property and nuisance already place upon land ownership'.[186] No compensation would be justified if a regulatory control merely made explicit some restriction which 'inhere[s] in the title itself'[187] and the 'proscribed use interests' were therefore 'not part of [the owner's] title to begin with'.[188] Where, however, a total prohibition of economically productive or beneficial land use went 'beyond what the relevant background principles would dictate', there was, in the view of the Supreme Court majority, no question: 'compensation must be paid to sustain it.'[189]

The hugely controversial ruling of the US Supreme Court in *Lucas* gave significant symbolic afforcement to an individualist rather than communitarian perspective on property holdings; and indeed the Court betrayed little awareness that community obligation—in the form of an inherent duty to avoid environmental degradation—might be a tacit qualification on title. Although again views may differ as to the correctness of the outcome, *Lucas* aptly illustrates the way in which social assumptions relating to the ambit of civic responsibility constantly exert a visible impact upon the definition of property in land. At stake is ultimately the boundary between the domain of the state and the domain of the individual citizen. In the words of a more recent American decision,[190] 'the question is simply one of basic

---

[185] 404 SE 2d 895 at 899 (1991). South Carolina's coastline was particularly susceptible to storm damage and in 1989 Hurricane Hugo had caused twenty-nine deaths and approximately $6 billion in property damage, some of it caused by the fact that beachfront homes were torn up and driven, 'like battering rams', into adjacent inland homes.

[186] (1992) 505 US 1003, *per* Scalia J at 1029.   [187] Ibid.

[188] Ibid., at 1027. Scalia J, although remanding to the state courts the identification of the relevant 'background principles of the . . . law of property and nuisance', added the gratuitous guidance that it 'seems unlikely that common-law principles would have prevented the erection of any habitable or productive improvements on petitioner's land' (ibid., at 1031).

[189] Ibid., at 1030. ' "A State, by ipse dixit, may not transform private property into public property without compensation . . . South Carolina must identify background principles of nuisance and property law that prohibit the uses [Lucas] now intends . . . Only on this showing can the State fairly claim that, in proscribing all such beneficial uses, the Beachfront Management Act is taking nothing' (ibid., at 1031–2).

[190] *Loveladies Harbor, Inc.* v. *United States*, 28 F. 3d 1171 at 1179 (Fed. Cir. 1994).

property ownership rights: within the bundle of rights which property lawyers understand to constitute property, is the right or interest at issue, as a matter of law, owned by the property owner or reserved to the state?' This inescapable engagement with the social and moral limitations of property ensures that private property can never remain truly private and that, in the end, all 'property' in land is inevitably infected with an extensive public law significance.[191]

CONCLUSION

This chapter has attempted to highlight three ways in which common law jurisprudence characteristically conceives of property in land. The chapter has also adumbrated some of the difficulties and challenges implicit in each of these divergent approaches. At different times and in many different contexts our notion of property has resonated with a varying sense that property emerges as a self-constituting fact or derives from some abstract jural entitlement or even emanates from the state control of socially responsible land use. The truth is, of course, that these alternative models of property do not exist in resolute opposition, for they are bound together in a creative tension which is part of the richness of our land law. Relativities of time and place certainly constrain the applicability of each of these modes of perception, and this chapter has pointed to some of the problems generated by the mismatching of sense and context. Each analysis nevertheless provides, in its own way, an important focus upon the essentially human institution of property, whilst reminding us of the ultimately elusive quality which still attaches to the core of the phenomenon.

---

[191] See Gray, 'Equitable Property', 211. 'The state takes on a critical, and so far little explored, role in defining the concept of "property". The state itself becomes a vital factor in the 'property' equation . . . in underpinning the law of "property" the state indirectly adjudicates an exceedingly broad range of the power-relations permitted within society' (Gray, 'Property in Thin Air', 304).

2

CRITICAL LAND LAW

Gregory Alexander

The purpose of this chapter is to summarize the main contributions of Critical Legal Studies (CLS) scholarship in the field of land law. Explaining the CLS perspective on land law is no easy task. To begin with, CLS itself is not easily explained. In general terms, about all that one can accurately say is that CLS is a highly diverse, largely unorganized group of progressive legal scholars committed to critiquing the political underpinnings of legal phenomena and developing alternative doctrines and institutions that instantiate progressive politics. Beyond that, there is little else uniting everyone associated with CLS.

Adding to the difficulty of the task, land law is notoriously complex in every country whose legal system is based on the common law. Modern statutory and judicial changes have created important differences in land law as it exists in the Commonwealth and the USA. Moreover, despite certain broad and obvious similarities in the political and economic systems that form the background for property law in the common law-based world, important differences exist between the political and economic cultures of, say, Canada and the USA. Progressive Canadian legal scholars can take certain assumptions for granted that their US counterparts cannot. The upshot of these legal and cultural differences is that there is no single project that globally unifies all Critical legal scholars who work on land law. These doctrinal differences in national systems have added to the differences among Critical property writings in the English-speaking world. Consequently, I will confine the scope of this chapter to US CLS scholarship and US land law.

The chapter is divided into two main parts. The first part briefly surveys some of the critiques that CLS scholars have made of existing doctrine and institutions of US land law, broadly defined. The second part turns from critique to construction, by describing three recent projects for reimagining the institutions and norms of property law in ways designed to promote progressive political values.

This way of proceeding in fact parallels the way in which CLS scholarship generally has developed. The first generation of CLS writing was

[1] For a general overview of US Critical Legal Studies, see Kelman, *A Guide to Critical Legal Studies* (Cambridge, Mass.: Harvard University Press, 1987).

devoted almost entirely to critiquing existing American legal norms and institutions, revealing their underlying, often unarticulated political presuppositions and internal structures. Subsequent generations of CLS scholarship have largely turned from critique to construction. Prompted perhaps by critics who wanted concretely to know (not unreasonably) just what CLS scholars were *for*, many progressive legal scholars began developing more programmatic and specific proposals for legal change. Some of these proposals operated strictly at the level of legal doctrine, while others' work was more broadly pitched. Some of the proposals represented fairly modest changes; others required more fundamental restructuring. Though much of the work was somewhat tentative and provisional, it was, and is, sufficiently detailed and rich to provide the basis for emerging alternative approaches to legal problems.

CRITIQUES

Problems with Property as a Baseline

The conventional, or Blackstonian, conception of property focuses on the concepts of title and ownership. It assumes that there is always one owner who has title to land giving him complete control over how the land is possessed, used, and transferred. This picture recognizes that government sometimes legitimately regulates how the owner exercises his power, but government regulation is the exception that proves the rule. Collective regulations must always be justified precisely because they encroach on the owner's autonomy.

An implicit function of this conception of property is to establish baselines in legal analyses of disputes among land-users. It defines what the relevant issues are, and it tips the balance among competing claimants by establishing certain presumptions and allocating burdens of proof. The claimant who is found to be the owner is presumptively favoured, while all others, as non-owners, carry a heavy burden of demonstrating why the owner's ordinary privilege should not prevail in this case.

Critical scholars have challenged this baseline-establishing function of the classical conception of property as both descriptively misleading and normatively flawed.[2] The descriptive critique makes several points. One is that

---

[2] The most important work explicitly dealing with the baseline problem in the law of property is that of Professor Joseph William Singer. See e.g. Singer, 'Property and Social Relations: From Title to Entitlement', in van Maanen and van der Walt (eds.), *Property Law on the Threshold of the 21st Century* (Antwerp: MAKLU, 1996), 69; Beerman and Singer, 'Baseline Questions in Legal Reasoning: The Example of Property in Jobs', 23 Georgia L. Rev. 911 (1989).

the classical conception rests on an erroneous assumption that there is
always a single owner of land. In fact, this is not the case. Indeed, frequently
even legal conventions make it difficult to tell who the owner is. Professor
Joseph Singer has pointed out, for example, that US mortgage law sometimes identifies the mortgage-holder as the title-holder to the mortgaged
property, while in other states the mortgagee is treated as merely a lien-
holder.[3] Similarly, formal title does not control the legal determination of
ownership of marital assets when the marriage dissolves either by divorce or
by death. Statutes commonly gives courts discretion to allocate assets to the
marital partner who is not the title-holder.

More generally, Singer and others have argued that the whole idea that
there exists a single owner in whom all rights, powers, and privileges are
legally vested is chimerical. Ownership of land and other resources is usually divided or shared. Many instances of divided or shared ownership are
routinely encountered in ordinary life: landlord and tenant, mortgagor and
mortgagee, life tenant and remainderman, trustee and beneficiary, servient
estate owners and easement owner, tenants in common, joint tenants.
When one adds up all of the forms of divided and shared ownership of land,
hardly any room remains for the classical unitary owner of land. Even
where legal convention recognizes only one owner, it is never the case
that that person has what Blackstone described as 'that sole and despotic
dominion which one man claims and exercises over the external things of
the world, in total exclusion of the right of any other individual in the
universe'.[4] Various legal norms constrain the freedom of owners to use or
dispose of their land: the law of nuisance, the rules against restraints on
alienation, the state's police power to regulate land, or anti-discrimination
statutes are only the most obvious legal constraints on individual freedom
of ownership.

The descriptively misleading character of the classical conception of
ownership creates a normative problem. The assumption that there is
always a single owner leads courts to frame issues of access to land exclusively in terms of the question, 'Who is the owner?' This way of framing
the issue has the effect of either totally ignoring competing public policy
concerns or minimizing those concerns out of deference to sanctity of private ownership. Thus, in one context thoroughly examined by Singer,[5] US
courts have held that employees, unions, and local communities cannot
object when a private company decides to close a plant that had long been
located in a small community and upon which the community's economic

---

[3] Singer, 'Property and Social Relations: From Title to Entitlement', 71.

[4] Blackstone, *Commentaries on the Laws of England* (Chicago: University of Chicago Press,
1979), ii. 2.

[5] See Singer, 'The Reliance Interest in Property', 40 Stan. L. Rev. 611 (1988).

survival depended.[6] Acknowledging that the plant closure would have a devastating blow to the community, the lower court stated that its hands were tied because 'unfortunately, the mechanism to reach th[e] ideal settlement, to recognize this new property right, is not now in existence in the code of laws of our nation'.[7] Singer argues that the fundamental error lies in the classical conception of property. Especially when applied to corporations, Singer contends,

Rather than ask who owns the property, we should ask who has a right to say something about the use or disposition of the property. If we ask this question, it turns out that *in every case* we will identify more than one person because property rights in corporate enterprises are *always* shared. Given this fact, the proper normative question then is how to allocate power among the persons with legally protected interests in the property.[8]

Freedom of Disposition versus Alienability

At least since Blackstone, legal writers have described the development of the common law of real property as organized around two central themes, the principle of individual freedom to use and dispose of property as one wishes and the policy of keeping land freely alienable. The principle of freedom of disposition and the policy of alienability are usually thought to be mutually reinforcing. The alienability of land is maintained just in so far as owners are free to dispose of it as they wish. The combined effect of this principle and policy is to make liberal land law appear to be a well-integrated, internally coherent system. Critical scholars have shown how misleading this picture is.

The principle of freedom of disposition follows from what Charles Donahue has called the 'agglomerative tendency' of Anglo-American land law,[9] or what Frank Michelman calls the 'policy of internalization.'[10] These terms refer to liberal property law's tendency to consolidate in a single legal entity (individual, corporation, or whatever) all of the relevant privileges and powers pertaining to the possession, use, and disposition of discrete ownership interests in land. But freedom of disposition also conflicts with

[6] The most notable of these cases is *Local 1330, United Steel Workers* v. *United States Steel Corp.*, 631 F. 2d 1264 (6th Cir. 1980).

[7] *Local 1330, United Steel Workers* v. *United States Steel Corp.*, 631 F. 2d 1264 at 1266 (6th Cir. 1980).

[8] Singer, *The Reliance Interest in Property*, 641.

[9] Donahue, 'The Future of the Concept of Property Predicted from its Past', in Pennock and Chapman (eds.), *Nomos XXII: Property*, (New York: New York University Press, 1980), 28.

[10] Michelman, 'Ethics, Economics, and the Law of Property', in Pennock and Chapman (eds.), *Nomos XXIV: Ethics, Economics, and the Law*, 1982 (New York: New York University Press, 1982), 8–12.

the agglomerative tendency. The dilemma is that an owner might wish to exercise her power to dispose of land in a way that excessively fragments ownership or impedes the land's alienability by transferring the land subject to a restraint on subsequent alienation. Now, the common law is more than a little familiar with this latter problem and has dealt with it by asserting a basic preference for the alienability policy over individual freedom where the two are in conflict. Direct restraints on alienation of land are generally void; indirect restraints on land, in the form of perpetuities, are also generally void. So far, there is nothing particularly surprising or problematic about this way of resolving the dilemma. The legal rules striking down restraints on alien-ation represent a fairly straightforward illustration of the common law's con-solidationist tendency—that is, the tendency to keep all of the relevant rights, privileges, and powers of ownership consolidated.

There are two problems with this explanation. First, descriptively, it is incomplete and misleading. The common law has long allowed individual owners to fragment ownership of land in ways that allocate rights, privi-leges, and powers among several individuals. This is precisely the point that Professor Singer makes when he criticizes courts and legal analysts for look-ing for 'the owner.'

Even with respect to the power of alienation, US law sometimes does allow one owner to deprive successive owners of the power to transfer their property. The obvious example is the US trust law doctrine known as the spendthrift trust.[11] Under this doctrine, a trust settlor may impose a valid direct disabling restraint on the alienation of any or all of the trust benefi-ciaries, including remainders in fee. The effect of such a restraint is to deprive, during the term of the trust, the future owner of an asset of pre-cisely the same power of disposition that the past owner had.

The logic by which American courts who developed this doctrine justi-fied the seemingly anomalous result reveals a deeper problem with the claim that the liberal conception of ownership is fully integrated and inter-nally coherent. In permitting settlors to impose direct restraints on alien-ation, the courts explained that they were merely following the bedrock principle of freedom of disposition. 'The decision in [the earliest of the spendthrift trust cases]', said one influential court, 'rests upon the doctrine that a testator has a right to dispose of his own property with such restric-tions and limitations, not repugnant to law, as he sees fit, and that his inten-tions ought to be carried out . . .'[12] Thus, the principle of individual freedom of disposition was used to justify an exercise of that power that effectively destroyed that power itself. By engaging in this sort of concep-tual casuistry, the courts avoided confronting the hard policy choice of

[11] See Alexander, 'The Dead Hand and the Law of Trusts in the Nineteenth Century', 37 Stan. L. Rev. 1189 (1985).

[12] *Claflin* v. *Claflin*, 20 NE 454 at 456 (Mass. 1889).

whose freedom should be protected—that of the donor or the donee. That choice cannot be made on the basis of any abstract neutral principle. It can be made only on the basis of a judgment, informed by some background social vision, about how relationships, particularly in generational terms, should be structured. The conventional approach to resolving questions like that in the spend-thrift trust cases hides this social aspect of the problem.

Coercion in the Private Sphere

A good deal of Anglo-American land law doctrine deals with land-use disputes between neighbouring landowners. This is the stuff of the law of nuisance, of lateral and subjacent support, of problems of access to light and air, and the like. The prevailing view is that negative interactions between neighbouring landholders are better resolved through private agreements rather than the alternatives, legislative regulation in the form of zoning and the life or judicial regulation through common-law doctrines like nuisance. The standard argument is that individuals know best what is in the self-interest and, as rational agents, they will act on self-interest to reach optimal solutions to land-use conflicts through private agreement in the absence of excessively high transaction costs. Private land-use agreements, that is, maximize both social utility and individual liberty.[13]

While private land-use agreements doubtless often do maximize preference satisfaction, this is not always the case. Especially in the context of land-use servitudes that regulate planned residential developments, such agreements are frequently the product of quasi-sovereign authority by powerful developers rather than by informed individual choice. Since servitudes are encumbrances upon the estate, they are binding not only on the original contracting parties but on all future purchasers who buy with notice of them. It is sometimes argued that this creates no problem of coercion because, so long as a purchaser had notice of the servitude, she presumably agreed to it.[14] Legal notice alone, however, does not guarantee free choice. Legal notice includes not only actual notice but, under US land law with its system of title records, also record notice. So long as the servitude is reflected in some legal instrument that has been properly recorded and is in the purchaser's chain of title, the purchaser is deemed to have been given notice of it. There is ample opportunity for a gap between record notice and actual notice. The quality of notice provided by the US recording system depends substantially on how each individual state defines the concept of chain of title. Some states have defined it so broadly as to put a purchaser on notice on the basis of instruments to individual parcels that the

[13] See e.g. Epstein, 'Notice and Freedom of Contract in the Law of Servitudes', 55 So. Calif. L. Rev. 1353 (1982).

[14] Epstein, 'Covenants and Constitutions', 73 Cornell L. Rev. 906 (1988).

developer transferred to persons other than the purchaser in question.[15] Purchasers who are unfamiliar with local practice are unlikely to discover the instrument that creates the servitude, yet they will still be held subject to it.

A second and more serious objection to equating consent with notice concerns the problem of imperfect preferences. The purchaser's 'revealed preference' for the servitude may in fact not be the product of autonomous choice. Rational-choice theorists have pointed out that revealed preferences are frequently only adaptations to what the agent regards as a *fait accompli*.[16] That is, the preference reflects not what the person wants but what she thinks she can get. In modern planned resident developments, purchasers acquire their property subject to many different servitude obligations. These obligations are memorialized in long, densely written deeds or 'Declarations of Uniform Conditions, Covenants, and Servitudes'. Housing purchasers frequently fail to read these documents altogether, or gloss over them with little or no understanding of what their legal consequences are.[17] Purchasers of lots in planned developments frequently make no attempt to negotiate over any single term other than price either out of ignorance or because they simply assume that these terms are non-negotiable. In complex transactions the failure of purchasers adequately to focus on servitudes means that they may not have been adequately compensated for an unwanted term. Had that term been negotiated individually rather than as part of a package of many terms, the purchaser would have required a very different level of compensation.[18]

The same problem occurs in landlord–tenant relations. An ongoing debate in US property law concerns compulsory terms in residential leases requiring landlords to maintain premises in habitable condition. Historically, US law did not imply a warranty or covenant of habitability except under very limited circumstances. As part of a so-called revolution in US residential landlord–tenant law, many courts have recognized such a term over the past two decades.[19] The most controversial aspect of this new

---

[15] See e.g. *Guillette* v. *Daly Dry Wall, Inc.*, 325 NE 2d 572 (Mass. 1975).

[16] This is the phenomenon that Jon Elster calls the 'sour grapes' syndrome. Elster, 'Introduction', in Elster (ed.), *Rational Choice* (New York: Cambridge University Press, 1986) 1, 15.

[17] For some empirical evidence of this, see Alexander, 'Conditions of "Voice": Passivity, Disappointment, and Democracy in Homeowner Associations', in Barton and Silverman (eds.), *Common Interest Communities: Private Governments and the Public Interest* (Berkeley: University of California Institute of Government Press, 1994), 145; Winokur, 'Choice, Consent, and Citizenship in Private Interest Communities', in ibid. 87.

[18] See generally Kelman, *A Guide to Critical Legal Studies*, 107–9; Alexander, 'Freedom, Coercion, and the Law of Servitudes', 73 Cornell L. Rev. 883 at 894–5 (1988).

[19] e.g. *Javins* v. *First National Realty Corp.*, 428 F. 2d 1071 (DC Cir. 1970); *Green* v. *Superior Court*, 517 P. 2d 1168 (Cal. 1974); *Hilder* v. *St. Peter*, 478 A. 2d 202 (Vt. 1984).

doctrine is whether the term should be waivable. Most of the decisions considering the question have held that it is not waivable. Critics of the doctrine have argued that compulsory lease terms violate the liberty interests of both parties and that they result in harming the very people they are intended to benefit. Faced with an unwanted duty of care, these critics contend, landlords will raise the rent, passing on the increased cost of the term to tenants. It will also lead to a reduction in supply of affordable rental housing as landlords respond to the increased cost by withdrawing their housing from the rental market.

Critical legal scholars have responded to these arguments in two ways. Responding to the argument that compulsory terms produce perverse economic consequences, critical scholars have pointed out that landlords will not be able to pass on to tenants the entire cost of the new duty because tenants will not be able to afford higher rents. Had tenants been able to pay, landlords would have had incentives to provide the term in the first instance. In the face of higher rents, at least some tenants will move to a cheaper location, double up with family or friends, or become homeless. The resulting decline in demand will limit landlords' ability to pass on the entire cost of the habitability duty. As a result, the compulsory term will produce a net redistribution of wealth from landlords as a class to tenants as a class, achieving precisely the desired result.[20]

Responding to the argument from individual freedom, critical scholars have argued that, far from being coercive, compulsory pro-tenant terms redress an imbalance of power between landlords and tenants. Housing is a necessity, not an amenity. This is reason alone why tenants as a group experience less choice than landlords do. Additionally, landlords often collude in ways detrimental to tenant choice. For example, in metropolitan areas, the common practice is for landlords to use standardized-form leases prepared by their industry associations and including terms favourable to them. Tenants would have no market power to reject these terms in the absence of legal protections such as the warranty of habitability. Compulsory pro-tenant terms, then, increase rather than decrease tenant choice and generally level the playing field between landlords and tenants.

The Critique of the Economic Efficiency of Private Ownership

A second major strand in Critical legal theory about land law concerns claims that private ownership of land is presumptively more economically efficient than alternative systems of ownership. The claim that a system of private property rights in land maximizes aggregate social wealth is now a

---

[20] The best single source here is Kennedy, 'Distributive and Paternalist Motives in Contract and Tort Law, with Special Reference to Compulsory Terms and Unequal Bargaining Power', 41 Maryland L. Rev. 463 (1982).

staple of the vast law-and-economics literature.[21] The arguments for private ownership's inherent economic superiority generally focus on the social waste that supposedly always besets communal forms of ownership and the need to keep land readily transferable so that it ends up in its highest valued use.

Critical scholars have attacked these claims on their own terms. One line of critique is that greatly different ownership regimes will appear to be economically efficient—that is, wealth-maximizing—depending on what assumptions are made regarding preferences and the initial assignment of actual entitlements.[22] For example, communal ownership and other property regimes with sharing obligations may be said to be efficient—that is, preference-maximizing—if there are people who have a strong preference for distributive fairness. In this situation, those who lose from this regime cannot successfully bribe those who gain from it to forgo their entitlements. By definition, then, the regime is efficient. On the other hand, a private-ownership regime with little or no sharing obligation may also be said to be efficient because those who are indifferent to distributive concerns and who have private ownership cannot be bribed to give them up to those who prefer distributive fairness. Both ownership regimes, then, may simultaneously be efficient despite the fact that they are otherwise vastly different.

The more general critique against the claim that private ownership of land is presumptively efficient is that the claim invariably rests on assumptions that are contingent and inherently contestable. Frank Michelman has argued, for example, that the belief that private property is good necessarily rests on some assumption in addition to the belief that people are rational maximizers of their own preferences.[23] These additional beliefs may be, as he calls them, 'quasi-empirical', such as the view that all well-adjusted individuals value security above all else. Or they may be distinctly moral, such as the view that 'irrespective of what various individuals may subjectively want, it is right that each person should be secured in the command over his or her own person'.[24] Michelman's point is not that these additional premises are wrong, but that they cannot be taken as given. Since they themselves require justification, they do not provide secure and rationally incontestable proof for the superiority of private property.[25]

---

[21] See e.g. Posner, *Economic Analysis of Law* (4th edn., Boston: Little Brown, 1992), 32–40; Demsetz, 'Toward a Theory of Property Rights', 57 Amer. Econ. Rev. (Papers & Proceedings) 347 (1967).

[22] See e.g. Kennedy, 'Cost-Benefit Analysis of Entitlement Problems: A Critique', 33 Stan. L. Rev. 387 (1981).

[23] Michelman, 'Ethics, Economics, and the Law of Property', 3.   [24] Ibid. 33.

[25] See also Kennedy and Michelman, 'Are Private Property and Contract Efficient?', 8 Hofstra L. Rev. 711 (1980).

Critical scholars have also shown that, even in legal systems nominally committed to private property, there are many pockets of collective property and of unregulated states of nature. In the USA, for example, an enormous amount of land is publicly owned and subject to public use. Similarly, many courts have recognized a public recreational easement in privately owned beaches.[26] Non-private forms of ownership are used in these instances to solve problems that private ownership would create. This is obvious in the case of national parks and the like, but it is also true with respect to commonses such as public rights to use beaches for recreational purposes. The beach easement is only one example of a successful commons that belies the claim that commons are invariably social 'tragic'.[27] Social wealth and the economic value of land are sometimes maximized by public rather than private ownership.

Engendering Land Law

Land law has not conventionally been considered from the perspective of gender. The emergence of feminist jurisprudence has begun to change that, however. Feminist scholars have shown how, both historically and currently, Anglo-American land law has treated men and women differently in ways that have nearly always disadvantaged women.

Legal historians have critiqued the common law's overt discrimination against women as property-owners. The most obvious example is the legal disability that it imposed on married women until the late nineteenth century. Under the institution of coverture, husbands held the exclusive power to use and control the profits on all land that a married couple owned. As Marylynn Salmon, Richard Chused, Norma Basch, and others have explained, coverture was the primary legal institution for maintaining the subordination of married women. The one exception to this picture was the equitable doctrine of the married woman's separate estate. Marriage settlements could give married women the power to act as *femes soles* with respect to managing settled property. Here again, though, the picture was far from one of independence and equality. The existence of the married woman's separate estate depended on either the husband's consent to the settlement or the willingness of a relative or friend to confer such an estate

---

[26] e.g. *Matthews* v. *Bay Head Improvement Ass'n.*, 47 A. 2d 355 (NJ 1984); *City of Daytona Beach* v. *Tona-Rama, Inc.*, 294 So. 2d 73 (Fla. 1974); *State ex rel. Thornton* v. *Hay*, 462 P. 2d 671 (Ore. 1969).

[27] The classical expression of the thesis that communal ownership is inherently socially wasteful is, of course, Hardin, 'The Tragedy of the Commons', 162 Science 1243 (1968). The thesis is superbly critiqued in Rose, 'The Comedy of the Commons: Custom, Commerce, and Inherently Public Property', 53 U. of Chicago L. Rev. 711 (1986).

on the woman. Either way, the wife was dependent on someone else.[28] In the USA, the situation did not fundamentally change later, when in the mid- to late nineteenth century state legislatures enacted statutes abolishing coverture and removing the legal disabilities imposed on married women as property-owners. Many women worked in the home for no wages, and the married women's property acts did nothing to grant them marital property rights on the basis of the labour they furnished at home. For wives who did domestic work in the home for wages, most of the statutes gave their husbands control over the wives' earnings. The statutes failed 'completely to achieve their supporters' stated objective of emancipating women's labor in the home as well as in the marketplace'.[29]

While women's status as property-owners has clearly improved in the late twentieth century, equality and independence still remain elusive goals for many women, married and non-married. US women are systematically worse off than men in terms of owning all forms of property, including land. Modern feminist legal scholars have extensively analysed the reasons why women continue to be poorer than men. One factor to which they have frequently pointed is the revolution in late-twentieth-century US marital property and divorce law. The combined effect of 'no-fault' divorce and so-called equitable distribution of property upon divorce statutes has been to entrench the impoverishment of many women. Indeed, scholars now perceive that divorce is a key path to poverty for women and children in the USA. Fully 40 per cent of divorced US women with children live below the poverty standard set by the federal government.[30] While the rules of property law alone have not brought this condition about, they have contributed to it.

Property and Race

In a racially diverse society like the USA with a long history of racism, it is hardly surprising that black Americans, Hispanic Americans, American Indians, and other people of colour continue to experience the property

---

[28] See e.g. Salmon, *Women and the Law of Property in Early America* (Chapel Hill, NC: University of North Carolina Press, 1986); Basch, *In the Eyes of the Law: Women, Marriage, and Property in Nineteenth-Century New York* (Ithaca, NY: Cornell University Press, 1982); Staves, *Married Women's Separate Property* (Cambridge, Mass.: Harvard University Press, 1990); Chused, 'Married Women's Property Law: 1800–1850', 71 Georgetown LJ 1359 (1983).

[29] See Siegel, 'The Modernization of Marital Status Law: Adjudicating Wives' Rights to Earnings, 1860–1930', 82 Georgetown LJ 2127 (1994); Siegel, 'Home as Work: The First Women's Rights Claims Concerning Wives' Household Labor, 1850–1880', 102 Yale LJ 1073 (1994).

[30] See Williams, 'Is Coverture Dead? Beyond a New Theory of Alimony', 82 Georgetown LJ 2227 (1994).

system differently from white Americans. Critical race theorists have taken the lead in describing and documenting just how different, and adverse, that experience has been. The USA's history of conquest, colonization, and chattel slavery must be the starting point for any such enquiry. For American Indians, the story begins with conquest.[31] The European invasion of North American began a long struggle over sovereignty and property rights.[32] Colonial theory held that conquest conferred title to land on the conquering nation. In the famous case of *Johnson* v. *M'Intosh*,[33] the US Supreme Court extended this theory to conclude that the property and sovereignty of American Indian nations was transferred from the colonial powers to the US government following independence. The Court held that title that traced from grants from the federal government was superior to title that traced from aborginal grants. In this way, US land law simply ratified the expropriation of the ancestral lands of American Indians. More fundamentally, as one critical scholar has stated, *Johnson* 'preserved the legacy of 1,000 years of European racism and colonialism directed against non-Western peoples', and it 'ensured that future acts of genocide would proceed on a rationalized, legal basis'.[34]

The Court in *Johnson* recognized that Indians had a possessory interest in tribal land, but that interest could be extinguished by purchase or by conquest. In fact, however, subsequent developments proved that the Indians' possessory interest was more tenuous than that. The federal government continuously expropriated possession of the lands of Indian nations which had never been conquered in military engagement. In 1955 (ironically, one year after the famous decision in *Brown* v. *Board of Education*), the Supreme Court held that native Alaskans had no constitutional right to compensation when the federal government extinguished their exclusive right to the timber on native land.[35] The Indians' right of occupancy, the Court reasoned, 'may be terminated and such lands fully disposed of by the sovereign itself without any legally enforceable obligation to compensate the Indians'. Had the claimants in the case been non-Indians, compensation would clearly have been constitutionally compelled. Critical scholars have pointed out that the upshot of these decisions is that constitutional protection of

---

[31] On the complex history of the relationship between the federal government and American Indians, see Prucha, *The Great Father* (Lincoln, Nebr.: University of Nebraska Press, 1984).

[32] Singer, *Property Law: Rules, Policies, and Practices* (2nd edn., New York: Aspen Publishing, 1997), 23.

[33] 21 US (8 Wheat.) 543 (1823).

[34] Williams, *The American Indian in Western Legal Thought: The Discourses of Conquest* (New York: Oxford University Press, 1990), 317.

[35] *Tee-Hit-Ton Indians* v. *United States*, 348 US 272 (1955).

possessory land interests in the USA is neither fixed nor neutral. At times at least, it has been conditioned on race.[36]

The experience of black Americans with the legal system of property is at least equally shameful. That experience began with them not only as legally incapable of owning land, but as property themselves. Patricia Williams has written insightfully about the modern legacy of that experience: 'one of the things passed on from slavery, which continues in the oppression of people of color', she writes, 'is a belief structure rooted in a concept of black (or brown, or red) anti-will, the antithetical embodiment of pure will. We live in a society in which the closest equivalent to nobility is the display of unremittingly controlled will-fulness. To be perceived as unremittingly will-less is to be imbued with an almost lethal trait.'[37] She sees the consequence of this history for her, as a black American, in the most profound terms. She states, 'I must assume . . . that, in the eyes of white culture, irrationality, lack of control, and ugliness signify not just the whole slave personality, not just the whole black personality, but me'.[38]

The legacy of this history of will-lessness has played itself out in many ways in twentieth-century US land law. Black Americans, along with other people of colour, have been widely discriminated against as tenants, as purchasers, and as occupants of land. To pick only one obvious example, throughout most of this century, deeds to residential lots very commonly included restrictive covenants explicitly prohibiting the sale or leasing of the lot in question to Blacks. No federal statute striking down such racially discriminatory covenants existed until 1968, when Congress enacted the Fair Housing Act, which expressly makes it unlawful to refuse to sell or rent residential property because of race.[39] Prior to that date, the only other weapon for attacking racially discriminatory deed covenants was the equal protection of the Fourteenth Amendment to the United States Constitution. The Supreme Court had held, in 1948, that judicial enforcement of such covenants constituted impermissible 'state action' for purposes of the Fourteenth Amendment.[40] Despite this decision, which formally made such covenant legally unenforceable, racially discriminatory

[36] See Ball, 'Constitution, Courts, Indian Tribes', 1987 American Bar Foundation Research J. 1; Newton, 'At the Whim of the Sovereign: Aboriginal Title Reconsidered', 31 Hastings LJ 1215 (1980). The Supreme Court has subsequently held that the federal government must pay compensation when it takes Indian tribal land that is recognized either by statute or by treaty. United States v. Sioux Nation of Indians, 448 US 371 (1980).

[37] Williams, 'On Being the Object of Property', 14 Signs: Journal of Women in Culture and Society 5 at 8 (1988).

[38] Ibid. 11.

[39] 42 USC §3604. In the same year, the US Supreme Court held that the generally worded Civil Rights Act of 1866 bars all racial discrimination, public and private, in the sale or rental of property (Jones v. Alfred H. Mayer Co., 391 US 409 (1968)).

[40] Shelley v. Kraemer, 334 US 1 (1948).

covenants and conditions continued to appear in leases and deeds.[41] Even where no racially discriminatory term appears, black Americans continue to experience discrimination in renting and buying real estate through a variety of other practices. It is no accident that large American cities such as Chicago, Philadelphia, and Boston remain heavily segregated in terms of housing on the basis of race. US land law is an important reason why racial injustice continues to be America's most intractable social problem.

FROM CRITIQUE TO RECONSTRUCTIVE THEORIES

More recently, critical scholars have turned from critiquing legal doctrines and institutions to developing constructive theories of law that offer the potential for realizing progressive goals. Some of the most interesting work in this vein has been in the area of property, including land, law. This part briefly describes three such theories.

All three theories represent an effort to develop a 'third way'—that is, a form of property ownership that is neither state socialism nor *laissez-faire* capitalism. At the same time, all three theories are committed to ownership that is private and liberal. In the West today, liberal ownership takes many forms, ranging from the Reaganite capitalism of the USA to the MITI capitalism of Japan. There is no single model of liberal private property. Nor does one model fit all. Some configurations of property rights suit some situations but not others. The question is *which* form of liberal ownership is appropriate in *which* situations.

The Social-Relations Model

Joseph Singer has recently developed an approach to thinking about property disputes that he terms the 'social-relations model'.[42] The basic point of this model is that it 'reconceptualizes property as a social system composed

---

[41] Clauses discriminating against black Americans, Jews, and other social groups continue to appear in title instruments. Incident to the confirmation hearings on his nomination as Chief Justice of the USA, for example, current Chief Justice William Rehnquist revealed that the deed to his summer house in Vermont contained a covenant barring sale to 'any member of the Hebrew race'. Rehnquist subsequently ordered his attorney to remove the covenant from his deed. See 'Rehnquist Alters Restrictive Deed', New York Times, 16 Nov. 1986, s. 1, pt. 2, at p. 50.

[42] Singer has developed his model in several papers. These include Singer, 'Property and Social Relations: From Title to Entitlement', 69; Singer, 'No Right to Exclude: Public Accommodations and Private Property', 90 Nw. U. L. Rev. 1283 (1996); Singer and Beerman, 'The Social Origins of Property', 6 Canadian J. of Law and Jurisprudence 217 (1993); Singer, 'The Reliance Interest in Property', 40 Stan. L. Rev. 611 (1988).

of entitlements which shape the contours of social relationships'.[43] Singer argues against focusing on individual property rights in isolation. He also stresses that property rights must be understood as contingent and contextual. The example of this model that Singer cites is the common-law doctrine of nuisance. Nuisance law explicitly recognizes and acts on the relational character of landownership by limiting a property-owner's rights in order to protect the interests of other owners and society as a whole. It also illustrates the contingency and contextuality of property rights by looking to the actual effects of land use in a particular time and place. Thus, using land to excavate gravel, though not in and of itself objectionable, may become publicly objectionable if the area in which the excavation occurs has developed residentially over time.[44]

To illustrate the practical difference that this ownership model makes, consider the much-discussed decision of the US Supreme Court in *Lucas* v. *South Carolina Coastal Council*.[45] That case involved a challenge to South Carolina's Beachfront Management Act under the Fifth Amendment of the Federal Constitution, barring 'takings' of 'property' for public purposes without payment of 'just compensation'. The statute severely restricted new construction or reconstruction of residential structures near the beach along South Carolina's 180-mile coastline. The purpose of the legislation was public safety and health: historically the coastal area was subject to substantial erosion and shifting shorelines. Certain high-erosion beach areas had beeen under water at least once during the previous forty years and were under a constant threat of hurricanes. In 1954, for example, Hurricane Hazel battered the South Carolina coast and destroyed twenty-seven of twenty-nine homes on the southern end of a barrier island near the city of Charleston.[46] The statute sought to prevent personal injury from such disasters, as well as to protect the ecological integrity of fragile barrier islands, by prohibiting construction or reconstruction of houses located less than 20 feet from the first row of dunes, or forty times the beach-erosion rate in the area, whichever is greater. Shifting shorelines, caused by beach erosion, over time changed the list of owners within the dead zone. David Lucas was one of those who found himself on the list.

Lucas, a real-estate developer, had purchased two lots for $1 million each, exclusively for the purpose of constructing luxury houses and condominiums on them. The Beachfront Management Act threatened to thwart his plans for commercial development, and he sued, claiming that the statute effected an unconstitutional taking of his property without compensation. The Supreme Court agreed. The Court held that land-use regulations that

---

[43] Singer, 'Property and Social Relations: From Title to Entitlement', 78.
[44] See *Hadacheck* v. *Sebastian*, 239 US 394 (1915).   [45] 505 US 1003 (1992).
[46] See Applebome, 'After Hugo, A Storm over Beach Development', New York Times, 24 Sept. 1989, at 1.

deny an owner all economically viable use of his land constitute takings unless they prevent nuisances as defined under local nuisance law.

Two aspects of the Court's reasoning merit special attention from the perspective of the social-relations model. First, the Court treated what it called the 'right to build on one's property' as the equivalent of ownership itself. It stated that the regulation in question had deprived Lucas of all economically viable use of his land, but this can be the case only if one assumes that commercial development is the only economically beneficial use of land. It ignores, for example, renting the beach for camping or fishing purposes.

The second aspect is the Court's refusal to acknowledge the prevention of social harms as a legitimate restriction on ownership rights. The Court stated that 'the notion . . . that title is somehow held subject to an "implied limitation" that the State may subsequently eliminate all economically valuable use is inconsistent with the historic compact recorded in the Takings Clause that has become part of our constitutional culture'.[47]

From the perspective of the social-relations model, this argument entirely mistakes both the character of landownership and the basis for the statute. The Court sought to define the essential nature of land title, determining that the right to build is somehow an inherent part of ownership. But, as Professors Singer and Beerman have pointed out, this reasoning 'assumes that the effect on others is irrelevant unless traditional nuisance tests are satisfied'. Such an approach 'relies on the nature of property rather than the interests at stake'.[48] Moreover, it ignores the fact that the statute represented a legislative determination about the proper balance to be struck between the competing interests. The democratically elected legislature determined that the individual owner's interest in commercial exploitation must give way to the public interest in protecting society and the environment against the effects of hurricanes. The Court's conceptualistic reasoning simply does not explain why that determination must, as a constitutional matter, be overturned or why the social interest at stake must be sacrificed.

Had the Court viewed the dispute through the lens of the social-relations mode, how would it have analysed the case? Singer and Beerman suggest the following two questions: 'Rather than asking whether a law imposes too great a sacrifice in the owner's property rights, the Court should ask whether the regulation in question deprives the owner of an entitlement which that owner could rightly have expected to enjoy. . . . Second . . . [i]s the owner being wrongly singled out or discriminated against to unfairly bear the burdens or costs of a project intended to benefit the community.'[49]

---

[47] 505 US at 1028.   [48] Singer and Beerman, 'The Social Origins of Property', 238.
[49] Ibid. 246.

While acknowledging some uncertainty, they suggest that the answers to both questions will be 'no'. More importantly, the questions will focus attention directly on the relevant conflict: the owner's obligation to protect the community of which he is a member versus the public's obligation to respect the owner's legitimate expectations. The classical theory of landownership, upon which the *Lucas* Court implicitly relied, fails to take adequate account of the social obligations of ownership.

Social-Republican Property

Another progressive model of ownership is that of social-republican property. Developed by William Simon, Duncan Kennedy, and others, the social-republican model is similar to the social-relations model in a number of respects.[50] The core idea behind the social-republican model is to combine private ownership with a commitment to participation and equality within discrete communities. Put differently, social-republican property structurally integrates the market and politics, fusing the roles of ownership and citizenship.

The defining characteristics of social-republican property are two conditions on ownership, an accumulation restraint and an alienation restraint. The alienation restraint limits control of property to active or potentially active participants in a community that itself is constituted by property. The accumulation restraint is intended to limit inequality among members of the relevant communities. Together, the two restraints limit the commodification of social relationships by restricting the extent to which individual owners are free to capitalize expected future returns on their investments. The idea is to 'encourage the owner to view her interest as a stake is a particular, long-term relationship'.[51]

Though not widely applied, the social-republican model has been implemented throughout the world in a variety of contexts. Perhaps the clearest example is the cooperative form of ownership, which exists in the industrialized countries of the West as well as in less-developed countries. Duncan Kennedy has recently shown how the cooperative form can be used in housing to realize the twin ideals of solidarity and participation.[52] He pro-

[50] See Simon, 'Republicanism, Market Socialism, and the Third Way', in Alexander and Skapska (eds.), *A Fourth Way? Privatization, Property, and the Emergence of New Market Economies* (New York: Routledge, 1994), 286; Kennedy and Specht, 'Limited Equity Housing Cooperatives as a Mode of Privatization', in ibid. 267; Simon, 'Social-Republican Property', 38 UCLA L. Rev. 1335 (1991).

[51] Simon, 'Republicanism, Market Socialism, and the Third Way', 287.

[52] See Kennedy, 'Neither the Market nor the State: Housing Privatization Issues', in Alexander and Skapska (eds.), *A Fourth Way? Privatization, Property, and the Emergence of New Market Economies* (New York: Routledge, 1994), 253; Kennedy and Specht, 'Limited Equity Housing Cooperatives as a Mode of Privatization', 267.

poses privatization of government-owned rental housing by transfer title in rental buildings to the current occupants organized into limited-interest joint tenancies. Occupants own shares in the joint tenancies. Share ownership entitles the owner to occupy a unit, modify it, lease it, transfer it to family members at death, or sell it at any time. Share ownership simultaneously makes occupants members of the joint tenancy, which manages and governs the property as a whole. Owner-members are free to sell their interests at any time. Upon sale, the owner-member recoups from the sale price his initial investment, which includes his initial cost plus the cost of his improvements plus a reasonable return on the investment cost. The return rate is based on either the bank rate on savings prevailing during the period of occupancy or the inflation rate, whichever is greater.

The extent of the owner-member's commodifiable interest is limited. If the market sale price is less than the initial investment, then the owner is entitled to the full proceeds of sale. However, if the sale price exceeds the initial investment, then the owner-member is entitled to recoup his initial investment plus the specified return rate. The joint tenancy receives the balance of the sale price. It must deposit this balance in a local development bank for the purpose of either improvements in the joint tenancy's common areas or retiring existing debt. This restriction on the owner's equity interest corresponds to what Simon calls accumulation restraints and is a defining characteristic of all exisiting limited-equity housing cooperatives.

Like Simon's model, Kennedy's plan also includes alienation restraints. In the initial joint-tenancy contract, the development bank retains a preemption right for all units. This right allows it to purchase the unit whenever the owner decides to sell. The purchase price is neither a fixed price nor a free market price. Rather it is based on economic inerests of the owner and the joint tenancy. Alternatively, the bank can consent to a proposed sale to someone else but require that the sale price be below the market price in order to assure that the partial commodification feature of the project not be undermined. The right of pre-emption does not, however, give the bank the right to determine who the buyer should be upon resale, once it has decided not to exercise the pre-emption right for itself. In this respect the arrangement remains a private, free-market form of ownership. Similarly, the owner remains free to relet the premises, subject to approval of the new lessee under the same procedures used to select the initial owner. The owner-lessor's ability to exploit housing shortages, however, is limited by the requirement that he share the rent with the joint tenancy and the bank according to a formula that grants him a fair return on his investment but does not allow him to appropriate the surplus of that amount.

The political, or participatory, norm of social-republican property is achieved in Kennedy's housing scheme through the organization of the joint tenancy, which manages the project. Participation by owner-members in the internal affairs of the joint tenancy may be either direct or representative, and individual owner-members may be given either strong or weaker control over decisions of the joint tenancy. For example, owner-occupants might be given strong or weaker powers of individual control over their interests, or some combination of varying degrees of power for particular issues. Moreover, owner-occupants might choose to delegate whatever powers they individually have to a management committee, members of which are democratically selected, or they might choose to retain their powers, making the arrangement more individualistic. The flexibility of the cooperative form permits considerable variation in the individual or collective character of the enterprise.

As Kennedy stresses, all of these variations constitute a liberal form of ownership. They are 'liberal' in the following senses. First, the cooperatives are created on a strictly voluntary basis. Secondly, the regime 'respect[s] freedom of contract, private property rights, and profit maximization'.[53] Finally, the state plays a modest, non-coercive role in the system. It neither owns any of the property in question, nor compels creation of the cooperatives. Rather its function is primarily facilitative. At the same time, the social-republican model, while liberal, seeks to enable individuals to infuse the communal values of participation and solidarity in institutions of private ownership. In this respect, the model is politically progressive and departs from more traditional forms of liberal ownership.

Civic Property

The final model is one that I have begun to develop in earlier work, a model that elsewhere I have called 'civic property'.[54] I can provide only the basic outline of this model here. Many of its details remain to be worked out, including its consequences for the use and distribution of various sorts of resources, including land, in different contexts. Still, enough of the general contours of the model is clear enough to see how it departs from the legal model of liberal ownership still dominant in the USA—the Blackstonian conception of ownership as 'that sole and despotic relationship between a person and thing'.

The civic-property model shares with both the social-relations and social-republican models the basic premiss that, within a liberal legal system, property performs many functions, not all of which are strictly economic. While certainly important from the vantage points of both allocative efficiency (i.e. wealth creation) and distributive justice, property has other,

[53] Kennedy and Specht, 'Limited Equity Housing Cooperatives', 268.
[54] See Alexander, 'Civic Property', 6 Social and Legal Studies 217 (1997); Alexander, 'Commodification, Housing, and Democracy', in van Maanen and van der Walt (eds.) *Property at the Threshold of the 21st Century* (Antwerp: Maklu Press, 1996), 537.

equally important purposes.[55] Among these non-economic functions of private property is the political goal of facilitating the active exercise of democratic citizenship. To see how private ownership can perform this political function, I must first sketch the conception of democracy on which the civic model of property is based. I will then explain, first, the role of civil society in creating and maintaining democracy and, secondly, the relationship between civil society and private ownership of property.

The conception of democracy that the civic model of ownership pre-supposes is one that Habermas calls 'discursive'[56] and that might also be called 'cooperative'. This theory of democracy can perhaps best be described in terms of what it is not. It is not the conception of democracy that public-choice theorists such as James Buchanan and Gordon Tullock have developed. Public-choice theorists depict democracy as essentially a matter of bargaining, or interest-group 'rent-seeking'. Politics is a market like any other market, they argue. Public-choice theory treats public values as mere preferences, fundamentally indistinguishable from other prefer-ences. Like preferences among cars, ice cream, and other commodities, public preferences are exogenous—that is, simply given and fixed. They are not a matter about which people deliberate, constitute, and reconstitute on a socially interactive basis, but instead are individual wants that people try to satisfy through the process of commodity exchange.

By contrast, the discursive theory of democracy conceives of democratic politics as the ongoing process of defining and pursuing the common good through 'public justification, communication, and deliberation'.[57] While public-choice theory conceives of politics as just another market, the dis-cursive theory of democracy views politics as the distinctive realm for the normative practice of collective deliberation about shared public values and conceptions of the proper social order. As an empirical theory, the discur-sive model considers preference satisfaction as no less an aspect of the polit-ical process than public-choice theory does, but it contends that preferences are more accurately understood as created rather than given, and dynamic rather than fixed. Moreover, the discursive model understands democracy to have a normative aspect that public-choice theory either overlooks or denies. This normative dimension requires that, in order for preference sat-isfaction in the political sphere to have legitimacy, political preferences be created, defined, and pursued through the process of public, collective deliberation rather than commodity exchange. The processes of collective

[55] On the multi-functional character of private property, see Baker, 'Property and its Relation to Constitutionally Protected Liberty', 134 U. Pa. L. Rev. 741 (1986).

[56] See Habermas, *Between Facts and Norms: Contributions to a Discourse Theory of Law and Democracy* (Cambridge, Mass.: MIT Press, 1996).

[57] See, generally, ibid. The phrase is borrowed from Justice Brandeis's concurring opin-ion in *Whitney v. California*, 274 US 357 at 375 (1927).

deliberation and justification, that is, are not only an available means for successfully achieving collective action; they are the only available basis for claiming legitimacy for collective action. Stated differently, collective deliberation and justification is the means of converting preference satisfaction into the common good.

In order for such a form of democracy to exist in any society, its citizens must possess a substantial capacity to trust others and cooperate with them. A society that is characterized by a high degree of distrust and cynicism is not one where citizens can legitimately claim to pursue the common good. Though democratic in a formal sense in so far as it is endowed with all of the relevant machinery of democracy (popularly elected legislatures, etc.), a society whose citizens routinely distrust others outside small closely knit, kin-like groups is one whose political life is in a substantive and normative sense undemocratic.

Examples of formally democratic but substantively undemocratic societies abound around the world today. One has only to look at political life as actually practised in countries such as Russia, Mexico, and Korea. Those are countries in which cynicism about collective action in the public sphere undermines the operation of democratic institutions to the point of threatening the future of stability of formal democracy. Even in some of the so-called advanced countries of the First World, including notably the USA, the democratic character of politics has declined to disquieting levels. Evidence of this fact is provided not just in the continuing decline in voting rates but in popular attitudes about politics and politicians. In the USA today, politicians rank in public esteem lower than all other professions, except lawyers and used-car salesmen. Americans widely expect that politicians at all levels routinely engage in corrupt practices. Whether or not true, that perception of politics is deeply threatening to democracy.

Why has democracy substantively declined or failed to strengthen in these countries? Recently there has been a revival of interest among US scholars in politics, sociology, and, to a lesser extent, law, in the topic of civil society. By 'civil society', I mean the social institutions and practices that mediate between the individual and the state. Churches, clubs, labour unions, neighbourhood organizations, and other voluntary associations are the paradigmatic examples of intermediate institutions that constitute civil society. That the civil-society revival has occurred when it has is no accident. As Tocqueville, Durkheim, and other great political sociologists told us long ago, a robust civil society is essential to democracy. The public and private spheres are fundamentally interrelated. Civil society represents that part of the private sphere in which individuals experience solidarity and participation, the same norms that are essential for democracy to succeed in the public sphere. The *praxis* of civil society creates what political theorists now call 'social capital', meaning trust, cooperation, and norms of reciprocity.[58] Recent empirical work by political sociologists has established that the the quality of democratic life in the public sphere is substantially dependent on the level of social capital existing in the private sphere.[59] A society that is poor in social capital—that is, one in which people are distrustful of others and unwilling to cooperate in social networks—is likely to be one where politics is relatively less democratic in a substantive sense, even if it possesses the formal machinery of democracy. Political decision-making becomes dominated by powerful individuals or interest groups as distrust and cynicism lead individual citizens to withdraw from collective life in both the public and private spheres.

What implications do this theory of civil society and its relationship to democracy have for private property? At first blush, one might suppose that civil society and private property have little, if anything, in common. Indeed, we are probably apt to suppose that private ownership of property is antithetical to the processes of collective deliberation and justification that are essential for the health of civil society. After all, many people today assume that the institution of private property is inevitably based on egoistic behaviour, hardly the stuff of social capital.[60] This is exactly the reason why some recent scholars have elaborated theories of civil society that explicitly exclude market relations from its realm.[61] They believe that the market and civil society must be kept apart somehow or else the egoism of the market will erode the capacity of individuals in civil-society institutions to deliberate and act cooperately. Since the market is based on the existence of private-property rights, those rights must themselves be threatening to civil society and ultimately to deliberative democracy.

The civic model of property is based on the view that the legal norms and institutions of private ownership are not inherently incompatible with the norms of civil society. The concept of private ownership is sufficiently indefinite to include norms, practices, and institutions that support rather

---

[58] See Coleman, *Foundations of Social Theory* (Cambridge, Mass.: Belknap Press, 1990), 300–21.

[59] See Putnam, *Making Democracy Work: Civic Traditions of Modern Italy* (Princeton: Princeton University Press, 1993); Putnam, 'Bowling Alone: America's Declining Social Capital', 6 J. of Democracy 65 (1995).

[60] This is the view, ironically enough, shared not only by neo-classical economists such as Ronald Coase, Gary Becker, and others, but also by many on the Left. See e.g. Nedelsky, *Private Property and the Limits of American Constitutionalism: The Madisonian Framework and its Legacy* (Chicago: University of Chicago Press, 1990); Abraham, 'Are Rights the Right Thing? Individual Rights, Communitarian Purposes and Crockpot Revolutions', 25 Conn. L. Rev. 947 (1993). Indeed, Marx himself held this view. See Marx, *On the Jewish Question*, in *Karl Marx: Early Writings*, ed. Bottomore (New York: McGraw Hill, 1964), 24–6.

[61] See Cohen and Arato, *Civil Society and Political Theory* (Cambridge, Mass.: MIT Press, 1995); Walzer, *Spheres of Justice: A Defense of Pluralism and Equality* (New York: Basic Books, 1983).

than undermine the social capital-creating function of civil society. For the balance of this chapter, I will sketch some ways in which this project has been, or might be, implemented at either or both of these levels, institutional and normative.

At the institutional level, there already exist examples of private landownership forms one of whose purposes is to advance the process of strenghtening trust and norms of reciprocity. Housing cooperatives, both of the conventional and the limited-equity varieties, are only the most obvious instance. Other housing arrangements, such as the common-interest developments or so-called private residential governments that have become so familiar in the USA today, also reflect the same vision of infusing private ownership with the social norms of collective deliberation, participation, and cooperation. Not all of these forms of housing have been equally successful in this regard, but the point is that, as existing institutions of private landownership, they illustrate the possibility of creating institutions of private property whose aim is to revitalize civil society without sacrificing the concerns with protecting individual autonomy and economic security.

A second existing ownership institution that is compatible with the civic model of private ownership is the land trust. Used for the purpose of preserving undeveloped land for recreation and other socializing activities, the land trust fully integrates the principles of private ownership with the democratic values of cooperation, participation, and sharing. In this respect, land trusts represent an important alternative to state ownership of recreational land in the form of national parks and natural-resources preserves. The state could take an active role in encouraging the creation of private land trusts without becoming 'interventionist' or violating the tenets of private ownership.

Beyond existing institutions, other institutional forms of private ownership can be imagined that potentially advance the goal of revitalizing civil society. One might consider, for example, ways in which the idea of a rotating capital fund, now used in many lesser-developed countries as a source of credit for otherwise non-creditworthy individuals, might be adapted to various uses of land, including agriculture and mining. Private ownership has adapted to many uses and institutional forms in the past. A hundred years ago, no one would have imagined that privately owned housing might take the form of condominiums. Today, we are barely aware of how innovative the condominium idea really is.

Shifting from institutions to legal norms, the civic perspective of ownership would not require any doctrinal revolution, but it would change the way in which courts analyse certain types of disputes concerning land use. In the area of constitutional protection of property, for example, the civic model implies important changes, both methodologically and substantively, under the so-called takings clause of the US constitution. It is worth paus-ing to consider some of these changes, since takings disputes have become the single most contentious area in all of US land law.

Without getting into the swamp of the details of that body of law,[62] the Fifth Amendment to the US Constitution provides that the state shall not 'take property' for public use without paying 'just compensation.' The neg-ative implication, of course, is that the state *can* take private property so long as it does so for some legitimate public purpose and so long as it pays just compensation. But just what does 'take property' mean? In the regulatory state, government enacts a great many measures that affect private-property rights without expropriating those rights. Are all of these regulations, which never provide compensation to the private owner who finds that the regu-lations have caused the market value of his land to decline, unconstitu-tional? The US Supreme Court has wrestled with that question since 1922, when it first announced that regulations would be held unconstitutional as uncompensated 'takings' if but only if they 'go too far', to use Justice Holmes's wonderfully murky phrase.[63] How does one go about deciding when a regulation goes too far, morphing into a 'taking'? Aye, there's the rub.

Take the 1990s dispute over wetlands regulations. State and local regula-tions in many US jurisdictions forbid private owners from draining the water from certain natural wetlands. Obviously, such restrictions are likely to depress the market value of the affected land because the land's highest and best use, as judged by the market, is some form of commercial exploita-tion, which is most likely to be either farming or residential development. Not surprisingly, many wetlands owners have been screaming that these wetlands regulations are outrageous and unconstitutional takings of their property. Are they right? Alas, there is no clear answer to the question as a matter of positive law, so the debate goes on. As a normative matter, how should courts go about analysing this dispute. More to the point, what questions would a court committed to the civic view of private property ask that are not asked under current constitutional doctrine?

The most important doctrinal difference is that a civic-minded court would construe the Constitution's vague language to imply what other lib-eral legal systems expressly provide, a social obligation of ownership. The Court would reason that both the textual reference to 'public use' and the background assumptions of the nature of property rights under private law provide grounds for implying an obligation similar to that expressly stated in the German Constitution (Basic Law). Article 14(2) of the Basic Law states that 'ownership imposes obligations' and that 'property should serve

---

[62] For a brief overview of recent developments in US takings law, see Alexander, 'Ten Years of Takings', 46 J. of Legal Educ. 586 (1996).

[63] *Pennsylvania Coal Co.* v. *Mahon*, 260 US 393 (1922).

the common good'. The relevant question would then become whether this social obligation of ownership requires that land owners forgo the opportunity to exploit the most economically valuable uses of their land in order to protect the public's interest in the environmental benefits of wetlands. While it is not entirely certain how the civic-minded court would answer that question, it is clear that the court would agree with the German Constitutional Court, which stated in a somewhat analogous case, 'The constitutionally guaranteed right to property does not permit the owner [of land] to make use of exactly that which promises the greatest possible economic advantage.'[64] On this view, the landowner would not prevail solely on the basis of his inability to put the land to its commercially most valuable use. This is generally true, but especially so in relation to wetlands. Land use that affects water invariably has intense public ramifications, and owners have a tendency to apply high discount rates to the future harmful effects of draining wetlands, aquifers, and other environmentally sensitive natural water sources.[65] The strength of the public stake in preserving wetlands, together with the substantial risk that the owner will not adequately take into account all of the social costs of his use of the land, means that the social obligation is especially weighty in this area.

At the same time, the social obligation clearly does have limits. The owner should not be required to forgo *all* commercially valuable uses, even conceding the strength of the public interest in preserving wetlands. The German Constitutional Court uses a legal norm of proportionality (*Verhältnismäßigkeit*) as the means of assuring that individual landowners do not bear undue burdens in the interest of the social obligation. Similarly, the civic model rejects the illiberal idea that the individual should be subordinated to the community. The civic norm of solidarity must be applied in a way that is compatible with liberal principles.

CONCLUSION

To conclude this chapter, which is being published as part of an international collection, I want very briefly to place the US CLS project in a broader context. Critics of CLS have often charged that CLS proposals concerning property such as those of Kennedy or Singer amount to abandoning the very idea of private ownership, or that they are 'collectivist' or 'statist' or even 'communist'. Nothing could be further from the truth. As

[64] The Wet Gravel Case (*Naßauskiesungsentscheidung*), 58 BVerfGE 300 (1981), Eng. trans. repr. in Kommers, *The Constitutional Jurisprudence of the Federal Republic of Germany* (Durham, NC: Duke University Press, 1997), 257, 260.

[65] For discussions of this points, see Freyfogle, 'Water Rights and the Common Wealth', 26 Environmental Law 33 (1996).

it actually operates around the world, the liberal concept of ownership permits a remarkably wide array of practices and norms, including practices and norms that are sometimes expressly predicated on the very norms that US CLS scholars wish to promote.

My own sense is that what makes the CLS project concerning property appear radical to many Americans is the fact that the dominant political baseline by which politics are judged in the USA is a view that most of the rest of world regards as extremist individualism. This is perhaps more true with respect to questions about property than any other area. One of the most enduring myths in American culture is the myth of absolute property rights. For most Americans, property is a cultural symbol as sacrosanct as the flag. It is regarded as the very foundation of individual liberty, the 'guardian of every other right'. No other legal system accords as much freedom to individuals in their possession, use, and disposition of all forms of property, but especially land. The truth is, though, that no system of private property can ignore the fact that property rights involve responsibilities to others as well as privileges. The American legal system in fact acts on this insight in a variety of ways. What is remarkable is how seldom that is acknowledged. In American political-legal discourse, the rhetoric about property is virtually entirely about individual 'rights', 'privileges', 'liberties', and so on. The rhetoric of 'responsibility', 'interdependency', 'cooperation', and the like is absent to a stunning extent. The rhetoric of 'solidarity' is missing altogether. These linguistic patterns reflect widely shared cultural assumptions. As I have already indicated, those assumptions are, to some extent, inaccurate; US land law certainly does not entirely ignore the responsibilities of landownership. But the assumptions still carry weight. The popular vision of the individual landowner as the unencumbered homesteader on the prairie (who, in truth, had plenty of encumbrances, including ones that the government directly imposed) creates a strong presumption against any collective restrictions on how to use or dispose of land. In the past we were able to absorb most of the social costs of the presumption—the degradation of soil conditions, pollution of water, air, and other essential resources, great disparities between possessors and non-possessors, and other costs. We no longer have that luxury. Without lapsing into the banal talk about 'globalization' that is all too common these days, it is still an ineluctable fact that social interdependency is increasing at an unprecedented rate. That interdependency will have profound consequences for most areas of US domestic law, of course, including land law. International environmental regulations, health and safety regulations affecting exports of agricultural products, and international human rights treaties and conventions are only some of the ways in which global interdependency will affect US landowners. Eventually, the mythic character of property rights as absolute will become too obvious to ignore, and Americans will join the rest of the

world in acknowledging that individual ownership entails social obligations. At that point Critical legal scholarship on property, far from appearing radical, will represent early attempts to harmonize American legal
consciousness with legal norms prevailing in the rest of the world.

PART TWO
LAND LAW IN HISTORY

3

ROMAN IDEAS OF LANDOWNERSHIP

Joshua Getzler

Roman jurisprudence invented many of the key concepts describing landownership that operate in the legal world today. It can no longer be doubted that the English common law of property was deeply influenced by the Roman doctrines of possession, title, and servitudes.[1] It follows that all cultivated law students in common law as well as Civilian jurisdictions should have some awareness of Roman and Civilian doctrines of landownership.[2] This chapter will describe the framework of Roman property theory and offer some assessments of its social and historical significance.

THE ROMAN JURISTS' ACHIEVEMENT

The Byzantine Emperor Justinian commissioned the jurist Tribonian in 530 to collate the fruits of classical Roman legal history and compile them into a great *Digest*. To this project was added the *Institutes*, a terse guide to the underlying principles of the law based on the earlier *Institutes* of Gaius. Justinian's *Institutes* and *Digest* were promulgated in 533, and turned out to be the most influential works of the Western legal tradition. During the Middle Ages and Renaissance, Institutionalist principles were cross-blended with the legal customs of different European countries to produce much of the law extant in the world today. If the Roman influence on English customary law was less overt, it was still powerful. The Roman ideas about private and public property provide a kind of DNA of legal ownership, the intellectual structure within which most later legal thought has developed.

---

[1] Bracton, Blackstone, Austin, Blackburn, and Gale are only a small sample of the generations of English jurists who openly avowed their debt to Roman law. See especially Blackstone, *Commentaries on the Laws of England* (4 vols., 1st edn., Oxford: Oxford University Press, 1765–9), i. 1–84; Helmholz, 'Continental Law and Common Law: Historical Strangers or Companions?', [1990] Duke LJ 1207; Jolowicz, 'Some English Civilians' (1949) 2 CLP 139.

[2] 'Civil law' means private law doctrines derived from the Roman legal system; 'Civilian' thus connotes a thing or person connected to Civil law. Civil law embraces German and French law, which in turn influenced continental European law and much of the private law elsewhere in the world—for example, in South America and Japan. See further Ibbetson and Lewis (eds.), *The Roman Law Tradition* (Cambridge: Cambridge University Press, 1994).

The technique of the classical Roman jurists was to describe categories into which different legal phenomena fell. Conceptual distinctions were evolved which aimed to show the law as rational, coherent, and systematic rather than haphazard and accidental. The jurists' approach to law adumbrated the techniques of modern natural and biological sciences. A vast material was observed, analysed, divided into interrelated categories of genus, species, and subspecies, and so brought within the grasp of the human mind. The Roman legal categories were not timelessly 'true'; but they had an elegance and facility encouraging the elaboration of legal thought for many centuries.

ROMAN PROPERTY CLASSIFICATIONS

The first book of Justinian's *Institutes* sets out the fundamental Roman distinction between private law and public law.[3] Book two makes a distinction between private things (wealth or assets of value) and things which could not be private wealth—that is, those things within and without patrimony.[4] Justinian states that 'most things belong to individuals';[5] and the Justinianic law creates an intricate structure of private-property rights embracing much of the physical world (including many human beings such as slaves).

Dominium as 'Absolute Right'

The central concept of Roman ownership was *dominium*. Classically this meant 'lordship', in the sense of sovereign, ultimate, or 'absolute' right to claim title and hence the possession and enjoyment of a thing. *Dominium* was absolute in the sense that one was either the owner or else not the owner. In classical law this implied—unlike in English law—that there was no relativity of title whereby one could be owner against some rivals but not against others.[6] Centuries later, *dominium* evolved into a mystical idea connoting complete and unchallenged domination and control of the land

---

[3] *Justinian's Institutes*, ed. Krueger, ed. and trans. Birks and McLeod (London: Duckworth, 1987) (cited as Inst.), Inst.1.1.4.

[4] Inst.2.1.pr.; Gaius, *Institutiones Iuris Civilis, The Institutes of Gaius*, ed. and trans. de Zulueta (Oxford: Oxford University Press, 1946) (cited as G.Inst.) G.Inst.2.1. See further Samuel, 'Roman Law and Modern Capitalism', (1984) 4 LS 185.

[5] Inst.2.1.

[6] This is doubted by Kaser, who believes that the early doctrines of negative prescription later developing into *usucapio* amounted to a system of relative land titles. See Jolowicz and Nicholas, *Historical Introduction to the Study of Roman Law* (3rd edn. by Nicholas, Cambridge: Cambridge University Press, 1972), 146–7, 153–5; Watson, 'Acquisition of Possession and *uscapion per servos et filios*' (1967) 78 LQR 205.

and other objects that were within one's property. Absolute ownership no longer meant a good legal title against all rivals, but was given a highly individualistic, anti-social, libertarian meaning as untrammelled ownership. The new-model *dominium* connoted absolute rights of private ownership free of inherent limitation or control by others, such rights being balanced only by the external restrictions and power of the impersonal state standing above all owners. This model of ownership was fundamentally political rather than legal. It was first propounded by Renaissance jurists as a polemic against feudal systems of multiple land titles distributed between lord and tenant and granting the lord power and jurisdiction over the economic and personal lives of the peasantry.[7] An allodial ownership system was propounded in order to cut the link between wealth and social-political power; allodial ownership requires that owners buy the labour power of workers in labour markets, rather than command the workforce to farm the landlords' demesnes as an incident of tenure. Thus Roman ownership ideas were claimed as a liberating ideology favourable to capitalism and hostile to feudalism.

In later capitalist societies, absolute property ideas served as a vehicle for debates concerning the ethical bases of capitalism and the relationship between communal and state interests and individual autonomy, notably in Germany in the nineteenth century.[8] Roman jurists of the classical period before Justinian were claimed as the first liberal sociologists and economists, thinkers who contributed to modernity by stressing the importance of clearly defined property rights and describing the conditions for their efficacious trade, freed of political and communal control.[9] Peter Birks has usefully summed up the political uses of the absolute property idea; he identifies 'the nineteenth-century tendency to exaggerate the independence of the Roman owner', 'the error of contrasting an autonomous Roman ownership with a socially-limited Germanic conception', and continues:

---

[7] See Schulz, *Principles of Roman Law* (Oxford: Oxford University Press, 1936), 151; Schulz, *Classical Roman Law* (Oxford: Oxford University Press, 1951), 338–55; Birks, 'The Roman Law Concept of Dominium and the Idea of Absolute Ownership' [1985] Acta Juridica 1 at 1, 19–20, 23–5.

[8] On the nineteenth-century debates between the German schools of von Savigny and von Jhering (and later between Windscheid and Gierke) concerning the ideological content of Roman private law and its bearing on Civilian codes, see John, 'The Peculiarities of the German State: Bourgeois Law and Society in the Imperial Era', (1989) 119 Past and Present 105; John, *Politics and the Law in Late Nineteenth-Century Germany: The Origins of the Civil Code* (Oxford: Oxford University Press, 1989); Jolowicz, 'Political Implications of Roman Law', (1947) 22 Tulane L. Rev. 62; Rodger, *Owners and Neighbours in Roman Law* (Oxford: Oxford University Press, 1972), 1–2 and ff., 34–7; Whitman, *The Legacy of Roman Law in the German Romantic Era: Historical Vision and Legal Change* (Princeton: Princeton University Press, 1990).

[9] See Galbraith, *A History of Economics: The Past as the Present* (Harmondsworth: Penguin, 1989), 18–19; Schulz, *Classical Roman Law*.

One source of the exaggeration was the desire, manifested in and after the French Revolution in 1789, to repress and draw a contrast with burdened and restricted feudal interests. The intention was to insist on equality before the law, not to make ownership absolute quoad the general law of the state but to free it from other personal superiorities. However, the reaction against feudalism is not the whole explanation of the absolute doctrine . . . We have to add in the rise of the nation state and the need to show that strong governments existed to defend property, not to imperil it.[10]

Legal analysis of the nature of Roman ownership suggests that this historical controversy is misplaced in focus. The pervasive and untrammelled nature of private-property rights in mature Roman law must be qualified carefully. Only in a formal or conceptual sense can Roman ownership be described as 'absolute'. The limited, strictly juristic nature of that 'absolutism' may be seen by contrasting Roman with common law ownership. First, *dominium* was a wholly exclusive, non-relative right, rather than a ranked title in a hierarchy of possessory rights;[11] a Roman owner could never be said to have a title good against later trespassers but void against some superior claimant from whom the land had wrongfully been taken.[12] Secondly, *dominium* was a right indivisible on the plane of time and subject to no doctrine of estates.[13] Unlike English law, there could be, for example, no *dominium* 'for life' (contrast the life estate), or *dominium* so long as a lineal descendant is alive (contrast the fee tail). Thirdly, it was a proprietary right independent of tenurial or contractual relations of superiority—an 'allodial' right created independently of any other person's lordship. There was never anything akin to the complex feudal doctrine of tenures which characterized English land law through the medieval ages. Notwithstanding these contrasts and the rhetoric of absolute ownership, there was, in fact, no principled regard for the absolute freedom of ownership in substantive content or practical exercise, beyond the uninformatively circular doctrine stating that owners were as free in their ownership as law permitted them; or so far as they did no legally wrongful harm to others.[14] Roman law, like English law, did not accept that ownership was unrestricted. An owner might be forbidden from building above a certain height, or within a certain distance of his boundary; he might not commit a nuisance against

[10] Birks, 'The Roman Law Concept of Dominium', 24.

[11] Buckland, *The Main Institutions of Roman Private Law* (Cambridge: Cambridge University Press, 1931), 93–4 and ff.; Buckland, *A Textbook of Roman Law fom Augustus to Justinian* (3rd edn., ed. Stein, Cambridge: Cambridge University Press, 1963), 186–8. Cf. the debate over the Kaser thesis, cited above at n. 6.

[12] Jolowicz and Nicholas, *Historical Introduction to the Study of Roman Law*, 142; Nicholas, *An Introduction to Roman Law* (3rd edn., Oxford: Oxford University Press, 1962), 154–7.

[13] Buckland, *The Main Institutions of Roman Private Law*, 100–1.

[14] This idea was expressed in the maxim *sic utere tuo ut alienum non laedas* ('so use your own as not to injure that of another'); Nicholas, *Roman Law*, 154–7.

neighbours or the public.[15] The later Civilians proposed a concept of *dominium* as '*ius utendi, fruendi, abutendi*', or the right to use, take profits, change, and alienate the thing, amounting to the fullest array of rights over a thing. But this model was an intellectual construction of what it meant in abstract to be an untrammelled owner, and was not part of classical law. The classical concept is that '*dominium* is the ultimate right, that which has no right behind it. It may be a mere *nudum ius* with no practical content . . . It is a "signoria" '.[16]

The doctrine of *dominium* implies that legal relationships between property-owners are horizontal, in the sense that each has an equivalent status as the sole lord of a piece of land, and none can legally claim jurisdiction over the others. By contrast, the English common law long viewed property relationships as vertical, in that landownership automatically bestowed political and judicial power over others. In the seventeenth century, lawyers such as Coke attempted to remodel the fee simple as something equivalent to *dominium*—a man's house as his castle against lords and kings. But this reading of the historical nature of Roman property-holding suggests that all ownership in Roman law was privatized, and this is not the case. Significantly, the *Institutes* commence discussion of things in book two with the categories of *non*-private wealth rather than with any discussion of the nature of *dominium*:

Things are either in the category of private wealth [*in patrimonio*] or not.[17]

Things can be: everybody's by the law of nature; the state's; a corporation's; or nobody's.[18]

The Romans were deeply conscious of the role of public goods as well as private goods in property law. They acknowledged that 'natural' or pre-state law allowed many non-private forms of property,[19] and they entrenched both within their fundamental jurisprudential categories. By contrast, the common law could only develop public proprietary interests by developing Crown ownership into a form of state control by a series of fictions and conventions; or by vesting a multitude of individuals with fragmentary feudal claims constituting a group or common right over a resource, such as a field for hunting or gleaning. Roman law was notably more direct in its recognition of state and communal ownerships.

---

[15] Rodger, *Owners and Neighbours in Roman Law*. Cf. English planning legislation.

[16] Buckland, *Textbook of Roman Law*, 185–8; cf. Buckland, *Elementary Principles of the Roman Private Law* (Cambridge: Cambridge University Press, 1912), 60–4.

[17] Derived from G.Inst.2.1., 2.10.; which draws a similar distinction; followed in de Bracton, *De legibus et consuetudinibus angliae*, c.1225 (4 vols., ed. Woodbine, trans. Thorne Cambridge, Mass.: Belknap Press, 1977), fo. 207, iii. 128.

[18] Inst.2.1.; Buckland, *Textbook of Roman Law*, 182–6.   [19] Inst.2.1.11.

The Institutionalist Analysis of Public and Private Goods

Gaius and Justinian's distinction between things *in patrimonio* and *extra patrimonium* suggested that private property was originally defined by heritability; but *in patrimonio* eventually came to be synonomous with *res* as any privately owned asset.[20] The usual legal term for a thing of economic value—the *res*—was ambiguous, meaning at once physical objects, property rights in those physical objects, and personal rights and obligations applying to economic assets such as personal claims to wealth or payment or compensatory damages. The term *res* had much overlap with the notion of a legal right—*ius*—which could often be classified as an economic asset or *res*.[21] Thus the Roman *res*, like the law French/common law term *chose*, may translate as either right or thing. *Corpus* was sometimes used to refer to the physical object subjected to legal control or to the physical control itself.[22] In what follows, *res* will tend to be used in the sense of a thing or right of property; and *ius* as all legal rights, proprietary or personal, which have economic value.[23]

The four categories of *res* or things not privately owned are elaborated in Roman law as follows:

1. *Res communes* (everybody's property)

'The things which are naturally everybody's are air, flowing water, the sea, and the sea-shore.'[24] This is a central text in the history of property law, and requires some exegesis. A right is 'natural' according to the Romans because all creatures instinctively recognize it.[25] In addition there is a natural law specific to humans: 'the law which natural reason makes for all mankind';

[20] See Buckland, *Textbook of Roman Law*, 182 n. 8, discussing D.50.16.5. (Paul). All references to D. are to *The Digest of Justinian*, ed. Mommsen and Krueger, ed. and trans. Watson (4 vols., Philadelphia: University of Pennsylvania Press, 1985).

[21] Personal status rights which were not quantifiable assets, such as family authority, were rights but not *res* (Nicholas, *Roman Law*, 98–9).

[22] For the development of the dual concept of *res* by Gaius, see Birks, 'The Roman Law Concept of Dominium', 4–7, 14, 25–7.

[23] Nicholas, *Roman Law*, 98 ff., 140 ff.; Buckland, *Main Institutions of Roman Private Law*, 143–4; Thomas, *Institutes of Justinian: Text and Commentary* (Amsterdam: North-Holland, 1975), 74; de Zulueta, G. Inst., 56–7.

[24] Inst.2.1.1.; and see D.1.8.2.pr., 1. (Marcian); Buckland, *Textbook of Roman Law*, 182 n. 9. See further D.1.8.2., 4.–6. (Marcian); D.1.8.1., 5. (Gaius); D.41.1.14.-15. (Neratius); D.41.1.50. (Pomponius); D.43.7.1. (Ulpian); D.43.8.1. (Paul); D.43.8.2. (Ulpian); D.43.8.3. (Celsus); D.43.8.4. (Scaevola); D.43.8.5. (Paul); D.43.8.6. (Julian); D.43.8.7. (Ulpian); D.43.12.1. (Ulpian); D.43.12.3. (Paul); D.43.13.1.; D.43.14.1.; D.43.15.1. (Ulpian). The modern English collective ownership concepts are broached in Gray, 'Property in Thin Air', [1991] CLJ 252.

[25] Inst.1.2.

this law 'is applied the same everywhere. It is called *ius gentium*, the law of all peoples', because it is common to every nation'.[26] In one application of this concept: 'The law of all peoples gives the public a . . . right to use the sea-shore, and the sea itself . . . The right view is that ownership of these shores is vested in no-one at all. Their legal position is the same as that of the sea and the land or sand under the sea.'[27] Thus ownership by everybody is stated to be a particular form of ownership by nobody, where things are naturally unowned by individuals yet in a sense owned by everybody because they are available for all to use and enjoy. *Res communes* can never be owned exclusively because they cannot (or should not, by natural law) be reduced to private control or possession. This contrasts with the specific category of *res nullius*, things naturally unowned which in some cases can be reduced to private ownership, such as wild animals upon capture. The *Institutes* also specify a type of mixed property where there is a private owner who must afford the public extensive use rights. The chief case was navigable rivers:

The law of all peoples allows public use of river banks, as of the rivers themselves: everybody is free to navigate rivers, and they can moor their boats to the banks, run ropes . . . and unload cargo. But ownership of the banks is vested in the adjacent landowners. That also makes them owners of the trees which grow there.[28]

This *res communes* can be seen as a type of common usufruct, a fraction of ownership or an incorporeal use right removed from private into public ownership, whilst leaving *dominium* intact as a residual private ownership.

Access to and use of *res communes* could be protected by interdicts akin to the common law's public nuisance writs: 'It is open to anyone to claim for public use what belongs to the use of all, such as public roads and public ways. Therefore, interdicts are available to safeguard these at anyone's demand.'[29]

---

[26] Inst.1.2.1. See Buckland, *Textbook of Roman Law*, 186 ff.

[27] Inst.2.1.5.; D.43.8.3.pr.−1., 4. (Celsus).   [28] Inst.2.1.4.; D.1.8.5. (Gaius).

[29] D.43.7.1. (Pomponius); Thomas, *Institutes of Justinian: Text and Commentary*, 75. Whilst English law has no direct parallels to *res communes*, ownership of many of the *res communes* is treated differently under English law than ownership of other—more private— things, perhaps making these things a little like the mixed property of Roman law. Airspace can be privately owned, but only up to a point—but there are conflicting views (see Gray, *Elements of Land Law* (2nd edn., London: Butterworths, 1993), 19 n. 12)—and probably not the air itself. Whilst flowing water may not be owned, the owner of adjacent land does have certain rights concerning the water such as rights of reasonable usufruct and navigation; the public has no such rights unless granted by statute or if the river has been dedicated as a public highway. Again with land adjacent to the sea, the foreshore (the land between high and low water mark) is owned not by the adjacent landowner but by the Crown, and the public have common law rights of navigation and fishing over the foreshore. The bed of the sea itself is owned by the Crown.

2. *Res publicae* (state property)

'Rivers and harbours are state property. So everybody shares the right to fish in them.'[30] This form of property resembles *res communes* in embracing natural resources, giving use rights to all, and excluding private or exclusive appropriations. Ownership, however, is not formally given to all private individuals as an incorporate group enjoying common use-rights, but to the state or communal body, as Gaius writes: 'Public things are regarded as belonging to no individual, but as being the property of the corporate body (*universitatis*).'[31] The line between this category and the *res communes* and *res universitatis* was not well drawn.[32]

3. *Res universitatis* (corporate property)

'Corporate, as opposed to individual, property consists in things in towns like theatres, racecourses and so on, in fact all things vested in the citizen-body.'[33] This category embraces fixed or built capital rather than natural resources owned by the local and municipal collective agencies of the people.[34] The jurist Paul explains the category as follows: 'Citizens of a municipality can possess nothing of themselves, because the consent of all is not possible. Hence, they do not possess the marketplace, public buildings, and the like, but they use them in common.'[35] The jurists Cebus, Celsus and Pomponius distinguished things in public appropriation as things in 'permanent appropriation to public uses'.[36] This included property and places: 'such are not the objects of commerce, but are public property, which, while they do not absolutely belong to the people, are used for public purposes, as for instance, the Campus Martius [the Field of Mars, used for military training and public events].'[37]

---

[30] Inst.2.1.2.; D.1.8.4., 5.; 41.1.65.1., 2. (Paul); D.43.12.1.3. (Ulpian). Paul alone treats the river banks as well as the waters as public property: D.41.1.65.1.; 43.12.3.pr. For references, see Buckland, *Textbook of Roman Law*, 185.

[31] G.Inst.2.11. Cf. Birks, 'The Roman Law Concept of Dominium', 10.

[32] de Zulueta (G. Inst., 56), notes that for Gaius the corporation lacked sufficient legal personality to be described as 'owner', so that *res publicae* were a type of *res nullius*. See also D.1.8.2.pr. (Marcian); Buckland, *Textbook of Roman Law*, 184–5; Thomas, *Institutes of Justinian: Text and Commentary*, 35; Sanders, *The Institutes of Justinian* (London: John W. Parker, 1876), 158; Schulz, *Classical Roman Law*, 340.

[33] Inst.2.1.6.

[34] Difficult jurisprudence surrounds this concept (see further Schulz, *Classical Roman Law*, 92–101). In the Christianized empire this category of ownership vastly expanded as significant wealth and social function accrued to the Church (see Birks, 'The Roman Law Concept of Dominium', 10–11).

[35] D.41.2.1.22. (Paul); cf. G.Inst.2.11., which treats these things as *res nullius*, implying that a corporation lacks sufficient personality to own.

[36] de Zulueta, G.Inst., ii. 56.

[37] D.18.1.6.pr. (Pomponius). English law has no such sophisticated division as between

4. *Res nullius* (Nobody's property)

There were two classes of unowned property within this category:

(i) res nullius, divini iuris. 'Sacred, religious, and sanctified things are owned by nobody. Things under divine law cannot belong to individuals.'[38] *Divini iuris* were a species of unowned property which could not be appropriated, nor used and enjoyed by persons either as private individuals or as members of the public; nor could *divini iuris* be subjected to partial ownership controls such as servitudes.[39] Within this class of *res*, the sacred things (*res sacrae*) were things consecrated, dedicated, or otherwise made sacred.[40] *Res religiosae*, religious things (such as tombs), were inherently sacred;[41] sanctified things were the city gates and walls, inherently sacred because of their civil importance rather than religious or other-worldly associations.[42]

(ii) res nullius, humani iuris. 'Wild animals, birds and fish, the creatures of land, sea and sky, become the property of the taker as soon as they are caught. Where something has no owner, it is reasonable that the person who takes it should have it.'[43] This principle dictated that uncaptured wild animals such as fish in a stream could not be owned. There was an elaborate set of rules defining when animals were to be regarded as wild and unowned, or captive and hence appropriated.[44] Another example of *res nullius, humani iuris* was abandoned property: 'if an owner abandons a thing the property passes straight away to anyone who takes possession of it. The law sees a thing as abandoned when the owner throws it away intending that it shall cease at once to be his property.'[45]

these previous three categories—*res communes, res publicae* and *res universitatis*. Many of the examples referred to are subject to ownership by private individuals. In relation to those privately owned there will generally be no public rights of access, even for buildings such as theatres which might be seen as 'quasi-public' (see Gray, 'Property in Thin Air', 286–92). Even in relation to things not privately owned, public rights to use may not be general but contractually licensed in order to prevent overcrowding and overexploitation.

[38] Inst.2.1.7.; G.Inst.2.2, 2.9.; D.1.8.1.,5. (Gaius); D.1.8.2.,4. (Marcian).

[39] D.8.4.4. (Javolenus); D.39.3.17.3. (Paul); cf. D.8.5.1. (Ulpian).

[40] Inst.2.1.8.   [41] Inst.2.1.9.

[42] Inst.2.1.10.; G.*Inst.* 2.8.; Buckland, *Textbook of Roman Law*, 183–4.

[43] Inst.2.1.12.; D.41.1.1.1. (Gaius); D.41.10.2. (Paul).

[44] e.g. Inst.1.12.–16. The English law took a very different course, with prerogative and feudal claims to wildlife trumping the *res nullius* doctrine; cf. *The Case of Swans* (1592) 7 Co. Rep. 156 at 176; see further Getzler, 'Judges and Hunters: Law and Economic Conflict in the English Countryside 1800–60', in Brooks and Lobban (eds.), *Communities and Courts in Britain 1150–1900* (London: Hambledon Press, 1997), 199–228.

[45] Inst.2.1.47. Cf. the case of treasure trove where there is no abandonment but no known owner, so that ownership passes in equal shares to finder and landowner (Inst.2.1.39.; Birks, 'The Roman Law Concept of Dominium', 15).

Res nullius embraced many disparate property forms; the defining quality of this type of *res* was that it could become privately owned—that is, unlike all the preceding categories of property, it was susceptible to appropriation by individuals as their exclusive property. Some texts state that public goods are capable of appropriation, blurring the line between communal and unowned goods; but this is against the main classical tradition of classification.[46]

The Primacy of Sacred and Communal Property in Early Law

The earlier *Institutes* of Gaius[47] describe the two classes of things 'subject either to divine right or to human' as 'the leading division of things', rather than the private/non-private division. After Gaius discusses the various divine categories in close detail, the non–divine are brusquely dealt with:

Now what is subject to divine right cannot belong to anyone, whereas what is subject to human right belongs in general to someone, though it may belong to no one . . . Things subject to human right are either public or private. Public things are regarded as belonging to no individual, but as being the property of the corporate body. Private things are those belonging to individuals.[48]

The emphasis on the divine/human distinction rather than the public/private distinction in the earlier Roman law provoked Durkheim to a brilliant anthropological speculation concerning the origins of property. He wrote:

There are things which are not the object of any kind of right of property . . . The sacred things [of Roman law] were in fact outside any transactions, absolutely inalienable and could not become the object of any real right or any obligation whatever. They were not owned by anyone. It is true we might say, and it was said, that they were the property of the gods. But the effect of this very formula is that they do not constitute human property, and we are concerned here with the rights of ownership exercised by men. This attributing of the sacred things to the gods was in reality only a way of declaring that they were not and could not be appropriated by any man. But that particular feature is not and could not be confined to

---

[46] See e.g. D.41.1.14.pr. (Neratius): 'What a man erects on the seashore are public, not in the sense that they belong to the community as such but that they are initially provided by nature and have hitherto become no one's property. Their state is not dissimilar to that of fish and wild animals which, once caught, undoubtedly become the property of those into whose power they have come.' Cf. D.41.1.50. (Pomponius) (administrative control of building on the seashore).

[47] Gaius, *Institutiones Iuris Civilis*. This work was only rediscovered in 1816, but its influence on European law is incalculable, as the Justinianic law is imbued with or founded upon Gaius's conceptions: see Jolowicz and Nicholas, *Historical Introduction to the Study of Roman Law*, 386 ff.; Honoré, *Gaius* (Oxford: Oxford University Press, 1962); *Justinian's Institutes*, ed. Krueger, ed. and trans. Birks and McLeod, Introduction, 16–18.

[48] G.Inst.2.9.–11.

this category alone. There was also what was called in Rome the *res communes* . . . things which belong to no one because they belong to all and by their nature elude any appropriation: the air, springs and streams and the sea. Everyone may use them, but no individual or group can be pointed to as owner. There exists today what is called property under public ownership—roads, highways, streets, the banks of rivers that are navigable . . . the shores of the sea. All these forms of property are administered by the State but they are not owned by it . . . What emerges from these facts is that the range of objects liable to appropriation is not necessarily settled by their natural composition but by the law of any nation. It is public opinion in every society that makes some objects regarded as liable to appropriation and others not: it is not their physical nature as natural science might define it, but the form their image takes in the public mind. A certain thing which yesterday could not be appropriated, may be so today and vice versa.[49]

Durkheim took the idea of sacred or taboo objects as the key to the emergence of all property forms. An examination of non-European societies suggested that 'to declare a thing taboo or to take possession of it are one and the same . . . During the harvest or fishing season, the river or the fields were declared taboo to protect the yield.' Durkheim observed that in all systems of law the right to exclude, rather than the rights to the use, the fruits or the disposal of assets, lay at the core of property institutions. The right to appropriate and exclude was based on a communal delegation of exclusory powers to the clan or family gods (and later to the desacralized individual who became a bearer of natural rights). In early societies these exclusive powers were in belief taboos ordained by gods; but in function, institutions by which society preserved and maintained itself:

The gods are no other than collective forces personified and hypostasized in material form. Ultimately it is the society that is worshipped by the believers; the superiority of the gods over men is that of the group over its members . . . If this interpretation is right, the sacred nature of appropriation had for a long time simply meant that private property was a concession by the collectivity.[50]

Durkheim argued that the high sanctity accorded to the walls of towns and the boundaries delimiting farming land in Rome[51] (and in other ancient cultures) was a form of taboo protecting the life of the community or family. It followed that in these societies exclusive rights upon appropriation were not based on some individual natural right to the product of one's labour or some utilitarian protection of and incentive for the individual's labour—the tradition of Hobbes, Locke, and Hegel which has so exercised the modern mind. Durkheim held rather that the concept of labour as the

---

[49] Durkheim, *The Nature and Origins of Property*, from Durkheim, *Professional Ethics and Civic Morals*, trans. Brookfield, repr. in Lukes and Scull (eds.), *Durkheim and the Law* (Oxford: Martin Robertson, 1983), 158–9.

[50] Lukes and Scull (eds.), *Durkheim and the Law*, 166, 182, 184.

[51] See D.8.2.14. (Papirus Justus, *Imperial Rulings*).

origin of property through appropriation was a very late philosophical theory not present in the history of property ideas until comparatively modern times—and then only through the rise of contractarian concepts.[52]

Thus Durkheim derived from early Roman law the theory that 'sacrosanct . . . communal property is the stock from which the other forms sprang'.[53] Durkheim's argument is useful as a corrective to the individualist stereotypes of Roman property law; his thesis suggests that the Justinianic law with its incorporation of the *extra patrimonio* idea of property inherited the collectivism of early law as well as the individualism of classical law. Moreover, Durkheim's ideas can suggest a different model of property institutions in general, across time and place. Non-private, *extra patrimonio* forms of property, appropriated for communal purposes, are seen to be analytically prior to the familiar natural and civil modes for acquiring and holding individual property developed by later law. The theory stresses the group mind over the individual will, communal solidarity and sentiment rather than rational individual utility-seeking, group action before cooperative transactions in pursuit of economic returns.[54] It is valuable to keep in mind these divergent social forms and practices contained within the institution of property as we further investigate the attempts of Roman and English jurists to define a regime of property rights for land resources.

Personal and Real Actions

Another divide in the Roman exegesis of the law of things was the split between rights *in personam* and *in rem*. Roman law did not speak strictly of personal rights binding specific obligated individuals, on the one hand, and real rights binding all persons, on the other; rather a distinction was made between *in personam* and *in rem* actions. According to the *Institutes*, an action was the 'right to go to court to get one's due', and 'every action which takes an issue between parties to a trial . . . is either real or personal'. Ulpian stated the principle as follows:

There are two kinds of action, real, which is called *vindicatio*, and personal, which is called *condictio*. A real action is one by which we claim our property which is in the possession of another; and it is always brought against the person who is in pos-

---

[52] Lukes and Scull (eds.), *Durkheim and the Law*, 189–91.

[53] Durkheim's theory remains to be empirically supported; modern scholarship investigating the emergence of property institutions in early Rome through reconstruction of the forms of action has not reached conclusions as to whether ownership developed from common property or from tribal territorial control (see discussions in Birks, 'The Roman Law Concept of Dominium', 3–7, and Diosdi, *Ownership in Ancient and Preclassical Roman Law*, (Budapest: Akadimiai Kiads, 1970), 19–30, 62–84, 121–7).

[54] For a fuller discussion of these points, see Getzler, 'Theories of Property and Economic Development', (1996) 26 J. of Interdisciplinary History 639.

session of the property. A personal action is one which we bring against him who is bound to do some act or give something to us; and it always has application against that person.[55]

A personal action typically asserted an obligation arising from contract or wrongdoing,[56] requiring the defendant to do something or give something to the plaintiff; a real action was a dispute not about the defendant's obligations but a real claim for a thing of value—for example, a claim for the possession of a corporeal thing or the exercise of an incorporeal property right.[57] There could be a personal obligation with real effects, such as a contractual obligation to deliver[58] or an obligation to surrender possession;[59] but these 'real obligations' were not to be confused with rights *in rem*: 'The essence of obligations does not consist in that it makes some property or a servitude ours, but that it binds another person to give, do, or perform something for us.'[60] This meant that Romans saw a gulf between contracts to convey land (*in personam*) and public actions that actually vested the land in the new owner (*in rem*). English law was far more lax in this territory, and allowed private obligations of sale and trust to have public effects in varying ownership; the resulting nightmare for conveyancers called the system of title registration into being.

At Roman law there was a parsimony of actions: 'if several actions arise from one obligation, one action alone and not all must be used.'[61] This meant that sometimes personal rather than real actions would be used in order to assert real rights. The distinction between the nature of a right asserted and the type of remedy sought to uphold the right was one of the Romans' most sophisticated legal innovations, and deeply influenced the English common law. Thus we use the ancient *in personam* wrong of trespass primarily to defend and assert *in rem* land rights, to take one important example.

Corporeal and Incorporeal Rights

Roman law did not make a primary distinction between objects in the world (land, water, and so on), and legal rights over those objects; instead there were the categories of corporeal and incorporeal things or rights. Corporeal things were physical, tangible objects;[62] the ultimate ownership right (*dominium*) of a physical object was identified with the object and was

---

[55] D.44.7.25.pr. (Ulpian).
[56] There were, of course, other categories: quasi-delict (Inst.4.5.) and quasi-contract (Inst.3.27.).
[57] Inst.4.6.pr.–1.; D.44.7.1.pr. (Gaius).
[58] D.44.7.1.1.–2. (Gaius).
[59] D.44.7.28. (Papinian); D.44.7.52. (Modestinus).
[60] D.44.7.3.pr. (Paul).
[61] D.44.7.53.pr. (Modestinus).
[62] Inst.2.2.2., borrowing directly from G.Inst.2.12.–14.

itself a *res corporalis*—the only corporeal right in the law.[63] All other real rights or things were incorporeal, as they were intangible rights that existed only in law; a right was incorporeal even if it brought with it control of physical things, such as a right of inheritance or a usufruct (the right to the use and produce of a corporeal thing).[64] Only corporeal rights could be possessed;[65] incorporeal rights could be used or exercised, but incorporeal things, according to post-classical nomenclature, could be 'quasi-possessed' only—possessed metaphorically through use or exercise of the incorporeal right.[66] This distinction has, of course, been adopted by common law systems—for example, the land itself is corporeal and a right of way over the land is incorporeal.[67]

Possession and Ownership

A defining feature of Justinanic property law was the strict insistence on the distinction between possession and ownership, or more accurately between the possessory actions and the actions to assert ownership.[68] We trade in similar ideas today with doctrines of prescription, estate contracts, and registration of possessory interests in conveyancing. The Roman concepts of possession and ownership were made up of a number of basic ideas including the following:

1. Possession at its simplest involves physical occupation

'Possession is so styled . . . from "seat", as it were "position", because there is a natural holding . . . by the person who stands on a thing.'[69] The idea of 'natural possession' or physical occupation was sometimes said to be the ultimate origin of ownership, and this idea survived as 'a relic . . . in the atti-

---

[63] Buckland, *Textbook of Roman Law*, 185–7.

[64] Inst.2.2.2.; Buckland, 'Interpolations in the Digest' (1923–4) 33 Yale LJ 343 at 359–60; Thomas, *Institutes of Justinian: Text and Commentary*, 84 (inheritance); Inst.2.4.pr.; D.7.1.1. (Paul); D.7.1.2. (Celsus); D.7.1.3.2. (Gaius); D.7.1.4. (Paul); Buckland, *Textbook of Roman Law*, 185–7 (usufruct).

[65] D.41.2.3.pr. (Paul).   [66] D.8.2.32.1. (Julian).

[67] See Gray, *Elements of Land Law*, 31–2.

[68] For the origin of this doctrine, see Jolowicz and Nicholas, *Historical Introduction to the Study of Roman Law*, 272 ff.; see further Barton, 'Animus and possessio nomine alieno'; Evans-Jones and MacCormack, *Iusta causa traditionis*; Gordon, 'The Importance of the *iusta causa* of *traditio*', all in Birks (ed.), *New Perspectives in the Roman Law of Property* (Oxford: Oxford University Press, 1989), 43, 99, 123. For comparisons with English law, see Pollock and Wright, *An Essay on Possession in the Common Law* (Oxford: Oxford University Press, 1888).

[69] D.41.2.1.pr. (Paul, Labeo); and note Nicholas, *Roman Law* 111 n. 1: *possessio* is 'sitting in power'; Thomas, *Institutes of Justinian: Text and Commentary*, 94–6: 'physical sovereignty'; Buckland, *Main Institutions of Roman Private Law*, 104: 'possession is . . . having effective control of a thing . . . *possessio* is a question of fact.'

tude to those things which are taken on land, sea, or in the air; for such things forthwith become the property of him who first takes possession of them.'[70] As rights and objects of property were defined outside the field of corporeal natural acquisitions, more complex ideas of possession and ownership than mere physical appropriation had to be developed. 'All in all, possession as such is one in nature, but its varieties are infinite' observed Paul.[71] Yet the physical nature of possession survived strongly in the exclusory rule that 'those things can be possessed which are corporeal'.[72] A number of results flowed from this doctrine. For example, possession as a physical occupation could only be an exclusive possession; and it followed that there could be joint, but not separate and simultaneous possessions: 'Only one person can possess exclusively; exclusive possessions cannot coincide, unless one is lawful the other(s) unlawful.'[73] Specific portions and undivided shares of an estate could be possessed and owned, but non-specific parts or appurtenances could not.[74]

2. A mental element goes to constitute possession

Both physical control and intention to possess—*corpus* and *animus*—had to be present to found a legal possession. Paul states the doctrine plainly: 'Now we take possession physically and mentally, not mentally alone and physically alone'[75] . . . One acquires possession by an act of the mind and an act of the body (*animo et corpore*); the act of the mind must be one's own, but the act of the body may be supplied by another.'[76] Hence a person who occupied land without the belief that he was taking an exclusive possession in the manner of an owner was not a possessor in law;[77] and an intention to possess in the absence of physical occupation was not enough to create a legal possession of a vacant or unowned *res*,[78] nor a factual possession sufficient to found *usucapio* of an owned *res*.[79]

---

[70] D.41.2.1.1. (Paul); see also D.41.10.2. (Paul). [71] D.41.2.3.21. (Paul).

[72] D.41.2.3.pr. (Paul). [73] D.41.2.3.5. (Paul).

[74] D.41.2.26. (Proculus); cf. 41.3.23.pr. (Javolenus); 41.3.26. (Ulpian). In modern trusts law this same attitude is reflected in the requirement of unity of possession for both forms of joint ownership, the tenancy in common and the joint tenancy.

[75] D.41.2.3.1. (Paul); D.8.6.9. (Javolenus) states a similar rule for servitudes.

[76] Cited in Nicholas, *Roman Law*, 112; and see D.41.2.3.pr.–1., D.41.2.3.12. (Paul).

[77] See e.g. D.41.2.6. (Ulpian).

[78] D.41.1.10.pr.–1. (Gaius). There could, however, be possession asserted through the physical occupation of land not by oneself but by another acting on your behalf (Inst.4.15.5.; D.41.1.10.2., D.41.1.32. (Gaius); D.41.2.49.2. (Papinian)).

[79] D.41.2.49.2. (Papinian). There are many echoes of this in English law, perhaps most obviously in the rules on adverse possession where both an *animus possidendi*, in the form of an 'intention for the time being to possess the land to the exclusion of all other persons' (see Slade LJ in *Buckinghamshire CC* v. *Moran* [1990] Ch. 623 at 643), and factual possession are required to acquire title.

Both *corpus* and *animus* were required to sustain as well as to commence possession; and absence of either element caused loss of possession: 'Just as no possession can be acquired except physically and with intent, so none is lost unless both elements are departed from.'[80] Some texts, however, emphasize either *corpus* or *animus* by themselves as the essential aspect of sustained possession: 'There is this difference between ownership and possession: that a man remains owner even when he does not wish to be, but possession departs once one decides not to possess. Hence if someone should transfer possession with the intention that it should later be restored to him, he ceases to possess.'[81]

Physical occupation, we have seen, was the factual foundation of possession; but as the law developed, the factor of intention or mental state was increasingly stressed. For example, once possession has been established, it seemed that the mental element alone was sufficient to terminate possession. 'Again, for the loss of possession, the possessor's mental attitude must be considered; if you are on a piece of land and lose the will to possess it, you immediately cease to possess it. Hence, possession can be lost, though it cannot be acquired, by will alone.'[82]

Conversely, intention could suffice to sustain a possession in law, even if the physical element of the possession had ended or was replaced by another's occupation:

But should you be in possession by will alone, you continue to possess the land, even though someone else be physically present on it.[83]

For summer and winter pastures of which possession is retained by intent . . . even though we have no slave or tenant there . . . the previous possessor is said to possess even though another has entered the pasture with the object of possessing it, so long as he is in ignorance of the entry. For just as the bond of an obligation is released in the same way that it is normally created, so also possession which is held solely by intention should not be taken away from one ignorant of the facts.[84]

The German jurists von Savigny and von Jhering differed over which element, mental or physical, should be emphasized in distinguishing Roman possession from mere detention;[85] and this ignited a celebrated controversy absorbing the attention of generations of nineteenth-century legal theorists. The whole issue may be circumvented by recognizing that a mental state of occupation is signalled by physical acts, just as the existence of acts of physical appropriation depends upon some state of mind on the part of the actor giving meaning and agency to that act. A good example of this dialectic between physical act and mental state was the important rule that a limited

---

[80] D.41.2.8. (Paul).   [81] D.41.2.17.1. (Ulpian).   [82] D.41.2.3.6. (Paul).
[83] D.41.2.3.7. (Paul).   [84] D.41.2.44.2.-4. (Papinian).
[85] See Nicholas, *Roman Law*, 112–24, esp. 112 n. 1; Thomas, *Institutes of Justinian: Text and Commentary*, 97.

act of appropriation could signal an occupation and intention sufficient to found a more extensive possession:

But when we say that we must take possession both physically and mentally, that should not be taken to mean that one seeking to possess an estate must go round every part of it; suffice it that he enters some part of the estate, but with the intent and awareness that thereby he seeks to possess the estate to its utmost boundaries.[86]

The civil mode of acquisition known as *traditio* exemplifies this principle, whereby property was transferred by informal, even symbolic delivery of the *res* or control thereof.[87]

3. Ownership may be asserted without possession

Ulpian states: 'Ownership has nothing in common with possession; hence, a man who institutes a *vindicatio* for land [a claim of *dominium*] will not be refused the interdict *uti possidetis* [a claim for restoration of possession]; for he is deemed not to have renounced possession by asserting ownership.'[88]

In the classical law a preliminary action was normal to determine possessory right before resort to a real action to vindicate ownership or *dominium*: 'The outcome of a dispute is simply this: that the judge makes an interim finding that one of the parties possesses; the result will be that the party defeated on the issue of possession will take the role of plaintiff when the question of ownership [*dominio*] is contested.'[89] In practice, a person seeking recovery would begin with the simpler possessory action, and leave his opponent to respond with an action of *vindicatio* asserting *dominium*.

The right to use a thing and enjoy its fruits—*usufruct*—could in a sense be 'owned' through possession alone. The principle of usufruct will further be analysed below as it casts light on fundamental aspects of the concept of *dominium*.

4. Possession may be defended without title

Ulpian states: 'If a person be evicted forcibly from possession, he is treated as still possessing, since he has the ability to recover possession. By the interdict *de vi*.'[90] The doctrine was sometimes expressed by the idea that possession is a fact, regardless of whether one has lost physical control; and that fact of possession is absolutely protected if physical control is lost.[91] The

---

[86] D.41.2.3.1. (Paul); also D.8.6.9. (Javolenus); D.41.10.1.pr. (Ulpian).

[87] Nicholas, *Roman Law*, 117–20.   [88] D.41.2.12.1. (Ulpian).

[89] D.41.2.35. (Ulpian); and see also Inst.4.15.4. In Justinian's law the interim interdict was assumed and the substantive issue of title decided directly: the post-classical law is set out in Inst.4.15.4a., 8.

[90] D.41.2.17.pr. (Ulpian).

[91] The distinction between the factual quality of legally protected possession and the legal quality of *dominium* was expressed in the dictum: 'Ownership has nothing in common with possession' (D.41.2.12.1. (Ulpian)).

chief concern of this doctrine was to prevent forcible dispossessions, even by a true owner reclaiming his land from a wrongful possessor; by the interdict *uti possidetis*,

the winner was the party in possession at the date of the interdict itself, as long as his possession had not been obtained from his opponent by force, stealth or licence [*nec vi, clam aut precario*]. It was irrelevant that the possessor had forcibly driven out a third party, had secretly usurped a third party's possession, or had obtained a third party's licence to possess.[92]

Thus immediate possession was generally protected from extra-legal interference, even if it was wrongful or vicious or based on a property-right relatively worse than the opponent's: 'It makes no difference in this interdict whether the possession against others is just or unjust. For every kind of possessor has by virtue of being a possessor more right than the non-possessor.'[93]

The interdictal protection of the possessor against all persons was qualified importantly by the rule that interdicts would protect only a possession that was *nec vi, clam aut precario* as regards one's opponent, though 'against third parties, even vicious possession is normally of avail'.[94] This rule meant that the immediate dispossessor of a claimant would lose possession because his possession fell into the *vi, clam aut precario* catogory. But an assignee of the immediate dispossesor, who had attained possession *nec vi, clam aut precario*, would retain possession under the interdict. Many of these rules were reproduced in the medieval English title actions of novel disseisin.[95]

5. Ownership must be proved as an absolute right, beyond disproof

In the post-classical law, a claimant who could not recover by possessory interdict would have to bring a *vindicatio* asserting not possession but *dominium*: 'I am the absolute owner.' He might then produce evidence towards establishing his *dominium*; the opponent in possession could defeat the claim only by proof that the claimant was *not* in fact the owner. In other words, to maintain a *vindicatio* restoring property, *dominium* had to be proved sufficiently so that the opponent could not disprove it by positive evidence. The action thus did not provide a procedure for asserting a *relative* title based on a superior ranked right to possession, as in English (and possibly earlier Roman law); *dominium* had to be proved absolutely (that is, ultimate ownership beyond the opponent's capacity to disprove it).[96]

---

[92] Inst.4.15.4a.

[93] D.43.17.2. (Paul).

[94] D.41.2.53. (Venuleius). For moveables, see Inst.4.1.4a.; D.43.31.pr.–1. (Ulpian).

[95] Sutherland, *The Assize of Novel Disseisin* (Oxford: Oxford University Press, 1973) 20–42.

[96] Nicholas, *Roman Law*, 108–9, 115.

'Roman law has an action asserting ownership and an action asserting possession but no action asserting merely a right to possession.'[97]

6. A derivative ownership must derive from causa or title, not from mere delivery of possession

Ownership or *dominium* could be constituted by possession, as through the natural or original modes of acquisition such as occupation of a *res nullius*. Derivative acquisition of an existing ownership required something more than possession: there had to be some recognized legal ground of title acquisition, some *iusta causa*. Where an existing ownership was to be transferred the rule was that 'bare delivery of itself never transfers ownership, but only where there is a prior sale or other ground [*iusta causa*] on account of which the delivery follows'.[98] Thus for contractual transfer it was delivery into possession, rather than the grant or contract or other *iusta causa*, which was the legal fact clinching the constitution of the newly transferred property right: 'the act which creates a right *in personam* does not create a right *in rem* . . . a contract creates rights in personam but cannot create or transfer rights *in rem*.'[99] But in all cases *causa* or independent source of title was the prerequisite to effective delivery; and it followed that: 'Delivery should not and cannot transfer to the transferee any greater title than resides in the transferor. Hence, if someone conveys land of which he is owner, he transfers his title; if he does not have ownership, he conveys nothing to the recipient.'[100] The principle can be expressed in more general terms as the distinction between contract and conveyance. There was *causa* or source of title in the form of a legal transaction dealing with ownership; and there was conveyance or constitution of the real right by delivery and possession. The doctrine is an instance of the idea of Roman law that property rights which bind all persons should not be transferred by private transactions alone, but by a public, apparent act. Hence some physical, ceremonial, and public act of delivery and appropriation was required to convey property additional to the legal act of contract and grant. The *Institutes* state the idea that a delivery executes and concludes a contractual transfer of property in the following terms:

Another natural law mode of acquisition is delivery. What could be more in line with natural justice than to give effect to a man's intention to transfer something of his to another? That is why the law allows all corporeal things to be delivered and all deliveries by owners to pass the property in the thing delivered.[101]

---

[97] Ibid. 154–7; Thomas, *Institutes of Justinian: Text and Commentary*, 94–6.

[98] D.41.1.31. (Paul); and see D.7.6.5. (Ulpian) for *usufruct*.

[99] Nicholas, *Roman Law*, 103.

[100] D.41.1.20.pr. (Ulpian). This doctrine—the *nemo dat* rule—survives in heavily qualified form in English sale law.

[101] Inst.2.1.40., and see Buckland, *Main Institutions of Roman Private Law*, 104–12; Buckland and McNair, *Roman Law and Common Law* (2nd edn. by Lawson, Cambridge: Cambridge University Press, 1952), 59; Nicholas, *Roman Law*, 103–5, 116–20.

The doctrine of *usucapio* employed the concept of *iusta causa* in a different sense to bridge the bright line between possession and ownership. *Usucapio* grounded new titles on the fact of long possession; but the doctrine formally preserved a requirement of *iusta causa* in conjunction with possession rather than taking factual possession as the foundation of the prescriptive ownership.[102] The later doctrines of bonitary ownership and good faith possession were derived from *usucapio* or long possession, and these doctrines created a further melding of possession and ownership rights. The law here provided protection to persons in possession who were on the way to gaining prescriptive titles, but had not yet completed the period of *usucapio*, thus vesting a proprietary right in any person who had good faith possession, a right good against all persons save the *dominus*. This development was transformative, giving rise in effect to a system of relative titles in the post-classical law.[103] But the relativity was restrained by the facility with which possessory titles could harden into species of *dominium*.[104]

Praedial servitudes

1. Servitudes as proprietary land-use rights.

Our next concern is with the category of real (not personal) servitudes (*servitutes*), known as praedial servitudes, '[t]he rights which belong to urban and rustic estates (*praediorum urbanorum et rusticorum*)'.[105] They may be defined as incorporeal rights *in rem* that gave some benefit to a dominant estate by restraining use of servient neighbouring land in some way, either by preventing the servient owner from pursuing certain actions, or by enjoining him to allow the dominant owner certain uses of his land.

2. The praedial doctrine

The *Institutes* state the following central doctrine delimiting the concept of servitude: 'The reason these rights are called servitudes belonging to land is that they cannot exist independently of land. Nobody can acquire a servitude of urban or rustic land unless he has land nor can one without land bear the liability implicit in a servitude.'[106] The praedial doctrine thus has two parts: for there to be a servitude there must be servient land burdened by a restriction; and there must be dominant land correspondingly benefited by the restriction. This dual doctrine had many implications, for example

---

[102] D.41.10.5.pr.-1. (Neratius).

[103] See further Nicholas, *An Introduction to Roman Law*, 3rd ed., 1962, (Oxford UP, Oxford) at pp. 125–8, 153–7.

[104] There are obvious parallels with modern English rules on adverse possession.

[105] Inst.2.2.3.; G.Inst.2.14., 14a. See generally Schulz, *Classical Roman Law*, 1951, (Oxford: Oxford University Press, 1951), 381–99.

[106] Inst.2.2.3.; see also G.Inst.2.29.; D.8.1.8.pr. (Paul); 15.pr. (Pomponius); 19. (Labeo); D.8.2.30. (Paul); D.8.2.32. (Julian); D.8.3.5.1. (Ulpian).

(1) there could be no servitude over one's own property as there was no servient tenement to be burdened;[107] (2) 'praedial servitudes are extinguished by merger if the same person becomes owner of both estates', for the same reason;[108] (3) the servitude could benefit only the dominant tenement as land; and could not benefit activities that happened to be conducted on the land,[109] nor benefit non-owners or adjacent lands,[110] so that water drawn under a right of *aquae haustus* could not be sold for industrial use.[111] The praedial doctrine also meant that the servitude right was appurtenant to exclusive ownership of particular land, and could not take effect as a right *in personam*; hence there was a rule that a stipulation to create part shares of a right of way or *aquae ductus* (the right to draw water) could create co-owners only of a single property right and not multiple obligations in many persons whether owners or not, 'because the exercise of such rights is indivisible'.[112]

The praedial rule did not apply in the case of personal servitudes, such as the right of usufruct over land which was enjoyed by the usufructary in person rather than as owner of benefited dominant land. Usufruct (being the 'right to the use and fruits of another person's property, with the duty to preserve its substance'[113]) was a means of providing income; it was not a transferable property right maintainable by real action, but was merely a personal right against the *dominus*. Later, a type of auxiliary or appurtenant servitude was annexed to the usufruct, giving the usufructary a real action to ensure physical possession or entry of the corpus in order to make good the right.[114]

---

[107] D.7.6.5.pr. (Ulpian); D.8.2.26. (Paul); D.8.6.1. (Gaius); see further Buckland, 'The Conception of Servitudes in Roman Law' (1928) 44 LQR 426. The rule entered into English land law through Bracton, *De legibus et consuetudinibus angliae*, at fo. 208; fo. 220c, iii. 130; 162; see e.g. *Sury* v. *Pigot* (1625) Popham 166; *Morris* v. *Edgington* (1810) 3 Taunt. 24.

[108] D.8.6.1. (Gaius). For English adoption of the Roman rule: *Tyringham's Case* (1584) 4 Co. Rep. 36b; *Sury* v. *Pigot* (1625) Popham 166.

[109] D.8.1.8.pr. (Paul); D.8.3.5.1.; D.8.3.3.2., 4., 6.pr.; D.8.4.13.pr. (Ulpian); a similar rule is followed in *Hill* v. *Tupper* (1863) 2 H & C 121.

[110] Buckland (*Textbook of Roman Law*, 263, and *Main Institutions of Roman Private Law*, 155) has perceived a possible variation of this rule in D.20.1.2. (Papinian), allowing the enjoyment of a rustic servitude to be pledged to a landed neighbour in security or part-payment of a debt, the pledge allowing sale of the right. English law early permitted profits *à prendre* to exist in gross.

[111] D.8.3.5.1. (Ulpian); D.8.3.24. (Pomponius).

[112] D.8.1.17. (Pomponius); see also D.8.4.5. (Javolenus); D.43.20.4. (Julian); Buckland, *Textbook of Roman Law*, 261–2; cf. D.41.2.43. (Marcian), allowing a part-owner to usucapt the other owner's shares by long possession.

[113] Inst.2.4.; D.7.1.1.(Paul).

[114] D.7.6.5.1.,6. (Ulpian). Buckland (*Textbook of Roman Law*, 268–76) notes that classification of *usufructus* as a personal servitude is post-classical. Another category of personal right with real qualities were restrictive covenants, described by Ulpian in D.8.4.13.; see further Rudden, 'Economic Theory versus Property Law: The *Numerus Clausus* Problem', in Eekelaar and Bell (eds.), *Oxford Essays in Jurisprudence* (3rd ser., Oxford: Oxford University Press, 1989), 239, 244–5.

The rustic praedial servitudes, by contrast, were originally conceived not as personal rights nor as abstract *res corporalis* or rights over land, but as a *corpus* or physical thing, owned and occupied separately from the land or soil itself. These rights could be described as an ownership of the defined way or watercourse being a physical structure on the land, or of the minerals and produce of the land—an ownership concurrent with the land itself. Hence the rustic servitudes were transferred by the same means as land, at first as *res mancipi* conveyed by a symbolic physical delivery;[115] in later law by *cessio in iure* (a form of conveyance) and *traditio* (delivery of the thing itself).[116]

The full list of mancipatible rustic servitudes includes rights of way and *aquae ductus* as well as various profits or rights to take elements of the land;[117] all the rustic servitudes exemplify the physical or material origin of such ancient rights in agricultural usage, such as rights to dig sand or to pasture cattle; and they tended to be positive rights. The urban servitudes governing the use of buildings in towns were later forms of more disembodied or intangible rights, and hence were not *res mancipi* but were real rights transferred by *cessio in iure*.[118] Most but not all urban servitudes were negative in nature, such as an obligation not to build higher.[119] By the time of the classical lawyers, the older rustic servitudes were also losing their 'physicalist' quality and were conceived as intangible *iure*, remaining within the class of *res mancipi* as an historical anomaly only.[120]

---

[115] G.Inst.2.14a., 28., 29.; Jolowicz and Nicholas, *Historical Introduction to the Study of Roman Law*, 158 ff.; Buckland, *Textbook of Roman Law*, 261–6; Birks, 'The Roman Law Concept of Dominium', 8–9. For a balanced criticism of the orthodoxy that servitudes originated as a form of corporeal ownership rather than as an independent class of incorporeal rights, see Diosdi, *Ownership in Ancient and Preclassical Roman Law*, 107–16.

[116] Buckland, *Textbook of Roman Law*, 264.

[117] See e.g. G.Inst.2.14.; D.8.3.1.1. (Ulpian); D.8.3.3. (Ulpian): 'Within the category of rustic servitudes must be included the right to draw water, the right to drive cattle to water, the right of pasture, the right to burn lime, and the right to dig sand.' See also discussion of D.8.3.30. (Paul), below n. 217. There are occasional references to *aquaeductus* as an urban servitude when appurtenant to houses: Buckland, *Textbook of Roman Law*, 262–3; D.6.2.11.1. (Ulpian).

[118] Personal servitudes such as usufruct or personal rights of way were originally nonassignable rights of user or enjoyment, enforceable only against the *dominus* of the burdened land. The personal enjoyment of these rights could be transferred contractually; and then, as the rights became more proprietary, there could be transfer by *quasi-traditio* or informal delivery: Buckland, *Textbook of Roman Law*, 268–76.

[119] English law tends to classify positive servitudes as easements and negative ones as restrictive covenants, each with different conceptual bases; Roman law used covenants annexed to land more sparingly.

[120] See e.g. D.8.1.14.pr. (Paul), stating that: 'Rustic praedial servitudes even though attached to corporeal property, are nevertheless incorporeal and so are never acquired by usucapion. Or the reason may be that the nature of these servitudes is such as not to engender clear and continuous possession.' See also D.8.5.4. (Ulpian) and D.8.1.20. (Javolenus), above; Jolowicz and Nicholas, *Historical Introduction to the Study of Roman Law*, 426–7.

Traces of the older corporeal conception may be seen in the idea that servitude rights were transferred formally by a metaphoric 'delivery' of possession;[121] and also in the rule that servitudes might survive the alienation[122] or abandonment[123] of a servient (or dominant) tenement to bind (or benefit) the next owner, as if the servitude maintained a physical existence in the land. However, upon merger of a dominant and servient estate, servitudes were extinguished and did not revive upon separation of the estates, because of the strong principle that servitudes as *iure* could not exist in one's own land; in this instance the abstract incorporeal quality of servitudes was more important than their physical, tangible qualities. According to Buckland,

A servitude is a burden on the land rather than on the ownership. It is an independent *ius* which must be thought of rather as parallel to ownership than as a burden on it. If we reflect on the fact that the earliest servitudes were *res mancipi*, capable of *usucapio* and pledge, the idea that they were thought of as physical things, actual visible tracks and channels, will account for those rules which may look anomalous in classical law.[124]

3. The *in rem* nature of servitude actions

The residual 'physicality' of servitudes and usufruct may partly explain why *in rem* or real actions came to be regarded as the proper procedure for claiming these rights. Incorporeal rights such as servitudes were certainly defended as proprietary *res* rather than as personal rights, by means of real actions:

The action was real . . . if someone claims to be entitled to a usufruct over some land or a house; or a right of way for man and beast over his neighbour's land; or a right to lead water from his neighbour's land. The same again with actions for the urban servitudes: claiming e.g. the right of building higher, of prospect, projection, or attachment to a neighbour's wall.[125]

In another sense servitudes were rights *in rem* because they were rights of property attached to land—rights which all persons were bound to respect independently of contractual or personal relations. This quality has two aspects: first, servitude rights followed or ran with the ownership of the land:

---

[121] D.8.1.20. (Javolenus); cf. D.8.3.14. (Pomponius) and D.39.3.11.pr. (Paul), on the *aquae ductus* as a physical right incompatible with the coexistence of a right of way along the same route.

[122] D.8.6.13. (Marcellus).

[123] Jolowicz and Nicholas, *Historical Introduction to the Study of Roman Law*, 427; Thomas, *Textbook of Roman Law* (Amsterdam: North-Holland, 1976), 195; Buckland, *Main Institutions of Roman Private Law* (Cambridge: Cambridge University Press, 1931), 113–14; Buckland, *Textbook of Roman Law*, 259, 268.

[124] Buckland, *Textbook of Roman Law*, 260, 268. [125] Inst.4.6.1.–2.

Now whenever ownership is transferred, it passes to the transferee in the same case as it was with the transferor; if the land was subject to a servitude, it passes with the servitude; if it was unencumbered, it passes in that state; and if, perchance, there should be servitudes due to the land, it passes with the servitudes due.[126]

And servitudes could be defended against all the world:

This [real] action can be brought not only against a man on whose land the source of the water is situated or across whose land it is channeled, but, in fact, against anyone at all who prevents one from channeling the water, as is the case with servitudes in general. In short, by means of this action, I can proceed against anyone who tries to stop me from channeling the water.[127]

There was a taboo against requiring a servient owner to perform positive actions of service as an indicium of their ownership; *dominium* of servient land was not to involve personal duties of servitude akin to slavery. Only tiny exceptions to this rule were allowed, such as the positive duty to keep a house support in good repair. By contrast, English law and other feudal systems commonly did annex personal burdens of service to servient tenements.[128]

4. *Ius and ius in re aliena*

The right of usufruct was eventually brought within the broader category of servitudes as a so-called personal servitude.[129] The notion of a unified law of servitudes embracing both usufructs and praedial servitudes can be seen as a move to generalize all rights over land amounting to less than full ownership as burdens upon or fractions of the ownership of another's land.[130] The humanist Civilians made this plain, using the general concept

---

[126] D.41.1.20.1. (Ulpian).

[127] D.8.5.10.1. (Ulpian). On the well-established application of real rather than personal actions for the maintenance of praedial servitudes, see also D.8.5.4., D.8.5.18. (Julian). The classical forms of action for asserting usufruct and servitude rights by *vindicatio* seeking real restitution through the personal sanction of a pecuniary condemnation are discussed in Buckland, 'The Protection of Servitudes in Roman Law' (1930) 46 LQR 447. Buckland also suggests that *iure in rem*, for the purposes of real procedure, were treated fictitiously as if they were a type of *dominium*: Buckland, *Main Institutions of Roman Private Law*, 160. Developments of the law after Justinian are traced in Kagan, 'The Nature of Servitudes and the Association of Usufruct with Them' (1947) 22 Tulane LR 94; Feenstra, '*Dominium* and *ius in re aliena*: The Origins of a Civil Law Distinction', in Birks (ed.), *New Perspectives in the Roman Law of Property*, 111.

[128] Cairns, 'Craig, Cujas, and the Definition of *feodum*: Is a Feu a Usufruct?', in Birks (ed.), *New Perspectives in the Roman Law of Property*, 76.

[129] D.8.1.1. (Marcian). Buckland states that *usufructus* is described as a servitude only six times, and suggests that this description was a late classical or Justinianic idea interpolated into *Digest* texts (Buckland, *Textbook of Roman Law*, 268).

[130] D.7.1.4. (Paul). Cf. definition of usufruct in Inst.2.4.pr. and D.7.1.1.; see Buckland, *Textbook of Roman Law*, 259; Buckland, *Elementary Principles of the Roman Private Law*, 92–114.

of *iura in re aliena*, incorporeal rights in the property of another, to describe the unified class of personal and praedial servitudes. *Dominium* was then redefined as the sum of the bundle of abstract rights over land—not the ultimate right of the owner to claim title, to have the thing in his property. The impulse behind this new conceptualization was not solely analytic. The humanist Civilians believed that *dominium* as absolute ownership summing all possible rights in land was the more modern institution, preferable to a concept of *dominium* as the superior right amongst many possible rights held over land, a concept too reminiscent of feudal lordship and inequality of status amongst right-holders.[131] These later categorizations were not, however, part of *Digest* law; both usufruct and servitude were seen simply as *iure*—abstract incorporeal rights entitling the holder to engage in certain uses of, or activities upon the land of another; rights which coexisted with the *dominus*'s ultimate right which was likewise a *ius* over the land. The special ultimate character of *dominium* was expressed in the rule that a *dominus* could not have a separate right of usufruct or servitude over his own land.[132]

THE ABIDING MARKS OF ROMAN LAW

Diosdi suggests it was not the case that sophisticated concepts of *iure* were developed as extensions of a more primitive concept of ownership as lawfully protected possession and control. Rather the reverse case held:

The creation of the notion of *dominium* was also dependent on the previous formation of the category of *servitus* and the appearance of the institution of *usus fructus*. A statue is only finished when the chisel of the sculptor has removed the superfluous marble. Likewise, the abstract notion of ownership can only be created after everything not belonging to ownership, has been stripped off. The classical Roman notion of ownership . . . is characterized by an utter disregard of those external appearances which represent the very idea of ownership to the layman. Thus *dominium* is not only clearly separated from possession, but also from the use of the thing and from enjoyment of its fruits.[133]

It was the drive to abstraction and technicality in the specification of property rights that made Roman law so significant in world history. Only the

---

[131] Cairns, 'Craig, Cujas, and the Definition of *feodum*: Is a Feu a Usufruct?', 76; Feenstra, '*Dominium* and *ius in re aliena*: The Origins of a Civil Law Distinction', 111. On the issues concerning *dominium* and relativity of titles, see Buckland, *Textbook of Roman Law*, 186–8; Diosdi, *Ownership in Ancient and Preclassical Roman Law*, 131–6, 180–5; Birks, 'The Roman Law Concept of Dominium', 25–31.

[132] D.7.6.5.pr. (Ulpian); D.8.2.26. (Paul); D.8.6.1. (Gaius); see further Buckland, 'The Conception of Servitudes in Roman Law' (1928) 44 LQR 426.

[133] Diosdi, *Ownership in Ancient and Preclassical Roman Law*, 131–6.

English common law developed a rival system of sophisticated, abstract, infinitely malleable and useful rules for the allocation and transformation of property rights. The common law system is still perceived as divided from Civilian law by a Chinese Wall of opposed concepts; the relativity of titles and the feudal inheritance of estates rather than dominion are prime examples. Yet, once we investigate the development of key English property doctrines such as possessory actions, prescription, and servitudes,[134] we discover powerful Roman influences that rob the common law of much of its originality.

[134] Key texts here include Gale, *Law of Easements* (1st edn., London: Sweet & Maxwell, 1839); *Benest* v. *Pipon* (1829) 1 Knapp 60 at 69–70 (PC, Jersey); *Dalton* v. *Angus* (1881) 6 App. Cas. 740 at 819, 822 (HL).

4

THE 1925 PROPERTY LEGISLATION:
SETTING CONTEXTS

Stuart Anderson

The 1925 legislation set English land law on a path quite different from that of other common law jurisdictions. One purpose of this chapter is to show how that happened, to enable students when considering the big ideas in land law to ground an understanding of the relation between law, time, and place. What was there about English society (and Welsh; but not Scottish or Northern Irish) that made its land law different? Was the law better for being different? Is it better still? For students lost in a maze of detail those questions may seem a luxury. But an ability to evaluate competing grand designs is part of understanding law as a whole, and one element of that may sometimes be an appreciation of how designs get invented. My second purpose is much more closely related to the day-to-day business of legal problem solving. It is to ask how far an understanding of the processes leading to the legislation can generate a preferred meaning to particular parts of the text, when that text comes to be tested in hard cases. Rather than attempting a single chronological account of the legislation's gestation, I shall offer three explanatory narratives leading to the legislation, in descending order of generality, followed by a postscript about its reception. The conclusion will then return to the themes sketched above. First, however, it is necessary to outline just what was different about the English path, what it is that needs explaining.

Suppose you are asked to sketch modern English land law for lawyers from a different common law jurisdiction—say the states of the USA or Australia, the Canadian provinces, or New Zealand. You would take a shared heritage for granted: that notions of tenure underly all land law;[1] that ownership is expressed through the concept of estates; that there are trusts; that things legal bind third parties; that things equitable bind with notice (which may be restricted to notice by registration); that registration of charges (or deeds, or incumbrances) is one thing and registration of title quite another. You might even take for granted some shared modernizations: gender equality in landownership, for example, or, with just slightly

---

[1] See *Wik Peoples* v. *Queensland* (1996) 141 ALR 129 for an illustration of how the concept may remain important in practice.

greater risk,[2] that land and other forms of property are inherited according to the same rules. Then you would come to England's divergences in 1925 from the underlying standard model. Broadly, they include:

1. Reduction of legal estates to the bare minimum: the fee simple absolute in possession and the term of years; no legal life estates, so no legal remainders or reversions. Save for the nearly universal abolition of the fee tail, you would have to search hard to find anything similar. Queensland comes nearest, requiring all future interests to be equitable only.[3]
2. Reduction of common law co-ownership to the joint tenancy; limitation of joint tenants to a maximum of four. This is unique. Elsewhere there is general, though not uniform, preference for the legal tenancy in common, unlimited as to number.[4]
3. Allowing abolished legal estates and forms of co-ownership to continue in equity behind a regime of trusts, giving trusts law a far greater role in land law than is common in other jurisdictions. This infusion of trusts law is unique for co-ownership. It is unusual for successive ownership, only Queensland and Western Australia having some similarities.[5]
4. Stipulating that the list of allowable equitable interests is closed. Elsewhere this is left to judicial decision.
5. Instituting a regime of overreaching, whereby on a sale of land many equitable interests are automatically and compulsorily shifted to the proceeds, subject to minimal safeguards and with exceptions for some registrable equitable interests. The nearest analogy is that most Australian jurisdictions and some Canadian copied the overreaching regime for successive estates from the English legislation of the 1880s.[6] The recently repealed regime of trusts for sale for co-ownership was unique, as indeed is its replacement Act.[7]
6. The consequent virtual abolition of the doctrine of notice. Curtailment is reasonably common elsewhere through various registration regimes. But some jurisdictions do allow notice from off the register, especially those in the USA.[8]

[2] Powell and Rohan, *Powell on Real Property* (rev. edn., New York: Matthew Bender, 1969–96), 16.§90.02[3].

[3] Bradbrook, MacCallum, and Moore, *Australian Real Property Law* (Sydney: Law Book Company Ltd., 1991), §§1.24, 12.06; Property Law Act 1974–86 (Qld), s. 301.

[4] Powell and Rohan, *Powell on Real Property*, 7.§602; Bradbrook, MacCallum, and Moore, *Australian Real Property Law*, §§9.23–9.27; Ziff, *Principles of Property Law*, (2nd edn., Scarborough, Ontario: Carswell, Thomson Professional Publishing, 1996), 295–8.

[5] Bradbrook, MacCallum, and Moore, *Australian Real Property Law*, §§12.06–12.08.

[6] Ibid., §12.07; Ziff, *Principles of Property Law*, 163–4.

[7] Trusts of Land and Appointment of Trustees Act 1996.

[8] Powell and Rohan, *Powell on Real Property*, 14.§82.02. In Torrens systems 'Land Transfer Act fraud' and the '*in personam* exception' raise related issues.

7. Mortgage by charge or long lease, but not by transfer. This is the usual position in Australasian Torrens regimes and, as the 'lien theory', in most states of the USA.[9] Canada shows no clear pattern.[10]

8. The existence, now being phased out, of two different land transfer systems, each fully modernized: private conveyance by deed and transfer by state-mediated registration of title. Lawyers from jurisdictions with registered title would be unsurprised by the need for a long transition period. For them the surprise would probably be that an indigenous title registration system was chosen at a time when the Torrens system had proved its worth elsewhere. The coexistence of two modernized systems was unique.

This pattern was unique in the common law world at the time, and has not been replicated. Indeed there is nothing even nearly the same. How did it come about?

NARRATIVE 1: AN INTELLECTUAL ACCOUNT

This account of the legislation's important structural changes stresses progress and simplification as an intellectual exercise related to broad political change. It was a sort of intellectual catch-up. At the beginning of the story, say in the early nineteenth century, ownership of land was the badge of full citizenship within a predominantly aristocratic political structure.[11] In the dominant ideology land alone gave men a permanent stake in the country, hence paternalist obligations, hence a set of entitlements to participate. The landed interest dominated both houses of the legislature and government in the countryside. To argue that land was just another form of wealth was to state a political position landowners regarded as dangerously radical. As late as 1887 one noble lord saw the onset of socialism in a proposal that the mechanism of land inheritance should be more like that for personalty.[12] The wealthy manipulated land law in such a way that succession from generation to generation was reasonably well guaranteed (since dynasty was important), and in such a way that ownership[13] was agglomerated into the

[9] Powell and Rohan, *Powell on Real Property*, 4.§439; Dukeminier and Krier, *Property* (3rd edn., Boston: Little, Brown & Co., 1993), 670.

[10] Ziff, *Principles of Property Law*, 372.

[11] The best introduction is Thompson, *English Landed Society in the Nineteenth Century* (London: Routledge & Kegan Paul, 1963), esp. chs. 1, 3.

[12] Lord Arundell of Wardour, Parl. Deb. (3rd series), 313 c. 1758, cited in Anderson, *Lawyers and the Making of English Land Law 1832–1940* (Oxford: Oxford University Press, 1992), 163.

[13] The term was used, albeit that we would say estate ownership was less than ownership of the land. See e.g. Williams, *Principles of the Law of Real Property*, (5th edn., London: Sweet, 1859), 352.

hands of the oldest male of each generation, but so that income from the land maintained many other members of the family. The documents that achieved these ends dealt in entitlements rather than discretions, resulting in a complex ownership structure, a form of fragmented ownership. The name commonly given to arrangements like this was settlement, and they were common.[14]

One point of settlements was to retain land, to discourage transactions in it.[15] So, if the ownership fragments were legal they would each have an independent existence such that someone wishing to acquire the land would need to acquire each fragment of the title.[16] If the fragments were equitable, the situation was more complex. It was possible for trustees of land to pass title clear of beneficial interests, but only if the trust said so, and only if any conditions imposed by the trust or by the general law were observed. Purchasers would almost certainly discover the trust's existence from the documents of title, and would then have to satisfy themselves that the trustees could pass a clear title. In practice risk lay with purchasers; that was the consequence of a fully developed doctrine of notice. Thus, in relation to purchasers, it need not much matter whether the fragments were legal or equitable; in practice both could be made equally secure. When manipulated in this way the devices of land law facilitated a form of family ownership suited to the complex ambitions of the wealthy.

Such fragmentation could be portrayed as a problem—though contestably so. Thus one could say that the complexity caused stagnation at worst, and high transaction costs at best. One could say that the ownership structure immunized families from the normal (contestable) consequences of risk-taking. The criticisms were inextricably bound up with the rise of a new class of industrial wealth, followed by middle class wealth, and were an aspect of a struggle for political power. That there was complexity is undeniable. How much flexibility there was in practice, how heavy the costs were, and whether they were worth paying, were contentious questions.

Political critics focused on what might be called external costs.[17] In their

---

[14] For a general account, see Thompson, *English Landed Society in the Nineteenth Century*, 64–70. For an exhaustive analysis of the estate system, see Habakkuk, *Marriage, Debt and the Estates System: English Landownership 1650–1950* (New York: Oxford University Press, 1994).

[15] Ibid., ch. 1.6.

[16] Where a legal fragment was held by trustees to preserve contingent remainders, i.e. to await the birth or coming of age of some would-be entitled person, a sale might be practically impossible. In those circumstances only a private Act of Parliament would do the trick, and, unless the land was to be sold to pay off debts, such an Act would usually be obtainable only on condition that substitute land be settled on the original terms. Sale was a sufficiently unusual event to warrant a separate chapter in Habakkuk, *Marriage, Debt and the Estates System* (ch. 5).

[17] For a summary of the land reform movement, see Habakkuk, *Marriage, Debt and the Estates System* 629–34, or Perkin, *The Origins of Modern English Society 1780–1880* (London:

eyes aristocratic manipulation of land law removed much needed land from the ordinary operation of the market; it perpetuated a useless class of rentiers; it raised land prices, with deleterious effect on housing conditions and on industrial costs and opportunities. Favoured remedies usually included abolition of entails and primogeniture, but, in the event, came to nothing. There were also what might be called internal costs, costs to those who engaged in these manipulations. On the one hand, there was reduced freedom of action—an opportunity cost, not necessarily experienced as a cost. On the other hand, there were increased transaction costs. Some of these can be seen as legal running costs of keeping the manipulative documents up to date. Others were more subtle. Families wanting flexibility could achieve it by yet further manipulation of legal devices.[18] They could fragment ownership as outlined above, but in addition they could build in various escape routes. Some of these were readily available—entails could be barred and the land could be resettled on new terms. Others needed planning: powers could be retained to shift interests around, for example. Sometimes legal devices created to provide security for family charges—income sometimes, capital allowances on marriage or coming of age more typically—could be kept artificially alive after their main purpose had been fulfilled. The usual form was a long lease, which, being a legal estate, would give possession, hence entitlement to rents of tenanted land. As legal estates they would prevail over subsequent interests. They could be kept alive to provide a form of legal back-up for purchasers of the land. Land sales were complex when the title had been fragmented, and it was always possible that some adverse interest had been overlooked. But if the purchaser took a conveyance of the long lease as well, then the probability was that it would act as a trump when the main conveyance proved inadequate. But, of course, transaction costs were high in setting all this up and then in handling the subsequent documentation. And they fell on the purchaser too. So quite apart from grumbles that participants may or may not have had, critics sometimes said that the high transaction costs were themselves a deterrent to investment in land, hence a clog on development.

In some respects land was less untypical of wealth in general than one might think. Settlements and trusts, as fragmented ownership structures, were not so very different from commercial companies. These had their directors, with powers to bind the company, and they had their shareholders, who drew an income and were ultimately the company's owners. Where landed owners had powers, companies had objects. Judges' reaction

Routledge & Kegan Paul, 1969), 451–3. Professor Perkin's views are elaborated in Perkin, 'Land Reform and Class Conflict in Victorian Britain', in Butt and Clark (eds.), *The Victorians and Social Protest* (Newton Abbot: David & Charles, 1973).

[18] For examples, see Habakkuk, *Marriage, Debt and the Estates System* ch. 1.6, and Spring, *The English Landed Estate* (Baltimore: Johns Hopkins University Press, 1963).

to corporate engagements outside the listed objects was to hold them *ultra vires* and void.[19] This rule existed, so it was said, for the benefit of shareholders and for outsiders dealing properly with the company. Outsiders penalized by the doctrine were told that it was their own fault: objects were listed in public registries where inspection was easy. The result, and to some extent the justification, were broadly similar to the land law.[20] Commercial values ensured that company law doctrine did not impede contracting for long. It was an easy matter to draft wide objects for companies, such that virtually all dealings became legitimate.[21] Thus freedom of action was enhanced, and hence the chance of profit. Loss through fraud, foolishness, over-optimism, or bad luck fell on the shareholders, save to the extent that shareholders' meetings may occasionally have prevented disaster.

For land a similar solution was not so easy. As time went on it did become usual to insert progressively wider powers into settlements.[22] But outsiders knew that normally the limited owners would be unable at law to engage in the transaction; so the special power would need to be proved. That would disclose the whole document, which would contain much sensitive information. Further, the power might be vested in the person who claimed it only if certain things had been properly done. He might be a replacement trustee, for example, who would need to have been properly appointed by someone with the power to do so. Or the power might exist only if some other power had not already been exercised—for example, a duty to sell might exist only if beneficiaries had not already opted to keep the land among themselves. A prudent outsider would need to be satisfied on these scores before concluding the transaction, since notice put the risk on him.[23] Thus even a wholesale movement towards extending the powers of limited owners might not affect transaction costs. The frequency of an undetected breach would be reduced, but the consequence of breach would remain. Time-consuming, and hence expensive, enquiries might still be needed, much harder than hiring an agent to scan the companies' register. One

---

[19] For a historical overview of the case law, see Cornish and Clark, *Law and Society in England 1750–1950* (London: Sweet & Maxwell, 1989), 259–61.

[20] The Land Registrar once put this argument to a Royal Commission (see Anderson, *Lawyers and the Making of English Land Law 1832–1940* (Oxford: Oxford University Press, 1992), 238–9.

[21] Cornish and Clark, *Law and Society in England 1750–1950*, 260–1.

[22] See e.g. the speech of N. T. Lawrence, President of the Incorporated Law Society, (1878–9) 23 Sol. J. 931, repr. as *Facts and Suggestions as to the Law of Real Property* (1880). Landowners dominated the Royal Commission on Agriculture, whose Report in 1882 reached the same conclusion (HCP (1882), xiv. 1).

[23] In practice it was documentary notice of trusts that caused conveyancing problems (see Anderson, *Lawyers and the Making of English Land Law 1832–1940*, 266–80). For a survey of the case law, see Jean Howell, 'The Doctrine of Notice: An Historical Perspective', [1997] Conv. 431.

might speculate that in a seller's market transaction costs increased the price of land, and that in a buyer's market they reduced the value of trust land compared with freely owned land.

A shift in thinking about landed wealth was accompanied by parallel changes in trusts law. Under the stimulus of expansion of safe but essentially passive forms of wealth, such as stock and shares, trusts became a vehicle through which relatively active trustees could manage a shifting fund for beneficiaries.[24] Their essence was flexibility and fluidity of assets—quite the opposite of settlements of land, which were primarily concerned with land-holding. Investment trusts might seek also to invest in land, or in mortgages, and when that happened the drafters of trusts did their best to retain flexibility. From the 1850s onwards it was common to find comparisons drawn between trusts of land, which protected beneficiaries by an extended doctrine of notice, and trusts of personalty which did not.[25] It was said that major defaults by trustees of personalty were rare, and virtually unknown where there was a plurality of trustees, thus that notice was an unnecessary protection. In this way limited ownership of land could be experienced as disadvantageous. Underlying this shift in perception were major shifts in the importance of land politically. It became easy for a cautious government to seek to head off hurtful reform with a limited assimilation of land law to personal property. In 1882 the Settled Land Act did for limited owners of land what lawyers were doing for companies, it gave them most of the powers of unfettered owners. The Act could be sold to political critics of the landed interest as removing artificial barriers to the operation of a free market in land, and to the landed interest itself as removing the opportunity costs and transaction costs that had hitherto fallen uniquely upon land. On the one hand, we have a further round in the class war; and on the other, we have a further successful adaptation by the wealthy. Either way, land was becoming just another form of wealth.

From there to the 1925 legislation is a short step. If limited owners have very nearly the powers of full owners, why not make them full owners in name too? So the reduction of legal estates, the relegation of many interests to equity, the introduction of a full-scale overreaching regime, can be seen as further steps down the road of assimilation of realty to personalty, differing from the earlier legislation more in intellectual elegance than in underlying aim. Part I of the Land Property Act 1925 can be seen as the logical outcome of a long process: so far as outsiders are concerned, convert all land ownership into unlimited ownership, or as near as can be.

---

[24] Chesterman, 'Family Settlements on Trust: Landowners and the Rising Bourgeoisie', in Rubin and Sugarman (eds.), *Law, Economy and Society, 1750–1914: Essays in the History of English Law* (Abingdon: Professional Books, 1984).
[25] For an early example, see (1857) 1 SJ. 886.

This is a neat, stylized narrative shorn of human agency. The changes seem to have a satisfying inevitability. But it shows only that the 1925 legislation fits with broader changes. It does not show who wanted it or why. It does not explain other features of the 1925 legislation—its co-ownership regime, for example. And it leaves us with a question why the 1882 legislation found ready emulation in the old colonies, but the 1925 legislation did not. A second narrative is needed, one that puts human agency back into law making.

NARRATIVE 2: THE MECHANICS OF LAND TRANSFER

This narrative concerns land transfers, professionals, professionalism, and the state. To start at the end, the 1925 legislation was the outcome of a prolonged struggle for control of the land transfer process between solicitors and the Land Registry. In solicitors' eyes, and to some extent also in the eyes of the specialist barristers whose creation the legislation was, the main objective was to make title registration less attractive.

Attorneys, as solicitors were then called, acquired a statutory monopoly of conveyancing in 1804, probably as a by-product of a revenue-raising measure.[26] Government had exacted the price in advance: heavy and unusual forms of professional taxation, unique to attorneys. This impost, greatly resented at the time, came in due course to symbolize for solicitors their special place in society. If they, alone, paid tax on their professional property, then they, alone, could claim rights even against the state. Put another way, the tax recognized a form of property; and property ought to be respected. What they got from it, the conveyancing monopoly, was certainly lucrative.[27]

As the century passed, attorneys renamed themselves solicitors, and conceptualized a profession with a distinctive role.[28] It had distinctive modes of organization, it had privileges, and it had responsibilities. It was as necessary and indispensable a part of modern living as the House of Commons or piped water. Its vocation was law, like barristers'; but, unlike barristers, solicitors saw themselves as men of business too. Part of their self-image lay

---

[26] Kirk, *Portrait of a Profession* (London: Oyez Publishing, 1976), 130–1.

[27] Offer, *Property and Politics 1870–1914: Land Ownership, Law, Ideology and Urban Development in England* (Cambridge: Cambridge University Press, 1981), ch. 4. For the origins of attorneys' dominance of the land transaction business see Holmes, *Augustan England* (London: George, Allen & Unwin, 1982), ch. 5, and, for eighteenth-century examples, Miles, 'Eminent Practitioners: The New Visage of Country Attorneys c.1750–1800', in Rubin and Sugarman (eds.), *Law, Economy and Society, 1750–1914: Essays in the History of English Law*.

[28] Anderson, *Lawyers and the Making of English Land Law 1832–1940*, 22–33.

in their relationship with the land laws (it appealed to the law part of their vision) and their brokering of land transactions (the business part). Their perfect land transaction law would necessarily include a major role for independent professional land law brokers. At the apogee of professionalism, what was ideal in a reformed land law was conceived in relation to the profession that would operate it: conveyancing Acts and professional organization can be seen as two facets of the same phenomenon. To understand this, and to understand this particular context for the 1925 legislation, it is helpful to consider solicitors' professionalism as a struggle for status.

Solicitors' most obvious struggle was to get out from under the barristers. Often it took the form of competition for work, or, more accurately, for monopoly of work and monopoly of the spoils and offices of the modern state. Linked with that, but separate too, was a competition for parity of esteem. The ideology of professionalism asserts that professionals serve their society; their privileges are earned.[29] They regard their service as public and unself-interested. For solicitors and their organizations, service operated at one level through an insistence on the virtues of education and coercive professional discipline, at another through intervention in public issues and participation in causes. To have a voice, or, better, a hand, in law-making was of great importance. That demonstrated public service and marked solicitors out as members of a learned profession, just like the barristers. For their hand in law-making to have been dominant would have been heaven indeed and, for just a moment, with the Conveyancing Act of 1881 the prize was grasped.[30] That Act streamlined the traditional method of land transfer, which was by private deed of conveyance between private citizens, mediated by their private advisers. The Act slashed the length and complexity of land transfer documents, and forbade time-wasting practices. Of the utmost importance to solicitors' self-image and to their pockets, scale fees were to be introduced which linked the cost of conveyancing to the value of the transaction.[31] Law societies saw that as protecting clients from damaging price competition between professional men, removing a temptation to sacrifice care. Further, now that land sales commonly proceeded in two steps—a detailed contract followed by a conveyance—law societies were busy standardizing the form of contract. It suited their public image

[29] The constitution of modern professions and the emergence of a pattern of professional career represented for the middle classes a novel possibility of gaining status through work. Larson, *The Rise of Professionalism* (Berkeley and Los Angeles: University of California Press, 1977), 5. See, generally, Perkin, *The Rise of Professional Society* (London: Routledge & Kegan Paul, 1989), esp. chs. 1, 4. For an extension of Perkin's analysis to solicitors, ironically somewhat different from his own, see Anderson, *Lawyers and the Making of English Land Law 1832–1940*, 314–23.

[30] Anderson, *Lawyers and the Making of English Land Law 1832–1940*, 146–56.

[31] Solicitors Remuneration Act 1881; Solicitors Remuneration Order, Statutory Rules and Orders Revised (1890) vi. 399.

to do so—they took advice on appropriate clauses from eminent barristers; but it reinforced their command of the process.[32] By chance the legislation coincided with the opening of the new law courts on the Strand, London, a project owing much to solicitors' leaders. In a fitting touch of theatre solicitors' achievement of élite status was recognized by the conferral of a knighthood on the President of the Law Society. Solicitors' contract with the state was ceremonially renewed.

The moment was all the sweeter because it promised a victorious end to the second struggle: the rout of the land title registration lobby.[33] It need not have been so. The originators of the first detailed schemes for land title registration had been solicitors, and solicitors' organizations had been used to lobby for implementation of the suggestions.[34] They had foundered partly because so many different schemes could be devised from the original set of ideas, partly because of fears for landowners' privacy, and perhaps ultimately their pockets, and partly because questions of the location of registries opened serious divisions between London and provincial solicitors. There were so many possible schemes because there were several competing visions of land law. Some proponents of title registration saw it as recording and ordering all that the present complex substantive land law made possible. Hence it must cope efficiently and faithfully with all the many variations of limited ownership and all that they entailed. But other proponents had in mind a vision of land law much more like the law of personal property—a relatively simple structure of ownership, where encumbrances would usually fall away on a sale. These latter schemes presupposed, with varying degrees of rigour, a regime that reduced competing interests in land and facilitated or mandated the overreaching of encumbrances. Between these two visions there was room for much argument, complicated by the political overtones of suggestions that land should be treated as much like personal property as possible.

There was another tension within proposals for title registration. In its origins title registration had appeared as an ancillary device to aid land transactions. Certainty of title would be increased, and transfers would be faster because there would be no place for repetitive re-examinations of a chain of title. With speed would come lower costs. In essence this is the title registration England has now: land transfer is private, but operates through

---

[32] Solicitors also had a major hand in the Settled Land Act (see Anderson, *Lawyers and the Making of English Land Law 1832–1940*, 146–52).

[33] The remainder of this narrative is taken from Anderson, *Lawyers and the Making of English Land Law 1832–1940*, which contains detailed references.

[34] Wilson, *Outlines of a Plan for Adopting the Machinery of the Public Funds to the Transfer of Real Property*, (1844); Sewell, *A Letter to Lord Worsley on the Burdens Affecting Real Property, with Reasons in Favour of a General Registry of Title* (1846); Select Committee on the Registration of Assurances Bill, Report, HCP (1852–3), xxxvi. 397, Report and evidence of Cookson, Field, and Williams.

a state-run register. The difficulty with establishing such a system lay in the politics of compulsion and in the setting of costs. If benefits are private, why should the scheme be compulsory? If the object is to save money, why should any of the Registry's costs fall on the taxpayer? Can the benefits be seen to be public? Perhaps, by arguing that wider ownership of land would be a public good, and that it would be stimulated by title registration. Such arguments lay behind the mid-century schemes, but they were not strong enough to ensure compulsion. Further, the first registration statute had opted for a full mirror-of-fragmented-title system, faithfully copying the full complexity of family ownership.[35] A voluntary system along those lines turned out to have little to offer.[36] Later amendments[37] shifted title registration back into simpler forms but, remaining voluntary, it still needed a firmer foundation to ensure its survival.[38] So its supporters would from time to time seek salvation by gripping firmly onto the coat-tails of political debate. When land was an issue, plans for taxation, rating, compulsory purchase, or whatever could be made to seem more easily attainable by grafting onto them the skills and facilities of the title registration office. At those times a political will to see title registration extended for those collateral purposes reinforced the continuous but relatively low-level demand for extension of registration for its own sake. The politics could be complex: sometimes a political faction might support extension of title registration as a sop to land reformers, hoping that would be enough to keep them away from substantively redistributive schemes; other factions would see title registration as a useful precursor, or a necessary concomitant; yet others would see title registration as wholly irrelevant to their plans, though that would not necessarily stop them supporting it in its own right.

If all that happened to come together, then the outcome would be a comprehensive registration system. And that is what would almost certainly

---

[35] Transfer of Land Act 1862 (25 & 26 Vict. c. 31).

[36] Report of the Royal Commission on the Operation of the Land Transfer Act and the Registry of Deeds for the County of Middlesex, HCP (1870), xviii. 595.

[37] Land Transfer Act 1875.

[38] England's experience with title registration is intermediate between its Australasian colonies and the states of the USA. In the former, stronger central government than was the case in England allied with the land-grabbing imperative of the new colonies and the relative shortage of private capital to make compulsion the norm. In the latter a tradition of weak government and incompetent bureaucracy made it impossible, generating a series of failed schemes and, eventually, private enterprise alternatives in the shape of title insurance companies and title abstract companies. Those companies then resisted proposals to revitalize title registration. For Australia, see Castles, An Australian Legal History (Sydney: Law Book Company Ltd., 1982), 458–61, Kercher, An Unruly Child (St Leonards, NSW: Allen & Unwin, 1995), 129–31, and Parkinson, Tradition and Change in Australian Law (Sydney: Law Book Company Ltd., 1994), 141. For the USA, see Shick and Plotkin, Torrens in the United States (Lexington, Mass.: D. C. Heath & Co., 1978), and Dukeminier and Krier, Property, 764–5.

have happened in the late 1880s, when all political parties agreed (for different reasons) and when lawyers' organizations appeared to acquiesce. There would have been registration, not quite along Torrens lines, though it was available for copying, nor along the lines that eventually we got, but a comprehensive scheme none the less. Significantly for the purposes of this chapter, the plan did not include any simplification of the underlying law— nor for that matter did Torrens legislation require it.[39] And the plan did not seek to oust solicitors from the process of conveyancing, though some thought in due course it would. But the moment passed, because the Liberal Party split over Ireland and its more radical land-reformers defected to the Conservatives.[40] The need for something to be done about land diminished, and title registration for the time being lost its connection with big political issues.

In 1897 registration became compulsory in London,[41] primarily for reasons concerning the conveyancing process for its own sake, hence connected with speed and cheapness. But, hemmed in by Treasury restrictions, the Registry made life difficult for solicitors. In a way, it had to. The benefits registration promised were essentially private, so the Registry must compete with an existing system that had been streamlined and modernized by the Conveyancing Act. And local compulsion was overtly seen as a trial, to pave the way for a national system only if successful. But Treasury control demanded that the Registry's large capital outlays be recouped. Price competiton was difficult, so difficult that in the eyes of the Registrar his scheme would succeed only if it replaced solicitors in the land transfer process, eliminating the legal middleman, as it was put. There is an air of fantasy to this claim, and so it was regarded by some Law Society leaders. There could be much more to a land transaction than the act of conveyance, especially with the recent stress on the pre-conveyance contractual stage of a sale. 'Every man his own conveyancer' was an unlikely outcome. Still, the threat was taken seriously, building as it did upon long-held fears, and a hard struggle eventuated. Even Law Society grandees were affected by the threatened diminution of their profession's empire, for it concerned more than just the pocket. At stake were two visions of society.

Solicitors held a professional/contract based view, where professions moderate and regulate a market in transactions, at the cost of sacrificing a market in brokering their own services. It was self-regulatory, market oriented in one sense, but protective in another. In opposition was a statist system operating through organizations of state employees. The former was epitomized by the Conveyancing Act 1881 and its associated institutions of

[39] Save for mortgage by charge, which does seem an inherent part of a Torrens system.

[40] For the significance of this event for the land reform movement, see Perkin, 'Land Reform and Class Conflict in Victorian Britain'.

[41] Land Transfer Act 1897.

law societies and rule making committees. The latter vision was quite different. The aggressive propagandists of the Registry promised that registration could enable even old-fashioned land transactions to continue, and that they would be quicker and cheaper, but with a sacrifice of a rule based system. There would be rules, but they would be internal Registry rules, to be waived, modified, and reissued by a benign official discretion preferably dealing directly with members of the public. Officials would operate like quasi-professionals, salaried, disciplined by internal codes, answerable to the public.

So it was that in 1896 the Law Society, with acute misgivings, advanced assimilation or simplification of the underlying land law as a last-ditch alternative to compulsory registration of title.[42] Its idea was to reshape land law so that traditional conveyancing operated by solicitors could be seen to be as quick and as cheap as that promised by universal and compulsory registration but free from the officious hand of bureaucracy. It lost, but, because of the sort of Registry instituted, and because of the deficiencies of the system it operated (some just teething troubles, some more fundamental to the variation chosen), the possibility of a rival reform of land transfer law remained open. When, in 1908, the time came for an inquiry into the 1897 Act, the plan was revived. That inquiry was broadly adversarial, a contest between Law Societies and Registry, largely on their own terms, with (as it turned out) expert barristers sitting in judgement. They were convinced by the solicitors that the Registry worked nowhere nearly as well as it claimed. By then, however, the principle of registration was generally acknowledged (and mandated by the inquiry's terms of reference), and the broad shape of the existing registration system had become institutionalized within the Registry. In 1911 the commission reported,[43] roughly, that both the registered and the unregistered systems of conveyancing were handicapped by the underlying state of the law, and that that should be reformed and tried out before a final decision was made. It should be said that the Registrar denied that there were problems, and denied that, if there were problems, they were caused by the underlying law. In his view, a Registry, free to operate with a proper mix of rule and official discretion, could handle all transactions efficiently no matter what the state of the underlying law. For a short while it looked as though the inquiry's diagnosis would be ignored, when once again registration became tacked onto more important redistributive questions concerning land and wealth. But the moment passed,

---

[42] The proposal originated with E. P. Wolstenholme, conveyancing barrister, in 1862 (Wolstenholme, 'Simplification of Title to Land: An Outline of a Plan' (1862) 2 Papers Read Before the Juridical Society). He redrafted his proposal for the Law Society in 1894 (see Anderson, *Lawyers and the Making of English Land Law 1832–1940*, 193–4).

[43] Royal Commission on the Land Transfer Acts, Second and Final Report, Cd. 5483, HCP (1911), xxx. 1.

and the question became one of land law: how to obtain the benefits of registration without the supposed disadvantages of a registry?

That is the end of the second narrative: the agenda remained like that through into the 1920s, though the Registrar made a further unsuccessful bid to link title registration with social progress in the aftermath of the war.[44] Only the obvious conclusion needs drawing at this stage: it was the rival professional concerns of solicitors and Land Registrar that generated the immediate need for a further revision of land law. That context would inevitably slant that law towards issues of land transfer.

NARRATIVE 3: GETTING A TEXT

The third narrative starts with the formulation of the project and ends with the final text of the legislation. This is the narrative of most interest to practitioners, because from it they may hope to build arguments about the preferred meaning of sections in disputed cases. And, because the narrative began with a sketch of an assimilation scheme way back in 1896 which, in 1925, made the statute book in recognizable form, it ought to be straightforward. Alas, it is not. The trail was contorted, and at times disappears from view. The goal was reasonably clear: a transfer of a fee simple by deed should be free from as many incumbrances as possible, and those that remained should be easily discoverable. But translating policy proposals into sound and principled legislation is not an easy task.

The first attempt to reformulate basic land law in the image of title registration, Lord Chancellor Haldane's, was aborted by the outbreak of war in 1914.[45] It had been ambitious, spelling out basic principles in considerable detail, wearing its theory on its face far more transparently than does the 1925 Act. And although it was inspired by the 1896 proposal that legal estates be reduced and an overreaching regime imposed, it went further by recasting estates and interests in functional terms. It began with the concept of 'proprietary estate', duly elaborated, which could be 'disposed of' in ways detailed. Naturally, spelling out what was already latent in property lawyers' minds led to a lengthy and complex text, and drew criticism for that. Estates and interests were then categorized according to the priority they were to receive in land transactions, and the principles on which they operated were all made explicit. Title registration was the conceptual

---

[44] Offer, 'The Origins of the Law of Property Acts 1910–25', (1977) 40 MLR 505 at 512.

[45] Real Property and Conveyancing Bill 1914. The bill was a revised and consolidated version of Conveyancing Bill 1913 and Real Property Bill 1913. The easiest introduction to the bill's principles is through professional commentary on the earlier versions: (1912–13) 57 SJ 682, 695, 713, 726, 737, 750, 761, 770, 781, 791, 797, 799, 807, 818, 832; (1913–14) 58 SJ 42, 79, 94, 115, 135, 151, 184.

model. For example, where title registration had overriding interests, the basic law would have paramount interests—a slightly different list perhaps, but the same idea. Where title registration had minor interests the basic law would have subordinate interests, which could be protected by cautions and inhibitions even though title was not registered. There was much public consultation before the final texts were promulgated as bills, with more small print appearing with each draft. Who can say whether the bills would have passed? But if they had, then England's basic land law would have been expressed quite differently, and writers applauding progress would have commented on how like a code the legislation was, and how it could form the foundation of a general scheme covering realty and personalty alike. Along with these mainstream provisions there was to be reform tidying up other aspects of property law—trustees, intestacy, copyhold, and settled land, in particular.

The barristers working on the ancillary provisions continued their planning during the war and, as it turned out, one of them became the guiding spirit of the post-war redrafting. He was Benjamin Cherry, and he steered the project away from the pre-war model and towards the stripped-down version we have today.[46] His vision may have been as comprehensive as Haldane's but his style was quite different: he sought to streamline unregistered land transactions by the shortest possible route. A masterful technician, he brought to legislative drafting the conveyancer's art of manipulating old devices for new purposes.[47] Cherry persuaded the guiding committee to drop the novel terminology and explicit code of categories and consequences, aiming for a simpler reduction in legal estates plus a watertight regime for overreaching equitable interests. He abandoned Haldane's proposed protection of beneficial interests by entry on a register. Instead nearly all equitable interests were to exist behind deemed trusts for sale or settlements, even if they were the sort of interest we would normally regard as informal—estoppels, for example. To make doubly sure, the permissible means of creating equitable interests were listed. There were to be no loopholes. This plan became the Law of Property Bill 1920, which was like the 1925 Act, but in exaggerated form. Its overreaching regime really was universal; commentators called it a universal curtain. In addition, to the committee's surprise and perhaps to its embarrassment, Cherry welded on to this basic outline all the ancillary bills which had been prepared during the war. Part of his plan was to modernize outlying areas of property law, and to bundle as much as possible together in one collection of statutes.

---

[46] This account of the post-war bills and the drafting process is based on Anderson, *Lawyers and the Making of English Land Law 1832–1940*, ch. 8, which contains detailed references.

[47] The phrase is Michael Chesterman's: Chesterman, 'Family Settlements on Trust', 166.

When reading the 1925 legislation it is important to know that the 1920 bill was rejected, and rejected because the universal curtain with its concomitant regime of deemed trusts for sale and settlements was unacceptable to Viscount Cave, a most conservative Conservative, powerful in the House of Lords.[48] Cherry and his supporters, who included just about every participant surviving from the project's inception in 1913, were outraged. But Lord Birkenhead, the Lord Chancellor, was adamant that support was needed from all sections of professional opinion, not just from those driving it. So a compromise had to be reached. It was embodied in the Law of Property Act 1922, sometimes (but wrongly) regarded as the immediate progenitor of the 1925 Act. In deference to Viscount Cave, the 1922 Act abandoned the universal curtain and the restrictions on establishing equitable interests. And, if the 1925 Act had been just a consolidation of the 1922 Act, then that would have remained the position today. But Cherry was not a man to give up. He was handicapped, unluckily, by Viscount Cave's appointment as Lord Chancellor during the ensuing consolidation period. Cave, so Cherry thought, did not trust him.[49] Perhaps Cave had good reason, for in the Law of Property Act 1924 Cherry managed to reinstate much of what he had lost. The committee drafting that Act consisted of Cherry's long-time collaborators, and it enjoyed wonderfully wide and vague terms of reference.[50] The enterprise could be presented to the public as though it were simply consolidating the 1922 Act, but in private the committee regarded itself as free to make significant changes. Cautiously, so as to ride both horses, it drafted legislation which smuggled back the gist of what had been rejected in 1920. So the committee implied a curtain without ever quite saying that there was one, a provision which is now section 2 of the Law of Property Act 1925. It could not quite limit equitable interests in the way the 1920 bill had done, but section 2, plus the detailed catalogue in the Land Charges Act, plus the bar on new equitable interests in the proviso to section 4 of the Law of Property Act gets almost all the way. It could not quite say that there could be no life interests outside the Settled Land Act, or that equitable co-ownership must always exist behind a deemed trust for sale, but it drafted legislation which made the most sense if those implications were made. As one of its drafters later commented, the 1924 Act was 'an act with a great number of schedules, and one which it was almost impossible to understand, and I do not think that anybody except those who drew [it] up ever read it'.[51] It was this Act, broken

[48] HL Deb. (1920), 39, c. 270 ff., HL Deb. (1920), 41, c. 486 ff. There was opposition from conservative conveyancing barristers too; see (1919–20) 64 SJ 741.

[49] Anderson, *Lawyers and the Making of English Land Law 1832–1940*, 309.

[50] HCP (1924), xi. 363.

[51] Topham, *The Law of Property Acts 1925: A Series of Lectures* (1926), 43.

into separate parts but with virtually no substantive amendments, which became the 1925 legislation.

Tracking down the reasons for particular textual formulations is a frustrating process; it is rare that one finds chapter and verse explaining the niceties of particular sections. Before the war, texts of proposals to make major change to land law or to title registration had been given wide public exposure. Even when the situation was charged with political or professional conflict, consultation was the norm. But the process from 1919 to 1925 was far more private. The work was done by a small and cohesive group of expert barristers in private practice, operating through closed departmental committees. Cherry's approach was to keep drafts private until they were complete, then to launch them as bills and put the onus on objectors. Opposition was regarded largely as political, in the sense that objections were weighed by the strength that they might have in Parliament. Concessions were made by private negotiations with those whom Cherry thought might be influential. The 1924 Act, critical in the legislative development of the project, had virtually no public input. It was drafted by Benjamin Cherry and his team, in private. Only they could have said why changes were made—and they did not. Nor did the planning and drafting teams often leave detailed accounts of their choices and values. A lot was left unsaid, or, at least, unrecorded, by men used to each other's ways of thinking and confident in their shared objectives. It is, for example, extraordinarily difficult to pin down what it was about the law of co-ownership that was thought to need such drastic reformulation.[52] There is no evidence of any conveyancing problems in any of the long investigations during the latter parts of the nineteenth century, nor any significant discussion in professional journals. The Registrar saw no difficulties. The Law Society thought procedures for partition of land in cases of dispute cumbersome, and flirted with the notion that co-owners might be given power to create an *ad hoc* trust for sale to force an end to their relationship without having to go to court. If that was the origin of the reform, the records of the relevant committee meetings do not disclose it. The Secretary of the Lord Chancellor' Office was on that committee, but when asked the reason his response was personal. His sad experience of a much-fragmented co-ownership of commercial property persuaded him that putting co-ownership behind a trust would solve management problems. His personal response reinforces the silence in the minutes and implies that the committee itself had not formulated its reasons. Similarly with the proviso to section 4 of the Law of Property Act, we just do not know exactly what the ambit of the prohibition on new equitable interests was thought to be. Nor do we know how its cryptic section 14 was thought to operate.

[52] The account that follows is based on Anderson, *Lawyers and the Making of English Land Law 1832–1940*, 286–90.

Even when the origin of a section can be identified, light is not necessarily shed on its meaning. Consider section 70(1)(g) of the Land
Registration Act, for example, a section well known to law students, and
one that may have generated more textbook pages than any other section
of the 1925 legislation.[53] It was first mooted by the Land Registrar in 1908
as a way of saving public money, to the astonishment of the Royal
Commission that heard him.[54] His reasoning had two stages. First, the risk
of an undiscovered overriding interest should fall on those acquiring the
land, not on the insurance fund. Secondly, occupiers' rights should override, since the Registry could not itself investigate the state of the land nor
its precise physical boundaries. He acknowledged that his proposal significantly reduced the security that title registration would bring, and that that
might make registration less attractive at a time when solicitors were arguing strenuously against its extension. But he clung to his point. One member of the commission at once drew the analogy with constructive notice,
which the Registrar accepted. The commission was content to let the
Registrar have his section, if that was what he really wanted. It had been
proposed as an absolute interest, but, much later, and without explanation,
Cherry's team added a defence: the interest would not override where
inquiry had been made.[55] Does this knowledge help us understand the Act?
On one level clearly not. Registrar Brickdale had a pragmatic rather than a
principled motive. But at once his proposal was slotted into a conceptual
background of constructive notice that at least one committee member
thought unexceptionable. Can we generalize, that the legislation as a whole
was about documents and documentary notice, not intended to touch possessory rights? Is section 14 of the Law of Property Act part of that same
assumption, an assumption so easily made and so generally shared that it was
never spelt out? It may have been so, but background assumptions can
scarcely stand against detailed text.

Finally, we must face judges' limitations on how they come to know
things. For a clear example, take the meaning of section 53(1)(c) of the Law
of Property Act. Cherry wanted the Acts to be modern and comprehensive, so he took the opportunity to update some of the old law. In some
cases, at least, he did not want to change its meaning—just express it

---

[53] For the uninitiated: s. 70(1) lists 'overriding interests', which have priority over the
register; s. 70(1)(g) includes in that list 'the rights of every person in actual occupation of the
land or in receipt of the rent and profits thereof, save where inquiry is made of such person
and the rights are not disclosed'.

[54] Royal Commission on the Land Transfer Acts, First Report, HCP (1909), xxvii. 733,
question 1407 *et seq*; Anderson, *Lawyers and the Making of English Land Law 1832–1940*,
277–9.

[55] Even by then its original purpose was fading from memory, witness Topham (*The Law
of Property Acts 1925,* 140), who could not see what s. 70(1)(g) of Land Registration Act 1925
added to s. 70(1)(k).

better. This, apparently, was how he saw his re-enactment of material from the Statute of Frauds, though we know it only from departmental correspondence.[56] But changing the statutory words raised a question about a change of meaning. And because the law-making enterprise was private there were no admissible *travaux préparatoires* to aid construction. And since both the 1922 and 1924 Acts changed the law, nothing could be made of the claim that the 1925 Act was just a consolidation. In 1960 the House of Lords had to make the best guess it could, quite unaided by any historical information about why the change had been made—and, in the historical sense, it got it wrong.[57]

That anticlimactic note is a fitting place to leave this narrative for the time being. Two points can be made. The first is that the drafters had acted like the conveyancing experts they were. Their procedures were essentially those of private law making—the law making that eventuates from the careful drafting of documents for the landowning or corporate client. So, they paid careful attention to the client's wants, which were themselves conceived on the basis of the advice the professionals gave; they drew texts to do the trick, using well-tested devices tailored to the new context; they perfected the texts between themselves; and they altered them to calm their client's doubts and questions. That the client was government made no difference. The process was essentially private. The second point is that, if hopes had been high that a rational and intelligible Property Act would eventuate, the texts that actually emerged were greeted with regret and disappointment at an opportunity missed. Writers now may see their virtues, but at the time commentators generally did not. Still, the Acts did not stand alone; they were quickly accompanied by explanatory texts. As a postscript to this narrative those texts will be described, before conclusions are finally drawn.

POSTSCRIPT: MAKING SENSE OF THE TEXT

This fourth and final narrative can be truncated, in part because it is much more tentative and in part because it has recently been eclipsed. It concerns the legislation's reception and transmission through books. That books were necessary could scarcely be doubted; it was obvious from the professional press and the files of letters in the Lord Chancellor's Office that even conveyancing experts found the Acts hard to grasp. What was less foreseeable was that the books that would emerge as the leading authorities would tend to paint the legislation in general terms, to stress its progressive

---

[56] Anderson, *Lawyers and the Making of English Land Law 1832–1940*, 311.
[57] *Grey* v. *IRC* [1960] AC 1.

tendencies, and to downplay, sometimes even ignore, the elements of compromise in the legislation that made such a characterization somewhat approximate. The emphasis was that conveyancing is the most important aspect of land law, and that progress requires it to be unimpeded.[58] For example, according to the books all co-ownership did exist behind a trust for sale,[59] no life estate could exist outside the Settled Land Act, overreaching of trusts for sale might even be unconditional, though that went beyond any of Cherry's texts. The main victims of this were to be the women who claimed that their interest in the family home should survive a covert sale or mortgage by the man of the house—not that that could have been foreseen in 1925 either.

Two reasons may be suggested for the laudatory treatment of the legislation, which tended to brush over its difficulties. First, even academic books were written with an audience of trainee or would-be conveyancers in mind.[60] University legal education between the wars was directed in large measure towards part-time students already working in offices, and partook very much of the 'what you need to know to get started in daily practice' philosophy. Secondly, however, there was a countervailing philosophy, which, paradoxically, in this context led to the same conclusion. Law was not firmly established as a subject worthy of university study. Some university law teachers would not have minded; they would have seen themselves primarily as practitioners who did some part-time teaching at the local university (and certainly no research). But others had different ambitions. For them it was important to demonstrate that English law was principled, rational, and good, worthy of study in universities for its own sake.[61] Their books, understandably, sometimes glossed over the niggling details that did not quite fit. And in due course judges filled many of the gaps anyway, because by then orthodoxy was that the gaps were illusions. When gaps appeared which judges would not plug, commentators attributed the problem to drafters' lack of foresight,[62] unaware, no doubt, of the Acts' flawed

[58] See Anderson, 'Land Law Texts and the Explanation of 1925', (1984) 37 CLP 63.

[59] The situation in *Williams & Glyn's Bank* v. *Boland* [1981] AC 487 is the one I have in mind here.

[60] See Anderson, 'Land Law Texts and the Explanation of 1925'.

[61] G. C. Cheshire spanned both schools. For an analysis of his *Modern Law of Real Property* see Anderson, 'Land Law Texts and the Explanation of 1925'. But he also wrote the pathbreaking volume ii of the 1928 (19th) edition of *Stephen's Commentaries*, treating property law as a coherent whole. For his influence, see the appreciation by F. H. Lawson, 'Geoffrey Chevalier Cheshire' (1979) 65 Proceedings of the British Academy 611, and Lawson's own book in a similar genre to *Stephen, The Rational Strength of English Law* (London: Stevens, 1951). Today's leading book, Gray, *Elements of Land Law* (2nd edn., London: Butterworths, 1993) is from a different mould—more critical, and far more inclined to see law as the transitory product of competing social forces.

[62] e.g. Burn, *Cheshire and Burn's Modern Law of Real Property* (14th edn., London: Butterworths, 1988), 94.

inception. Law-as-principle had taken over from law-as-political-compromise. That too is understandable, since law societies and Land Registrar had long since shared out the land transaction business between them in a way that kept both interests happy. The 1925 legislation became the final settlement of their turf war, and not merely its penultimate stage. In retrospect, then, it could be reclothed as an exercise in law reform.

CONCLUSIONS: READING LAND LAW IN THE 1990s

From my first narrative one may easily see that any one of a wide range of schemes assimilating land law to the law of personal property would have fitted with the times. It could have been a series of *ad hoc* technical amendments like the reforms of the 1880s, or a property code based upon ownership. Perhaps a short statute could just have deemed realty to be personalty, a trick proposed from time to time.[63] What we got was something in between. But, as my third narrative demonstrates, the texts were, in a sense, accidental, the product of Lincoln's Inn talking to itself. It could easily have been Haldane's version that was enacted, or the quite different version first proposed by Cherry. So in drawing morals about the fit between text and time, in tracing themes of law and wealth, too much should not be made of the text itself.

Secondly, an understanding of the historical processes leading to the texts will very rarely yield an obviously preferable reading in a hard case. Because the legislation had a limited objective (my second narrative) and because it was not a code, broad issues which might help in statutory interpretation did not have to be aired. So, for example, the relation between section 14 of the Law of Property Act, section 70(1)(g) of the Land Registration Act, and a possible privileging of persons lawfully in possession cannot be elucidated from the surviving documents. But, seeing the same point from a different angle, the *ad hoc* nature of the legislation makes grand principles for its interpretation suspect. Take Land Registration Act, section 70(1)(g), as an example again. Registrar Brickdale, title registration's main champion and *bête noire* of the solicitors, would no doubt have supported a mirror principle if asked, but from the beginning he knew that the Registry must balance its books. He did not seek an Act embodying the mirror principle without a counterbalancing set of overriding interests off the register; his Act always was a compromise.

This last point can be taken a stage further. Contrary to the general laudatory statements preferred by text writers until quite recently, it is rarely possible to move from a general statement such as the 1925 legislation was

---

63 And once even enacted, in Newfoundland in 1834 (Ziff, *Principles of Property Law*, 71).

meant to simplify conveyancing to a conclusion that the drafters intended
one particular operation for a section rather than another. The reason is
quite simple: to get any Act at all the drafters had to compromise. The
intentions of those who forced the compromise are just as much a part of
the legislative process as the intentions of those who did the writing. From
the nature of the process, the fact of the compromise and the terms on
which it was reached will not appear in the official record. Indeed, because
the drafting moved from objectives (my second narrative) to techniques,
without going though an intermediate stage of principles, the accommodation might be quite invisible. All that one may see in the Act is a device
which appears not quite to do the job that one might expect it to do. Yet a
judge who uses the general slogan to make a sense of the Act that would
have appealed to the drafter is tacitly undoing the compromise that was
reached. There may be good reasons for doing that, seventy years on, but
an appeal to the intentions of the people on one side of the bargain is not
one of them.

Consideration of what would be a good reason for preferring one reading to another should lead to an analysis of what the Acts' role should be
today. Are the reasons why simplification was sought still important and, if
so, should they outweigh competing considerations in the case in hand?
Remember that simplification was always a strategy; it never had an empirical underpinning. Indeed, as a strategy it was something of an embarrassment to the law societies, whose main attack on title registration was that
the reforms of the 1880s already enabled them to beat the Registrar in the
'service to clients' game. To this end they adduced pages of evidence detailing small land transactions speedily conducted at modest cost.[64] Even the
sort of complexity associated with family settlements was not usually an
obstacle to the efficient operation of the land market, as the land sales
between 1918 and 1921 show. During those few years aristocratic families,
their sons killed in the trenches and their fortunes threatened by taxation,
sold off their ancestral lands as if there were no tomorrow[65]—but all before
the 1925 simplifications took effect. And, to return to my starting point, the
lack of a 1925–style simplification does not seem to have impeded the operation of land markets in Sydney, Auckland, or Toronto. So it should be possible to conclude today that simplification always was a strategy rather than
a cure for an acknowledged ill, that it was a strategy in a contest between
law societies and Land Registrar long since resolved, that because of the
need for *ad hoc* compromises the texts were anyway flawed, and that in so
far as complexity had been a real problem it arose from the activities of a
landowning aristocracy which long ago changed its game, well ahead of the
legislature. It does all seem peculiarly English.

[64] Anderson, *Lawyers and the Making of English Land Law 1832–1940*, 233.
[65] Thompson, *English Landed Society in the Nineteenth Century*, 329–37.

5

EVIDENCING OWNERSHIP

Alain Pottage

This chapter considers the notion of title to land, focusing on the techniques which are used to evidence or identify ownership of land. The approach taken is somewhat different from that encountered in traditional land law textbooks, which seek only to set out the rules determining what counts as good title to an ownership interest. Instead of beginning with these rules—the set of prescriptions which define what written formalities or investigative procedures are necessary to protect or transfer an interest— this chapter deals with what might be called practices or technologies. This shift in perspective results from a particular understanding of the 'substance' of property rights, which begins with practical expectations rather than formal legal rules. Life is not lived in accordance with textbook rules and categories. Even where transactions are made in deliberate reliance on these rules, legal criteria are thoroughly reconstructed by practical expectations and objectives. Legal forms might be presupposed by domestic relationships or commercial projects, but they are translated into practical logics that have little in common with the logic of the textbook. Indeed, judges often have to reach into these practical understandings when they determine the rights or obligations of those who hold interests in land. The concepts which lawyers use to make sense of ownership disputes are parasitic upon practical senses of entitlement: the 'right' answer cannot simply be derived mechanically from the application of a formal distinction to the facts of a dispute. For example, the bare form of the legal distinction between joint tenancies and tenancies in common takes on a quite different colour and content depending on whether it is used to make sense of an occupation contract or an informal agreement as to a savings account.[1] In recovering practical expectations, the judges are not referring to some generalized idea of ownership; rather, they are reaching into understandings which are specific to particular social activities and to particular historical periods.

Rules of title presuppose these same networks of practical expectations. Just as the contents of textbook rules are responsive to the understandings of people 'on the ground', so rules as to the proof of ownership are

---

[1] Cf. *Antoniades* v. *Villiers*, *AG Securities* v. *Vaughan* [1989]1 AC 417 with *Paul* v. *Constance* [1977] 1 WLR 527.

parasitic upon those modes of seeing and doing which make the production and reproduction of documents possible. The general nature of these practices is clearest in the case of simpler uses of legal writing. For example, throughout the medieval period, the value or validity of a legal document depended upon the testimony of those individuals who had been present at its making. Anyone who wanted to prove the transaction symbolized by a document would have to call these individuals and ask them to bear witness to what had been done. This imposed some limitations on the practical value of writing. Given that paper served only as a mirror of memory, no document could outlive the individuals who might be called to bear witness to it. There were ways of addressing this problem. For example, lawyers in medieval and early modern France enhanced the life expectancy of their documents by using infants as witnesses. Each child was given a firm slap, thus ensuring that they had good cause to remember the event.[2] This illustration shows that in itself a written document was nothing. It derived its function and value from a discreet practical knowledge of the world. Many seemingly obvious and routine legal procedures in fact depend upon the evolution of such deeply rooted cultural practices. For example, the idea that a document might be authenticated by reference to a signature presupposes a number of specific cultural achievements. First, the use of signatures was made possible only by the change in naming practices which occurred in later medieval Europe, which allowed individuals to be known by transmissible family names rather than simple Christian names. Similarly, a signature could work only after the demise of the medieval idea that individuals could speak as such only if their status or identity was affirmed by a body of witnesses. Thirdly, one might point to the development of techniques for the production of documents, which made possible the distinction between author and scribe which is essential to the functioning of signatures.[3] These simple examples suggest how paper documents and other evidential signs exist only within a fabric of practical rationalities, which attribute personal roles and capacities, distribute learning or authority, and supply codes for the interpretation of written and other signs.[4]

This chapter is concerned less with these basic practical rationalities than with the concepts and techniques of proof which they support and reproduce. Rules about the proof of title presuppose specific techniques for the production and reproduction of legal documents, and these techniques in turn presuppose specific patterns of ownership expectations. The modern system of proof by registration emerged from a transformation in this asso-

---

[2] For the use of documents in medieval England, see Clanchy, *From Memory to Written Record* (2nd edn., Oxford: Blackwell, 1993).

[3] Fraenkel, *La Signature: Genèse d'un signe* (Paris: Gallimard, 1992).

[4] Associated with these developments, there are various complex transformations, such as the shift from orality to literacy, the invention of printing, and so on.

ciation between techniques of documentation and understandings of ownership. The traditional regime of conveyancing was adapted to the needs of an élite class of property-owners. It worked with criteria of proof, and documentary techniques, which were dependent upon the expectations of a small and homogenous class of owners, and upon stable resources of local knowledge. The modern system of registration of title evolved as a solution to the problems of proof which emerged when landownership took on a more complex form, with the result that these resources were eroded, leaving land transfer law to develop modes of proof which were largely independent of the situation 'on the ground'. This relative autonomy is the basis of a new association of techniques of proof and practices of ownership.

TITLES AS STATUS INDICATORS

It is difficult to give a simple and unproblematic definition of the notion of title in English land law, not least because different texts accord different meanings to the word.[5] However, for the purposes of this chapter, the most important element of the notion lies in the conventional distinction between ownership and possession. Ownership describes a normative condition, and possession a state of fact. To be an owner is to enjoy a set of abstract legal powers or faculties; to possess a thing is to have factual, physical, control of it.[6] In practical terms, a buyer of land concerned to ensure that his seller has good title has to look for something other than mere factual possession.[7] Title is an abstract quality, which depends upon an interpretation of rights rather than the identification of physical facts. Ownership consists not in a physical relation to things, but in a socially constructed

[5] See Rudden, 'The Terminology of Title', (1964) 80 LQR 63.

[6] This distinction can become quite complicated. The main difficulty is that possession is not a brute state of fact but a legal description or qualification of facts. There are legal rules which stipulate that a given set of facts should count as possession, and which then go on to attribute legal consequences to those facts. Indeed, one of the most important consequences of possession might be ownership. For example, the right to enjoy the powers and faculties of an owner may be derived from the fact of possessing land, and acting *as if* one were the owner of it (see *Buckinghamshire County Council* v. *Moran* [1990] 1 Ch. 623). By the same token, title to land in English law is relative; title is never anything more than a *better* right (based on prior possession) to enjoy the powers of ownership (see Hargreaves, 'Terminology and Title in Ejectment' (1940) 56 LQR 376).

[7] Indeed, this distinction is implicit in the traditional formulation of the traditional maxim that *nemo dat quod non habet* ('no one can give what they do not have'), according to which a buyer can have no better right than that held by the seller; the buyer can acquire good title to an interest only if his seller had good title. This maxim presupposes a distinction between ownership and possession: 'how can you get something (ownership) from a person who does not have it, even if you do get something he does have (possession)?' (Weir, 'Taking for Granted: The Ramifications of *Nemo Dat*', (1996) 48 CLP 325 at 329).

condition or status, that of being the rightful owner. For that reason, title might be described in terms of a 'status indicator':

I can wear my shirt, drive my car, even carry my computer, but when it comes to my house and land, maintenance of my possession requires status indicators . . . Institutional structures enable brute physical possession in the case of property to be replaced by a recognized set of relationships whereby people can own property even though the property is far away from them . . . Even when I am a long way from my house, the institutional structures enable me to remain an owner, and, if need be, to demonstrate that position to others through the use of status indicators.[8]

This concept of status indicators should be qualified in two respects. First, it is important to clarify the role of documents as modes of indicating or evidencing ownership. Secondly, it is appropriate to say something about how title relates to the broader social roles of ownership. These qualifications arise because in practice the relation between the 'evidence' (paper title) and what it 'points towards' (ownership rights) is considerably more complex than this concept suggests.

The most familiar indicators of ownership are documents, usually title deeds or certified copies of entries in a register. The obvious but essential observation is that these documents do not of themselves constitute title. They are merely a provisional 'map' of title. A document is a piece of evidence from which one might infer or deduce that the seller has good title. Even if a set of title deeds or a copy of an entry in a register is genuine, it may no longer describe the location of rights. A squatter may have acquired title by adverse possession, or the occupier of a domestic home may have acted in such a way as to acquire a share of the beneficial interest behind the legal title, and so on. In other words, ownership rights may be transferred or divided up by means of processes which leave no documentary traces. The structure of a title changes unnoticed, as a result of the law's recognition of practical ownership expectations. And, the social practices and expectations which the law treats as the substance of ownership are always more complex and elusive than the available techniques for representing them. So, even if a documentary 'status indicator' does initially represent the state of ownership expectations, as and when social practices change, the document loses its grip on the facts. The 'status indicator' then becomes inaccurate. Even where documents are supplemented by other evidential signs (such as traces of occupation) the law has to negotiate a balance between the indicative function of a status indicator (what would be visible to a buyer) and the substance of what it indicates (the basis or legitimacy of the occupier's expectations).[9] The difficulty is that the quality of 'title' con-

---

[8] Searle, *The Construction of Social Reality* (London: Allen Lane, 1995), 84–5.
[9] See generally the decisions interpreting Land Registration Act 1925, s. 70(1)(g).

sists neither in status indicators nor in ownership expectations. Even the most formal regimes of land law do not allow buyers to take documents at face value; rarely are status indicators allowed to supplant the expectations which they are meant to indicate. On the other hand, a title is not merely a mirror of ownership expectations. Owners are expected to identify their rights to outsiders. The upshot is that the quality of title seems to be suspended between status indicators and the reality towards which they point.

A status indicator is therefore a peculiar form of evidence. As with all other forms of evidence, it is inherently suspicious and uncertain. So, again, as with other forms of evidence, one might seek to reduce these uncertainties by corroborating the contents of the document with other pieces of evidence (an inspection of the land, an assessment of the owners, and so on). In other words, in using the document as proof of title, one cannot simply follow a set of rules as to what counts as 'title'. Even if the rules are adjusted to practice, as they were in the traditional doctrine of notice, it is still necessary to hold a document to the light of practical knowledge, or to set up a system for producing and interpreting documents which works in such a way as to provide practical certainty. How, then, does one know whether a particular document can be trusted? The traditional regime of conveyancing in the eighteenth and nineteenth centuries was obsessed with this question, and devised increasingly complicated ways of preserving and evaluating documents. Ultimately, however, even this attempt to reduce proof to documentation had to concede that proof was practical. Further on, it is suggested that proof of a title involved holding a document up to the light of circumstances 'on the ground', asking whether its content was consistent with the conveyancer's interpretation of a particular pattern of land use. In this way, practices of title (the set of techniques which sustained the reproduction of documents and rules about title) were coupled to practices of ownership (the expectations associated with particular forms of land use). The story of the transformation of English land law shows how a change in land use and expectations necessarily brought with it a change in the techniques for the proof of title. As landownership expanded beyond a small class, and became differentiated into more complex commercial and residential uses, the traditional techniques were no longer reliable. It became necessary to find a way of evidencing ownership which was not dependent upon local knowledge, but which could work with an autonomous set of documentary techniques. The solution was found in the scheme of registration of title, which transferred the confidence of owners to a set of bureaucratic techniques—namely, the sort of 'precise practice of craftsmanship and knowledge' that is discreetly at work in the organization of lists, files, indexes, diagrams, and bureaucratic formulas.[10] This does not mean

[10] Latour, 'Visualization and Cognition: Thinking with Hands and Eyes' (1986) 6 Knowledge and Society 1.

that the basic relation between practices of title and practices of ownership has dissolved. Rather, the relative autonomy of the registration system allows for the development of increasingly complex forms of landowner-ship.

This suggests the second qualification to the concept of titles as status indicators. If the nature of practices of title depends upon the social roles and distributions of ownership, it becomes difficult to insist on a crisp sep-aration of title and ownership.[11] One of the more interesting things about the history of English conveyancing practice is the practical and conceptual difference between the grammar of nineteenth-century land law, in which legal title was often fragmented into shares held by a number of dispersed owners, their common denominator being an abstract and often uncertain 'root of title', and the modern scheme of registration, which, buttressed by a novel use of the distinction between law and equity, adopts a grammar in which interests in land are indexed by reference to a fictitious owner. Each of these grammars involves a different concept of title, and a different way of ordering the various interests than can cluster around a good root of title or a fictitious owner. In conceptual terms, the implication is that each grammar models a different structure of ownership as a social function, adjusted to the character and complexity of practical social expectations about land. To draw a crisp distinction between title and ownership is to obscure the subtle articulation of this structure. In practical terms, the implication is that a buyer is generally concerned not only with title in the narrow sense of a 'status indicator', but also with the question whether title is accompanied by certain ownership rights. Again, the history of land transfer shows a change in the way in which the 'ownership scope' of a title was understood, and hence a change in the techniques for ensuring that a title was accompanied by the appropriate ownership rights.

How did an effective scheme of registration of title emerge at the end of the nineteenth century? Why did it take so long to establish a reliable and routine method of evidencing ownership, and how did the process of con-veyancing manage until that point?

---

[11] Title is sometimes distinguished from ownership, the difference being that the former is a credential or qualification which authorizes the holder to exercise the faculties or pow-ers of an owner. Thus, to have title to land is to satisfy the conditions for enjoyment of the relevant ownership rights, but the criteria by which one recognizes that someone has title are quite different from the criteria which determine the content or exercise of their own-ership (see Harris, *Property and Justice* (Oxford: Oxford University Press, 1996), 39–40, 80–1). This analytical distinction is somewhat too crisp. The discussion in this chapter sug-gests that, although one might distinguish between the figure of the owner and the faculties of ownership, different regimes of land law have blended these components in different ways.

THE PRACTICAL FOUNDATIONS OF CONVEYANCING

A reading of nineteenth-century conveyancing manuals might suggest that, at least in that era, status indicators could be taken at face value. The relentless concern of these manuals was to set up and maintain a system to ensure that documentary indicators could be taken as proof of title. However, to the extent that this system worked, it did so not because documents spoke for themselves, but because they were sustained by a tightly woven set of documentary techniques. The factor which allowed for this close definition was the fact that conveyancing was adjusted to the needs of an élite class. The basic paradigm of landownership was the aristocratic strict settlement, which bound the devolution of land to the career of a family and its fortunes. Land was the most essential component of status, and the ambition of aristocratic families was to achieve social promotion by accumulating land through successive generations.[12] Because commercial interests in land, such as leases and mortgages, were usually understood to be parasitic upon settlements, this model of inheritance had some considerable influence upon understandings of property in land. Aristocratic owners took a long view of their landholdings: 'they planted trees that only their descendants would see in full splendour; they granted building leases for ninety-nine years in the confident hope that their grandchildren would enjoy the reversion; and they entailed their estates so as to safeguard them for as long as possible.'[13] These projects depended upon a particular use of legal writing. Documentary technologies were supposed to project a stable grid of reference points into the future, which could be used to make reliable provision for future events. Whereas it is now quite common to deal with uncertainty by taking out insurance, for much of the period of traditional conveyancing it was understood that the contingency of the future should be met by anticipating events, and by making the appropriate provision in writing. Everything had to be provided for by careful estate-planning, and the stability of the proprietary grid was essential to the continuity of expectations. Writing stored up the past and projected it into the future. One should not exaggerate this obsession with writing. In practice, settlements afforded a good deal of room for manœuvre, and one prominent conveyancer advised landowners that, ultimately, if something had been overlooked, one might 'with ease get the omission supplied by a private act of parliament'.[14] Nevertheless, the basic aspiration was that there should be a reliable measure of long-term certainty.

[12] See, generally, Habakkuk, *Marriage, Debt, and the Estates System. English Landownership 1650–1950* (Oxford: Oxford University Press, 1994).

[13] Cannadine, *The Decline and Fall of the British Aristocracy* (London: Yale University Press, 1990) 24.

[14] Sugden, *A Series of Letters to a Man of Property* (London, 1809) 85.

How were documents supposed to provide certainty over time? For judges and conveyancers, this was to be done by establishing and maintaining 'landmarks': 'where certain words have obtained a precise technical meaning, we ought not to give them a different meaning; that would be . . . removing landmarks'.[15] In pursuit of this objective, they adopted strict rules as to the interpretation of documents. Precedents, once they had become established, served as the elements of a code which landowners could use to compose and record their projects. If there were any dispute in the future, one could be sure that this code would have the same meaning for later judges and conveyancers. How was this code sustained? First, looking at the formal rules of interpretation, judges and conveyancers insisted that the words used in documents should be given only the meaning fixed by precedent. Documents were not seen, as they might be today, as clues to the 'real' intentions of individuals.[16] The use of the parol evidence rule (according to which one could not refer to evidence of unformalized acts or words in interpreting documents) allowed the judges to disqualify appeals to 'real' intention. Thus, the semantic value of words and phrases was held constant, by ensuring that documents referred to other documents, and not to external acts or events. Indeed, this was one of the essential aspirations of early schemes of registration: 'the policy of the law provides that the title to land shall depend as far as possible on written instruments—which excludes as far as possible the necessity of resorting to parol evidence, or to inferences from equivocal facts and circumstances—is founded on the same motives and principles which lead to the recommendation of a register'.[17] The result was to insulate titles from land in such a way that transactions could be made almost without regard to what happened 'on the ground'. Paper title, rather than land itself, was the commodity that landowners bought and sold. The material fabric of the paper was, in some respects, more significant than the features of the land. For example, the most direct evidence of fraud was to be gathered from the document itself, either from the style or layout of the writing, or from the way in which a document had been folded or endorsed.[18] This example is symptomatic of a conveyancing procedure in which the primary reason for investigating the land itself was to gain a different perspective on a paper title rather than to look for interests which might contradict or qualify the paper title.[19] The purpose of the inspection was to corroborate the claims of a paper title.

[15] *Lane* v. *Stanhope* (1795) 6 TR 345 at 354.

[16] Contrast *Jones* v. *Lock* (1865) LR 1 Ch. App. 25 with *Paul* v. *Constance* [1977] 1 WLR 527.

[17] 'Report of the Commission on Registration and Conveyancing' HCP (1850) xxxii. 27.

[18] *Kennedy* v. *Green* (1843) 3 My. & K 699.

[19] Pottage, 'The Originality of Registration' (1995) 15 OJLS 371 at 398–400.

One of the reasons why paper could be insulated from activity on the ground was that the position of the landowning class allowed it to maintain a distinction between the 'estate' as an income-producing unit and the practical relationships which generated that income. Indeed, it may be that landowners enjoyed a form of economic power which allowed them to impose leases which insulated them from the risks of agriculture.[20] In short, estates could be bought for their rental income without it being necessary for the buyer to enquire too closely into the practices which produced those rents. The tenants of the land disappeared into the opaque sphere of people and events which were not worth recording directly, and which historians are now keen to reconstruct by pursuing such clues or fragments as remain. In summary, although conveyancers insisted that there was 'no such thing as an abstract acre of land',[21] they could nevertheless convey title without being much concerned by the realities of land use and occupation.

This seems to come close to the ideal model imagined by the conveyancing manuals: a formal scheme in which status indicators effectively supplanted the interests which they were supposed to represent and protect. However, as with any enterprise of codification, this appearance was the product of an ongoing process of codifying meanings, and designating authorized interpreters. The substance of the conveyancing code lay not in the formal precedents or rules of evidence which defined intention or which gave shape to the parol evidence rule, but in the set of interpretive techniques which were codified and in the interests and expectations to which those techniques were adapted. One important element consisted in the sort of practices for making and deciphering signatures, or for producing and indexing documents, which are sketched out in the introduction to this chapter. More important, however, there were networks of practical relationships which bound expectations to documents. First, there was a partnership between solicitors and landed families, which ensured that estate owners acted with property codes in mind. Secondly, there was a partnership between judges and conveyancers in which the latter shaped precedents which were endorsed and maintained by the former. The most important thing about this relationship was that it was not founded in rules; rather, it was the foundation and constitutive medium of formal rules and principles. The system depended not on the propositional content of the words used, but on the fact that words were embedded in a fabric of practical understandings about the uses of documents. Indeed, returning to the idea that documents are nothing without the technologies that give life to

[20] Offer, 'Farm tenure and land values in England, c.1750–1850' (1991) Economic History Review 1.
[21] Royal Commission on the Operation of the Land Transfer Act, Report, Minutes of Evidence, HCP (1870), xviii, appendix, at para. 65.

them, the point is that the formal, textual, language of conveyancing and adjudication was 'machined' by these practical technologies.

This dependence upon practice is evident in the way in which the parol evidence rule was used to police the boundary between 'formal' and 'substantive' intentions. The principle of the rule was that landowners should be bound only by what they had put in formal writing, precisely because formal legal acts were the only ones which a man of property would expect to have binding effect. This insistence on formality could catch people out. Yet the judges were prepared to maintain this principle counterfactually, by applying it even in cases where it was clear that the document did not carry the 'real' expectations of those who had made it. Nevertheless, where the divergence of real and written intentions was the result of some 'accident', a whole battery of exceptions was available: latent ambiguity,[22] relief against specific performance,[23] *non est factum*, mistake, surprise, and a general category of fraud.[24] Each of these notions offered a way of upholding a rule while avoiding its effects. For example, although parol evidence could not be used by someone seeking specific performance of an agreement, it could be used by a defendant resisting a bill for specific performance. What was going on in those cases in which the parol evidence rule was circumnavigated? One interpetation is that these were cases in which the rationale of the code had evaporated, and the particular expectations of landowners could be salvaged. For example, where a contract had been drawn up by a conveyancer according to a misunderstanding of his instructions, the effects of the parol evidence rule could be mitigated by treating the event as a species of fraud. The exercise of striking a balance between the integrity of the code and the legitimate interests of disappointed landowners was dependent upon a quite sophisticated reflection on the relation between documentary techniques and ownership understandings. The code was parasitic upon the expectations of landowners, as much when the parol evidence rule was asserted as when it was avoided.

FORMAL AND PRACTICAL PROOFS OF TITLE

In what sense was this fabric of understandings essential to proof of title? In what senses was the articulation of the rules of good title dependent upon the same complicity between lawyers and landowners, and judges and con-

---

[22] *Shelburne* v. *Inchiquin* (1784) 1 Bro. CC 338.

[23] *Clarke* v. *Grant* (1807) 14 Ves. Jun. 519; *Higginson* v. *Clowes* (1808) 15 Ves. Jun. 516; *Winch* v. *Winchester* (1812) 1 V & B 375; *Clowes* v. *Higginson* (1813) 1 V & B 524; *Besant* v. *Richards* (1830) Tam. 509; *London & Birmingham Rly. Co.* v. *Winter* (1840) Cr. & Ph. 57; *Martin* v. *Pycroft* (1852) 2 De GM & G 785.

[24] *Ramsbottom* v. *Gosden* (1812) 1 V & B 165.

veyancers? The answer lies in the formal definition of a good root of title. This theoretical ideal of good title forced conveyancers to look to practical expectations rather than theoretical ideals. Formally, a title was sound if it could be traced to a 'good root of title'. A good root of title was 'an instrument of disposition dealing with or proving on the face of it (without the aid of extrinsic evidence) the ownership of the whole of the legal and equitable estate in the property sold, containing a description by which the property can be identified, and showing nothing to cast any doubt on the title of the disposing parties'.[25] Until 1874, the traditional common law rule was that this 'instrument of disposition' should be at least sixty years old if the buyer was to meet their contractual obligations to the buyer.[26] Why was good title defined in this way, what does the definition mean, and how did it work in practice?

The definition presupposes the common-sense logic of the *nemo dat* rule, according to which property in land is a finite quality, which might be distributed in different ways but cannot be created out of nothing. Traditional conveyancing supposed that new owners emerged either when a subsidiary interest was carved out of a larger, pre-existing, entitlement or when one person succeeded another as the owner of an interest. In both cases, present ownership was founded upon past ownership. To prove title, one had to trace the 'parentage' of an interest back through each of its predecessors to an ultimate root of title. Transmission of ownership was understood in genealogical terms. When conveyancers sat down to investigate a title, they would set out the interests as though they were reconstructing a family tree or pedigree, ordering each interest in such a way that, by working backwards, 'the course of each separate portion [could] be traced until the ownership of the whole of them [united] in a single party'.[27] The organizing function of this ideal is less apparent in cases where a title had remained intact for some time, so that retracing its devolution was simply a process of reconstructing a linear sequence of transactions. However, this function becomes more obvious, and somewhat more problematic, where the title in question was a fragment which had to be traced back to some obscure parent interest. In the latter case, the proof of title depended upon an understanding of how the structure of ownership fitted together—how mortgages related to fee simples or life estates, leases to mortgages, and so on. These understandings of the relation between whole and part, or centre and periphery, were linked to title as an abstract ideal, and, beyond that, to a practical understanding of ownership as a general structure of title credentials and ownership faculties.

[25] Williams, *Vendor and Purchaser* (3rd edn., London: Stevens, 1922), 98.

[26] The stipulated period was reduced to forty years by the Vendor and Purchaser Act 1874.

[27] Hughes, 'The Law of Contracts Relating to Real Property', (1846) 7 Law Times 246.

Although the theory of proof conceded that a seller might begin the pedigree of title with a document that was no less than sixty years old, rather than some ancient entitlement, in practice things were not so simple. The first difficulty was that the *nemo dat* rule opened up an infinite regression of proof. One could show that a particular candidate for the status of good root of title was the real thing only by retracing its pedigree back to some (impossible) ultimate ground. Here, the courts were prepared to help out by holding sellers to a standard of 'moral certainty', it being 'impossible in the nature of things [that] there should be a mathematical certainty of a good title'.[28] This meant that a buyer would have to presume that some documents or acts were in order. However, even assuming that this lower standard could address the problems posed by regressive proof, it could not dispose of the more serious problem of documents as evidence of title. The problem lay not so much in the spectre of forgery as in the difficulty that, even if the available documents were genuine, it was impossible to be sure that their effect had not been modified by transactions or events which had been suppressed or overlooked. For example, settlements of titles usually provided for a set of quite remote contingencies, so that their effect depended upon potentially obscure facts about the birth of children within an extended family group, or the question whether a testator had made a new will, and so on. The subtle complexities of these contingencies will be familiar to readers of Wilkie Collins; indeed, it may be the case that these hazards were usually more fictional than real. However, conveyancing theory was unhelpfully clear about the risks: 'if the event be such that its occurrence must necessarily have rendered the title different from that stated, the purchaser is entitled to require some evidence from which its absence may be inferred.'[29] The upshot was that the certainty sought by the theoretical buyer was negative; it was a certainty that particular documents had not been made or that particular events had not happened. Paradoxically, the very ideal of title as something transmitted from owner to owner made the effective proof of title impossible. This was an organizing ideal which committed the process of proof to the pursuit of its own tail.

If formal proof was impossible, how then could titles be proved? The solution was to make proof a matter of consent rather than an objective standard. The measures of proof—the documents which were to count as the foundation of title and the evidence which was to count as proof of their tenor—were agreed between buyer and seller as part of the contract of sale. The buyer would negotiate the standard of proof with the seller, enter into a contract, and pay a deposit on that basis, and then, if the agreed standard

[28] *Lyddall v. Weston* (1739) 2 Atk. 19. See also *Hillary v. Waller* (1805) 12 Ves. Jun. 239, and *Emery v. Grocok* (1821) 6 Madd. 54.

[29] Williams, *Vendor and Purchaser*, 121.

of proof had been satisified, would pay the balance of the purchase price in return for a formal conveyance of title. These 'special contracts' were the ordinary currency of conveyancing. Often, the status of a title seemed so secure that it could be sold without any proper investigation. For instance, one witness to an inquiry into the operation of conveyancing described how a well-known title could be divided up and sold for house-building: 'we should probably have precluded a purchaser from making any requisitions at all; we should have started with the purchase deed, and precluded the purchaser from taking any other title, and he would have been quite satisfied.'[30] Similarly, a witness to a later inquiry said of sales made by the Grosvenor Estate in London that buyers would happily take a conveyance without insisting upon anything approaching formal proof.[31] In such cases, the reputation of a family and the continuity of its holdings would be sufficient to establish the validity of a paper title. These are somewhat extreme examples of a mode of proof which was used in almost all transactions. Conveyancing was a practical art, in which documents were evaluated by holding them to the light of local knowledge of the history of a family, the management of an estate, or the reputation of the conveyancer who had conducted earlier transactions. These practical proofs were sufficient to validate a title. In less straightforward cases, the skill of the conveyancer was to make informed inferences about the movement of title from facts about the career of a family, or from a pattern of past transactions. As with the operation of the code of conveyancing, the homogeneity of property practices within a relatively small landowning class made these inferences from documentary evidence possible. The conditions for the operation of this practical art were secured by the judges, who would hold buyers bound by the terms of a special contract so long as the stipulated measures of private proof were clear and unequivocal.[32] Thus, proof of title could be left to private agreement.

A conveyancer was supposed to obtain 'not only such title as will effectually protect his client from eviction, but also such a title as a subsequent purchaser or mortgagee may be compelled to accept'.[33] In practice, this meant securing a title which would appear sufficiently sound that it could be sold on by special contract to a subsequent buyer. No one expected that he would have to sell his land under the theoretical standard of proof which applied to so-called open contracts. As one nineteenth-century commentator put it, 'owing to refinements in modern conveyancing, and the infinite

[30] Royal Commission on the Operation of the Land Transfer Act, Report, Minutes of Evidence, HCP (1870), xviii. 529.

[31] Royal Commission on Land Transfer and Titles, Second Report, Minutes of Evidence HCP (1911), xxx. question 10153.

[32] *Southby* v. *Hutt* (1837) 2 My & Cr 207.

[33] Hughes, 'The Law of Contracts Relating to Real Property' (1845–6) 6 Law Times 289.

. multiplication of questions upon titles, special conditions have, to a certain extent, become absolutely necessary in putting up almost every title for sale'.[34] In any case, conveyancing was so expensive that it would rarely have been tempting for a buyer to invest in the pursuit of something more than a practical standard of proof. Again, as the parallel example of the conveyancing codes suggests, the basic fabric of ownership in this era of land law was composed, not of formal rules and principles, but of practical techniques and expectations. Ownership was secured, not by documents, but by the techniques which brought them to life. Only as these practical foundations were eroded did registration come to seem an attractive method of land. This change in the patterns of landownership has been amply described;[35] here, the focus is on the implications of these transformations for proof of title.

THE EMERGENCE OF REGISTRATION

In retrospect, the value of registration of title seems irresistibly obvious. Instead of having a system of archaeological proof, in which the task of the conveyancer was to sift through many layers of paper title, establishing which interests were still relevant or effective, and ensuring that there was no danger of hidden documents surfacing in the future, one would have a much simpler scheme of tabular proof, in which all effective interests would be visible at a glance. The accuracy of the table would be maintained by a simple process of updating. Interests and owners would be added or subtracted as appropriate, and any mistakes caused by the administration of registration would be guaranteed by an indemnity fund. Proof would be simple, effective, and cheap. Why then did it take so long to implement a working scheme of registration of title?

The idea of registration, and the sort of administrative framework which it implied, had been familiar for many decades before the first effective scheme of registration of title was introduced by the Land Transfer Act 1897. During that period there were various attempts to implement systems of registration, and as many inquiries into the failure of these tentative schemes.[36] These moves were played out against the background of progress in other areas of property law. In relation to patents and copyright in designs, schemes of registration had been established even before the end of the eighteenth century, and many of the legislative efforts of the nine-

[34] Anon. (1843) 1 Law Times 189, at 190.

[35] For an overview, see Murphy and Clark, *The Family Home* (London: Sweet & Maxwell, 1983), ch. 1.

[36] See Anderson, *Lawyers and the Making of English Land Law 1832–1840* (Oxford: Oxford University Press, 1992).

teenth century were aimed at the improvement of existing systems. It is true that such forms of intangible property present different questions of priority and identity, but these parallel systems of registration offered working models of bureaucratic property. Moreover, the aspiration of early reformers was indeed that land should be treated as a quasi-intangible, which could be traded in the same way as stocks and shares. Further from home, but closer to the question of land transfer, the colonial experience of India held out the promise of a thoroughgoing cadastral register of property holdings. The 1853 Settlement in the Panjab shows how regulations made as early as 1822 came to be realized in a complete topographical survey of village fields, made to a scale of four inches to the mile, upon which were recorded all landholdings, the boundaries between them, and a fiscal classification of soil quality.[37] This particular example, more perhaps than the domestic issues surrounding the collection of tithes, suggests the intimate connection between the question of registration and some broader questions concerning government and administration. At a general level, those questions concern a transformation in the way in which the task of government was conceptualized, and the role of law and administration within that conception.[38] More specifically, it may be that nineteenth-century models of bureaucratic property were informed by a movement towards administrative reform that began in 1780, committed to the ideals of 'speed, precision, impartiality, uniformity and accountability' in adminstration.[39] If that is so, then perhaps public officials rather than private practitioners would have seemed the most appropriate and trustworthy agents of land transfer: 'mid- and late-Victorian society, which had escaped from "Old Corruption", was inclined to place high trust in incorruptible public servants'.[40] Cumulatively, these factors confirm the obviousness of registration.

There are a number of reasons why it took so long for these strands to be bound into an effective scheme of registration of title. First, a good deal of time was wasted on experiments with deeds registration. The difference between registration of title and registration of deeds was that, whereas the former was a register of conclusions, the latter was only a register of the material from which conclusions might be drawn.[41] Conveyancers would still have been expected to sift through accumulated layers of paperwork to

[37] Smith, *Rule by Records: Land Registration and Village Custom in Early British Panjab* (Delhi: Oxford University Press, 1996).

[38] For a discussion of some of these themes in relation to law, see Murphy, 'The Oldest Social Science? The Epistemic Properties of the Common Law Tradition' (1991) 54 MLR 182.

[39] Torrance, 'Social Class and Bureaucratic Innovation 1780–1787' (1978) 78 Past and Present 56.

[40] Offer, 'Lawyers and Land Law Revisited' (1994) 14 OJLS 269 at 275.

[41] Anderson, *Lawyers and the Making of English Land Law 1832–1940*, ch. 3.

extract relevant interests, and so on. Secondly, there were some outstanding technological problems to be overcome, not least that of finding an effective method of identifying and indexing landholdings.[42] Most contentious, and most important, there is the question of economic self-interest.[43] The question is whether, or to what extent, the slow evolution and final configuration of registration should be attributed to the success of a campaign of resistance to reform, mounted by the conveyancing profession in the defence of its monopoly. This chapter identifies a different issue. Given that titles depend upon practical techniques and networks for their existence and effectiveness, and given that registration presupposes a fabric of practical techniques which is thoroughly unlike the practical foundation of traditional conveyancing, one of the most basic difficulties of the transition is that of undoing one set of embedded expectations and replacing it with another. The scope of this transformation was such that the shift from contractual proof to bureaucratic proof could not have been straightforward.

Again, the contrast between the progress made with cadastral schemes in India and the difficulties experienced in England is instructive. Although the cadastral scheme imposed in the Panjab in 1853 was supposed to be sensitive to the fine-grained texture of local customs, administrative representations of land and ownership thoroughly reconstructed local society. Specifically, the genealogical accounts of entitlement which accompanied the 1853 Settlement imposed a model of kinship, status, and social reciprocity which supplanted local understandings with a new understanding of land and its social value: 'what might seem mere technicalities of the new system—the fixing of boundaries, the absolute measurement of area and the classification of soils—entailed the most radical change in the concept of land.[44] The same was true of registration of title in England, the important difference being that what had been done so deliberately and effectively in the Panjab had to be left to a slow and capricious process of social evolution.

The transformation implied by the project of registration reached the deepest layers of practical understanding. First, it implied a thorough alteration in the conveyancer's notion of certainty in property. Any workable scheme of registration of title required that certainty be produced in the registry, by techniques of indexing and recording supervised by an administrative official. The security of titles depended entirely on these tech-

---

[42] Pottage, 'The Measure of Land' (1994) 57 MLR 361.

[43] See Offer, 'The Origins of the Law of Property Acts 1910–1925' (1977) 40 MLR 505; Offer, *Property and Politics, 1870–1914: Land Ownership, Law, Ideology and Urban Development in England* (Cambridge: Cambridge University Press, 1981); Offer, 'Lawyers and Land Law Revisited'; Anderson, *Lawyers and the Making of English Land Law 1832–1940*.

[44] Smith, *Rule by Records: Land Registration and Village Custom in Early British Panjab*, 241.

niques. For the nineteenth-century conveyancer, it was no easy thing to entrust their clients' expectations to a registrar. The measure of proof in traditional conveyancing being contractual, every potential hazard or loophole had to be identified and sealed by the conveyancer. So, despite (or because) the basic validity of a title was a matter of practical judgement rather than 'mathematical certainty', conveyancers took it that they were responsible for ensuring that a conveyance was made only when they had accounted for ascertainable risks and secured priority over other interests and transactions. The idea of trusting a third party to evaluate title, safeguard priorities, and ensure closure was entirely contrary to this understanding of proof as a private standard achieved through self-reliance. The tensions between private and public certainty became especially acute during the early stages of registration of title. The process by which titles were transcribed from deeds to registers was entirely in the hands of the administration of the Registry. Some aspects of the administration were unclear to the conveyancers, and perhaps the bureaucrats: would the registrar interpret and validate titles in such a way as to preserve existing expectations? might the existing rights of mortgagees and lessors be affected by new structures of title and ownership? how could one organize the timing of transactions so as to ensure that a buyer's application for registration would retain priority over other, possibly fraudulent, applications?[45] More important, the nature of these uncertainties was such that the registrar was required to use his discretion to adjust rules and procedures to difficulties thrown up by practical experience. For conveyancers, this made the basis of registration so uncertain that they were reluctant to abandon measures of private proof. Even the insurance provision, which was supposed to secure registration, was ineffective because the rules which determined who might qualify for compensation were still unclear. So, rather than transfer their trust to the register, conveyancers carried on making and securing conveyances in the old way, treating registration as an annoying and superfluous bureaucratic routine.

These questions about certainty accentuated another tension between the old and the new. The scheme of tabular title introduced a novel organizing principle for interests in land. Whereas in the old scheme interests were organized around the ideal of a good root of title, the new scheme replaced this somewhat elusive practical standard with a fixed index. This pivotal indexing role was occupied by the figure of a fictitious owner, 'created for the purpose of registration'.[46] The role of the registered owner is fictional in the sense that it serves primarily as the key to the grammar of interests in registered land, or a reference point organizing the priorities and

---

[45] Pottage, 'The Originality of Registration'.

[46] Select Committee on Land Titles and Transfer, Reports, HCP (1878–9), xi, at para. 13.

relationships between those interests. The nominal registered owner might indeed be the beneficial owner of the relevant interests (after all, the scheme was designed on the basis that the registered owner should as much as possible be the 'real' owner of the land), but it is important to distinguish the office from the office-holder. As an abstract office, the registered owner serves only to frame the structure of formal interests, the indexing of those interests to the registry map, and the techniques of recording which establish how each interest should be protected. This raised the question whether the new system offered quite as effective protection as the old. In recent years this has become especially problematic because the sphere of relevant rights has come to include interests that were all but ignored in 1925—namely, the informal rights of those in occupation. Because the scheme of registration was formulated in the late nineteenth century, it incorporated traditional assumptions about the separation of ownership and occupation, the result being that no effective provision was made for the recording and indexing of such interests.

However, in this vital transitional period, the question was somethat different. Conveyancers were anxious about how the fictional powers of the registered owner would relate to the practical structure of ownership expectations, which had in their view been properly represented in the old scheme of conveyancing. Again, these anxieties reveal the difference between the conceptual and practical structures of registration and traditional conveyancing. For example, the coherence and continuity of the register's index could be maintained only if mortgagors remained as the registered owners of 'their' title. This undermined the old assumption that a mortgagee should gain control of the legal title. The difficulty was that in the traditional scheme the powers of the mortgagee to defend and realize his security were tied to his control of the legal estate. How could one be sure that the new grammar of fictitious powers would offer equivalent protection?[47] Questions such as this were complicated by the fact that, in working out a new grammar of ownership, registration was also working out a way of (re)distributing conveyancing functions between the registry and the legal profession. Given that registration could not easily make conveyancers redundant—'there were simply too many aspects to a land transaction other than the act of transfer for solicitors to be ousted'[48]—the new grammar had to be adjusted to a distinction between the function of providing certainty of title (which was the job of the registry) and that of fashioning ownership powers to suit the projects of individuals (which was to be the job of the conveyancing profession). This is why registration implied a novel play on the distinction between title credentials and ownership powers.

[47] Hogg, 'The Mortgage Charge of the Land Transfer Acts' (1907) 59 LQR 68.
[48] Anderson, *Lawyers and the Making of English Land Law 1832–1940*, 228.

This sketch of the difficulties encountered by registration in its most important formative period (1897–1930) exposes not only the contingency of the practices of traditional conveyancing, but also the extent to which the routines of registration, which in the late twentieth century seem to work in an almost mechanical fashion, are in fact adjusted to, and dependent upon, many layers of practical expectations. The story of this episode shows how such things as indexes and recording techniques are not simply mechanical devices, which work like clockwork, but are distilled or 'materialized' forms of practical learning—just the sort of 'precise practice of craftsmanship and knowledge' which characterizes documentary technologies.

How was the gap closed? How did conveyancers come to accept the model of certainty proposed by registration and the division of labour that went with it? Perhaps the answer is that, although the introduction of registration sharply accentuated the differences between old and new, those differences were so acute because matters had reached the point at which one model had to give way to the other, and, thanks to developments generated by the conveyancing profession itself in response to changing structures of landownership, registration held a decisive advantage.[49] The argument is that registration was favoured by the gradual but inexorable convergence of a movement towards standardization which was taking place inside and outside the profession. In the traditional model of practical proof, each title was unique in the sense that it rested upon a specific, local, measure of proof. There could be no standardized measure of proof (which was precisely why people made 'special', rather than 'open', contracts). For the same reason, it would have been pointless to impose a standard scale of fees for conveyancing. The old idea was that each title required a different method or degree of investigation, and the conveyancer should be paid accordingly. Yet, the internal development of the profession, because it imposed standardization on quite different grounds, effectively undermined the process of practical proof.

Stuart Anderson suggests that the movement towards standardization emerged from the promotion of local interests. Local law societies introduced standard conditions of sale so as to make their auction rooms fairer and more efficient than their competitors in adjacent districts. These conditions were often tailored to patterns established by the management practices of local estates.[50] However, as the profession began to fashion itself into a more uniform and cohesive body, and as statutes began to standardize practices, local conditions of sale were merged into more general conditions of sale, leading to the emergence of a common measure for proof of

---

[49] Pottage, 'The Originality of Registration', 388–93.
[50] Anderson, *Lawyers and the Making of English Land Law 1832–1940*, 122, 154.

title. This in turn made a standard fee scale seem less objectionable. Not only were these politically desirable for a profession which was accused of overcharging, but there were economic advantages:

Fixed scale fees did not abolish bargaining altogether, but they provided a high reference point to anchor concessions. Furthermore, once scale fees had been fixed, agents were in a position to appropriate any increase in productivity. Hence the great attractions of 'simplification' reforms, which acted to reduce uncertainty and cost for the agents.[51]

The difficulty for the profession was that it was committed to a process of proof whose viability decreased in direct proportion to the success of the process of standardization. The upshot was that the movement towards standardization and simplification eased the profession into the very scheme of registration which it found so objectionable. Precisely because it held out the promise of a standard measure of proof, backed by an indemnity fund, it offered a more viable solution to the paradox created by professional standardization. Only in the scheme of registration was the statutory imposition of a standard range of inquiries supported by a common measure of certainty.

ARTICULATING EXPECTATIONS

By way of conclusion, it is appropriate to say something about how this particular episode in the history of English land transfer practices relates to a broader transformation in the function of titles, or of legal writing in general. The conventional understanding of the function of titles is to see them as credentials of ownership, which might be tendered to a future buyer or asserted against an intruder. The idea is that paper titles are instruments of transfer; they shift land from one owner to the next, or, more precisely, they shift the powers and faculties of ownership from one owner to the next. The central function of title is indeed to indicate or prove ownership, or to serve as 'status indicators'. From this perspective, the conceptual and functional core of title lies in the evidential relation between title (paper) and land (ownership powers). It may be that this is no longer the most accurate representation of the functional logic of titles. Transformations in the use of land, and of property in general, suggest that the role of title—or paper titles—is changing as land more obviously becomes a quasi-intangible form of property. Even in the traditional framework of landownership, a paper title was not so much a surrogate for land as a way of indexing expectations which built up around land. Land was supposedly the exclusive foundation of wealth and political competence; landed men were the 'true owners of

---

[51] Offer, 'Lawyers and Land Law Revisited', 276.

our political vessel' and moneyed men 'no more than passengers in it'.[52] The reality was that the myth of 'land' was simply a way of representing wealth and status, or a way of distinguishing some forms of wealth from others, and titles were the means by which people and events were bound to that representation. These expectations, rather than the material substance of land itself, were the correlates of titles. Now, land is much more densely shrouded in intangible expectations.

The familiar example of the contemporary domestic mortage offers an example of this phenomenon. In its basic form, the mortgage seems to resemble the classical form of a security transaction. The title carries with it a set of rights to the income and capital of the land, and the function of a registered title is to define the rights of borrowers, lenders, and occupiers to draw on the commercial value of the land which the title represents. However, if one includes the other elements of a modern mortgage transaction, the picture becomes somewhat more complex. First, financial regulatory principles may require a lender to take out some form of insurance to guarantee loans which exceed a certain percentage of the purchase price of the home. The title, and the rights and obligations which it organizes, serves primarily to structure the relationship between lender and insurer, or to make the title a suitable investment for a company which is notionally accountable to its shareholders. Neither of these relationships is more than obliquely or residually dependent upon the traditional function of a title as an index to land. Secondly, a borrower may be required or induced to take out various forms of insurance, or to subscribe to a pension or endowment fund linked to the duration of the mortgage. One component of the long-term transaction may be insurance premiums to cover repayments if the borrower becomes ill or unemployed. Again, the rights and obligations attached to title are used mainly to structure a relationship between borrower and insurer, or borrower and institutional investor. The result of transferring so many of the day-to-day risks of the mortgage relationship to insurance is to emphasize that the primary role of the mortgage transaction is to structure a relationship between the borrower as employee and the lender as a provider of credit. More abstractly, or more cynically, the transaction is one in which the wish to secure personal expectations and relationships is exploited in such a way that the borrower serves as a nexus between labour markets and financial-services markets. In any case, so long as the transaction works in this way, with insurance as the primary safeguard, the title functions as a nexus of expectations in a way which differs substantially from its traditional role. The traditional security function of the mortgage becomes only a last resort, which is itself a factor in insurance calculations.

[52] Bolingbroke, *Some Reflections on the Political State of the Nation*, cited in Langford, *Public Life and the Propertied Englishman, 1689–1798* (Oxford: Oxford University Press, 1991), 59.

The expectations articulated by title are therefore of many different sorts. Perhaps one could characterize some of these distinctions in terms of a difference between commercial, fungible, property, and 'personhood-constituting' property.[53] In any case, however the differences are explained, the difficulty for technologies of title is that they can no longer resort to the sort of coherent, homogenous, expectations which underpinned traditional conveyancing. Rather, they have to offer a measure of certainty which can be incorporated into a wide range of social activities. Whether or not it is part of the explanation for the consolidation of registration, the point is that traditional practical proof is now impossible. A title has to be produced by techniques which are largely self-sufficient, and this self-sufficiency is precisely what allows title to be coupled to social practices. The question of overriding interests shows that the relationship between ownership expectations and documentary techniques of title is still inherently problematic, but, in making technologies of title yet more discreet and self-reliant, registration has allowed for much greater complexity in transactions.

[53] Radin, 'Property and Personhood', 34 Stan. L. Rev. 957 (1982).

6

THE LAW COMMISSION AND THE
REFORM OF LAND LAW

Charles Harpum

This chapter is a modest attempt to assess the contribution that the Law Commission for England and Wales has made to the reform of land law since it was set up by the Law Commissions Act 1965.[1] Such an assessment is not easy to make, because there is no single yardstick by which that contribution can be judged. There are however a number of possible criteria that can be employed. These include—

1. the number of reform proposals that the Commission has made and the success or otherwise that it has enjoyed in securing their implementation;
2. the critical reception given to the Commission's reforms when they have been implemented;
3. the extent to which the changes have worked well in practice (itself rather a difficult assessment to make);
4. the impact of the proposals on the structure and content of land law; and
5. the effectiveness of the Commission's contribution as against other bodies that have brought about statutory reform.

This list of indicators is not in any sense a comprehensive one. Nor would it be possible in an essay of this kind to attempt a full survey of the Law Commission's Reports on land law judged against these and other possible criteria. What follows must necessarily be an impressionistic view, coloured by examples rather than by any exhaustive analysis. The materials on which it is based are drawn entirely from sources that are in the public domain.[2]

Charles Harpum is a Law Commissioner for England and Wales and Fellow of Downing College, Cambridge. Although the author is a serving Law Commissioner, it must be emphasized that the views expressed in this chapter are wholly personal and are not in any sense those of the Law Commission.

[1] For these purposes, 'land law' has been taken to include conveyancing law and landlord and tenant law, but not family property law. Also excluded are matters such as powers of attorney, inheritance, and points of pure trust law.

[2] Most of the archive which covers the history of the Law Commission, except the papers concerning its creation and its first two years, are, of course, subject to the thirty-year rule. For Stephen Cretney's important analysis of the origins of the Law Commission, which does

The chapter begins with an account of the way in which the Law Commission works. This is followed by an assessment of the Commission's record in relation to land law in terms of the production of reports and their implementation—the first of the criteria above. There are then studies of four of the aspects of land law which the Commission has addressed—landlord and tenant law, land registration, conveyancing law, and trusts of land.[3] These are considered with regard to the other criteria mentioned above. The conclusion attempts to answer the question posed by the chapter. Finally, there is an appendix consisting of two tables which supplement the material in the text.

THE LAW COMMISSION: ITS STATUTORY POWERS AND DUTIES AND THE WAY IN WHICH IT WORKS

The Statutory Framework

For many, the Law Commission is something of a mystery.[4] The founding statute, the Law Commissions Act 1965, imposes a statutory duty upon the two Law Commissions[5]—

to take and keep under review all the law with which they are respectively concerned with a view to its systematic development and reform, including in particular the codification of such law, the elimination of anomalies, the repeal of obsolete and unnecessary enactments, the reduction of the number of separate enactments and generally the simplification and modernisation of the law . . .[6]

The Act then specifies the six ways in which this can be done.[7] In summary these are:

---

take into account archive material that is now available at the Public Record Office, see 'The Law Commission: True Dawns and False Dawns' (1996) 59 MLR 631.

[3] These are chosen as illustrative only. There are many aspects of the Commission's work on land law that have necessarily had to be excluded by constraints of space.

[4] There is, of course, a substantial literature about the Law Commission. For a selected list of publications prior to 1985, see Cretney, 'The Politics of Law Reform: A View from the Inside' (1985) 48 MLR 493 at 515. Later writings include Gibson, 'The Law Commission' (1986) 39 CLP 57; Zellick (ed.), *The Law Commission and Law Reform* (London: Sweet & Maxwell, 1988); and Ogus, 'Economics and Law Reform: Thirty Years of Law Commission Endeavour' (1995) 111 LQR 407.

[5] Namely, for England and Wales and for Scotland. There are five Law Commissioners in each jurisdiction. The Chairman, who is one of the Commissioners, is always a High Court Judge in England and Wales, and a Judge of the Court of Session in Scotland. In England and Wales the other Commissioners usually consist of a barrister, a solicitor, and two academic lawyers.

[6] s. 3(1).   [7] Ibid. The most important of these are explained more fully below.

1. to consider proposals for reform in response to a reference made to the Commission;
2. to prepare programmes for the reform of different branches of the law;[8]
3. to make proposals for reform under such programmes;
4. to undertake programmes of consolidation and statute law revision;[9]
5. to provide advice and information to government departments for the reform or amendment of the law; and
6. to obtain information as to foreign legal systems to facilitate the Commissioners' functions.

A Typical Law Commission Project

The usual way in which the Commission proceeds is either pursuant to a reference or under one of the Law Commission's Programmes of Reform. The work is undertaken by one of the four law reform teams at the Commission.[10] Typically a Law Commission project will take the following course. First, a Consultation Paper is written and published. The Paper introduces the topic under consideration, gives a detailed statement of the law and why it needs to be changed, and then offers a range of options for reform. After wide public consultation,[11] the Commissioners decide on the policy to be adopted in the light of the responses received. The final Report is then prepared and Parliamentary counsel at the Commission are instructed to draft a Bill which is appended to the Report. After the Report has been agreed by Commissioners and published, there is usually a period of consideration and consultation by the government department whose concern it is.[12] If the Report is accepted, the next step is to try to secure its

---

[8] These programmes must be agreed with 'the Minister', which means the Lord Chancellor in relation to the Law Commission for England and Wales, and the Lord Advocate as regards the Scottish Commission. The Lord Chancellor's Department is the sponsoring department for the Law Commission for England and Wales.

[9] These programmes are to be undertaken at the request of the Minister.

[10] These teams are headed by a Law Commissioner and usually consist of three other lawyers (from the Government Legal Service) and three research assistants (often some of the ablest recent law graduates in the country). They specialize in particular areas of the law. The present author is head of the Property and Trust Law Team. There is a fifth team, statute law revision, which is headed by a lawyer from the Government Legal Service. There are also a number of parliamentary counsel at the Commission. They draft law reform and consolidation Bills.

[11] The Commission targets particular persons and bodies likely to be able to offer authoritative and informed comment. It also receives comment from others. Its papers are now being published on the Internet as well as in hard copy, which will, it is hoped, lead to a wider circulation. The Commission's website is http://www.gtnet.uk/lawcomm/homepage.htm.

[12] In property matters it will usually be the Lord Chancellor's Department. If it concerns leases, the Department of the Environment will also have an interest. The Commission is generally involved in discussions with the relevant department.

implementation. If a means can be found to take the Bill through Parliament,[13] the Commission usually provides assistance to the government department that is supporting the Bill.[14]

Principal Types of Law Reform Work Undertaken by the Commission

(1) References are invariably concerned with a specific issue, often quite a narrow one. There have been just four references in matters of land law since the founding of the Commission, of which three have led to legislation.[15]

(2) Programmes have had a much larger role to play. The Commission is currently in the middle of its Sixth Programme of Law Reform.[16] There are four items in that programme which touch on the contents of this chapter. The most important, Item 6, 'Transfer of Land', is, in sweeping terms, 'that an examination be made of the creation, transfer and extinction of rights in or over registered and unregistered land with a view to the modernisation and simplification of the law'.[17] The transfer of land has in fact been a programme item since the creation of the Law Commission in 1965. Although originally restricted to unregistered land, it was widened in January 1966 to cover the whole law relating to transfer of both registered and unregistered land.[18] Another item that had in all previous Programmes been of major importance, Item 5, 'The Law of Landlord and Tenant', is now included on a mere 'care and maintenance' basis—to do what is necessary to facilitate the implementation of earlier Reports but no more.[19] The reasons for this

[13] A variety of means have been employed to secure implementation. Of the four most recent Acts in property law, the Law of Property (Miscellaneous Provisions) Act 1994 was run by means of a special procedure (called the 'Jellicoe' procedure), by which most of the work is done by Committee in the House of Lords, the Landlord and Tenant (Covenants) Act 1995 was introduced as a Private Members' Bill (under the 'Ten Minute Rule'), the Trusts of Land and Appointment of Trustees Act 1996 was run as a government programme Bill, and the Land Registration Act 1997 as a Private Peers' Bill.

[14] The Commission has always given assistance with implementation: see the comments in Law Commission, *Fifth Annual Report 1969–1970*, Law Com. No. 36 (1970), para. 4. The work involved can be considerable.

[15] The relevant Acts are the Charging Orders Act 1979, the Reverter of Sites Act 1987, and the Access to Neighbouring Land Act 1992. See Appendix, Table 2.

[16] Law Commission, *Sixth Programme of Law Reform*, Law Com. No. 234 (1995), published on the thirtieth anniversary of the establishment of the Commission. This will be the Commission's agenda until the end of 1998.

[17] Ibid. 31.

[18] See Law Commission, *First Annual Report 1965–1966*, Law Com. No. 4 (1966), para. 70.

[19] Law Commission, *Sixth Programme of Law Reform*, 30. At the time when the *Sixth Programme* was published, the Commission's final Report on Landlord and Tenant Law, *Landlord and Tenant: Responsibility for State and Condition of Property*, Law Com. No. 238 (1996), had not been completed. Item 5 also made express provision for it.

are explained below.[20] Item 7, 'The Law of Trusts', is not an open-ended item, but consists of such aspects of trust law as are agreed by the Law Commission with the Lord Chancellor's Department.[21] A number of specific topics have been agreed, of which the first, the rule against perpetuities and excessive accumulations, has obvious implications for land law.[22] Finally, Item 8, 'Family Law', includes, as its only substantive item, an examination of the property rights of homesharers.[23]

(3) Consolidation is a valuable but little-appreciated instrument of law reform. To reduce many statutes to one and rationalize them in the process[24] makes the law more usable and more accessible. Parliamentary counsel working at the Law Commission have undertaken a number of major consolidations of property legislation, including the Rent Act 1977, the Housing Act 1985, the Landlord and Tenant Act 1985, and the Agricultural Holdings Act 1986.[25]

(4) The repeal of obsolete legislation is undertaken on the basis of the work of the Statute Law Revision Team at the Commission.[26] This can have a greater importance in relation to land law than might be expected. For example, there are a number of ancient rights over or connected with land that are now no longer in practice extant. The repeal of legislation that relates to such rights eliminates doubts and the need for unnecessary enquiries on the purchase of land that might otherwise be thought necessary.

(5) The Law Commission has throughout its history given advice to government departments on a wide variety of subjects. For example, although the Law Commission has had an active role in the reform of the law of land registration under its programme on transfer of land,[27] it has also given advice to the Lord Chancellor's Department to assist it with other legislation on the subject.[28]

---

[20] See p. 162.   [21] Law Commission, *Sixth Programme of Law Reform*, 32.

[22] A final Report is in preparation and is likely to be published early in 1998.

[23] Law Commission, *Sixth Programme of Law Reform*, 36. A Consultation Paper is likely to be published in 1998.

[24] It is sometimes necessary to pass 'paving legislation', ironing out inconsistencies and amending the legislation in issue before its consolidation can be undertaken.

[25] On this aspect of the Commission's work, see *Landlord and Tenant: Reform of the Law*, Law Com. No. 162 (1987), para. 1.9.

[26] One of its recent victims was the Land Registration Act 1966: see Statute Law (Repeals) Act 1995, sch. 1, part VI. For the irony of this, see below.

[27] See the Land Registration Acts 1986, 1988, and 1997.

[28] See below, p. 164.

THE PRODUCTION AND IMPLEMENTATION OF
LAW REFORM PROPOSALS

In its *Twenty-Fifth Annual Report, 1990*, the Law Commission commented that 'however well received our reports may be, the ultimate proof of the value of our work comes only when Parliament decides to give legislative effect to our recommendations'.[29] In assessing the effectiveness or otherwise of the Law Commission's contribution to the reform of land law, the extent to which its proposals have been implemented must therefore be a relevant criterion. To assess this, it is convenient to start with some simple statistics set out in Table 1 of the Appendix. That reveals that twenty-three of the forty Reports published on land law have been enacted in whole or part to date.[30] That is, however, a misleading picture, because the number of those Reports that *could* have been enacted was thirty-six.[31] On that basis, nearly two-thirds of them were enacted and that percentage is likely to rise, because a number of outstanding Reports are still very much in contention.[32] The figures also show that while the decade 1971–80 was an unfruitful period for the Commission in relation to land law, the fifteen years that followed were very productive.[33] In the first of the two periods, the Commission was heavily involved in work on family law and this diverted resources from other work on land law.[34] It also expended much effort on an ultimately abortive project to codify the law of landlord and tenant.[35] By contrast in the period 1984–8 there were two Commissioners who devoted themselves exclusively to land law.[36] Since 1994, although the Commission has maintained a land law programme, its new property

[29] Law Com. No. 195 (1991), para. 1.5.

[30] Taking April 1997 as the cut-off date. In some cases only a small part of a Report's recommendations have been implemented.

[31] Five of the forty Reports did not contain draft Bills. Of those, one was in fact enacted in part, two made no recommendations for legislation, and two were followed by later Reports which contained Bills for their implementation.

[32] Certain Reports have been expressly rejected, such as *Transfer of Land: Obsolete Restrictive Covenants*, Law Com. No. 201 (1991). Others are now so old that they will not be implemented, such as *Codification of the Law of Landlord and Tenant: Report on Obligations of Landlords and Tenants*, Law Com. No. 67 (1975).

[33] They were also a period of success in terms of implementation, even though a substantial number of property reports remain unenacted.

[34] See e.g. Law Commission, *Ninth Annual Report 1973–1974*, Law Com. No. 64 (1974), para. 11.

[35] See p. 157.

[36] Professor Julian Farrand (Commissioner 1984–8) and Mr Trevor Aldridge (Commissioner 1984–93). When Professor Farrand left the Commission, it was decided that the Commission should turn its attention to the reform of the common law (Law Commission, *Twenty-Fourth Annual Report 1989*, Law Com. No. 190 (1990), para. 1.4).

work has shifted away from landlord and tenant law (which had enjoyed some prominence) to trust law instead.

CASE STUDY 1: LANDLORD AND TENANT LAW

The Experiment with Codification

The codification of the law is part of the Law Commission's statutory duty.[37] However, its attempts to reform and codify the law of landlord and tenant have been amongst its least successful ventures.[38] As is well known, Item VIII of the Law Commission's *First Programme of Law Reform*[39] was the 'Codification of the Law of Landlord and Tenant'. For these purposes, 'codification' was not just 'a comprehensive restatement of the law as it is, with the object of giving ready access to rules until then only available from studying the cases which have built up the common law'.[40] Instead, the law was to be clarified and, where necessary, reformed, as part of the process of codification.[41] After thirteen years, the Commission admitted defeat, and attempts to codify the law were, for practical purposes, abandoned.[42]

As a result of considerable labour by many hands[43] over a lengthy period,[44] the Commission produced three Reports under the codification rubric. The first, *Codification of the Law of Landlord and Tenant: Report on Obligations of Landlords and Tenants*,[45] proposed that certain obligations between landlord and tenant should be implied into leases, though some obligations were to be capable of variation. The Report contained a draft Bill to give effect to its proposals, but it has never been (and plainly never will be) implemented.[46] The second Report, *Codification of the Law of*

---

[37] Law Commissions Act 1965, s. 3(1); see above, p. 152.

[38] For an excellent summary of the position as it stood in 1986, see Gibson, 'The Law Commission', 68–70.

[39] Law Com. No. 1 (1965).

[40] Law Commission, *Landlord and Tenant: Reform of the Law*, para. 3.2.

[41] Law Commission, *Codification of the Law of Landlord and Tenant: Report on Obligations of Landlords and Tenants*, para. 5.

[42] See Law Commission, *Thirteenth Annual Report 1977–1978*, Law Com. No. 92 (1978), para. 2.34.

[43] Much use was made over the years of a working party which had a very distinguished membership.

[44] 'The work of the Law Commission upon landlord and tenant law over a period of about ten years has made slow and unsatisfactory progress' (*Nineteenth Annual Report 1983–1984*, Law Com. No. 140 (1985), para. 2.49.

[45] The Report contained a draft Bill. The basis for the Report was a working paper, *Provisional Proposals Relating to Obligations of Landlords and Tenants*, Law Com. WP No. 8 (1967).

[46] Cf. Law Commission, *Landlord and Tenant: Reform of the Law*, para. 1.6(3).

Landlord and Tenant: Covenants Restricting Dispositions, Alterations and Change of User,[47] contained two main recommendations. The first was to prohibit the use of absolute covenants against the disposition of leases (subject to certain exceptions),[48] a proposal that was not accepted. The second was to give tenants remedies against landlords who either unreasonably withheld their consent to an assignment or failed to give it within a reasonable time, or only on conditions that were unreasonable. A draft Bill was subsequently prepared to implement this second recommendation.[49] and this was enacted as the Landlord and Tenant Act 1988. This Act has not been the cause of any particular difficulty to date,[50] though its impact has been subsequently blunted by the Landlord and Tenant (Covenants) Act 1995, as is explained below.[51]

The final codification Report was *Codification of the Law of Landlord and Tenant: Forfeiture of Tenancies.*[52] This also contained two principal recommendations. First, it proposed the replacement of the notoriously complex and unsatisfactory law on the forfeiture of leases for breach of covenant by a simpler and more rational system. Secondly, tenants were to be given a right to terminate a lease for breach of covenant by the landlord. Once again, the Report did not contain a draft Bill. However, the Commission subsequently produced a draft Bill to implement the first of its recommendations,[53] giving this a greater priority than the possible enactment of the second recommendation.[54] In practice, the second is never likely to be enacted, nor may it be needed. There are welcome signs that the courts, by emphasizing the contractual nature of leases, will give tenants the right to terminate a lease where the landlord commits a repudiatory breach of the

---

[47] Law Com. No. 141 (1985). This grew out of a working paper, *The Law of Landlord and Tenant: Working Party's Provisional Proposals Relating to Covenants Restricting Dispositions, Parting with Possession, Change of User and Alterations,* Law Com. WP No. 25 (1970). The draft of the Report was first submitted to the Department of the Environment for its views in 1979. A response was eventually received in 1982.

[48] The effect of the proposals would have been that a covenant which prohibited any disposition of the lease by the tenant would in fact have taken effect as a qualified covenant not to make any disposition without the landlord's consent, which could not be unreasonably withheld.

[49] See Law Commission, *Leasehold Conveyancing,* Law Com. No. 161 (1987).

[50] The Act has been judicially considered on a number of occasions: see e.g. *Dong Bang Minerva (UK) Ltd.* v. *Davina Ltd.* [1995] 1 EGLR 41 (HC); [1996] 2 EGLR 31 (CA).

[51] See p. 159.

[52] Law Com. No. 142 (1985). This is the Law Commission's longest running project. It originated in a working paper, *Provisional Proposals Relating to Termination of Tenancies,* Law Com. WP No. 17 (1968).

[53] Law Commission, *Landlord and Tenant Law: Termination of Tenancies Bill,* Law Com. No. 221 (1994).

[54] Ibid., para. 1.7.

terms of the lease.[55] There is a real prospect that this Report may be implemented, though it will probably be necessary to modify some of its recommendations to take account of concerns within the property industry.[56] It is significant that, in the absence of new legislation, the courts have taken the initiative and have boldly reinterpreted a number of the existing statutory provisions which govern forfeiture in an attempt to meet a number of the deficiencies which the Commission's proposals address.[57]

Other Work: The Landlord and Tenant (Covenants) Act 1995

In 1987 the Law Commission published an intriguing Report in an attempt to revive the process of reform in landlord and tenant law.[58] It contained no proposals for reform, and its avowed objective was 'to survey the existing law of landlord and tenant in order to identify areas which require reform and the work which needs to be done'.[59] A series of new projects followed which eventually resulted in five Reports.[60] Of these, one has been enacted, but in substantially amended form,[61] two were accepted in whole or part by the government of the day but have not yet been implemented,[62] and decisions are awaited on the others.

The one Report that was enacted was *Landlord and Tenant Law: Privity of Contract and Estate*.[63] It reached the statute book as the Landlord and Tenant (Covenants) Act 1995 in an extraordinary way, but one which reveals some

[55] See the important decision of Stephen Sedley, QC, in *Hussein* v. *Mehlman* [1992] 2 EGLR 87.

[56] There has been no full consultation on this subject since 1968 and landlord and tenant law and practice have changed fundamentally in that period. The Commission's proposal to abolish landlords' rights of peaceable re-entry—which are now widely used in relation to business premises—has proved to be particularly controversial.

[57] See, in particular, *Billson* v. *Residential Apartments Ltd.* [1992] 1 AC 494 (giving rights to relief in cases where the lease had been forfeited by peaceable re-entry); *Escalus Properties Ltd.* v. *Robinson* [1996] QB 231 (extending the range of relief open to those with derivative interests under the forfeited lease); *Savva* v. *Houssein* [1996] 2 EGLR 65 (restricting to just one the situations in which, for the purposes of Law of Property Act 1925, s. 146, a breach of covenant is as a matter of law incapable of remedy by the tenant).

[58] Law Commission, *Landlord and Tenant: Reform of the Law*.

[59] Ibid., para. 1.2.

[60] Law Commission, *Landlord and Tenant Law: Privity of Contract and Estate*, Law Com. No. 174 (1988); *Landlord and Tenant: Compensation for Tenants' Improvements*, Law Com. No. 178 (1989); *Landlord and Tenant: Distress for Rent*, Law Com. No. 194 (1991); *Landlord and Tenant: Business Tenancies—A Periodic Review of the Landlord and Tenant Act 1954 Part II*, Law Com. No. 208 (1992); *Landlord and Tenant: Responsibility for State and Condition of Property*, Law Com. No. 238 (1996).

[61] Law Commission, *Landlord and Tenant Law: Privity of Contract and Estate*; see Landlord and Tenant (Covenants) Act 1995, considered below.

[62] Law Commission, *Landlord and Tenant: Compensation for Tenants' Improvements* and *Landlord and Tenant: Responsibility for State and Condition of Property*.

[63] Law Com. No. 174 (1988).

of the problems that attend the reform of landlord and tenant law.[64] What was at issue was the ancient common law rule by which the original tenant under a lease remained primarily liable on the covenants under the lease for the duration of the lease, notwithstanding subsequent assignments of it.[65] The landlord for the time being could sue him for any breach of covenant committed by the tenant for the time being. The Law Commission recommended the abolition of the rule, but it considered that in certain circumstances the outgoing tenant should be obliged to guarantee the performance of the covenants by the assignee of the lease for the period until the lease was further assigned.[66] There was considerable pressure for this reform from those who supported tenants' interests because of the hardship that the rule caused. There was an equally strong lobby against on behalf of landlords. Attempts to enact the Commission's proposals through the medium of Private Members' Bills were twice unsuccessful.[67] The situation, in short, encapsulated the essential problem of attempting any major reform of landlord and tenant law. The point was summarized succinctly by a former Commissioner: 'any change of substance, however minimal, is likely to alter the balance between landlords and tenants, and if you make things easier for tenants, you are by the same token probably making things harder for landlords—scarcely a technical or non-controversial or apolitical matter.'[68]

In the end a much-publicized understanding was reached within the property industry (often referred to thereafter as the 'concordat') by which landlords agreed to accept the abolition of original tenant liability,[69] in return for a weakening of tenants' rights to assign. In leases in which the landlord's consent to assignment was required, landlords were to be permitted to attach conditions to the giving of such consent. A refusal of consent because of non-compliance with any such condition would not be regarded in law as unreasonable.[70] Although the abolition of original

[64] For accounts of the Act and its background, see Law Commission, *Thirtieth Annual Report 1995*, Law Com. No. 239 (1996), paras. 5.5–5.9; Bridge, 'Former Tenants, Future Liabilities and the Privity of Contract Principle: The Landlord and Tenant (Covenants) Act 1995' [1996] CLJ 313; Davey, 'Privity of Contract and Leases—Reform at Last' (1996) 59 MLR 78.

[65] *Walker's Case* (1587) 3 Co. Rep. 22a.

[66] The circumstances were (i) that the landlord's consent to assignment should be required; and (ii) that it should be reasonable to require such a guarantee in the particular case.

[67] In 1993 and 1994 respectively (see Law Commission, *Thirtieth Annual Report 1995*, para. 5.7).

[68] Diamond, 'The Law Commission and Government Departments', in Zellick (ed.), *The Law Commission and Law Reform* (London: Sweet & Maxwell, 1988), 23–4.

[69] Or 'privity of contract' as it is often misleadingly known.

[70] Under Landlord and Tenant Act 1988, s. 1(4), giving consent subject to any condition that is not a reasonable condition is a breach of the statutory duty cast upon landlords by that Act, the breach of which is actionable in damages.

tenant liability was to apply only to leases granted after any legislation came into force, a number of concessions were offered to tenants under existing leases as part of the package.[71]

The Lord Chancellor's Department consulted on the proposals, which were found to enjoy strong support. In the light of this, the Government decided to give its support to a third attempt to introduce the Commission's proposals which was then before Parliament.[72] To that Bill it was necessary to add two elements. The first was the terms of the concordat between the British Property Federation and the British Retail Consortium. The second was a new code of rules devised by the Law Commission for the transmission of leasehold covenants, which were designed to harmonize with the new law as to the termination of a tenant's liability on assignment.[73] In the six weeks that followed the Government's decision, the eighty-nine amendments that were needed to achieve these were drafted by Parliamentary Counsel at the Commission, working under exceptional pressure.[74] Although the Commission was opposed to significant elements in the concordat,[75] it gave substantial assistance to the Lord Chancellor's Department in preparing the legislation.[76] The Bill cleared Parliament on the last day for Private Members' business before Parliament rose.

The passage of the Landlord and Tenant (Covenants) Act 1995 demonstrates that law reform legislation, like any other, is subject to the buffets of

---

[71] For example, an original tenant who had to pay up because of a default by an assignee would be entitled to an 'overriding lease'—a lease of the reversion immediately expectant upon the term of the defaulting assignee. That would both enable the original tenant to terminate the lease of the defaulter and give him a lease which he could exploit.

[72] Introduced by Mr Peter Thurnham MP.

[73] For these rules, see Landlord and Tenant Covenants Act 1995, ss. 3, 4, 15, 23. They grew out of a draft Consultative Document prepared by the Law Commission that had in fact been sent to press on the day that the Government decided to support Mr Thurnham's Bill (and had to be recalled). The Commission's document contained proposals that would have codified and clarified the law for *existing* leases as well as making provision for new leases. It proved to be possible to enact only the latter: see Law Commission, *Thirtieth Annual Report 1995*, paras. 5.7–5.8.

[74] It transpired that many details of the concordat between the British Property Federation and the British Retail Consortium had not been fully worked out. As a result, the passage of the Bill was in the balance until the very end.

[75] See HC Deb. (14 July 1995), 263, c. 1264, where the Parliamentary Secretary, Mr John Taylor MP, explained that 'the Law Commission had reservations, and expressed them eloquently'.

[76] Criticisms are made from time to time because the Commission has been critical when its proposals have been rejected or have been implemented in a modified form: see e.g. Cretney, 'The Law Commission: True Dawns and False Dawns', 655–6. On this occasion, the Commission adhered to what the present writer believes to be a correct view of its own position—namely, as a body which merely proposes, leaving it to Ministers and Parliament to dispose. It accepted that its concerns were not shared by the majority of consultees and gave advice and assistance notwithstanding.

politics—interest group rather than party politics on this occasion. It is not a perfect piece of legislation because of the circumstances under which it was enacted. An existing Bill had to be amended. It was simply not possible to draft a new one from scratch, which in the circumstances would have been the ideal solution. Issues of detailed policy were in the process of evolving even as the drafting went on. Much difficult and highly technical work had to be done within a tight deadline. That the Act has been criticized comes as no surprise.[77] But the question has to be asked whether it was better to have an Act that was in some respects imperfect rather than no Act at all for the foreseeable future—which was in practice the alternative.

Why has Reform Proved so Elusive?

The Commission's lack of success in securing landlord and tenant reform has much to do with its status as something of a square peg within the round hole of the structure of government. It is not an institution that is really understood in Whitehall. Law reform can take place only if it has the support of the relevant government department. However, in such departments policy tends to be driven either by political imperatives, or by pressure from the public,[78] or from representative bodies.[79] Government departments also tend to have their own sounding boards, formal or informal, which can influence policy.

The Law Commission does not, of course, conform to this pattern. Although it is commonly perceived to be concerned with 'lawyers' law',[80] there is in reality little worthwhile law reform that is purely technical and which does not have a significant element of policy in it.[81] But the policy-makers—the Commissioners—are not only lawyers; they are also *not* civil

---

[77] See e.g. Walter, 'The Landlord and Tenant (Covenants) Act 1995: A Legislative Folly' [1996] Conveyancer 432. Mr Walter's predictions that the Act would lead to the creation of non-assignable leases may have given insufficient weight to the impact of rent review clauses on how parties negotiate leases. Leases with restrictive terms are likely to have unattractive returns on rent review. On the information that the present writer has received from practitioners in East Anglia, the only conditions that many landlords insist upon as a condition of assignment is that the tenant should enter into an authorized guarantee agreement. The practice may be different elsewhere.

[78] MPs' postbags can be important. A campaign led by the *Evening Standard* recently secured the enactment of part III of the Housing Act 1996, which places restrictions on landlords' powers to forfeit leases for non-payment of service charge.

[79] For example, the Party Wall Act 1996 was enacted in response to an initiative from within the surveying profession, particularly those who specialize in party wall work in London (where there has been local legislation for centuries). They have their own club—the wittily named Pyramus and Thisbe Club.

[80] Something that probably does not exist in reality.

[81] Diamond, 'The Law Commission and Government Departments', 23–4.

servants.[82] Furthermore, the priorities that may encourage law reform, such as problems encountered by legal practitioners, or the unsatisfactory and incoherent nature of some particular legal doctrine, are often not those which are of primary concern to Whitehall policy-makers. Although the Law Commission can and does respond swiftly to circumstances where legislation is required urgently, this is the exception rather than the rule. Projects tend to be long-term ones dealing with major subjects. Law Commission papers are highly regarded within the legal profession and amongst law teachers for their enormous thoroughness, but they do not conform to the normal model that is adopted by government departments. Their consultation papers and reports tend to be shorter and to be focused more exclusively on issues of policy.

The political nature of landlord and tenant law reform[83] creates an additional problem. Law reform can pass through Parliament only if it enjoys consensus on both sides of the House, unless it is a government programme Bill. As all departments are in competition for programme Bills, which are not easy to obtain, few law reform measures can hope to pass into law that way. In these circumstances, it is not entirely surprising that so few of the Commission's proposals have been enacted.[84]

The Law Commission has recognized that the way forward lies in making both the nature of its work and the potential benefits that flow from it better understood within government departments.[85] There are now regular meetings with those departments with which it works most closely. This leads to a better understanding of the priorities (and the concerns) of each. This process of working more closely with government is likely to cause the Commission to scrutinize more carefully its choice of law reform projects to ensure that they meet genuine needs. It should also lead to a wider input from outside the Commission into the contents of its programmes of law reform.

CASE STUDY 2: LAND REGISTRATION

The Law Commission has been more successful in its endeavours to reform the law on land registration than it has been in the field of landlord and tenant law. To date all the reforms have been the results of a series of comparatively limited projects. Their cumulative effect has however been significant. Three Land Registration Acts—those of 1986, 1988, and

---

[82] See p. 152.   [83] See p. 162.

[84] A similar problem exists in relation to the Commission's proposals for the reform of the criminal law.

[85] For example, in March 1997, it hosted a well-attended afternoon conference for Permanent Secretaries.

1997—enact Law Commission Reports.[86] Furthermore, the Commission made contributions to both the Land Registration Act 1966[87] and the provisions of the Administration of Justice Act 1977[88] which amended the Land Registration Act 1925.[89] Four of the reforms are particularly noteworthy. First, the Land Registration Act 1966 removed the restrictions on the extension of compulsory registration of title in the 1925 Act.[90] By 1 December 1990[91] the 1966 Act had done its work and the whole of England and Wales was subject to compulsory registration. Secondly, as a result of the Land Registration Act 1988, the register became a public document.[92] Any person may search any title on the register. The effects of this are very far reaching, particularly when it is coupled with the computerization of the register.[93] It is now possible to have direct access to the register by computer, so that a solicitor can inspect the title to a property from the terminal in her office at the press of a button. Another advantage is the additional security (and therefore marketability) which this brings to leasehold title where the superior title is registered. The general rule is that the grantee of a lease is not entitled to see the landlord's freehold title.[94] If that title is registered, he can now inspect it and can be assured of the title that he will obtain. Thirdly, one result of the Land Registration Act 1997 is that almost but not quite all dispositions[95] of unregistered freehold or leasehold land with more than twenty-one years to run—including a first legal mortgage—will trigger the compulsory registration of that title.[96] Finally, the

[86] See respectively Law Commission, *Property Law: Land Registration*, Law Com. No. 125 (1983); *Property Law: Second Report on Land Registration*, Law Com. No. 148 (1985); *Transfer of Land: Land Registration. First Report of A Joint Working Group on the Implementation of the Law Commission's Third and Fourth Reports on Land Registration*, Law Com. No. 235 (1995).

[87] See Law Commission, *First Annual Report 1965–1966*, para. 69.

[88] Namely ss. 24, 26.

[89] See Law Commission, *Twelfth Annual Report 1976–1977*, Law Com. No. 85 (1977), para. 20.

[90] Prior to the 1966 Act, the decision whether or not compulsory registration should be extended to a particular county had effectively rested with the county council (see Land Registration Act 1925, ss. 121, 122 (which the 1966 Act repealed)). Thereafter it rested with the Lord Chancellor. The Law Commission specifically advised on this point (see its *First Annual Report 1965–1966*, para. 69).

[91] The date on which the last Registration of Title Order took effect.

[92] Land Registration Act 1925, s. 112, substituted by Land Registration Act 1988, s. 1(1).

[93] As a result of Administration of Justice Act 1982, s. 66(1) (substituting a new Land Registration Act 1925, s. 1), the register is not required to be kept in documentary form.

[94] Law of Property Act 1925, s. 44(2).

[95] The appointment of a new trustee of unregistered land will not (for example) trigger compulsory registration. Where unregistered land passes by gift or inheritance it will have to be registered.

[96] Land Registration Act 1925, ss. 123, 123A, substituted by s. 1 of the 1997 Act. These provisions are likely to be brought into force on 1 April 1998.

provisions for indemnity have been recast[97] in order to correct certain deficiencies that had come to light,[98] to introduce a principle of contributory negligence (so that some negligence on the part of a claimant was no longer a complete bar to the recovery of indemnity), and to improve the Land Registry's rights of recourse against those whose conduct was the cause of the need to rectify the register.

There are two major Reports on land registration that have not been implemented except in very small part. Those are *Property Law: Third Report on Land Registration*,[99] and *Property Law: Fourth Report on Land Registration*.[100] The *Third Report* was unusual in two respects. First, it contained no draft Bill and, secondly, it did not derive directly from any consultation paper. It addressed the issues of overriding interests, rectification and indemnity, and minor interests, and represented a radical rethink of much of the land registration system. The *Fourth Report* consisted of a draft Land Registration Bill that was intended to replace the entirety of the Land Registration Act 1925. What happened thereafter was summarized in one of the Law Commission's Annual Reports: 'During the Lord Chancellor's Department's usual consultations on our Third and Fourth Reports it became clear that there was significant opposition to some of their principal recommendations not least from HM Land Registry'.[101] On the Second Reading of what became the Land Registration Act 1997, the view was expressed that the two Reports 'had proved too ambitious for early implementation'.[102] The upshot was the creation of a Joint Working Group, with representatives from the Law Commission, HM Land Registry, and the Lord Chancellor's Department.[103] This is examining the future of land registration legislation both against the background of the *Third* and *Fourth Reports*, and in the light of further developments, such as the computerization of the register and the real prospect of electronic transfer of title to land. The draft Bill attached to its first Report[104] has already been enacted as the Land

---

[97] Land Registration Act 1997, s. 2, substituting a new s. 83 of the Land Registration Act 1925.

[98] For example, where a person obtained rectification of the register he was unable to recover indemnity as well, even though he had suffered loss (see *Freer* v. *Unwins Ltd.* [1976] Ch. 288).

[99] Law Com. No. 158 (1987).   [100] Law Com. No. 173 (1988).

[101] Law Commission, *Twenty-Ninth Annual Report 1994*, Law Com. No. 232 (1995), para. 2.67. The reference is to HM Land Registry, *Annual Report 1988–1989* (1989), para. 48.

[102] HL Deb (18 Nov. 1996), 575, c. 1159, Lord Browne-Wilkinson.

[103] For the background to its formation, see Law Commission, *Twenty-Ninth Annual Report 1994*, para. 2.67.

[104] Law Commission, *Transfer of Land: Land Registration. First Report of A Joint Working Group on the Implementation of the Law Commission's Third and Fourth Reports on Land Registration*.

Registration Act 1997. Its second Report, which will be in the form of a consultation paper, will be much more substantial and will contain proposals for the complete replacement of the Land Registration Act 1925. If this leads to legislation of the kind visualized, it will be the most substantial reform of the law of property in which the Law Commission has been involved. The existence of the Joint Working Group reflects the Commission's concern to work closely with relevant government departments. The experience of the Group has demonstrated that the Commission can work in this way without any compromise of its independence.

CASE STUDY 3: CONVEYANCING LAW

In terms of securing the implementation of its recommendations, the Law Commission has also enjoyed considerable success in relation to its Reports on a number of aspects of conveyancing law.[105] Five Acts of Parliament[106] have implemented nine Law Commission reports on conveyancing law,[107] and their impact has been significant. One of these Acts has become particularly well known and merits specific attention.

The Law of Property (Miscellaneous Provisions) Act 1989 contains three elements. First, it significantly amended the law on the execution of

---

[105] It should also be recorded that there was in existence for four years a Conveyancing Standing Committee. This was established by the Lord Chancellor 'to consider matters relating to conveyancing practice and procedure, to advise the Law Commission on reform of conveyancing law, and to promote changes in practice and procedure necessary to create and maintain a cheap, simple and effective conveyancing system from the point of view of buyers and sellers of land' (*Conveyancing Standing Committee: First Annual Report 1985–1986*, in Law Commission, *Twenty-First Annual Report 1985–1986* Law Com. No. 159 (1987), para. 1.3. The Committee covered much ground (as its Annual Reports record) and produced a variety of documents and recommendations. Its demise is recorded in the Law Commission's *Twenty-Fourth Annual Report 1989*, para. 1.9.

[106] This disregards the Landlord and Tenant Act 1988, which implemented Law Commission, *Leasehold Conveyancing*. See above, p. 158.

[107] Namely, Law of Property Act 1969 (enacting, *inter alia*, *Transfer of Land: Interim Report on Root of Title*, Law Com. No. 9 (1967); *Transfer of Land: Report on Land Charges Affecting Unregistered Land*, Law Com. No. 18 (1969)); Local Land Charges Act 1975 (*Transfer of Land: Report on Local Land Charges*, Law Com. No. 62 (1974)); Rentcharges Act 1977 (*Transfer of Land: Report on Rentcharges*, Law Com. No. 68 (1975)); Law of Property (Miscellaneous Provisions) Act 1989 (*Deeds and Escrows*, Law Com. No. 163 (1987); *Transfer of Land: Formalities for Contracts for Sale etc. of Land*, Law Com. No. 164 (1987); *Transfer of Land: The Rule in Bain v. Fothergill*, Law Com. No. 166 (1987)); and Law of Property (Miscellaneous Provisions) Act 1994 (*Property Law: Title on Death*, Law Com. No. 184 (1989); *Transfer of Land: Implied Covenants for Title*, Law Com. No. 199 (1991)).

deeds.[108] Secondly, the Act abolished the notorious rule in *Bain* v. *Fothergill*,[109] which limited damages recoverable against a vendor of land who could not complete because she was unable to show title to the land in question. It is the third element of the Act that has occasioned the greatest interest—and controversy. Section 2 laid down new formal requirements for contracts for the sale of land, sweeping away more than three centuries of learning. Although this section of the 1989 Act was based upon the Law Commission's recommendations,[110] the Bill that was eventually enacted differed from the one that had been attached to the Commission's Report.[111] The reasons for the differences are not known to the present writer,[112] but the courts have attached great importance to them in interpreting the section.[113] What the Law Commission undoubtedly intended[114] was that:

1. all contracts for the sale or other disposition of an interest in land should have to be *made* in writing (and not merely *evidenced* as before[115]) and signed by all the parties to the contract;
2. the contract should contain all the terms agreed, though it would still be possible to incorporate them by reference; and
3. agreements which did not comply with these requirements would be void (unless it was possible to rectify the contract). This would mean

---

[108] s. 1. This provision appears to have worked reasonably well: such difficulties as have arisen in relation to deeds in recent years have tended to be the result of Companies Act 1989, s. 130(2) (inserting a new s. 36A into the Companies Act 1985) concerning the execution of deeds by companies (see Law Commission, *The Execution of Deeds and Documents by or on behalf of Bodies Corporate*, Law Com. CP No. 143 (1996)).

[109] (1874) LR 7 HL 158.

[110] Law Commission, *Transfer of Land: Formalities for Contracts for Sale etc. of Land*.

[111] The crucial difference between the two is that cl. 1(1) of the Law Commission's draft Bill provided that all the express terms of the contract had to be incorporated in one document 'or each of two or more documents', whereas s. 2(1) of the 1989 Act provides that the contract must incorporate all the terms which have been expressly agreed 'in one document or, *where contracts are exchanged*, in each' (emphasis added). The latter is considerably more restrictive than the former.

[112] When it is decided to implement a Law Commission Report, the draft Bill attached to that Report is reviewed in the light of comments that have been received since it was published. A parliamentary draftsman is assigned to the Bill while it is in passage through Parliament. In making any amendments to the Bill, the draftsman will act on the instructions of the department sponsoring the Bill.

[113] See *Commission for New Towns* v. *Cooper (Great Britain) Ltd.* [1995] Ch. 259 at 287; *McCausland* v. *Duncan Lawrie Ltd.* [1997] 1 WLR 38 at 46–7.

[114] See Law Commission, *Transfer of Land: Formalities for Contracts for Sale etc. of Land*, pt. VI.

[115] See Law of Property Act 1925, s. 40 (now repealed).

that the doctrine of part performance would cease to have any effect because a void agreement could not be partly performed.[116]

The effect of the section as enacted, however, has been to impose a higher requirement of formality than the Law Commission had intended.[117] It has been held that there will be a contract only if either both parties sign one document or there is an exchange of contracts.[118] Indeed, the courts have interpreted the Act as a major break with the past.[119] The old learning on what constitutes a signature has been rejected and mortgages by deposit of title deeds will be valid only if they are made in compliance with section 2.[120]

The Act has given rise to a number of doubts in addition to the points mentioned above.[121] Initially there was some uncertainty as to the transactions to which it applied, but this was clarified by judicial decision.[122] The abolition of the doctrine of part performance—which the present writer does not lament[123]—has not in the eyes of some commentators been matched by a clear definition of the role of proprietary estoppel.[124] It has been observed that '[a] question which the statute leaves unanswered is whether it is legitimate, in the light of the statutory provision, for the court, by invoking the equitable doctrine of estoppel by acquiescence, to compel the vendor to convey the land to, or declare him a trustee of the land, for the purchaser'.[125] Ineffective transactions are, of course, always notoriously

---

[116] This fundamental point has been accepted by the Court of Appeal (see *Firstpost Homes Ltd.* v. *Johnson* [1995] 1 WLR 1567 at 1571; *United Bank of Kuwait plc* v. *Sahib* [1997] Ch. 107 at 140; cf. *Singh* v. *Beggs* (1995) 71 P & CR 120 at 122 (where this point is overlooked)).

[117] *McCausland* v. *Duncan Lawrie Ltd.* at 47.

[118] *Commission for New Towns* v. *Cooper (Great Britain) Ltd.* There will not normally be a contract, therefore, as a result of an exchange of correspondence.

[119] *Firstpost Homes Ltd.* v. *Johnson* at 1571.

[120] *United Bank of Kuwait plc* v. *Sahib*.

[121] For a concise survey, see Smith, *Property Law* (London: Langman, 1996), 85–93.

[122] Specifically in relation to options (see Hoffmann J's masterly judgment in *Spiro* v. *Glencrown Properties Ltd.* [1991] Ch. 537). The position in relation to rights of pre-emption remains uncertain—as does the status of such rights (see *London & Blenheim Estates Ltd.* v. *Ladbroke Retail Parks Ltd.* [1994] 1 WLR 31 at 38). There are obvious dangers in making specific legislative provision for rights where their status is uncertain, and they might be recharacterized in a subsequent decision.

[123] After *Steadman* v. *Steadman* [1976] AC 536, the ambit of the doctrine was extremely uncertain. One of the real difficulties about the doctrine was that it was in some senses a rule of evidence and in others an equitable rule about preventing fraud that was akin to proprietary estoppel. See Thompson, 'The Role of Evidence in Part Performance' [1979] Conveyancer 402.

[124] See Davis, 'Estoppel: An Adequate Substitute for Part Performance?' (1993) 13 OJLS 99. For the Law Commission's own comments on this point, see *Transfer of Land: Formalities for Contracts for Sale etc. of Land*, paras. 5.4–5.5.

[125] Goff and Jones, *The Law of Restitution* (4th edn., London: Sweet & Maxwell, 1993), 470.

difficult because of the conflicting policies which they generate, and it has been necessary to legislate in regard to a number of them.[126] In fact the Law Commission did address these issues in its Report and gave some guidance on them. It certainly appeared to recognize that an application of the principles of proprietary estoppel would not be inconsistent with the policy of the Act.[127] The difficulty that arises is that the Act requires a higher degree of formality than the Commission itself had intended. It is not possible to be certain whether this has affected the issue.[128] In any event, there must be some doubt whether it would have been either appropriate or indeed possible to legislate for all such contingencies with a sufficient degree of flexibility. There is certainly a defensible case for leaving such matters to common law development, as the Commission itself advocated.

CASE STUDY 4: TRUSTS OF LAND

The Trusts of Land and Appointment of Trustees Act 1996

In terms of its effect on the conceptual scheme of land law as a whole, the Trusts of Land and Appointment of Trustees Act 1996, which implements a Law Commission Report,[129] is the most significant measure of property law reform since the legislation of 1925. Not only does the Act prospectively abolish one of the three estates of freehold—namely, the entail[130]— but it also creates a unitary method of holding land upon trust.[131] This new concept—called the trust of land—applied retrospectively to all trusts for sale and bare trusts that were in existence on 1 January 1997 (when the Act

---

[126] See e.g. Law Reform (Frustrated Contracts) Act 1943; Minors' Contracts Act 1987.

[127] Law Commission, *Transfer of Land: Formalities for Contracts for Sale etc. of Land*, paras. 5.4–5.5. This was accepted by Peter Gibson LJ in *United Bank of Kuwait plc* v. *Sahib* [1997] Ch. 107 at 141, but on the facts before the court in that case, estoppel could not be established.

[128] Though it is clear that the courts will examine the policy of the Act to decide whether a claim based upon estoppel is consistent with it (see *United Bank of Kuwait plc* v. *Sahib* at 142).

[129] Law Commission, *Transfer of Land: Trusts of Land*, Law Com. No. 181 (1989). The Act also implements a subsidiary part of *Transfer of Land: Overreaching: Beneficiaries in Occupation*, Law Com. No. 188 (1989). The Bill upon which the Act was based is not that which was attached to Law Com. No. 181. A number of difficulties were identified in that Bill (principally in the transitional provisions) and, as a result, the Law Commission was asked to redraft the Bill: see *Twenty-Seventh Annual Report 1992*, Law Com. No. 210 (1993), paras. 2.63–2.64; *Twenty-Eighth Annual Report 1993*, Law Com. No. 223 (1994), para. 2.73. It was that revised Bill that formed the basis of the 1996 Act. For comment on the Act, see Oakley, 'The Trusts of Land and Appointment of Trustees Act 1996' [1996] Conveyancer 401; Nicholas Hopkins, 'The Trusts of Land and Appointment of Trustees Act 1996' [1996] Conveyancer 411.

[130] Sch. 1, para. 5.   [131] ss. 1(1), 1(2).

came into force)[132] and prospectively to *all* trusts of land[133] created in any way thereafter,[134] subject only to one minor exception.[135] Strict settlements in existence at that date are left untouched,[136] but the effect of the Act is that no new settlements may now be created under the provisions of the Settled Land Act 1925.[137] Three elements in the Act call for particular comment because they have all in some way or another attracted adverse comment. What is disappointing is that little of the critical analysis appears to take into account the clear principles on which the Act is based.

The Prospective Abolition of Settled Land

The first of these elements is the prospective abolition of strict settlements under the Settled Land Act 1925.[138] The Law Commission offered two reasons for this course.[139] The first was that such settlements, which were developed for use in relation to large landed estates,[140] could be created by accident very easily,[141] even as a result of an informal transaction, and might apply to very small landholdings.[142] The law reports are littered with examples of where this happened.[143] The Commission noted the unfortunate conveyancing consequences that could flow from this.[144] The second was that the structure of a strict settlement was inherently unsatisfactory. This is because the life tenant is invested with a dual role. He is, of course, the beneficiary entitled in possession under the settlement.[145] However, in addition, the legal title to the land and the powers of management and disposition are vested in him as trustee.[146] This situation is one in which

---

[132] s. 1(2)(b).

[133] Strictly, a 'trust of land' means 'any trust of property which consists of or includes land' (s. 1(1)(a)) and may, therefore, include personal property. However, the powers that are given to trustees of land (by s. 6(1)) are only 'in relation to the *land* subject to the trust'. They do not, therefore, apply to any personalty held as part of the trust of land.

[134] s. 1(1)(a).

[135] Namely, land to which the Universities and College Estates Act 1925 applies (Trusts of Land and Appointment of Trustees Act 1996, s. 1(3)).

[136] s. 1(3).   [137] s. 2(1).

[138] Criticized by Matthews in 'If it ain't broke, don't fix it' (1996) 10 TLI 97, on the basis that it is inherently wrong to 'prevent settlors from deliberately creating Settled Land Act settlements in future'. Mr Matthews does not examine any of the reasons why the 1996 Act has taken this course.

[139] See Law Commission, *Transfer of Land: Trusts of Land*, paras. 4.1–4.4.

[140] See e.g. the definition of 'principal mansion house' in Settled Land Act 1925, s. 65(2).

[141] For example, under a home made will, by which a testator left land to his or her spouse for life, thereafter to a son or daughter absolutely.

[142] As in *Bannister* v. *Bannister* [1948] 2 All ER 133; *Binions* v. *Evans* [1972] Ch. 359.

[143] For two modern instances, see *Ungurian* v. *Lesnoff* [1990] Ch. 206; *Costello* v. *Costello* (1994) 27 HLR 12.

[144] Law Commission, *Transfer of Land: Trusts of Land*, para. 4.1.

[145] Cf. Settled Land Act 1925, s. 19(1).   [146] See ibid., s. 107(1).

there necessarily exists a conflict of duty and interest. The Commission noted that 'although the life tenant may be a trustee, there are indications that the duties which attach to this role will not be as rigorously enforced as they are in other trust situations'.[147] In short, the life tenant can with comparative impunity favour his interest at the expense of the remainderman. The Commission might also have added that life tenants, unlike trustees, are born to their role and cannot be readily removed or replaced if they turn out to be unsuitable.[148] The Act does provide a means by which the trustees can, by power of attorney, delegate any of their functions to one or more of the beneficiaries entitled in possession.[149] This reflects the thinking behind the Settled Land Act 1925 that the current occupier of the land may be the most appropriate person to exercise the powers of management over the property, and it provides a means of replicating that aspect of the strict settlement. But the potential dangers of such a situation are recognized: the Act enables any one of the trustees to revoke the power of attorney.[150] The trustees are, therefore, in a much better position to protect the interests of the remaindermen from abuse by the life tenant than are the trustees of the settlement where the Settled Land Act 1925 still applies.

The Prospective Abolition of Entails

The second element of the Trusts of Land and Appointment of Trustees Act 1996 that has attracted comment is its abolition of the ancient and extraordinary estate tail and of the more recent entails of personalty.[151] It is remarkable that the entail had survived so long. Sir William Blackstone, writing in 1776, was critical of entails and advocated the enlargement of every entail into a fee simple. His reason for so doing is revealing. It was because 'the ill consequences of fettered inheritances are now generally seen

[147] Law Commission, *Transfer of Land: Trusts of Land*, para. 4.4. See too *Trusts of Land*, Law Com. WP No. 94 (1985), para. 3.16.

[148] Though the court is not powerless in such circumstances: see *Hambro* v. *Duke of Marlborough* [1994] Ch. 158 (which concerned the heir-apparent to the Blenheim estates, Lord Blandford, whose 'unbusinesslike habits' and 'lack of responsibility' prompted the trustees to make an application to the court).

[149] s. 9. The section was much amended during its passage through Parliament. In particular, trustees are not vicariously liable for the acts of the delegate, but will be responsible for his defaults only if they did not exercise reasonable care in deciding to delegate the function to the beneficiary: s. 9(8).

[150] s. 9(3). The appointment of a new trustee also revokes the power (ibid.).

[151] Sch. 1, para. 5. It has been suggested to the present writer by a member of a well-known firm of solicitors with a large private client practice that it is 'still possible' to create an entail of personalty orally, because the Act deals only with purported dispositions by *instrument*. Why anyone would wish to do anything so strange is not apparent, but, in any event, it has *never* been possible to create an entail of personalty orally (see Law of Property Act 1925, ss. 130(6), 205(xxvi); Settled Land Act 1925, s. 1(1)).

and allowed'.[152] In other words, entails offended the same principles that had led to the evolution of the rule against perpetuities. In its Consultation Paper, *The Law of Trusts: The Rules against Perpetuities and Excessive Accumulations*,[153] the Law Commission explained that 'the fundamental justification for the rule against perpetuities is that it restricts the ability of a property owner to "reach out from beyond the grave" to control the actions of his successors in title'. The rule against perpetuities strikes a balance between the living and the dead, and its continued existence is widely supported. It is at the very least inconsistent to retain a rule against perpetuities while allowing the continued creation of entails, which can and do endure for centuries.[154] The most distinguished legal historian of our time has commented that 'unbelievably, the structure of entails and their barring is with us yet'.[155] It is, therefore, somewhat puzzling to find recent criticism of 'the foolish policies behind this Act[156] . . . to prevent settlors from creating entails if they wish to (even for *personalty*!)'.[157] Properly understood, those policies are anything but foolish, but are rooted in some of the most fundamental principles of English property law.

The Abolition of the Doctrine of Conversion

The third element that calls for comment is the abolition[158] of one aspect of the doctrine of conversion—namely, the rule that interests under a trust for sale were for some (but not all) purposes[159] to be regarded as interests in the proceeds of sale of land and not in the land itself. The abrogation of this form of the doctrine of conversion is one of the most welcome features of the Act, given the very considerable difficulties to which it gave rise.[160] It

---

[152] *Commentaries on the Laws of England* (4 vols., 1st edn., Oxford: Oxford University Press, 1765–9), ii. 360.

[153] Law Com CP No. 133 (1993), para. 1.12.

[154] Thus the statutory entail created in 1704 for the Duke of Marlborough is still in existence and the present tenant in tail in possession is the eleventh duke (see *Hambro* v. *Duke of Marlborough* [1994] Ch. 158).

[155] Milsom, *Historical Foundations of the Common Law* (2nd edn., London: Butterworths, 1981), 189.

[156] That is, the Trusts of Land and Appointment of Trustees Act 1996.

[157] Matthews, 'If it ain't broke, don't fix it'. It came as quite a surprise to the present writer to discover that there was at least one firm of solicitors in the north-east of England that still created entails fairly regularly—and arranged for resettlements every generation in the traditional way.

[158] By Trusts of Land and Appointment of Trustees Act 1996, s. 3(1).

[159] One of the main difficulties with the doctrine of conversion is to know when it applied and when it did not.

[160] The uncertainties as to the applicability of the doctrine is apparent from a comparison of the remarks of Lord Wilberforce in *Williams & Glyn's Bank Ltd.* v. *Boland* [1981] AC 487 at 507, with those of Lord Oliver in *City of London Building Society* v. *Flegg* [1988] AC 54 at 82.

might have been expected to be welcomed. Instead it has prompted criticism or comment on three fronts. It is suggested that this criticism is unwarranted.

First, the side note to the relevant section in the Act—'Abolition of doctrine of conversion'—has excited some attention amongst academic commentators. More than one has observed that it is only one aspect of the doctrine of conversion that has been abolished.[161] The doctrine of conversion that applies where a vendor contracts to sell land, so that he is deemed to hold it on some kind of trust for the purchaser,[162] is unaffected. This is of course correct, but:

1. it is well settled that 'side notes cannot be used as an aid to construction';[163]
2. a side note is necessarily conditioned by the long title of the Act, which states that its purpose is 'to make new provision *about trusts of land* including . . . abolishing the doctrine of conversion';[164] and
3. there is nothing in the Law Commission's Report to suggest that the doctrine was intended to be abolished except in regard to trusts for sale.[165]

Secondly, it has been suggested that the doctrine of conversion has not been abolished in all cases.[166] This is apparently because the relevant section of the Act[167] does not cover the case where money is directed by a settlor to be applied in the purchase of land, but only 'where personal property is subject to a trust for sale in order that the trustees may acquire land'. On a purposive interpretation of the section this view is hard to maintain.[168] But even a literal interpretation points to the same result. If personal property is sold to enable land to be purchased, it would defeat the section if, as soon as it had been converted into money, the doctrine of conversion then applied. A direction that money should be applied in the purchase of land is, therefore, an *a fortiori* case.

---

[161] See e.g. Pettit, 'Demise of Trusts for Sale and the Doctrine of Conversion?' (1997) 113 LQR 207 at 209. His suggestion that 'the Act itself is positively misleading' is, with respect, incorrect, for the reasons stated below.

[162] See e.g. *Re Cary-Elwes' Contract* [1906] 2 Ch. 143 at 149.

[163] *Chandler* v. *DPP* [1964] AC 763 at 789, *per* Lord Reid. See too *Uddin* v. *Associated Portland Cement Manufacturers Ltd.* [1965] 2 QB 15 at 23.

[164] Emphasis added. The side note to s. 6 is 'General powers of trustees'. Nobody would suggest that that section was concerned with anything other than the powers of *trustees of land*.

[165] See Law Commission, *Transfer of Land: Trusts of Land*, para. 3.6; *Trusts of Land*, para. 3.18.

[166] See Matthews, 'If it ain't broke, don't fix it'.   [167] s. 3(1).

[168] Purposive rather than literal interpretation of statutes is now accepted as the normal canon by the judiciary.

Finally, it has been suggested that trusts for sale could be overreached only because of the doctrine of conversion, and that, now conversion has gone, 'there is nothing to enable the beneficial interest under a trust of land to be overreached'.[169] This seems to be derived from a view current amongst some textbook writers.[170] However, an authority on the doctrine of conversion has suggested that we should drop 'the dogma that conversion is, or once was, necessary to explain overreaching. That has never been true; nor could it ever have been true . . .'.[171] One reason why it could never have been true stems from the nature of overreaching itself. The Court of Appeal has recently accepted that 'overreaching is the process whereby existing interests are subordinated to a later interest or estate created pursuant to a trust or power', and that 'a transaction made by a person within the dispositive powers conferred upon him will overreach equitable interests in the property the subject of the disposition . . .'.[172] It has indeed long been settled that the exercise of a mere *power* of sale will overreach an interest under a trust.[173] If that is so, trustees of land must be able to overreach, as they have the dispositive powers of a beneficial owner.[174] The view that trustees of land cannot overreach is also at variance with the stated intention of the legislature[175] that the 1996 Act was intended to implement not only the Law Commission's Report, *Transfer of Land: Trusts of Land*,[176] but also the subsidiary recommendation in its Report, *Transfer of Land: Overreaching: Beneficiaries in Occupation*,[177] that bare trusts should be overreachable.[178]

[169] Hopkins, 'Overreaching and the Trusts of Land and Appointment of Trustees Act 1996' [1997] Conveyancer 81 at 83.

[170] See Megarry and Wade, *The Law of Real Property* (5th edn., London: Stevens, 1984), 403–4. The notion that overreaching depended on the doctrine of conversion has been expressly rejected by Burn, *Cheshire and Burn's Modern Law of Real Property* (15th edn., London: Butterworths, 1994), 238. It was in any event inherently improbable: see the last part of the now repealed Law of Property Act 1925, s. 28(1).

[171] Anderson, 'The Proper Narrow Scope of Equitable Conversion in Land Law' (1984) 100 LQR 86 at 109.

[172] *State Bank of India* v. *Sood* [1997] Ch 276 at 281, *per* Peter Gibson LJ. See Harpum, 'Overreaching, Trustees' Powers and the Reform of the 1925 Legislation' [1990] CLJ 277 at 282.

[173] See *Wheate* v. *Hall* (1809) 17 Ves. 80 at 86, where Grant MR observed that 'it is clear, this Power of Sale in the Settlement of 1793 was introduced with reference to those Limitations, which would have made a sale impracticable, if a Power, over-reaching those Limitations, had not been introduced . . .'.

[174] Trusts of Land and Appointment of Trustees Act 1996, s. 6(1).

[175] See the remarks of the Lord Advocate, Lord Mackay of Drumadoon, speaking on behalf of the Government in the Second Reading Debate: HL Deb. (1 Mar. 1996), 569, cc. 1717–19.

[176] Law Com. No. 181 (1989).   [177] Law Com. No. 188 (1989), para. 4.27.

[178] There had been a doubt whether bare trusts were overreachable. See Harpum, 'Overreaching, Trustees' Powers and the Reform of the 1925 Legislation', 294, 303.

CONCLUSIONS

How successful has the Law Commission been as an instrument of reform and development in land law? In the field of landlord and tenant law, the Commission cannot claim any great measure of success for the reasons that have been explained in this chapter. However, within the wider field of land law, it has produced a significant number of reports covering a broad range of subjects of which a substantial proportion have been enacted. At least until recently, the Commission's reforms have tended to be modest measures rather than the replacement of major tracts of the law. This has begun to change, however, with the enactment of legislation such as the Landlord and Tenant (Covenants) Act 1995 and the Trusts of Land and Appointment of Trustees Act 1996. There are real prospects that legislation on a significant scale may yet occur in relation to matters such as land registration,[179] the transmission of freehold covenants,[180] and the forfeiture of leases.[181] It should also be noted that some of the reforms that have appeared modest, have had a significant impact in practice, notably in relation to land registration.

Any effective law reform will create changes to the law that, in the short term, will be disruptive to and demanding for those who have either to apply it or to advise clients upon it. It comes as no great surprise that, in the aftermath of the Commission's reforms, there has generally been some hostility from certain sectors of the legal profession.[182] Such hostility is not necessarily a reflection on the quality of the reform.[183] Some of it is ill-founded and is simply an understandable reaction to the disruption of change. But the Commission cannot afford the luxury of complacency. It does take its critics seriously and, at least on an informal basis, it monitors the interpretation of legislation that has resulted from its proposals and any

---

[179] See p. 166.

[180] See Law Commission, *Transfer of Land: The Law of Positive and Restrictive Covenants*, Law Com. No. 127 (1984).

[181] See p. 159.

[182] The 1925 property legislation received a hostile reception from the profession.

[183] A case in point is the critical reception given by the legal profession to the overhaul of covenants for title in the Law Reform (Miscellaneous Provisions) Act 1994. Under the old law, covenants for title provided scant protection for purchasers and they were, in consequence, seldom considered during the conveyancing process. The Law Commission's proposals addressed the well-documented defects in the law. As a result of the Act, a vendor of land will, in practice, be liable if she sells land with a defective title in exactly the same circumstances *after* the land has been transferred as she would have been between contract and completion. The issue of covenants for title has become a live one as a result of the Act, at least for the time being. The benefits flowing from the Act are, of course, a greater security of title. The concomitant of that is that vendors have to be certain of their title before they market it.

comments that are made upon it. Whatever the attractions of trying to create coherent legal structures, the Commission needs to be sure that it is
tackling those areas of the law where reform is really needed. While views
will inevitably differ as to which aspects of the law fall within that umbrella,
the present writer's experience has been that the Commission takes very
seriously its need to select areas of law that are in urgent need of review and
where the prospects of legislation are reasonable.

It is certainly possible to think of measures of law reform in the field of
land law over the last thirty years or so in which the Law Commission
played no role.[184] But they are few and far between. It may be that, if the
Commission had not existed, other bodies such as the Law Reform
Committee[185] might have brought about at least some of the reforms that
it has achieved. But it seems very unlikely that very much would have been
done, or that it would have been done with the same thoroughness and care
that it has been by the Law Commission as an established body specifically
dedicated to law reform.

APPENDIX

The Appendix consists of two tables. Table 1 sets out the number of Acts of
Parliament which have implemented Law Commission Reports on Land Law as
against the total number of such Reports. It also indicates the number of Reports
published within a given period which were eventually enacted. Table 2 lists those
Acts of Parliament and indicates the Reports which were enacted in whole of part.
It also indicates whether the Report in question arose under one of the
Commission's Programmes of Law Reform or on a reference from a government
department or other body.

---

[184] For example, the Land Registration and Land Charges Act 1971 or the Housing Act
1996, pt III.

[185] Which consisted of judges and practitioners and did its work outside office hours.

Table 1. *The number of Reports on Land Law published and the number of Acts of Parliament implementing such Reports*

Years	Number of Reports published	Number eventually enacted[a]	Number of Acts of Parliament
1965[b]–70	5[c]	4	1[d]
1971–5	4[e]	2	1
1976–80	1	1	2
1981–5	9[f]	5	1
1986–90	13[g]	9	4[h]
1991–5	7[i]	2	3[j]
1996–7[k]	1	0	2[l]
TOTALS	40[m]	23	14

a   In whole or in part. It is likely that a number of Reports that are listed will be enacted at a future date.

b   The Law Commission was founded on 14 June 1965.

c   Two of these Reports did not contain a draft Bill, though one of them was subsequently enacted in part.

d   Implementing in whole or part four Reports

e   One of the Reports contained no recommendations for legislation.

f   Two of the Reports did not contain draft Bills.

g   Two of the Reports contained no recommendations for legislation. One further Report contained no draft Bill to implement its proposals, but another Report consisted just of the draft Bill.

h   Implementing in whole or part seven Reports.

i   One of the Reports consisted of a draft Bill in respect of an earlier Report.

j   Implementing in whole or part four Reports.

k   The cut-off date taken for this table is 1 April 1997.

l   Implementing in whole or part four Reports.

m   Of these, three Reports contained no recommendations for reform, a further five did not contain a draft Bill.

Table 2. *Acts of Parliament, the Reports which they implemented, and whether the Report arose under one of the Programmes for Reform or from a Reference*

Act of Parliament	Reports enacted in whole or part	Programme or Reference
Law of Property Act 1969	*Transfer of Land: Interim Report on Root of Title*[a] *Transfer of Land: Report on Restrictive Covenants*[b] *Landlord and Tenant: Report on the Landlord and Tenant Act 1954, Part II*[c]	All programme items

Act of Parliament	Reports enacted in whole or part	Programme or Reference
	Transfer of Land: Report on Land Charges Affecting Unregistered Land[d]	
Local Land Charges Act 1975	*Transfer of Land: Report on Local Land Charges*[e]	Programme item
Rentcharges Act 1977	*Transfer of Land: Report on Rentcharges*[f]	Programme item
Charging Orders Act 1979	*Charging Orders*[g]	Reference
Land Registration Act 1986	*Property Law: Land Registration*[h]	Programme item
Reverter of Sites Act 1987	*Property Law: Rights of Reverter*[i]	Reference
Land Registration Act 1988	*Property Law: Second Report on Land Registration*[j]	Programme item
Landlord and Tenant Act 1988	*Codification of the Law of Landlord and Tenant: Covenants Restricting Dispositions, Alterations and Change of User*[k] (in part only) *Leasehold Conveyancing*[l]	Both programme items
Law of Property (Miscellaneous Provisions) Act 1989	*Deeds and Escrows*[m] *Transfer of Land: Formalities for Contracts for Sale etc. of Land*[n]	All programme items
	Transfer of Land: The Rule in Bain v. Fothergill[o]	
Access to Neighbouring Land Act 1992	*Rights of Access to Neighbouring Land*[p]	Reference
Law of Property (Miscellaneous Provisions) Act 1994	*Property Law: Title on Death*[q] *Transfer of Land: Implied Covenants for Title*[r]	Both programme items
Landlord and Tenant (Covenants) Act 1995	*Landlord and Tenant Law: Privity of Contract and Estate*[s]	Programme item
Trusts of Land and Appointment of Trustees Act 1996	*Transfer of Land: Trusts of Land*[t] *Transfer of Land: Overreaching: Beneficiaries in Occupation*[u] (subsidiary recommendation only)	Programme item

Act of Parliament	Reports enacted in whole or part	Programme or Reference
Land Registration Act 1997	*Transfer of Land: Land Registration. First Report of A Joint Working Group on the Implementation of the Law Commission's Third and Fourth Reports on Land Registration*[v]	Programme item

[a] Law Com. No. 9 (1967).
[b] Law Com. No. 11 (1967).
[c] Law Com. No. 17 (1969).
[d] Law Com. No. 18 (1969).
[e] Law Com. No. 62 (1974).
[f] Law Com. No. 68 (1975).
[g] Law Com. No. 74 (1976).
[h] Law Com. No. 125 (1983).
[i] Law Com. No. 111 (1981).
[j] Law Com. No. 148 (1985).
[k] Law Com. No. 141 (1985).
[l] Law Com. No. 161 (1987).
[m] Law Com. No. 163 (1987).
[n] Law Com. No. 164 (1987).
[o] Law Com. No. 166 (1987).
[p] Law Com. No. 151 (1985).
[q] Law Com. No. 184 (1989)
[r] Law Com. No. 199 (1991).
[s] Law Com. No. 174 (1988).
[t] Law Com. No. 181 (1989).
[u] Law Com. No. 188 (1989).
[v] Law Com. No. 235 (1995).

PART THREE
LAND LAW AND CITIZENSHIP

7

THE HOME-OWNER: CITIZEN
OR CONSUMER?

Lisa Whitehouse

Land Law is often viewed as a distinct area of academic study. In undertaking the difficult task of deciphering the complex web of statutory provisions which regulate dealings with land, the law student is often unaware of the relationships which exist between Land Law and other subjects. This chapter, in analysing the mortgage repossession process, aims to highlight the interdisciplinary nature of Land Law by drawing on principles which are often reserved for Public Law, the Law of Contract, and Housing Law courses.

A recurrent theme in the policies of central government since the late 1970s has been the withdrawal of direct state intervention in preference for the regulation offered by the market system. This reliance on market forces as the vehicle for the regulation of the supply of goods and services has altered our conception of the individual in society, demoting him from 'citizen' to 'consumer'. This shift in emphasis may seem uncontroversial, particularly as the term 'consumer' is often combined with concepts such as 'rights', 'protection', and 'choice'. An examination of the mortgage repossession process, however, suggests that reliance on an 'idealistic' view of consumerism is denying mortgagors their civil entitlement to due process.

The fundamental nature of housing demands that it should no longer be viewed in the same manner as other commodities. Housing is not a consumer good but a prerequisite for the attainment of the status of citizenship. The home-owner is, therefore, entitled to the highest degree of procedural stringency within the repossession process. Its failure to adhere to this requirement of due process suggests that the legal process of possession stands in need of reform. In order for reform to prove effective, however, we must reappraise our conception of the individual in society, shifting the emphasis away from consumerism, with affordability as its main focus, and towards the entitlements of citizenship which are universal.

DEFINING TERMS

Citizenship

At its most fundamental level, citizenship is concerned with the entitlements and obligations of the individual within society and the relationship
between the individual and the state. In terms of specifying the particular
entitlements and obligations of the individual, the literature concerning the
concept of citizenship presents a number of conflicting views. This is due,
to a large extent, to the inherently political nature of citizenship. As
Blackburn notes, 'The particular interpretation of citizenship taken by each
person will reflect his or her own ideology in general about the proper relationship between the individual and society.'[1]

It is possible, however, to set the boundaries of the debate on citizenship
by reference to those characteristics which distinguish citizenship from
other concepts. Our task in this respect is assisted by the work of T. H.
Marshall.[2] His essays on citizenship, first published in 1950, continue to
make a significant contribution to the debate on the nature of citizenship.
The relevance of his work derives from its attempt to define the universal
elements of citizenship, which Marshall divides into three—namely, the
civil, the political, and the social. Marshall traces the historical development
of these elements and claims that the formative period in the life of civil
rights can be assigned to the eighteenth century. The freeing of men from
servile labour enabled them to obtain the civil element of citizenship which
Marshall describes as 'the rights necessary for individual freedom—liberty
of the person, freedom of speech, thought and faith, the right to own property and to conclude valid contracts, and the right to justice'.[3]

Built upon this foundation, during the nineteenth century, was the
development of the political element. This element encompasses the entitlements most commonly associated with citizenship—namely, the 'right to
participate in the exercise of political power, as a member of a body
invested with political authority or as an elector of the members of such a
body. The corresponding institutions are Parliament and councils of local
government.'[4]

The final element essential to the status of citizenship forms the focus of
much of the debate on citizenship. The social element, according to
Marshall, provides the foundation upon which the individual can undertake

---

[1] Blackburn, 'Introduction: Citizenship Today', in Blackburn (ed.), *Rights of Citizenship*
(London: Mansell, 1993), 3.

[2] Marshall, *Citizenship and Social Class and Other Essays* (Cambridge; Cambridge University
Press, 1950); and *Sociology at the Crossroads and Other Essays* (London: Heinemann, 1963).

[3] Marshall, *Citizenship and Social Class*, 10–11.   [4] Ibid.

the effective exercise of her civil entitlements and obligations. This can be seen in the definition, provided by Marshall, of the social element as,

the whole range from the right to a modicum of economic welfare and security to the right to share to the full in the social heritage and to live the life of a civilised being according to the standards prevailing in the society. The institutions most closely connected with it are the education system and the social services.[5]

It may be argued that, in addition to the education system and the social services, a necessary component of the social element of citizenship is the entitlement to 'decent' housing. Attempting to define 'decent' in relation to housing is a difficult task, but, at the very least, it would include those factors necessary for the individual to function effectively as a citizen—for example, heating, sanitation, privacy, and a degree of security. Without the security and stability offered by housing, the citizen will find it difficult to exercise his civil entitlements, particularly the right to 'live the life of a civilised being according to the standards prevailing in society'. Access to decent housing is, therefore, a necessary precondition for the attainment of the status of citizenship.

The civil, political, and social elements, as constructed by Marshall, constitute the fundamental determinants of citizenship. Beyond these basic factors, however, the concept of citizenship can take many forms. One of the principal variants within the concept concerns the role of the state. Civil entitlements are universal; therefore, those who do not have the ability to provide those entitlements for themselves must have provision made from some other source. The obvious candidate for the provision of civil entitlements in a liberal democracy is the state. Commentators differ in their views regarding the extent to which it is the responsibility of the state to ensure that all members of society have access to the entitlements and obligations of citizenship. In England and Wales, however, central government has promoted a particular view of citizenship which emphasizes the individual's responsibility to provide for his own civil entitlements. The following section of this chapter examines the impact of this new conception of citizenship on the social entitlement to decent housing.

The New Concept of Citizenship: The Consumer-Citizen

A recurrent theme in the policies of the central government since the late 1970s has been the 'rolling back of the state' in preference for the regulation offered by a market system. This reduction in direct state intervention required a new conception of the relationship between the individual and the state which emphasized individual responsibility as opposed to reliance on state-funded services. The means by which this has been achieved has

[5] Ibid.

included the introduction of policies which emphasized particular aspects of the civil element of citizenship, rather than the political or social elements.[6]

The preference for the civil element of citizenship derives from its emphasis on 'individualism' and 'negative' entitlements. Taking Marshall's definition of civil entitlements, liberty of the person, for example, requires that the individual is not prevented by others from exercising his freedom to partake in lawful activities. In contrast, the political, and, particularly, the social elements of citizenship require some degree of positive state intervention to ensure that all members of society have access to the necessary entitlements.[7] The most common example of a social entitlement is access to the welfare system for those who cannot obtain 'the modicum of economic welfare' from other sources.

One of the most obvious methods adopted by central government to shift the emphasis in our conception of the citizen and the role of the state was to encourage an increase in home-ownership, whilst reducing support for other tenures. The right to own property and to conclude valid contracts is, according to Marshall, an essential entitlement of the civil element of citizenship. Home-ownership was, therefore, useful in terms of focusing attention on the civil entitlements of citizenship, but, more importantly, it also proved useful in redefining the role of the state in relation to the provision of social entitlements.

In order to reduce the direct intervention of the state within the housing system in England and Wales it was necessary to reduce the state's role as a 'provider' of housing. One of the most successful policies, in this respect, was the introduction of the council tenant's 'right to buy' in the Housing Act 1980. This enabled a council tenant of three years' standing to purchase her home from her local council at a substantial discount, regardless of whether the council wished to sell or not. The Housing and Building Control Act 1984 and the Housing and Planning Act 1986 were introduced to encourage further sales by increasing discounts and reducing the qualifying period for tenants from three to two years. By the end of 1996 more than 2.2 million public-sector dwellings had been purchased under the 'right to buy'.[8]

The significance of the 'right to buy', in terms of its impact on the housing role of local authorities, can be understood only in the light of the financial changes which were made during the same period. During 1979/80–1993/4, public expenditure on housing decreased in real terms by

[6] Bellamy and Greenaway, 'The New Right Conception of Citizenship and the Citizen's Charter' (1995) 30 Government and Opposition 469 at 472.

[7] Van Steenbergen, 'The Condition of Citizenship: An Introduction', in Van Steenbergen (ed.), *The Condition of Citizenship* (London: Sage, 1994), 3.

[8] *Social Trends* (London: HMSO, 1997), 179.

approximately 60 per cent.[9] In addition to these cuts, the government introduced a new financial regime for local authorities in the Local Government and Housing Act 1989. In relation to the 'right to buy', the Local Government and Housing Act 1989 restricted the ability of local authorities to use the receipts from the sales of council houses. In effect, local authorities were required to set aside 75 per cent of receipts from housing to redeem their debts. The ability of local authorities to undertake new house-building completions was, therefore, severely restricted and led to a decrease from 108,700 in 1978 to only 4,600 in 1992.[10] This decline in new house-building by local authorities has continued, with the majority of new constructions within the public sector since 1992 being undertaken by housing associations.[11]

In providing council tenants with the right to purchase their home, central government managed to redefine the role of local government, converting it from provider to enabler of housing. The reduction in state expenditure within the public-rented sector significantly diminished the ability of local authorities to replace the homes purchased under the 'right to buy'. Local authorities, therefore, had to seek alternative methods of meeting housing demand, including the use of bed-and-breakfast accommodation.[12] The increased use of temporary accommodation, combined with the large number of dwellings purchased under the 'right to buy', has served to make the public-rented sector less attractive to those seeking decent housing. Not surprisingly, properties purchased under the 'right to buy' constituted the better-quality dwellings purchased by those local-authority tenants who could afford owner-occupation. Coupled with the reduction in new house-building completions, the quality of local-authority housing has been significantly reduced.[13]

The outcome of these housing-policy initiatives, as regards the public-rented sector, has been marginalization, or what writers such as Murie and Forrest term 'residualization'—namely, making the public-rented sector a 'welfare net' for those who cannot afford home-ownership.[14] In relation to the concept of citizenship, the residualization of the public-rented sector has engendered the view that it is not the responsibility of the state to play a significant role in the provision of the social entitlement to decent housing. Instead, it is the responsibility of individual households to obtain that

---

[9] Wilcox, *Housing Finance Review 1993* (York: Joseph Rowntree Foundation, 1993), 47.

[10] Balchin, *Housing Policy: An Introduction* (London: Routledge, 1995), 37, table 3.4.

[11] *Social Trends* (London: HMSO, 1997), 175.

[12] Foster, *No New Homes* (London: Shelter, 1990).

[13] See Forrest and Murie, *Right to Buy? Issues of Need, Equity and Polarisation in the Sale of Council Houses* (Bristol: School for Advanced Urban Studies, 1984), and Malpass and Murie, *Housing Policy and Practice* (Basingstoke: Macmillan, 1994).

[14] Ibid. 147.

entitlement for themselves. For the majority of households in England and Wales, the outright purchase of accommodation is beyond their means. This obstacle has been overcome, however, by the increased use of the mortgage device. The classic description of a mortgage was given by Lindley MR in *Santley* v. *Wilde*[15] in the following terms: 'A mortgage is a conveyance of land or an assignment of chattels as a security for the payment of a debt or the discharge of some other obligation for which it is given.'

As with other forms of money-lending, the prospective home-owner will enter into a contract with the lender which will specify terms regarding the repayment of the loan and the interest which is to be charged. The unique aspect of the mortgage transaction, however, relates to the rights of the mortgagee as opposed to other forms of creditor, as Gray notes: 'For the purpose of recovering the amount of his loan, the mortgagee enjoys not merely a personal right based on his contract of loan with the borrower, but also a proprietary right, potentially enforceable against third parties, to realise the value of the mortgaged property.'[16]

In seeking to utilize the mortgage device, prospective home-owners will, in most cases, be undertaking the largest single debt that they are ever likely to encounter. They will also be aware that if they fail to meet the payment terms set out in their mortgage contract, they will be liable to be repossessed by their mortgagee. In the light of these factors, it may be surprising to note that the number of dwellings within the home-ownership sector have increased by 12 per cent since 1979.[17] An influential factor in this increase may be argued to be the implementation of policies by successive governments which have promoted home-ownership as the tenure to be preferred. An example of the attitude adopted in respect of the advantages to be gained by entering into home-ownership was provided by John Stanley MP, in 1980, the then Minister for Housing and Construction, when he stated that 'It provides a measures of independence, choice and financial benefit that for most people cannot be achieved to the same degree by renting.'[18]

The outcome of these and other housing-policy initiatives has been to create a housing system dominated by home-ownership. In 1996, over 68 per cent of all dwellings in England and Wales were owner-occupied, with 42 per cent subject to an outstanding mortgage debt.[19] The reliance placed on mortgage finance, as the means of gaining access to the social entitlement of decent housing, is indicative of the new conception of the individual in society as 'consumer-citizen'. In addition to placing the burden of

---

[15] [1899] 2 Ch. 474.

[16] Gray, *Elements of Land Law* (2nd edn., London: Butterworths, 1993), 931–2.

[17] *Social Trends* (London: HMSO, 1997), 169.

[18] Stanley, 'Government Policies on Home Ownership in the 1980s', in *Home Ownership in the 1980s* (London, Shelter Housing Aid Centre, 1980), 6.

[19] *Social Trends* (London: HMSO, 1997), 170.

housing costs on to individual households, the promotion of home-ownership has allowed central government to replace direct state intervention with the regulation offered by a market system. The private contractual basis of mortgage finance makes it eminently suitable for regulation by a market. Because of the varied types of accommodation available within the owner-occupied sector and the wide range of mortgagees willing to offer different types of mortgage products, the state could reduce its intervention within the housing system and allow market forces to regulate the activities of mortgagors and mortgagees.

The justification for the reduction in direct state intervention within the housing system is based on an 'idealistic' view of consumerism which extols the benefits of market forces as the guardians of choice, competition, and accountability. The shift in emphasis away from citizenship and towards consumerism may seem uncontroversial, particularly as the term 'consumer' is often combined with concepts such as 'rights', 'protection', and 'legislation'. The rhetoric of consumerism implies that, where the market fails to provide a sufficient degree of choice and accountability, the state will intervene, on the consumer's behalf, by implementing legislation which corrects the failings of the market. The 'protection' afforded to the home-owner, therefore is claimed to derive from a combination of market regulation and direct legal intervention.

Many of the policies implemented by central government since the late 1970s have attempted to ensure that the mortgage market operates effectively, whilst avoiding the need for any substantial increase in state expenditure. As Lewis notes, 'the justification for markets is a human rights/choice justification so that where markets impede effective choice then it follows that the constitution is obliged to restore choice and freedom; to regulate markets, especially where competition, and therefore choice, is impeded'.[20]

Choice is a fundamental aspect of the 'idealistic' view of market regulation promoted by the rhetoric of consumerism. If consumers can exercise choice, then they can also determine which suppliers survive within the market. This provides consumers with a degree of influence which ensures that suppliers of goods and services operate according to the demands of consumers. In order for there to be choice, however, there must be a range of goods and services offered by different suppliers. In other words, competition is essential to the effective operation of a free market. In order to ensure competition, the former Conservative government sought to 'deregulate' the mortgage market, thereby encouraging financial institutions other than building societies to offer mortgage finance.[21] In order to

[20] Lewis, *Choice and the Legal Order* (London: Butterworths, 1996), 12.

[21] In addition to building societies, mortgages are now offered by, for example, banks, 'centralized' lenders, and insurance companies.

ensure that building societies could compete on an equal footing with these 'new' mortgagees, the government introduced the Building Societies Act 1986, which allowed building societies to offer services similar to those offered by other financial institutions. The former Economic Secretary to the Treasury (Mr Ian Stewart) summarized the main objective of the Building Societies Act 1986:

In today's fast-changing markets, societies need to be able to offer a wide range of facilities to an increasingly sophisticated public if they are to continue to compete effectively. New technology and greater customer awareness are posing a new challenge for all financial institutions, but I believe that, by allowing the societies more scope, we will not only enable them to develop their business but will bring extra healthy competition into housing and finance.[22]

An increase in competition should lead to an increased choice and a more effective voice within a market for consumers. This is due to the belief that effective choice based on sufficient information makes suppliers of goods and services accountable to the consumer. The nature of accountability requires that, where decisions are made which affect the interests of individuals, information regarding how those decisions were taken should be made available to the individual in question. As Lewis notes, 'It is inherent . . . in the nature of choice that those in authority should render an account to those who chose them in the first place.'[23]

Accountability also implies that sanctions should be imposed where the decision-making processes, adopted by those in authority, fail to meet the required standards. The only published standards which concern the process by which the decision to repossess is taken are contained in the Council of Mortgage Lenders' *Statement of Practice*[24] on the management of arrears and repossessions. This encourages its members to assist mortgagors who are experiencing arrears by entering into 'forbearance agreements'. These include measures such as 'freezing' the arrears for a short period or allowing the mortgagor to repay the arrears over a certain period.

In seeking to make accountable the decisions of mortgagees regarding repossession, the 'self-regulatory' scheme operated by the Council of Mortgage Lenders in the form of their *Statement of Practice* is combined with direct legal intervention, the most significant provision being section 36 of the Administration of Justice Act 1970. This provision provides district judges with a discretion to adjourn, postpone, or suspend a possession order where the mortgagor can show an ability to clear the arrears within a 'reasonable' period. The objective of section 36 of the Administration of Justice Act 1970, as amended by section 8 of the Administration of Justice Act 1973, was recognized by Griffiths LJ: 'It is the intention of both sections to

---

[22] HC Deb. (1985–6), 89, c. 592.   [23] Lewis, *Choice and the Legal Order*, 24.
[24] (London: Council of Mortgage Lenders, 1995).

give a measure of relief to those people who find themselves in temporary financial difficulties, unable to meet their commitments under their mortgage and in danger of losing their homes.'[25]

The protection offered by section 36 of the Administration of Justice Act 1970, combined with the effective operation of the mortgage market based on competition and choice, serves to protect the mortgagor, it is claimed, from unnecessary and unjustified claims for repossession. The mortgagor, as 'consumer-citizen', is, therefore, said to enjoy the protection often associated with consumerism. The following section of this chapter questions whether this is the case through an examination of the practical operation of the repossession process.

THE LEGAL PROCESS OF POSSESSION

As all students of Land Law will know, the mortgagee has an inherent right to possession,[26] the classic pronouncement of which was made by Harman J in *Four-Maids Ltd.* v. *Dudley Marshall (Properties) Ltd.*: '[the mortgagee] may go into possession before the ink is dry on the mortgage unless there is something in the contract, express or by implication, whereby he has contracted himself out of that right.'[27] An aspect of the repossession process which is less well known relates to the factors which influence the decisions of mortgagees and district judges regarding repossession. The most obvious factor would appear to be the ability of the mortgagor to meet his mortgage payments, the principal reason underlying the majority of repossessions being arrears in mortgage payments. A closer examination of the practical operation of the legal process of repossession, however, suggests that a more fundamental factor relates to the terms of the mortgage contract.

As Harman J made clear, mortgagees may contract themselves out of the inherent right to possession in the mortgage contract. In practice, the majority of mortgagees do restrict their ability to repossess by inserting a term which states that they reserve the right to seek possession should the mortgagor breach the mortgage contract. Once the mortgagor has broken

---

[25] *Bank of Scotland* v. *Grimes* [1985] 2 All ER 254 at 259b.

[26] The qualitative data used in this chapter were collected during a series of semi-structured interviews involving: representatives of thirteen lenders; six district judges; a representative of the Council of Mortgage Lenders; two officers of the Building Society Ombudsman; and two lawyers who undertook repossession work for two of the lenders. Data regarding the views of mortgagors were obtained through the secondary analysis of research undertaken by consumer organizations and other researchers. Owing to the economic and political sensitivity of repossession, the respondents requested, and have been granted, anonymity.

[27] [1957] Ch. 317 at 320.

the contract, the decision as to whether to seek possession is entirely at the discretion of the mortgagee.

The only form of regulation in this respect is the Council of Mortgage Lenders' *Statement of Practice*, which encourages its members to seek repossession only as a last resort. Mortgagees are not, however, under any obligation to adhere to the guidelines set out in the *Statement of Practice*. It has no legal force and the Council of Mortgage Lenders cannot impose any sanctions on those who do not follow it. As a representative of the Council of Mortgage Lenders stated, 'We hope that they do but in detail many wouldn't because they are generalized recommendations and the reality of mortgagees is that they have a different approach and an obvious difference is the speed with which they take possession.'

The majority of mortgagees interviewed stated that they did adhere to the guidelines set out in the *Statement of Practice*. The most important factor which they claimed influenced their decision to seek repossession concerned the willingness of the mortgagor to enter into a forbearance arrangement with the mortgagee. If the mortgagor refused to enter into such an arrangement or failed to meet the terms of the arrangement, then the majority of mortgagees interviewed stated that they would feel obliged to seek possession. As one mortgagee stated, 'We only take legal proceedings if everything else fails and even if we have a hearing date then we will cancel it if circumstances change.'

There were, however, some mortgagees who considered that possession should be sought immediately upon the mortgagor falling three months into arrears with her mortgage payments, regardless of whether there was a forbearance arrangement or not.[28] They considered that seeking a possession order, even though they knew it would be suspended by virtue of section 36 of the Administration of Justice Act 1970, would ensure that the mortgagor understood the nature of her obligations under the mortgage contract. As one mortgagee noted, 'Although we may have a lot of repossession orders in a year the bulk of them don't lead to repossession, they lead to the borrower realizing that there is a commitment to be undertaken and with the power of the law behind it, it does assist. But if people haven't got the money then it will lead to repossession.'

The different approach adopted by mortgagees in respect of the decision to repossess results in a situation where mortgagors in similar circumstances are not treated in similar ways. Mortgagors with mortgagee X may be liable to possession proceedings after three months' default whereas, if they were with mortgagee Y, they would be allowed more time to clear their arrears

---

[28] The ability of some mortgagees to seek a possession order immediately upon three months' default is assisted by the fact that they do not have to serve notice either before entering, *Birch* v. *Wright* (1786) 1 Term. Rep. 378 at 383, or commencing proceedings, *Jolly* v. *Arbuthnot* (1859) 4 De G & J 224 at 236.

without reference to the court. This inconsistency in the treatment of mortgagors in similar arrears situations may be justified by reference to the fact that mortgagors know, before entering into their mortgage contract, what the repossession policy of the mortgagee is. This is not the case, however, for mortgagees do not publish their repossession policies. The mortgage contract will merely state that the mortgagee reserves the right to seek possession should the mortgagor breach the mortgage contract. Information regarding how or when that decision will be taken is not made available to a prospective mortgagor. Mortgagors cannot therefore make an informed choice of mortgagee on the basis of the repossession policies operated by different mortgagees.

Choice in this respect may be argued to be irrelevant on the basis that mortgagors do know that if they fail to pay their mortgage payments, they will be subject to repossession. The inconsistency in the repossession policies operated by different mortgagees can, however, prove crucial in relation to the mortgagor's ability to avoid repossession. Those mortgagors who are subject to legal proceedings for possession will find it more difficult to avoid repossession than those who are allowed to clear their arrears without reference to the court, for the reason that they will additionally be liable for the costs of those legal proceedings.

The majority of mortgage contracts state that the mortgagor will be liable for all costs incurred as a result of the enforcement of any of the mortgagee's rights under that contract. Where a mortgagee seeks to enforce their contractual right to possession, therefore, the mortgagor will have to pay the costs of the possession hearing, which on average amount to approximately £600. The imposition of these costs on a mortgagor who is already experiencing financial difficulties, evidenced by the arrears in her mortgage payments, will obviously restrict her ability to clear those arrears. More significantly, however, liability for the costs of legal proceedings is also seen to exert a considerable degree of influence on the exercise of discretion by district judges within the repossession process.

Where a possession order is sought in respect of a dwelling house, the district judge may: give an outright possession order, which will be delayed for twenty-eight days in most cases; suspend the possession order on specified payment terms; or adjourn the hearing. Section 36 of the Administration of Justice Act 1970 allows the judge the discretion to adopt any one of these options if 'it appears to the court that in the event of its exercising the power the mortgagor is likely to be able within a reasonable period to pay any sums due under the mortgage or to remedy a default consisting of a breach of any other obligation arising under or by virtue of the mortgage . . .'.

The term 'any sums due' in section 36 of the Administration of Justice Act 1970 now relates merely to the contractual payments and arrears existing at the time of the hearing.[29] The district judge, therefore, has the discretion to suspend a possession order where the mortgagor can show an ability to clear her arrears, whilst maintaining the contractual payments, within a 'reasonable period'. In exercising this discretion, district judges will take into consideration the mortgagor's liability for legal costs' as one district judge made clear, 'I have to take that into account if the arrears are X pounds they will be X pounds plus £600 each time the case comes back.'

The addition of legal costs to the debt already incurred by the mortgagor has particular significance where the mortgagor has failed to meet the specified payment terms under a suspended possession order. In this case, the mortgagee can seek a warrant for eviction and, in turn, the mortgagor can request that it be suspended. In determining whether to suspend the warrant, district judges made it clear that, in many cases, they consider it to be in the best interests of the mortgagor to grant possession. The basis for this belief is that the continued involvement of mortgagors in legal proceedings for possession will only increase the debt they already face and as a result, it may prove to be in their interests to grant possession immediately.

District judges do have the power to award costs against the mortgagee but they may do so only where the case has been brought 'unreasonably'.[30] Owing to the fact that, in most cases, the mortgagor will be in breach of his mortgage contract, it is extremely difficult for district judges to determine that the case has been brought 'unreasonably'. As one district judge stated,

It is very difficult if a borrower is behind to say that a case has been brought 'unreasonably'. Where costs usually come in is where the information is not to hand and the borrower comes in time and time again saying this amount is wrong and you get sick to death of the mortgagee and you make an order that no part of the costs will fall against the borrower. Very rarely if there are arrears can you say that proceedings have been brought unreasonably.

The mortgagee is therefore said to be acting 'reasonably' in seeking an order for possession for the reason that the mortgage contract states that he may seek such an order should the mortgagor fail to meet the specified payment terms. In addition, the contract will also state that it is the responsibility of the mortgagor to meet the costs of the legal proceedings involved. District judges recognize that costs are a major hurdle in the mortgagor's attempts to avoid repossession but they feel unable to interfere with the contractual relationship between the mortgagor and mortgagee. This is due to their adherence to the principle of freedom of contract.

The principle of freedom of contract is based on the assumption that the parties entered the contract on a voluntary basis and were free to negotiate its terms. The parties should, therefore, be bound by the terms of that contract. This assumption is, however, misplaced within the mortgage market.

---

[29] Administration of Justice Act 1973, s. 8.   [30] RSC Ord. 62, r. 6[2].

In practice, the mortgagor rarely has the ability to influence the contractual terms, regardless of the mortgage product or mortgagee chosen. Mortgagees offer standard terms throughout the industry and, as one mortgagee stated, they offer 'Non-negotiable standard terms. If you want to borrow then these are the terms.' A prospective mortgagor is, therefore, obliged to accept these standard terms, which are similar throughout the mortgage market, including liability for costs, if they wish to obtain mortgage finance. District judges do not recognize the inability of the mortgagor to exercise a choice within the mortgage market and so they continue to apply the principle of freedom of contract to the disadvantage of the mortgagor.

It is the inability of the mortgagor to exercise an effective choice within the mortgage market which enables mortgagees to impose terms which favour them. This is particularly apparent in relation to the imposition of additional costs on the account of a mortgagor in arrears. The types of additional costs imposed by mortgagees upon a mortgagor in arrears include, for example, £10 for each telephone call, £30 for a home visit, and £50 for the issue of a solicitor's letter.[31] The amount of additional charges imposed on a mortgagor in arrears is entirely at the discretion of the mortgagee. In addition to the charges imposed for these types of services, the mortgagor will also be liable to pay interest on his arrears.

A justification which may be made for the lack of direct legal intervention in the setting of additional charges is that competition within the mortgage market ensures that mortgagees will set only charges which reflect the actual cost of the service involved. This justification, however, is undermined by the fact that different mortgagees impose different charges for the same service. As one mortgagee stated, 'The scale of fees that we charge in terms of letters are used to provoke a response from the customer.' Borrowers with this mortgagee were charged higher amounts for each subsequent letter, indicating that a charge higher than that necessary to cover administrative costs was imposed. Other mortgagees stated that they charged the same amount for each letter regardless of how many had been sent previously. The significance of this inconsistency in the amount of charges that will be imposed is that those mortgagors who are subject to higher charges will find it more difficult to avoid repossession than those who are subject to lesser charges. A mortgagor who has been subject to large amounts of additional charges will find it more difficult to convince the court that he has the financial funds necessary to clear his arrears within a reasonable period. This fact was made apparent by the district judges. They stated that they limit the extent of the reasonable period under section 36 of the Administration of Justice Act 1970 so as to avoid the mortgagor falling further into debt as a result of additional costs.

---

[31] National Association of Citizens' Advice Bureaux, (London: NACAB, 1993), 11.

The most significant aspect of the repossession process relates to the definition applied to the term 'reasonable period'. The amount that the mortgagor will have to pay each month will depend on the length of suspension. A mortgagor who owes £500, for example, may find it difficult to convince the court that he will be able to clear that amount in three months, but, given three years, the court may be more willing to suspend the possession order. This fact has been recognized by the Court of Appeal in *Cheltenham and Gloucester Building Society* v. *Norgan*.[32] The Court of Appeal held that, when assessing a 'reasonable period' for the purposes of section 36 of the Administration of Justice Act 1970 for the payment of arrears by a defaulting mortgagor, it was appropriate for the court to take account of the whole of the remaining part of the original term of the mortgage and, accordingly, the existing practice of imposing a shorter fixed period of two or more years should no longer be followed.

The decision of the Court of Appeal is indicative of the general acceptance that repossession should be avoided wherever possible. District judges, however, have indicated that, despite the decision in *Cheltenham and Gloucester Building Society* v. *Norgan*,[33] they feel unable to suspend possession orders for the remaining term of the mortgage. This is due to the fact that a mortgagor will be liable for the costs of the legal proceedings and will be subject to additional charges while she remains in arrears with her mortgage payments. If the district judge were to suspend the possession order for twenty years, for example, the mortgagor would be subject to increasing financial debt as a result of the imposition of additional costs. District judges, therefore, believe that a shorter period than that of the remaining term of the mortgage is in the best interests of the mortgagor. As one district judge noted, 'we started with a couple of years and it went to three and now it's gone to five. I'll go to five. I haven't gone over the whole length of the mortgage, because I think anyone who needs to do that is in real trouble.'

In restricting the extent of the reasonable period to a period shorter than that of the remaining term of the mortgage, district judges are attempting to ensure that mortgagors are not subjected to years of ever-increasing debt and that mortgagees are not burdened by unpaid debts. The difficulty with this proposition, however, is that it is the mortgagee who imposes these costs on the mortgagor through a contract which did not involve equal bargaining power or free negotiations. The principle of freedom of contract demands, however, that the district judges apply and uphold the terms of that contract. If additional costs were not imposed, district judges could suspend orders for possession for longer periods, allowing many more mortgagors the opportunity of avoiding repossession.

[32] [1996] 1 All ER 449.   [33] [1996] 1 All ER 449.

The Rhetoric of Consumerism

The withdrawal of the state from the provision of housing and its replacement by a market system has been instrumental in altering our conception of the individual in society. Rather than the emphasis being on the individual as 'citizen', it is now on the individual as 'consumer'. The significance of this shift in emphasis concerns the entitlements which may be legitimately claimed by the individual. As stated above, citizenship implies that every member of society is entitled to have access to all entitlements of the civil, political, and social elements of citizenship. The consumer-citizen, however, can only expect to have access to those entitlements which he can afford.

The justification put forward for this aspect of consumerism is that the millions of transactions entered into by consumers determine the price and quality of goods and services. The market will, therefore, offer a range of goods and services which vary in price, thereby allowing all consumers, regardless of their financial status, to exercise some degree of choice. The fact that some consumers will have a wider choice than others is merely an outcome of market forces which is beyond the control of central government. As Saunders argues, 'In a privatized system of provision based upon the principles of market exchange, access to resources is governed by a different principle, namely, the ability (and willingness) to pay for the good or service demanded.'[34]

The inability or unwillingness of district judges to intervene in the contractual relationship between the mortgagor and mortgagee is indicative of the reliance placed on this aspect of consumerism within the repossession process. The home-owner is viewed as an individual consumer, operating within the mortgage market, with the ability to influence the terms of the mortgage contract by exercising his choice. If he cannot afford to meet the payment terms, which he agreed to, then he should not be entitled to remain in home-ownership. As one district judge stated,

If I make an order to pay X amount per month off the arrears and it is consistently flouted I persistently say to borrowers who aren't towing the line, I'm sorry but a time must come when the mortgagee can be reassured that when he goes to court exercising the right which *you* gave him on *your* security by *your* contract under *your* hand, he must be reassured at some stage that the court will say of course you are entitled to that.

What this approach does not take into account is the imbalance in the strength of the bargaining positions of the respective parties. Mortgagors are not free to negotiate the terms of their mortgage contract but must accept

[34] Saunders, 'Citizenship in a Liberal Society', in Turner (ed.), *Citizenship and Social Theory* (London: Sage, 1993), 63.

standard terms which make them liable for all costs incurred in the enforcement of the mortgagee's rights under that contract. The mortgage market
is, therefore, failing to operate effectively on the basis of choice and competition, but district judges do not have or are unwilling to exercise the
power to intervene in the contractual relationship between the mortgagor
and mortgagee to redress this imbalance.

The Need for Reform

The claims made by central government regarding the benefits to be gained
from the regulation offered by the market, a market which they sought to
ensure operated effectively, have not been met in practice. The reliance on
aspects of consumerism within the repossession process is misplaced, for the
mortgagor does not have the ability to exercise choice within the mortgage
market owing to the lack of information which mortgagees provide. The
offer of standard terms obscures the difference in approach adopted by
mortgagees, and, without information relating to repossession policies or
additional charges, the mortgagor cannot exercise an effective choice. As
Lewis states, 'It needs to be underlined that accessible information is a precondition for choice to be effectively exercised.'[35]

The lack of information available to mortgagors denies them the ability
to make an effective choice of mortgagee, which in turn denies the
accountability of mortgagees. This has implications for the home-owner,
his ability to avoid repossession is significantly restricted as a result. More
important, however, is the fact that the current repossession process denies
home-owners a fundamental civil expectation—namely, the entitlement to
due process and decent housing. Marshall's definition of the civil element
of citizenship includes the 'right to justice', which he defines as 'the right
to defend and assert all one's rights on terms of equality with others and by
due process of law. This shows us that the institutions most directly associated with civil rights are the courts of justice.'[36]

In order to satisfy this fundamental requirement of justice, therefore, the
legal process of repossession must allow equal access to those who seek to
utilize its mechanisms for grievance redress. As has already been indicated,
mortgagors are not allowed equal access to the protection afforded by section 36 of the Administration of Justice Act 1970 for the reason that particular mortgagees who seek repossession as a matter of course on three
months' default significantly reduce the ability of their mortgagors to avoid
repossession.

The basis of the protection afforded by section 36 of the Administration
of Justice Act 1970 is that it allows the mortgagor to avoid repossession if

[35] Lewis, *Choice and the Legal Order*, 7.
[36] Marshall, *Citizenship and Social Class*, 10–11.

he can show an ability to clear his arrears within a reasonable period. His ability to do so is dependent on the decisions taken by his mortgagee regarding repossession and the imposition of additional costs. The more costs that are imposed, the more difficult it will be for the mortgagor to avoid repossession. The ability of mortgagors to question these decisions is hindered by the fact that mortgagees refuse to provide any relevant information. By failing to provide any information regarding the decision to repossess or to impose additional charges, mortgagees are ensuring that their decisions are not made accountable to mortgagors.

Transparency within the decision-making processes adopted by mortgagees is, therefore, avoided by their refusal to make available any information regarding how their decisions are made. The mortgagor will, therefore, find it extremely difficult to challenge the decision to repossess on the basis of procedural propriety. Their difficulty in this respect is exacerbated by the lack of any enforceable standards requiring procedural fairness. The *Statement of Practice* published by the Council of Mortgage Lenders constitutes guidelines only, with no sanctions for non-adherence. Mortgagees are, therefore, able to operate unaccountable decision-making processes in respect of the withdrawal of the mortgagor's civil entitlement to decent housing.

It may be argued, however, that repossession does not deny this entitlement, for there are alternative means of gaining access to decent housing. This argument is undermined by the fact that the only alternative available to home-owners in most cases is the public-rented sector. The residualization of this sector by central government means that it cannot offer the same quality of housing as home-ownership. More importantly, the burden placed on local authorities to house the homeless means that some home-owners may find it extremely difficult to obtain accommodation in the public-rented sector. The report by Ford, Kempson, and Wilson highlights the problems faced by those who have been repossessed in seeking alternative housing; 'It was clear that some local authorities took, or had to take, a fairly hard line on intentional homelessness so that even with a possession order families would not necessarily be rehoused straight away.'[37] The repossession process, in failing to make accountable the decisions of mortgagees and to ensure that mortgagors receive equal protection under section 36 of the Administration of Justice Act 1970, therefore appears to stand in need of reform.

[37] Ford, Kempson, and Wilson, *Mortgage Arrears and Possessions; Perspectives from Borrowers, Lenders and the Courts* (London: HMSO, 1995), 95.

AN ALTERNATIVE APPROACH?

In seeking to reform the repossession process, it is necessary to reappraise our conception of the individual in society. A conception which views the individual as consumer leads to social exclusion, because those who cannot afford the goods and services which the majority enjoy are excluded from the standards which prevail in society. By returning to the conception of the individual as citizen, it will be possible to ensure that all citizens receive the entitlements which attach to that status, including decent housing.

The justification for this reform of the repossession process based on a new conception of the home-owner as citizen is that decent housing is a necessary precondition of citizenship. As with education, decent housing is fundamental to the individual's ability to exercise the entitlements which attach to the status of citizenship. It should not, therefore, be dependent on whether the individual can afford it or not, for 'the principle of universality demands access to certain basic things irrespective of ability or performance. Drinking water, food, shelter, and also elementary education and primary health care should be universally available to all, and in their case questions of merit do not arise.'[38]

It must be accepted, however, that the housing system does operate within a market system. We cannot, therefore, ignore the consumerist perspective, but we can shift the emphasis in favour of citizenship and reintroduce the element of universal entitlements. By shifting the emphasis in favour of the citizen, it may be possible to reform the legal process of repossession without denying mortgagees the ability to recover their debt via repossession. It must be accepted that the majority of home-owners in England and Wales have entered into contracts which allow the mortgagee the ability to seek repossession. It may be argued, therefore, that this contractual entitlement should not be denied. By viewing the home-owner as citizen, however, we can at least demand that the contractual entitlement to repossession is undertaken with procedural fairness. As Dahrendorf argues, 'Civil rights are the key to the modern world. They include the basic elements of the rule of law, equality before the law and due process.'[39]

By focusing on the individual as citizen, the home-owner will be able to claim the highest degree of procedural stringency within the repossession process. The legitimacy of this proposition derives from the concept of judicial review, which Lewis and Birkinshaw define as 'the process by

[38] Beteille, 'Equality and Universality: The Best-Off and the Worst-Off', The Times of India, 8 Mar. 1995, quoted in Lewis, Choice and the Legal Order, 13.

[39] Dahrendorf, 'Citizenship and Social Class', in Bulmer and Rees (eds.), Citizenship Today (London: UCL Press, 1996), 37.

which judges keep powers exercised on behalf of the public within their allotted legal bounds'.[40] The limitation of judicial review to the discretion exercised by public bodies would appear, superficially, to make it unsuitable for application within the mortgage market. Following the decision in *R. v. Panel on Takeovers and Mergers, ex p. Datafin plc*,[41] however, it is possible for a non-governmental body to be subject to judicial review if it operates as part of a regulatory framework established by government, and the government would have set up a similar body had it not existed.

There are aspects of the position of mortgagees which could equate them with other non-governmental bodies which have been subject to judicial review. These bodies include private organizations which determine whether an individual should have the ability to gain entry to a trade or profession. The justification for the application of judicial review in relation to these bodies is that they make decisions which affect the livelihood of an individual.[42] As Cane notes, 'The basis of such decisions is that bodies of this sort exercise great, and often monopoly, power over some area of social or economic activity in which not only participants in the activity but also the wider public have an interest.'[43]

With over 42 per cent of all dwellings in England and Wales currently subject to an outstanding mortgage debt,[44] mortgagees exercise a significant degree of power within the housing system. Their decision regarding repossession has significant implications for the welfare of home-owners, for it constitutes the withdrawal of their civil entitlement to decent housing. The repossession process should, therefore, ensure that correct procedures are followed, for, as Megarry VC held in *McInnes* v. *Onslow-Fane*,[45] the 'forfeiture' of an already acquired interest requires a high degree of procedural protection.

The major obstacle in the application of judicial review to the decisions of mortgagees concerns the contractual nature of the relationship between mortgagor and mortgagee. Where the powers exercised by a body derive from a contract, its decisions remain a matter for consideration under the principles of private law and are not open to judicial review.[46] This approach has been criticized for failing to recognize that the exercise of contractual powers may have a significant impact on the public.[47] It is

---

[40] Lewis and Birkinshaw, *When Citizens Complain* (Buckingham: Open University Press, 1939), 200–1.

[41] [1987] QB 815.   [42] *Nagle* v. *Fielden* [1966] 2 QB 633.

[43] Cane, *An Introduction to Administrative Law* (Oxford: Oxford University Press, 1996), 21.

[44] *Social Trends* (London: HMSO, 1997), 170.   [45] [1978] 1 WLR 1520.

[46] *R.* v. *Lloyd's of London, ex p. Briggs* [1993] 1 Lloyd's Rep. 176 and *R.* v. *Football Association, ex p. Football League* [1993] 2 All ER 833.

[47] Cane, *An Introduction to Administrative Law*, 21.

possible to argue, however, that the nature of the powers exercised by mortgagees equates them with bodies which have been subject to judicial review. They should, therefore, adopt decision-making processes which satisfy requirements as to procedural fairness.

Procedural fairness in this respect requires that the decisions of mortgagees are made accountable to the mortgagor and the court. Only where the court has some knowledge of the decision taken by the mortgagee is it possible to question whether a procedure, acceptable within the law, has been adopted. This would require, at the very least, the publication of the repossession policies of mortgagees. As Lewis, argues,

The classical market only makes sense in terms of signals, wants and preferences in a situation of assumed knowledge. Therefore, the information available to seller and purchaser needs to be roughly in balance if the transaction is to be free and if fairness and equality are to prevail. There needs therefore to be very good reason for non-disclosure or non-accessibility if the whole 'free speech' paradigm is to be satisfied.[48]

The publication, by mortgagees, of their repossession policies might also ensure the effective operation of the mortgage market. It would enable mortgagors to exercise an effective choice based on relevant information. In turn, this would lead to consistency in the treatment of mortgagors in similar circumstances, for mortgagees who sought to impose higher additional costs or to repossess at an earlier stage than other mortgagees, would not survive in the competitive mortgage market. In addition, transparency within the contractual relationship would provide an opportunity for a more active review of unfair terms by virtue of the Unfair Terms in Consumer Contracts Regulations 1994,[49] which came into force on 1 July 1995. Unlike the Unfair Contract Terms Act 1977, the 1994 Regulations *do* apply to contracts concerning land.[50]

Under these Regulations, any 'unfair' term in a contract concluded between a seller or supplier and a consumer, where the said term has not been individually negotiated,[51] shall not be binding on the consumer.[52] The Regulations define an 'unfair term' as 'any term which contrary to the requirement of good faith causes a significant imbalance in the parties' rights and obligations under the contract to the detriment of the consumer'.[53]

The Regulations provide guidance on the assessment of 'good faith', stat-

[48] Lewis, 'Markets, Regulation and Citizenship: A Constitutional Analysis', in Brownsword (ed.), *Law and the Public Interest* (Stuttgart: Franz Steiner, 1993), 127.

[49] SI 1994/3159.

[50] Department of Trade and Industry, *The Unfair Terms in Consumer Contracts Regulations 1994. Guidance Notes* (London: DTI, 1995), 7–8.

[51] UTCCR 1994, para. 3(1).   [52] UTCCR 1994, para. 5(1).

[53] UTCCR 1994, para. 4(1).

ing that regard shall be had in particular to: the strength of the bargaining positions of the parties; whether the consumer had an inducement to agree to the term; whether the goods or services were sold or supplied to the special order of the consumer; and the extent to which the seller or supplier has dealt fairly and equitably with the consumer.[54] As this chapter has already illustrated, the non-negotiable standard terms offered by mortgagees, which impose additional costs on the mortgagor and do not provide sufficient information regarding repossession, cause a 'significant imbalance in the parties' rights and obligations under the contract to the detriment of the consumer'. Mortgagors and interest groups will, however, face difficulties in bringing an action under these Regulations for the reason that they do not have sufficient information regarding the repossession policies adopted by mortgagees. If these policies were published, both mortgagors and interest groups could challenge their 'fairness' under the Unfair Terms in Consumer Contracts Regulations 1994, thereby ensuring a degree of accountability within the repossession process.

Procedural fairness within the repossession process must be ensured if justice is to be achieved, and, furthermore, it must also be accepted that the state has some part to play in assisting home-owners in their attempts to avoid repossession. The objective of successive governments during the post-war period has been to encourage households to enter into home-ownership. The policies implemented to achieve that aim have promoted home-ownership as the tenure which provides a degree of security in excess of that offered by other tenures. This necessarily engendered expectations on the part of home-owners that these claims would be met. Research undertaken by Nixon, Smith, Wishart, and Hunter, published in 1996, suggests, however, that, in practice, home-owners are more likely to be repossessed than public-rented-sector tenants in similar circumstances.[55]

The protection afforded to home-owners by virtue of section 36 of the Administration of Justice Act 1970, fails to provide any practical assistance. It merely allows the mortgagor more time to clear her arrears, the onus being on the mortgagor to find sufficient funds to do so. The state does provide assistance with mortgage interest payments for those with low incomes, but these benefits have been the subject of reform under the Social Security (Income Support and Claims and Payments) Amendment Regulations 1995.[56]

Under these new rules, borrowers who took out their mortgage before 2 October 1995 and who claim Income Support after that date will not receive mortgage-interest payments for the first eight weeks of their claim;

[54] UTCCR 1994, sch. 2.
[55] Nixon et al., *Housing Cases in County Courts* (London: The Policy Press, 1996).
[56] SI 1995/1613.

for the next eighteen weeks, they will receive half of the amount otherwise payable; full payments will then be made. Those who entered into a mortgage after 2 October 1995 will not receive any mortgage-interest payment for the first thirty-nine weeks of their claim; after that time they will receive full payments.

It would appear that the government, having encouraged people to undertake owner-occupation, the majority of which could do so only with the aid of mortgage finance, has left mortgagors to fend for themselves in times of financial difficulty. It is necessary, therefore, to introduce financial assistance for mortgagors who are experiencing difficulties in meeting their mortgage payments. A number of commentators have called for the introduction of a 'mortgage-benefit' scheme similar to the payment of Housing Benefit received by tenants.[57] It would appear that the introduction of such a benefit would assist mortgagors in avoiding falling into arrears in the first instance and would therefore avoid the possibility of repossession.

In demanding procedural fairness within the repossession process coupled with support for home-owners in financial difficulties, it is assumed that some mortgagors will still be subject to repossession. In order to satisfy the requirements of citizenship, however, these mortgagors must have access to a similar standard of decent housing from alternative sources. This would not necessarily involve a substantial increase in government expenditure, particularly if it was achieved in partnership with private bodies, including, for example, an extended role for housing associations.

CONCLUSION

Housing, as a necessary precondition of citizenship, should no longer be viewed in the same respect as other commodities. It is a factor fundamental to the exercise of civil entitlements. If we are to ensure that all citizens have access to decent housing, then we must begin by imposing procedural fairness in the legal process of repossession and introducing alternative tenures which offer a decent standard of housing. In order to do this, however, we must shift the emphasis away from consumerism and towards citizenship. As Dahrendorf notes,

Citizenship rights are at the heart of the open society. They need to be reformulated by precise minds who do not use them for devious ends or to cloak vested interests. They need to be reasserted by those who recognize that reform is the only

[57] Ford, *Which Way Out?* (London: Shelter, 1995); Ford and Wilcox, *Reducing Mortgage Arrears and Possessions: An Evaluation of the Initiatives* (York: Joseph Rowntree Foundation, 1992); and Foster, *Mortgage Rescue: What Does It Add Up to?* (London: Shelter, 1992).

hope of liberty. And they need to be extended to cope with the new challenges. Who said that there is no longer an agenda for change?[58]

That change must reassert the entitlements of citizenship. It is to be hoped that governments, regardless of their political persuasion, will undertake this challenge.

[58] Dahrendorf, 'The Changing Quality of Citizenship', in Van Steenbergen (ed.), *The Condition of Citizenship* (London: Sage, 1994), 19.

8

WOMEN AND TRUST(S): PORTRAYING THE FAMILY IN THE GALLERY OF LAW

Anne Bottomley

IN LAW AS IN ART?

I would contend that neither the Courts of Law nor the Courts of Criticism could continue to function if we really let go of the notion of an intended meaning.[1]

I was reading Gombrich on problems associated with the study of iconography when it struck me that this assertion (which he does not at this point in his text expand upon) summed up the basic thesis I want to develop in this chapter; in which I propose to revisit the law on disputes over family property, and specifically role played by 'intention' in the law of imputed trusts. Gombrich, in accepting that a work of art may 'hold' many readings, recognizes a more complex picture of the artist/author than one which assumes that authorial knowledge or control is absolute. Value may be given to a work in a series of readings which 'mean' more than the artist/author might have intended or foreseen. However he is holding, as a historian, to a basic need to attempt to draw a distinction between drawing a meaning from a work of art and attributing that meaning to the creator. In a sense it is a recovery of the artist, but with a clear recognition that this is only one mode of analysis, of normative and functional value, rather than a simple reality to be asserted (imposed) to the exclusion of all else.

Gombrich is, of course, struggling with the problem encountered in all academic disciplines of dealing with the issue of subjectivity. The notion of the unitary subject, to whom can be attributed full and rational control over her actions and her products, has been under attack in the academic world for more than a century. And yet, as Gombrich so neatly suggests, it remains fundamental to the operation of the 'Courts of Law'. Much work, within both feminist and postmodernist critiques of law, has focused on the costs involved in constructing and sustaining the image of the unitary subject. However, as the project of critique has developed and has led to fundamental questioning as to the viability of either academic disciplines or

---

[1] Gombrich, *Gombrich on The Renaissance*, ii (3rd edn., London: Phaidon, 1984), 4.

social/cultural practices, which seem dependent on the need to believe in the fully autonomous rational subject, so a *via media* seems to have emerged—one which might be seen as a compromise but which, I believe, is much more than that. It is a turning-back to find, and give credit to, the cluster of values associated with the idea of a fully autonomous rational subject, as a way or ordering our understanding of our worlds, our choices, and our value judgements. What, however, is radically different is that we neither assume this as a reality nor, necessarily, prefer it as the 'best' way of ordering our understanding and our actions. They are as ideas to be interrogated and as maps available for use. The questions we always pose in relation to them are: what exactly is their use to us and where might they lead us?[2] The fundamental issue for us, as critical lawyers, is, therefore, not simply the frailty of such concepts as 'responsibility' but rather their potential utility.[3] That potential can be explored only if one has a political project for law: an idea, however incomplete and inchoate, of a more just society.

On a much smaller canvas, I want to use and examine the issue of 'intended meaning' as attributed to the parties of legal actions concerning disputes over domestic property, specifically the issue of 'intention' in implied (that is unwritten) trusts.[4] In as far as I have space, I would also like to extend this into the issue of 'intended meaning' as attributed to judges in the records of previous cases (which actually brings me much closer to the issues which concern Gombrich).

FRAMING 'INTENTION'

This appeal, concerning the disputed beneficial interests in a matrimonial home, was heard during the week in which the Law Commission published its Sixth Programme of Law Reform (Law Com. No. 243). Item 8 of the programme recommends an examination of the property-rights of home-sharers. The report comments (pg 34): 'The present legal rules are uncertain and difficult to apply and can lead to serious injustice.' Though this was a reference to the problems of unmarried home owners, the rights of married occupiers can be equally problematic—as the present case shows—when the claims of third parties such as creditors or mortgagees become involved. The economic and social significance of home-ownership in modern society, and the frequency with which cases involving disputes as to the

---

[2] See e.g. Braidotti, *Nomadic Subjects* (New York: Columbia University Press, 1994).

[3] This theme is evident in the papers in Bottomley (ed.), *Feminist Perspectives on the Foundational Subjects of Law* (London: Cavendish Publishing, 1996).

[4] I have not outlined the law in this area, presuming that most readers are familiar with it. However, for more detail, I suggest Gray, *Elements of Land Law* (2nd edn., London: Butterworths, 1993).

property rights of home-sharers (married or unmarried) are coming
before the courts, suggest that the Law Commission's intervention is
well-timed and has the potential to save a lot of human heartache as
well as public expense.'[5]

As is reflected in the quotation Waite LJ takes from the Law Commission,
he is giving judgment in an area in which the 'rules are uncertain and difficult to apply'; for, despite the welcome given by many commentators, to
the seemingly restrictive and clarifying judgment given in the leading case
of *Rosset*,[6] not only do many issues remain unclear (in that they were not
fully addressed in the judgment) but subsequent judgments have also found,
in the text of *Rosset*, room for manœuvre. Indeed it could be argued that
Rosset exemplifies how obfuscation can be found, or created out of, a judgment which attempts to be (too) simple. However, this is to rest a critique
of *Rosset* purely at the level of doctrinal clarity. What must be read in *Rosset*
are other registers of authority, narratives lying behind and informing the
doctrinal foreground, and then themselves sustained through the doctrinal
nexus. Thus, central to the judgment, but not immediately within the doctrinal nexus, is the authority found in *Rosset* for drawing a sharp distinction
between an intention to share ownership of specific property as opposed to
simply the sharing of lives (and the use of property): 'I pause to observe that
neither a common intention by the spouses that a house is to be renovated
as a "joint venture" nor a common intention that the house is to be shared
by parents and children as the family home throws any light on their intentions with respect to the beneficial ownership of the property.'[7]

I have argued elsewhere that this insistence on a specific agreement as to
ownership is not only unreal in the context of sexual–domestic arrangements, but is also likely to discriminate against women.[8] In this context, I
want to emphasize a related thread in Lord Bridge's argument which further disadvantaged Mrs Rosset: it was her role as a wife. Commenting on
the work she undertook in organizing the renovation of the property, Lord
Bridge said:

It was common ground that Mrs Rosset was extremely anxious that the new matrimonial home should be ready for occupation by Christmas . . . in these circumstances it would seem to be the most natural thing in the world for any wife . . . to
spend all the time she could spare . . . in doing all she could to accelerate progress

---

[5] *Midland Bank plc* v. *Cooke* [1995] 4 All ER 564, *per* Waite LJ 564–5.

[6] *Lloyds Bank* v. *Rosset* [1991] 1 AC 107. See e.g. O'Hagan 'Quantifying Interests under
Resulting Trusts', (1997) 60 MLR 420.

[7] *Lloyds Bank* v. *Rosset* [1991] 1 AC 107, *per* Lord Bridge at 130.

[8] Bottomley, 'Self and Subjectivities: Languages of Claim in Property Law', in Bottomley
and Conaghan (eds.), *Feminist Theory and Legal Strategy* (Oxford: Blackwell, 1993).

of the work quite irrespective of any expectation she might have of enjoying a beneficial interest in the property.[9]

This figure of 'the wife' operated not only to disadvantage Mrs Rosset in terms of possible 'contributions' made to the improvement of the property, but equally disadvantaged her in relation to the finding of an 'intention'. Lord Bridge makes clear in his judgment that no account will be taken of the context and likely consequences of a marital relationship. In making the marital relationship irrelevant he is able to require, in doctrinal terms, a need to prove discussions which are more likely, and more suitable, to relations between strangers, or at least those not living within a sexual–domestic nexus.

So later:

The first and fundamental question which must always be resolved is whether, independently of any inference to be drawn from the conduct of the parties in the course of sharing the house as their home and managing their joint affairs, there has at any time prior to acquisition, or exceptionally at some later date, been any agreement, arrangement or understanding reached between them that the property is to be shared beneficially. The finding of an agreement or arrangement to share in this sense can only, I think, be based on evidence of express discussions between the parties, however imperfectly remembered and however imprecise their terms may have been.[10]

The terrain is then limited, not only by ignoring the interrelations between sharing, using, or owning in this kind of relationship, but ignoring also the very implausibility of what he seeks: a specific discussion on ownership. It seemed very much that this judgment brought to an end any search for a notion of 'family assets' as part of a modified area of trusts law.

The focus insisted upon in *Rosset* on express(ed) intention, irrespective of the sexual–domestic context to the relationship, has become the subject of a great deal of criticism: both in terms of doctrinal clarity and in terms of whether this reflects the policy stance the law ought to take in relation to such disputes. A certain discomfort with the decision, especially as it remains to date the most recent House of Lords authority in the area, must in part lie behind the lengthy introduction given by Waite LJ as a context for his decision in *Cooke*.

Cooke involves a number of tropes (including issues of repossession of the property by the mortgagee and the successful pleas of undue influence in relation to the signing of a 'consent form'), but the major focus for the Court of Appeal, and indeed for this chapter, is the quantification of the beneficial interest. Although the matrimonial home had originally been

[9] *Lloyds Bank* v. *Rosset* [1991] 1 AC 107, *per* Lord Bridge at 132.

[10] Ibid. It must be then supported by evidence that the claimant has acted to her detriment or significantly altered her position on the basis of this agreement.

bought in Mr Cooke's name alone, legal title was later, on the insistence of Mrs Cooke, transferred into joint names. In fact Mrs Cooke had gone to the length of initiating court proceedings (under the Married Women's Property Act 1964) to achieve this: by a consent order the parties then held the property as joint tenants in law and as tenants in common in equity. It seems that at no point was the quantification of the beneficial interest discussed.

The Cookes' story bears many of the usual features of such case histories but with one major modification. Mrs Cooke was clearly quite an independent lady who was able and willing to act, as far as she thought she could, in the interests of herself (and her children). She had been a student away at college when her fiancé made the arrangements to purchase what was to become the matrimonial home, in preparation for the marriage. In the accounts he gives in evidence to Hitchin County Court of this period, two factors become very clear. First, that he was doing it 'for them', helped by moneys provided as a marriage gift from his parents but otherwise by arranging a mortgage based on his salary. In reproducing sections of the evidence Mr Cooke gave, Waite LJ brings into the court arena (and the record) the difficulties in looking for intention. In response to the question: 'So far as you were concerned, at the time you were signing the conveyance, going through with the legalities with the solicitors, whose house did you think this was to be once the transaction was completed?', Mr Cooke answers: 'To be truthful, I can't actually remember, but I always thought of it as "our house". It was just because I did—Jane was away at teacher training college in Eastbourne. . .'.

Then he is asked: 'Do you remember anything in relation to the building society and obtaining the mortgage—any problems which arose there?' To which he answers: 'Only in respect of when I told them Jane was a student and they said they didn't want that on the form, basically because she had no income, you see, so . . . .'.[11]

Waite LJ introduces this as

a vivid illustration of the difficulties which these cases pose for the honest recollections of witnesses and the barrenness of the terrain which the judges and district judges who try them are required to search for the small evidential nuggets on which such issues as to the existence—or the proportions—of beneficial interest are liable to depend.[12]

As a Family Division judge, Waite J (as he then was) was one of the first to have to deal with *Rosset*, in the case of *Hammond* v. *Mitchell*.[13] The necessity for a 'painfully detailed retrospective'[14] was followed by Waite J, but in so doing he made clear the difficulty and cost this puts the legal system

---

[11] *Midland Bank plc* v. *Cooke* [1995] 4 All ER 564, at 567–8.

[12] Ibid., at 567.   [13] [1991] 1 WLR 1127.   [14] Ibid., *per* Waite J at 1129.

through, particularly when adjustments have to be made to having the hearing in the Family Division.[15]

Further, in actually analysing the result of his judgment it is clear that he took a far more flexible approach to the use of 'express intention' than might have been expected from *Rosset*. Posing the question 'Is there any . . . property which has been the subject of some agreement, arrangement or understanding between the parties on the basis of express discussion to the effect that such property is to be shared beneficially . . .?', he answers 'yes': 'In relation to the bungalow there was express discussion on the occasions I have already described which, although not directed with any precision to the proprietary interests, were sufficient to amount to an understanding at least that the bungalow was to be shared beneficially . . .'.[16]

It is actually six pages earlier that Waite J records the relevant evidence:

Shortly before completion of that purchase the couple visited the property and were walking in the garden of what was about to become their new home when the following conversation took place. He said to her spontaneously: 'I'll have to put the house in my name because I have tax problems due to the fact that my wife burnt all my account books and my caravan burned down with all the records of my car sales in it. The tax man would be interested, and if I could prove my money had gone back into property I'd be safeguarded.' Later that same day he mentioned to her that he was going through a divorce and it would be in his best interests if he was to put the property in his name. Soon after completion he said to her, 'don't worry because as soon as we are married it will be half yours anyway and I'll always look after you and (the boy)'.[17]

This suggests a very flexible approach to the use of 'express intention'; if no assault is made directly on the doctrine itself, it is made indirectly through its application.[18] (One cannot help thinking that Mrs Rosset would have received a quite different result from Waite J from the one she received in the House of Lords.) The judgment in *Hammond* v. *Mitchell* is made more controversial in that Waite J then used this evidence of intention to include a sharing of the beneficial interests in the enlargement of the property holding by the purchase of adjoining properties, and, in so

---

[15] This is not to suggest that he was against such hearings being brought in this Division; on the contrary, he seems to welcome it as the proper forum for couples who also have to make provision for children of the relationship.

[16] *Hammond* v. *Mitchell* [1991] 1 WLR 1127, *per* Waite J at 1137.

[17] Ibid., *per* Waite J at 1131 (He does not comment on the presumed veracity of Mr Hammond's statements.)

[18] In parenthesis . . . the detail of 'walking in the garden' rather reminds me of the 'human touches' in narratives introduced in many of Lord Denning's judgments, especially when he was furthest away from orthodox law. I am also intrigued by the 'spontaneous' aspect of the little speech. Put together these would suggest a rather romantic setting in which the 'right thing' was said; quite the opposite from the more orthodox picture of carefully thought-out and expressed intentions.

tracking these developments, by extending his brief to cover 'the whole course of dealings between the parties'.[19] It is rather as if, having satisfied himself that he has found an original agreement, he can then extend this, by a process of analogy, to any related properties (a line is drawn, however, and not all property acquired during the relationship is deemed to be jointly owned).

Waite J's judgment in *Hammond* can be approached as an example of the classic problem of dealing with an unmarried couple who do not have the benefit of access to the divorce courts; the subtext is of a judge attempting to deal with the issue of division of property at the end of a relationship (with the implications of provision for children).[20] *Cooke* introduces a rather different set of problems which form a subtext to the judgment. By citing the evidence of the husband in *Cooke* (referred to above), Waite LJ illustrates not only the implausibility of looking (and finding) express discussions ('however imperfectly remembered and however imprecise their terms may have been . . .[21]), but also the very fact (although he does not express it) that for many people the very notion of a beneficial interest is remote. It is clear from the evidence Mr Cooke gave that the process of acquiring the mortgage determined the way in which the property was held. However, it is equally clear that this did not, in his mind, finally determine the property as simply 'his'. He was 19, about to be married, and clearly pleased to have been able to buy a house at all. Did any solicitor sit him, or them, down and explain the notion of a beneficial interest? The building society set the scene; who was able to pay? They were not interested in her[22] and it is unlikely that either party to the marriage would have, at this point, even been interested in such a discussion: they wanted a mortgage with which to be able to purchase a house. Later, when title to the house was transferred into joint names, the beneficial interest was referred to: but only as being held as tenants in common. Was this explained to the couple?[23] Neither do we know why there seems to have been no discussion about quantum.

[19] *Hammond* v. *Mitchell* [1991] 1 WLR 1127, *per* Waite J at 1137.

[20] A subtext foregrounded in Lord Denning's judgment in *Eves* v. *Eves* [1975] 1 WLR 1338.

[21] *Hammond* v. *Mitchell* [1991] 1 WLR 1127, *per* Waite J at 1137.

[22] This would have been very different by the end of the decade.

[23] The problem here, of course, is the *ius accrescendi*, and it is likely that the parties, already having been in dispute their legal advisors, and /or the court, would have considered a joint tenancy inappropriate. However, it is this aspect of the joint tenancy which seems closest to most people's idea of 'matrimonial property'. One of the greatest problems with discussions of 'matrimonial property' in this country is that they almost invariably focus on either the divorce courts or the problems of cohabitees without benefit of access to divorce law; a much more fruitful (and historically correct) starting point would be to look at the rules on death and work from that basis. One would then have directly to confront the issue of freedom of testation, supported, at present, by a liberal interpretation of the severance rules as

What can we conclude from looking at the process which led to the need for the court to adjudicate the proportion of the beneficial interest held by Mrs Cooke? First, and simply, that all the indications are that this couple neither 'knew' the law nor made clear decisions about their 'ownership' of the property based on clear legal advice. They responded to external contingencies (the mortgage) whilst holding a notion that they were purchasing a matrimonial home 'for them'. When Mrs Cooke took steps to have the property placed in their joint names, she must have thought that this was now clarified, and, of course, to some extent it was, but not to the extent of the crucial question of the holding of the beneficial interest. Did she think that she now simply 'owned' the property? Was she advised as to what would happen if one of them died? Did her lawyers fail her? It does seem that the failure to address these questions arose from lack of knowledge about law (and lack of legal advice) rather that simply lack of 'intention'. Not knowing the question makes it impossible to begin to formulate an answer. Seeking 'intention' in these circumstances is, therefore, a double bind: it requires some knowledge of law, as well as dealing with the problem that couples in sexual–domestic relationships often find such discussions difficult.

Looking back at *Hammond*, another confusion that many couples operate under is, I believe, alluded to. The man said 'as soon as we are married (the property) will be half yours anyway . . .'; what did he mean by this? Could this be an example of a common idea I have found many people hold: that on marriage a couple automatically share their property in law? If you force the question and ask them to distinguish between 'use' and 'ownership', they often become confused. They also often hold a presumption that spouses (and children) have a right to inherit. These presumptions are often reinforced in practice by the use of joint tenancies and the operation of intestacy rules in the absence of wills, but the point is that we too often fail to deal with issue of the lack of knowledge amongst ordinary people when dealing with the complex(ity) of legal title, beneficial interests, marriage, and death.

Onto this grid of muddled ideas, we place a compass of 'intention' as the guide for judicial decision-making. It is all too easy to dismiss the use of 'intention' when placed against these contingencies, as neither practicable nor 'fair' (to the individual or as social mores). It can be used as a clear example of the importation of doctrines and standards which make more sense in a world presumed to be populated with strangers entering into financial/legal relations with each other based on clear objectives and supported with sound legal advice. These standards applied to sexual–

favoured in equity. Denning's vain attempt to reintroduce tenancy by entireties in *Bedson* v. *Bedson* (1965) 2 QB 666 has been rightly criticized for the legal argument, but has not been used to reconsider the policy objective.

domestic relations seem too harsh, too unreal, and particularly to the disadvantage of women.

The penalties of separate property, and of entering into juridical capacity as 'equal to men', have operated harshly for women who still have (on the whole) less financial weight than men and who still (on the whole) bear the primary responsibility in the home for domestic labour and the care of children and continue (on the whole) to give a value to the domestic sphere which remains (except in very limited circumstances) unvalued in economic/legal terms. The status of marriage has very little effect on property relations, except on divorce, and, if we are to follow *Rosset* closely, neither the status of marriage nor the context of a sexual–domestic relationship is at all relevant in the trust cases. Indeed, it can be argued that *Rosset* makes the status of marriage, as well as the relationship of marriage, a positive disadvantage in trying to establish an 'intention'. However, *Hammond* and *Cooke* (although the product of one judge and indeed of a judge coming from the Family Division) display an unwillingness to ignore the context of the sexual–domestic relationship and a willingness to deal creatively with the doctrinal nexus of *Rosset* in order to challenge the policy implications of the judgment.

THE LANDSCAPE OF A RELATIONSHIP BROUGHT INTO THE PICTURE

In both *Hammond* and *Cooke* Waite LJ signals in his introductory comments the importance of taking into account the sexual–domestic setting in his analysis and application of trusts law. In *Cooke* he is quite clear about the need to take into account 'the relationship':

> the duty of the judge is to undertake a survey of the whole of the course of dealings between the parties relevant to their ownership and occupation of the property and their sharing of its burdens and advantages. That scrutiny will not confine itself to the limited range of acts of direct contribution of the sort that are needed to found a beneficial interest in the first place . . .[24]

so neatly avoiding being blocked by *Rosset*, and looking rather at the context of the sexual–domestic setting:

> One could hardly have a clearer example of a couple who had agreed to share everything equally: the profits of his business while it prospered, and the risks of indebtedness suffered through its failure; the upbringing of their children; the rewards of her own career as a teacher; and, most relevantly, a home into which he had put his savings and to which she was to give over the years the benefit of the maintenance and improvement contribution. When to all this is added the fact (still

---

[24] *Midland Bank* v. *Cooke* [1995] 4 All ER 564 at 547.

an important one) that this was a couple who had chosen to introduce into their relationship the additional commitment which marriage involves, the conclusion becomes inescapable that the presumed intention was to share the beneficial interest in equal shares.[25]

Waite LJ is transparent in his concerns, as well as in his sidestepping of the thrust of *Rosset* by doctrinal nicety. The narrative of such an approach was prefigured for him in *Springette* v. *Defoe*[26] where Dillon LJ takes a much more conventional approach to the material: 'The court does not as yet sit, as under a palm tree, to exercise a general discretion to do what the man in the street, on a general overview of the case, might regard as fair . . .'. He holds to the need for 'a common intention between the parties (which) must in my judgment mean a shared intention communicated between them. It cannot mean an intention which each happened to have in his or her own mind but had never communicated to the other.'[27]

In the absence of such communication, in *Springette* the judges found/made a division of the beneficial interest based solely on financial contributions. The presumption of a resulting trust was not displaced by intention. Dillon LJ's judgment is as robust as it is conventionally sound, yet he notes, and it is given prominence in the headnote, that the parties were both of 'mature years' when they began to cohabit (first in her flat and later in the acquired property which was held in joint legal title). It is almost as if this statement of age (we are never told their actual ages), and the fact that they both had adult children, are used to justify the court in taking a commercial reading of their dealings. Their 'relationship' is noted but downplayed. In *MacHardy* v. *Warren*,[28] the history of a relationship between a much younger couple (married at 20 and 19) is given a much fuller account by the very same judge, who then upholds the court of first instance in awarding an equal division of the beneficial interest. Throughout a long marital history the matrimonial homes had been held in the husband's name alone, but the first property was bought partly with the down payment of a wedding gift and subsequently mortgage repayments were made out of joint bank accounts. In a very brief judgment Dillon LJ (citing only *Grant* v. *Edwards*[29] and *Rosset*) found an intention to share equally without any reference to a need to communicate such intention, the use of joint accounts leading him to conclude: 'I find it irrational to conclude that the intention was that the entire beneficial interest . . . should belong solely to the husband . . .'[30].

Waite LJ, in *Cooke*, expresses some surprise at the different approaches in the two cases, attempting to reconcile them doctrinally through the use of

---

[25] Ibid., at 576.　　　　[26] [1992] 2 FLR 388.　　　　[27] Ibid., at 393.

[28] [1994] 2 FLR 338.　　　　[29] [1986] Ch. 638.

[30] *MacHardy* v. *Warren* [1994] 2 FLR 338, at 340. (Or indeed that the wife's interest should be limited to a proportion based on the initial wedding gift.)

Lord Diplock in *Gissing* v. *Gissing*.[31] Using *MacHardy* to escape the confines of *Springette* is an audacious doctrinal move, but in another register it simply picks up a subtext provided by the juxtaposition of the two cases: one is dealing with a couple whose relationship, through its timing, length, and focus, allows for a quasi-matrimonial analysis; the other in contrast appears more as a business affair. The operative presumption allows a focus on presumed intention (albeit arising from joint bank accounts) in one, whilst, in the other, the judge refuses to displace the resulting trust through lack of evidence of communicated intention.

Critics may doubt the doctrinal plausibility of *Cooke*, and I do not mean to underestimate this, but for me the interesting point is that Waite LJ, in both *Hammond* and *Cooke,* is clearly pushing at doctrine to achieve a policy end: the recognition of the context and logic of sexual–domestic relationships. In *Hammond* he relies heavily on his audacious use of the evidential material to push at the doctrinal limitations, but he also limits the effect of *Rosset* by linking the *Rosset* criteria with an initial agreement rather than tracking it through the course of the dealings. In *Cooke* he manages to limit the effects of *Rosset* via *Springette* by this concentration on *MacHardy* (downplaying the specific point in *MacHardy* of the joint bank account) and thus further drives a wedge between an initial intention and later issues such as quantum. However plausible this limitation exercise on the doctrinal heritage of *Rosset*, what is much more sustainable as an analysis of these cases is a refusal to let go of the issue of the context of the sexual–domestic relationship. In *Hammond* the immediate context was the break-up of the relationship; the classic figure of the cohabitee without benefit of the powers of the divorce regime to reallocate property on criteria which may include both a broader reference to contributions and, more importantly, future need. In *Cooke* the context is rather the lack of knowledge and foresight that could have been utilized to determine the division of the beneficial interests as well as the context of a marriage, in which so often such questions are simply not raised. My argument is simply that the doctrinal subtleties are being played out through a register which is primarily concerned with limiting the impact of *Rosset* at a rather more abstract level: that is the taking into account of the sexual–domestic relationship. This has to take form in two ways to counter the full import of *Rosset*. First, that one *can* take it into account, and, secondly, that it can, and *will*, be taken into account as a positive aspect rather than a negative one. I believe that Waite LJ is fully aware of this but that other judges are also influenced by similar concerns, although perhaps less consciously so in their own thinking and certainly less transparently so in their judgments. In this light, despite the much more conventional reasoning of Dillon LJ, I do think it important that the narratives

[31] [1970] 2 All ER 780. This section of his judgment is subjected to particular criticism in O'Hagan 'Quantifying Interests under Resulting Trusts'.

of his judgments involved a cohabiting couple of mature years and brief cohabitation as opposed to a lengthy and rather conventional marriage.

What seems to me to be emerging in these post-*Rosset* cases is a concern to mitigate the harshness of the relationship blindness of the reasoning: either in terms of simply refusing to take it into account or in its implicit negative value. Attempts at specifically limiting the doctrinal impact of *Rosset* are really only evidence of this broader concern: one might almost name it as 'middle-order' reasoning, the hinge between policy and doctrinal detail. The informing policy requires that the sexual–domestic relationship is not ignored, even more so not treated negatively. Therefore the 'middle-order' reasoning of the judgment is fundamentally under attack, but played through (in Waite at least) in a series of doctrinal moves aimed at limiting the requirement for expressed intention. It is both the broader sweep of the brush as well as the detail of the work which must be examined.

PORTRAITS OF MARRIAGE AND OF LAW

In what has become an influential article, Simon Gardner critiques the focus on intention in three ways. First, 'doctrines which rely on the parties' thinking are, in fact, inappropriate to this area of law, since by the nature of the relationships in question, the parties deal with each other more by trust and collaboration rather than by organised thinking about their respective rights.'[32] Secondly, that, despite this focus and, necessarily, because of it, 'there is a gap between the articulated doctrines and the manner in which cases are actually decided'.[33]

Thus behind the use (and misuse?) of doctrine lie policy decisions. The extent to which any individual judge allows himself to be influenced by factors extraneous to a strict interpretation of judgment means not only that these are aspects of policy reliant on a judge being willing to utilize doctrine within a broader context but also that these aspects 'beyond doctrine' are not fully articulated and therefore not explored or subject to a close scrutiny, which might allow a judgment as to their appropriateness as policy.

And thirdly, then, that what is required are doctrinal forms which do articulate the policies which society and law deem appropriate for such relationships: 'the law must adopt different values when it comes to family

---

[32] Gardner, 'Rethinking Family Property', (1993) 109 LQR 263, at 263, the paper is developed from a chapter in Gardner, *An Introduction to the Law of Trusts* (Oxford: Oxford University Press, 1990).

[33] Gardner, 'Rethinking Family Property', 279. He includes in his critique developments in other jurisdictions (Australia, Canada, and New Zealand) which he argues (controversially) remain plagued by the same problems.

property cases. For the values which society expects to characterise the dealings between parties to an emotional partnership are not those of individual autonomy and discrete responsibility, but those of trust and collaboration.'[34]

Gardner then seeks 'defensible doctrinal vehicles by which the law can overcome the lack of thinking associated with emotional relationships, and provide remedies instead on the basis of trust and collaboration which characterise such relationships'.[35]

The first, and most obvious, point to make is that Gardner's concern with the limitations of the focus on intention, and also the values he commends of 'trust and collaboration', are going to be attractive to me as a feminist. It is as if, on both points, his argument is congruent with feminist critique and with feminist aspirations. I was fascinated then by my own initial response on first reading his article, which was one of discomfort and ambivalence.

I think that, in part, I am ambivalent to Gardner's position because of the very fact that it is both so plausible and so attractive. This derives from two aspects: the assertiveness of his mode of writing and the assertiveness of the high moral ground of this ethical position. As Moffat writes, in his review of Gardner's book on trusts law,[36] his 'evaluative approach carries within it the seeds of prescription'.[37] Embedded within his text are assertions of values of law as well as societal values: legal doctrines must be transparent both in themselves and in their application; they must be open to rigorous examination in terms of both their internal logic and the policy values they carry and articulate; they must, therefore, be defensible. The values expressed in law must be congruent with the values society upholds and seeks to uphold. In other words, everything can, and must, fit. We may, must, expect in, and of, law a clear reproduction and reflection of clear societal values. Leaving aside for the moment this particular jurisprudential conception of law, let us take a step back from his article and situate it within the context of his book.

In the second chapter of his book he outlines justifications for imposing restraints upon the right of a property-holder to dispose of his (sic) property as he wishes; in other words restraints upon liberty and the corollary of rights to privacy. He lists them (and he notes that the list may not be exhaustive) as paternal, communitarian, utilitarian, and a rights-orientated approach. He expresses a communitarian approach as those times when 'the trust concept, with its legal rights and obligations, should not be allowed to intrude into, and so contaminate, contexts, such as family relationships, in which the governing influence should be love'.[38]

---

[34] Gardner, 'Rethinking Family Property', 286.   [35] Ibid. 289.
[36] Gardner, *An Introduction to the Law of Trusts*.
[37] Moffat, 'Trusts Law: A Song Without End?', (1992) 55 MLR 123 at 133.
[38] Gardner, *An Introduction to the Law of Trusts*, 14.

Later, in further exploring this, he says: 'One thrust of communitarianism is a concern to protect and foster such institutions as the family, which are the preserve of humane influences like love',[39] so, we have to be careful about 'the intrusion of stiff legal rights and obligations into love-orientated contexts at all . . .'.[40]

In his article, Gardner directly embraces communitarianism, the values of trust and collaboration, as being central to the family and therefore central to any 'defensible doctrinal vehicle' which might import 'stiff legal rights and obligation'. His problem is an old one. It is how one deals with a vision of 'the family' which presumes 'love' (trust and collaboration) and views law as an external force intruding on/into familial privacy. Gardner in effect tries to bridge this gap by looking for a way to articulate 'love' in 'law'. That is, trying to find within 'defensible legal doctrines' a way of upholding a moral scheme which overcomes individualism, specifically the individualism presumed in the need for 'express intentions'.

LOVE IN LAW?

There is no doubt that many commentators, in both land law and equity and trusts, have felt uncomfortable with 'family' situations as part of their area of legal study. There is often a sense that not only are these situations awkward in themselves but that they (to twist Gardner's allusion) 'contaminate' the law by bringing in extra problems which dissipate doctrinal purity and clarity. Too often one has a sense that, rather than wrestling with the problems involved, it would be easier to designate these as somehow 'special cases' and move them into a different picture, a different frame of reference. The most obvious manœuvre is to argue for their designation as 'family law' and therefore as subject to a regime which directly, centrally, addresses the familial relationship. Gardner at least avoids this, by arguing within the frame of equity and trusts for 'defensible legal doctrines' which will reflect not merely a relationship but the values presumed of that relationship. His commitment to communitarian ideals, 'trust and collaboration', lead him to construct a continuum in which,

so far as marriage is concerned, communality seems incontestably the right approach. But it is wrong to think communality is never appropriate to unmarried relationships. The idea of equivalence to marriage is in fact something of a red herring . . . that communality is the right analysis in marriage . . . does not prevent it from also being apt for unmarried relationships, if in fact the requisite values are present. Unmarried relationships form a continuum, and at its end are cases where the parties adopt such values.[41]

---

[39] Ibid. 16.   [40] Ibid. 17.   [41] Gardner, 'Rethinking Family Property', 291.

Thus the status of marriage is presumed to involve the 'requisite values', but a regime based on communality is not to be limited to marriage status, but extended to cover those relationships which display the 'requisite values'. This end of the continuum is recognized in those relationships, when in deciding (for instance) 'to pool belongings and efforts towards a shared well being . . . a more active form of collaboration (then) enters the picture, giving each a claim to the resources of the other'.[42] Gardner finds a doctrinal home for this in 'in effect a mutually fiduciary relationship . . . so gain(ing) access to the law's existing learning about fiduciaries. It is thus able to give the parties relief by way of either a half share in, or adequate support from, each other's assets.'[43]

This does have the major advantage of 'access to the law's existing learning about fiduciaries', but otherwise seems a simple reinvention of community of property (however, neatly avoiding the problem of leaving it status based). However, at this point, it is the route by which Gardner gets to his doctrinal home which interests me. The presumption of the values of trust and collaboration become, in a rather muddled way, fixed in marriage and otherwise recognized in non-marital relationships by their very presence. How are we to find them? Gardner gets caught in exactly the same conundrums as the very doctrines he critiques:

The problem is that the parties' ideas may . . . vary through time; and one party may have had a different view from the other. The solution lies in taking an objective approach. That is to say, the law should recognise a relationship of trust and collaboration not simply by how the parties see it in their hearts, but also where their external behaviour seems to be upon that basis.[44]

Therefore, one form of external behaviour, marriage, seems readily to give rise to the presumption. In other relationships the courts would have to look at such factors as shared finances. Two major problems arise. First, it is unlikely that cases which reach the courts will offer up a simple scenario of 'trust and collaboration'; that is the whole point. It is in the very cases in which 'trust and collaboration' have been absent or been betrayed that we have to find the nexus which allows us to justify 'intrusion' into the property relations of the parties. It is then, unfortunately, a short step to imposing onto the relationship our vision of what it should have been. The 'objective' approach can become very quickly a prescriptive approach, one in which 'trust and collaboration' are presumed to be right for certain types of relationships. Despite Gardner's criterion of pooled financial resources, I suspect that finding the most 'marriage-like' relationships may well become a way of establishing a rationale for imposing communality in those relationships in which, firstly, there are classic gender roles and, secondly, the female partner (as the more vulnerable economically) is the claimant.

---

[42] Gardner, 'Rethinking Family Property', 292.   [43] Ibid. 298.   [44] Ibid. 294.

Gardner's solution in emphasizing the mutuality of communality may be more informed by an ideal of what should be, rather than by a struggle to deal with the real issues of complex and often transient relationships, and the particular problems of economically and emotionally vulnerable women.

The problem is that behind the search for a defensible rational for intervention lies a simple figure; it is the wronged woman. Gardner refers to her only obliquely, yet, I believe, she is central to his text. For some, the solution has been to award her rights based on status, or an equivalent to status. Gardner does not take this route, although I believe he is not wholly avoiding it. For others, a solution has been sought in emphasizing contributions to the domestic economy, and rewarding these. The ultimate scenario here is rewarding domestic or sexual labour with economic value, an exchange relationship. Gardner seemingly opens up a third route; the recognition of mutuality. But, in fact, this route is likely to lead us back to looking at the status of marriage and the relations of marriage-like relationships; it is likely that, in practice, what would be awarded the claim of communality are those relationships which seem to conform to our expectations of marriage. It is most likely that in court the good 'wife' would receive the recognition of betrayed trust and be awarded for her services based on trust. Is that really so different? What makes it compelling is that it seems so much cozier and so much more progressive because it is based on an ideal of mutuality.

What Gardner is really doing is taking an image of commitment and trust, which has been betrayed, or that one party is now attempting to avoid, and using that as a starting point for the redistribution of property on separation (he does not deal with the issue of death). For some relationships this narrative will be appropriate, but they are by their very nature the relationships which are least likely to require the assistance of legal dispute resolution at the end of them; they are likely to be those relationships where parties, in the context of their commitment to each other, have already taken the legal steps which result in communality of property. It is those relationships which never went through a threshold of commitment, but rather let drift an emerging relationship, without any clear future commitment, that are our real problem. Gardner places these relationships into a section of his continuum which would still allow for legal intervention and resolution, through the development not of rights in property but rather of claims under a modified form of unjust enrichment. This is quite logical within his frame of reference, but I suspect that in practice a slippage would emerge. The 'wronged-woman' figure could be used; indeed her very presence could insist upon a rather different claim—that is, that she was entitled to a relationship of 'trust and confidence' because of her commitment and her role in the relationship. The very lack of mutuality might become a fulcrum for an argument that the image of mutuality should be imposed, that she has a right to more than merely a claim within unjust enrichment.

The wronged and deserving woman is likely to present herself within a narrative which draws from the discrepancy between her role and her rights. As Eekelaar says, in his critique of Regan's argument for communitarian ideals in family law:

individuals are primarily perceived, and socially evaluated, according to their role performance: so a person is not so much a good (or bad) woman or man as a good or bad mother, wife, father, husband . . . communitarian approaches accept presently-defined social roles and give individuals less scope to bargain over their enforcement.[45]

Gardner's text, with his very liberal emphasis on mutuality arising literally out of a shared commitment, does not consider this problem, and he manages to avoid it by not dealing head on with the issue of power in relationships, specifically power between the genders. He is uncritical of his ideal of mutuality; he assumes it not merely as an ethical base but as proper and achievable social practice, which it is simply up to the law to confirm. But, as the law must not get in the way of it, so the law must facilitate it. Therefore, should the law impose it? The slippages in the seeming logic are all too easy. The quandary becomes even more problematic if we place his argument within the context of his book. Gardner is concerned to uphold liberty, the right to deal with one's property, to follow through one's intentions, except when there is a justification against individualism. In his article he is forced to confront one aspect of the tension between mutuality and individualism when he deals with the possibility of opting out of communality. It is only here that he faces directly the problem of power:

It follows from the overall notion that the rules in this area will derive from the nature of the parties' relationship. So where both parties agree that the otherwise relevant rules should not apply, that should be the position. Attending to the nature of the relationship requires us to respect their agreement, since it is part of the definition of the relationship . . . The agreement could emanate from both parties equally, or from the initiative of one and acquiescence of the other: so if one party announces to the other that he (*sic*) does not intend to concede a share of the property . . . and the other enters or continues in the relationship and makes contributions in the face of this announcement, she (*sic*) can be regarded as agreeing to the exclusion . . .[46]

He goes on to recognize that there may be a problem of 'oppression' in this context, and, looking back at cases, says:

---

[45] Eekelaar, 'Family Justice: Ideal or Illusion?', (1995) 48 CLP 191 at 203–4.
[46] Gardner, 'Rethinking Family Property', 295.

Those cases all involved the situation of one party taking the initiative—saying that the property will not be shared—and the other merely acquiescing. This is what one would expect: if there is oppression to be found, it is more likely to be associated with this situation than with that where both parties play equally active parts. Then, the cases all involved a man denying a claim to a woman . . . although it seems a crude generalisation, it is more likely that men oppress women in these matters than visa versa.[47]

What is being recognized here is that the law does need to recognize the position of the individual within the relationship as well as the relationship *per se*. Within this context issues of power within sexual–domestic scenarios become crucial. To give such preference to mutuality may not give enough space to this crucial point.

Gardner, in his critique of 'intention', gives great weight to the point that 'the relationship' (sexual–domestic), by its very nature, is unlikely to give rise to the form of individualistic behaviour which is seemingly required by law (thus leading the judges to the need to invent agreements for women who work inside the home and have no financial contribution to make). He presumes it is the mutuality (trust) of the close emotional relationship which gives rise to this, and is the basis for the contributions made by the woman to the domestic economy (collaboration). What does not enter into this analysis is a follow-through to issues of economic dependency and power. It is as if by asserting the moral value of mutuality we will create it, either through the facilitation of law or through the imposition of it. Because *that* is the paradox: will individuals opt for mutuality or do they need to be forced into it? Is the family a private autonomous sphere ruled by love into which law intrudes? As Eekelaar says of the delegalization debate in family law:

On the one hand, freedom from lawyers and the claims of 'legal rights' seem to open out a more caring ethic, when responsibilities will replace self-interest. But the goal of self-determination can also promote individual assertion . . . unfettered by law, 'rights' or the assertion of 'obligations' in this context may amount to little more than the exercise of power.[48]

Eekelaar's argument is that the communitarian approach leads to a fundamental paradox: either towards more legal intervention (to uphold and confirm the ideals of the roles required for the image of the family idyll) or towards delegalization—that is, an emphasis on private agreements and settlements through mediation. One confirms the role models within the family, the other the privacy of the family. If we follow through Gardner's logic we become caught in the same dilemma: how far should the law intervene to enforce a model of good ethical practice, through compensation for its abuse or loss? Because of the elision between ethics (the ideal) and actual

---

[47] Ibid. 296.   [48] Eekelaar, 'Family Justice: Ideal or Illusion?', 205.

practice (the presumption of the ideal as operative), the pressure either to impose more law or to deregulate is a very likely future. A critique of Gardner requires a closer look at family relations than this simple assertion of the ideal of mutuality, as well as a closer look at the presumption that all one requires of law is a sustainable doctrinal home for the ethical values he lays claim to. What is missing in his work is a real concern with power, power in the family and power in law:

Communitarianism lacks a theory of power. It pre-supposes a model of the self and society which is either radically post-modern—so fragmented as to be incoherent and chaotic—or neo-romantic—unrealistically homogeneous and static, allowing for the possibility of only the most modest, incremental change. Largely as a consequence of these features, in so far as any substantive political implications flow from communitarianism, they tend to be conservative ones. Although feminist thought is sympathetic to the insights of 'constitutive communitarianism' in . . . its advocacy of genuinely inter-subjective values, the communitarian alternative to liberalism is far from qualifying as a potentially feminist political theory.[49]

Gardner, as a neo-romantic, does not provide a sustainable approach for a feminist because he does not deal with the issue of power. His ethical stance may appeal, but it does not correspond to the real dilemmas of sexual–domestic relations. His brief references to power within the context of opting out of mutuality need to be taken far more seriously and applied far more extensively within the overall schema of his argument. However, they do offer clues as to what needs to be recovered; it is the aspect of individualism and rights. Eekelaar says: 'rights-based arguments allow for more scope for individuals to decide which roles they wish to pursue and greater freedom whether or not to pursue claims arising out of the socially-defined roles of others.'[50]

In other words, the classic liberal concern with freedom of choice. As Frazer and Lacey make clear in their critique of liberalism, such freedom is illusory if not matched by real equality and by shared values. Hence, one level of an appeal in communitarianism for feminists. But, further, the classic conception of liberalism rests on a claim to a unitary, rational, subject. Communitarianism, by its very emphasis, tends to downplay the problem of subjectivity, emphasizing roles and relations rather than the individual. But the problem remains that, as we have begun to understand the fragility of the notion of a unitary subject, and as we have also appreciated the limitations of arguments based solely on individual rights and liberties, we have also begun to appreciate the value of the idea, not as a descriptive reality but as an organizing proposition. The frame of critique has to be a threshold—

[49] Frazer and Lacey, *The Politics of Community* (Brighton: Harvester Wheatsheaf, 1993), 161.
[50] Eekelaar, 'Family Justice: Ideal or Illusion?', 204.

a quite different way of appreciating what seems to a be familiar picture. In terms of my discomfort with Gardner, it can be drawn in this way. Gardner gives a predominance to roles and relations; in so doing, he seems to offer a scenario favourable to women, and certainly attractive in its ethical stance to feminists. But in so doing he is also ascribing to relationships an ethic which ties individuals into patterns which are likely simply to confirm existing social relations rather than challenge them. In this he is in part a liberal and in part a communitarian: a liberal in that he presumes choice and equality, a communitarian in that he is willing to make the presumed choices, for mutuality, and impose them as a claim to equality. What he ignores is both the problem of gendered power relations and the reality that most of us live our lives within a continuum of a relationship which is based on a precarious balance between the need for individuality as well as the need for communality. Thus we recognize a split subjectivity, ourselves as individuals (however fragile this account may be) and ourselves as related to others.[51] Therefore, my resistance to Gardner stems from the very same source as my attraction to an ethics of responsibility and caring. I see behind Gardner's emphasis on 'trust and collaboration', the potential loss of individually based rights arguments.

The implication of Gardner's argument is that the individualistic approach, which informs 'express intention', has not served me, the family, and the community well. This suggests that 'me', 'the family', and 'the community' are all easily identifiable and at one, or should be. I do not think that it is that easy. Whilst I accept that, in particular, *Rosset* has been extremely restrictive, it does not follow that the idea of 'intention' as being central to the law is, of itself, a problem, either as policy or as doctrine. Indeed I believe it is important to argue to retain it.

INTENDED MEANINGS

The simplest narratives are those which have a beginning, a middle, and an end. However, few narratives conform easily to this lineal pattern, being more often dependent on a series of circular movements onto which is imposed the orthodox and prescriptive pattern. What would I say is Gardner's beginning: his critique of the present law, or his commitment to the values of communitarianism? My own beginning, within this text, became the middle of the text, and now, as I approach an end, I return to re-encounter what became my beginning. I have used Gardner in two ways. First, to explore how and why one method of valuing relationships, in this case communitarianism, may lead to a loss of the value of the

[51] See e.g. West, 'Jurisprudence and Gender', 55 U. of Chicago L. R. 1 (1988).

individual. I recognize that it is not simply, and never can be, a stark choice between one or the other but rather a need to recognize the tension between the two. In fact, in many ways, this tension runs through Gardner's work, although it remains unexplored. But, secondly, in reading back through the cases, and in the development of the case law since Gardner wrote his article, I wanted to reconsider the critiques which Gardner makes of the focus on 'intention'.

Gardner's first argument on the plausibility of expecting, and then seeking, 'expressed intention' is well taken, and indeed echoed in the judgments given by Waite LJ, although I differ from Gardner in presuming that it is simply the mutuality of 'trust and collaboration' which gives rise to this. Rather one must add to the picture the aspect of power which arises in an economically and emotionally dependent relationship. Further, his second point of critique—that the judges are reaching decisions despite doctrine rather than through doctrine—also seems well founded, and again confirmed in the processes which Waite LJ uses to limit both the doctrinal nexus of *Rosset* and the middle-order authority found in *Rosset* for ignoring the context of the sexual–domestic relationship. I have argued above that, in the post-*Rosset* cases I have looked at, there seems to be a recognition of marriage-like relationships which then seem to give a different slant to judgments and hence to decisions made by the judges. That this is neither fully articulated in judgments, nor therefore justified, seems to confirm Gardner's fears. However, this is to accept Gardner's claim that legal judgment should, or indeed could, be formed through a pattern of reasoning which deduces the answer from the rigorous application of transparent doctrine.[52] In fact, his own proposals for the use of fiduciary relations and unjust enrichment are unlikely to deliver this aspiration with ease, but, at this point, the question is, rather, is this a sound criterion by which to judge and condemn the present law?

The Law Commission's comment that 'the present legal rules are uncertain and difficult to apply and can lead to serious injustice'[53] is, of course, incontestable. They do require more clarity, and limiting the effects of *Rosset* through creative decision-making will not remove all the problems and issues associated with this judgment. However, Waite LJ's judgments in particular display one of the aspects of the richness of common law reasoning: it is the ability to find a number of 'intended meanings' within previous cases and many different registers of possibilities rather than simply seeking and applying doctrinal authority. As Waite LJ, and others, struggle with the heritage of the case law they are continually finding and testing aspects of policy, as well as of doctrine, which in a muddled, inchoate way

[52] For a fuller account of the richness of legal reasoning, see e.g. Goodrich, *Languages of Law* (London: Weidenfeld & Nicolson, 1990).

[53] *Midland Bank plc* v. Cooke [1995] 4 All ER 564, *per* Waite LJ at 564.

reach out towards a muddled and incoherent social existence. I have argued that Gardner's image of the family, or at least of sexual–domestic relationships, is too simple and absolutist. Only if one has a clear image of the social scenario can one demand that image is reflected, clearly, in law. A more realistic approach would be to recognize the plurality of relationships, and plurality in relationships, and therefore not to seek simplicity in law. However, to take Gardner's third point: that the law should reflect, in its doctrinal base, policies the law seeks to support. The question then is, what should the entry point of the law be? In one way Gardner, in the end, is simply reversing the present entry point. Rather than opting into mutuality, a couple must opt out. Presumptions are reversed. This then, finally, becomes a simple issue of policy. Should we seek to displace the seeming individualism of 'intention' with a form which privileges a relational aspect?

If this is premised on an account of familial relationships which presumes mutuality and ignores power, then I believe that the attractions of this are outweighed by the dangers. I also believe that taking this as the entry point will not avoid the problems of the muddled relationships which do not easily fit and which still leave us with the figure of the 'wronged woman'. In fact, in practical terms, it is likely that cases would simply reach a shared terrain of trying to determine a rationale and outcome for situations of unilateral trust and confidence, whichever entry point is chosen. But there still remains the basic policy question of whether 'intention' remains a valid starting point.

The value of intention returns us to the value of 'intended meaning'. It focuses on a need to try and attribute to actors a purpose to their actions which was within their own foresight. As policy in law, this gives credence to individuals and also, as a broader statement, encourages in individuals the need to take responsibility for their actions. It does not ascribe to them roles or make presumptions of them as to how they should lead their lives. It is quite clear that, following *Rosset,* the need in present law that this intention be communicated is too onerous. Sexual–domestic relationships, as a result either of true mutuality or of power (or very likely a mixture of both), too often do not produce the kind of specific discussions about specific property that *Rosset* requires. That is already being recognized in post-*Rosset* decisions. Looking at ways to open up the idea of 'intention' by taking into account both the fact of the relationship and the interrelations between the couple leads one back to the argument against a subjective test which Lord Read expressed in *Pettitt* v. *Pettitt*[54] and *Gissing* v. *Gissing.*[55] None of these modifications, however, removes the basic idea that one should start with what the parties intended, or might have intended on the evidence of their actions, if they had addressed their minds to the issue.

[54] [1970] AC 777 at 795.   [55] [1971] AC 886 at 897.

The importance of holding to the idea of 'intended meaning' seems, to me, to be crucial both for women and for feminists when faced with the alternatives of being rewarded (protected) on the basis of status or arguments based on economic exchange or presumed mutuality. It ascribes to us the freedom we seek to make our own decisions; what the law must act to mitigate are those situations which circumscribe our freedom through the power relations emanating from, and creating, economic or emotional dependancy.

Patterns already present in land law and the law of trusts allow for finding a precarious balance between the aspirations of individuals and recognizing patterns of power within relationships. Continuing to explore the particular problems of sexual–domestic relationships with the tools offered by these areas of law is likely to be, and should be, an open-ended project. As we continue to explore, attempt to understand, and seek better relationships between men and women, we cannot expect of law a simple solution. However, central to our project must be seeking policies and doctrines which facilitate choice and encourage discussion, without penalizing those who were unable to exercise choice or enter into discussions.

In fact, but coming from a different place, I find Gardner's use of fiduciary relations (and unjust enrichment) full of potential. The question one has to ask, within my frame of reference, is whether as a policy, or as a cluster of doctrinal concepts, it will 'simply entrench inequality further, or does it offer a remedial structure progressive forces can deploy?'[56]

Our portraits of the family in the gallery of law cannot be premised on the presumption of an idyll of family life, a rather pastoral vision of home and hearth. Rather we must struggle to find a way of reflecting the tensions, the jagged edges, and the complexity of modern relationships. We may yearn for the simple beauty and balance of mutuality, but our experiences tell us that the picture is far more complex than that. The figure of the wronged woman compels us towards compassion. The idyllic image of the family offers hope. But both are romantic icons, pulling us back in time rather than moving us forward. We seek pictures for a future and, ironically, they are to be found in re-viewing the very images, the ideas, which once seemed so constraining. We seek to be seen as citizens rather than to be continually portrayed as wives.

[56] Cooper, 'Fiduciary Government: Decentring Property and Taxpayers' Interests' (1997) Social and Legal Issues 234 at 235.

9

CITIZENS AND SQUATTERS: UNDER THE SURFACES OF LAND LAW

Kate Green

My aim in this chapter is to carry out a kind of archaeological enquiry: I want to explore beneath the surfaces of land law and uncover the connections between the character of the 'ideal English landowner' in the law of adverse possession and that of the 'citizen'. Further, I want to expose the limitations and exclusions inherent in the character of the landowner and citizen: that is, I want to show who does not fit the stereotype. In the traditional world of land law, there is no place for such an examination of the relationship between the 'private' rights of a person who gains landownership through adverse possession and the 'public' rights of a citizen against the state. Nevertheless, a space can be opened up: as in the adverse possession of land, it is possible to change the map by making a new claim.

In order to stake this claim, I have adopted the route of Deleuze and Guattari, the twentieth-century French philosopher and psychoanalyst respectively, who aimed to revolutionize thinking. Their writings are vast: I am merely using fragments. One of these is the idea of 'nomadism', of the world as founded on movement not fixity:

In the figure of the 'nomad', they see embodied all the fugitive forces that European states since the early modern period have sought to contain and destroy. The nomadic sums up everything that has remained counter to the state, including knowledges that resist bureaucratic codification . . . peoples that defy national concentration (think of Jews, gypsies, indigenous tribes) . . . [1]

Nomads raise questions for those who sit still; they question settled ideas. Thus, rather than follow the usual (Platonic) tradition which is based on defining the permanent 'essence' of a concept, Deleuze and Guattari were interested in constantly changing relationships. Following their approach, you do not ask, 'What *is* it?', but 'What does it *do*?': 'The question is not,

---

[1] Richards, *The Imperial Archive—Knowledge and the Fantasy of Empire* (London: Verso, 1993), 19–20; for details of their work, see Massumi, *A User's Guide to Capitalism and Schizophrenia: Deviations from Deleuze and Guattari* (Cambridge, Mass.: MIT Press, 1993). More generally along the way, I am relying on contributions from critical, feminist, and postcolonial theorists.

Is it true? But, Does it work? What new thoughts does it make possible to think?'[2]

Following their approach, I therefore asked the question, 'What does the law of adverse possession of land *do*?', and then I found an intimate connection between 'private' land law and 'public' citizenship:

1. the rules of adverse possession construct and reflect the political concept of an 'ideal English landowner'; and
2. this landowner is also 'the citizen'.

In each case of adverse possession, the judges have to decide whether what the claimant did to the land amounts to possession of it. In making these decisions, they are, little by little, fleshing out the character and activities of 'the landowner', while at the same time his pre-existing mythical figure is affecting their decisions. This is because such mythical figures as 'the landowner' 'resonate across space and over time' to anchor a philosophy of having and being 'which can influence events, behaviour and perception'.[3] The judges are thus stabilizing and making transparent the boundaries not only on the surface of the land but also in the ideology of ownership.

The law of adverse possession is, therefore, not merely a historical curiosity which operates as a technical convenience in the modern world of land registration. It does more than Kevin Gray, for example, suggests when he describes it as 'an important check on immense social and legal costs which would otherwise be incurred in endless litigation over matters of title'.[4] One of the roles of adverse possession, even today, is to maintain within the law the mythic character of the ideal English landowner.

The case law shows this character to be a self-interested and rational individual who makes a permanent mark on the landscape. He is a slippery amalgam of various notions of the yeoman, the small farmer, the market gardener, leaning on his gate in leather boots and gaiters in some Golden Age in the English countryside. His location there is not fortuitous, for, as John Rennie Short points out:

At its simplest, the countryside becomes the image of the country, indeed the term 'country' has the double meaning of 'rural land' and 'native land'. It becomes the scene of national harmony, peace and stability . . . the countryside has become the embodiment of the nation . . . a combination of nature and culture which best represents the nation-state.[5]

---

[2] Massumi, *A User's Guide*, 3.

[3] Short, *Imagined Country: Society, Culture and Environment* (London: Routledge, 1991), p. xvi.

[4] Gray, *Elements of Land Law* (2nd edn., London: Butterworths, 1993), 285.

[5] Short, *Imagined Country*, 34–5. He also points out that the more uncertain the future, the more the golden rural past offers a retreat (at p. 31). See generally also on the 'countryside' the writing of Williams, *The Country and the City* (London: Hogarth Press, 1993). In

It is important to recognize, first, that this character has been formed by the nature of English land, by the fertile agricultural earth of large areas of England rather than, say, the deserts of Australia or the lush forests of the South Pacific. That is, it is the physical nature of the land itself which has created and continues to create the ideal landowner.

In England, he has to work over the years to make and keep the land productive, while, in the desert, no matter how hard or how long he worked, he could produce little, and, in a Pacific island, the earth produces sufficient for life without any long-term investment. This continuing commitment to the land ensures the cultivation of its owner's character: patient, honest, hard-working, and exhibiting a sense of solidarity with those whom he identifies as similar to himself.

It is also important to observe, secondly, that it is the land itself which is the evidence of the owner's good husbandry: a bad potter can throw mistakes into the dustbin, but a bad farmer's incompetence is (while making allowances for different fertility and the weather) demonstrated simply by the productivity of the earth and the livestock it supports. Well-cared-for English land sings out to the world, 'I am owned.'

The characteristics of the ideal landowner as a permanent, rational, and self-interested countryman matches those of the citizen, for both figures emerge from a particular understanding of human nature. However, they are more than merely surface projections of an underlying ideological geology. The model citizen bears a special relation to the model landowner, for, as will be shown, only the *land*owner has the necessary moral stability to fulfil the standards of citizenship.

However, the ideal English landowner/citizen represents only one kind of human being; many others tend to be excluded because they fail to match the model's characteristics. (Such exclusions operate in complex ways, especially when there are multiple intersecting factors on the grounds of class, sex, race, sexuality, or age.) First, there are those who are seen as transient: the travellers who move from one piece of land to another. Secondly, there are those shut out by reason of their 'irrationality'—as defined by the rational owners and citizens. Thirdly, and of course closely connected, there are those defined as not 'self-interested'—members of families and other communities which put social before individual well-being. It is possible to list the 'outsiders'—in no particular order, children, women, 'natives', homosexuals, workers—so that, in the end, the real image of the ideal English landowner appears: he is the middle-aged, middle-class, heterosexual white man.

this 'country', there is also an interesting confusion between England (or Wales or Scotland, and so on), Britain and the UK: the slippage between these locations makes it difficult to use any of the terms accurately.

In the first section of this chapter, I sketch out this character as drawn by the judges in decided cases on adverse possession, and also uncover those who do not qualify. The following section connects the ideal landowner to the ideal citizen, and links together all those who are likely to be excluded, those who tend to be disqualified from both landownership and citizenship.

My archaeology thus exposes the connections between a tenancy and a passport, a mortgage and voting rights, which, under the surface of the law, are inextricably linked. English land law's ideal owner, the successful adverse possessor, and the political world's ideal citizen construct and are constructed by one another in a continuing circulation of the ideology of liberalism, the all-pervasive set of ideas within which English lawyers perceive their world. Indeed, the two have been intimately bound together since the seventeenth century, when the foundations of modern views of property and citizenship were laid in the early growth of capitalism.[6] Initially, however, it is necessary to explore the challenge to land law of the squatter–citizen link.

THE CHALLENGE TO LAND LAW

As I have suggested, linking squatters and citizens is a challenge to the accepted boundaries of land law, since the rules of adverse possession and the notion of citizenship appear to operate in quite separate spheres. Normally, land law seems to be concerned with the private world, with one individual enforcing rights against others, while citizenship is about the public world, the reciprocal rights and duties of citizen and state. Land law, it would seem, has nothing at all to do with such politics.

Other writers have also recognized this division between the lateral relations of individuals with one another, and the hierarchical relations of individuals with the state. For example, Bonaventura de Sousa Santos has described the modern world as resting upon two structural 'pillars'—the pillar of regulation (roughly, law) and the pillar of emancipation (liberty).[7] These two pillars are in permanent tension, but, ultimately, liberalism promises to resolve this by guaranteeing liberty under the law, in the 'rule of law' which treats everyone equally.

Santos's 'pillar of regulation' consists in three separate principles: one is

---

[6] See e.g. Anthony Arblaster, *The Rise and Decline of Western Liberalism* (Oxford: Blackwell, 1984). This liberal ideology has nothing to do with party politics, but is the shared belief system of the major British political parties; it resembles a roundabout in perpetual motion—politicians may get on and off the dancing horses but the horses seem to gallop on round and round for ever.

[7] De Sousa Santos, *Toward a New Common Sense: Law, Science and Politics in the Paradigmatic Transition* (London: Routledge, 1995), 2.

the principle of the state, which consists in 'the vertical political obligation between citizens and state'; the second is the market, which refers to the 'horizontal self-interested or antagonistic political obligation between market partners'. The first is the place of the citizen, and the second, quite distinct, that of the landowner. (The third principle, which does not concern me until later, is the principle of community, which is also horizontal, but participatory rather than competitive like the market.)

To put it another way, people play various, apparently separate, roles in their lives, such as 'citizen' and 'home-owner', and these roles feel quite unconnected. In a person's sense of herself as the monthly tenant of a flat, she is more concerned about the landlady repairing the central-heating system than her right to a British passport. Similarly, a voter in a non-marginal constituency may care deeply about his effective disenfranchisement, but this seems to have nothing to do with what will happen if he fails to pay the mortgage.

It would have been fairly straightforward to write a chapter on 'squatters and citizens' at the boundary of land law, in relation to 'public order and land issues' such as New Age travellers or roads protesters—but this would not really be 'land law'. I wanted to discover what could be said about citizenship *within* the boundaries of the subject, even though at first sight it seems less promising terrain than rights of protest or freedom of movement on the highway and their relevance to participation in the state. I wanted to uncover something of the hidden public politics of private land law.

The general understanding in traditional land law would seem to be that the state's power is only tangentially relevant to rights in land: it matters only when a paper owner needs public enforcement of these private rights. When this does arise, land law itself withdraws from the issue because it is immediately translated into one of constitutional, tort, or criminal law. Thus, in the law of adverse possession, textbooks restrict themselves to a discussion of the limitation of the rights of the landowner, and, when the state is drawn in through questions of enforcement or policy, readers are automatically referred elsewhere, to constitutional texts on civil or human rights, or to the new criminal laws of trespass.

On the surface of things, the whole question of the politics of private land would appear not to have been voiced since the Levellers 300 years ago.[8] The relocation of such issues out of land law to other, more 'public', areas of law is part of the great achievement of modern academic law: the extraction of politics from the subject. Within the traditions of land law, questions of democracy and state power vanish beneath the black letters of the laws. Challenges to the status quo—whether or not successful—are swiftly diminished into footnotes to this real law and are presented as part

[8] See e.g. Hill, *The World Turned Upside Down: Radical Ideas during the English Revolution* (London: Martin Temple Smith, 1972).

of the natural and inevitable evolution of land law to its true and perfect condition.[9]

This traditional view of the 'unbroken development of land law' matches the 'countryside' home of the ideal landowner–citizen. It is a view of an unchanging and timeless idyll of rural England placed somewhere between the novels of Goldsmith and Dickens, between the painted landscapes of Constable and the poetic and musical ones of Wordsworth and Elgar. It is the home of folk dance and nursery rhyme and television's costume dramas. In the idyllic world of the land law textbook, both the law and the surface of the land barely change as time passes—the feudal farming strips are still visible, ancient boundary hedges mark out the old estates. As Anne Bottomley comments:

Real property books are characterised by a focus on landscape. Indeed landscape in the sense in which it is most often and most evocatively used in this country—rural. Other images could have been chosen . . . Instead the dominant iconography has utilised not only rural landscape but also the major English artists who have been themselves melded into a tradition of 'Englishness'.[10]

This is of course not unique to Land Law, but is shared by other kinds of knowledge, which tend to

transmute history itself into a seamless evolutionary continuum, endowing social institutions with all the stolid inevitability of a boulder. Society itself, in this view, becomes a marvellous aesthetic organism, self-generating and self-contained . . . the sense that history is less something you strenuously fashion than spontaneously transmit, a lineage powered by its own inscrutable autonomous laws.[11]

So, both citizenship and landownership, like the image of land law in the texts, inhabit a Garden of Eden in which the earth and the nation are united and unchanging. However, under the surface of the sunlit pictures lie the histories of great political struggles over the boundaries—histories which continue today even beneath the apparently settled ground of adverse possession. As Raymond Williams commented in regard to the eighteenth-century myth of the English countryside:

[9] Indeed, this is necessary: for modern law to inspire our trust it must appear to provide stability and continuity; and see below. See too De Sousa Santos, *Towards a New Common Sense*, 105: 'The Western legal tradition has . . . been marked by recurrent revolutions out of which new systems of law have emerged which, once established, negate or minimize the occurrence or the impact of the previous revolution.'

[10] Bottomley, 'Figures in a Landscape: Feminist Perspectives on Law, Land and Landscape', in Bottomley (ed.), *Feminist Perspectives on the Foundational Subjects of Law* (London: Cavendish Publishing, 1996), 109 at 117. See also Tomkins, 'Public Order Law and Visions of Englishness', in Bentley and Flynn (eds.), *Law and the Senses—Sensational Jurisprudence* (London: Pluto Press, 1996), 80, quoting, for example, Stanley Baldwin (p. 83).

[11] Eagleton, *Heathcliffe and the Great Hunger* (London: Verso, 1995), 4, 14, writing on parallels between the English view of land, the Irish people, and Charlotte Brontë's Heathcliffe.

a moral order is abstracted from the feudal inheritance and break-up and seeks to impose itself ideally on conditions which are inherently unstable . . . An idealisation, based on a temporary situation and on a deep desire for stability, served to cover and to evade the actual and bitter contradictions of the time.[12]

Similarly today: despite the image of timeless continuity, no boundary (either of the land or of the law or of the state) is for ever. State, law, and land are always changing. Each fence, case, or election is just a frozen moment, a snapshot of the surface which has changed as soon as the film has been exposed. As Williams concludes the first chapter of his book:

The life of country and city is moving and present: moving in time, through the history of a family and people; moving in feeling and ideas, through a network of relationships and decisions.

A dog is barking—that chained bark—behind the asbestos barn. It is now and then: here and many places. When there are questions to put, I have to push back my chair, look down at my papers, and feel the change.[13]

And today, I would add, it is the histories of different families and different peoples, and there are infinite networks of relationships and decisions in motion. An excavation beneath the surface of squatting and citizenship exposes many layers of life, and many possible futures.

THE IDEAL LANDOWNER

I am not going to repeat the rules of adverse possession here, nor analyse the cases in the usual way: textbooks do this very well in their fashion. Rather, I am going to use a few cases simply to show what the law of adverse possession *does*.

The Adverse Possessor

The analysis of adverse possession in textbooks and modern cases is based on a notional divide between body and mind, between what is done and what is thought. Thus, the first question which is supposed to be answered in adverse possession cases is, 'what did the adverse possessors do?' The second question is, 'what did they think about what they were doing?' (the *animus possidendi*). However, these separate questions are merely devices to help students understand and predict legal decisions. In reality, the human body and mind, actions and thoughts, are fully interdependent: interpretation of the one is dependent on an understanding of the other. An ambiguous action may be given unambiguous meaning when viewed in the light of the intention with which it is done, and the interpretation of an action

---

[12] Williams, *The Country and the City*, 45.   [13] Ibid. 7–8.

which appears to have an unequivocal meaning may be changed by the addition of a particular human will. On their own, neither actions nor intentions have any necessary meaning.

Precisely this kind of complexity lies at the core of adverse possession disputes. For example, *Littledale* v. *Liverpool College*[14] illustrates how an act which would normally be sufficient without any more to ground a claim to land may be reinterpreted in the light of an intention. Here, the would-be adverse possessor, Littledale, sought an injunction to prevent the College, the paper owner, from entering the disputed strip of land in Liverpool. The grassy strip of land connected Penny Lane to a field owned by Littledale. Littledale had a legal easement to cross the strip to get to his field, but now was claiming that he had become the owner of it because: 'Many years ago the plaintiffs [Littledale] or their predecessors put up two gates, one at each end of the strip of land in question, and they put locks on these gates, and they were kept locked until recently, when disputes arose. The plaintiffs . . . have kept the keys.'[15] An act of exclusion—fences, gates, keys—is usually the best proof of adverse possession. However, as Sir F. H. Jeune spelt out in the Court of Appeal:

I should have though that, when a man puts gates at each end of a strip of land and locks them, he has done as strong an act as he could do to assert his right to the ownership of the land. Such an act, which is, in fact, an inclosure, has always been held to be one of the strongest things that can be done to assert ownership. But when you find that the man who has done this has a right of way over the land . . . the erection of the gates and the locking and keeping them locked would appear referable rather to the exercise of the undoubted right of way than to acts of user such as to constitute dispossession.[16]

The analysis is thus much more complex than the two simple questions would suggest, for each item of evidence—whether actions or intentions—is to be weighed simultaneously with, and in relation to, all the others in order to decide whether there was an adverse possession. The real key to adverse possession lies not in discrete acts and intentions but in the effect of the claimant on the object of the claim (the land), and on the world beyond. As Carol Rose points out in relation to possession generally in the law:

Possession . . . means a clear act, whereby all the world understands that the pursuer has an 'unequivocal intention of appropriating . . . [the land] to his individual use . . . Possession as the basis of property ownership, then, seems to amount to

---

[14] (1900) 1 Ch. (CA).   [15] *Per* Lindley MR at 22.
[16] At 25–6. Lindley MR at 23 commented, 'I am myself convinced that the gates were put up, not to exclude the defendants, but to protect the plaintiff's right of way, and to prevent the public from going along the strip of land now claimed by the plaintiffs.'

something like yelling loudly enough to all who may be interested. The first to say, 'This is mine', in a way the public understands, gets the prize . . .[17]

It is clear, therefore, why 'exclusion of the world including the paper owner' is a crucial question: the successful adverse possessor must have kept out 'the world' in a way which demonstrated to everyone who might be interested that he was 'being an owner of the land'. Thus, in the *Littledale* case, if everyone had known of the right of way, they would not have assumed that the locked gates were an assumption of ownership and possession.

In some cases the padlocked gate has, of course, been definitive. In the current leading case, *Buckingham County Council* v. *Moran*[18] Slade LJ said:

On evidence it would appear clear by 28 October 1973 the defendant had acquired complete and exclusive physical control of the plot. He had secured a complete enclosure of the plot and its annexation to Dolphin Place [his own neighbouring land]. Any intruder could have gained access to the plot only by way of Dolphin Place, unless he was prepared to climb the locked gate fronting the highway or to scramble through one or other of the hedges bordering the plot. The defendant had put a new lock and chain on the gate and had fastened it . . .[19]

Similarly in *Williams* v. *Usherwood*,[20] the claimant relied partly on a fence and a gate which had not been merely locked but nailed up. In *Treloar* v. *Nute*,[21] too, fencing was an important element in the success of the claim:

In the summer of 1963, i.e. after the commencement of the limitation period, the defendant's father erected a fence along the western boundary of the disputed land. The plaintiff protested by letter dated August 14, 1963, and had the fence moved. The defendant's father re-erected it and it remains in position [thirteen years later].[22]

In *Boosey* v. *Davis*[23] however, the claimant adverse possessor's fence was less equivocal evidence of a loud yell of 'Mine!':

although in some cases the erection of a fence can be very significant, it seems to me that that was not so here. The fence was erected in order to reinforce a fence which had already been put there by the . . . [paper owner's] predecessors in title, and it did not in any event enclose the disputed land from Inglefield Road.[24]

This case illustrates also the importance of the stability and continuity of the claim. This is essential in the cry, 'This land is my land': the successful adverse possessor must have shown some serious commitment to the land

---

[17] Rose, 'Possession as the Origin of Property', 52 U. of Chicago L. Rev 73 at 81 (1985). She is dealing with the ownership of animals but the same principle holds for the possession of land.

[18] (1989) 2 All ER 225 (CA).

[19] Ibid., at 236.

[20] (1982) 43 P & CR 235.

[21] (1976) 1 WLR 1295 (CA).

[22] Ibid., at 1298.   [23] (1987) 55 P & CR 83.

[24] *Per* Lord Mustill at 87.

in question. Usually, this is through improving the land, visibly investing his labour and/or money in order to make it more productive or more convenient. In *Moran* the wasteland was adjoined to his carefully cultivated garden: 'They had incorporated it into the garden of Dolphin Place. They had planted bulbs and daffodils in the grass. They had maintained it as a part of that garden and had trimmed the hedges . . . It is hard to see what more he could have done . . .'.[25] In *Usherwood* again the court found sufficient improvement: 'In 1974, the defendants paved an area with decorative crazy-paving stones, at some expense, which went beyond any normal maintenance requirements, replacing the tarmacadam surface . . . this work clearly pointed to an assertion of exclusive possession.'[26] And in *Treloar*:

spoil taken from a well dug on land of the defendant's father to the south of the disputed land was placed in the gully, thus partially filling it up . . .

Much more important, in our view, is the change in the surface of the land by placing soil in the gully, thereby setting in train the levelling of the land upon which a bungalow could be built.[27]

In *Boosey* v. *Davis*, on the other hand, where the fencing had been held to be more ambiguous, the claimant failed also on the count of improving the land: 'Nor do I think that the cutting down of the scrub . . . add[s] very much. The cutting down of the scrub was merely to facilitate the minimal use by the goats—it was not for any wider purpose.'[28]

In *Ocean Estates Ltd* v. *Pinder*[29] the claimant had certainly worked hard for many years upon the land. However, he failed. He was claiming a large estate, in which he had worked different plots at different times:

from 1940 until the date of the hearing the defendant had cultivated and grown vegetables on various plots on the land, none of which had exceeded 20 acres. Between 1954 and 1956 he had also planted some fruit trees on part of the land. His system of farming vegetables was to clear a piece of land, grow vegetables on it for a year or 18 months, then give it up, let it go back to scrub and in due course return and clear the land and cultivate it again. According to the findings of the learned judge no single area of the land was cultivated by the defendant more than three times in the 27 years in which he carried on this peripatetic system of farming.[30]

Activities such as grazing animals (*Boosey*), or children playing,[31] also fail. This is because there is nothing out of the ordinary in it: the natural activities of animals or children do not send the required message of ownership. Similarly, merely living on the claimed land will not in itself ground a claim.

---

[25] (1989) 2 All ER 225 at 236.
[26] (1982) 43 P & CR 235 *per* Cumming Bruce LJ at 252.
[27] (1976) 1 WLR 1295 at 1297, 1300.   [28] (1987) 55 P & CR 83 at 87.
[29] (1969) 2 AC 19, PC.   [30] (1969) 2 AC 19 *per* Lord Diplock at 23.
[31] As in *Powell* v. *McFarlane* (1977) 38 P & CR 452.

In *Miller* v. *East Sussex County Council*,[32] a student squatting in a council flat and paying the rates and other bills and maintaining the property failed in his claim:

At no stage did the appellant attempt to assert a title or to exclude the representatives of the respondent from the premises . . . I do not have to decide this point (that is, the question of the existence of the necessary *animus*) but I think I would just have decided that there was not quite sufficient *animus possidendi* bearing in mind all the circumstances of this case.[33]

In *Pollard* v. *Jackson*,[34] however, a successful claim was based on a tenant's clearing out and cleaning up an upstairs flat which had been lived in by an elderly man (the claimant's landlord), and adjoining it to the downstairs flat:

Mr Bennett's condition at the latter part of his life was pretty squalid. The evidence was that Mr Jackson [the claimant] had tried to get various public agencies interested in the squalid state of the upper part of the property, but the Environmental Health Department took no action, so Mr Jackson burnt the clothes—'old rags, old cloth, crawling things, and nothing of value'. The judge commented: 'If his description is right—and I have no reason to doubt it—that was the most sensible thing he could have done.' Having done that, he cleaned the upper part of the property, and he and his family moved into it.[35]

Finally, a person described as a gypsy living in a caravan pitched in a corner of a large area of land has also been held not to be an adverse possessor of the occupied land. *In R.* v. *Environment Secretary ex p. Davis*[36] the claimant stated:

I submit that my openly moving onto the land and openly maintaining exclusive possession of it without interruption or acknowledging any one else's rights constitutes adverse possession . . . This is a God made Quarry not man made. And God has not told me to move off. [37]

She claimed a right of appeal as an owner of an interest in land against the planning authority. However: 'the Secretary of State was, in my judgement, entitled, indeed, right, to conclude that the applicant had not established adverse possession of her caravan pitch. She was not in fact in adverse possession but was a mere trespasser . . .'.[38]

Adverse Possessors, Squatters, and Trespassers

Strictly, there is no difference between the terms 'adverse possessor', 'squatter', and 'trespasser': all adverse possessors are squatters and all squatters are

[32] (1991) 26 April, unreported (CA).
[34] (1993) 67 P & CR 327.
[36] (1989) 59 P & CR 306.
[38] *Per* McCowan J at 314.

[33] *Per* Farquaharson LJ.
[35] *Per* Dillon LJ at 329.
[37] *Per* McCowan J at 308, 312.

trespassers. However, a closer look shows that there is a hidden hierarchy in the language: 'adverse possessors' are fairly respectable; 'squatters' may have some lingering rustic charm but their status, especially in an urban context, is somewhat ambivalent in the modern world;[39] 'trespassers'— 'sinners', after all—pose a direct threat to a modern civilized society. The first term is usually reserved for those who are likely to gain landownership through their activities, and the second for those less likely to win. 'Trespassers' is used to refer to the entirely undeserving users of other people's land: they are the ones who are—like Swampy, the Newbury road protester in his earth tunnels—hidden under the surface of land, relegated to criminal or constitutional law. The categories are not fixed, however, for the use of the different labels varies over time and place. One generation's trespasser is another's respectable citizen, as can be shown in the changing popular judgements on environmental or animal-rights activists.

Most successful 'adverse possessors' are already owners of land, and are trying to extend their boundaries: 'to them that hath . . .'. Examples of neighbours extending their boundaries include *Moran*, with his garden, *Williams* with his paved driveway, and *Treloar* with his filled-in gully. Also included here is *Pollard*, who was already a tenant of the downstairs flat when he took over the first floor. A number of cases have also already been cited where a stranger to the land tried and failed to get ownership: *Pinder* with his peripatetic farming, *Davis* with her caravan, *Boosey* with his goats, and *Miller* in the council flat. It is evidently easier for an existing landowner—providing he appears hard-working—to gain adverse possession of a neighbour's land than it is for a stranger.[40]

In addition, the existing landowner, whether he has made a mistake—to his own benefit—as to the extent of his boundaries, or has deliberately taken advantage of a neighbour's laxness, will find it easier to prove the necessary elements of adverse possession. Perhaps this is because he is already—clearly—a believer in permanent and exclusive individual occupation of land, and is used to shouting it loudly, while his neighbour is, for whatever reason, not shouting loudly enough.

The second term, 'squatters', includes people who are not neighbours: the have-nots who want to join the haves. By definition, they share the belief that permanent and individual exclusive possession of land is a Good Idea. However, the courts seem to be less sympathetic to their claims and it seems to be far more difficult for them to succeed. They are 'merely squatters', and may even be 'trespassers'—as in the *Davis* case.

[39] See e.g. Hardy and Ward, *Arcadia for All: The Legacy of a Makeshift Landscape* (London: Mansell, 1984), esp. 12.

[40] Of course, some neighbours fail, as in *Littledale* v. *Liverpool College* (1900) 1 Ch. 19 and, notoriously, *Wallis's Cayton Bay Holiday Camp Ltd.* v. *Shell-Mex and BP Ltd.* (1975) QB 94 (CA).

This term also includes others, those who *use* someone else's land but who do not necessarily want to become the 'owners' of it. Their message to the world says perhaps, 'I am here for the moment but I will be moving on'. In this category would fall the urban squatters of the 1960s and 1970s who agreed licences with local authorities for temporary housing. Traditionally gypsies and other travellers would also be included.[41] However, in the traditions of land law, travellers are always 'trespassers'. For example: 'Public concern has been particularly aroused where a trespass takes the form of occupation by a mass motorized convoy of squatters who swarm locust-like from the land of one innocent owner to that of another, or who invade ancient monuments . . .'.[42] The imagery of these motorized plagues of modern locusts threatening the peace of land law's idyllic rural landscape, or, worse still, of nomadic tribes who might desecrate some 'ancient monument', some essential part of 'our national heritage', indicates the level of the danger they apparently pose to the eternal truths of land law. Such seductive trespassing must be kept out.

The Ideal Landowner

The ideal landowner constructed by the laws of adverse possession is clearly no threat to civilized society. On the contrary, he is settled and stable, and honours both man-made and natural laws. His cultivation involves hard work. The sturdy figure of the ideal English landowner as reflected and maintained in adverse possession law invests his physical, intellectual, and emotional energies in the ground: he has entirely committed himself, through his engagement with the earth, to his plot of land. He wants to be a fixture in the landscape. He fences his land and locks his gates in order to exclude those who might detract from his hard labour—addressing the world outside as well as the land within his boundaries.

His moral justification is equally plain. He may be apparently 'stealing' land from his neighbour, but in practice he can do so only if the neighbour is a bad owner, a waster of the natural national resource. Clearly, he cares

---

[41] Sandlands 'The Real, The Simulacrum, and the Construction of "Gypsy" in Law', (1996) 23 JLS 383 at 385 argues that the legal term 'gypsy' 'is best understood as a projection of our own profound sense of ambiguity . . . a fantastical category invented within the sedentary population, which functions as a metaphor for the ambivalence with which such "civilized" societies regard themselves'. See too Shurmer-Smith and Hannam, *Worlds of Desire, Realms of Power: A Cultural Geography* (London: Edward Arnold, 1994), 149.

[42] Short, *Imagined Country*, 306. Tomkins ('Public Order Law and Visions of Englishness') quotes Anne Winterton MP, who described the groups at whom Conservative goverment public order legislation was directed as, 'hooligans, thugs, vandals and anarchists who, disguising their malice and anti-social tendencies with a thin cloak of compassion for animal welfare, delight in bringing havoc, injury and fear to . . . many law-abiding citizens . . .' (p. 83).

more for the country than the mere holder of a piece of paper; his possible small dishonesty is justified by his reliability as a natural guardian of English earth.

As already suggested, this mythical figure is yeoman, farmer, gardener. He plants, fertilizes, and ploughs the earth, keeps away the rabbits and vermin who would take advantage of his honest toil. Probably, he inherited the land from his father, who was himself the successor to generations of solid Anglo-Saxons. In the natural order of things, he harvests his wheat and milks his cows to provide his own bread and butter: self-sufficient to himself, he is beyond the influence of the trivial or transitory. He also takes his surplus to the market place, where he makes rational and self-interested contracts with others like himself. In this way, he also provides for his family, for those hidden behind his individual public face of ownership. He is a pillar of the community, the backbone of the country, the salt of the earth.

The qualities of this model owner match those of the possessive individual in the philosophy of John Locke, one of the founding thinkers of English liberalism in the seventeenth century. As Margaret Davies has stated: 'what the predominant paradigms of identity in law, property and personality emphasize are delimitation, exclusion of the other, the notion of essential properties, and mastery—of the self and of objects.'[43] The rational and self-interested property-owner from Locke's *Two Treatises*, who fences in the land and farms it well, is recognizable in the modern law of adverse possession, even in the apparently different worlds of *Moran's* daffodil garden or *Pollard's* flat.

Locke argued in revolutionary terms that land belonged to the cultivator and not automatically to the king: it was proper that it should be the property of the one who made the land more productive. This was naturally taken up by the accumulators of capital in, for example, the enclosures of common lands in the eighteenth century. As Short points out:

It is ironic that the typical English countryside, the supercharged image of English environmental ideology, which can still conjure up notions of community, unchanging values and national sentiments, is in reality the imprint of a profit-based exercise which destroyed the English peasantry and replaced a moral economy of traditional rights and obligations with the cash nexus of commercial capitalism . . .[44]

These same groups of people exported such values into 'un-owned' lands of empire. Both conquest and enclosure were said to be justified in Locke's

---

[43] Davies, 'Feminist Appropriations: Law, Property and Personality', (1994) 3 Social and Legal Studies 365 at 371. She parallels property, personality in law, and modern knowledge as sharing these characteristics, and as constructing as Other those who do not: primarily her Others are women, but of course many other Others must also be included as the dispossessed of property, personality, knowledge, and law.

[44] Short, *Imagined Country*, 67; also, it is 'a landscape which carries the imprint of power' (p. 71).

insistence on the moral understanding that gifts from God, including the earth itself, should be used and not wasted: increasing the productivity of land in this philosophy is not greed but Christian self-discipline: 'uncultivated or 'waste' land represented a failure to realize God's intentions that individuals should engage in productive labor.'[45]

In addition, it is explicit in Locke's justification of property, in his definition of the good landowner, that God's gift of the land should not be used in a way which left others hungry: some may be excluded from ownership, but should not therefore starve. Thus, the model moral cultivator would also look after his family, and will give to charity, especially to those whom he recognizes are like himself but have fallen on hard times through no fault of their own.

To summarize, therefore, the ideal English landowner is constructed through, and reflected in, cases on adverse possession. This mythical character, a rational and self-interested individual who invests in the land for profit, masters the earth, and bargains in the market place is a fixed feature of the timeless English countryside. The actions of successful adverse possessors reinforce the law's subterranean foundations in the ideology of private landownership, just as the judges maintain the fences on the surface of the ideology of ownership.

Not the Ideal Landowner

Every definition creates a boundary between those inside and those outside, even though, as in hard cases, the boundary may be somewhat opaque and even though it may on occasion be moved. From the foregoing discussion of adverse possession case law, it is clear who is 'inside' the ideal landowner: it may also be becoming clear who is 'outside'.

To take the first area of activity and exclusion: those who do not seek to make their mark on, to master, the landscape. As already suggested, the myth of the English countryside as the home of a 'simple, organic and classless society'[46] covers up the power struggle which produced the real landscape. It is implicit in the writing of Locke that the land belongs not to the workers on the land itself, the servants, but to their master. The ideal landowner is not a tenant or a member of the working class: he is an autonomous, independent figure.

Furthermore, in most cultures, the work of one sex is usually adjudged superficial, trivial, and transient—and thereby invisible: the farmer clears

[45] Ashcraft, 'Lockean Ideas, Poverty and the Development of Liberal Political Theory', in Brewer and Staves (eds.), *Early Modern Conceptions of Property* (London: Routledge, 1995), 43 at p.51; see also p. 162.

[46] Ching-Liang Low, *White Skins Black Masks: Representation and Colonialism* (London: Routledge, 1996), 18.

the forest and ploughs the field while the farmer's wife feeds the chickens and makes the butter—there is no nursery rhyme about the farmer's husband. Women's energies on the land are notoriously unrecognized by the law—for example, in cohabitation–constructive trusts cases—as well as by many husbands. Thus, his husband-ry gives him title to land while she plays at being the housewife.

At another level too, women are themselves merely the fertile earth which men own and seed, for women have been rather objects in the market place than its subjects. Also, the beauty of the English landscape is a reflection of the beauty of the 'virtuous Englishwoman': 'Wordsworth's landscape is beautiful because it provides "intercourse" between man and nature . . . Women, too, perform a similar function for Wordsworth; they are . . . the transparent medium through which the poet can reach a higher Self.'[47]

There are also others who walk outside the boundaries of the Masters of the Earth. The first imperialists, the explorers, set out to map the unknown world. In their charts, the world is simply a resource for their exploitation, a gold mine, so that the next generation, the settlers, can transport their little England to the new world:

> We wrought with a will increasing,
> We moulded, and fashioned and planned,
> And we fought with the black, and blazed the track
> That ye might inherit the land.[48]

In order to achieve this, some 'native' relations to the land had to be defined by the incoming settler as 'being owned' rather than 'owning'; more recently, this has been played out in stories like that concerning Western-style mining and aboriginal peoples in Australia.[49] Such native occupants of land, designated as non-owners by the sedentary farmers, are neither controlled by land nor seek to control it and so—like the Highlanders in Scotland—they had to be 'cleared off'. As Gail Ching-Liang Low comments in her analysis of the 'African' writings of Rider Haggard: 'The presence of the white man domesticates the wild country into a safe pastoral one; here a man may live and work like an original Adam, creating and refashioning an Eden—trapped in a time warp—to his own image.'[50]

[47] Grewal, *Home and Harem: Nation, Gender, Empire, and the Cultures of Travel* (London: Leicester University Press, 1996), 44, 33. See too Rose, *Feminism and Geography: the Limits of Geographical Knowledge* (Cambridge: Polity Press, 1993), ch. 5.

[48] Hudson, *Pioneers* (1908), quoted by Short, *Imagined Country*, 126. See too Pugh, *Geography II*, quoted in Lim and Green, *Cases and Materials in Land Law* (2nd edn., London: Pitmans Publishing, 1995), 27.

[49] See Short, *Imagined Country*, 129–30.

[50] Ching-Liang Low, *White Skins Black Masks*, 38. Also, for the natives invisible in the landscape, see p. 76.

It must be emphasized, therefore that it is not the mere fact of labour that differentiates the ideal landowner from all the Others—workers, women, and natives all work the land, but, as in the *Ocean Estates* case, it is the White Man's failure to notice the work at all, or his designation of it as 'peripatetic', which disqualifies it as a basis of ownership. As Rose comments:

We may enjoy nature and enjoy wildness, but those sentiments find little resonance in the doctrine of first possession. Its texts are those of cultivation, manufacture, and development. . . This may be a reward to useful labor, but it is more precisely the articulation of a specific vocabulary within a structure of symbols approved and understood by a commercial people . . .[51]

Mastery, therefore, is not just about work, but about class, sex, and race. It is also about sexuality: it is implicit in the myth that the ideal landowner is the father of a family. He appears in public as the owner of the land, and his wife, children, and servants (black and white) are hidden behind his title.

This issue of mastery, the perceived impact of the landowner on the land, leads to the question of the individual. The ideal landowner is clearly an individualistic human being with a unique and separate 'public' outward appearance concealing and excluding others from a 'private' inside. As Mark Wigley commented in relation to the early development of the architecture of the private house:

The first treatise on the interior of the body, which is to say, the treatise that gave the body an interior, written by Henri de Mondeville in the fourteenth century, argues that the body is a house, the house of the soul, which like any house can only be maintained as such by constant surveillance of its openings.[52]

This 'boundaried' individual in the modern world involves a particular sense of identity:

Graphically, the individual might be pictured as a closed circle; its smooth contours ensure its clear division from its location as well as assuring its internal coherence and consistency. Outside lies a vacuum in which objects appear within their own bubbles, self-contained but largely irrelevant to this self-sufficient ego. Will, thought, perception might be depicted as rays issuing outward to play over the surface of Objects, finally rejecting them in order to reaffirm its own primacy. Objects that are accepted are pulled in through the walls of the subject and assimilated, restoring the interior to homeostasis.[53]

Here again, women are largely excluded. Mondeville again: 'The woman's body is seen as an inadequate enclosure because its boundaries are convoluted.

---

[51] Rose, 'Possession as the Origin of Property', 88.

[52] Wigley, 'Untitled: the Housing of Gender', in Colomina (ed.), *Sexuality and Space* (Princeton: Princeton Architectural Press, 1992), 327 at 358.

[53] Kirby, 'Re: Mapping Subjectivity: Cartographic Vision and the Limits of Politics', in Duncan (ed.), *Body Space: Destabilizing Geographies of Gender and Sexuality* (London: Routledge, 1996), 45. See too her references to Luce Irigaray at p. 68.

While it is made of the same material as a man's body, it has been turned inside out. Her house has been disordered, leaving its walls full of openings . . .'.[54] It is the male body which is 'individual', for not only are women's bodies naturally and obviously divisible in reproduction, but also their lives are stereotypically connected with the needs of others. As a result, they do not necessarily live with a sense of separate identity and autonomy: 'Throughout the world, women generally don't *want*, they *need* or they *desire*, and this is why so many women's lives are seen to be such a curious mixture of mundane practicality, with no room for manoeuvre, and dreamy fantasy or petulant yearning.'[55]

The traditional stereotype of women, on the whole, thus has difficulty in coming within the definition of the individual, but here again the Woman is not the only one who is excluded, for outside the individualist boundary travel some surprising companions. Members of any group which prefers 'community' to individualism will find themselves outside the model of the ideal landowner. (It may be remembered here that the principle of community is the third separate principle of de Sousa Santos's 'pillar of regulation': it describes the 'horizontal, solidary, political obligation among community members and associations' as opposed to the hierarchical relations of citizen and state or competitive lateral relations of citizens with one another.[56])

Perhaps the most famous communal claimants of land in this country were the seventeenth-century 'Diggers, or True Levellers'. Their manifesto was to

lay the foundations of making the earth a common treasury for all . . . that everyone is born in the land, may be fed by the earth his mother that brought him forth . . . Not inclosing any part into a particular hand, but all as one man, working together and feeding together as sons of one father, members of one family . . .

As Gerard Winstanley, their spokesman, reaffirmed when the Diggers started work on the land: 'For the earth, with all her fruits of corn, cattle and such like, was made to be a common storehouse of livelihood to all mankind . . .'.[57]

Traditional ownership of land in Nigeria is also communal:

The cardinal principle of all customary land tenure in Nigeria is that land belongs to all the people . . . The right of access to land is based on the privilege of being

---

[54] Wigley, 'Untitled', 358.

[55] Shurmer-Smith and Hannam, *Worlds of Desire*, 120.

[56] De Sousa Santos, *Toward a New Common Sense*, 2. He sees the current imbalance between 'regulation' and 'emancipation' to be resolved in part by elevating to greater significance the principle of community.

[57] Both quotations are taken from Partridge, 'Enclosures, Clearances and the Diggers', in Girardet (ed.), *Land for the People* (London: Crescent Books, 1976), 62 at 66.

a member of the family or community. As was stated by the West African Lands Committee, 'Land belongs to a vast family of whom many are dead, a few are living, and countless numbers are still unborn.'[58]

The shared interests of other families or tribes are also to be rendered invisible in land law. The old aristocracy of land in England, in which land and family are united through the continuing generations, share this philosophy of community rather than individual ownership, but they too have been a threat to a civilized use of land.[59]

Many travellers too may be excluded from the ideal by their lack of individual self-interest. Such occupiers of land are often interested only in use of the land for a time, threatening the committed work ethic of the settled farmers, and it is in part this threat which recent public order legislation reacted against.[60] In addition, temporary occupants may not mind sharing the land with others: the individual for them may be merely one element of a close and cooperative community in which the concerns of that community are supreme. But, in the world of the landowner there is only one owner: the farmer whose woman, children, and servants are hidden beneath the surface.

Finally, the ideal landowner is the rational man who trades in the market. Some native peoples, and white women, as well as children, have been defined out of rationality. In different imperial territories, for example, some 'natives' were shut out of rationality by orientalism, and in others by 'naturalizing'; Donna Haraway refers to the way that, in Africa, 'the form of intellectual colonialism is in terms of the primitive',[61] and Kobena Mercer writes of 'the logic of dehumanization in which African peoples were defined as having bodies but not minds'.[62]

As Genevieve Lloyd concludes in relation to women:

It is not a question simply of the applicability to women of neutrally specified ideals of rationality, but rather of the genderization of the ideals themselves. An exclusion or transcending of the feminine is built into past ideals of Reason as the sovereign human character trait . . .[63]

---

[58] Yakubu, *Land Law in Nigeria* (London: Macmillan, 1985), 6.

[59] See Offer, *Property and Politics, 1870–1914: Land Ownership, Law, Ideology and Urban Development in England* (Cambridge: Cambridge University Press, 1981).

[60] See Tomkins, 'Public Order Law and Visions of Englishness'.

[61] Haraway, 'Shifting the Subject', in Bhavnani and Phoenix (eds.), *Shifting Identities, Shifting Racisms: A Feminist and Psychology Reader* (London: Sage, 1994), 19 at 30.

[62] Mercer, *Welcome to the Jungle: New Positions in Black Cultural Studies* (London: Routledge, 1994), 138.

[63] Lloyd, *The Man of Reason: 'Male' and 'Female' in Western Philosophy* (London: Methuen, 1984), 37. See too Gatens, *Feminism and Philosophy: Perspectives on Difference and Equality* (Cambridge: Polity Press, 1991).

One may add, it is also the racialization of the ideals, and the transcendence of other races, which is built into the very notion of rationality.

Thus, to summarize: the ideal English landowner in the law of adverse possession appears in more material detail. He is an adult Anglo-Saxon male, and at least of average mental and physical competence. He is the heterosexual father of the family. He sees himself as a free and rational individual who makes a permanent mark on the world.

THE CITIZEN

Citizenship

The 'citizen' has a long history in both political and sociological theory in the West: 'Out of . . . [the] alliance of the state with capital, dictated by necessity, arose the national citizen class, the bourgeoisie in the modern sense of the word.'[64] Essentially, the concept originates from a particular view of the nature of a human being. For example: 'There is probably no other idea in human history which combines the aspiration of man's need for equality and man's desire for liberty as does that of citizenship.'[65] Thus here again are de Sousa Santos's two pillars of the modern world, regulation and emancipation: the modern citizen enjoys his freedoms under the rule of law.

The standard analysis of citizenship in Britain was provided by T. H. Marshall in the middle of this century.[66] On the basis of this, and—again, following Deleuze and Guattari—asking the question, 'What does citizenship do?', the concept can be viewed as a gate in the fence around the nation which admits certain people to certain sets of rights—and excludes others. These sets of rights, and the groups admitted or excluded, vary over time. In the seventeenth and eighteenth centuries, according to Marshall, citizenship was a qualification for the *civil* rights necessary for individual freedom—liberty of the person, freedom of speech, thought, and faith, the right to own property and to conclude valid contracts.[67] In the nineteenth century, it came to include *political* rights, including 'the right to participate in the exercise of political power, as a member of a body invested with political authority . . .',[68] while in the twentieth it extends to a range of

---

[64] Weber, quoted by Heater, *Citizenship: The Civic Ideal in World History, Politics and Education* (New York: Longman, 1990), 162.

[65] Dahrendorf, 'Citizenship and Beyond: The Social Dynamics', in Turner and Hamilton (eds.), *Citizenship: Critical concepts Volume I/II* (London: Routledge, 1994), 292 at 294. He also points out that citizenship is the 'institutional counterpart of rationality . . . the crystallization of rationality into a social role' (p. 294).

[66] Marshall, *Class, Citizenship and Social Development* (London: Greenwood Press, 1964).

[67] Ibid. 71.   [68] Ibid. 72.

social rights, from the 'right to a modicum of economic welfare and security to the right to share in full in the social heritage and to live the life of a civilized being according to the standards prevailing in society'.[69]

At the end of the twentieth century it is the third range of rights which is in contention: in simple terms, politics centres around the assumption that (good) citizens are entitled to benefits and the others (scroungers) must be locked out. There is a similarity here with the law of adverse possession and its implicit categorization of claimants. Thus, adverse possessors parallel acceptable entrants into the territory, those who are going to increase the cultivation of the nation—some athletes leap to mind. Then there are those who are somewhat less desirable but who retain associations which make them barely acceptable—the squatters, parallel to refugees, or, now, 'asylum-seekers'. At the bottom of the heap lie the trespassers, the undesirables, aliens to be kept out or removed at the first opportunity.

From a legal perspective, the state operates as an ideal landowner, maintaining the boundaries and at the same time improving the productivity and cultivation of the land.[70] As de Sousa Santos suggests: 'the control over national boundaries as a major prerogative of territorial sovereignty has been growing steadily since the mid-nineteenth century as a central dimension of the consolidation of the nation-states and of the modern interstate system.'[71]

Indeed, in the UK, the concept of citizenship has been employed directly to control access and settlement, so that, as Ann Dummett remarks, 'Since 1962, immigration law and nationality law have been so closely and confusingly entangled that it is difficult to describe them separately'.[72] A highly complex series of statutes has used the concept of the citizen as the base on which to construct a range of categories which are supposed to guarantee various rights of entry or abode to some, and to exclude others.

Even the most cursory glance through the texts demonstrates that the tendency throughout the legislation, both primary and secondary, has been to ensure that certain groups retain their rights of access and abode and that other groups are excluded. The very first immigration control, the Aliens Act 1905, did not yet adopt the concept of citizenship as a tool for ensuring border control, but was designed to keep out those who did not own property: only those travelling by the cheapest means and arriving in

---

[69] Ibid. Cf. the Hayek view of citizenship, as explained for example by Barron and Scott, 'The Citizen's Charter Programme', (1992) 55 MLR 526 at 535–7.

[70] For details, see e.g. Heater, *Citizenship*, 103.

[71] De Sousa Santos, *Toward a New Common Sense*, 305.

[72] Dummett, 'Immigration and Nationality', in McCrudden and Chambers (eds.), *Individual Rights and the Law in Britain* (Oxford: Oxford University Press, 1995) 335 at 341. In other jurisprudential traditions, the concept of citizenship and citizens' rights are fundamental to the written constitution.

certain ports were to be kept out. Subsequent legislation has restricted the access of the inhabitants of former imperial territories and those relying on a maternal connection with the 'mother country' by requiring a link between the would-be entrant and the UK either by place of birth or by paternal inheritance. Thus, the Immigration Act 1971 laid down a test of 'patriality' which would entitle only some 'British subjects' to a right of abode in the UK; it was limited to those born in the UK or whose father or grandfather had been born in the UK.[73]

Although the 1981 Immigration Act abolished the concept of patriality, its effects have remained embedded in the new law. In addition, some of the more detailed provisons of the later Act have continued the tradition of a discriminatory law of citizenship. The long-standing discrimination between husbands joining wives with a right of abode, and wives joining husbands,[74] was notorious, like the rule that a man could give citizenship to his spouse by marriage, but a woman could not. There are other examples too. For instance, within the definition of a 'head of household' for the purposes of special voucher entry from Hong Kong, a male must simply be over 18, while a female must be over 18 *and* single or married to a man who has some medical disability which prevents his being the head of household.[75] Another example can be found in the rules relating to deportation: the wife and children of a male deportee can be deported with him, but only the children of a female deportee can be deported with her; her spouse is immune.[76]

More recently in Britain, citizenship has been adopted as a political device to legitimate the privatizing of the public sector. As Ann Barron and Colin Scott point out, the citizen is becoming a consumer, a paying customer for state services, who—in a new, private social contract—has some sort of entitlement to redress for a breach of 'charter': 'the achievement of contemporary New Right thinking has been to reinterpret the identity of the citizen in terms of the capacity to own and exchange property, and to reduce the rights of the citizen to one: the right to buy.'[77] Thus, the citizen is explicitly now conceptualized as the Man of Contract. However, as Barron and Scott point out, 'the precise legal status of these documents [charters] is difficult to ascertain. Formally, they are of no legal effect . . . '.[78]

---

[73] See Supperstone and O'Dempsey, *Immigration: The Law and Practice* (London: Longman, 1994), ch. 2.

[74] In *Abdulaziz, Cabales and Balkandali* v. *UK* [1985] 11 EHRR 459 the European Court of Human Rights found that rules which made it harder for a woman than a man to join her/his spouse were discriminatory and unlawful.

[75] See Supperstone and O'Dempsey, *Immigration*, 193.

[76] Dummett, 'Immigration and Nationality', 352.

[77] Barron and Scott, 'The Citizen's Charter Programme', 545.   [78] Ibid. 529.

Clearly, it is easier for a property-owning adult white male to qualify for the 'best' kind of citizenship, which entitles the holder to enter and live in the country, than it is for anyone else. Equally, as shown above, this white man is the epitome of the rational citizen wielding his charter of rights. However, although, in law, citizenship may be used as the test of the right of access and abode, and it may have been at the centre of the Conservative government's attempts to legitimate privatizations, nevertheless, for the many (white) people who have never had to argue about their right to enter the country at Heathrow the question of citizenship seems to have become an irrelevancy, less important than the mortgage interest rate or the national lottery.

The Ideal Citizen

As already suggested, in popular understandings the term 'citizen' (like 'adverse possessor' in law) is a positive one: there may be bad citizens around, but the language admits only adjectives to describe the good—active, upright, God-fearing: 'the ideal good citizen must be a paragon of multiple virtues, who brings to the fore different qualities according to circumstances . . . loyalty, responsibility and respect for political and social procedural values . . .'.[79]

St Just's famous comment contains many of the features of the ideal citizen: 'If each person comes out of his cottage with a rifle in his hand, the *patrie* will be saved . . .'.[80] The late twentieth century equivalent of this is perhaps the 'cricket' test of citizenship propounded by 1980s Conservatives: the good citizen is one who comes out to support the English cricket team.

However, at a deeper level, the citizen *is* the soldier, ready to defend family and nation. He is an able-bodied man, tied to the land, for his blood is nourished by English earth (*Natio* is the goddess of birth and origin). In the national mythology, if the English soldier dies abroad, 'there's some corner of a foreign field That is forever England.' The law of nationality too relies on genetic inheritance, as in the 1971 invention of 'patriality' as a means of indirectly discriminating on racial grounds. Inherited religious ties are also significant—Roman Catholics struggled for centuries to achieve political citizenship with the vote, and Muslims are still suspected by some of a divided loyalty.

However, not only inheritance but also an individual's permanence and stability are important: 'Citizenship is a relationship between an individual and a state involving the individual's full political membership in the state

[79] Heater, *Citizenship*, 193: the good citizen is he who queues?

[80] Quoted by Leca, 'Individualism and Citizenship', in Turner and Hamilton (eds.), *Citizenship: Critical Concepts Volume I*, 148 at 173.

and his *permanent* allegiance to it . . . the status of citizen is official recognition of the individual's integration into the political system.'[81] Thus, the ideal citizen is evidently male, able-bodied, and permanent, without any religious or other deviations from his inherited loyalty to the Crown. He can trace close links between his blood line and the land. Furthermore, he is a property-owner, for it is *his* cottage from which he runs with *his* rifle. As a property-owner, the ideal citizen is also necessarily—as in the Citizen's Charter of the 1990s—a rational contract-maker. However, the citizen is not just any old property-owner: the old direct link between real property and citizenship may have been untied legally by the successful struggles for the franchise, but it remains beneath the surface. This is because:

Civic virtue and public action were shown to be founded on the ownership of land, which ensured independence and responsibility. The interests of the whole country could best be directed by those not in the pocket of the financier and by those far removed from commercial operations based upon credit and speculation . . .[82]

As Lawrence E. Klein also points out:

land was seen as a form of wealth that insured the reliability of the owner. The permanence of land and its tangible reality were a guarantee of the owner's commitment to the nation since his wealth was physically a part of the nation . . . Second, the fact that land was physically part of the nation meant that the land owner's wealth was entirely of a piece with the security and well-being of the nation. The landowner was ineluctably drawn to consider his own interests in the context of the interest of the nation as a whole.[83]

Thus, the ideal citizen *is* traditionally the same person as the landowner: the man with a fixed stake in the country, for any other property-owner could pick up his money and run. Today, this connection between good citizenship and land has also been employed in reverse: twentieth-century government has encouraged landownership, since it makes for permanence, reliability, and hard work, the required qualities of good citizenship.

The landowner and citizen are, therefore, not merely different expressions of the same underlying understanding of the nature of the human being, but are linked by the way in which the cultivation of English agricultural land constructs a human character. The moral and physical character of both landowner and citizen are formed by the necessities of work on the land: the civilized person today is he who cultivates and is cultivated by English land.

---

[81] Murray Clark Haven quoted by Heater, *Citizenship*, 246 (emphasis added).

[82] Raven, 'Defending Conduct and Property: The London Press and the Luxury Debate', in Brewer and Staves, (eds.), *Early Modern Conceptions of Property*, 301 at 305.

[83] Klein, 'Property and Politics in the Early Eighteenth Century Whig Moralists: The Case of *The Spectator*', in ibid. 221 at 223.

As in the case of the ideal landowner, the boundary around the ideal citizen has been drawn by those on the inside, largely in response to the military and economic needs of the nineteenth- and early twentieth-century nation state. And, again, it is fairly easy to recognize the ideal citizen: the soldier, whose forebears probably fought at Agincourt, and who is ready to pick up his rifle and run into battle to defend his country, land, and family. As the needs of the nation state change, citizenship may have become more inclusive on the surface, but immigration law ensures that the 'real citizen' is more likely to be a white male property-owner.

Not the Ideal Citizen

Since the landowner and the citizen now appear as the same person, clearly the same groups of people tend to be excluded from both. Those who are—at least in relation to the ownership or use of land—more interested in the social than the individual, and those who are defined as irrational, are all 'outside': women, 'natives', and children and others who cannot or will not fight are likely to be outside the notion of citizenship.

Those defined as transitory in particular must be kept out; anyone who seeks to move from one country to another is, by definition, suspect:

A person who resides in a society for a particular purpose, and who must depart from it once his business there is concluded, is not a *citizen* of that society but only a temporary subject. A person who makes his home there, but does not partake of its rights and privileges, is similarly not a *citizen* . . . Women, young children and servants are only granted the title as members of the family of a citizen properly so-called; they are not true *citizens* themselves . . .[84]

Women have always been vulnerable to exclusion for their nomadism. Traditionally, they moved at marriage to their husband's home, they gave up their name and took his, and even their children were his children: 'In lineage, descent, the patrilineal system, inheritance, the monarchy, succession to title and nobility, men define the family. There is a nexus of masculinity, authority, the bloodline, *pater familias*, public representative of the family . . .'.[85] Thus, as Carole Pateman concludes:

Women . . . are incorporated into the civil order differently from men . . . Women have never been completely excluded from participation in the institutions of the public world—but women have been incorporated into public life in a different manner from men. Women's bodies symbolize everything opposed to political

---

[84] Diderot, 'Citoyen', in Turner and Hamiton (eds.), *Citizenship: Critical Concepts Volume I*, 318.

[85] O'Donovan, 'A New Settlement Between the Sexes? Constitutional Law and the Citizenship of Women', p. 243 in Bottomley (ed.), *Feminist Perspectives on the Foundational Subjects of Law*, 243 at 252.

order, and yet the long and often bitterly contested process through which women have been included as citizens has been structured around women's bodily (sexual) difference from men.[86]

To summarize then, the landowner and the citizen are the same person and he is the White Man who rules at the centre of his boundaried world. Only those who most nearly match the model's patrial blood ties to the land, and its capacity for rational contract-making will enjoy the benefits of 'real citizenship'. The English cricket test tends to exclude from participation in civil, political, and social rights many so-called citizens who choose to support a team whose origins match their sense of a home where they are not treated as second-class human beings, as well as those many other 'citizens' who do not, or are not allowed to, enjoy 'English boys' games'.

THE FUTURES

My aim in this chapter has been to dig beneath the surface of land law in order to expose the connections between a mortgage and a vote, a tenancy and a passport, by enquiring, 'What does the law of adverse possession do?' I wanted to think of the law of adverse possession differently, to open up a new space in land law, because 'unauthorized but perfectly possible readings open the possibility of new forms of living'.[87] In the course of my excavation I have also exposed three less frequently observed features of adverse possession:

1. adverse possession is not just about questions of 'action plus intention', but concerns a cry of 'I possess the land' to the world;
2. adverse possessors are more likely to succeed if they are neighbouring landowners;
3. 'adverse possessor' is the label judges give to likely successful claimants of land through long use; 'squatters' are less likely to win their cases; 'trespassers' will lose.

Private land and public politics may seem to operate in separate spheres but they are united beneath the surface: to misquote Bentham, 'Land ownership and citizenship were born together . . .'. As land and nation are indivisible, so too are landownership and citizenship, and, to the extent that non-owners/non-citizens are more likely to be excluded from the one, they are also more likely to be excluded from the other. The connection between the two is necessarily invisible: neither landownership nor citizen-

[86] Pateman, *The Disorder of Women* (Cambridge: Polity Press, 1989), 4.

[87] Douzinas and Warrington, *Justice Miscarried: Ethics, Aesthetics and the Law* (Brighton: Harvester Wheatsheaf, 1994), 309.

ship may be allowed to become popular political issues, for the prevailing liberal ideology, through the public/private divide, must conceal the links between property and state in order to legitimate the accumulation of capital. It also conceals sex, class, race, and postcolonial politics in order to ensure that there is no disturbance of the particular understanding of the human being which justifies capital's circulation.

And this is not merely history: the ideal types are daily at work in the law, silently excluding other ways of having and being than that of the possessive individualist. The rule of law may promise equality of treatment to all, but many are still treated unequally. Beneath the surface of formal equality, the actions and intentions of women, children, 'natives', homosexuals, and others are kept out of the underlying models, and are more likely to be locked out of ownership and citizenship. Even when the rules are changed to allow entry to members of a previously excluded group, the stereotype ensures that they are included only to the extent that they can pretend to fit the mould.

Landownership and citizenship thus have long been two sides of the same coin of membership of the political world. It may be that liberal land law can continue its success in keeping its excluded classes hidden beneath the surface, civilizing—'citizenizing'—its subjects by the dead hand of the mortgage in the same way as English fields are cultivated by English farmers. However, excluded outsiders are now becoming more visible in relation to citizenship:

> Modern issues in citizenship will increasingly embrace the problems of stateless persons, and refugees, where the question of human rights in relation to citizenship will become highly problematic. In addition, it is difficult to isolate or separate the debate about global responsibility from the ecological crisis . . .[88]

Western history has mostly been written by the sedentary landowners, but, as Deleuze and Guattari suggested, we need a 'nomadology',[89] to hear the voices of those long silenced in the histories. When the stories of the non-landowners, non-citizens, are told and heard, then our understanding of the world changes, because nomads challenge the underlying stereotypes, and especially at the end of the Western millennium, a moment which inspires reflection on pasts and futures. Such millennial 'extra-consciousness' focuses more sharply many people's understanding of their own identity, including their sense of belonging to a particular community or place. Homi Bhabha, for example, identifies a particular 'sense of disorientation, a disturbance of direction'[90] which is accentuated by the feeling

---

[88] Turner and Hamilton (eds.), *Citizenship. Critical Concepts Volume I*, 9.
[89] Massumi, *A User's Guide*.
[90] Bhabha, *The Location of Culture* (London: Routledge, 1994), 1.

of accelerating change in the Western world. Linda McDowell makes a similar argument:

we have seen both a speeding up of the interconnections and new sets of configurations that connect spatial scales, particularly the global with the local in new and unexpected ways . . . What distinguishes the world at the end of the twentieth century is the transnational attenuation of 'local' space, and this breaking of space into 'discontinuous realities' which alters our sense of ourselves as individuals, members of various groups and communities, as citizens of a nation state . . . Men and women, divided or united by age, by class, or by beliefs, are differentially affected, and the links between identity and a sense of belonging to a particular territory or place are being remapped. [91]

When 'nomadology' exposes the 'citizen' as a limited and limiting model of the human being, there may be unforeseen repercussions on his counterpart, the ideal English landowner, for, to misquote Bentham again, 'Land ownership and citizenship are born together and die together.' What may change when old myths are brought into the light, and judges must decide new cases about environmental concerns or shared enterprises or city living? Above all, the globalizing city pushes at the boundaries of the notion of ideal landownership: as Williams pointed out, while the countryside looks back to a nostalgic harmonious past, the concept of the city looks forward to a future where anything may be built or moved.[92]

[91] McDowell, 'Spatializing Feminism: Geographic Perspectives', in Duncan (ed.), *Body Space*, 28 at 30, 38.
[92] Williams, *The Country and the City*, ch. 23.

10

HOMELESSNESS

David Cowan and Julia Fionda

English law recognizes no rights, fundamental or otherwise, which guarantee access to housing. No matter how needy a person, the housing welfare legislation of England and Wales does not allow automatic access to housing. That legislation is, and always has been, founded upon the distinction between the deserving and undeserving, not upon the basis of housing need.[1] The modern homelessness legislation, the Housing (Homeless Persons) Act 1977 and its successors, has required those administering it to make moral judgements, not about a person's housing need, but about why they became homeless in the first place.[2] Once it is acknowledged that there are differences of opinion as to why a person becomes homeless, one is halfway to appreciating the statutory mishmash that has been created.[3]

Until 1977 (and possibly even beyond this), state assistance penalized those who required it. For example, recipients of Poor Law relief at one time had to wear the letter ' "P" on the right shoulder of their uppermost garment'.[4] Even though the National Assistance Act 1948 abolished the old poor law, the ethic (as well as the dormitory-style accommodation) remained, as was exposed by the BBC play *Cathy Come Home*.

In the current homelessness legislation, the Housing Act 1996, part VII (hereafter 'the 1996 Act'), the deserving/undeserving distinction is

---

[1] We are using the word 'need' in an absolute sense here. We accept (for the purposes of this chapter) that need can be interpreted from a political perspective in line with the divide between the deserving and undeserving. In this latter sense, the Conservatives, no doubt, would have argued that single mothers had no housing 'need' but to do so sounds unnecessarily constraining (and dismissive).

[2] For further discussion of this, see Cowan, *Homelessness: The (In-)Appropriate Applicant*, (Aldershot: Dartmouth, 1997), ch. 2.

[3] There are, in fact, a number of statutory and quasi-statutory attempts purporting to formulate the principles, all of which are now in operation: the Housing Act 1996, part VII, (the homelessness legislation); the Children Act 1989, part III; LAC 93(10), under powers given to the Secretary of State by virtue of the National Health and Community Care Act 1990 (a replica of National Assistance Act 1948, s. 21(1)(b); National Assistance Act 1948, s. 21(1)(a); Asylum and Immigration Act 1996.

[4] Cranston, *Legal Foundations of the Welfare State*, (London: Weidenfeld & Nicolson, 1985), 35.

enforced through obstacles[5] over which the homeless must jump before they are able to access even short-term accommodation.[6] In order to access accommodation through the homelessness legislation, a person must be found to be (*a*) homeless, (*b*) eligible, (*c*) in priority need, and (*d*) not intentionally homeless.[7] Furthermore, the criteria governing the definitions of homelessness and intentional homelessness are specifically related to the supply and quality of accommodation.[8]

If there is little available accommodation in a particular area, people will be expected to occupy lower quality accommodation, often an insecure tenure such as a licence, and if they leave it they may not expect the state to assist them. The unfortunate starvation of local authorities[9] from building new housing since the 1970s, as well as the effects of various privatization initiatives over this period, have led one of the most respected commentators to describe the homelessness legislation as 'an exercise in legislative deceit'.[10] Put simply, there is insufficient available accommodation and this impacts harshly upon the implementation of the homelessness legislation.[11]

Our exploration of the issues begins by locating homelessness as one of the contexts of land law. Commonly ignored within land law teaching, we argue that this is an unfortunate omission, for homelessness provides a useful context for discussion. We go on to argue for a greater conceptual development of land law thinking to include the teaching of issues of access to accommodation for the marginalized. The following section analyses three overlapping causes of homelessness: structural factors created by housing

---

[5] This adopts the terminology used by writers considering the modern homelessness legislation in 1977: Watchman and Robson, 'The Homeless Persons' Obstacle Race' (1980) 2, Journal of Social Welfare and Family Law 1 (pt. 1), (1980) 2, Journal of Social Welfare and Family Law 65 (pt. 2).

[6] The 1996 Act enables successful applicants to access accommodation for a minimum period of two years (s. 193(3)).

[7] See below for discussion of these concepts.   [8] 1996 Act, s. 177(2).

[9] Local authorities are responsible for the interpretation of the homelessness legislation as well as being the providers of much of the accommodation to successful applicants.

[10] Loveland, *Housing Homeless Persons* (Oxford: Oxford University Press, 1995), 331. This also impacts upon the collation of statistics of homelessness in England and Wales. These statistics are drawn up on the basis of returns made to the Department of Environment by local authorities as to the numbers of people they have accepted as homeless. The result is that, paradoxically, a fall in the statistics can be more representative of a deeper housing crisis than the success of rehousing policies.

[11] The homelessness legislation enables local authorities explicitly to *ration* accommodation (see Lidstone, 'Rationing Housing to the Homeless Applicant', (1994) 9 Housing Studies 459); for a more theoretical analysis, see Carlen, 'The Governance of Homelessness: Legality, Lore and Lexicon in the Agency-Maintenance of Youth Homelessness' (1994) 41 Critical Social Policy 18. Carlen identifies bureaucratic or professional procedures which have the effect of deterring applicants, denying applicants, and disciplining applicants into withdrawing their status.

policy which hasten the downward spiral; precipitating factors, such as gender and race; and, finally, the theory that responses to homelessness paradoxically cause homelessness. We turn to the 1996 Act in our final section. That section first outlines some general perspectives on the new legislation, secondly considers how the various definitions are framed, and finally considers the results of some of the empirical investigations conducted into the administrative decision-making process. It is argued that often that decision-making bears little relation to the law. Two specific examples are used briefly to illustrate these points: violence to women; and children.

HOMELESSNESS AND LAND LAW

An Uncontroversial Approach

Homelessness is rarely taught within traditional land law courses.[12] An attempt to locate homelessness within a coherent structure for the teaching of land law was made by Professor Gray in the first edition of his important textbook on land law.[13] However, most other textbooks have tended to avoid the issue[14] or relegate it to footnote status.[15] Our purpose in this section is to remedy this deficiency, albeit briefly, by locating homelessness law as a context of land law.

In fact, this is not as ambitious as might have been anticipated. First, the indirect effect of much discussed in traditional courses is homelessness. The most obvious example of this would be mortgage repossession. At the height of the recession in the early 1990s when mortgage repossessions reached their zenith, it was no surprise that there was a commensurate increase in the numbers of people accepted as homeless.[16] Further, the breakdown of a relationship often leads to an order for sale of the accommodation, which might

[12] One possible rationale for this is that it forms a core part of Housing Law courses which often adopt a welfarist approach. Possibly also, land lawyers perceive homelessness law as fitting within the discourse of public law. Homelessness does, however, form part of the options within the land law course taught at King's College London; no doubt there are other exceptions.

[13] Gray, *Elements of Land Law* (1st edn., London: Butterworths, 1987), ch. 21. The chapter did not, however, appear in the second edition (1993), which was a disappointing (although, no doubt, justifiable within the constraints of the vast amount of material covered) omission.

[14] Texts in this category include MacKenzie and Phillips, *A Practical Introduction to Land Law* (6th edn., London: Blackstones, 1996); and, possibly more notably, Megarry and Wade, *The Law of Real Property* (5th edn., London: Stevens, 1984).

[15] See e.g. Burn, *Cheshire and Burn's Modern Law of Real Property*, (15th edn., London: Butterworths, 1994).

[16] The peak of homelessness acceptances came in the first quarter of 1992, during which 38,150 acceptances of families and single people were made.

cause homelessness (or at least an application by one or both parties as home-less).[17] The thin distinction between exclusive possession and non-exclusive possession also masks the distinction between property rights and impending homelessness as non-exclusivity enables speedier eviction.[18]

Land law also creates practical problems which can govern difficult questions surrounding the allocation of accommodation. One example of this is the well-known rule, enshrined in section 1(6) of the Law of Property Act 1925, that a minor cannot hold a legal estate. A minor cannot take a tenancy at law. There are, of course, methods of circumventing this problem, but it has undoubtedly created difficulties.[19] Furthermore, this was one of the reasons given by the Housing Minister in the debates leading to the Housing Act 1996 for excluding minors from priority categories governing allocation.

Finally, as might be expected, the homelessness legislation adopts and adapts principles of land law to its own ends. For example, part of the statutory definition of homelessness requires a person to have no accommodation which that person

(a) is entitled to occupy by virtue of an interest in it or by virtue of an order of a court,
(b) has an express or implied licence to occupy, or
(c) occupies as a residence by virtue of any enactment or rule of law giving him the right to remain in occupation or restricting the right of another person to recover possession.[20]

Those administering the homelessness legislation are often called upon to make the most difficult judgements as to whether a person does have an interest in property, as well as occasionally quantifying that interest. Most officers make these judgements without legal qualification.[21]

Developing Controversies

In contrast to the approach taken in the previous section, a more threatening stance should be adopted requiring land lawyers to justify the conceptual boundaries of their subject. If land law is the law about land, then it is inconceivable that land law should not cover issues of *access* to land. The

---

[17] For discussion, see Bull, *Housing Consequences of Relationship Breakdown* (London: HMSO, 1993).

[18] See e.g. the difficult case of *Westminster City Council* v. *Clarke* [1992] 2 AC 288, and Cowan, 'A Public Dimension of a Private Problem', [1992] Conveyancer 288.

[19] See e.g. Thornton, *The New Homeless* (London: SHAC, 1990), 44–7; Goss, 'Can Children be Tenants of their Homes?', (1996) May Childright 5.

[20] Housing Act 1996, s. 175(1).

[21] See Loveland, *Housing Homeless Persons*, 131—only two out of the forty officers in that study had legal qualifications.

creation of rights in land is often covered only through a consideration of the boundaries between property and personal rights. In doing so, we (as land lawyers) mislead our students into believing that issues of access are routine matters which are outside the domain of land law.

Put another way, land lawyers concern themselves with the 'included' and not the 'excluded'. Land law is a subject where we consider the rights of the included, as consumers, but those unable to consume do not feature. The challenging notion of 'citizenship', which might be defined in this context as 'the ability to consume',[22] assists us in our appreciation of a more radical approach. This preoccupation with consumerism is at odds with the more traditional socialist view of citizenship as social inclusion—a preoccupation with the welfare of the most marginalized and poverty-stricken in society in order to ensure their inclusion in the mainstream of society; that is, empowerment through social unity.[23]

In recent years the consumerist view of citizenship was resurrected under the Thatcher regime. A welfarist view of citizenship threatened the government's commitment to creating an enterprise culture in which, in theory, social equality could be achieved through the equality of opportunity for each citizen to strive to maintain their own wealth. Trying to achieve economic and social equality through a redistribution of wealth, via a welfare system which offered handouts to those unable to fend for themselves, was not only at ideological cross-purposes with this ideal, but could even be counter-productive. Welfare benefits were seen as anathema to the enterprise culture because they encouraged dependency and discouraged self-sufficiency.[24]

A more thematic, political, and ideological approach to land law is within our grasp. If we develop land law through the notion of citizenship, we should automatically also consider the non-citizens or those who are seeking to participate in the benefits of citizenship. Within this approach, the causes of—and responses to—homelessness, rather than being part of the context of land law, become a central focus. Then the aim of land law is not

---

[22] This might be derived from, for example, the approach of *The Citizen's Charter* (London: HMSO, 1991)—note the individualization of the Citizen through the apostrophe—which discussed citizenship in the context of the relationship between the individual and the state by reference to the quality of public services, choice between competing providers of public services, expected minimum standards of public services, and efficiency in their provision.

[23] Peter Mandelson touched on this idea when he outlined New Labour's plans to eradicate social exclusion: 'Our vision is to end social exclusion. Our priority is to redirect and reform social programmes and the welfare state towards that goal. Our strategy is to build a broad ranging political consensus for action' ('Labour's Next Steps: Tackling Social Exclusion', unpublished lecture to the Fabian Society, 14 Aug. 1997).

[24] Loney, 'A War on Poverty or on the Poor?', in Walker and Walker (eds.), *The Growing Divide: A Social Audit 1979–1987* (London: Child Poverty Action Group, 1989).

to provide students with the law of land but to provide them with a comprehensive analysis of the forces of social inclusion and social exclusion.

CAUSES OF HOMELESSNESS

In past centuries, many believed that homelessness was a result of fecklessness and personal inadequacy. Responses were therefore harsh and punitive. This view also permeated the response to homelessness provided by the National Assistance Act 1948. However, a series of influential reports in the early 1970s provided alternative rationales.[25] There are at least three other current rationales explaining why people become homeless. These relate, first, to the consequences of *structural* inequalities in housing; secondly, to the fact that inequalities in society act as *precipitating* causes; and, finally, to the view that any response to homelessness encourages people to make themselves homeless in order *to (ab-)use the legislation*. We shall outline and analyse each in turn.

Structural Causes

The first is that homelessness is a result of structural inadequacies and imbalances in the housing market which particularly affect lower socio-economic groups—these have been termed structural causes of homelessness.[26] Bramley provides the following list:

- demographic change, especially greater household formation due to age structure and fission, including rising rates of divorce and relationship breakdown;
- the rising cost of housing and problems of access and affordability, particularly in high demand regions (London and the South) in the late 1980s;
- greater economic inequality in terms of both income and wealth over the 1980s;
- the continued decline of the private rented sector;
- the diminished supply of social rented lettings and lowered access through traditional waiting list channels;

[25] Greve, Page, and Greve, *Homelessness in London*, (Edinburgh: Scottish Academic Press, 1971); Central Housing Advisory Committee, *Council Housing Purposes, Procedures and Priorities*, (London: HMSO, 1969); Seebohm, *Report of the Committee on Local Authority and Allied Personal Social Services*, Cmnd. 3703 (London: HMSO, 1968). Each of these reports argued that homelessness was essentially a housing problem.

[26] Carlen, 'The Governance of Homelessness'.

- changed attitudes and expectations, particularly with regard to living separately, among certain groups or society generally.[27]

This is not the place to provide a broad sweep of housing and social policy.[28] However, some extrapolation is essential in order to appreciate these structural causes.

At the outbreak of the First World War, 90 per cent of the population rented privately in some form or other. However, in 1997, only about 10 per cent remain in this tenure. The major explosion has been in the form of home-ownership—now accounting for about 70 per cent[29]—whilst local authority tenure increased from 2 per cent in 1913 to 32 per cent in 1979 and has reduced to around 20 per cent in 1997. There have been dramatic movements in housing tenure which have had a concomitant effect on the supply of low-cost housing. For many, home-ownership is out of the question, or the reason why they have become homeless in the first place (for example, as a result of mortgage arrears—'the new poor').[30]

The reasons for the overall decline in the market share of private renting have been subjected to rigorous analysis within the housing studies movement,[31] and a number of different factors have contributed to this downslide. For example, the impact of increased taxation of residential rental income, decreased subsidies and allowances, increased security of tenure including rent control until 1988 (under, for example, the Rent Act 1977), together with the more recent unattractiveness of being known as a 'landlord' have all been cited as causes. Basically, renting was not a sound investment for potential landlords. Further, low interest rates together with individual subsidies in the form of mortgage tax relief strengthened the desire to own property. There are more general influences, as Malpass and Murie argue: 'The decline of [private renting] reflects its economic obsolescence in the twentieth century . . . Private renting can be seen as giving way to home ownership as a form of housing provision that is more appropriate to the capitalism of the twentieth century.'[32]

[27] Bramley, 'Explaining the Incidence of Statutory Homelessness in England' (1993) 8 Housing Studies 128 at 129.

[28] See, further, Malpass and Murie, Housing Policy and Practice (Basingstoke: Macmillan, 1994); Balchin, Housing Policy: An Introduction, (London: Routledge, 1995); Pascall, Social Policy: A New Feminist Analysis (London: Routledge, 1997) esp. ch. 5; Williams (ed.), Directions in Housing Policy (London: Paul Chapman, 1997).

[29] See Malpass and Murie, Housing Policy and Practice (Macmillan); Balchin, Housing Policy.

[30] We do not propose to discuss this further, as this volume already contains a chapter on mortgage repossession (see Chapter 7).

[31] See e.g. Kemp, 'The Ghost of Rachman', in Grant (ed.), Built to Last (London: Roof, 1992); Crook, 'Private Rented Housing and the Impact of Deregulation', in Birchall (ed.), Housing Policies in the 1990s (London: Routledge, 1992); Crook and Kemp, 'The Revival of Private Rented Housing in Britain' (1996) 11 Housing Studies 51; for a less contextual approach, see Balchin, Housing Policy, 92–5.

[32] Malpass and Murie, Housing Policy and Practice, 14.

The statutory regime governing private rented accommodation developed in the Housing Act 1988 and extended by the 1996 Act relies on free-market principles.[33] There is little rent control, and security is commonly granted only for six months. The private rental market has slightly increased its tenure size since the adoption of this approach, although it is unclear whether this is a result of deregulation and decontrol (exemplified by the Housing Act 1988) or whether this was a temporary stopgap during recession.

Deregulation and decontrol have meant higher rents and higher rental deposits. Initially, a form of direct subsidy, housing benefit, was meant 'to take the strain', but two problems have resulted, illustrating the oft-repeated comment in newspaper letting advertisements 'No DSS'.[34] First, there is now a considerable body of literature which suggests that many landlords do not wish to let their properties to recipients of housing benefit, or to the home-less—to do so appears to be a last resort.[35] Secondly, changes in housing benefit regulations in the 1990s, imposing ceilings on the applicable payment (on the basis of shared accommodation) for the under 25s as well as payment now being made in arrears, are likely to have a significant impact. All of these factors operate to exclude many from private rented accommodation.

The increasing numbers marginalized from the private sector therefore need to rely on the public sector (local authorities) and quasi-public sector (registered[36] social landlords, formerly known as housing associations). The rise and fall of public sector housing has been well documented.[37] It has been argued that housing was the weakest link in public sector provision and, therefore, ripe for Thatcherite reforms.[38] So, for example, until 1980,

[33] The market, however, depends on housing benefit being granted. Attempts to control the upward spiral of housing benefit through local authority rent assessment officers have been an implied control on market value (see Crook and Kemp, 'The Revival of Private Rented Housing in Britain').

[34] In the *Bristol Evening Post*, 9 Sept. 1997, twenty-six private advertisements of proper-ties to let were available only to students (who are not entitled to benefit), 'professional per-sons', or explicitly said 'no DSS'; three included the phrase 'DSS welcome'; twenty-four offered no preference (although twelve of these included rents over £500).

[35] Kemp and Rhodes, *Private Landlords in Scotland* (Edinburgh: Scottish Homes, 1994); Crook, Hughes, and Kemp, *The Supply of Privately Rented Homes* (York: Joseph Rowntree Foundation, 1995); Bevan, Kemp, and Rhodes, *Private Landlords and Housing Benefit* (York: University of York, 1995), where it is suggested (p. 53) that: 'These [reasons] are mainly concerned with difficulties surrounding the administration of housing benefit; the undesir-able image which a number of landlords have about tenants on housing benefit; and the financially insecure position of the people receiving such payments.'

[36] Registration is with a publicly funded body, known as the Housing Corporation. Registration carries the advantage of being able to apply for public funding (although this is now limited—see below). Many social landlords, however, are not registered and there are little data available as to their operation.

[37] The central texts are: Forrest and Murie, *Selling the Welfare State* (London: Routledge, 1991); Cole and Furbey, *The Eclipse of Council Housing*, (London: Routledge, 1994).

[38] Ibid.

local authorities rarely made contracts with their tenants;[39] tenants rarely had a say in the construction, design, development, and management of their estates;[40] allocation of accommodation was on a discretionary basis creating no rights to enforce;[41] there was little, if any, method of redressing grievances.[42] Council housing could therefore have been portrayed generally as an unresponsive monolith.

Thus, it was the first to be attacked by the Thatcher governments, even though the process of dismantling council housing began some time before the Thatcher government's first term in 1979 because of changes in the relationship between central and local government, involving harsher fiscal priorities and increased judicialization.[43] The result was a fourfold attack during the successive Conservative governments from 1979 to 1997: implementation of the right of certain tenants to buy their council houses including, when demand weakened, increasing sweeteners to tenants through ever larger discounts;[44] financial controls preventing local authorities from building more accommodation as well as increasing rent levels of the remaining housing;[45] financial incentives to sweeten large-scale transfers of council

[39] The difficulties faced by the House of Lords in *Liverpool City Council* v. *Irwin* [1977] AC 239 are a more than adequate reflection of this. The Housing Act 1980, which first provided a 'tenants' charter', in fact met with an uneven response from local authorities, some of which attempted to avoid its implementation because of the other obligations imposed by that Act: Loveland, 'Square Pegs, Round Holes: The 'Right' to Council Housing in the Post-War Era', (1992) 19 Journal of Law and Society 339 at 350–3.

[40] See Cole and Furbey, *The Eclipse of Council Housing*, pt. II. They also suggest that these difficulties could be overstated. For example, the design of council housing was uneven—some good, some bad.

[41] See Loveland, *Housing Homeless Persons*, ch. 1. For discussion of the issue of racism in housing allocation as well as the numerous Commission for Racial Equality reports, see Ginsburg, 'Racism and Housing: Concepts and Reality', in Braham, Rattansi, and Skellington (eds.), *Racism and Antiracism* (London: Sage, 1992), 109; Smith, *The Politics of 'Race' and Residence* (Cambridge: Polity, 1989), ch. 4.

[42] This was the case even in 1986 (Lewis, Seneveritane, and Cracknell, *Complaints Procedures in Local Government* (Sheffield: University of Sheffield, 1987)).

[43] The literature here is extensive, although see (controversially), Loughlin, *Legality and Locality*, (Oxford: Oxford University Press, 1996); also Loughlin, *Local Government in the Modern State* (London: Sweet & Maxwell, 1986).

[44] Housing Act 1980, part I; consolidated in the Housing Act 1985, part V, as amended by the Housing and Planning Act 1986. The current discount begins at 32% in the case of houses, and increases by 1% for each year of occupation; for flats, the initial discount is 44% (because few were initially bought), and increases by 2% thereafter. The maximum discounts available are 60% for houses and 70% for flats. In addition to the two works by Loughlin, see also Hughes and Lowe, *Social Housing Law and Policy* (London: Butterworths, 1995), ch. 2; Balchin, *Housing Policy*, ch. 8.

[45] For a summary of the plethora of measures and their effects, see Loveland, *Constitutional Law: A Critical Introduction* (London: Butterworths, 1996), ch. 11; Loughlin, *Legality and Locality*.

housing to housing associations[46] as well as forced transfers of council housing to Housing Action Trusts;[47] finally, local authority housing management
was required to be put out to tender.[48] This was not so much a 'New Right'
agenda as attempts at populist housing policies.[49]

The effects of these policies have been (at least) threefold. The obvious
result was a general decline in local authority stock (although this differed
from area to area) which now houses the marginalized socio-economic
groups.[50] Local authority tenure has decreased. Mainly the better quality
accommodation has been sold off. Hardly any accommodation is now built
by local authorities. Housing studies characterize the effects of the sales as
'residualization' and 'marginalization'.[51] Secondly, the paradoxical effect
has been the rise of the tenant's movement as a direct result of the initial
opposition to the policies (particularly exemplified by the Housing Act
1988), and there now remains a substantial tenant input into local authority policy and practice.[52]

The third effect has been a significant jump in the tenure share of registered social landlords, which were supposed to fill the void left by the withdrawal of local government.[53] These are a curious mix of public and private
in the sense that they receive public money through their central organiza-

[46] These powers were created by the Housing Act 1988, although it was not immediately obvious that the general powers did enable this approach to be taken. The movement
in this direction, ironically, seems to have developed first from local authority housing man-
agers themselves (who subsequently largely staffed the housing associations): see Mullins,
Niner, and Riseborough, 'Large-Scale Voluntary Transfers', in Malpass and Means (eds.),
Implementing Housing Policy (Buckingham: Open University Press, 1993), 169.

[47] Created by the Housing Act 1988. Once again, ironically, the government failed in its
first attempts to set up the Trusts partly because of local opposition (see below). However,
local authorities were then able to negotiate from a position of strength and gained a substantial financial advantage for some of their estates, which occasionally have been of the bet-
ter-off variety (contrary to the original policy): see Karn, 'Remodelling a HAT: the
implementation of the Housing Action Trust legislation 1987–92', in Malpass and Means
(eds.), *Implementing Housing Policy*, 74.

[48] SI 1994/1671; see, for discussion, Vincent-Jones and Harries, 'Tenant Participation in
Contracting for Housing Management Services: A Case Study', in Cowan (ed.), *Housing:
Participation and Exclusion* (Aldershot: Dartmouth, forthcoming).

[49] Cole and Furbey, *The Eclipse of Council Housing*.

[50] Forrest and Murie, *Selling the Welfare State*.   [51] Ibid. 65–85.

[52] See Woodward, 'Mobilising Opposition: The Campaign against Housing Action
Trusts in Tower Hamlets' (1991) 6 Housing Studies 44; the aftermath is considered by
Gilroy, 'Bringing Tenants into Decision Making', in Cowan (ed.), *Housing: Participation and
Exclusion*.

[53] This was signalled by the government's 1987 White Paper: Department of the
Environment *Housing: The Government's Proposals*, Cmnd. 214 (London: HMSO, 1987),
which announced that local authorities were to be the 'enablers', whilst providing would be
handed over to housing associations. For an excellent summary, see Stewart, *Rethinking
Housing Law* (London: Sweet & Maxwell, 1996), ch. 5.

tion—the Housing Corporation—but let accommodation on private sector assured tenancies within the regime prescribed by the Housing Act 1988.[54] This has caused differential rent rates and security between public and quasi-public sectors.[55] However, this regime was introduced to facilitate the phased withdrawal of central government for the phased influx of private sector finance. Private sector finance has brought with it the risk of insolvency.[56] Finally, there is also a belief that the quasi-public movement simply cannot cater for the mass of unmet housing need. This is because the construction of new housing by the sector currently accounts for only about a half of the estimated need. Further, the need to reduce the public sector borrowing requirement has resulted in a reduction of the budget due to the Housing Corporation.[57]

Precipitating Causes

This is the phrase given to the more systemic inequalities in society which have an impact upon the housing opportunities of certain groups of people. So, for example, there is a wealth of evidence suggesting that ethnic minorities are at a disadvantage in the allocation of housing by the public and private sectors.[58] Women have similarly been marginalized by the design and allocation of accommodation,[59] which has a particular impact after relationship breakdown.[60] Recent literature has argued that female homelessness can be viewed as a response to cycles of abuse.[61] Other examples

[54] This provides a contrast with the regime for council tenants. Bearing in mind the fact that each tenure broadly has the same aims, this distinction is difficult to justify (although see below) (Miller, 'Time to end the two-tier tenancies', (1997) Sept.–Oct. ROOF 12–13).

[55] See Mullen, Scott, Fitzpatrick, and Goodlad, *Tenancy Rights and Repossession Rates: in Theory and Practice*, (Edinburgh: Scottish Homes, 1996).

[56] See, generally, Randolph, 'The Re-Privatization of Housing Associations', in Malpass and Means (eds.), *The Implementation of Housing Policy*, 39.

[57] For further discussion, see Balchin, *Housing Policy*, 151–9.

[58] See Loveland, *Housing Homeless Persons*, Ginsburg, 'Racism and Housing', and Smith, *The Politics of 'Race' and Residence*.

[59] Pascall, *Social Policy* 138–51.

[60] There is an immense literature here, of which the following edited collections exemplify the research tradition: Gilroy and Woods (eds.), *Housing Women* (London: Routledge, 1994); Booth, Darke, and Yeandle, *Changing Places: Women's Lives in the City* (London: Paul Chapman, 1996). More specific research includes: Bull, *Housing Consequences of Relationship Breakdown*; Malos and Hague, *Domestic Violence and Housing* (Women's Aid Federation England: School of Applied Social Studies, University of Bristol, 1993); Moroney and Harris, *Relationship Breakdown and Housing: A Practical Guide* (London: Shelter, 1997).

[61] See Tomas and Dittmar, 'The experiences of homeless women: an exploration of housing histories and the meaning of home' (1995) 10 Housing Studies 493; more generally, see Watson with Austerberry, *Housing and Homelessness: A Feminist Perspective* (London: Routledge, 1986); Lidstone, 'Women and homelessness', in Booth, Darke, and Yeandle

include the problems caused by discharge from hospital or institutional care,[62] children (in particular those leaving care or who have been subject to abuse),[63] some older people,[64] and alcoholism and drug abuse.[65] Clearly, these are not mutually exclusive (nor the only) categories and the homeless themselves often encounter multiple other precipitating events.

The Homelessness Legislation

The third cause of homelessness has been said to be the very existence of legislation which enables people to access accommodation. The argument is based firmly on 'New Right' ideology and, to a degree, was the rationale behind the significant amendments to the Housing (Homeless Persons) Bill in 1977,[66] as well as having been accepted by the Conservative government at least from 1993. The argument is a simple one—people make themselves homeless in order to access accommodation through the homelessness legislation. As Charles Murray evocatively argued, the 'system [had been] designed to be exploited'.[67] This is often a precursor to a general diatribe linking the legislation with a breakdown in the *mores* of society.

This was what explicitly occurred in the period between 1993 and 1995, beginning with a speech made by John Redwood, then Secretary of State for Wales, linking teenage pregnancies with access to housing. It was argued that women, usually teenagers, became pregnant in order to access accommodation. There is, however, no empirical evidence to justify this assertion; indeed, the weight of evidence suggests the opposite.[68] A national debate ensued, given force by the 'back to basics' motif of the Conservative party conference that year. Cowan argues that this debate, which mainly took

(eds.), *Changing Places*, 72; Woods, 'Women and housing', in Hallett (ed.), *Women and Social Policy* (Brighton: Harvester Wheatsheaf, 1996), 65.

[62] See Means and Smith, *Community Care: Policy and Practice* (Basingstoke: Macmillan, 1994); Cowan, 'Accommodating community care' (1995) 22 Journal of Law and Society 212; Cowan, *Homelessness: The (In-)Appropriate Applicant*, ch. 3.

[63] Thornton, *The New Homeless*; Malpass, 'Housing and Young People', in Malpass (ed.), *The Housing Crisis* (London: Routledge, 1986); as well as various publications from the Campaign for the Homeless and Rootless.

[64] Hawes, *Homelessness and Older People* (Bristol: Policy Press, 1997).

[65] These are often cited as a cause of street homelessness: see e.g. Department of the Environment, *Rough Sleepers Initiative: Future Plans* (London: DoE, 1995), paras. 2.5–2.7.

[66] See Loveland, 'Legal Rights and Political Realities: Governmental Responses to Homelessness in Britain' (1991) 18 Law and Social Inquiry 249.

[67] Murray, *Underclass: The Crisis Deepens* (London: Institute for Economic Affairs, 1994), 22.

[68] See Ermisch, *Household Formation and Housing Tenure Decisions of Young People* (Colchester: University of Essex, 1997); Institute of Housing, *One Parent Families: Are they Jumping the Housing Queue?* (Coventry: IoH, 1994); Green and Hansbro, *Housing in England 1993/4* (London: HMSO, 1995), ch. 8.

place in the media, overshadowed the reality of the government's reforms to the legislation, which involved a more general policy of penalizing the homeless.[69]

The government's Consultation Paper, issued in early 1994, provided an example both of the belief that the legislation caused homelessness as well as the resultant general policy shift towards exclusion.[70] The argument was that, as local authority waiting lists were substantially oversubscribed, the homelessness route became 'the more attractive way into subsidised housing for those wishing to be rehoused . . . The current legislation creates a perverse incentive for people to have themselves accepted by the local authority as homeless . . .'.[71] One possible method of curing this perverse incentive might have been to build more accommodation but the Consultation Paper expressed the view that, were this to be done, 'future generations may not thank us if we continue to devote scarce natural resources to producing ever more dwellings.'[72] Instead, the government canvassed methods of reducing demand through a crude reduction in obligations to the homeless as well as narrowing the definitions in the original homelessness legislation.[73] Most of these changes have now been implemented within the 1996 Act, to which we now turn for detailed analysis.

THE HOUSING ACT 1996: PRINCIPLES, LAW, AND PRACTICE

Principles

As might readily be appreciated, bearing in mind the previous section, the homelessness legislation[74] is a mishmash of different ideologies.[75] However,

---

[69] Cowan, *Homelessness: The (In-)Appropriate Applicant*, ch. 8.

[70] Department of the Environment, *Access to Local Authority and Housing Association Tenancies* (London: DoE, 1994).

[71] Ibid., paras. 2.7–2.8.   [72] Ibid., para. 2.3.

[73] For a withering critique of these proposals, see Loveland, 'Cathy Sod Off! The End of the Homelessness Legislation' (1994) 16 Journal of Social Welfare Law 367; also Cowan and Fionda, 'Back to Basics: The Government's Homelessness Proposals' (1994) 57 MLR 610.

[74] For greater detail, see Cowan (ed.), *The Housing Act 1996: A Practical Guide* (Bristol: Jordans, 1996); Arden and Hunter, *Homelessness and Allocations* (London: Legal Action Group, 1997). For a comparative analysis of definitions of homelessness taken in Britain, the USA, and Canada, see Daly, *Homeless* (London: Routledge, 1996)—readers of this text should, however, beware the author's lack of legal training.

[75] The most recent example of this new housing exclusion involves the use of the powers given to local authorities to exclude certain people from the housing register. It has been reported that some authorities have excluded paedophiles in this way, or are considering doing so: Tendler, 'Council refuses to house sex offenders', The Times (6 Mar. 1997); Ford, 'Council considers ban on housing paedophiles', The Times (9 Jan. 1997).

the fundamental principle underlying the homelessness provisions in the 1996 Act was that homelessness is only a short-term reflection of housing need and not a symptom of it. Consequently, the response contained in the 1996 Act was that the legislation should provide only a short-term solution through the provision of accommodation for a minimum period of two years.[76] Long-term tenancies were to be allocated through a housing register (or waiting list) kept by the local authority.[77] The Act prescribes certain groups to whom a 'reasonable preference' is to be given on that register, which are supposed to reflect long-term housing need.[78] Naturally, homelessness was not one of these categories. This controversial move by the Conservative government has since been overturned by the New Labour government, so that those accepted under the homelessness provisions are also entitled to this preference.[79] The Blair government has made a small amendment to the even more controversial change made by the 1996 Act, which requires local authorities to provide advice and assistance to successful homeless applicants in order to secure accommodation in other sectors.[80] This accommodation now has to be provided for a minimum of two years.[81] The principle of diverting successful applicants to an inadequate private sector remains, though.

Two other significant amendments reinforce the move towards housing exclusion. First, asylum seekers and their dependants are made ineligible, subject to certain inclusions.[82] Secondly, those who collude to make themselves homeless cannot expect to be successful, as they will be found intentionally homeless (potentially involving a return to the old, discredited practice of requiring parents to obtain a court order evicting their children).[83] Other amendments strip away the loopholes from the old legislation, narrowing its scope, as well as increasing the level of fine for the provision of false information.[84]

This move towards housing exclusion has required myopic vision. Many of the lessons of the past twenty years were also forgotten. This has particularly involved undermining the effects of earlier legislation, such as the Children Act 1989 and part III of the National Health Service and

---

[76] s. 193(3). It has been argued that case law had erroneously reached that view within the old legislation, more on the basis of then current government policy than on that which underpinned the old legislation: see R. v. *London Borough of Brent ex p. Awua* [1996] 1 AC 55; Cowan, 'Doing the Government's Work' (1997) 60 MLR 276; for a slightly different interpretation, see Hunter and Miles, 'The Unsettling of Settled Law on "Settled Accommodation" ' (1997) 19 Journal of Social Welfare and Family Law 267.

[77] 1996 Act, part VI.

[78] Cf. Cowan, *Homelessness: The (In-)Appropriate Applicant*, 193–6.

[79] SI 1997/1902.   [80] s. 197.   [81] SI 1997/1741.

[82] s. 185–8; SI 1996/2754.   [83] s. 191(3).

[84] s. 214(4). A lexis search found no cases under the former provision (Housing Act 1985, s. 74).

Community Care Act 1990. Each of these, as well as other aspects of social policy (such as racial harassment and domestic violence), involves different organizations working together. However, the new Act provides no method of enforcing the obligation to work with other agencies.[85] The government successfully argued that encouraging collaboration was a matter for the Code of Guidance, to which local authorities are required only to have regard, and not for enforceable duties.[86] On the other hand, the policies of exclusion towards asylum seekers are backed up by statutory duties on the local authority to consult the Home Office at almost every turn.[87]

Law

A successful applicant under the 1996 Act must be found (*a*) homeless, (*b*) eligible, (*c*) in priority need, (*d*) not intentionally homeless. From this quadruplet of obstacles, it is manifest that homelessness itself does not guarantee access to housing.

'Homeless'
Broadly, this definition is predicated on the lack of any property or personal rights to occupy accommodation.[88] This definition was narrowed by the 1996 Act so that homelessness occurs only when a person[89] has no such rights anywhere in the world.[90] It has always been accepted that this definition is broader than mere rooflessness.[91] So, Lord Brightman observed that

[85] See e.g. *R. v. Northavon District Council ex p. Smith* (1994) 26 HLR 659 at 666, where Lord Templeman argued that 'Judicial review is not the way to obtain co-operation'. Local housing authorities were already tending to ignore the corporate response to domestic violence (inspired by the Home Office): Hague, Malos, and Dear, *Multi-Agency Work and Domestic Violence* (Bristol: Policy Press, 1996), 24. On this issue, see Cowan, *Homelessness: The (In-)Appropriate Applicant.*

[86] s. 182(1). The 1996 Act repeats the ineffectual duty to cooperate with other authorities, contained in the original legislation, provided it is 'reasonable in all the circumstances' (s. 213(1)).

[87] s. 187.

[88] The Act also makes provision for those 'threatened with homelessness' within twenty-eight days (ss. 184, 196). As these are broadly the same as the provisions for those already homeless, with tense changes only, no account is given here.

[89] The word 'person' bears a wider meaning in the 1996 Act (as in earlier versions) to cover any person who normally resides, or might be expected to reside, with the person (s. 176). This reflects the desire to stamp out the previous practice of splitting families.

[90] This amendment to the original definition was an attempt to cure an apparent defect that a person could have accommodation in (say) Italy, but be homeless because he did not have accommodation in the UK (see *R. v. London Borough of Camden ex p. Aranda* (1996) 28 HLR 672, and Doran, 'Tenants' £20,000 Worth of Cheek', Daily Mail (19 Feb. 1996)).

[91] Some situations are deemed homeless, such as travellers with no place for their mobile home (s. 175(2)). Cf. the government's original proposal to reduce the definition to

Diogenes' barrel would not have been 'accommodation' within the meaning of the Act.[92] However, his Lordship did not accept that a married couple with two children, living in one room in a guest house without cooking or laundry facilities, were homeless.

The uproar resulting from that decision led to amendments being made to the definition, which have been transferred into the 1996 Act. These amendments require a test of relative accommodation standards to be made. First, it is provided that 'A person shall not be treated as having accommodation unless it is accommodation which it would be reasonable for [that person] to continue to occupy.'[93] Secondly, in determining reasonableness, 'regard may be had to the general circumstances prevailing in relation to housing in the district of the local housing authority to whom [that person] has applied . . .'.[94] As Lord Hoffmann has shown, these amendments have not had much effect.[95] There is a delicate balancing act required of homelessness officers, which has been made all the more difficult because of the general lack of available, low-cost, accommodation as well as the poor quality of housing stock which might be offered to a successful applicant.

It has always been the case that those subject to violence within the home have been deemed homeless on the grounds that it is unreasonable to continue to occupy that accommodation. The distinction between violence in and outside the home was never convincing and led to some bizarre results. Amendments have widened this provision, in line with the Family Law Act 1996, so that the distinction is now based upon the person who commits the violence. If an 'associated person' commits the violence, then the applicant is homeless.[96] However, those subjected to racial harassment or violence still need to depend upon the 'reasonableness' criterion.

Eligibility

Any person who is 'subject to immigration control within the meaning of the Asylum and Immigration Act 1996' is ineligible for assistance under the 1996 Act.[97] Those asylum seekers not caught by this provision are never-

---

rooflessness with one or two exceptions (Department of the Environment, *Access to Local Authority and Housing Association Tenancies* para.5.1).

[92] *R. v. London Borough of Hillingdon ex p. Puhlhofer* [1986] AC 484.

[93] Housing Act 1985, s. 58(2A) inserted by Housing and Planning Act 1986, s. 14(6); now Housing Act 1996, s. 175(3) and SI 1996/3204.

[94] Housing Act 1985, s. 58(2B), inserted by Housing and Planning Act 1986, s. 14(6); now Housing Act 1996, s. 177(2).

[95] 'A local housing authority could take the view that a family like the Puhlhofers, put into a single cramped and squalid bedroom, can be expected to make do for a limited period. On the other hand, there will come a time at which it is no longer reasonable to expect them to continue to occupy such accommodation' (*R. v. London Borough of Brent ex p. Awua* [1995] 1 AC 55 at 68).

[96] ss. 177–8.   [97] s. 185(2). See also SI 1996/2754; SI 1997/631.

theless ineligible 'if [they have] any accommodation in the United Kingdom, however temporary, available for [their] occupation'.[98] This exclusion was a response to two interconnected facets of immigration policy: the desire to stop people coming to England and Wales to 'take advantage of the welfare system', as well as a money-saving operation.[99] In 1997 the courts agreed that homeless, penniless asylum seekers may seek accommodation under the National Assistance Act 1948.[100]

Priority Need

The 1996 Act retained the notion and definition of priority need from its predecessors without amendment. The following are the list of those with priority need:

(a) a pregnant woman or a person with whom she resides or might reasonably be expected to reside;

(b) a person with whom dependent children reside or might reasonably be expected to reside;

(c) a person who is vulnerable as a result of old age, mental illness or handicap or physical difficulty or other special reason, or with whom such a person resides or might be expected to reside;

(d) a person who is homeless or threatened with homelessness as a result of an emergency such as flood, fire or other disaster.[101]

Those not pregnant or without dependent children can receive a priority need only on the basis of the last two paragraphs. However, the courts have adopted a restrictive interpretation on paragraph (d).[102] The critical paragraph has become the third, relating to vulnerability.[103] As the specific consequential examples of vulnerability are narrow, some attention has recently focused on the meaning of 'other special reason'. These words 'require examination of all the personal circumstances of an applicant, including physical or mental characteristics or disabilities, but not so

---

[98] s. 186(1). Others are ineligible because of their exclusion from housing benefit, SI 1996/2754.

[99] The policy was announced by Michael Howard, then Secretary of State at the Home Office, in 'Britain should be haven not a honeypot', Daily Mail, 12 Dec. 1995.

[100] See R. v. London Borough of Hammersmith and Fulham ex p. M, (1998) 30 HLR 10; see also, R. v. Secretary of State for Health ex p. London Borough of Hammersmith and Fulham, The Times, QBD, 31 July 1997; see also SI 1998/628.

[101] s. 189(1). Note that pregnancy only gives priority need and does not guarantee access, for the person must also cross the other obstacles in the Act.

[102] R. v. Bristol City Council ex p. Bradic (1995) 27 HLR 584.

[103] Defined as 'less able to fend for oneself [in housing terms] so that injury or detriment will result where a less vulnerable [person] will be able to cope without harmful effects' (R. v. Waveney District Council ex p. Bowers [1983] QB 238; R. v. Bath City Council ex p. Sangermano (1984) 17 HLR 94).

limited; accordingly, impecuniosity will be relevant as will be opportunities to raise money . . . or—put another way—"utter poverty and resourcelessness" '.[104]

Intentional Homelessness

This provision was introduced into the original legislation to respond to fears that people would make themselves homeless in order to jump the housing waiting list. There are four elements to intentional homelessness: the applicant must have deliberately[105] done or omitted to do something; that act or omission must have caused the loss of accommodation; that accommodation must, however, have been available for the applicant's occupation at the time of the act or omission; and it must have been 'reasonable to continue to occupy' the accommodation but for the act or omission.[106] An additional example of intentional homelessness occurs when the applicant has colluded with another person to make themselves homeless.[107]

The intentional homelessness provisions have caused, and will continue to cause, the most difficulty both for local authorities and the courts. It is the most highly litigated concept within the legislation and much of the decision-making has broadened its scope. A few examples should suffice to illustrate its operation.

Example 1: The applicant left secure accommodation for a winter let which automatically terminated. It was held that the applicant's deliberate act of leaving the secure accommodation for insecure accommodation caused the homelessness.[108]

Example 2: The applicants were incurring substantial arrears of rent on their accommodation. They were advised to await the result of possession proceedings by the local authority but they left before those proceedings had begun. The House of Lords upheld the local authority's finding of intentional homelessnes because the voluntary decision to leave the accommodation was the cause of the homelessness (not the substantial arrears of rent).[109]

---

[104] Arden and Hunter, *Homelessness and Allocations*, para. 6.28, referring to *R. v. Royal Borough of Kensington and Chelsea and others ex p. Kihara and others* (1996) 29 HLR 147.

[105] Acts or omissions in good faith are not deliberate (s. 191(2)).

[106] s. 191(1).

[107] s. 191(3).

[108] *Dyson v. Kerrier District Council* [1980] 1 WLR 1205.

[109] *Din v. London Borough of Wandsworth* [1983] 1 AC 657; cf *R. v. London Borough of Wandsworth ex p. Hawthorne* (1994) 27 HLR 59 (family unable to pay rent because of inadequacy of resources, not intentionally homeless).

Example 3: Deliberate failure to pay rent or mortgage payments which results in eviction is also likely to lead to a justifiable finding of intentional homelessness.[110]

Local Authority Duties

The main housing duty owed to successful applicants is to provide 'suitable accommodation' for a minimum period of two years. If the successful applicant has no 'local connection' with the authority to whom the application was made, that authority can refer the applicant to another authority with which such a connection exists.[111] However, such applicants can be diverted into the private sector to take an assured shorthold tenancy (provided the minimum term is two years).[112] The two-year period can be extended only if there is no other accommodation available in the private sector as well as there being a continuing priority need.[113] Failure to accept offers of accommodation in either sector results in a finding of intentional homelessness or a discharge of the authority's duty.[114]

The penalties for failing to meet the criteria are harsh. If an applicant is unsuccessful, the duties are reduced to the provision of temporary accommodation (usually for a period of 4–12 weeks), and/or the provision of advice and assistance.[115] The latter has, in the past, sometimes taken the form of 'sign here and sod off'.[116]

Practice

Socio-legal research has expertly uncovered much substantive illegality in homelessness decision-making. In particular, Professor Loveland's in-depth analysis of policies, practices, and decision-making in three local authority homelessness departments has shattered any belief in the substantive legality of much decision-making.[117] Decision-making tends to be conducted on the basis of resource pressures, both as a result of limited accommodation as

---

[110] *Robinson v. Torbay Borough Council* [1982] 1 All ER 726. This principle has controversially been extended to a paedophile who gave up accommodation because housing benefit was not payable in prison (*R. v. London Borough of Hounslow ex p. R*, The Times, QBD, 25 Feb. 1997).

[111] Complex provisions govern this (ss. 198–200); see also Loveland, 'Irrelevant Considerations?', in Richardson and Genn (eds.), *Administrative Law and Government Action* (Oxford: Oxford University Press, 1994), 211.

[112] s. 197 and SI 1997/1741.

[113] s. 194(2), reflecting concerns that successful applicants might, for example, put their baby up for adoption after securing accommodation.

[114] ss. 191(4) and 193(5)–(7).   [115] Detailed in ss. 190 and 192.

[116] See Loveland, 'Administrative Law, Administrative Processes and the Housing of Homeless Persons: A View from the Sharp End' (1992) Journal of Social Welfare Law 4.

[117] Loveland, *Housing Homeless Persons*.

well as the staffing of these departments. Some decision-making also rests on perceptions of the desirability of housing certain applicants, some of whom might be perceived as potential trouble-makers. Moreover, often concentration is upon the use that applicants would make of property were they to be successful. Administrative expediency is often the constraining factor in decision-making. These studies took place before the introduction of the 1996 Act. However, it has been argued that, if anything, administrative practice will become harsher as a result of its implementation.[118] In this section we concentrate on two particular examples through which we illustrate the practical operation of the homelessness legislation: violence to women; and children. In doing so, we draw on empirical research conducted by ourselves and others.

Violence to Women

As we have seen, the homelessness legislation has always responded to violence which takes place within the home through the definition of homelessness (although not through the other concepts). The Code of Guidance, which expands on the legislation, suggests that authorities should also consider whether single women fleeing violence or abuse are vulnerable as a result of that violence.[119] Authorities' practices, in fact, vary widely and advisers have become skilful in filtering potential applicants to authorities with more generous policies. However, this may have an effect on those more generous authorities which are subject broadly to the same constraints as the less generous ones. Policies are often changed unfavourably where the authority perceives it is too generous.

One early study suggested that 73 per cent of applicants from women's refuges were unsuccessful on one or more of the criteria.[120] Recent studies have shown how local authorities sometimes avoid taking applications from some women claiming homelessness by invoking threshold tests.[121] The most significant of these has been the requirement imposed by many authorities on women fleeing violence to seek legal advice and obtain an injunction.[122] Problems noted by other recent research include narrow definitions of violence, poor and occasionally antagonistic interviewing technique by local authority officers, as well as findings of intentional

---

[118] Cowan, *Homelessness: The (In-)Appropriate Applicant*, ch. 9.   [119] Para. 14.17.

[120] Binney, Harkell, and Nixon, *Leaving Violent Men* (Women's Aid Federation England, 1981), 78–85.

[121] Cowan, *Homelessness: The (In-)Appropriate Applicant*, 126–31.

[122] There is plenty of evidence to suggest that women have difficulties in obtaining injunctions and the like as a result of violence and these are often not enforced: Barron, *Not Worth the Paper . . .?* (Women's Aid Federation England, 1990). For similar examples, see Loveland, *Housing Homeless Persons*, 180–90; Malos and Hague, *Domestic Violence and Housing*, paras. 3.44–3.50.

homelessness.[123] Threshold tests were designed to test the genuineness of applicants, as the common fear was that a suggestion of violence was regarded as the 'easiest' way of gaining access to accommodation. One reason for this fear was that officers reported that cases of violence to women made up 15–30 per cent of their caseload. Occasionally, officers believed that some women would return to a violent situation (and not make use of any accommodation offered by the authority).

Children

The position adopted by land law that minors cannot take a legal estate, as well as the fact that the 1996 Act makes no provision for youth homelessness, mark an unpromising beginning to our consideration. However, two recent developments have significantly altered the position, as well as some attitudes, within local authorities. First, the Children Act 1989 created new obligations on housing authorities to house children assessed by social services departments as being in need of accommodation.[124] Secondly, the Code of Guidance recognizes that some children may be 'vulnerable . . . for some other special reason'. This includes those children 'at risk' through, for example, sexual exploitation, as well as other particular problems such as leaving local authority care.[125] A result of both these developments was a move within local government to negotiate agreements between the different arms responsible for children.

Initial research concluded that professional hostilities were still evident despite agreements. The clear problem which developed was that the different pieces of legislation had different frameworks as well as the departments having 'unclear and limited perceptions of their respective roles.'[126] In particular, few social services departments felt it was their role to house homeless people.[127] Subsequently, it appears that joint working arrangements have tended to break down for these reasons as well as because of their lack of enforceability.[128] This has had a consequential effect on homelessness decision-making. The principal concern of many homelessness officers appears to be that they do not wish to allocate accommodation to young people who have no support for it is feared that this will create a 'revolving doors' situation (that is, reapplication as homeless after eviction), which would help nobody. Decisions may be made accordingly as well as depending upon whether the social services departments will offer the requisite support. In these cases, the homelessness legislation often takes

---

[123] In addition to Cowan, *Homelessness: The (In-)Appropriate Applicant*, see Malos and Hague, *Domestic Violence and Housing*, esp. paras. 4.17–4.31; Thornton, 'Homelessness through Relationship Breakdown' (1988) 10 Journal of Social Welfare Law 67.

[124] Children Act 1989, ss. 17(10), 20(1), 27. [125] Paras. 14.10–14.17.

[126] McCluskey, *Acting in Isolation* (London: CHAR, 1994) 39. [127] *Ibid.* 45.

[128] R. v. *Northavon District Council ex p. Smith.*

second place to more practical requirements.[129] Carlen, drawing on an empirical study which suggested that many homeless young people were deterred from applying as homeless,[130] argues: 'By implying that truly homeless young single people necessarily have some problem other than homelessness, the law and local authorities together manage to deter [the] young single homeless from applying to them for accommodation at the same time as producing legitimate statistics indicating that young single homelessness is less than it is.'[131]

CONCLUSION

It has been our aim in this chapter to analyse how land law can be provided with an alternative focus through a consideration of the causes of, and responses to, homelessness. Our analysis has brought us to the conclusion that certain people are excluded from all types of housing, as a result of the causes of homelessness and homelessness policies. Professor Rutherford has termed these causes and effects as the pursuit of an 'eliminative ideal'. He argues that to be excluded is social death:

Members of a society conceive of the socially dead as being bereft of some essential human attributes and undeserving of essential social, civil and legal protections. Furthermore, they are treated in a manner that denies them the possibility of receiving social honour, which is a requisite for becoming a recognised and full member of a social community.[132]

We have argued that social death should be an essential part of the land law syllabus.

[129] Cowan, *Homelessness: The (In-)Appropriate Applicant*, ch. 3.

[130] Carlen and Wardhaugh, *Shropshire Single Homelessness Survey* (Keele: Shropshire Probation and University of Keele, 1992), including the comment by one interviewee: 'they haven't got anything to offer—whether they accept you as being homeless or not'.

[131] Carlen, *Jigsaw: A Political Criminology of Youth Homelessness* (Buckingham: Open University Press, 1996), 62.

[132] Rutherford, *Criminal Policy and the Eliminative Ideal* (Southampton: University of Southampton, 1996).

11

LAND LAW AND DISPOSSESSION: INDIGENOUS RIGHTS TO LAND IN AUSTRALIA

Shaunnagh Dorsett

The history of Indigenous land rights in Australia is one of denial. From the first settlement of the colony of New South Wales, Indigenous Australians were seen as trespassers. Around the Empire, Indigenous peoples were continually denied status or protection unless they fitted within narrow categories of political and social organization and land use.[1] Aboriginal Australians were no different.

The image of the ideal owner/user[2] of land has always influenced the law's recognition and protection of interests. Those who conform to the expected and idealized use of land will receive the law's protection, while those who do not will be excluded as 'other'. In the case of Indigenous Australians, their failure to conform to the ideal has led to their continued legal dispossession of land. Although the image of the ideal Australian land owner/user now bears little resemblance to the English agrarian ideal from which it sprang, that image still has no place for Indigenous Australians' relationships with the land.

The purpose of this chapter is to examine the ways in which the law has dispossessed Indigenous Australians, and how it has justified that dispossession. In order to do this, it will be necessary to consider the ideal Australian land owner/user and the history of Indigenous land rights in Australia. The chapter begins by considering the settlement of Australia, and the importation of the common law into the colony of New South Wales, as dispossession began with an application of the rules relating to acquisition of sovereignty and consequent acquisition of land. The recent High Court decisions in *Mabo v. State of Queensland (No. 2)*[3] and *The Wik Peoples v. Queensland*,[4] as well as the Commonwealth Native Title Act[5] are also

---

[1] Anaya, *Indigenous Peoples in International Law* (Oxford: Oxford University Press, 1996), 19.

[2] The term 'user', as well as 'owner', is used here to reflect the fact that substantial parts of Australia have been held for generations under statutory pastoral leases, rather than under freehold title.

[3] *Mabo v. State of Queensland (No. 2)* (1992) 175 CLR 1 (*Mabo (No. 2)*).

[4] *The Wik Peoples v. Queensland* (1996) 141 ALR 129 (*The Wik Peoples*).

[5] Native Title Act 1993 (Cth).

examined. They reveal a change in rhetoric, but a continuing exclusion of native title interests by defining Indigenous Australians as 'other', and relegating native title to a matter of evidence and priorities. Although, since *Mabo (No. 2)*, the common law recognizes the continued existence of native title interests, applicants will be able to prove native title only if they can demonstrate that their relationship with the land fits within a narrow category of circumstances in which such rights will be recognized. Native title interests remain subordinate to those of white Australians. It is telling that in the five years since the decision in *Mabo (No. 2)* there have been no other successful determinations of native title through the courts, although two claims have been determined through negotiation.

INHERITED LAND LAW

Australia's legal institutions are built on the inheritance of English law. The first fleet brought with it not only tools, provisions, and weapons, but also the great birthright of the English colonist, the common law. According to Blackstone, on settlement of a colony as much of the common law as was applicable to the circumstances of the colony was to be imported.[6] Thus laws which were neither 'necessary nor convenient' were excluded.[7] The rules applying to a settled, rather than a conquered colony, were applied on the basis that the Australian continent was *terra nullius*, or uninhabited,[8] and the importation of English law was legislatively confirmed by the British Parliament.[9] Australia, of course, had an indigenous population whose existence could not be factually ignored. Legally, however, it could be, provided that there was sufficient justification for such action. A ready justification was provided by the writings of international jurists, such as those of Emer de Vattel, in whose opinion: 'every nation is . . . bound by natural law to cultivate the land which has fallen to its share, and it has no

---

[6] Blackstone, *Commentaries on the Laws of England* (14 vols., 1st edn., Oxford: Oxford University Press, 1765–9), 107–8. The *Commentaries* were published twenty years before first settlement of Australia, and were highly influential in the early days of the colony. David Collins, a marine officer with no legal training, was Judge Advocate for the first eight years of the colony. He relied on his store of legal books: *Statutes at Large*, Reeve's *History of English Law*, Jacob's *A New Law Dictionary*, Burn's *The Justice of the Peace and Parish Officer*, as well as Blackstone's *Commentaries on the Laws of England* (Kercher, *Debt, Seduction and Other Disasters* (Sydney: Federation Press, 1996), 23).

[7] *Cooper* v. *Stuart* (1889) 14 AC 286, at 292.

[8] *Terra nullius* literally translates as 'no one's land'. If the new colony were acquired by conquest, rather than by settlement, the laws in force would be respected by the conqueror, and could be changed only by the King.

[9] See the Australian Courts Act 9 (Geo. IV c. 83), which declared that the laws of England in force at the date of the statute (1828) applied to the colony of New South Wales so far as they were applicable to the circumstances of the colony.

right to extend its boundaries or to obtain help from other nations except in so far as the land it inhabits can not supply its needs'.[10] Thus, if the indigenous inhabitants of the new territory do not cultivate their land, then:

in establishing the obligation to cultivate the earth, [tribes] cannot exclusively appropriate to themselves more land than they have occasion for, or more than they are able to settle and cultivate. Their unsettled habitation in those immense regions cannot be accounted a true and legal possession; and the People of Europe, too closely pent up at home, finding land of which the savages stood in no particular need, and of which they made no actual and constant use, were lawfully entitled to take possession of it, and settle, with colonies.[11]

Similar views inform the writings of John Locke, who was one of the most influential figures in the defence of colonialism as Secretary of the Council of Trade and Plantations from 1673 to 1675. As is well known, Locke's justification of private property centres around the notion of labour. Man, by his labour, can appropriate the fruits of the earth as his own. Locke states the origins of property in land thus: 'as Much Land as a Man Tills, Plants, Improves, Cultivates, and can use the Product of, so much is his Property. He by his Labor does, as it were enclose it from the Common.'[12]

Locke's *Second Treatise* is littered with references to the land and Indians of North America. Locke clearly believed that land in the colonies would be more valuable if it were to be farmed, rather than left to the Indigenous inhabitants:

I ask whether in the wild woods and uncultivated waste of America . . . without any improvement, tillage or husbandry, a thousand acres will yield the needy and wretched inhabitants as many conveniences of life as ten acres of equally fertile land down in Devonshire where they are well cultivated.[13]

Thus, the Devon farmer, and English agricultural methods, exemplify the agrarian ideal. By contrasting the unproductive occupation of North America by the Indians with the fruitful labour of the Devon farmer, the appropriation of Indian land could be justified in terms of bringing unproductive land into proper economic use: 'where there being more land, than the Inhabitants possess, and make use of, any one has liberty to make use of the waste.'[14]

Based on the above justification, it was easy to disregard the existence of Indigenous Australians. The colonists neither understood, nor wanted to understand, the complexities of Aboriginal Australians' relationship with

---

[10] Vattel, *Droit des gens ou principles de la loi naturelle appliqués aux affairs des nations et des souvrains*, ed. Chitty (1758; Philadelphia: T. & J. W. Johnson & Co., 1863), 35.

[11] Ibid. at 100.

[12] Locke, *The Second Treatise of Government*, ed. Peardon (Indianapolis: Bobs-Merrill Educational Publishing, 1952), para. 32.

[13] Ibid., para 37.   [14] Ibid., para 184.

the land. Rather, they labelled them 'indolent' or 'lazy' for their failure to conform to the English agrarian ideal. This failure to conform allowed Indigenous Australians to be disregarded, and the colony to be legally declared uninhabited, or *terra nullius*. Early judicial opinion confirmed the colony's status as a settled, rather than conquered colony.[15] Aboriginal people were, therefore, declared to be British subjects, although the persistent refusal to recognize Aboriginal rights made a mockery of their status as subjects.[16] Ironically, had the colony been classified as conquered, with Indigenous Australians considered enemies, rather than British subjects, they might have had a better claim to recognition of their local laws and customs.

Importation of the common law under the rules of settlement entailed the importation of the English land law system. Such a system was considered both necessary and convenient. These imported laws included the fundamental doctrines of English land law, although they arguably had nothing to do with the circumstances of a colony which had no direct feudal heritage. In particular, the doctrine of tenure, with its fiction that all land is held of the Crown, found its way to Australia. It is perhaps ironic that the doctrine of tenure, which had largely lost all meaning in the country of its origins, should become the instrument of dispossession in Australia.

Although there was some question as to the applicability of principles of English land law to the new colony, an English trained legal profession could not conceive of excluding the doctrine of tenure. The consequence of characterizing Australia as a settled colony, and the consequential importation of the doctrine of tenure, was an assumption not only that the Crown acquired sovereignty, but also that all lands in the new colony were immediately vested in it, much the same as supposedly occurred in 1066 as a result of Harold's defeat at the Battle of Hastings. This assumption was confirmed by the judiciary. In the early case of *Attorney-General (NSW)* v. *Brown*,[17] Stephens CJ dismissed an argument that title to land in Australia was allodial, and confirmed that the 'feudal fiction' had been adopted in land, so that all land was held by Crown grant. The Privy Council further confirmed in *Cooper* v. *Stuart*[18] that the Australian colonies were settled and

---

[15] *Cooper* v. *Stuart* (1889) 14 AC 286.

[16] Notably, however, Aboriginal Australians were not included in the census until the Constitutional Referendum of 1967. In 1967, 91% of Australians voted to give the Federal Government power to make laws with respect to Aboriginal Australians, which had previously resided with the states. Further, s. 127 of the Constitution was repealed, which provided that: 'In reckoning the numbers of the people of the Commonwealth, or of a State or other part of the Commonwealth, aboriginal natives shall not be counted.' Indigenous Australians did not receive the vote until the 1960s.

[17] (1847) 1 Legge 312.

[18] 14 A.C. 286. Allodial land is land which is not held of any superior lord. The holder of allodial land owns it absolutely, rather than merely holding an estate in the land. Consequently, the owner is not subject to any rent or tenurial obligations.

that the doctrine of tenure formed the fundamental basis of land law in those colonies.[19] This case did not concern Indigenous rights to land, but was seen as setting in place the foundation for the subsequent legal denial of rights. The case actually considered the applicability of the rule against perpetuities to New South Wales, and concerned a Crown grant which contained a reservation to the Crown of timber and water rights, as well as the right to resume up to ten acres of the land for public purposes if needed. The Governor resumed the land for a public park and the applicant brought an action for a declaration that the resumption was void as the reservation violated the rule against perpetuities. The applicability of the rule against perpetuities depended on whether New South Wales was a settled or conquered colony. If settled, then it would have been introduced into the colony with the reception of the common law. The Privy Council held that New South Wales 'consisted of a tract of territory practically unoccupied, without settled inhabitants or settled law, at the time when it was peacefully annexed to the British dominions . . . There was no land law or tenure existing at the time of its annexation to the Crown.'[20] As a result, the rule against perpetuities, which was described as 'an important feature of the common law',[21] was found to be operational in New South Wales.

Combining the propositions that the Crown obtained title to all lands on acquisition of sovereignty, and that the doctrine of tenure provides that valid title to land can be acquired only by Crown grant, led to the conclusion that in 1788 Indigenous Australians were immediately dispossessed of all interest they may have had in lands. This view received judicial sanction as recently as 1971 in *Milirrpum v. Nabalco*, the first land rights case:

all the Australian cases to which I was referred . . . affirm the principle, fundamental to the English law of real property, that the Crown is the source of title to all land; that no subject can own allodially, but only an estate or interest in it which he holds mediately or immediately of the Crown. On the foundation of new South Wales, therefore, and of South Australia, every square inch of territory in the colony became the property of the Crown. All titles, rights and interests whatever in land which existed thereafter in the subjects of the Crown were the direct consequence of some grant from the Crown.[22]

In general, colonial laws were designed to be applicable across all the colonies. Once it was determined into which category—settled or conquered—a colony was to be placed, the common law applied the appropriate rules relating to importation of the common law, and protection of

---

[19] See also *Wade v. New South Wales Rutile Mining Co. Pty. Ltd.* (1969) 121 CLR 177, per Windeyer J at 194; *New South Wales v. The Commonwealth (The Seas and Submerged Lands Case)* (1975) 135 CLR 337, per Stephen J at 438.

[20] *Cooper v. Stuart* (1889) 14 AC 286 at 291–2.   [21] Ibid., at 293.

[22] *Milirrpum v. Nabalco* (1970–1) 17 FLR 141 at 245.

existing interests. Cultivation was the yardstick by which a colony was categorized. This remained the accepted view of the law until the High Court's decision in *Mabo (No. 2)*.

CHANGING IMAGES OF THE IDEAL LAND-USER

From the above it can be seen that the law relating to acquisition of territory and land reflected the Anglocentric view of intense small scale cultivation as the superior use of land. However, the first colonists in Australia faced environmental conditions vastly different from those of the mother country. England is small and fertile with good rainfall. Australia, by contrast, is large and arid. Of all the colonies, Van Diemen's Land (Tasmania) most resembled England. Although agricultural pursuits can be, and are, undertaken in coastal areas, the nearer one approaches the centre of the continent, the more sterile, and the less suitable, it becomes for traditional English agriculture. In addition to this, transportation is difficult. The main river system, the Murray system, is not navigable for its entire length.

Early land grant practices reflect those of the newly departed mother country. Grants of small plots of land were made, largely for agricultural purposes. However, the discovery of the lushness of the native grasses in the colony led to the introduction of wool growing at the end of the eighteenth century, and hence the need for more land. Despite this, the first two Governors attempted to restrict land grants to small allotments with some allowance for common areas for pasturage. Official policy was to allow no settlement outside of a surveyed area known as the 'Limit of Settlement', beyond which settlers were not allowed to pass. Officials were afraid that, if colonists moved beyond a safe area, they would lose their civilization: 'concentration produces civilisation'.[23] Such a view was, for example, loudly espoused by Wakefield, the head of a prominent school of economists, who believed that the selling of public land of Australia in small contiguous areas at high prices would bring about the conditions that prevailed in the mother country. The money derived from these sales could be used to bring out agricultural labourers from England, thus both providing some relief from continuing protests by the post-industrial English working class against poverty, and perpetuating the agricultural class in Australia.[24]

[23] Wakefield, *A Letter from Sydney and Other Writings* (London: Dent, 1929), 47. A predecessor to the 'Limits of Settlement Line' is to be found in the experiences of the American colonies. In Virginia, Massachusetts, and Connecticut authorities also prescribed penalties for those who moved ahead of the line of settlement.

[24] Lines, *Taming the Great Southern Land: A History of the Conquest of Nature in Australia* (Sydney: Allen & Unwin, 1991), 64.

Of course, policies to limit settlement were doomed to failure, as were attempts to recreate an English agrarian society based on that of England. Environmental and geographical conditions simply were not appropriate. While the Colonial authorities in London preached the virtues of intensive cultivation and mixed farming,[25] the colonists were breaking the bounds of settlement and squatting on vast tracts of land.[26] Local officials quickly realized the futility of attempting to halt the rapidly expanding pastoral industry. In the late 1830s Governor Gipps rejected Wakefield-style plans for land allocation which were designed to ensure the emergence of land-use patterns based on those of England.[27] As Gipps noted:

The Theory of forcing persons to cultivate, or even to occupy lands in the order of their natural advantages, seems altogether to fail in Australia, where not the hundredth part of the land sold by the Government is purchased with any intention of cultivating it, and where scarcely one acre in a thousand is cultivated, of the land that is occupied without being purchased . . .'[28]

This is not to suggest that small scale agriculture was not undertaken. In fact, much of Australia's history of land use is one of the battle between small scale agriculturalists (or 'selectors'[29]) and the pastoralists. Landless immigrants questioned the right of the squatters to maintain their occupancy of large tracts of land,[30] while squatters agitated to be given security of tenure over those areas of land which they had settled. Eventually, because of their wealth, and hence political influence, the squatters prevailed. As a means of delivering security of tenure, while retaining the Crown's ability to utilize lands if necessary, a system of granting leases for pastoral purposes arose. At the same time, land was opened for granting for

[25] Powell, *Environmental Management in Australia: 1788–1914* (Oxford: Oxford University Press, 1976), 23.

[26] The word 'squatter' originated in the USA, where outlaws referred to themselves as 'squatters'. In Australia the term was first used in the 1830s to refer to those who occupied vacant Crown lands without authorization.

[27] Powell, *Environmental Management*, 25.

[28] *Historical Records of Australia*, I, vol. xxi (Library Committee of Commonwealth Parliament, 1918), 127.

[29] Early legislation allowed for the conditional purchase of land. Although legislation varied between jurisdictions and over time, the general pattern was that a deposit was required, usually between 10 and 25%, and the purchasers were obliged to fulfil conditions relating to fencing, building of dwellings, and cultivation within a prescribed period of time. Failure to fulfil these conditions led to forfeit of both land and deposit. The holders of land under conditional purchase were known as 'selectors'. See e.g. the Agricultural Reserves Act 1859 (Qld).

[30] For example, James Walker of Willerowang, New South Wales, held, by virtue of a single ten pound licence, which allowed him to live beyond the 'Limits of Settlement', twenty-seven stations totalling 2.02 million hectares in 1845. By 1849, 1019 squatters held nearly 17.7 million hectares in eastern Australia.

agricultural purposes. However, owing not in inconsiderable part to fraud, much of the land set aside in New South Wales, and later Queensland, for agricultural purposes ended up in the hands of graziers. The pastoral lease system still exists today, and much of Australia is still held under pastoral lease.[31] For over a century, pastoralism was to be the backbone of the Australian economy, [32] hence the well-known statement that Australia developed 'riding on the sheep's back'. Notably, all land grants, in the form of either freehold or pastoral leasehold, were made to settlers despite the fact that the land was inhabited. A case in point is provided by the *South Australia Constitution Act*,[33] which declared in the preamble that South Australia was wasteland and uninhabited and therefore open for colonization. The Colonization Commission of South Australia, established by the British Parliament to oversee the colonization of the new colony, was aware that the colony was inhabited, but colonists claimed the land on the basis of the 'law of nature', content in the knowledge that the labour of industrious farmers and pastoralists would advance the colony from a barbarous wilderness to civilization.[34]

The image of the ideal user of land, and accepted patterns of land use, metamorphosed in a short period of time from the English agricultural labourer, who intensively cultivated small scale lots, to the Australian pastoralist, whose cattle and sheep either roamed over vast tracts of arid land or grazed in dense flocks in fertile southern areas.[35] Despite the fact that pastoralism is largely unprofitable in the 1990s, the image of the successful pastoralist is so central to Australian culture that we seem unable to escape its grasp. Although graziers hold under statutory leases, their right to the land is as unquestioned to many as the rights of urban Australians to their freehold suburban lots. However, just as Indigenous Australians did not conform to the legally and socially accepted ideal of the cultivator of the soil, nor do they conform to the image of the successful Australian pastoralist.

Indigenous Australians had inhabited the mainland of Australia for almost 60,000 years prior to settlement. Estimates as to the number of Indigenous Australians prior to contact suggest a figure of approximately 750,000 to 900,000,[36] although any estimation is likely to be inaccurate. It is impossible to make generalizations about Indigenous use of land prior to 1788.

[31] See e.g. the provisions of the Land Act 1994 (Qld).
[32] For example, by 1851, Australia supplied over 50% of Britain's wool needs.
[33] South Australia Constitution Act (4 & 5 Will IV c. 95 (1834)).
[34] Lines, *Taming the Great Southern Lands*, 66.
[35] By 1860 there were approximately 20 million sheep and 4 million cattle in eastern Australia, with several million in Tasmania alone.
[36] Davies, 'The First 150 Years', in Berndt and Berndt (eds.), *Aborigines of the West* (Nedlands: UWA Press, 1980), 78.

However, the complex relationship which Aboriginal groups have with the land was, and is, central to their culture and spirituality. Many Aboriginal groups were nomadic, and their land-use patterns reflect a relationship with the land which is characterized by a sense of obligation to the land. Aboriginal people see themselves as custodians of the land, duty bound to care for it and to ensure that it thrives for future generations. Land, or 'country' continues to be central to Aboriginal self-identity and spiritual well-being. Land not only provides physical sustenance, but is a crucial link with the Dreamtime and spiritual ancestors.

Most mainland Indigenous Australians did not practise agriculture in the accepted English sense, although they clearly did practise 'land management'. For example, use of regular low-intensity 'burn-offs' ensured regeneration of the bush, as many Australian species flourish after fire. Some groups planted yams, while others practiced river control, building dams and traps.[37] However, they did not practise English-style agriculture.[38] The 'failure' of Indigenous Australians to practise agriculture was commented on adversely as early as 1770, by Joseph Banks, botanist on James Cook's voyage of 'discovery'. He conjectured of the inhabitants of the new land that, because they did not practise agriculture, 'their reason must be supposed to hold a rank little superior to that of monkies'.[39]

The failure of Indigenous Australians to conform to accepted and 'civilized' patterns of land use, and the law's protection of those who conformed to these patterns, led to a state of perpetual otherness for 200 years and continued to justify their dispossession. The superiority of cultivation justified the initial classification of the colony as settled, the assumption that the Crown owned all land, and the grant of Crown land on the basis that it was vacant. After *Cooper* v. *Stuart* little attempt was made to argue Indigenous rights to land, although Imperial policies, and to some extent colonial policies, after responsible government, attempted to force civilization on Aborigines by teaching them the arts of cultivation.[40] However, under the influence of enlightenment thinking and social-Darwinism, or Spencerism,

[37] Lines, *Taming the Great Southern Lands*, 10.

[38] This is in direct contrast to a number of North American Indian groups. For example, the Huron and Five Nations practised a sedentary form of slash-and-burn agriculture prior to contact: see Dickerson, *Canada's First Nations: A History of Founding Peoples from the Earliest Times* (Norman: University of Oklahoma Press, 1994), 69.

[39] *The Endeavour Journals of Joseph Banks, 1769–1771*, ed. Beaglehole (Sydney: Angus & Robertson, 1962), ii. 122–3.

[40] For example, in 1814, Governor Macquarie established a programme of civilization which in part consisted of the granting of small plots of land to Aboriginals in order to teach them farming. The programme was a failure (Governor Macquarie to Earl Bathurst, despatch marked 'No. 15 of 1814' per ship Seringapatam, *Historical Records of Australia*, I, vol. VIII, July 1813–Dec. 1815 (Library Committee of Commonwealth Parliament, 1916), 369–70).

even these attempts slowly ceased. The 100 years between *Cooper* v. *Stuart* and the High Court decision in *Mabo (No. 2)* were characterized by racially discriminatory governmental policies, forced removals from land, and, in many cases, the opening of land for settlement by extermination of the original inhabitants.[41]

MABO (NO. 2)

In 1982 Eddie Mabo and four other plaintiffs commenced an action in the High Court of Australia for a declaration that they were entitled to the Murray Islands as owners, possessors, occupiers, or persons entitled to use and enjoy the islands. In 1992, after ten years of litigation, the majority of the High Court in *Mabo (No. 2)* held that the common law of Australia recognizes a form of customary native title which continues to exist where indigenous people have maintained their connection with the land and their title has not been extinguished by acts of Imperial, colonial, Commonwealth, state, or territory governments. The Murray Islands were chosen as a test case because the landholding patterns of the Meriam people and their relationship to their land resembled the kinds of Western interests in land and traditional agrarian patterns of land use that would be most familiar to the court.

The Murray Islands are located in the Torres Strait between Australia and Papua New Guinea. The total land area is only about nine square kilometres. The largest island is Mer, or the Murray Island. The other two islands, Dauar and Waier, are separated from Mer by a nine-hundred-metre channel. All three islands are surrounded by reefs. The Meriam people probably came to the Murray Islands from Melanesia via Papua New Guinea. There was only occasional contact with Europeans prior to the 1870s. In 1879 the Queensland Governor declared by Proclamation that the Murray Islands were annexed to Queensland, and that the Islands were subject to Queensland law.

In reply to the plaintiff's claims, Queensland argued that:

1. on annexation of the Murray Islands, the Crown acquired sovereignty over the islands and that the common law of Queensland became the law of the islands;

---

[41] For example, it is estimated that on establishment of the first settlement in Tasmania there were approximately 4,000 Tasmanian Aboriginals. By the 1870s virtually all had perished. Methods used by the settlers included decoy juts containing arsenic-laced flour and sugar, as well as disguised steel man-traps. Official policies included the notorious 'black line'. Governor Arthur of Tasmania mustered 2,200 armed men and attempted to drive all of the Aboriginal inhabitants onto the Tasman Peninsula, where they could be kept imprisoned until they naturally died out. All except an old man and a boy slipped through the cordon.

2. by virtue of the common law, the Crown acquired the 'radical' or 'ultimate' title to the islands;
3. as a result of acquisition of sovereignty, all the land in the islands was vested in the Crown to the exclusion of all others.

Of course, Queensland's argument exactly follows the decision of the Privy Council in *Cooper* v. *Stuart*, the result of this chain of reasoning being that all Indigenous rights to land were extinguished in 1788.

The first two of the above contentions were accepted by the High Court. However, the third—that on acquisition of sovereignty all lands were vested in the Crown—was rejected, along with the view that Australia was *terra nullius* in 1788.[42] Brennan J held that the doctrine of tenure does not compel the Australian legal system to disregard indigenous people's rights and interests in land. Although the Crown did acquire radical title, that did not automatically lead to the conclusion, as previously believed, that the Crown also gained full ownership of land:

By attributing to the Crown a radical title to all land within a territory over which the Crown has assumed sovereignty, the common law enabled the Crown, in exercise of its sovereign power, to grant an interest in land to be held of the Crown or to acquire land for the Crown's demesne. The notion of radical title enabled the Crown to become Paramount Lord of all who hold a tenure granted by the Crown and to become absolute beneficial owner of unalienated land required for the Crown's purposes. But it is not a corollary of the Crown's acquisition of a radical title to land in an occupied territory that the Crown acquired absolute beneficial ownership of that land to the exclusion of the indigenous inhabitants.[43]

However, just as the Crown's sovereign power enables it to grant interests in land, it also gives it the ability to extinguish native title.[44] Native title will be extinguished by a legislative enactment which exhibits a clear and plain intention to extinguish such rights.[45] However, this does not mean that extinguishment must be express. It can be implied. For example, native title can be extinguished by a grant of land pursuant to a valid enactment which is inconsistent with the continued existence of native title. In other words, grant of an estate in fee simple with respect to land subject to native title will extinguish that native title.

In order to prove that native title exists, it is necessary to show that the plaintiff group are biological descendants of the original inhabitants, that they have maintained an ongoing connection with the land, and that they exercise substantially the same customs as at the Crown's acquisition of sovereignty.[46] The result of this is that Aboriginal groups who were forcibly removed from their land will be unable to claim native title, as they will have lost their ongoing connection with the land.

[42] *Mabo* v. *State of Queensland (No. 2)* (1992) 175 CLR 1 at 41–3.   [43] Ibid., at 48.
[44] Ibid., at 63.   [45] Ibid., at 64.   [46] Ibid., at 61.

So what is native title? According to Brennan J, 'Native title has its origins in and is given its content by the traditional laws acknowledged by and the traditional customs observed by the Indigenous inhabitants of a territory. The nature and incidents of native title must be ascertained as a matter of fact according to those laws and customs.'[47] Thus, the content of native title varies depending on the customs and traditions of the particular plaintiff group. Native title may, for example, be a possessory right analogous to full ownership (as in *Mabo (No. 2)* itself), or a right to hunt in a particular area, or even the right periodically to enter land to conduct certain ceremonies or rituals. The fact that native title is determined according to the customs and traditions of the particular indigenous plaintiffs would appear to be to their advantage. However, although customs and traditions may be determined in part by the oral evidence of elders or other members of the clan, most evidence is by way of (white) anthropological expert evidence. That evidence will then be interpreted by a court and placed into a legal context. The Court, not surprisingly, tends to assess these customs and traditions which originate outside the common law by reference both to its own institutions and the social mores of the dominant culture. Native title is communal in nature, although individual ownership is possible if it is a facet of tradition and custom.

In *Mabo (No. 2)*, there is no question that the Court was influenced by certain of the trial judge's findings of fact. Notably, the Murray Islanders' agricultural lifestyle closely resembled white land-use patterns, as a result of which, in contrast to many mainland groups, the Islanders lived in settled villages. Further, their relationship to the land was one which was familiar to the court: it was based in economic need, and resembled the traditional English agrarian ideal of agricultural pursuits on small plots of land.

The findings of fact in the *Mabo* case came to over 400 pages. Finding of Fact 75 stated, *inter alia*,

Gardening was of the most profound importance to the inhabitants of Murray Island at and prior to European contact . . . Gardening was important not only from the point of view of subsistence, but to provide produce for consumption or exchange during the various rituals associated with different aspects of community life. Marriage and adoption involved the provision or exchange of considerable quantity of produce. Surplus produce was also required for the rituals associated with the various cults at least to sustain those who engaged in them and in connection with the various activities associated with death.[48]

---

[47] *Mabo v. State of Queensland (No. 2)* (1992) 175 CLR 1 at 58.

[48] *Determination Pursuant to Reference of 27 February, 1986 by the High Court of Australia to the Supreme Court of Queensland to hear and determine all issues of facts raised by the pleadings, particulars and further particulars in High Court action B12 of 1982*, unpublished findings of fact by Moynihan J, volume 1, at 110–111. Finding of Fact 75 comprises chapters 7–10 of volume 1.

Further, cultivation was undertaken on small, individually owned plots:

> There is no doubt that the evidence established that Murray Islanders recognise the continuance of claims to garden plots and recognise or dispute claims of entitlement by individuals in respect of those plots. It seems that an islander who claims a garden plot will generally be able to identify the person entitled to any adjoining garden plot, albeit that there may be a dispute with that person in respect of boundaries.[49]

This evidence of a relationship with the land akin to a proprietary relationship also extended to the villages:

> The evidence seems to establish that within the boundaries of a village the land continues to be divided into what in modern town planning jargon might be referred to as single residential lots or house sites upon which is erected a single unit dwelling . . . Each site was and is divided from the adjoining site by a boundary defined by some geographical or artificial feature, although on occasion adjoining occupiers might share some facilities . . . The rights associated with a site include a right to use it for domestic residence to the exclusion of others and an entitlement to determine the disposition of the land, either during life or as a consequence of death.[50]

The trial judge, Moynihan J, specifically held that the relationship of the Meriam to their land was not primarily of a spiritual nature or religious nature, as, for example, characterizes that of many mainland Aboriginal groups.[51]

The land-use patterns of the Meriam people can be contrasted with those of the plaintiffs in the earlier, and unsuccessful, case of *Milirrpum v. Nabalco*. In *Milirrpum*, representatives of several clans sued a mining company (Nabalco) and the Commonwealth, claiming the possession and ownership of areas of Arnhem Land in the Gove Peninsula over which mineral licences had been granted by the Commonwealth to Nabalco. The plaintiffs failed both in fact and at law to prove native title. Blackburn J held that the doctrine of native title had never formed part of the law of Australia. Even had it been part of the law, the clan also failed to show on the balance of probabilities that their ancestors had, at the time of annexation of New South Wales, the same links to the same areas of land as were now claimed.[52] Blackburn J noted the relationship of the clans to the land was largely spiritual, rather than economic in nature:

> As I understand it, the fundamental truth about the aboriginal's relationship to the land is that whatever else it is, it is a religious relationship . . . It is not in dispute that each clan regards itself as a spiritual entity having a spiritual relationship to each particular place or areas and having a duty to care for that land by means of

---

[49] Ibid., at 178.   [50] Ibid., at 173–4.   [51] Ibid., at 155.
[52] *Milirrpum v. Nabalco* (1970–1) 17 FLR 141 at 198.

ritual observances . . . The clan had little significance in the economic sense; indeed it was a matter of dispute whether it had any such significance, The economic relationship between the aboriginals and the land is not easy to describe. It seems that at any given time there would be various groups of aboriginals in various places about the land, each group living in a particular area, hunting animals, obtaining food, getting materials for clothing and ritual observances and moving from area to area as the economic exigencies required.[53]

In response to paragraph 4 of the pleadings in *Milirrpum*, which claimed that the clan's interest in the land was proprietary in nature, Blackburn J specifically examined the nature of the clan's interest. His Honour found that the elaborate system of social rules and customs by which the community lived was recognizable as a system of law.[54] However, he concluded that their interest in the land was not proprietary in nature. This decision was based partially on the fact that the relationship with the land was not economic in nature,[55] but primarily on the fact that it failed to exhibit the generally agreed indicia of a proprietary interest. Blackburn J noted that:

I think that property, in its many forms, generally implies the right to use or enjoy, the right to exclude others, and the right to alienate. I do not say that all these rights must co-exist before there can be a proprietary interest, or deny that each of them may be subject to qualifications. But by this standard I do not think that I can characterise the relationship of the clan to the land as proprietary.

It makes little sense to say that the clan has the right to use or enjoy the land . . . The greatest extent to which it is true that the clan as such has the right to use and enjoy the clan territory is that the clan may . . . perform ritual ceremonies on the land. That the clan has a duty to the land—to care for it—is another matter. This is not without parallels in our law, which sometimes imposes duties of such a kind on a proprietor. But this resemblance is not . . . an indication of a proprietary right.[56]

Blackburn J also found that the clan had no right to exclude and that the right to alienate was expressly repudiated by the plaintiffs in their statement of claim.[57]

It is uncertain what would have happened had the plaintiffs in *Milirrpum* chosen to appeal. On the one hand, the High Court had already recognized customary title to land in the then Territory of Papua, now part of Papua New Guinea, in the case of *Geita Sebea*.[58] On the other hand, the facts in *Milirrpum* were not as strong as those of *Mabo (No. 2)*, which provided an easy test case for the High Court. The institutions and land-use patterns of the Meriam resembled white land use and common law institutions. Their

---

[53] *Milirrpum* v. *Nabalco* (1970–1) 17 FLR 141 at at 167–8.   [54] Ibid., at 268.
[55] Ibid., at 270.   [56] Ibid., at 272.   [57] Ibid.
[58] *Geita Sebea* v. *The Territory of Papua* (1941) 67 CLR 544. The High Court again recognized customary title to land in Papua two years after the decision in *Milirrpum* in *Administrator of Papua and New Guinea* v. *Daera Guba* (1973) 130 CLR 353.

economic reliance on the land, individual, non-communal landholding, and market garden economy marked them as a civilized people with a recognizable entitlement to land.

THE TRIUMPH OF THE COMMON LAW

The decision in *Mabo (No. 2)* has been described as revolutionary.[59] In reality, however, it is a triumph for traditional property rights and common law methodology. In many ways, the Court performed a 'sleight of hand'. On the one hand, the Court acknowledges the law's shameful treatment of Indigenous peoples, while at the same time it constructs the rules for the recognition of native title so narrowly that it seems unlikely that there will be many successful claims through the courts. Negotiation between all the groups with interests in a particular native title claim may, in the end, be more fruitful than litigation.

The Court's powerful rhetoric distracts the reader from the reality of its decision. An example of rhetoric used by the Court includes the following statement by Deane and Gaudron JJ: 'The acts and events by which . . . dispossession in legal theory was carried into practical effect constitute the darkest aspect of the history of this nation. The nation as a whole must remain diminished unless and until there is an acknowledgment of, and retreat from, those past injustices.'[60]

On a more specific level, the Court also refers to the inappropriateness of forcing aboriginal interests in land to conform to Western ideals, citing the famous statement of Lord Haldane in *Amodu Tijani*, where his Lordship notes 'a tendency, operating at times unconsciously, to render [native title] conceptually in terms which are appropriate only to systems which have grown up under English law. But this tendency has to be held in check closely.'[61]

Unfortunately, having decried such an approach, the Court implicitly adopts it by classifying native title according to traditional methodology, but more importantly, by making it subservient to interests derived from Crown grant. To acknowledge past injustices is one thing: however, to modify the shape of the common law in order to address those wrongs is clearly another. Native title can be recognized only if it does not alter the shape of the common law:

[59] See, generally, Stephenson (ed.), *Mabo: A Judicial Revolution* (Brisbane: University of Queensland Press, 1993).

[60] *Mabo v. State of Queensland (No. 2)* (1992) 175 CLR 1 at 109.

[61] *Amodu Tijani v. Southern Nigeria (Secretary)* [1921] 2 AC 399 at 403; *Mabo v. State of Queensland (No. 2)* (1992) 175 CLR 1 at 84.

In discharging its duty to declare the common law of Australia, this Court is not free to adopt rules that accord with contemporary notions of justice and human rights if their adoption would fracture the skeleton of principle which gives the body of our law its shape and internal consistency. Australian law is not only the historical successor of, but is an organic development from, the law of England.[62]

As a result, native title must be 'squeezed' into the existing framework of the Australian Legal System. The following two examples serve to illustrate this point.

Extinguishment of Native Title

As noted above, native title is extinguished by adverse Crown grant. Thus, a grant of freehold title will always extinguish native title, even if that land granted remains vacant and unused. This is because the key feature of an estate in fee simple is that it gives the holder exclusive possession. According to the court, exclusive possession is *legally* inconsistent with continued Aboriginal land use, although the *factual* reality may be quite different. The holder of an estate in fee simple may not even be using the land. This has two results. The first is that the Court has made an implicit value judgement as to the relative worth of indigenous and non-indigenous interests in land, and has chosen to elevate interests derived by Crown grant above those derived from custom or tradition. Secondly, in deciding whether native title has been extinguished, the Court does not consider what use of land is actually occurring (although it will consider this when it decides whether native title exists at all), or the relationships between the parties claiming interests to the land, but merely the nature of the Crown derived interest which is claimed to extinguish native title. Therefore, if a fee simple interest was granted over land last century, and that interest was resumed by the Crown so that it again became Crown vacant land, native title would nevertheless be extinguished.

The High Court had an opportunity to reconsider the rules on extinguishment in the recent case of *The Wik Peoples*. Soon after the decision in *Mabo (No. 2)*, the Wik People commenced proceedings in the Federal Court of Australia against Queensland and the Commonwealth for a declaration that they had native title rights over an area of land and waters in far north Queensland. The Thayorre People were later joined to the action, as the legal questions facing them were virtually identical. In both cases, the lands claimed included parcels either presently subject to a pastoral lease, or which had been subject to a pastoral lease in the first part of the century, but was now again Crown land. The major issue before the Court was whether or not native title was extinguished by pastoral lease. As expected,

---

[62] *Mabo v. State of Queensland (No. 2) (1992) 175 CLR 1*, per Brennan J at 109.

the trial judge, Drummond J, found that the pastoral leases had extinguished native title because they confer exclusive possession. The Wik and Thayorre appealed and the matter was removed to the High Court.

Most people confidently predicted that the High Court would uphold the trial judge's decision. Dicta by Brennan J in *Mabo (No. 2)* indicated that the grant of a leasehold interest would extinguish native title. His Honour reasoned that although the Crown had mere radical title, the granting of a lease would create a reversionary interest in the Crown, which at the expiration of the lease would expand the Crown's interest from radical title only to full ownership.[63] A reflection of this as the accepted view is found in the preamble to the *Native Title Act*, which states, *inter alia*, that:

The High Court has:
  (b) held that native title is extinguished by valid government acts that are inconsistent with the continued existence of native title rights and interests, such as the grant of freehold or leasehold estates.

Instead, the High Court held by a 4–3 majority that native title is not extinguished by statutory pastoral leases, a decision which has caused as much political furore as did the original decision in *Mabo (No. 2)*. Almost 70 per cent of the Australian continent is held under some form of statutory lease. The majority[64] held that pastoral leases are not common law leases, as they do not confer exclusive possession. Rather, they are a creature of statute, and no exclusive possession was granted to the lessees by the statutes which authorized the granting of the lease.[65] Native title will be extinguished only if it cannot coexist with rights granted under the pastoral lease.[66] The flip side of this, of course, is that, in the event of an inconsistency between native title rights and the rights granted to pastoralists under the lease, native title rights must 'yield' to the pastoralists' rights.[67]

This decision was hailed by Indigenous groups as a victory. Pastoralists, stunned by the Court's decision, denounced it as 'judicial activism'. The public's reaction was polarized, just as it was over the original decision in *Mabo (No. 2)*. Concerned at what they see as a threat to their security of tenure, pastoralists have demanded that the government secure their interests by legislating to ensure that pastoral leases do extinguish native title,

---

[63] Ibid., at 73.

[64] The majority consisted of Gummow, Toohey, Gaudron, and Kirby J.J. Notably, membership of the High Court changed between *Mabo v. State of Queensland (No. 2)* (1992) 175 CLR 1 and *The Wik Peoples v. Queensland* (1996) 141 ALR 129. Mason CJ and Deane J retired and were replaced by Gummow and Kirby JJ.

[65] The Acts at issue were the Land Act 1910 (Qld) and the Land Act 1962 (Qld). The successor to these acts is the Land Act 1994 (Qld). All states have similar legislation.

[66] *The Wik Peoples v. Queensland* (1996) 141 ALR 129 at 184.

[67] Ibid. 190.

preferably by upgrading their tenure to freehold.[68] This has led to enormous pressure being placed on the Federal Government, as one partner to the Liberal/National coalition, the National Party, draws its support base from the rural sector and particularly from those most affected by the High Court's decision.

Implicitly, arguments for the precedence of pastoral leases over native title are a retake of ones we have considered earlier: namely, that a spiritual, non-economically based interest in land cannot be allowed to stand in the way of pastoralism, which, according to a Western viewpoint, is an economically and culturally superior mode of land use. Pastoralists draw strength in their argument from their association with the dominant and idealized pattern of land use in Australia. They point to the fact that their leases have been in the family for several generations, while ignoring the length of association that an indigenous group must demonstrate with regard to the same land in order to be able to prove native title. In fact, the arguments being put forward for security of tenure by the pastoralists mirror those invoked by squatters for recognition of their tenure in the early 1800s. The High Court's crucial holding that native title must give way to pastoral interests where they cannot coexist has been sidestepped in the debate. Even a claim as strong as that of the Meriam people, with their agrarian land-use patterns, would not stand up to the claims of the holder of a pastoral lease to the same land.

There is no doubt that the High Court's decision that native title can coexist with pastoral leases is of vital importance, as it allows an enormous number of claims to proceed.[69] However, it is questionable whether it adds anything to the decision in *Mabo (No. 2)* as regards the place of native title within the Australian Legal System, except perhaps to confirm both that native title will always be subordinate to interests derived from the Crown, and that the law will continue to favour those who conform to expected and 'ideal' patterns of land use. It is true that the Court's analysis of the nature of pastoral leases by reference to the historical and political context in which they first arose does show signs that the Court is attempting to reconnect the notion of property with other (non-legal) discourses. However, this reconnection does not appear to extend to native title.

---

[68] The Federal Government has recently ruled out the upgrading of pastoral leases to freehold: *The Australian* (31 May 1997). However, this is largely due to the enormous compensation payout that would accompany mass extinguishment of native title.

[69] Pastoral leases, for example, cover 41% of South Australia, 49% of the Northern Territory, 37% of Western Australia, and 65% of Queensland.

Classification of Native Title

The second example of how the law attempts to 'squeeze' native title into its existing framework considers the common law's classification of native title. According to the common law, we have two classifications of interests: proprietary or non-proprietary (personal). With very few exceptions, all interests fit within this dichotomy. Proprietary interests are generally seen as 'better' interests, which the law will protect with a wide range of remedies. So where does native title fit within this dichotomy? As noted above, the High Court cautions against forcing native title to conform to Western notions of property. As a result, the Court is reluctant to classify native title as either. However, common law methodology demands that the court find a category for native title. The problem is that native title simply does not exhibit the traditional criteria of a property interest. For example, the law deems that native title is not freely alienable. Rather, it can be alienated to the Crown or another Indigenous group only if this is traditionally allowed. If anything, according to older precedents, native title resembles a personal interest.[70] However, the Court recognized that to classify native title as such would be politically and culturally inappropriate because it implicitly down grades native title. As a result, the Court determined, in line with the Privy Council and the Supreme Court of Canada, that native title is best classified as unique or *sui generis*.[71] This, however, amounted to a judicial 'sleight of hand'. On the one hand, the Court claimed that, by determining native title is a *sui generis* interest, it avoided the culturally inappropriate action of forcing native title to be recognized as a Western institution.[72] On the other hand, the Court turned around, and did in fact treat native title in just that manner. In an exercise of traditional common law methodology, the Court created a category for native title. By claiming native title was *sui generis*, it allowed the Court to place particular rules on both the recognition of native title, and its priority when compared with other interests. Thus, as depicted by the High Court, native title is an anomaly, to be categorized as something other than a property interest, and to be accorded less protection than property interests. Native title has been effectively placed in the 'too-hard basket' and subsumed into the common law in a way which does not disturb the traditional hierarchy of rights. Just as indigenous rights were historically denied by defining Aboriginal people

---

[70] *St Catherine's Milling Case* (1888) 14 AC 46 at 54. An example of a personal interest in land is a licence.

[71] *Mabo v. State of Queensland (No. 2)* (1992) 175 CLR 1 at 89. See *Guerin v. The Queen* (1984) 13 DLR (4th), 321 at 339, per Dickson J (Supreme Court of Canada) and *Amodu Tijani* (1921) at 409–10 (PC).

[72] *Mabo v. State of Queensland (No. 2)* (1992) 175 CLR 1 at 89.

and their use of land as other, in *Mabo (No. 2)* native title is defined by what it is not.

A preferable course of action might have been to rethink what is meant by 'property' in order to recognize the social, political, and cultural aspects of 'property'. The traditional liberal notion of property is no longer relevant to Australian society (assuming it ever was). Furthermore, property law remains rooted to structures of a society that no longer exists. The rigid rules of property law have increasingly little relevance to current structures, and have virtually no relevance to Aboriginal peoples and their traditional relationships with the land. Classifying something as 'property' tells us nothing about the complex social fabric in which those interests are located. However, the question remains whether even a more fluid rereading of property could encompass the special nature of Indigenous relationships with the land. We need to consider whether property can ever escape its cultural origins, or whether it is destined to remain the product of a Western, medieval society. On a more fundamental level, we need to question whether it is even appropriate to locate native title within any notion of property, even an expanded and more fluid one.

The problems of first proving that this *sui generis* interest exists, and then of demonstrating that it has not been extinguished by subsequent government action, are legion. To date there have been hundreds of claims for native title. *Mabo (No. 2)* remains the only successful determination of native title through the court process.[73] While this is in part due to the cumbersome application process under the *Native Title Act* (discussed below), it is also due to the strict criteria and requirements of proof placed on any recognition of native title by the common law.

THE GOVERNMENT SOLUTION: THE NATIVE TITLE ACT

Not surprisingly, the High Court decision in *Mabo (No. 2)* led to considerable public reaction, not least from the natural resources sector, which was concerned about both the validity of leases and the impact both on future exploration in the mining industry and development in the pastoral industry. Mining industry lobbies placed considerable pressure on both parties to legislate a solution in the federal election campaign held some eight months after the decision in *Mabo (No. 2)* was handed down. A further problem was that the public generally did not, and to a large extent still do not, understand the decision in *Mabo (No. 2)*. Hype by the media, politicians, and in

---

[73] However, there have been two subsequent determinations, the Dungutti and Hopevale claims, based on a mediated process.

some cases Indigenous Australians themselves[74] did not help matters. The Prime Minister, Paul Keating had indicated prior to the election that he intended to do more than merely validate titles in response to the resource sector's concerns. He stated that *Mabo (No. 2)* should be 'an historic turning point, the basis for a new relationship between indigenous and non-aboriginal Australians'.[75]

After winning the election, Paul Keating's government committed itself to a schedule of consultations over a six-month period, to culminate in a bill to go before parliament. The negotiation period was intense and often bitter. It was not merely Aboriginal peoples and the mining lobbies which could not agree on the best way to deal with the High Court's decision, but also the state governments, some of whom managed simultaneously to deny during negotiations with the Federal Government that *Mabo (No. 2)* had any legal implications for mainland Australia, while at the same time warning the public of the dangers to their security of tenure.

The negotiations culminated in the passing of the Native Title Act 1993 (Cth.), which came into operation on 1 January 1994.[76] The Act is wide-ranging in nature and purports to treat native title in a non-discriminatory way. To summarize, the Act provides for:

- the establishment of a claims process for native title;[77]
- the establishment of the National Native Title Tribunal,[78] which provides a mediation service for all parties to a native title claim, but does not have the power to make a determination of native title, as such determinations can be made only by a court;
- the validation of governmental actions prior to 1 January 1994 which may have affected native title.[79] The Act designates governmental actions as category A, B, C, or D 'past acts', each of which has a different effect on native title. For example, a category A past act wholly extinguished native title, while a category C act suspends native title for the duration of act.[80] Notably, only pastoral leases in force at the date of commencement of the Act were caught by the past act provisions, leaving the way open for the Wik and Thayorre People;

---

[74] For example, at the end of 1992, the South East Queensland Aboriginal and Islander Legal Service revealed that it would claim Brisbane's central business district, although it later withdrew this claim.

[75] Keating, 'Redfern Park Speech' (1993) 3(61) Aboriginal Law Bulletin 4 at 5.

[76] The High Court upheld the constitutional validity of the Act (excepting s. 12) in *Western Australia* v. *The Commonwealth (The Native Title Act Case)* (1995) 183 CLR 373.

[77] Part 3 Native Title Act 1993, part 3.   [78] Ibid., s. 107.

[79] Ibid., part 2, division 2.

[80] An example of a category A past act is the grant of an estate in fee simple (Native Title Act 1993, s. 229(2)), while an example of a category C past act is the granting of a mining lease (Native Title Act 1993, ss. 231, 238).

- the protection of native title by restricting the circumstances in which native title may be extinguished. Native title may now be extinguished only in accordance with the Act.[81] In general, native title is now not extinguished by adverse governmental action, but 'suspended' for the term of the Act.[82] This results, however, in the unsatisfactory situation where native title can be 'suspended' for the entire term of a ninety-nine-year mining lease, with the land returned to the traditional owners in a condition vastly different to that at the outset of the lease;
- the setting-up of a 'right to negotiate' procedure, under which mining companies can negotiate with Aboriginal groups for the right to explore or mine on land subject to native title.[83] This procedure was the subject of much criticism at the time of the enactment, because it fails to give Aboriginal peoples a right to refuse to allow mining on their land. The Act mandates negotiations between mining companies seeking access to land and native title owners. If negotiations for mining access fail, the matter can be arbitrated by the Federal Court. If the Federal Court finds for the native title holders, this decision can be overturned by the Federal Minister in the 'national interest'.[84] Under the present Liberal/National coalition government which is presently considering allowing new uranium mines in Kakadu National Park in the Northern Territory, it seems likely that the Minister would find in favour of the mining company.

The definition of native title in the Act is the same as at common law.[85] In fact, the Act is largely procedural, except for its limitation on future extinguishment. However, despite these limitations, the status of native title as subordinate to other interests—for example, an estate in fee simple, or a statutorily derived mining lease—does not change. It is true that native title is suspended, not extinguished, but that is of little comfort to the holder of a native title interest who may be unable to exercise that interest in her life time.

Further, it leaves native title as largely a concern of evidence or priorities. The underlying substance of the decision in *Mabo (No. 2)* is not changed. If the applicant can both furnish sufficient and appropriate evidence that its interest conforms to the High Court's requirements in *Mabo (No. 2)*, and demonstrate that the interest has not been extinguished at some point in the past, then the applicant will succeed. Just as the High Court did, the government sidestepped the difficult issues raised and left unanswered by *Mabo (No. 2)*. The Act ignores the consequent questions as to the

[81] Native Title Act 1993, s. 11.

[82] See the 'future act provisions', Native Title Act, ss. 22, 23, 233, and the 'non-extinguishment principle', ibid., s. 238.

[83] Ibid., ss. 26–44.   [84] Ibid., s. 42.   [85] Ibid., s. 233.

place of Indigenous peoples and native title rights in the Australian legal and political system. 'Protection' of native title rights does not take place in the context of a large land-reform issue. Nor does the Act address the problem of the thousands who were dispossessed by various governments and have lost their traditional connection to the land. In the end, the Act entrenches the common law's view of native title as an anomaly or exception and merely adds a procedural layer to an already cumbersome process of proof.

CONCLUSION

It is uncertain what the future holds for native title. The euphoria which for Indigenous Australians accompanied the decision in *Mabo (No. 2)* has abated, as the reality of trying to prove native title has set in. Legal recognition of traditional Aboriginal rights to land has had little impact on the lives of most Indigenous Australians. The rhetoric has changed, but they remain dispossessed by the law. The law's original dispossession was justified by reference to the specific social and political organizations and land use of the colonists. The social fabric of society has changed, but the position of Aboriginal Australians on the outskirts has not. Apparently, they still fail to conform to the expected and accepted standards of the majority of society. Native title is the ultimate example of how property is socially constructed, and how it legitimizes social power relationships. If property institutions reflect social values and power,[86] then the time has come for us to consider whose social values are being reflected, and why.

[86] See Gray, 'Equitable Property', (1994) 47(2) CLP 157 at 160.

12

LAND AND POST-APARTHEID RECONSTRUCTION IN SOUTH AFRICA

Michael Robertson

> The primary reason for the government's land reform measures is to redress the injustices of apartheid and to alleviate the impoverishment and suffering that it caused . . . Resentment over land dispossession runs deep in society . . . Without a significant change in the racial distribution of land ownership, there can be no long-term political stability and therefore no economic prosperity.[1]

This chapter examines the role of land in post-apartheid 'reconstruction' in South Africa. In particular it seeks to examine how post-apartheid South Africa is trying to find a workable, justifiable mix of social and private needs in land, given the apartheid legacy and the stated goals of social reconstruction. The distinctive feature of the reform so far, it is suggested, is the attention being paid to the conception of land as a social commodity whose role is linked to the provision of material support and the opportunity for civic participation in a democratic culture.

Limited reference will also be made in the chapter to land-reform attempts in Latin America, principally in order to make a distinction between the *social function* of landownership evident in the Latin American region, and the *social purpose* approach to land which is emerging in the new South Africa. Although the social role of property—and land in particular—assumes great significance in both contexts, the 'social purpose' approach in South Africa (emphasizing the community's interest in having land shared as widely as possible) is indicative of a policy which appears to be more equitable, coherent, and practicable than the Latin American 'social function' approach (which places use obligations upon the owner). The social purpose theme is explored in the latter half of the chapter.

Land reform, sometimes referred to as agrarian reform,[2] has been a global

---

[1] South African government, Department of Land Affairs, Green Paper on South African Land Policy, Pretoria (Feb. 1996), 5–6.

[2] Derived from the Spanish *reforma agraria*. The term implies that other institutions must be reshaped in concert with changes to the actual land system in order to allow the reform to be successful (see Thiesenhusen, 'Introduction: Searching for Agrarian Reform in Latin America', in Thiesenhusen (ed.), *Searching for Agrarian Reform in Latin America* (Boston: Unwin Hyman, 1989), 7–8).

issue for at least the second half of the twentieth century. Identifiable and frequently well-documented reform programmes exist or existed in Europe, Asia, Latin America and Africa. While a definition of 'land reform' is elusive, one suggestion is that it is 'invariably a more or less direct, publicly controlled change in the existing character of land ownership, and it normally attempts a diffusion of wealth, income or productive capacity'.[3]

The main arguments for land reform are generally couched in terms of goals of social equity or as economic necessity (for individuals or as part of a development policy). Other arguments scarcely conceal ideological or political dogma. The presence of these social, economic, and political dimensions indicate why land reform is an interdisciplinary topic embracing concerns of property (in law), production and capital (in economics), social security (in social psychology), culture (in anthropology), social systems (in sociology), and soil use (in agriculture). It is also fertile terrain for political philosophers.[4]

Most approaches to land reform emphasize the need for improved economic conditions in the rural sector. Scholars speak of agrarian reform being integral to the whole process of agricultural development; or about making profound changes to the agrarian structure; or about increasing agricultural output; or about ensuring that the rural poor benefit from the process.[5] Sometimes land reform is also a 'popular slogan for redistribution of wealth and promotion of economic development'.[6]

In order to be able to make sense of the dimensions and significance of post-apartheid land reform which began in 1994, the chapter begins by summarizing the apartheid legacy and examining developments in land affairs in the final few years of apartheid rule.

PRE-DEMOCRACY LAND LAW HISTORY IN SOUTH AFRICA

Indigenous peoples of Southern Africa occupied and utilized land under various tribal practices when colonial settlement began in 1652. An early explanation of the nature of customary land tenure, given in 1883, was that the land belonged to the tribe and that the chief had the right of giving

[3] King, *Land Reform: A World Survey* (Boulder, Colo.: Westview Press, 1977), 5, relying upon Carroll, *The Concept of Land Reform* (New York: FAO, 1955), 25.

[4] King, *Land Reform*, 3–4.

[5] Thiesenhusen, 'Introduction', 7; Thome, 'Agrarian Reform Legislation: Chile', in Dorner (ed.), *Land Reform in Latin America* (Madison, Wis.: Land Tenure Center, University of Wisconsin, 1971), 81 at 99; Chonchol, *El Desarrollo de America y la Reforma Agraria* (Madison, Wis.: Land Tenure Center, University of Wisconsin, n.d.); Oliart, *El legalismo como ideologia politica en las leyes de reforma agraria latinoamericana* (Bogota, 1970), 26–9; trans. M. Ocran.

[6] King, *Land Reform*, 3.

occupation to members of the tribe. Headmen had the right of subdividing it subject to an appeal to the chief. Land was, however, regarded as the property of the chief.[7]

The early European settlers, and later colonists, brought with them a variety of Roman and Roman–Dutch legal principles applicable to the acquisition, use, and disposal of land.[8] These principles together reflected a classical view of property[9] and were accompanied by remedies recognizing, in appropriate circumstances, the right of the holder to exclude others and to vindicate.[10]

It has been suggested that the imposition in Africa of European colonists' property principles was not simply the substitution of private property for non-private or communal property concepts. It was, rather, the application of a specific form of private property that was functional to capitalism and imperialism. Although capitalist property and property relations were underdeveloped prior to colonial domination of African society, they were not unknown. Precolonial social systems also manifested instances of social-class stratification and gender discrimination in property access.[11]

From the time of the first recorded land 'deal' in 1672 between the Dutch East India Company and indigenous Cape inhabitants, a process began which would ultimately alter traditional Southern African tenure forms forever. It is probably now only of historical significance that the integrity of these early land treaties is questionable,[12] as is the issue of whether the tribal leaders, to whom the notion of sale was unknown, possessed the authority to sell off tribal land.[13]

---

[7] Evidence of Theophilus Shepstone in Minutes of Evidence, Cape Native Laws Commission, 1883, 55–6.

[8] *Dominium, emphyteusis,* possession, *usufruct, fideicommissum, commadatum, precarium,* and *locatio conductio rei*: Buckland, *The Main Institutions of Roman Private Law* (Cambridge: Cambridge University Press, 1931), 93 ff.; and Roman–Dutch forms such as *leen goed, eigen goed,* and quit-rent (e.g. *tijnsrecht*): Lee, *An Introduction to Roman-Dutch Law* (5th edn., Oxford: Oxford University Press, 1953), 150.

[9] Described e.g. by Cohen, 'Property and Sovereignty' in Macpherson (ed.), *Property: Mainstream and Critical Positions* (Toronto: University of Toronto Press, 1978), 155 at 159.

[10] 'An owner may always vindicate his property wherever it is found' *per* de Villiers CJ in *Salvage Association of London* v. *SA Salvage Syndicate Ltd.* 23 SC 171); the main remedies, still evident in the modern legal system, were *rei vindicatio, mandament van spolie,* and *actio ad exhibendum.*

[11] Gutto, *Property and Land Reform: Constitutional and Jurisprudential Perspectives* (Durban: Butterworths, 1995), 13. The patriarchal nature of customary land tenure was noted also in the Mandela government's Green Paper on South African Land Policy, 21.

[12] The present government believes that it is not possible to entertain land claims which rely on dispossession by colonial authorities or settlers prior to 1913 (Green Paper on South African Land Policy, 37).

[13] Davenport and Hunt (eds.), *The Right to the Land* (Cape Town: David Philip, 1974), 9–10.

By the time of the formation of the Union of South Africa in 1910, the four colonial legislatures, acting separately, had established a system of laws and practices that regulated the acquisition and occupation of land by indigenous people throughout the region. These controls were, in large measure, racially discriminatory. They placed heavy restrictions on indigenous land occupation, although the extent of their coercive content was inconstant. The controls included the establishment of 'reserves' for indigenous inhabitants under different 'models' of land use and containment.[14]

The general lack of uniformity of law and practice was to create something of a challenge for the first Union parliament. The resulting Natives' Land Act of 1913[15] was perceived at the time to be a major legislative achievement and was destined to have a profoundly significant impact on South African society over nearly eight decades. It was augmented in the 1940s by Group Areas legislation and many other laws which together constituted the system of government that would become known as *apartheid*. The restrictive and racist land legislation would be seen by many to provide the core of the apartheid system. And, unlike the Roman and Roman–Dutch legal principles that continued to operate except where displaced by the apartheid laws, the latter reflected the very antithesis of the classical view of property. The land laws of apartheid, being statutory in origin, effectively 'trumped' the Roman–Dutch principles. Freedom, individualism, and autonomy, implicit in the liberal view of property, were anathema to the laws of apartheid.

Summarized, it is possible to identify three major streams of white parliamentary activity that together provided the system of legal, race-based land control under the apartheid system. The first stream consisted of the many statutes that decreed physical racial segregation over the bulk of the land mass of South Africa. This suite of laws was anchored by the Natives' Land Act 1913 and applied to all areas that were not subject to urban controls (the second category) and the Group Areas legislation (the third category). The second category consisted of laws aimed at controlling the entry and residence of Africans in urban areas. For many years the linchpin was the Natives (Urban Areas) Act 1923.[16] Controls and restrictions were loosened in the final few years of apartheid, but for decades these laws effectively prevented the establishment of a stable, permanent African urban population. The third category, the Group Areas system, was used in

[14] On the social and economic significance of reserves see Robertson, 'Segregation Land Law: A Socio-Legal Analysis' in Corder (ed.), *Essays on Law and Social Practice in South Africa* (Cape Town: Juta, 1988), 285.

[15] Act 27 of 1913.

[16] Act 21 of 1923, replaced in 1945 and superseded by the Black Communities Development Act 4 of 1984.

practice to designate areas, for both residence and business activity, for persons classified as 'white', 'coloured' and Asian (but not African).

All these many laws, taken together, were preoccupied with racial classification of individuals, designation of geographical race zones for residential and commercial activity, and mechanisms (including penal provisions) for enforcement. But they manifested at least one other significant component: the power of officials, acting often with extensive discretion, who were immune from judicial scrutiny. This was the power to order the removal and resettlement of people whose occupation or ownership of land was offensive to the grand plan. In many cases land was expropriated; in others the victims did not have expropriable rights and their removal and relocation presented less difficulties for the authorities. In excess of three million South Africans were removed, sometimes forcibly, by the early 1980s[17] and the practice continued well into the decade. Their land, once acquired by the state, was frequently made available to white beneficiaries. A programme of restitution[18] for those dispossessed during the greater part of the century was to become a central plank of the Mandela government's immediate post-election land-reform policy.[19]

Despite the grand plan, many black persons resided in the comparatively huge white zones, frequently as farmworkers serving the labour needs of white agriculture. Together with their families they occupied land which, in some instances, had been occupied by their forebears for many generations. However, they lacked tenure security, possessing no legally recognizable rights in the land. The real homes of all black people were seen by the authorities to be in the homelands, the areas which originated in the pre-Union reserves and which constituted less than 20 per cent of all the land in South Africa.[20] These ten homelands—or *bantustans*—were supposed ultimately to become independent states. Four did, but their sovereign status was never recognized by any government outside South Africa.

The homeland (or reserve) system together with the labour policies of both colonial and apartheid governments have provoked a considerable body of literature and debate.[21] While the extent of poverty and 'underdevelopment' in the homelands has been widely recognized, explanations differ as to the significance of *bantustans* for the wider South African economy over that period. One view is that the impoverishment of these areas,

[17] Platsky and Walker, *The Surplus People: Forced Removals in South Africa* (Johannesburg: Ravan, 1985), 9.

[18] In this context 'restitution' is used to denote a category of land reform in terms of which land is returned to formerly dispossessed people.

[19] See below.

[20] Frequently this figure was put at 13%, but it was probably slightly larger than this following the addition of more lands to the homelands in the consolidation process in the 1970s and 1980s.

[21] For a summary of some of these issues, see Robertson, 'Segregation Land Law', 285.

together with the social systems they barely supported, was directly functional (beneficially) to the development of the white economy. The homeland system, involving the allocation of plots of land to families under delegated legislation schemes (which were ostensibly based on customary tenure principles), were intended to provide a welfare net for residents[22] and returning migrant workers, thereby relieving the white government of responsibility for these functions. In this perspective it also seems plausible that the retention of a one-person-one-(small)-plot land-allocation system (a derivation of the customary tenure scheme) was a convenient device.[23] Not only did the size of the allotments ensure that a subsistence economy would never be possible, and therefore that there would always be a steady stream of work-seekers in the white economy, but the land-allocation system could utilize traditional tribal structures to reinforce the social system. This thesis leads to the conclusion that land was a profoundly important commodity in economic and political control under apartheid.

In February 1990 de Klerk (the last apartheid head of state) announced the white government's intention to introduce significant political reforms. A year later a White Paper on land reform[24] announced a series of legislative changes. The most significant was the intended abolition of the Acts that held together the apartheid land edifice. These various laws, including the Land Act and the Group Areas Act, were repealed later in the year.[25] Other reforms were simultaneously introduced.[26]

These repeals were an important step in dismantling formal, geographical apartheid. In one assessment they were an attempt to defuse the complex and controversial racial politics of the land issue by placing land rights at the mercy of the market.[27] However, given that a legacy of extensive and racially skewed land-occupation patterns had already been engineered under apartheid land law, it was highly unlikely that the free-market 'solution' would be seen to be sufficient reform by the government in waiting.

The de Klerk reform package included the introduction of a commission on land allocation.[28] Although, in principle, this body was empowered to identify state-owned land for restitution purposes, the life of the commission

[22] See also the discussion below, p. 322, on the place of customary land practice in post-apartheid reform.

[23] Tribal chiefs were given powers over land 'beyond those normally sanctioned under customary law' (Green Paper on South African Land Policy), 9.

[24] South African government, White Paper on Land Reform, B-91, Cape Town (1991).

[25] Abolition of Racially Based Land Measures Act 108 of 1991.

[26] Upgrading of Land Tenure Rights Act 112 of 1991 and Less Formal Township Establishment Act 113 of 1991.

[27] Roux, 'Property, Land as Property, and the Interim Constitution' (Cape Town: University of Cape Town, n.d.).

[28] Under Abolition of Racially Based Land Measures Act 108 of 1991, ss. 89–96.

was short and unremarkable. Its achievements were insubstantial and its work was overtaken by the process of political change itself.

At this time the African National Congress (ANC) was beginning to publish its own land-reform proposals. One manifestation of the views within the ANC appeared in a draft bill of rights for the new society.[29] Article 11, seemingly qualified elsewhere in the document, presented the right to property, including land, as a fundamental human right. It stated that all persons would have the right to acquire, possess, own, or dispose of property without distinction based on race or gender, etc. Article 13, dealing with affirmative action, provided that the future constitution would not, however, prevent the enactment of laws designed to procure land for persons who in the past had been disadvantaged by discrimination. This was a clear and direct signal of the likelihood of the introduction of land-reform programmes driven by a concern to reverse centuries of racial discrimination.

Simultaneously, the ANC was also formulating a major policy document that would become known simply as 'RDP' (Reconstruction and Development Programme). The initial RDP proposals stated that a national land reform programme was needed to redress the injustices caused by forced removals and the historical denial of land access. Land reform, in this view, should supply residential and productive land to the rural poor and also address the issue of insecurity of land tenure.[30] The ambitious and far-reaching social-reconstruction policy proposals, designed ultimately to be a blueprint for the transformation of South African society, would later surface as the Mandela government's White Paper on Reconstruction and Development.[31]

During 1993, in the year prior to the first democratic elections, South Africa's main political groups negotiated an interim constitution containing a bill of rights.[32]

Section 28 of the interim constitution provides that every person has the right to acquire and hold rights in property and that no deprivation of any rights in property is permitted except by law. Where any rights in property *are* expropriated by law, such expropriation will be permissible only for public purposes and will be subject to payment of compensation. This section became known as 'the property clause' in the Act's chapter on Fundamental Rights (chapter 3). The question of whether a property-

[29] African National Congress, *A Draft Bill of Rights for a New South Africa* (Cape Town: Center for Development Studies, University of Western Cape, 1990).

[30] Van der Walt, 'Land Reform in South Africa since 1990—an Overview' (1995) 10 SA Public Law 1 at 17–18.

[31] South African government, White Paper on Reconstruction and Development, Cape Town, 15 Nov. 1994, in *Government Gazette*, No. 16085, 23 Nov. 1994.

[32] Constitution of the Republic of South Africa Act 200 of 1993.

protection provision should be included in the final constitution would engender much political debate during 1996.

The interim constitution also contains three sections under the heading 'Restitution of Land Rights'.[33] In terms of these sections, a future Act of Parliament will provide avenues for the restitution of land rights to persons or communities who have been dispossessed of their land (1) at any time after a date to be fixed in the legislation, and (2) under a law which was racially discriminatory. The Mandela government was to waste no time enacting a restitution law (which was passed before the end of 1994).[34]

The interim constitution also required the passing of a 'new constitutional text' within two years from the date of the first sitting of the final constitution-making body, the Constitutional Assembly.[35]

On the eve of the first democratic elections in 1994 a number of important questions about the land issue were calling for and receiving urgent attention. Some of these were:

1. How should the first post-apartheid government approach the issue of property generally, and land in particular, in its social, economic, and legal policy-planning?
2. What role, if any, should (or could) land and land reform play in the process of social reconstruction and development of the society generally?
3. Ought property in general, and land in particular, to receive protection in the final constitution or bill of rights?
4. Assuming the promulgation of a law to permit and facilitate restitution of land (as envisaged in the interim constitution) what should the content of the law be?[36]
5. Besides restitution, should there be a broader land-reform programme, involving the *redistribution* of land to persons disadvantaged, but not directly dispossessed, under the laws of apartheid and the social systems which preceded the apartheid era?
6. Assuming the adoption of various land-reform measures, should South Africans in future be entitled to expect constitutionally protected *security of tenure* in their occupation of land? (This issue was prompted by a number of factors, including the plight of farmworkers, the survival of customary tenure practices in various areas, and, perhaps, the recognition that the sometimes brutal removal practices of the past should under no circumstances be repeated.)

---

[33] ss. 121, 122, 123.   [34] Restitution of Land Rights Act 22 of 1994.
[35] s. 73 (1). The new Constitution (Act 108 of 1996) was adopted in October 1996 and came into effect in July 1997 (s. 243).
[36] Who would benefit, in terms of what principles, by what processes, and so on?

POST–APARTHEID LAND REFORM

The magnitude of the social-reform process, as seen by the Mandela government, is evident from the President's own preamble to the White Paper on Reconstruction and Development ('RDP').[37] In it the President claims that his government has been elected because people want change involving a 'profound transformation of all levels of government and society'. The government, he states, is committed to address 'the problems of poverty and the gross inequality evident in almost all aspects of South African Society'. The key policy formulation through which transformation will be attempted is the RDP itself.[38]

The contents of the White Paper leave no doubt about the enormous sense of mission in the process of change. For example, the government states a commitment to redistributing resources to address inherited inequalities following 'centuries of oppression and decades of formal apartheid'.[39] The RDP is presented as a policy framework for 'integrated and coherent socio-economic progress' aimed at developing democratic institutions, ensuring participation, non-racialism, and non-sexism, and creating 'a sustainable and environmentally friendly growth and development path'.[40]

One of the 'key programmes' of the RDP is agrarian reform, because 'no political democracy can survive and flourish if the majority of its people remain in poverty, without land, without their basic needs being met and without tangible prospects for a better life'.[41] The initial RDP policy document, a forerunner to the White Paper, stated that the abolition of the apartheid land legislation would simply not constitute sufficient reform in that persons who were previously disqualified from landownership in the elaborate racial zones were mostly unable to afford to purchase land in a new, free land market.[42]

A detailed presentation of land reform was omitted from the White Paper, but was spelt out in another important policy document, a Green Paper, which was published by the Department of Land Affairs early in 1996.[43]

---

[37] Cape Town, 15 Nov. 1994 in *Government Gazette*, No. 16085 (23 Nov. 1994).
[38] White Paper on Reconstruction and Development, 4.
[39] Ibid. paras. 0.3, 0.1.   [40] Ibid., para. 1.1.1.
[41] Ibid., paras. 1.4.1, 1.4.3, 1.2.7. The White Paper does not seek to describe land-reform policies. That detail was left to the Department of Land Affairs in its own policy contribution to the RDP (see below). As a matter of general economic policy goals, however, the White Paper includes reference to the need for 'less concentrated, more racially and gender inclusive [land] ownership patterns' (para. 3.1.4).
[42] Green Paper on South African Land Policy.   [43] Ibid.

In the Green Paper the Department's 'goals and vision' proceed from the basis that land is 'an important and sensitive issue to all South Africans. It is a finite resource which binds all together in a common destiny' and is 'a cornerstone for reconstruction and development'. The goal of the land-reform programme is to contribute to 'reconciliation, stability, growth and development in an equitable and sustainable way'. Land in urban and rural contexts has a central role to play in 'achieving a better quality of life for the most disadvantaged'.[44]

This perception of land as a necessary precondition for an individual's quality of life rests upon a view that land has a broad, welfare function. It is a view echoed elsewhere in other important and contemporaneous policy documents. For example, a statement on rural development strategy from the Ministry in the Office of the President states that the government's vision is that by the year 2020 rural people will have dignity, security, freedom from poverty, full and productive employment, a more diverse agriculture, and a healthy and productive environment.[45] Likewise, the developing policy on housing, in recognizing that housing is a basic entitlement ('a basic human right')—which apartheid has ignored (one of the 'most visible and destructive legacies of the past')—states that housing is necessary to achieve 'a safe and healthy environment', 'viable communities' and an 'integrated society'.[46]

The main principles of land reform are stated in the Green Paper to be the following: social justice (to deal with the apartheid land legacy); overcoming poverty; responding to expressed needs (as opposed to government-designed plans); government intervention in reform processes; flexibility in approaches; gender equality (so that women have equal opportunity in land access); economic viability and environmental sustainability; and democratic processes (involving participation and accountability at all levels).[47] Similar general principles relating to land development began to emerge in the new government's statutory reforms. For example, policy, administrative practice, and laws should 'contribute to the correction of the historically distorted spatial pattern of settlement in the Republic . . . and encourage environmentally sustainable land development practices and processes'.[48]

---

[44] Ibid., para. 1.1.

[45] Ministry in the Office of the President, The Rural Development Strategy of the Government of National Unity, Oct. 1995, in Government Gazette, No. 16679, 3 Nov. 1995, 9. Other goals listed included 'fewer, healthier, safe, well nourished children, with access to well resourced schools'.

[46] South African government, Department of Housing, White Paper on a New Housing Policy and Strategy for South Africa, in Government Gazette, No. 16178, 23 Dec. 1994, 4, 21, 22.

[47] Green Paper on South African Land Policy, para. 1.5.

[48] Development Facilitation Act 67 of 1995, s. 3(1)(c)(vii), (viii).

In practical terms the land-reform programme is seen to have three distinct aspects: restitution, redistribution, and tenure reform.[49] The main features of each of these three elements will be summarized.

Restitution

As stated above, the interim constitution required the new government to enact restitution legislation in accordance with specified principles. However, the detail of the law was to be determined by the ANC government itself. Detailed restitution principles first appeared in a party policy document[50] and later, in more comprehensive form, in the Green Paper.[51] There, the restitution of land to persons dispossessed by racially discriminatory legislation is linked directly to the whole process of reconciliation, reconstruction, and development.[52]

The Restitution of Land Rights Act,[53] which appeared soon after the elections, applies to certain claimants who were dispossessed of rights in land after 19 June 1913[54] in terms of racially discriminatory legislation (and to persons not paid just compensation under an earlier expropriation Act).[55]

Claims are to be directed to a special Commission in the first instance. Once the Commissioner is satisfied that the claim is valid, a negotiation process (including mediation if necessary) is put in motion in an effort to reach agreement between the parties to the disputed land. Only upon failure of the negotiation process can the dispute be submitted to the specialist Land Claims Court.[56]

Restitution by order of the court may involve the restoration of land from which the claimants were dispossessed, the provision of alternative land, or payment of compensation.[57] A court order to restore land which is held by a private owner may not be made unless it is 'just and equitable' to do so. Some of the factors relevant to this enquiry include: the history of the dispossession, the hardship caused, the use to which the property was being put, the history of its acquisition by the owner, and the interests of the dispossessed.[58]

Expropriation of the land necessarily requires the payment of compensation under section 28 of the interim constitution. The factors relevant in determining what compensation is appropriate include enquiries into the

---

[49] Green Paper on South African Land Policy, para. 1.1.
[50] African National Congress, 'Restitution of Land Rights Policy' (n.d.).
[51] Green Paper on South African Land Policy, 34–42.
[52] Ibid., para. 3.10.   [53] Act 22 of 1994.
[54] A symbolic day: the date of promulgation of the Natives' Land Act of 1913.
[55] Restitution Act, s. 2, read with Interim Constitution, s. 121.   [56] ss. 4–14.
[57] Interim Constitution, s. 123(3), which also contemplates 'alternative relief'.
[58] Interim Constitution, s. 123(2).

use to which the property was being put, the history of its acquisition, its market value, and the interests of those affected.[59]

Redistribution

Land-redistribution policy differs in scope and purpose from restitution. The latter aims to provide redress for victims of dispossession, while redistribution is conceived as a wider land-reform programme 'to provide the poor with access to land for residential and productive uses, in order to improve their livelihoods'.[60]

Broadly stated, the Mandela government's redistribution programme aims to distribute land 'to the needy, [while] at the same time maintaining public confidence in the land market'.[61] The approach is to encourage voluntary transactions between willing buyers and sellers with expropriation being used only in the final resort.[62] The intended 'outputs' of the programme include: more equitable land distribution patterns (and a public perception that this is so); a contribution to national reconciliation; a substantial reduction in land-related conflict; and a solution to the problem of landlessness.[63]

The land-redistribution strategy will involve two categories of activity. First, the programme will involve land acquisition (presumably from both public and private sources—although this is not clearly stated). Secondly, the programme will contain an efficient 'delivery system', providing mechanisms for coordination, planning, implementation, and financial management in relation to land delivery.[64] The policy document also affirms the viability of smallholder agricultural production on land which has been redistributed.[65] A land-reform pilot programme, seeking to give effect to these and other redistribution-policy objectives, was launched late in

---

[59] Interim Constitution, s. 28(3). In the new Constitution, adopted by the Constitutional Assembly in Oct. 1996, the compensation provisions in section 28 are replaced by enlarged provisions in section 25(3) which requires the court to consider also the extent of direct state investment and subsidy in the land as a factor affecting the amount of compensation payable: subsection (d).

[60] Green Paper on South African Land Policy, para. 3.1.

[61] Ibid., para. 3.2. This approach differs significantly from that stated in the Freedom Charter, the inspirational charter of popular rights formulated in the 1950s and which, for many years, was held out to be the ANC's guiding set of principles awaiting the new order. The Charter proclaimed that 'The land shall be shared amongst those who work it.'

[62] Green Paper on South African Land Policy, para. 3.2.

[63] Ibid. 26.

[64] Ibid. Elsewhere the Green Paper sets out guidelines for the provision of financial assistance for beneficiaries of land redistribution (p. 53).

[65] A commitment to smallholder production and a belief in its importance for the agricultural economy is a significant aspect of policy but is beyond the scope of this chapter.

1994.[66] Under this scheme, the government identified rural land suitable for redistribution to an estimated 13,500 beneficiary households.[67]

The first major redistribution law passed by the new government was the Development Facilitation Act.[68] This was described as a measure to facilitate and hasten the RDP itself, and to lay down general principles governing land development throughout the country. The Act sets out principles and procedures to facilitate the designation and development of land for settlement.

Tenure Reform

The third aspect of land reform, as perceived by the new government, is reform of land tenure. As with restitution and redistribution, the Green Paper on land policy provides an initial insight into the way in which tenure issues are likely to be perceived and legislated.

The ultimate goal is to 'extend security of tenure to all South Africans under diverse forms of tenure' to overcome 'widespread tenure insecurity' under the apartheid system. Reform should 'enable citizens to hold and enjoy the benefits of their land . . . without fear of arbitrary action by the state, private individuals or other institutions'. Thus, security of tenure is seen as a necessary ingredient of 'personal security and social stability'.[69]

Among the objectives of land tenure reform strategy are 'mechanisms' for the recognition of various kinds of tenure (including communal or group tenure), and the improvement of tenancy laws to ensure greater fairness in the system of tenancy.[70] Alongside this is a belief in the principle that, while the content of land rights will vary, they will all nevertheless 'be clearly defined and as such enjoy the protection of the legal system'.[71]

Other aspects of policy, revealed in this context, seem significant. First, the policy document advocates an approach to questions of tenure which it describes as 'rights based'. In one sense this is obviously a commitment to the legal enforceability, before the courts, of rights in land whether those rights amount to ownership rights[72] or farmworker, tenancy or communal land rights (which received little or no legal recognition previously). It is also to be noted in passing that the 'property clause' in the new Constitution (formulated after the Green Paper under discussion) enjoins parliament to enact legislation to 'secure' the land rights of persons or communities whose tenure in land is 'legally insecure'.[73]

---

[66] Using the mechanisms provided in one of the de Klerk Reform Acts: the Provision of Certain Land for Settlement Act 126 of 1993.

[67] As described in the Green Paper on South African Land Policy, 4.

[68] Act 67 of 1995.   [69] Green Paper on South African Land Policy, para. 3.12.

[70] Ibid. 45.   [71] Ibid., para. 3.13.1.

[72] As understood in the context of South African Roman–Dutch legal principles.

[73] Constitution of the Republic of South Africa Act 108 of 1996, s. 25(6), (9).

Secondly, this commitment in the policy document to a 'rights-based' approach seems also to reflect a wider interest in the application of the legal culture, with all its paraphernalia, to land matters.[74] This is revealed in the stated preference for 're-establishing the rule of law in relation to land transactions'. This statement, while not altogether clear, is made in the context of needing 'to create a legal mechanism for transforming current *de facto* relationships to land into formal legal rights to land.'

Perhaps the policy is intended to convey merely the belief in the appropriateness of regulating land use (even under customary land practices) by and through usual legal property norms. However, these statements may signify a more extensive commitment to a legally regulated society. Such a conclusion seems plausible in the light of the final remark in this section of the policy document, which is to decry 'extra legal unstable and sometimes violent land transactions'.[75] Perhaps, also, there is nothing remarkable in this, given the commitment to constitutional democracy in the new South African political order.[76] But this level of commitment to law and legal process was not previously transparent in the views of all ANC-aligned anti-apartheid activists in debates over the land question.[77]

The new government has already begun to pay attention to tenure reform in a number of ways. For example, the Development Facilitation Act, dealing with the wider process of land redistribution (as noted above), provides that in certain circumstances informal settlements—involving loose, unregulated tenure forms—may be converted into ownership in the manner prescribed.[78] A more obvious example of land tenure reform is to be found in the legislation (some of which emerged late in the de Klerk era) which seeks to provide avenues to 'upgrade' informal tenure holdings.[79] Even more recent proposals deal with principles and mechanisms to 'provide security of [land] tenure for vulnerable occupiers'[80] such as farmworkers whose practical and historical links with the land, while extensive, have not previously been recognized.

---

[74] In the pre-reform era, ANC-aligned critics of apartheid land policies were generally ambivalent about the role of law in land reform. See e.g. Robertson, 'Land and Rights in South Africa' (1990) 6 'South African Journal on Human Rights', 215.

[75] Green Paper on South African Land Policy, para. 3.13.1.

[76] See e.g. du Plessis and Corder *Understanding South Africa's Transitional Bill of Rights* (Cape Town: Juta, 1994), 1–22; and also sections 1 and 2 of the new Constitution.

[77] Robertson, 'Land and Rights in South Africa', 215.

[78] Development Facilitation Act 67 of 1995, s. 63.

[79] Upgrading of Land Tenure Rights Act 112 of 1991 and Upgrading of Land Tenure Rights Amendment Act of 1996. See also Land Reform (Labour Tenants) Act 3 of 1996: 'to provide for security of tenure of labour tenants.'

[80] South African government, Department of Land Affairs, Executive Summary of the Extension of Security of Tenure Bill, Pretoria, 29 Jan. 1997.

The Bill of Rights

Finally, in seeking to summarize policy and legislative developments in the reform era so far, it is necessary to highlight the main features of the property clause in the Bill of Rights which is incorporated in the new Constitution (which will come into operation in 1997). Unlike its predecessor[81] the property clause contains no umbrella protection for private property, or 'rights in property' as it was styled. However, the proscription against property deprivation otherwise than in accordance with law is retained, together with an added protection that reads 'and no law may permit *arbitrary* deprivation of property'.[82]

The section also permits expropriation 'for a public purpose' subject to the payment of compensation but adds 'the public interest' as another ground for taking. Moreover, the section provides that the public-interest ground 'includes the nation's commitment to land reform, and to reforms to bring about equitable access to all South Africa's natural resources'. (The predecessor section permitted expropriation 'for public purposes only' but was qualified by the restitution provisions elsewhere in the Act.)[83]

It is noteworthy that the section also imposes three sets of obligations on the state. First, the state is required to take reasonable legislative steps 'to foster conditions which enable citizens to gain access to land on an equitable basis'; secondly, to pass laws designed to secure tenure which is 'legally insecure';[84] and, thirdly, to provide legislation enabling persons to gain restitution or other relief in circumstances where they were dispossessed under discriminatory laws in the past.[85] The latter provision is not dissimilar from the provision in the interim constitution requiring parliament to pass a restitution law (which parliament subsequently did[86]).

THE ROLE OF LAND IN SOCIAL RECONSTRUCTION

The degree of commitment in South Africa to constitutional government, the rule of law, the protection of individual liberty (in a bill of rights), and the maintenance of a market economy all point to a political order which is liberal-democratic in orientation. Like other societies in this mould, South Africa will not escape the private-property dilemma, described by Macpherson as 'an insoluble difficulty' and the 'central problem' of liberal-democratic theory. Stated briefly, it is 'the difficulty of reconciling the liberal property right with that equal effective right of all individuals to use

---

[81] Act 200 of 1993, s. 28, and see above, p. 308.   [82] s. 125(1) (emphasis added).
[83] ss. 121–3.   [84] See the discussion above, pp. 314–15.
[85] s. 25(6), (7), (8).
[86] See Restitution of Land Rights Act 22 of 1994 discussed above.

and develop their capacities which is the essential ethical principle of liberal democracy'.[87]

The 'central problem' arises when the legal protection of property, including that gained through the market system (itself a feature of liberalism), leads to a *concentration* of property ownership and power which 'negates the ethical goal of free and independent individual development'.[88] Thus, the protection of property in an absolute sense must result, ultimately, in 'detriment' to the lives of others.[89]

Where the acquisition of private property *is* to be recognized and, to an extent, protected (as it must be[90] in a liberal democracy), the *appropriate* line of enquiry, it has been said, is to determine exactly where 'private enterprise must be given free scope and where it must be restricted in the interests of the common good'.[91]

South Africa is presently engaged in a process of reconstruction of what has been a dysfunctional society. RDP[92] is a massive undertaking. Land reform is seen to be a central plank of the entire programme which is concerned with the high policy goals of overcoming poverty, equity, reconciliation, production, growth, social integration, and democracy. In designing the land-reform programme to fit with these objectives, and identifying its own main goals (restitution, redistribution, and tenure security), the society is simultaneously and necessarily formulating its position on the institution of property in relation to land. In summary, the agenda involves (1) state manipulation of rights in land in order (2) to ameliorate highly undesirable social conditions and (3) to contribute to the reconstruction of the society and the economy in general.

It is helpful, at this point, to recall,[93] in summary, some of the key features of the South African property legacy. Roman–Dutch property law—containing classical principles[94]—accompanied the expansion of white settlement across the territory which became the Union of South Africa in 1910.[95] Later, the statutory land laws of apartheid (which had their origins

---

[87] Macpherson, 'Liberal-Democracy and Property', in Macpherson (ed.), *Property: Mainstream and Critical Positions* (Toronto: University of Toronto Press, 1978), 199. The dilemma is evident in this question by Honoré: 'Is it inconsistent or morally obtuse to recognize the value of the [property] institution and at the same time to argue that each member of a society is entitled to an equal or approximately equal standard of living?' (Honoré, 'Property, Title and Redistribution', in Held (ed.), *Property, Profits and Economic Justice* (Belmont: Wadsworth Publishing Company, 1980), 84).

[88] Macpherson (ed.), *Property*, 200.

[89] Cohen, 'Property and Sovereignty' in Macpherson (ed.), *Property*, 155 at 167.

[90] 'The protection and regulation of some variety of property is central to the purposes of every modern state' (Macpherson (ed.), *Property*, 13).

[91] Cohen, 'Property and Sovereignty', 167.   [92] See above, p. 310.

[93] See above, pp. 303–9.   [94] Cohen, 'Property and Sovereignty', 167.

[95] For a Continental view of the application of Roman law in South Africa, see Zweigert and Kotz, *Introduction to Comparative Law*, trans. Weir (2nd edn., Oxford: Oxford University

in the Dutch and British colonial systems, and also the settler republics[96])
displaced Roman–Dutch principles which were inconsistent with the
objects of racial segregation and domination. The criteria upon which classical property rights were removed were entirely arbitrary, based upon
racial appearance, culture, and morals. For example, persons deemed 'non-
white' were prevented from acquiring rights in land in areas set aside for
persons regarded as 'white', while land which was provided in the crowded
black areas was granted on limited and precarious statutory title and was
subject to administrative discretion. Persons who were otherwise the beneficiaries of the political system also suffered restrictions. For example, they
were prohibited from disposing of rights in land to persons deemed not to
be of the same racial category; nor could they acquire land in areas set aside
for persons not white. Under apartheid, therefore, land was subject to
extensive state control. It was, however, a complex mix of freedom (for
some) and restraint: while strong private-property freedoms were accorded
white landowners, the great majority of the population were disqualified
from any participation in the land market.

Although direct state intervention in the distribution and role of land is
a feature both of apartheid and of the new democracy, the similarity ends
there. Whereas the apartheid system set extensive limits on the traditional
individual power over land in order to benefit a minority social group, the
post-apartheid reform programme is apparently concerned to set limits on
private-property power for the benefit of the community at large.
Furthermore, unlike the old, the new social programme is rooted in a
democratic mandate, is not based upon arbitrary racial distinctions, and is
being implemented in a single political entity.

The restitution and redistribution goals in the reform programme do not
in themselves necessarily indicate anything remarkable about post-apartheid
land policy, or that the reformers are looking beyond liberal property principles to guide the reform programme. For instance, although the liberal
conception of ownership involves 'a permanent, exclusive and transmissible interest in property', expropriation by public authority, in the interests
of the community rather than the individual, is not inconsistent with liberal
property principles.[97] Furthermore, state-initiated expropriation of private
property which has been gained in a manner properly regarded as 'unjust'
(for example, through confiscation on racial or religious grounds) does not
offend the liberal tradition.

What, if anything, is distinctive about the treatment of land in this period
of post-apartheid social reconstruction and land reform? Considering both

Press, 1987): 'Roman law has shown a greater vitality in South Africa than anywhere else in
the world by surviving to the present day . . .' (p. 240).

[96] Natal, Transvaal, and the Orange Free State.

[97] See e.g. Honoré, 'Property, Title, and Redistribution', 86–7.

the policy statements and laws until the end of 1996, it is the emphasis being placed on the *social purpose* of land which is standing out. This social purpose perspective, involving the seemingly unquestioned belief that land can serve a vital role in both the normalization and development of a new society, consists of three distinct but related components. These are (1) the welfare, (2) the economic, and (3) the political. Each is considered below. In addition, it is suggested, this teleological approach carries with it a strong moral justificatory component which is a consequence of South Africa's apartheid history.

Latin America and the Social Function Approach

Before examining these three components, a brief comparison will be made with the Latin American experience and the predominance there of the 'social function of property' concept. This assists in gaining a fuller perspective on the South African approach. It will be suggested that, although the social-function approach shares some common elements with the 'social purpose' approach, it amounts, ultimately, to a different way of treating property.[98]

The French philosopher, Duguit, is regarded as having been influential in the formulation of the social function of property concept in Latin America. He was highly critical of the 'rigid legal construction' of the Roman *dominium*, which involved an absolute right to property, including the right to use, benefit, and disposal (together with the right *not* to use it, to derive benefit from it, or to dispose of it). Because the individual was 'only a wheel of a huge mechanism, the body social', it was wrong that property should be protected exclusively for individual use, rather than for society (the social function). Continued respect for strong individual property rights was 'in open opposition to the temper of the modern conscience'.[99] Duguit did not, however, advocate the abolition of private property, but insisted that the highly individualistic approach to its use and misuse be modified.[100]

One consequence of his view of property having a social function was the notion that there is a responsibility on the owner to cultivate land properly,[101] failing which the land may become susceptible to expropriation.

---

[98] There is no semantic significance in the use of these terms. The 'social purpose of land' could just as easily be referred to as the 'social function of land', but the latter phrase has acquired a particular meaning in international land-reform literature. However, the South African approach, it is suggested, is not the same, for reasons which emerge in the text below.

[99] Reproduced in Karst, *Latin American Legal Institutions: Problems for Comparative Study* (Berkeley and Los Angeles: University of California Press, 1966), 501.

[100] Duguit in ibid. 501.   [101] Duguit in ibid. 502.

The essence of this view, therefore, is that, although property in land confers *rights*, it also imposes *obligations*, on the owner, in the public interest.[102] It was this principle which appeared in many Latin American legal texts.[103]

The view that property (and particularly land) involves obligations as well as rights is not inconsistent with the general principles in the new South African Constitution.[104] But there is no direct endorsement of the social function principle, nor any suggestion in the policy documents that a penalty or forfeiture should apply where an owner fails to use land productively, for example.[105] However, in a recent development the Minister of Land Affairs has stated that 'ownership of land carries with it both rights and duties . . . owners must exercise their rights in a way which respect [*sic*] the human dignity and basic human rights of all the people who live on the land.'[106] These remarks were made concerning a proposal to introduce legislation to provide greater tenure security to rural dwellers.

Although the social function concept in Latin America has tended to emphasize owners' obligations to use land productively, failing which tenure security would not be guaranteed, some laws simultaneously emphasized a 'welfare' dimension of land in the context of rural poverty. Obligations sometimes included the responsibility to respect laws designed to protect the interests of rural workers and to respect the tenure-security interests of customary communities. In other cases the reform programmes

---

[102] The notion of *functionality* and *conditionality* of land is echoed, for example, in the work of Reich. In the context of a discussion about property as 'government largess', he suggests that all property is 'given on condition and subject to loss'. It is not a natural right, but a (social) 'construction designed to serve certain functions'. The conditions that can be attached to ownership and its use depend upon what functions it should perform (Reich, 'The New Property', in Macpherson (ed.), *Property*, 179 at 189.

[103] See e.g. Frei and Trivelli, 'Mensaje del ejecutivo al Congreso proponiendo la aprobacion del proyecto de ley de reforma agraria', in Vodavonic, *Ley de reforma agraria* (Santiago: Editorial Nascimento, 1967), 5; trans. P. Hazleton. And see Act No. 4504 (Brazil) of 30 Nov. 1964; FAO translation in *Food and Agricultural Legislation*, 14/2 (Dec. 1965). Karst's text on 'the social function of ownership' includes a translated extract of a judgment in a Venezuelan court in 1961, where it was found that an owner of land, who was failing to use his land beyond about 10% of its productive capacity, was not fulfilling the social function. The land was therefore subject to expropriation (Karst, *Latin American Legal Institutions*, 495).

[104] s. 125.

[105] Were there such a Constitutional provision, it would, presumably, need to apply both to current holders of land *and* to future beneficiaries under restitution or redistribution schemes. It is not difficult to imagine the practical and political difficulties this would involve. But extinction of title by prescription is still possible in South Africa. Although not of much contemporary, practical significance, prescription embodies the idea that the owner who *neglects* property may be deprived of it (Honoré, 'Property, Title and Redistribution', 86). In South Africa the historical justification for prescription is an injury caused to the state through uncertainty over who is owner and the attendant lawsuits this entails. (Kleyn and Boraine, *The Law of Property* (3rd edn., Durban: Butterworths, 1987), 223.

[106] Press Statement on the Extension of Security of Tenure Bill, Pretoria, 29 Jan. 1997.

themselves made clear the welfare goals. For example, in Peru, land-reform laws were designed to provide social security, freedom, and dignity to the rural community by granting small landholdings to the landless.[107]

The Social Purpose Approach in South Africa

Strictly speaking, there is a difference between the social function of property (as understood in the Latin American context) and the 'social purpose' as the term is being used here. Although both are concerned with the necessity of private power over property yielding to wider social interests, they suggest different juridical relationships. Social function is primarily about the obligations of the owner and therefore concerned with the *user's obligation to the community*. Social purpose, on the other hand, is about the utilization of land for individual (and ultimately community) interests (welfare, economic, and political) and the state's role in facilitating these purposes; hence, the *community's obligation to the user*.

Although the South African community has an 'obligation' to provide land to the landless, this does not, it seems,[108] give rise to an actionable legal right, despite the relevant Constitutional provision which enjoins the state 'to foster conditions which enable citizens to gain access to land on an equitable basis'.[109] The most that can be said is that certain (identified or unidentified) potential beneficiaries have a contingent expectation that land might be provided as a result of state intervention. The expectation is contingent upon state acquisition and redistribution of land in terms of the enabling laws.

Social Purpose 1: Welfare

The land-as-*welfare* notion—being the first component of the social purpose approach—occupies a significant place in the new concept of land which is emerging in South Africa. In constitutional terms, the notion is exemplified in the emphasis being placed upon security of tenure ('no one may be deprived of property', etc.) and the attendant state responsibility to take steps which enable citizens to gain access to land. The same approach is evident in respect of the provision of housing: all have the right to adequate housing, and the state must take reasonable legislative measures to achieve the 'progressive realisation of this right'.[110]

---

[107] Act No. 15.037 of 21 May 1964 and Act No. 17.716 of 24 June 1969; FAO translations in *Food and Agricultural Legislation*, 13/4 (June 1965) and 19/1 (June 1970) respectively.

[108] In time it is probable that the new Constitutional Court in South Africa will be called on to clarify what rights, if any, flow from the relevant Constitutional provision.

[109] s. 25(5).   [110] s. 26.

Some of the numerous policy statements which make clear the importance of the welfare purpose of land have been noted above.[111] Stated shortly, the role of land is perceived as crucial in the fight against poverty. Land will provide income and food security[112] and this will lead to 'a better quality of life for the most disadvantaged'.[113]

Closely connected with the welfare purpose is the role of land in providing 'dignity'. The word is used frequently in the policy documents[114] and was an element of Latin American policy.[115] The concept of property and dignity is also evident in the work of property theorists. For example, Reich states that 'property performs the function of maintaining independence, dignity and pluralism in society by creating zones within which the majority has to yield to the owner'.[116]

The belief that land is necessary to provide zones of security[117] and dignity is also clearly demonstrated in the emerging policy on the recognition of customary tenure systems. The Green Paper first notes that under precolonial communal land practices 'qualified landholders'[118] 'often enjoyed highly secure tenure rights to land'.[119] The document then acknowledges the importance of rejuvenating, where appropriate, the system which had in many instances been distorted by colonial and apartheid laws.[120] This endorsement of the individualistic (but limited[121]) property values inherent in the customary land system can be seen as an indication of the broader policy interest in emphasizing the social purposes of land, and may assist in explaining the general approach. Land in customary society, to which all families were entitled, fulfilled certain essential social functions including security, subsistence, and signification of community membership. These elements parallel the ingredients of the social purpose of land approach identified above: welfare, economic, and political.

[111] See above, pp. 310–11.

[112] Green Paper on South African Land Policy, 5, and the more emotive 'the absence of household-level food security has devastating consequences, most notably on the physical and mental development of children' (ibid. 6).

[113] Ibid. 1, 6 'Access to productive land will provide the opportunity for putting more food on the table and providing cash for the purchase of food items.'

[114] See e.g. the statement on rural development from the Ministry in the Office of the President quoted above, p. 311.

[115] Frei and Trivelli, 'Mensaje', 16.   [116] Reich, 'The New Property', 180.

[117] The idea that property is part of the necessary human entitlement has provided the basis for the traditional justification for the institution of property (see Macpherson (ed.), *Property*, 12).

[118] A category which excluded women. For this reason the policy proposals to recognize the rights of communities to maintain communal land practices are careful to include proposals which avoid support for continued gender discrimination.

[119] Green Paper on South African Land Policy, para. 2.13.2.   [120] Ibid. para. 2.13.3.

[121] Despite the high degree of security, landholders were generally not able to sell their lots, for example.

Social Purpose 2: Economic

In the climate of reconstruction, land also has an *economic* purpose, in relation not only to the individuals who use it (the welfare purpose), but also to the wider society. This is the second ingredient of the social-purpose concept. Land is seen as integral to 'national economic development',[122] which is assisted by stimulating agricultural production based upon a small-scale production model.[123] This model proceeds on the belief that 'an area of high-potential arable farmland normally produces considerably more livelihoods if divided into small family-operated farms' (and this has a 'multiplier effect on the local economy'). Land used in this way (together with support services from government) 'is central to the government's employment strategy' and also reduces 'the mounting cost of the welfare budget'.[124] Also, land reform contributes to economic development 'by giving households the opportunity to engage in productive land use and by increasing employment opportunities through encouraging greater investment'.[125]

Social Purpose 3: Political

Finally, land is seen to have a *political* purpose, the third ingredient of the social-purpose doctrine. In Latin America one of the goals of land reform was the integration of the new landowners into the social and economic life of the country.[126] In South Africa land access is seen to be a key to building democratic institutions and achieving 'a more secure and balanced civil society'.[127] RDP policy makes the point clearly: 'No political democracy can survive and flourish if the majority of its people remains in poverty, without land . . . .'.[128]

Other political 'roles' for land include equity (redressing the wrongs of the past through restitution and redistribution of land, and tackling gender discrimination issues in land allocation, including those in customary law) and, consequently, political reconciliation.

It must be acknowledged, however, that much of this political dimension could be perceived merely as rhetoric, as an exercise in slogans designed to satisfy the aspirations of a significant constituency. Even if this

[122] White Paper on Reconstruction and Development, 43.
[123] Green Paper on South African Land Policy, 7.   [124] Ibid.
[125] Ibid. 1–2. For an international perspective on land reform and economic development, see Thiesenhusen, 'Introduction', 9: when reform succeeds 'the resource and income-distribution patterns are improved and rural people have the opportunity to become a more productive workforce'.
[126] Thome, 'The Process of Land Reform in Latin America,' Wisconsin Law Review 15 (1968).
[127] Green Paper on Land Affairs, para. 1.5.3.
[128] White Paper on Reconstruction and Development, para. 1.2.7.

is so, and whether or not there is substance to the slogans (or the views which inform them), it could be suggested that land in this social setting has a powerful, popular mobilizing function.

CONCLUSION

Land has been designated a central role in the reconstruction of South African society. Given the injustices of the past, and the prominent use which was made of land in the systems of political control which formally ended in 1994, this is hardly surprising. South Africa's unusual if not peculiar history provides, in part, the moral justification[129] for the clear emphasis which is being placed on the social purpose of land. In this teleological perspective land is no longer perceived as a haven for exclusionary individual freedom and power. Rather, it is seen as a finite, legitimate, and necessary social commodity, to be shared out in a manner which enables the achievement of a secure and dignified existence for its beneficiaries, who, in turn, are therefore able to contribute to and participate in the social, economic, and political life of the community.

The global experience shows, though, that land reform, even when inspired and driven by high ideals, is not necessarily a panacea: 'there is no necessary correlation between land reforms, economic betterment and democratic forms of government.'[130]

Sounding a note of caution seems entirely apposite. Post-apartheid reconstruction was destined, always, to be lengthy and arduous.

---

[129] Property, and land in particular, always calls for justification by reference to basic human or social purposes (Macpherson (ed.), *Property*, 11–12).

[130] The conclusions of two leading land reform scholars on land-reform attempts in East and South-East Asia: Dorner and Thiesenhusen, 'Selected Land Reforms in East and Southeast Asia: Their Origins and Impacts' (1990) 4(1) Asian-Pacific Economic Literature 65 at 92.

PART FOUR
POLICY ISSUES IN LAND LAW

13

LAND, LAW, AND THE FAMILY HOME

John Dewar

The English law concerning the family home is difficult to grasp in all its aspects. This reflects the fact that English law has no coherent regime of family or matrimonial property comparable to civilian community property regimes.[1] Instead, the relevant legal rules must be picked out from the law of conveyancing, real property, trusts, and contract, and from statutes dealing with divorce, children, domestic violence, insolvency, trusts of land, tenancies, and creditor protection. Rarely are these rules considered in the round. The purpose of this chapter is to counter this tendency by drawing some of these threads together and subjecting them to critical scrutiny.

English law starts from the principle of separation of property.[2] This means that husband and wife are treated as strangers to each other in terms of their capacity to acquire and own property, and marriage itself confers no property rights in jointly used property.[3] What is true of the married is true equally of the unmarried. As Lord Upjohn put it in *Pettitt* v. *Pettitt*,[4]

the rights of the parties must be judged on the general principles applicable in any court of law when considering questions of title to property, and though the parties are husband and wife these questions of title must be decided by the principles of law applicable to the settlement of claims between those not so related, while making full allowances in view of that relationship.[5]

This remark expresses, perhaps in its purest form, the implications of the principle of separation for family property disputes; but it also begs the question of just what 'allowances' English law has made, and should make, for the needs of family members when it comes to claims to or over property, and for the fact that land (usually the land on which sits a dwelling serving the function of a family home) is used for a family purpose.

---

[1] See Glendon, *The Transformation of Family Law: State, Law and the Family in the United States and Western Europe* (Chicago: University of Chicago Press, 1989), 116–40 for a comparative survey.

[2] For a historical account of the nineteenth-century legislation, see Shanley, *Feminism, Marriage and the Law in Victorian England* (Princeton: Princeton University Press, 1989).

[3] *National Provincial Bank* v. *Ainsworth* [1965] AC 1175, where it was held that any right a wife might have to be housed by her husband was not proprietary and was therefore not capable of binding a third party.

[4] [1970] AC 777.   [5] Ibid., at 813D.

The view that that there should be some allowances made was most forcefully put by Otto Kahn-Freund, a lawyer from the civil law tradition, and a stern critic of the English principle of separation of property. For him, the principle of separation presupposes, unrealistically, that spouses have an equal ability to acquire property in legally recognized ways: and, given the tendency to ascribe legal ownership on the basis of money contribution to acquisition,[6] and the continuing evidence that men and woman are very unequal in their abilities to contribute in this way,[7] the net result of separation is 'to treat as equal that which is unequal [which] may . . . be a very odious form of discrimination'.[8] Others, though, have suggested that the principle of separation does indeed form a satisfactory basis for the law, and that to confer some sort of special legal treatment on family members in their acquisition of property rights, through a community regime or otherwise, would be a retrograde step—either because economic reality will in due course match the legal assumption of equality, or because equality of the sexes is itself a desirable premiss for legal policy in this area.[9]

This chapter will show that 'allowances' have indeed been made for the fact that land is used as a family home, and that the principle of separation, although notionally still the basis of the law, is more honoured in the breach than the observance. Indeed, I will argue that the law concerning the family home has developed into a highly complex and specialized branch of the law.[10] But this development has been pragmatic and piecemeal, with apparently little cross-flow of concepts or policies between different legal conceptual categories.

I will trace two parallel tendencies. The first is what I will call the 'familialization' of the general law of trusts and real property. By this, I mean the process by which both judges and the legislature have modified general principles of land law or trusts to accommodate the specific needs of family members. We have now reached the stage, for example, at which it is possible to point to sub-branches of the law of real property and the law of implied trusts which have no application outside the context of the family home. This process has been spurred in part by a desire to curb the worst consequences of the separation doctrine. So far as the judges are concerned,

---

[6] A tendency which may have been diluted since Kahn-Freund wrote these words: see below.

[7] Summarized in Moffat with Bean and Dewar, *Trusts Law: Text and Materials* (2nd edn., London: Butterworths, 1994), 443–9.

[8] Kahn-Freund, 'Matrimonial Property and Equality before the Law: Some Sceptical Reflections' (1971) 4 Human Rights Journal 493 at 510.

[9] Deech, 'A Tide in the Affairs of Women' (1972) 122 New Law Journal 742; Glendon, 'Is there a Future for Separate Property?' (1980) 14 Family Law Quarterly 315.

[10] For a related argument in a New Zealand context, see Peart, 'Towards a Concept of Family Property in New Zealand' (1996) 10 International Journal of Law, Policy and the Family 105.

this has really been a process of judicial legislation, governed by an identifiable policy of what I shall call 'give and take': that is, the broadening of the grounds for claiming ownership informally, while preserving as far as possible the position of creditors whose debts are secured by a charge or mortgage over the family home. As we shall see, this process has been an uneven one, with some significant disagreements emerging between judges about what the policy should be.

The second tendency has been the slow accretion of legislation singling out the family home for special treatment: the development, in other words, of a nascent statutory regime for the family home. Good examples of this would be the Family Law Act 1996 code governing the occupation of the family home; the Insolvency Act 1986, which provides separate criteria for applications by creditors' representatives for sale of the family home; the Trusts of Land and Appointment of Trustees Act (TOLATA) 1996, which confers a broad jurisdiction for resolving disputes over co-owned land that enables the courts specifically to refer to 'family' considerations in the exercise of their discretion; and, of course, the powers of the divorce court under the Matrimonial Causes Act 1973 to make orders transferring property between spouses on divorce. But I shall argue that the picture that emerges from this legislative activity is complex: its applicability may turn on status (married, unmarried, a parent, bankrupt) or on the procedural context (divorce or separation, bankruptcy or the enforcement of security), and the prescribed criteria may overlap or simply contradict each other.

The result of both these tendencies is complexity and internal inconsistency, as well as a failure to deliver a just regime of family property. English law has proceeded inductively, from a variety of starting points, and has ended (so I will argue) in a muddle. So what is to be done? Law reformers, after all, have hardly been idle. The Law Commission has tried on a number of occasions to introduce a comprehensive legal regime of matrimonial property, but failed, and has now given up;[11] it will instead be proposing yet another statutory regime to resolve the ownership problems of 'homesharers', a social category that goes beyond the married. This chapter does not propose any final solutions; but it will suggest that some progress might be made if we ask what rights family members need in or over the family home. It will suggest that reform of the law has been sidetracked by treating ownership of the family home as the only, or the main, vehicle by which those needs are to be satisfied.

---

[11] Law Commission, *Third Report on Family Property: The Matrimonial Home (Co-Ownership and Occupation Rights) and Household Goods*, Law Com. No. 86 (London: HMSO, 1978); *Family Law: Matrimonial Property*, Law Com. No. 175, (London: HMSO, 1988).

'FAMILIALIZING' THE GENERAL LAW OF REAL
PROPERTY AND TRUSTS

The conceptual framework supplied by the law of real property , and especially that of co-ownership of interests in land under the 1925 Law of
Property Act 1925, was not created to deal with the problems of a modern-
day owner-occupying population; nor to resolve the problems created by
the widespread use of mortgage capital secured on family property to fund
personal consumption or to finance businesses. Instead, it has been largely
left to the judges[12] to refashion a conceptual framework devised in the early
twentieth century to deal with the problems created by the altered demo-
graphics of the late twentieth.

I want to suggest that, in doing so, the judiciary have 'familialized' these
areas of legal doctrine in ways just described. This has been an attempt to
hold a line between avoiding the worst excesses of a strict application of the
principle of separation, while ensuring that family property retains its attractiveness to mortgage-lenders as security for mortgage loans.

When Does Ownership Matter?

Before going further, it is worth reminding ourselves of when ownership
will be important in resolving disputes over family property, and why. A
simple answer is that ownership now plays a default role: that is, it will be
called into play when there are no other (statutory) means available to
resolve matters. So, for example, whereas married couples who are getting
divorced can have property questions dealt with by the divorce court exercising its discretionary powers under the Matrimonial Causes Act 1973,
unmarried couples have no equivalent jurisdiction to turn to, and will
instead be forced to debate their claims in the language of ownership. This,
in turn, entails examining written documents, such as conveyances or declarations of trust, or, in their absence, asking what understandings (if any)
have been arrived at between the parties with regard to property ownership, or tracing the convoluted history of the parties' financial dealings. In
some cases, this can be a long and expensive business.[13]

Similarly, when a dispute arises between an occupier of a family home,
and a creditor with a security interest (such as a mortgage) in the same
home, the question of whose interest takes priority will be resolved using

---

[12] Though not exclusively: the Trusts of Land and Appointment of Trustees Act
(TOLATA) 1996 substantially reforms the law on co-ownership by replacing the settlement
and the trust for sale with a single trust of land (see Sydenham, *Trusts of Land—The New Law*
(Bristol: Family Law, 1996)). The implications of these changes are considered later.

[13] e.g. *Hammond* v. *Mitchell* [1992] 1 FLR 233.

the technical and conceptual language of trusts and real property (and, in particular, that of trusts for sale, now trusts of land, and overreaching), or, depending on the circumstances, of joint legal ownership, notice, and undue influence.[14] In the landmark case of *Boland*, for example, the wife's successful claim to resist an application for possession by a mortgage-lender depended on her being able to show, first, that she was a co-owner in equity of the house behind a trust for sale and, secondly, that she satisfied the definition of 'actual occupation' for the purposes of section 70(1)(g) of the Land Registration Act 1925 at the date of the mortgage. In the equally important case of *Lloyds Bank* v. *Rosset*,[15] the wife failed to repel the lender because she was *unable* to prove that she had acquired an ownership interest in the house. As the facts of both these cases imply, ownership will play a role in such cases whether the parties are married or not, since there is no other legal framework for resolving these issues, even for the married.[16]

I want now to substantiate the claim that the law of real property and trusts have been 'familialized' in ways already outlined.

A Specialized Body of Doctrine?

The law on implied trusts has been considerably developed in the context of family property disputes: old concepts, such as resulting trusts, have been pressed into new service; and new concepts, in particular the constructive trust, have appeared, or have been considerably developed in the crucible of family property disputes. In both cases, the relevant doctrine as it now stands has no significant application outside the family context.

The modern formulation of the relevant doctrine, in Lord Bridge's speech in *Lloyds Bank* v. *Rosset*,[17] lays down two circumstances in which implied trusts of family property arise. The first is where there has been some express 'agreement, arrangement or understanding' between the

---

[14] *Barclays Bank* v. *O'Brien* [1994] 1 AC 180, where the wife was joint legal owner of the home and had agreed that her share of the house could be used as security for the husband's business loans. Such cases will usually arise where the wife is a legal co-owner of the property, so that her agreement to such loans is required; but the principle of undue influence has been applied to letters of postponement, by which non-legally owning spouses agree to postpone priority of any interest they have in the property to that of the lender (see e.g. *Halifax BS* v. *Brown* [1996] 1 FLR 103). For an assessment of the effectiveness of this form of protection, see Fehlberg, *Sexually Transmitted Debt: Surety Experience and English Law* (Oxford: Oxford University Press, 1997).

[15] [1991] 1 AC 107.

[16] Ownership may have a bearing on other matters: for example, on death, where the size of the deceased party's estate may be in issue; or in divorce proceedings, where the extent of property owned by one party to a marriage may need to be decided before the divorce court can exercise its discretion to make orders for distribution of property.

[17] [1991] 1 AC 107 at 132–3.

parties on which the claimant has relied to his or her detriment. According
to Lord Bridge, this gives rise to a 'constructive trust or proprietary estoppel'. The second—and it is in 'sharp contrast' to the first—is where there is
no evidence of any express discussions between the parties, where the
courts have to go entirely on inferences from conduct. The relevant conduct for these purposes is the making of direct financial contributions to the
acquisition of property, whether to the purchase price or subsequently to
mortgage instalments. This too will justify the inference of a 'constructive
trust'.

As for the first category, the requirement that the courts can act only on
evidence of a common intention that has been detrimentally relied on is
one that seems specific to family cases: indeed, it is common to see the
'common intention' constructive trust treated in texts as having no application beyond the immediate context of the family home.[18] Dissatisfaction
with the search for common intention[19] may lead English courts in due
course to assimilate the first *Rosset* category with a broader doctrine of
estoppel (as Australian courts have begun to move towards unconscionabil-
ity[20] and the Canadian courts towards unjust enrichment[21]), a move foreshadowed by Lord Bridge's formulation in *Rosset*, and which I will argue in
a moment would be consistent with the policy of 'give and take'. But, for
the time being, it seems that the sort of constructive trust Lord Bridge refers
to is peculiar to family cases.

There is some disagreement as to the proper description of Lord Bridge's
second category of trust. Lord Bridge himself described it as 'constructive',
although there is some support in post-*Rosset* case law for the proposition
that the amount recovered under such a trust will be dictated by the amount
of the claimant's contribution:[22] in other words, that the trust is 'constructive in name, but resulting in pattern'.[23] However, Lord Bridge's formulation is some way from what would be conventionally recognized as a
resulting trust, since the contributions that count towards building a share
include direct contributions to mortgage repayments made *after* acquisition;
conventionally, such post-acquisition contributions should be relevant only
to equitable accounting between the parties, and should not affect their
underlying shares. This is the Australian view.[24] But all of this has now to

---

[18] For the argument that 'there is no need for a special jurisprudence in this area', see
Glover and Todd, 'The Myth of Common Intention' (1996) 16 LS 325.

[19] Expressed by both judges and academics: see Waite J in *Hammond* v. *Mitchell* [1991] 1
WLR 1127; Gardner, 'Rethinking Family Property' (1993) 109 LQR 263; Glover and Todd,
'The Myth of Common Intention'.

[20] *Baumgartner* v. *Baumgartner* (1987) 164 CLR 137.

[21] *Peter* v. *Beblow* (1993) 101 DLR (4th) 601.

[22] *Huntingford* v. *Hobbs* [1993] 1 FLR 736; *Springette* v. *Defoe* [1992] 2 FLR 388. See
O'Hagan, 'Quantifying Interests under Resulting Trusts' (1997) 60 MLR 420.

[23] Moffat, *Trusts Law*, 463.   [24] *Calverley* v. *Green* (1984) 155 CLR 242.

be read in the light of the Court of Appeal's decision in *Midland Bank* v. *Cooke*,[25] which suggests that there will be no necessary link between the amount put in and the amount received back, although Waite LJ appeared to recognize that such a link might be appropriate in some cases.[26] The result is a form of trust, whatever its proper name, that has no counterpart, nor any obvious application, outside the immediate context of the family home.

'Give and Take'

Alongside this development of a unique body of equitable doctrine has been the emergence of a distinctive policy of give and take.[27] That is, the courts have exploited the unique body of doctrine just discussed to increase the flexibility available to them in deciding property disputes, and in particular to expand the range of contributions that qualify for a share of the property to include non-financial contributions ('give'). At the same time, they have developed techniques for ensuring that these interests do not adversely affect third parties, such as mortgage-lenders ('take').

On the 'give' side, there has been a willingness to move beyond just money contributions in determining property rights, either by taking non-financial contributions into account as evidence of reliance on an 'agreement, arrangement or understanding', as in cases such as *Grant* v. *Edwards*[28] or *Hammond* v. *Mitchell*,[29] or by generous approaches to valuation, such as *Midland Bank* v. *Cooke*.[30] Admittedly, these cases are all ones in which the successful claimant had clearly made a financial contribution (although in *Cooke* the contribution was small by comparison with the share awarded), and where non-financial contributions had the effect of increasing the share rather than founding it; and it remains true that cases where shares have been awarded on the basis of non-financial contributions alone are rare.[31] Nevertheless, the trend, perhaps most noticeable in *Cooke*, seems to be towards greater generosity.

On the 'take' side has been the development of various means by which equitable interests of family members can be defeated by third parties, usually mortgage-lenders whose security is the family home itself (and especially where the mortgage is an acquisition mortgage rather than a second

---

[25] *Midland Bank plc* v. *Cooke* [1995] 2 FLR 915.

[26] Waite LJ distinguished *Springette* v. *Defoe* as a case 'relating to the part-pooling of resources by a middle-aged couple already established in life whose house purchasing arrangements were clearly regarded by the court as having the same formality as if they had been the subject of a joint venture or commercial partnership' (p. 928).

[27] The argument is pursued in greater detail in Dewar, 'Give and Take in the Family Home' [1993] Family Law 231.

[28] [1986] 1 Ch. 638.   [29] [1992] 1 FLR 233.   [30] [1995] 2 FLR 915.

[31] *Eves* v. *Eves* [1975] 1 WLR 1388 remains the best example of such a case.

mortgage or remortgage). This process has to be seen against the background of a judicial retreat from the landmark decision of *Williams & Glyn's Bank* v. *Boland*,[32] which, in retrospect, represents the high water mark of protection for occupying family members against lenders. In that case, the House of Lords found that a wife in occupation of the family home at the date of execution of a second mortgage over the home could assert that her equitable interest in the home took priority over the lender's security. In technical language, she had an overriding interest under section 70(1)(g) of the Land Registration Act 1925 by virtue of her equitable share in the house, held behind a trust for sale, that had not been overreached by the mortgage, which had been executed by the husband as sole legal owner of the property.

Since then, the courts have found ways of retreating from *Boland* without actually overruling it. In *City of London Building Society* v. *Flegg*,[33] for example, in circumstances not unlike those in *Boland*, it was held that, where two legal owners execute the mortgage (as in *Flegg*), instead of one (as in *Boland*), the overreaching guarantee contained in the Law of Property Act 1925[34] is triggered and protects the mortgagee.

In *Abbey National Building Society* v. *Cann*,[35] the House of Lords found a number of other ways of giving a lender priority over an occupying family member with an equitable share. First, where a mortgage is executed at the same time as the conveyance of the property the purchase of which is being funded by the mortgage, and which is itself the mortgage security, the legal owner does not at any time acquire any equitable estate in the property against which any occupier's claim for an equitable interest can bite. Instead, the purchaser merely acquires an equity of redemption, subject to the mortgagee's interest. In these circumstances, any claim against the purchaser's interest under an implied trust will be subordinate to the lender's mortgage.

Secondly, the House of Lords appeared to give approval to a line of reasoning, developed by the Court of Appeal in decisions such as *Bristol and West Building Society* v. *Henning*[36] and *Equity and Law Home Loans* v. *Prestidge*,[37] that, wherever a person with an equitable interest in the home knows about, and actually or impliedly consents to, a mortgage being raised in order to purchase the property in which the interest is to be claimed, then that person's interest is subordinated to that mortgage. It is unclear whether this stems from concepts of agency or estoppel, or from the nature of the equitable interest itself: either way, the result is that, where the requirement of knowledge (whatever it might be) is satisfied, the lender takes priority.

---

[32] [1981] AC 487.   [33] [1988] AC 54.
[34] LPA 1925, ss. 2(1), 27(2) (as amended by TOLATA 1996, sch.3).
[35] [1991] 1 AC 56.   [36] [1985] 1 WLR 778.   [37] [1992] 1 WLR 137.

One explanation of the pattern in these cases is that the courts are drawing a distinction between first (or acquisition) mortgages (that is, the mortgage used to purchase the property in which the interest is claimed) and second mortgages (which may be used to fund home improvements or to run a business). Protection for family members, it seems, is more likely to be forthcoming in cases of second mortgages. *Boland* itself (where the bank lost) was a case of a second mortgage, while *Cann* and *Henning* (where the lenders won) were cases of a first mortgage. *Prestidge* was a case of both, and the result was that the bank obtained priority only over the first mortgage, not the second.[38]

The policy of give and take has conceptual consequences. What seems to be happening is that two functions of equitable interests in property—to provide claims between co-owners and to offer protection against third parties—are being decoupled from each other. While claims between co-owners are being strengthened, those made against lenders are being attenuated. This trend seems likely to strengthen further. For example, if, as seems possible, the courts move to assimilate implied trusts of family property to the more general principle of estoppel, the decoupling will be almost complete: for it is generally accepted that an inchoate estoppel claim does not have proprietary status until it is recognized as such by a court.[39] The courts will then have a free hand to resolve claims between co-owners without placing third party interests at risk. A similar policy seems to be at work in TOLATA 1996. As we shall see later, that legislation strengthens the claims of beneficiaries of trusts of land against their trustees, while retaining and strengthening the overreaching guarantee to purchasers.

I have argued, then, that allowances have been made by judges in these cases for the fact that they relate to the family home. I have suggested that this has had two consequences: first, the development of a specialized set of techniques for resolving disputes over ownership that have no application outside the social context of the family home; and, secondly, the emergence of a specific policy of extending claims between family members, drawing on those specialized techniques, while not disrupting the priority of mortgage-lenders' interests, at least in cases of first (or acquisition) mortgages.

---

[38] *Flegg* does not fit the pattern, although the mortgage in that case was partly a remortgage and partly a second mortgage. This pattern is confirmed by the line of cases stemming from *Barclays Bank* v. *O'Brien,* most of which involve second or subsequent mortgages, usually for the husband's business purposes, where the courts have been willing to devise means of protecting 'sureties' or guarantors (see Fehlberg, *Sexually Transmitted Debt*).

[39] See the discussion in Moffat, *Trusts Law,* 458–62.

A STATUTORY REGIME?

So far, I have suggested that English law has made allowances for family property by a process of internal, and largely judicial, development. I now want to suggest that legislative enactments over the last quarter of the twentieth century have created a nascent statutory regime of family property, especially for the family home, but that this has been a piecemeal and haphazard process. This is partly because attempts, most notably by the Law Commission, to address the issue of family property *as such* have met with little or no success. As a result, legislation has addressed family issues obliquely, on a case-by-case basis, with little or no sense of overarching purpose, nor according to any grand plan.

Most of this legislative activity has taken place since 1970. Questions concerning the family home that were once resolved under the general law are increasingly being 'syphoned off' into specialist statutory jurisdictions. This section will consider the most significant of these provisions, with an eye on drawing out the piecemeal nature of this inchoate statutory regime of family property. An important question of policy must be whether English law will continue down this *ad hoc* route, or whether something more coherent will emerge.

Disputes between Co-Owners: TOLATA 1996

The Trusts of Land and Appointment of Trustees Act (TOLATA) 1996 substantially recasts the legal framework of co-ownership of land.[40] Although not directed primarily at co-ownership between family members, its provisions will have direct application to families where the family home is co-owned; and there is one respect in which the Act makes explicit acknowledgement of the 'family' character of land held on trust.

The 1996 Act abolished the old 'dual system' of trusts for sale and settlements of land as the legal framework for the co-ownership of land. Instead, all instances of co-ownership will, in effect, be brought within the new statutory trust of land.[41] The most important features of this new concept include the abolition of the doctrine of conversion,[42] the removal of any overriding duty to sell trust land, the express declaration of a beneficiary's right of occupation of trust land,[43] the grant of broad powers to trustees to decide various matters between beneficiaries, such as occupation,[44] and a

---

[40] It is based on proposals contained in Law Commission, *Transfer of Land: Trusts of Land*, Law Com. No. 181 (London: HMSO, 1989).

[41] TOLATA 1996, ss. 1, 2, 4, 5; existing settlements under the Settled Land Act 1882 will not be brought within the new framework.

[42] Ibid., s. 3.   [43] Ibid., s. 12.   [44] Ibid., ss. 6, 12.

correspondingly broad jurisdiction in the courts to settle disputes over the exercise of these functions by trustees.[45] In short, the Act seeks to simplify the trust of land framework, to strengthen the position of the beneficiary, while allowing for greater flexibility in the creation of express trusts of land. What are the implications of this new regime for the family home?

It is unlikely that the new Act will have much impact on the question of priorities between co-owners and mortgage-lenders: despite the improvement of the beneficiary's rights under a trust of land, none of the judicial techniques for subordinating those rights to security interests, just discussed, is likely to be impaired. For example, the abolition of the doctrine of conversion would make no difference to the outcome in cases like *Flegg*, since the statutory overreaching guarantee is preserved for the benefit of the purchaser.[46] The Law Commission's recommendation that overreaching should be conditional on the consent of full age beneficiaries in occupation has not been implemented.[47] Where there is only one trustee, so that overreaching cannot occur, the old case law continues to apply; but TOLATA amends the Land Registration Act 1925 to make it virtually compulsory to register equitable interests behind trusts of land as restrictions,[48] thereby increasing the chances that overreaching requirements will be complied with. Further, there is nothing in TOLATA to cast doubt on the techniques for deciding priorities between interests of the sort at work in *Henning* and *Cann*. If anything, this serves to emphasize the notion of 'de-coupling', discussed above: the improvement of the beneficiary's position brought about by the 1996 Act is only as regards the trustee.[49]

The main impact of the new regime on family property is therefore likely to be in cases where there is a dispute *between* co-owners over the exercise of trustees' powers. There are three reasons for this. The first is the removal of the primary obligation to sell trust land. Under the old section 30, the jurisprudence was strongly flavoured by the background duty to sell land held on trust for sale: judges had to have some justification for refusing a sale, usually found in the notion of 'underlying purpose' of the trust.[50] The removal of that substratum duty leaves the courts with a freer hand. The second is that the court's jurisdiction is not limited to hearing only applications for sale, as it was under section 30. Instead, the court has jurisdiction

---

[45] Ibid., ss. 14, 15.

[46] LPA 1925, ss. 2(1), 27(2) (as amended by TOLATA 1996, sch. 3).

[47] See Law Commission, *Transfer of Land: Overreaching: Beneficiaries in Occupation*, Law Com. No. 188 (London: HMSO, 1989). It would be possible for the settlor to incorporate such a consent requirement expressly into the trust instrument.

[48] TOLATA 1996, para. 5, sch. 3, inserting a new s. 94(4) and (5) of the LRA 1925.

[49] There may be some cases where the removal of the doctrine of conversion will have a substantive impact: in charging order cases, for example.

[50] e.g. *Jones* v. *Challenger* [1961] 1 QB 176. This requirement came to be generously interpreted in family home cases (see *Re Evers* [1980] 3 All ER 399).

to resolve disputes over the exercise by trustees of *any* of their functions.[51]
So, it would now be possible for either a joint legal owner or a trust beneficiary[52] to apply for an order *preventing* sale, or to require the trustees to
exercise any of their other powers in a particular way.

The third is that the new powers vested in courts are now governed for
the first time by a statutory list of criteria, contained in section 15:

    (a) the intentions of the person or persons (if any) who created the trust,
    (b) the purposes for which the property subject to the trust is held,
    (c) the welfare of any minor who occupies or might reasonably be expected to
        occupy any land subject to the trust as his home, and
    (d) the interests of any secured creditor of any beneficiary.

While paragraphs (a) and (b) arguably codify the old 'purpose' doctrine,
paragraph (c) represents an explicit acknowledgement of the family dimension of many disputes between co-owners, and resolves what had been an
uncertainty in the previous case law.[53] Particularly striking is the fact that
children will rarely be owners of any interest in the home in question, so
this section represents the explicit intrusion of welfarist considerations into
deliberations about property rights and their effects.

By way of example, it is now possible for a court to make an order
restraining a sale, perhaps in the interests of the children, while at the same
time directing that one or other beneficiary be entitled to occupy to the
exclusion of the other, and imposing conditions on that exclusive occupation (e.g., as to outgoings or rent). These are all matters that are within the
power of the trustees themselves to determine,[54] and therefore fall to be
resolved by a court in cases of dispute. Given that married couples will usually take their disputes to the divorce court, this provision is likely to be
most relevant to cohabitants.

Nevertheless, it has to be remembered that, for section 15 to come into
play at all, there must be co-ownership of the family home; and the person
applying must have some ownership interest in the property subject to the
trust. Section 15 will have no relevance to those cases where the family
home is owned entirely by one party, because there will be no trust of land.
Where there is co-ownership, so that these provisions are available, they
will sit alongside the powers to make occupation orders under the Family
Law Act 1996, discussed later. The criteria for making occupation orders

---

[51] TOLATA 1996, s. 14(2)(a).

[52] Applications under s. 14 may be brought by trustees or beneficiaries of trusts of land,
or by any other person with 'an interest in property subject to a trust of land', which would
include, for example, secured creditors of the beneficiaries (TOLATA 1996, s. 14(1)).

[53] *Burke* v. *Burke* [1974] 1 WLR 1063 with *Re Evers Trust* [1980] 1 WLR 1326.

[54] See s. 6 (general powers of trustees) and s. 13 (exclusion and restriction of right to
occupy).

are different from those in section 15, just as the courts' powers are defined differently. To the extent, therefore, that occupation is the issue, there is likely to be an element of jurisdictional arbitrage as litigants seek to argue their case under whichever statutory jurisdiction they consider most favourable to their cause.

Indebtedness and the Family Home

A family home can often become the target of a creditor seeking repayment of a debt. We have already seen that this may occur in the context of mortgages, and that the courts have been careful to maintain the mortgage-lender's priority over off-title claims (especially in the context of acquisition mortgages). But indebtedness may arise in many other ways: and, if the debtor is ultimately unable to repay those debts, then the creditor may, by invoking bankruptcy procedures, seek to recover the sums owed by appointing a trustee in bankruptcy, whose job is to realize (sell) the debtor's assets and repay the creditors out of the proceeds.[55] Where those assets include a family home, the trustee in bankruptcy in effect steps into the shoes of the debtor and becomes entitled to the same rights or remedies—including the right to seek the sale of any co-owned land.[56] Before the Insolvency Act 1986, such applications were made under section 30 of the Law of Property Act 1925, and the courts developed a specialized jurisprudence for dealing with them. With some notable exceptions, the court's stance was heavily pro-creditor: the courts took the view that the interests of the creditors must prevail on applications under section 30, unless there were 'exceptional circumstances'.[57] It was extremely rare for 'exceptional circumstances' to be found.

The Insolvency Act 1986 now provides special criteria according to which applications in bankruptcy proceedings for sale of the family home must be decided.[58] A court must make such order as it thinks 'just and reasonable' having regard to:

(a) the interests of the creditors;
(b) where the application is made in respect of land which includes a dwelling house which is or has been the home of the bankrupt or the bankrupt's spouse or former spouse:[59]

[55] Insolvency Act 1986, s. 305(2).   [56] Ibid., s. 306.

[57] See *Re Citro (A bankrupt)* [1991] 1 Ch. 142.

[58] Applications are brought under TOLATA 1996, s. 14, but must be made to the court with jurisdiction in the bankruptcy and must be decided according to the criteria set out in Insolvency Act 1986, s. 335A (amended by TOLATA 1996, sch. 3). The IA 1986 provides other protection for *spouses* or *parents* by according them the limited protection of the statutory 'matrimonial home rights' against a trustee in bankruptcy (ss. 336, 337).

[59] The phrase 'home of the bankrupt' is wide enough to include a non-marital home; it is only where the home is that of a bankrupt's partner that the protection is confined to spouses or former spouses.

    (i)   the conduct of the spouse or former spouse, so far as contributing to the bankruptcy,[60]

   (ii) the needs and financial resources of the spouse or former spouse; and

  (iii) the needs of any children; and

(c) all the circumstances of the case other than the needs of the bankrupt.

The legislation goes on to say that, once a year has elapsed since the initiation of the bankruptcy, the courts must assume that the interests of the creditors outweigh all other considerations, unless there are 'exceptional circumstances'.

Once again, this amounts to a recognition of the special nature of family property and that the claims of non-owning family members merit some special consideration in a bankruptcy context: but there are two important limits to the impact of this provision. The first comes from the Court of Appeal decision in *Re Citro*,[61] in which it was suggested that the new provision had the effect of merely codifying the pre-1986 law, which dictated that it would be very rare for 'exceptional circumstances' to exist after the expiry of a year. As one commentator has suggested, 'the effect of the 1986 legislation seems likely to be that the bankrupt's family will in practice be given one year's grace but (in the absence of truly exceptional circumstances) no more before sale'.[62]

The second is that these criteria are only as wide in scope as section 14 itself: and, since section 14 applies only where there is some co-ownership of the land between family members, they will have no application where the bankrupt is the sole legal and beneficial owner of the home.[63] Once again, property ownership, or co-ownership, is the fulcrum on which the jurisdiction turns: no weight is attached to preserving the family home *as such*.

The pro-creditor approach evident in *Re Citro* is not universal, however, and some differences of approach are evident in closely related contexts. For example, there may be cases where a creditor is seeking to sell the family home by means other than bankruptcy proceedings, perhaps by exercising rights under a charge or mortgage. A chargee of a co-owner's share in a family home would have standing under section 14 to seek an order for

---

[60] It is unclear whether this provision is relevant only where it is the spouse's or former spouse's home that is the subject of the application, or generally; and if the latter, why there is no reference to unmarried partners' contributions to bankruptcy who, after all, may still be in the bankrupt's home. The same point may be made with respect to para. (b)(ii).

[61] [1991] Ch. 142.

[62] Cretney and Masson, *Principles of Family Law* (6th edn., London: Sweet & Maxwell, 1997), 168.

[63] Strictly speaking, no application will be necessary by a trustee in bankruptcy where the bankrupt is the sole trustee (legal owner) of the land; but a beneficiary of a trust of land could in these circumstances apply under the new s. 14 to *restrain* any proposed sale, in which case the s. 335A criteria would presumably also apply.

sale of trust land as a 'person interested'; and a mortgagee would have the remedy of possession in the event of a borrower's default. In both contexts, the courts have recently shown signs of a pro-debtor stance at odds with that of *Re Citro*.

In the context of chargees, for example, in *Abbey National Building Society* v. *Moss*,[64] a building society with a charge over the equitable tenancy in common of one of two co-owners was refused an order for sale under the old section 30. The Court of Appeal distinguished *Re Citro*. According to Peter Gibson LJ, cases of bankruptcy are distinguishable because any sub-sisting collateral purpose that might justify postponement of a sale is brought to an end by the bankruptcy of one of the co-owners: the bankruptcy brings co-ownership to an end, and co-ownership is the necessary foundation for a collateral purpose of shared occupation. In cases not involving bank-ruptcy, therefore, it is open to a court to find that a collateral purpose is still subsisting, and thus to refuse an order for sale. In *Moss* itself, the collateral purpose in question was to provide an elderly parent with a home for her lifetime, a purpose that had not been brought to an end by the daughter's charge over her equitable share in the property.[65]

The pattern with respect to chargees is not consistent, however. In *Barclays Bank* v. *Hendricks*,[66] for example, a Chancery Division judge, fol-lowing *Re Citro*, held that the interests of a chargee must prevail in an appli-cation under section 30 unless there are 'exceptional circumstances', just as those of a trustee in bankruptcy would have done before the introduction of section 335A IA 1986. The Court of Appeal decision in *Lloyds Bank* v. *Byrne*[67] is to much the same effect. However, both *Hendricks* and *Byrne* were cases in which the collateral purpose was one of joint rather than sole occupation, a fact which might explain the difference in outcome, at least if Peter Gibson's explanation of *Citro* in *Moss* is taken seriously. Either way, the results are peculiar: if *Moss* prevails, then there will be some circum-stances in which co-owners are better protected than others (although pre-cisely what those circumstances are remains obscure).

What is common to all of these cases, however, is the fact that an appli-cation for sale by the creditors or their representatives will be necessary only where there is shared ownership between the debtor and another family member. As already suggested, there is no concern to protect the family home as such, merely to protect the interests of the other (non-debtor) co-owner. These provisions, therefore, do not amount to anything like the 'homestead' legislation encountered in other jurisdictions, designed to

---

[64] [1994] 1 FLR 307.

[65] It is possible that this logic extends to some bankruptcy cases as well, wherever the col-lateral purpose is not joint occupation of the co-owners, but the sole occupation of only one of them—that is, of the one who is neither bankrupt nor has charged her share.

[66] [1996] 1 FLR 258.   [67] [1993] 1 FLR 369.

protect the debtor's family home from creditors irrespective of the ownership of it.[68]

In the context of mortgagees' actions for repossession following a borrower's default, the Court of Appeal has recently taken a much more
expansive view of its powers under section 36 of the Administration of
Justice Act 1970 than previously. This section confers on a court the power
to adjourn a mortgagee's possession proceedings, or to stay, suspend, or
postpone an order for possession for such period as the court thinks
reasonable, if the court is of the view that the borrower is 'likely within a
reasonable period to pay any sums due under the mortgage' or to remedy
any default. The phrase 'any sums due under the mortgage' refers, in effect,
to periodic instalments of interest, or (depending on the mortgage) capital
and interest, and not to the entire mortgage debt: it is payments of arrears
of periodic instalments that the borrower must be likely to repay within a
reasonable period.[69] In *Cheltenham and Gloucester Building Society plc v.
Norgan*,[70] evidence was provided that the standard period of time given for
repaying arrears by county courts is between two and four years;[71] yet the
Court of Appeal in *Norgan* found that a county court judge who had made
an order under section 36 in accordance with this usual practice had fallen
into error. According to Waite LJ, the court should take the full term of the
mortgage as its starting point and ask whether there is a reasonable prospect
of the borrower making full repayments of all arrears by the end of the term.
This is a considerably more 'pro-borrower' approach to section 36 than the
one it replaces.

The cases discussed in this section, all of which deal with substantially the
same issue of whether a family home should be sold to repay debts, reveal
that there is considerable disagreement between judges as to proper policy,
with some judges being far more pro-creditor than others. This could be
attributed in part to the lack of any coherent legislative guidance where the
family home is concerned. As already noted, existing legislation falls some
way short of a comprehensive code for dealing with such matters; and what
legislation there is points to substantially different treatment for those borrowers whose family home is mortgaged, and therefore subject to section
36, as compared to those whose lenders have charges over a part of the
equity and who can seek an order for sale under section 14. The legislative
policy is different again where the creditors have initiated bankruptcy proceedings. This state of affairs stems from a failure to see all these procedural
options 'in the round' and as essentially touching on the same issue—

---

[68] For a discussion of 'homestead' legislation', see Gray, *Elements of Land Law* (2nd edn.,
London: Butterworths, 1993), 604–6.

[69] Administration of Justice Act 1973, s. 8.   [70] [1996] 2 FLR 257.

[71] See Whitehouse, in this volume, for empirical evidence concerning the operation of
s. 36.

namely, whether the consequences of family indebtedness are to be visited on the family home, and, if so, how.

Occupation Orders: Family Law Act 1996, Part IV

So far, we have been looking at legislation that seeks to resolve the competing claims of co-owners of land, or those who claim through them such as creditors. The logic at work has been one of property: that is, the jurisdiction arises only where ownership of family property is shared in more than one person, and the purpose of the relevant provisions is to work out the implications of that co-ownership in particular circumstances. We have seen that some family considerations have been allowed to intrude, but only where there is already some form of co-ownership.

By contrast, Part IV of the Family Law Act 1996 creates a framework for the regulation of the occupation of the family home, whether the home is co-owned or not.[72] It is concerned with the use rather than the ownership of the family home. As such, it is part of the law's response to the problem of violence by men against women in the home, and the new Act represents both a clarification and an extension of the previous law in this respect;[73] but the new Part IV goes wider than cases of violence, and confers extensive powers on the courts to grant orders regulating the use of the home over the short to medium term, often as a prelude to divorce or other final proceedings between the parties.[74] In constructing this code, the Act draws on a complex web of statuses, including marriage, cohabitation, parenthood, and property ownership. Its logic is largely, though not exclusively, a family rather than property one: that is, its remedies turn on familial status rather than property ownership (although property ownership, as we shall see, is still accorded some pre-eminence).

For our purposes, the most relevant aspect of the new legislation is that dealing with occupation orders. An occupation order is an order regulating the occupation of the family home.[75] An occupation order may have both positive and negative aspects: it may enforce or confer an applicant's right to enter or remain in the home; and it may restrict or terminate the

---

[72] Only a very brief summary of the legislation is possible here. For more detail, see Bird, *Domestic Violence: The New Law*, (Bristol: Family Law, 1986).

[73] Part IV replaces the Domestic Violence and Matrimonial Proceedings Act 1976, the Matrimonial Homes Act 1983, and the relevant provisions of the Domestic Proceedings and Magistrates' Courts Act 1978, and for practical purposes supersedes the inherent powers of the High Court to grant injunctions in domestic violence cases.

[74] The new Part IV is based on the recommendations of the Law Commission, *Domestic Violence and Occupation of the Family Home*, Law Com. No. 207 (London: HMSO, 1992).

[75] The term 'family home' is used loosely. In fact, the legislation employs a number of different terms, depending on the status of the applicant (see n. 80).

respondent's rights to occupy the home.[76] As we shall see, the court's powers are more extensive where the applicant has some pre-existing right to
occupy the home (such as an ownership interest): but the legislation does
more than merely give effect to those rights, since the orders that may be
made could go beyond anything that might be described as enforcement.[77]
Property ownership is relevant only in deciding the extent of the court's
powers: the court is not confined by the limits or extent of those rights in
exercising its jurisdiction under the Act.

The Act draws a central distinction between entitled and non-entitled
applicants. Into the entitled category fall those who are entitled to occupy
the home in question by virtue of some pre-existing legal entitlement, such
as legal or beneficial ownership, a tenancy or contractual licence ('person
entitled'); and spouses, who may either be entitled in any case, or who will
be deemed to be so entitled by virtue of their 'matrimonial home rights'
conferred by the Act itself (see below). Non-entitled applicants are those
who are neither spouses nor owners of the property in question but who
have lived in a family home with the respondent.[78] This non-entitled
category is further subdivided into former spouses, on the one hand, and
cohabitants and former cohabitants, on the other.

The Act thus sets up a hierarchy of applicants. At the top are those with
property rights or with current marital status; those who are neither married to the respondent nor co-owners of the relevant property are in an
inferior position, but with former spouses being treated more generously
than non-owning cohabitants or non-owning former cohabitants. Much of
this reflects political concern, loudly voiced during the passage of the Act,
that the legislation should not undermine the institution of marriage by
treating cohabitants in the same way as married or formerly married
couples.[79]

The chief point of distinction between entitled and non-entitled applicants lies in the duration of any occupation order that may be made: for
entitled applicants, there is no limit to the length of time a court may make
an order governing the parties' occupation. For non-owners and non-
spouses, there is an initial limit of six months on orders; but, in keeping
with the policy of differentiating between former spouses and former or

---

[76] The legislation spells out in detail the contents of any occupation order, provides for
ancillary orders concerning such matters as repairs and payment of outgoings, and sets out
criteria for making orders (see Bird, *Domestic Violence*).

[77] Cretney and Masson, *Principles of Family Law*, 245. For example, an occupation order
may have the effect of excluding a joint tenant from the property, something which, under
general principles, one joint tenant cannot do to another.

[78] The Act also makes provision for those cases where *neither* party is entitled, again distinguishing between spouses and cohabitants: see ss. 37 and 38.

[79] See Eekelaar, 'The Family Law Bill: The Politics of Family Law' [1996] Family Law
45.

current, but non-owning, cohabitants, orders made in favour of the former can be renewed for any period not exceeding six months, whereas for the latter only one such renewal is possible.[80]

The significance of these status-based categories is less where there is a threat of 'significant harm' to any child of the family if the order is not made. In such cases, the court has no discretion whether to make the order—it must do so. To that extent, status-based thinking is displaced by a child-centred protectionist logic; but, even here, distinctions of status retain their grip where the applicant is a non-entitled cohabitant or former cohabitant, since in such cases the court is not obliged to make the order, but is required merely to 'have regard' to the threat of significant harm as a factor in the exercise of its discretion.[81]

The new Part IV represents the most significant attempt to date to codify an important aspect of family property, the use of the family home. In doing so, as we have seen, it draws on a number of different statuses: marriage, property entitlement, cohabitation, and parenthood. It seeks to knit together this hierarchical, status-based logic, according to which the claims that may be made are dictated by the status category into which an applicant falls, with a more traditional welfarist or needs-oriented logic, that seeks to achieve certain welfare outcomes regardless of the parties' status. This complexity is reflected in the contorted drafting of the legislation, described by one commentator as a 'parliamentary dog's breakfast'.[82]

The scope of the legislation is limited: it deals only with temporary use or enjoyment, rather than long-term ownership, of the family home; but, in doing so, it exemplifies a trend of thought about family property, a shift away from ownership to function, that may be worth developing further. I will return to this later.

---

[80] Another distinction lies in the property with respect to which the orders may be made: for entitled applicants, the court has jurisdiction over any dwelling that the applicant has shared with an 'associated person', a term that is broadly defined in s. 62(3); non-entitled applicants may seek orders only with respect to the former matrimonial or family home. There is further differentiation within the non-entitled category between former spouses and cohabitants: for example, in deciding whether to make an occupation order in favour of a non-entitled cohabitant or former cohabitant, the court is directed to take account of 'the nature of the parties' relationship' and in doing so is required to 'have regard to the fact that they have not given each other the commitment involved in marriage' (s. 41 FLA 1996). This is clearly an attempt to accord the never-married lesser treatment than the formerly-married, although that distinction is already enshrined to some extent in the difference in the duration of orders that the courts are empowered to make.

[81] FLA 1997, ss. 33(7), 35(8), 36(7), (8).

[82] Murphy, 'Domestic Violence: The New Law' (1996) 59 MLR 845, at 859.

Matrimonial Home Rights

One of the earliest statutory responses to the special needs of family members with respect to the family home was the Matrimonial Homes Act 1967. The immediate stimulus for this legislation was the decision of the House of Lords in *National Provincial Bank* v. *Ainsworth*,[83] in which it was held that the status of marriage conferred no automatic proprietary claims to the family home on an otherwise non-owning spouse. This raised the possibility that a husband could enter transactions involving the matrimonial home which could ultimately threaten a wife's continued occupation, such as a mortgage, without her knowledge or consent. The statutory solution was to confer on a non-owning spouse statutory rights of occupation in a matrimonial home that were exercisable against the other spouse and which were capable of binding a third party when protected on the register in a prescribed manner. The scope of the legislation was subsequently expanded by later statutory amendment[84] and by judicial interpretation;[85] and is now contained in Part IV of the Family Law Act 1996.[86]

The legislation now defines 'matrimonial home rights' as (*a*) the right, if in occupation, not to be evicted except by court order and (*b*), if not in occupation, the right, with leave of court, to enter and occupy.[87] These statutory rights arise where one spouse has a right to occupy a dwelling house and the other does not:[88] in these circumstances, the latter has the statutory rights, provided that the house in question is one that the parties have used, or have intended to use, as their matrimonial home.[89] It will be noted that the exercise of these rights between spouses is heavily dependent on the exercise by a court of its order-making discretion: and, for these purposes, the exercise by spouses of their matrimonial home rights against each other is subsumed within the general jurisdiction to make occupation orders (discussed above). A spouse with the statutory rights will be deemed to be an 'entitled' applicant for those purposes. The statutory rights take effect as a charge on the owning spouse's estate in the house, but will have priority against third parties only if registered (either as a notice or Class F land charge) before the third party's interest in the land is created.[90]

The legislation, and its conceptual apparatus, sits uneasily with the exigencies of family life. In particular, the adoption of a conveyancer's logic—that enforceability against third parties depends on registration—confers

---

[83] [1965] AC 1175.

[84] Matrimonial Homes and Property Act 1981; Matrimonial Homes Act 1983.

[85] Esp. *Richards* v. *Richards* [1984] 1 AC 174.   [86] FLA 1996, ss. 30–1 and sch. 4.

[87] Ibid., s. 30(2).

[88] Ibid., s. 30(1); for these purposes only, an equitable interest in land is not deemed to carry with it a right of occupation (s. 30 (9)).

[89] Ibid., s. 30(7).   [90] Ibid., s. 31.

protection that manages simultaneously to be too weak and too strong. For example, a non-owning spouse will not be able to claim priority for his or her statutory rights over those of a mortgagee lending on an acquisition mortgage, since there will be no 'moment in time' at which the owning spouse has an unencumbered estate against which the statutory charge can bite.[91] Yet, registration of a statutory charge after purchase can confer a powerful veto on the non-owning spouse over any later transactions involving the property: after registration of the statutory rights, no potential purchaser or mortgage-lender will enter a transaction with the husband in the knowledge that the wife has matrimonial home rights that will bind them; and, as one well-known case has illustrated,[92] the legislation permits the wife potentially to block a conveyancing transaction to which she is opposed, even after contracts have been exchanged and have become binding.

The legislation reaches towards a regime of cooperation and consultation between spouses in dealings with the family home, but manages instead to create the legal conditions under which one spouse is potentially always at the mercy of the other. Indeed, it is arguable that the shortcomings of this regime have been tolerated only because they have been obscured by later judicial developments, especially *Boland* and *O'Brien*, which between them have arguably been far more effective in ensuring spousal cooperation and consultation, mainly by visiting the consequences of their absence on the mortgage-lenders themselves.[93] But the effectiveness of these doctrines depends, as we have seen, on the ownership of the home being joint.

Property Distribution on Divorce: Matrimonial Causes Act 1973

Perhaps the best example of specific statutory provision for family property are those sections of the Matrimonial Causes Act 1973[94] empowering a divorce court to make orders transferring property between divorcing spouses, or between divorcing spouses and their children, or both. Unlike occupation orders, these powers affect ownership of family property as well as its enjoyment.

A 'property adjustment order', as defined by the Act, is an order that one spouse transfer or settle property to or for the benefit of the other spouse or a child of the family, or that interests under marriage settlements be varied

---

[91] *Abbey National Building Society* v. *Cann* [1991] AC 56.

[92] *Wroth* v. *Tyler* [1974] Ch. 30; see now FLA 1996, sch. 4, paras. 3, 5.

[93] Perhaps the most practically valuable aspects of the legislation are those enabling the spouse with the statutory rights to step into the shoes of the other spouse for certain purposes, such as the discharge of liabilities or for the purposes of the Rent or Housing Acts (see FLA 1996, ss. 30(3)–(6)).

[94] Most importantly, MCA 1973, s. 21(2).

or extinguished. These property adjustment powers are exercisable along-side powers to make 'financial provision orders', which are orders for regular periodical payments out of income or lump sums of capital. The discretion to make both types of order is governed by the factors set out in section 25 (and now section 25A) of the Act, of which more in a moment.

These powers originated in the Matrimonial Proceedings and Property Act 1970. The 1970 Act was a pragmatic response to two factors. The first was the decisions in *Pettitt* v. *Pettitt*[95] and *Gissing* v. *Gissing*,[96] which over-ruled the earlier case law seeking to establish a doctrine of 'family assets' in English law, and which sought to give the courts a discretion to deal with the property consequences of divorce under section 17 of the Married Women's Property Act 1882.[97] Instead, as we have seen, the House of Lords ruled that family property cases had to be resolved by the application of general rules of property law (with due 'allowances'), and that section 17 was declaratory only. The second was the need to ensure the safe passage through Parliament of the Divorce Reform Act 1969. Wide property distribution powers were seen as a necessary *quid pro quo* if the grounds for divorce were to be broadened to include no-fault divorce.[98] That is what resulted: the Act confers on the courts what has been described as a wide-ranging 'power of appointment' over spousal property.[99]

As originally drafted, the legislation directed the courts, in section 25, to have regard to a number of general factors (such as the parties' respective needs and resources) and then to exercise their powers in such a way as to place the parties, so far as possible, in the position they would have been in if the marriage had not broken down (subsequently christened 'the principle of minimal loss'[100]). This part of the Act was amended in 1984 to direct the courts instead to have regard as their primary consideration to the welfare of any minor child of the family; and also to the desirability of terminating financial relations between the parties as soon as possible (the so-called 'clean break').[101]

These powers are wide-ranging, and even after the 1984 reforms continue to give the courts a wide discretion to resolve the financial consequences of divorce. Any asset that is owned beneficially by one or other party is potentially within the scope of these powers, including the freehold of a family home (if there is one).[102] So far as the family home is concerned,

---

[95] [1970] AC 777.   [96] [1971] AC 886.

[97] e.g. *Fribance* v. *Fribance* [1957] 1 WLR 384.

[98] Cretney and Masson, *Principles of Family Law*, 424–5.

[99] Gray, 'Equitable Property' (1994) 47(2) CLP 157 at 171.

[100] Eekelaar, *Family Law and Social Policy* (London: Weidenfeld & Nicolson, 1978), ch. 9.

[101] Matrimonial and Family Proceedings Act 1984, introducing a new s. 25 and s. 25A.

[102] Leaseholds may also be 'property' available for distribution under the MCA 1973; but there is now a comprehensive statutory code for transferring family home tenancies in sch. 7 to the Family Law Act 1997, which is considered further below.

it is difficult to generalize about how the courts use these powers in practice: the whole point of a wide discretion is to enable the courts to fine-
tune outcomes to the facts of each case and to the needs of the parties.
Nevertheless, some general trends can be identified.

The most important of these is the priority the courts attach to retaining
the former family home as a home for the children. This can be justified in
terms of the legislation as giving priority to the welfare of the children, but
it was a well-established practice of the divorce courts even before the 1984
reforms.[103] There are a number of means by which the courts can achieve
this objective: by an outright transfer to the primary caring parent, perhaps
with a compensating money payment to the transferor, immediate or
deferred;[104] or by a settlement of the property on trust for sale, with sale
(and distribution of proceeds) postponed until the children reach a certain
age or have completed their education, or until the parent remarries or no
longer wishes to remain in the house.[105]

Despite their breadth, these provisions by no means amount to a comprehensive statutory regime of family property. For one thing, they apply
only on divorce.[106] This means that they have no application during a marriage, and have no relevance at all to the unmarried either during their relationship or at its end.[107] The legislation is thus status based (i.e. available
only to the married-but-divorcing); and 'pathological', that is, it is triggered
only when there is a family breakdown leading to the formal step of
divorce. Furthermore, it could be said that the legislation contains very few
general statements of principle about the nature and purpose of property
adjustment and financial provision: the emphasis is on retaining a broad discretion so as to do justice on the facts. As such, it is scarcely a model for any
overarching framework of family property relations in law.[108]

---

[103] e.g. *Browne* v. *Pritchard* [1975] 3 AER 721; Eekelaar, *Regulating Divorce* (Oxford:
Oxford University Press, 1991), 70–3.   [104] e.g. *Hanlon* [1978] 1 WLR 592.

[105] e.g. *Mesher* [1980] 1 All ER 126; *Clutton* [1991] 1 FLR 42. The existence of child-
support liabilities under the Child Support Act 1991 will influence the use of these orders,
since it is no longer as easy as it once was for spouses to 'trade' reduced child support for a
transfer of the family home (see *Crozier* [1994] 1 FLR 126). Some such arrangements may
be retrospectively accommodated under the Child Support Act 1995.

[106] Amendments introduced by the Family Law Act 1996 make it clear that any property
adjustment order can take effect only on divorce, and only in exceptional cases earlier (MCA
1973, s. 22B); and a divorce will itself be conditional on the parties making satisfactory financial arrangements (see FLA 1996, ss. 3, 9).

[107] We have seen that the courts adapted their powers under the old LPA 1925, s. 30 to
achieve similar ends with respect to the family home where unmarried couples with children were concerned, but their ability to do so depended on the unmarried couple being
co-owners of the property in question (see *Re Evers*, above).

[108] There is a related power to order parents to make financial provision, or transfer property to, their children under Children Act 1989, sch. 1 (see e.g. *A.* v. *A. (Minor)(Financial
provision)* [1994] 1 FLR 657).

ATTEMPTS AT REFORM

This brief survey of legislative developments affecting the family home bears out the claim that there is a growing body of what can only be described as a distinctive law of the family home; but that, at the same time, there is no single model, or set of concepts, underlying all these instances of it. Instead, as we have seen, rights and obligations turn on different types of familial status (marriage, parenthood, cohabitation) and are context- or procedure-specific: they arise only on the occurrence of certain legally relevant events, such as divorce or family breakdown, bankruptcy, and so on, and have no application beyond that specific context. The criteria governing their operation vary from context to context, and may sometimes overlap.

English law has proved stubbornly resistant to the introduction of a single legal regime for the family home that would answer all these questions in one go; and the introduction of a civil law-style community of property regime covering *all* family property, real and personal, has only rarely been considered seriously. Instead, law reformers have tended to assume that the main problem in family property is the family home. Thus, the chief protagonist of reform in this area, the Law Commission, has for some time been pressing for the introduction of statutory co-ownership of the matrimonial home. This suggestion was first made in 1973, then set out in more detail in 1978,[109] and reiterated in 1982[110] as a response to the conveyancing 'problem' presented by *Boland*: but no legislation was forthcoming, and the scheme has now been abandoned. Instead, the Commission has since turned its attentions to matrimonial property other than land, and to the broader issue of the property rights of 'home-sharers'. It is instructive to examine, briefly, why this has been the case.

The Commission's main reason for recommending its scheme was that the rules governing acquisition of interests in the family home were unfair. Ownership depended too heavily on financial contributions to property acquisition, something which discriminated against women, because their contributions were more likely to be non-financial. As the Commission argued, 'Husband and wife each contribute to the home in their different ways—the wife's contributions are no less real because they may not be financial—and the home is essential to the well-being of the family as a whole. In our view these factors make the matrimonial home a unique item of family property, and one to which a unique law of co-ownership should apply'.[111] The 'unique law' proposed was one under which a matrimonial

[109] Law Commission, *Third Report on Family Property*.

[110] Law Commission, *Property Law: The Implications of Williams & Glyn's Bank v. Boland*, Law Com. No.115 (London: HMSO, 1982).

[111] Law Commission, *Third Report on Family Property*, para. 0.9.

home would, subject to a contrary agreement, be automatically co-owned by both spouses in any case where there was not already co-ownership. This would take the form of a statutory joint tenancy of the equitable interest in the property: in a sense, a forced transfer of a share of the owning spouse's rights to the other. In all cases of co-ownership, statutory or otherwise, spouses would have the right to veto any sale or other disposition (such as a mortgage) of the property, a veto that would prevent title passing to a third party. However, the effectiveness of that veto would depend on the protection of the co-ownership interest by registration of a statutory charge. Failure to protect the interest would mean that a third party could ignore it, even where the equitable interest arose from the general law rather than the statute.

The scheme was roundly criticized from a number of different quarters. First, it was argued that there was no obvious reason why a non-contributing spouse should be put on an equal footing in all respects with a contributing one. On this view, the proposals ran the risk of entrenching rather than alleviating female dependency on men and of rewarding economic inactivity.[112] Secondly, it was suggested that, in view of the rapid rise of cohabitation outside marriage, it was arbitrary to confine the scheme to married couples, just as it was arbitrary to confine the scheme to the matrimonial home.[113] Thirdly, it was suggested that the scheme was unnecessary, since it is increasingly common for family homes to be held in joint names, and that in any case decisions such as *Boland* had substantially increased the protection available to those wives whose names did not appear on the legal title.[114] In other words, the problem to be solved was simply too small to warrant such a complex scheme. Fourthly, it was argued that the scheme did not go far enough, either because it had no application on death or divorce (where, arguably, a principle of equal co-ownership, and thus of equal sharing, would make the greatest difference), or because its protection depended too heavily on the inappropriate device of registration.[115] Indeed, the Law Commission's scheme would actually decrease the protection afforded in those cases where a spouse would have an interest under general law principles, since protection turns on registration, whereas *Boland* depends simply on actual occupation.[116] In attempting to strike the

---

[112] Deech, 'Williams and Glyn's and Family Law' [1980] New Law Journal 896.

[113] Scottish Law Commission, *Family Law: Report on Matrimonial Property*, Scot. Law Com. No. 86 (Edinburgh: HMSO, 1984).

[114] Deech, 'Williams and Glyn's and Family Law'.

[115] Murphy and Rawlings, 'The Matrimonial Homes (Co-Ownership) Bill: The Right Way Forward?' [1980] Family Law 136; Murphy, 'After Boland: Law Com. No.115' (1983) 46 MLR 330.

[116] The Law Commission would have exonerated third parties from the consequences of non-compliance with the two-trustee rule in cases of non-registration: hence the criticism that the proposals were more attuned to the needs of conveyancers than anything else, since

balance between protecting occupation of the matrimonial home, on the one hand, and removing any uncertainty from conveyancing transactions, on the other, it was argued that the proposals tilted the balance too far towards the latter.[117]

The Law Commission proposals represented a curious compromise between property and status thinking: certain policy objectives were to be pursued by conferring property rights by statute, but only on those who possess a certain status (marriage). Yet it is difficult to see why a more direct approach could not have been taken—that is, of conferring a consent right on spouses, cutting out the language of ownership altogether. The Law Commission's reasons for routing all this through ownership were (i) that granting a mere consent right would not cure uncertainties about the extent of a spouse's ownership interest; (ii) that a consent right was not a big enough *quid pro quo* to spouses for the registration requirement; and (iii) that to confer a consent right on a non co-owning spouse would represent a 'drastic inroad into accepted concepts of property'.[118] None of these is especially persuasive—the last in particular, since it is difficult to imagine circumstances where a spouse would not also be a co-owner either under the general law or under the proposed statute. As Tim Murphy pointed out, 'a certain amount of casuistry is involved here. There is of course a difference between a consent requirement derived from status and a consent requirement annexed to a property right derived from status. But it is a rather nice difference'.[119] It is difficult not to read the anxiety to cast the consent rights in terms of ownership as a way of defusing the threat posed to third parties by off-title interests in the family home.

These criticisms, combined with a lack of political support for the proposal, have ensured that the scheme has never seen the legislative light of day. It seems likely, therefore, that, subject to whatever emerges from the Law Commission's home-sharing project, English law will continue down the piecemeal and pragmatic path identified in this chapter. In the final section, I want to suggest ways in which that pragmatic tradition might be exploited.

WHAT IS NEEDED?

The Law Commission's scheme, in its successive versions, took co-ownership as its conceptual starting point. The detailed workings out of

even a spouse who had contributed to acquisition would lose priority to a third party through a failure to register the necessary charge.

[117] Murphy, 'After Boland'.

[118] Law Commission, *Property Law: The Implications of Williams & Glyn's Bank* v. *Boland*, para. 110.

[119] Murphy, 'After Boland', 335.

that starting premiss have been intricate and problematic. This starting point has also been reflected in doctrinal theorizing about the family home. Simon Gardner,[120] for example, has suggested that there are existing conceptual resources available within legal discourse to enable judges to arrive at equal ownership, at least for those couples who are either married or who display the necessary qualities of 'trust and collaboration'; for the rest, a restitutionary model is preferred. In either case, we are invited to accept that, once the issue of ownership is resolved, by whatever doctrinal means, everything else will fall into place.[121]

I want to suggest that, in devising a legislative strategy in this context, we need not think exclusively in terms of ownership; and that ownership thinking may have become a bit of a strait-jacket. Instead, I want to suggest that, in line with the English tradition of pragmatism in this area, we should think functionally. Thinking functionally about the family home means asking what rights family members need in relation to it. If we can identify what those are or might be, we can set about conferring them directly, without necessarily invoking the language of ownership. This means avoiding the Law Commission's strategy of creating equal ownership in order to confer rights incidental to that ownership. The focus would be on status as the mechanism for conferring the necessary rights, not on property. Of course, this begs the questions of what we mean by familial 'status' for these purposes, who would qualify for it, and how the different interests of family members and third parties would be weighed against each other: but at least the strategy would be clear.[122]

In order to get discussion going on these lines, I suggest that there are four broad rights that family members need in relation to the family home: a right of *control over dealings* (such as mortgages or sales); a right of *occupation or enjoyment*; a right of *capital entitlement on sale*; and a right, on the termination of the relationship, to have *basic needs met out of the family resources represented by the family home*.

We have seen that the incidents of property ownership have been developed judicially in such a way that co-owners of a family home already have many of these rights secured to them—through what I have called the 'familialization' of property law. An equitable interest in land, for example,

---

[120] Gardner, 'Rethinking Family Property' [1993] 109 LQR 263, discussed by Bottomley, Chapter 8, this volume. An interesting feature of Gardner's argument is that it amounts to a proposal for an explicitly 'familialized' set of principles for dealing with family property disputes.

[121] Gardner suggests that his principle of communality would lead either to a half share in communal assets, or to 'adequate support from [the] other's assets' (ibid. 298)—but he leaves the mechanisms of that support unspecified.

[122] A 'status-based' approach would not find favour with everyone (see e.g. Bottomley, Chapter 8, this volume.

can form the basis of securing the first two rights of consent to dealings and enjoyment through occupation;[123] and ownership remains pre-eminent in determining the third right, at least where there are no statutory alternatives available for doing so. But, in a family context, or more specifically a context of gender inequality, it needs to be asked whether ownership is a sufficient or necessary basis for securing these rights.

I would suggest that it is neither. It is not necessary, because there are existing instances in which some of these rights are secured to family members *as such*, regardless of their rights of ownership (for example, occupation orders under the Family Law Act 1996, or property distribution orders under the Matrimonial Causes Act 1973); and there is no reason why a status-based logic, which bypasses ownership, could not be extended to securing the other rights mentioned.

Nor is it sufficient, given the weight of evidence suggesting that, despite judicial development, the rules of ownership acquisition operate unfavourably in a family context, especially against women, by according pre-eminence to money contributions to acquisition; and in the light of the fact that ownership is a very crude device for securing all four of the rights mentioned above, especially the fourth. For example, an a priori assumption of equal ownership would translate into a principle of equal division on separation, yet that is a rule that legislatures have generally avoided, on the basis that equal distribution can lead to serious post-separation inequality.[124] Instead, distribution of property has to be seen in the light of the parties' post-relationship needs and of other powers concerning maintenance for spouses and children. Vindication of the fourth right therefore requires more than a simple rule about ownership.

We should not forget that there is a sense in which all four of the rights mentioned are already secured, to some degree, by means of existing legislation—what I have called the nascent statutory regime governing the family home. To that extent, we might say that ownership is in any case fast becoming obsolete as a significant conceptual category in this area; and that, in its pragmatic way, English statute law is groping towards a satisfactory regime for the family home, despite its continuing theoretical attachment to the doctrine of separation. But, as this chapter has sought to demonstrate, that statutory regime has arisen piecemeal, and varies significantly in its

[123] See *Boland*, discussed above; but note the inroads made into *Boland* by *Cann* and *Flegg*, as discussed above. Cases such as *O'Brien* seek to make the consent requirement a real one.

[124] Even those jurisdictions whose family law statutes enshrine a principle of equal sharing of matrimonial property on divorce do so only as a starting point that may be departed from (see for example, Family Law (Scotland) Act 1985, s. 9, or the Matrimonial Property Act 1976 (New Zealand)). A rule of formal equality has been rejected in Australia (see Australian Law Reform Commission, *Matrimonial Property*, Report No. 39 (Canberra: AGPS, 1987), especially at para. 273: 'equal sharing of property at the end of a marriage is not necessarily fair sharing').

application according to status or the procedural context in ways that are not obviously justified.

If, instead, we were to view the current maze of the law relating to the family home through the grid of the four rights mentioned above, and at the same time reduce our attachment to ownership as the sole vehicle for attaining these rights, we might get some greater clarity about proper policy in this important area of social and economic life.

14

EUROPE, THE NATION STATE, AND LAND

Christopher Bright and Susan Bright

The regulation of landownership and use is generally perceived, in the context of Europe, to be a matter for the nation state and not an area for which membership of supranational groupings, such as the Council of Europe and in particular the European Union,[1] has any major significance. The European Union is perceived primarily as focused on the supranational goals of market integration embodied in the European Community. At first blush it may seem that land and the law relating to it have little connection with this. Land is immoveable and consequently not something that itself requires market-opening measures to allow cross-border trade. In fact the European Community has as its goals, set out in Article 2 of the Treaty of Rome,[2] the bringing-about of a common market and economic and monetary union, the promotion of harmonious and balanced development, economic convergence and growth, employment and social protection, economic and social cohesion, and the somewhat nebulous concept of raising the standard of living and quality of life.[3] It does not take huge skills in textual exegesis to see the wide scope of these. Taken together with the fact that land is both a core part of most enterprises and an essential aspect of the quality of life for individuals, the likelihood of European Community law being applied to land-related issues may seem less surprising. Land, and

Our thanks to Sonya McNulty for her assistance with the preparation of this chapter.

[1] There is a confusion of terms for the European Union. The Union was created by the Treaty of Maastricht (1992). It has three pillars: the three European Communities (being the European Community established and governed by the Treaty of Rome in 1957 (originally named the European Economic Community), the European Coal and Steel Community established under the Treaty of Paris in 1952 (which expires in 2002), and the European Atomic Energy Community), provisions on justice and home affairs, and provisions on a common foreign and security policy. Consequently we will use the term 'Union' as the generic description and 'Community' when dealing particularly with Treaty of Rome matters. Issues relating to land arise within the European Union principally under the Treaty of Rome.

[2] The Treaty of Rome, as amended by the Single European Act 1986 and the Maastricht Treaty 1992, is referred to in this chapter as the Treaty.

[3] The Treaty of Rome is to be further amended by the Treaty of Amsterdam 1997 and will result in a renumbering of the Articles referred to throughout this chapter. The Treaty of Amsterdam will enter into force after it has been ratified by all Member States, which is not likely to be before 1999.

rights relating to it, can have a significant impact on the objectives of the European Community. Apart from the European Union itself there are other issues arising from Europe that have a potential impact in this area— notably the European Convention on Human Rights and the growing Europeanization of English law generally. The aim of this chapter is to discuss the areas in which the Union has competence to regulate land matters and the extent to which there is a protected core of property rights which are left to national regulation and, secondly, to examine some of the areas in which European law has already had an impact in relation to land.

COMPETENCE OF THE UNION AND LAND

Whilst argument abounds about the political and social aims of the Union, the economic goal of creating a single market is long-established and common ground among the protagonists in the European debate. This market is an 'area without internal frontiers in which the free movement of goods, persons, services and capital is ensured' (Article 7a) and it is these four freedoms that were at the heart of developments in the first three decades following the founding of the Community. The Treaty as originally drafted has been revealed over time as concerned with issues going significantly beyond the creation of a single market and the four freedoms. The competence of the European Community was expanded by the Single European Act of 1986 and by the Maastricht Treaty of 1992. It is no longer the case, if ever it was, that the Union has competence only in relation to matters affecting trade. This is evident from the goals in Article 2 of the Treaty and from Article 3, which sets out twenty activities of the Community. These activities also reveal great diversity: establishing the internal market, the approximation of national laws to ensure the proper functioning of the common market, an environmental policy, a common agricultural policy, and the strengthening of consumer protection. What must also be borne in mind is that not only are the goals and activities widely crafted, but the Treaty has created independent insititutions and an independent legal system which work together in a creative way. In essence, as time goes on, the European Community under the umbrella of the European Union is gaining all the hallmarks of a fully fledged government concerned with most aspects of the human condition. Consequently it should not be surprising that European Community law is increasingly impinging on land.

When the wider goals and activities of the Community, as set out in Articles 2 and 3, are taken into account, the idea that it lacks the potential for intervention in the area of land rights and usage can be seen to be wholly illusory. Intervention can take two forms. The subtle form of intervention emerges from the direct application of the Treaty. The principles enshrined in the Treaty are already effective and can crystallize when action is brought by an individual based on the Articles of the Treaty or by Community enforcement action. This 'passive intervention' has already had an impact upon land issues. The other form, 'active intervention,' stems from Community legislative action in pursuit of Community goals. Again, active intervention has begun to impact upon land.

LIMITS ON THE COMPETENCE OF THE UNION AND LAND?

The notion that the European Community is constrained in its approach to land comes from a number of sources. The early focus upon the 'four freedoms' created a climate in which Community law was seen as only to do with cross-border activities and property which is moveable across borders, which, of course, land itself is not. Two provisions of the Treaty lend legal credence to this observation of early practice. First, the principle of subsidiarity enunciated in Article 3b is commonly understood to stand for the view that the Community is able to act only if an issue cannot be adequately regulated at national level. Matters affecting land use, given its immoveable status, seem eminently suited to national regulation. Secondly, Article 222 refers specifically to property and states that the Treaty 'shall in no way prejudice the rules in Member States governing the system of property ownership'. This appears to create a 'no-go' zone for the Union. In fact, neither of these provisions provides much of a barrier to Union intrusion into land issues.

Subsidiarity as a Limit on Union Competence

Subsidiarity understood in the sense outlined above—that decisions and measures should be taken and implemented at the level closest to the ordinary citizen and that the Community should act only if an objective can be better achieved at the level of the Community than at the level of the nation—would seem to give strength to the idea that issues relating to immoveable property are for the nation state, or indeed levels of government lower in the normative hierarchy where they exist (such as the proposed Scottish Assembly and Welsh Assembly). This picture of how subsidiarity works is more political rhetoric than legal reality. The principle of subsidiarity states

In areas which do not fall within its exclusive competence, the Community shall take action, in accordance with the principle of subsidiarity, only if and in so far as the objectives of the proposed action cannot be sufficiently achieved by the

Member States and can therefore, by reason of the scale or effects of the proposed action, be better achieved by the Community.[4]

It is crucial to note that the principle of subsidiarity does not apply in relation to areas which fall within the 'exclusive competence of the Community'. Unfortunately the Treaty does not attempt to define the division of competences. Nevertheless, it is clear that the areas in which the Community is taken to have exclusive powers are wide-ranging; an internal report prepared by the European Commission ('the Commission') refers,[5] for example, to the establishment of an internal market and a common organization of agricultural markets as areas of exclusive powers. Further, in relation to competence shared with Member States, the Community is still able to act if the objectives cannot be achieved sufficiently by the Member State.

The resultant picture is one of the Community free to act, notwithstanding the principle of subsidiarity, in relation to wide-ranging matters which can have a considerable impact upon land. Of course, this discussion relates to active intervention. Passive intervention through the directly applicable provisions of the Treaty in any event prevails over national law.

Article 222 as a Limit on Union Competence

The origins of Article 222 are to be found in Article 83 of the Coal and Steel Treaty.[6] This was designed to permit nationalization of the relevant industries, without fear that the nationalization programmes might be branded as barriers to trade and anti-competitive. When the Treaty of Rome was adopted, the wording was amended, and again it is clear that one of the designs was to make clear that nationalization of industry was permitted.[7] Viewed in this light, Article 222 could be said to have a very narrow objective, which is to enable Member States to permit public or private holding of property. If this were the case, the Union would clearly be competent to regulate land without risk of infringing Article 222.

What has emerged, however, from a string of cases relating to industrial property is that Article 222 has a wider import.[8] The European Court of Justice (ECJ) clearly perceives Article 222 as protecting more than the Member State's right to determine the simple form of property ownership (whether it is private or public). In the context of intellectual property

---

[4] Treaty of Rome, Article 3b, inserted by the Maastricht Treaty in 1992.

[5] Annexed to a Communication of the Commission to the Council and the European Parliament dated 27 Oct. 1992.

[6] The Treaty of Paris, 1952, established the European Coal and Steel Community.

[7] Case C–41/90, *Hofner and Elser* v. *Macrotron GmbH* [1993] 4 CMLR 306, *per* Jacobs AG at 325.

[8] See Case 58/64, *Grundig-Verhaufs GmbH* v. *Commission* [1966] ECR 299, esp. at 345.

rights, there has been a distinction made between the existence of a right, which is taken to be a matter for Member State determination and protected from Union control, and the exercise of a right, which must be consistent with the provisions of the Treaty. The result is that Member States are able to decide what sorts of rights can be created or recognized but that the exercise of those rights is a matter of concern to the Union.

There are two aspects to this that inform our debate on Union competence in relation to land. First, Article 222 may create a zone of protection, preserving for Member States the ability to create and recognize real property rights, which the Union does not have competence to enter. But, secondly, even though there may be a 'no-go' zone, the use and exercise of the recognized property rights must still comply with other Union goals. Of course, neither is necessarily true if the ECJ were to interpret Article 222 differently in relation to immoveable property than for industrial property but there is no obvious reason why it should do so and there are indications that the ECJ does propose to treat land in a similar manner to other forms of property where Article 222 issues arise. In *Fearon* v. *Irish Land Commission*[9] a challenge was made in relation to the compulsory purchase powers of the Irish Land Commission, which exempted certain categories of persons from being liable to compulsory purchase. It was claimed that this was discriminatory. In an unusually self-denying manner, the Commission, in evidence to the ECJ, contended that compulsory acquisition by public bodies was part of the system of property ownership in Ireland and that Article 222 precluded the application of the free movement rules. The ECJ ruled that the Commission's approach could not be accepted. It held that, 'although Article 222 . . . does not call in question the Member States' right to establish a system of compulsory acquisition by public bodies, such a system remains subject to the fundamental rule of non-discrimination . . .'(para. 7). On the facts, the policy could be justified as it applied equally to Irish nationals and non-nationals and consequently no discrimination arose.[10] From this it appears that although the ECJ recognizes that certain aspects of property-ownership are a matter for Member States, their application must still be consistent with Union goals.

The emerging picture is that Article 222 ring-fences the creation of rights as a matter for Member States, whilst the exercise of those rights is of interest to the Union. It is probable that the existence/exercise distinction will

[9] Case 182/83, *Fearon* v. *The Irish Land Commission* [1984] ECR 3677.

[10] It is unclear that this decision sits easily alongside other cases concerning the promotion of local interests, see Case 31/87, *Gebroeders Beentjes BV* v. *The Netherlands* [1988] ECR 4635, and Case 3/88, *Commission* v. *Italy* [1989] ECR 4035, which indicate that provisions of national law which, while applicable without distinction to nationals of all Member States, in fact hinder or disadvantage primarily nationals of other Member States fall foul of the Treaty.

also be adopted for rights in land, with 'existence' issues being matters for Member States alone under Article 222. This can be done only if the concept of 'existence' is given some clear meaning, a task that cannot be achieved without a value judgement being brought into play. It is artificial to talk of 'a right' existing unless the right-holder is able to exercise the right in some manner. It is nonsensical to recognize, for example, an easement of way if it is not permissible for the right-holder to exercise that right by crossing the servient land. The fact that a right cannot be easily separated from its exercise has led the ECJ, in the context of intellectual property rights, to extend the notion of existence of a right to include its exercise where that relates to the 'specific subject matter of the property'—namely, 'those powers which, *in the Court's view*, the holder must be able to exercise if the right is to retain any meaning at all'.[11] To identify this it has extracted one of the rights of ownership—the liberty to put a product into first circulation—as the substance of the right. In doing so the ECJ has made a policy decision about the extent to which the right is permitted to be exercised.

Applying this approach to rights in land raises novel challenges. With intellectual property rights, the reason why the right is given is to encourage and reward the creative process of invention, and in so doing to create an incentive to invest in research. In effect, what the ECJ has done in identifying the specific subject matter of the property is to extract the perceived primary *purpose* of the right and ring-fence this as the zone protected by Article 222. Interests in relation to land cannot be so readily reduced to sharing a common purpose. There is a huge variety of interests recognized as proprietary interests in land, ranging from ownership interests in the form of freeholds and leaseholds to permission to use another's land, such as a right to lay sewers, or even a right to control the use another makes of his land, as with covenants. There are also non-proprietary interests in land, such as a licence to stay in a hostel. There is no one purpose or liberty that can unify rights in land and be used to define their essential 'existence'. Is there in relation to land another way of defining the existence of the right?

In the context of fundamental rights,[12] there has been an attempt to

---

[11] Friden, 'Recent Developments in EEC Intellectual Property Law: The Distinction between Existence and Exercise Revisited' (1989) 26 CML Rev. 193 at 194; see also Case 192/73, *Van Zuylen-Freres* v. *Hag AG (Hag 1)* [1974] ECR 731, and Case 15/74, *Centrafarm BV* v. *Sterling Drug* [1974] ECR 1147.

[12] Many jurisdictions respect the 'right to property'. Article 1 of the First Protocol to the European Convention for the Protection of Human Rights provides, *inter alia*, 'Every natural or legal person is entitled to the peaceful enjoyment of his possessions. No one shall be deprived of his possessions except in the public interest and subject to the conditions provided for by law and by the general principles of international law.' The right to property has been recognized by the ECJ as forming part of the Community legal order (see text accompanying n. 16). Article 5 of the American Constitution provides, 'No person shall . . .

produce an objective test of the 'specific subject matter of property', linked to the right to realize appreciable economic value from the property. In both US and European 'Takings' cases, landowners have challenged governmental acts which have interfered with the owner's ability to use the property, arguing that these restrictions amount to an unlawful taking of property in violation of the right to property. In the US case of *Kaiser Aetna*[13] the government proposed to turn a private marina into one open to the public. In *Hauer*[14] the landowner had been refused permission to plant new vines on her land following the implementation of a Union measure designed to reduce overproduction of wine within the Union. In each case the relevant court treated the question of whether the 'right to property' had been infringed as bound up with the question of whether there had been a permanent deprivation of the economic potential of the land. Whilst this might have been appropriate in the particular contexts, it would not suit to link the protected zone of Member State control for Article 222 purposes to the economic potential of land. It simply would not work as a test. Much land is used and valued for non-economic activity and the interpretation given to Article 222 must respect such uses. Moreover, given the economic goals of the Union, it is improbable that the ECJ would accept that the existence of a property right incorporates the right to exploit the property—this would concede too much to the protected zone of Article 222.

An alternative approach would be to say that Article 222 protects only the ownership of the right itself, and that the enjoyment of rights in land is to do with the exercise of rights and so is not protected. Support for this view can be gleaned from the *Masterfoods*[15] case involving a claim by Mars that the competition provisions of the Treaty were breached by an ice-cream supplier (HB), who provided display cabinets on loan to retailers on condition that only HB's goods were displayed. Keane J regarded these cabinets as the property of HB and, as they were supplied for one purpose alone, the storage and display of their products, to allow Mars to display in them would erode HB's property rights in violation of Article 222.[16] Keane J contrasts the ice-cream cabinets with pub leases containing a tie covenant. To end the exclusivity tie in a lease affects only the exercise of a right, leav-

---

be deprived of life, liberty, or property, without due process of law; nor shall private property be taken for public use without just compensation.'

[13] *Kaiser Aetna* v. *United States* 100 S.Ct. 383 (1979).

[14] Case 44/79, *Hauer* v. *Land Rheinland Pfalz* [1979] ECR 3727.

[15] *Masterfoods Limited T/A Mars Ireland* v. *H.B. Ice Cream Limited* [1992] 3 CMLR 829, a case in the Irish High Court.

[16] The Commission seems to have had some regard to this issue when it has reviewed the relevant agreements. For a comment, see Maitland-Walker, 'Ice-Cream Wars: An Honourable Peace or the Beginning of a Greater Conflict?' (1995) 8 ECLR 451.

ing intact the 'essential right of ownership'. The assumption appears to be that 'ownership' can be separated from the rights exercisable by virtue of the ownership (a view argued above to be nonsensical), and only if ownership itself is threatened will the substance of the right be affected. This, as can be seen from the 'Takings' cases, is not so. 'Ownership' cannot be separated from the bundle of rights that it confers on the owner, and this is why there is so much difficulty in determining exactly what Article 222 protects.

At the end of the day, it must be conceded that, whilst Article 222 purports to preserve for Member States' control an ill-defined area relating to the 'existence' of property rights, the distinction between existence and exercise is malleable. Furthermore, it is likely that in applying the distinction the ECJ will give priority to Union goals, as can be seen in some of the cases earlier discussed. In *Fearon* v. *Irish Land Commission*,[17] it was held that the compulsory acquisition policy must not violate the non-discrimination goals of the Treaty. In *Hauer*,[18] the legitimacy of the restriction on growing vines was determined by reference to the Union goal of reducing overproduction of wine. However the 'existence' of the right is defined, it will be surprising if in most cases the ECJ does not regard most issues as matters within the competence of the Union.

Fundamental Rights as a Limit on Union Competence

A further check on Community action might be the 'right to property', prohibiting action which violates established property rights. Even though the 'right to property' is not referred to in the Treaty, the ECJ has accepted that such a right does form part of the Union legal order, reflecting the constitutional positions in most Member States and international treaties to which Member States are parties.[19] Not only do fundamental rights form part of the Union order but it was held in *Wachauf* that national measures implementing Union measures must also respect these fundamental rights.[20]

In practice, this apparent check on Union competence provides only a flimsy shield against Union action and can easily be penetrated. Although the language of fundamental rights is used, this does not mean that the rights

---

[17] Case 182/83, *Fearon* v. *Irish Land Commission* [1984] ECR 3677.

[18] Case 44/79, *Hauer* v. *Land Rheinland Pfalz* [1979] ECR 3727. See also Case 5/88, *Wachauf* v. *Germany* [1991] 1 CMLR 328.

[19] Case 44/79, *Hauer* v. *Land Rheinland Pfalz* [1979] ECR 3727.

[20] Case 5/88, *Wachauf* v. *Germany* [1991] 1 CMLR 328 at 349, para. [19]. See also Coppel, and O'Neill, 'The European Court of Justice: Taking Rights Seriously?' (1992) CML Rev. 669 esp. at 681. Cf. the challenge brought by the Trustees of the Duke of Westminster's Estate before the European Court of Human Rights alleging that the Leasehold Reform Act 1967 breached Article 1 of Protocol 1 to the European Convention on Human Rights, *James* v. *United Kingdom* (1986) 8 EHRR 123.

are given greater weight within Union law than the objectives of the European Union. This is illustrated by the judgment in *Wachauf*, where the ECJ referred to the fact that restrictions could be placed on the right to property so long as those restrictions implemented Union goals.[21] On closer examination, the factors constraining the Union's competence in relation to land issues are unlikely to provide much of an obstacle in a legal order which is growing apace and proactively pursues the wide goals of political, social, and economic union. Subsidiarity, Article 222, and the right to property all qualify the Union's power, but there remains a far-reaching potential for Union action before these limits are reached.

PASSIVE INTERVENTION AND LAND

As indicated earlier, there are two processes of application of European Community law: through what we have called passive intervention—being the operation of existing Community law whether applied judicially or administratively—or through active intervention—being the creation of new legal principles through legislative action. The two major areas of passive intervention are through the four freedoms and the competition rules of the Treaty, which are directly applicable and effective provisions giving rise to legal rights and remedies.

The Four Freedoms and Land

The four freedoms—the free movement of goods, persons, services, and capital—are at the heart of Union objectives and activities. Given that in the scheme of the Treaty these freedoms amount to fundamental rights, it is not surprising that they are interpreted widely and guarded jealously. Action or imposition by the nation state which limits these freedoms without justification will infringe the Treaty and lead to those actions or impositions being qualified or overridden. It is clear from Union legislation, the case law of the ECJ, and the actions of the Commission that national treatment of land can infringe the four freedoms.

Turning first to the Treaty, the provisions on free movement of capital in Article 73c expressly include ' investment in real estate' within the mean-

---

[21] Case 5/88, *Wachauf* v. *Germany* [1991] 1 CMLR 328 at 349, para. [18] 'restrictions may be imposed on the exercise of those rights, in particular in the context of a common organisation of a market, provided that those restrictions in fact correspond to objectives of general interest pursued by the Union and do not constitute, with regard to the aim pursued, a disproportionate and intolerable interference, impairing the very substance of those rights.' See also Case 44/79, *Hauer* v. *Land Rheinland Pfalz* [1979] ECR 3727 at 3746–7, paras. [19]–[23].

ing of that freedom. Article 73c allows Member States to restrict that freedom in relation to investment in or from third (i.e. non-member) countries.[22] By implication,[23] rules restricting who can invest in land, when, or on what terms are capable of infringing the provisions on free movement of capital when they affect investment flows between Member States. This can be a difficult issue, particularly for countries that have a high influx of people from other parts of the Union, such as Greece in respect of the Greek Islands. It will also be relevant to rural or cultural protection schemes. There are often calls, for instance, to protect Welsh-speaking communities from the influx of non-Welsh speakers. Policies such as this can founder on the free movement of capital principle.

The Treaty is silent on the application of the other three freedoms to issues relating to land. Whilst the link between these freedoms—goods, services, and persons—and land is less obvious than in relation to free movement of capital, there are nevertheless significant points of contact.

Taking the last of these first, it is apparent that impediments to the ownership of land will affect the ability of workers[24] to move around the Union. The right to obtain housing is essential to quality of life—without this ability foreign workers would be no more than transient migrants and free movement would have little reality. This is specifically recognized in Regulation (EEC) No. 1612/68 on freedom of movement for workers,[25] Article 9(1) of which provides: 'A worker who is a national of a Member State and who is employed in the territory of another Member State shall enjoy all the rights and benefits accorded to national workers in matters of housing, including ownership of the housing he needs.'

Free movement of persons also entails the right of establishment (Article 52), which entitles nationals from one Member State to establish themselves (for business purposes) in another Member State. Article 54(3)(e) specifically requires the Commission and the Council to enable a national of one Member State to acquire and use land and buildings in another Member State for the purpose of establishment. Freedom to provide services from one Member State to another (Article 59) can raise similar issues. Guidance issued by the Council in 1961 illustrates some of the outworkings of the freedom of establishment and provision of services, to include the right to purchase, exploit, and transfer real and personal property and the right to obtain loans.[26]

All these issues came together in *Commission* v. *Greece*.[27] The Commission brought an action under Article 169 of the Treaty to bring to an end

---

[22] The EEA Agreement extends the freedom to Norway, Iceland, and Liechtenstein.
[23] And as elaborated by Directive 88/361, OJ L178, 8 July 1988, 5.
[24] Article 48 specifically refers to the free movement of workers.
[25] OJ L257, 19 Oct. 1968, 2.   [26] [1962] JO 32/62 and 36/62.
[27] Case 305/87, *Commission* v. *Greece* [1989] ECR 1461.

an infringement by Greece of the rules on free movement of persons and services. For decades before it joined the Union, Greece had had a decree in existence prohibiting the acquisition by foreigners of ownership of real estate or real property rights in property situated in its border regions. Almost 55 per cent of its territory had been designated as 'border regions'. The ECJ found that the Greek legislation was an obstacle to the free movement of workers, the freedom of establishment, and the freedom to provide services.[28]

This is not to say that all controls on the purchase of interests in land fall foul of these provisions. In *Fearon* v. *Irish Land Commission*,[29] the claim that the compulsory purchase powers of the Irish Land Commission were discriminatory was based on the fact that the powers could not be exercised against individuals who had resided for more than one year within three miles of the land or against bodies corporate all of whose shareholders met the same conditions. The five shareholders of the company in question in the case were all British. The ECJ held that the use of the powers did not infringe the freedom of establishment principle provided that Irish nationals were subject to the same rule and that the powers were not in practice exercised in a discriminatory way.

These various freedoms concern not only property directly related to the establishment of the business but also the general facilities which assist these activities, including access to housing. In *Re Housing Aid: EC Commission* v. *Italy*,[30] the ECJ considered Italian legislation allowing only Italians to purchase or lease housing built or renovated with public funds or to obtain reduced-rate mortgage loans. The ECJ held that housing legislation, even where it concerns social housing, was subject to the freedom of establishment rules. Access to the benefits must be given not only to nationals but also to those people with a principal place of business in another Member State whose business required such an extended stay in Italy that a need for permanent housing arose.

The principle of the free movement of goods in Article 30 is likely to have a more limited application to land than the other freedoms. This is not because land is incapable of being characterized as goods in a European Community law context,[31] but because, even if it is, land and interests in

---

[28] See paras. [19]–[27].

[29] Case 182/83, *Fearon* v. *Irish Land Commission* [1984] ECR 3677; see n. 8 above and accompanying text.

[30] Case 63/86, *Commission* v. *Italy* [1989] 2 CMLR 601. See also *R.* v. *City of Westminster ex p. Castelli* (1996) 28 HLR 616, where the English Court of Appeal held that an Italian lawfully present in the UK had a right to be considered for temporary housing under the Housing Act 1985.

[31] See Bright and Bright, 'Unfair Terms in Land Contracts: Copy Out or Cop Out?' (1995) 111 LQR 655, for a discussion of this. In English legislation land is not normally treated as a good.

land are not capable of circulating as, for example, consumer products or construction products are.

Competition Law and Land

The impact of competition law on land often comes as more of a surprise than that of the four freedoms. The competition rules have three areas of application: the rules on the abuse of a dominant position under Article 86, the rules on anti-competitive agreements under Article 85, and the rules on state aids under Article 92.

Article 86

Landownership clearly confers a monopoly and gives the proprietor the ability to decide what use should be made of the land and who is permitted access to the land. It may be that the proprietor has identified a significant opportunity and developed an economic activity on the land. For European Community law to be concerned this activity would need to be economically significant and would need to affect trade between Member States of the European Community. Consequently, issues relating to land most often arise in relation to facilities affecting the movement of people or goods, notably airports, ports, and railways. In these areas the concept of an 'essential facility' has arisen.[32] Where a land facility is regarded as essential, and confers dominance on the owner/operator of the facility, Community law requires that access to the facility be given on non-discriminatory terms.

So, for instance, if a port-owner operates a port and runs services from that port, competing services may need to be given access to the port on terms no less favourable than the services of the owner. This occurred in *Euro-Port* v. *Denmark*, where the port authority owned and operated routes from Rodby in Denmark but refused permission for competing shipping companies to make use of the port facilities. This refusal was held by the ECJ to be an abuse of its dominant position,

an undertaking that owns or manages and uses itself an essential facility, i.e. a facility or infrastructure without which its competitors are unable to offer their services to customers, and refuses to grant them access to such facility is abusing its dominant position.

Consequently, an undertaking that owns or manages an essential port facility from which it provides a maritime transport service may not, without objective justification, refuse to grant a shipowner wishing to operate on the same maritime route access to that facility without infringing Article 86.[33]

[32] See Temple Lang, 'Defining Legitimate Competition: Companies' Duties to Supply Competitors and Access to Essential Facilities' (1994) 18 Fordham International Law Journal 437.

[33] *Euro-Port A/S and Scan-Port GmbH* v. *Denmark*, 94/119/EEC, [1994] 5 CMLR 457 at 464, para. [12].

Another example is the Commission decision that the French authorities could not persist in a policy of refusing air traffic rights on the Paris (Orly)–London route to Union airlines.[34]

Article 85

Article 85 also impacts on the use that a proprietor may make of land. The major area that has been affected in the UK is the leasing of land on terms that the lessee must purchase goods from the lessor. This has particularly been in the area of the tying of beer purchases by publican tenants to brewery-owners. These ties may well be in breach of the Treaty if their effect is, taken together with similar clauses in other leases from the same landlord, to affect trade between Member States. The issue of validity of the lease has arisen,[35] as Article 85(2) provides that agreements that contravene the prohibition on anti-competitive agreements in Article 85(1) are void. Issues of severability and enforceability of the remainder of the lease have also arisen.[36] Indeed, in some cases rights of repossession of the property by the lessor turn on the impact of Article 85 on the lease. It is clear from these cases and from so-called 'block exemptions' issued by the Commission that the rights of landlords can be constrained by Article 85.

Article 92

The rules on state aid impact on the sale of land where it is transferred out of the public sector at an undervalue or where state financial inducements or support are given on any disposal. In the Mainz case[37] the Commission found that the sale of land by the City of Mainz to the Siemens group was at an undervalue and consequently involved state aid. The sale formed part of an inner-city regeneration scheme involving the purchaser building an office complex. The aid, amounting to DM 4.9 million, was regarded as distorting intra-Community competition in the data processing sector by advantaging one company with lower than normal costs to the disadvantage of other companies. Such findings lead not only to a finding of infringement of Community law for the public authority involved but also require the repayment of the aid by the recipient. The Commission has now issued guidelines on land sales by public authorities to prevent such situations arising.[38]

---

[34] Commission decision of 27 Apr. 1994, OJ L127/22, 19 May 1994, Case VII/AMA/II/93—TAT–Paris (Orly)–London, 94/290/EC.

[35] *Inntrepreneur Estates (GL) Limited* v. *Boyes* (1993) 47 EG 140.

[36] *Inntrepreneur Estates Limited* v. *Mason* [1993] 2 CMLR 293.

[37] Commission decision of 17 July 1996, OJ L283/43, 5 Nov. 1996.

[38] Communication from the Commission to Member States, 20 Nov. 1996, 'Aid elements in land sales by public authorities'.

ACTIVE INTERVENTION AND LAND

Having assessed the potential of the four freedoms and Treaty competition rules to act as constraining influences on national law, it is necessary to look at the issue of the competence of the institutions of the Union to act in an active or formative way with respect to land. Perhaps the most active way would be for the Union to try and create a single or parallel system of property ownership. Is this possible or likely?

Harmonization, New Property Forms, and Land

One manner in which the Union acts is through the introduction of 'harmonization' or 'approximation' measures that aim to bring national laws into line with one another. Action is taken under Article 100 to issue directives approximating national laws where necessary for the establishment or functioning of the common market. These provisions require the Council to be unanimous—i.e. for all Member States to agree. Very often unanimity is difficult to obtain. The Single European Act inserted Article 100a into the Treaty allowing decisions in respect of approximations necessary for the completion of the internal market, other than those relating, *inter alia*, to free movement of persons, to be taken by qualified majority vote. Approximation initiatives in respect of some issues are consequently now more easy to take. In relation to land, one such measure has been the Timeshare Directive.[39] The Unfair Terms Directive adopted under this process also potentially applies to land.[40] Approximation measures in relation to land have, however, been limited.

The use of harmonization powers in relation to other property rights has not always been successful. In the context of trade mark laws, it proved to be impossible to break down national barriers through harmonization measures. Consequently, a Community Trade Mark has been introduced.[41] The Regulation recites that ' the barrier of territoriality of rights conferred on proprietors of trade marks by the laws of Member States cannot be removed by approximation of laws' and that 'in order to open up unrestricted economic activity in the whole of the common market for the benefit of undertakings, trade marks need to be created which are governed by

---

[39] Directive 94/47, OJ L289/83, 29 Oct. 1994. This requires contracts for the purchase of property on a timeshare basis to contain certain minimal elements of protection. The Directive has been adopted in the UK by the Timeshare Regulations 1997, SI 1997/1081.

[40] Directive on Unfair Terms in Consumer Contracts, 93/13/EEC, OJ L95/29, 21 Apr. 1993, see Bright and Bright, 'Unfair Terms in Land Contracts: Copy Out or Cop Out?'.

[41] By Council Regulation (EEC) No. 40/94, OJ L11/1, 11 Jan. 1994; Council Regulation (EEC) No. 3288/94, OJ L349/83, 31 Dec. 1994; adopted under Article 235. Given effect to in the UK by The Union Trade Mark Regulations 1996, SI 1996/1908.

a uniform Community law directly applicable in all Member States'. It was also necessary to break down barriers to free movement and to create the legal conditions 'which enable undertakings to adapt their activities to the scale of the Union'. The Regulation introduced a new form of property into the Union and national legal orders: the Community Trade Mark. The existence of a Community Trade Mark enables undertakings to operate quite freely within different Member States taking advantage of one identical means of trade-mark protection.

There are also proposals to create a European Company.[42] This follows much of the reasoning on trade marks.[43] The draft Regulation recites:

Whereas the legal framework in which business still has to be carried on in Europe, being still based entirely on national laws, thus no longer corresponds to the economic framework in which it must develop if the objectives set out in Article 8a of the Treaty are to be achieved; whereas this situation forms a considerable obstacle to the creation of groups consisting of companies from different Member States;

Whereas it is essential to ensure as far as possible that the economic unit and the legal unit of business in Europe coincide; whereas for this purpose provision should be made for creating, side by side with companies governed by a particular national law, companies formed and carrying on business under the law created by a Community regulation directly applicable in all Member States . . .

Both initiatives, on trade marks and companies, propose the creation of a parallel form of property right. National equivalents would not be extinguished. They are designed to make life simpler for those operating cross border in the Union who wish to take advantage of them.

Looking at these initiatives, it is not impossible to imagine an activist approach in Brussels pushing for a common form of regulation of land. This possibility is compounded when the Timeshare Directive is examined. This recites:

1. Whereas the disparities between national legislations on contracts relating to the purchase of the right to use one or more immovable properties on a time share basis are likely to create barriers to the proper operation of the internal market and distortions of competition and lead to the compartmentalization of national markets . . .[44]

The explanatory memorandum on the Commission's proposal for the Unfair Terms Directive took this idea further by indicating that: 'It cannot be assumed that consumers who cross frontiers . . . to invest or acquire property in other Member States, have understood and agreed the terms of

---

[42] See Com. (89) 268 (OJ C263 of 16 Oct. 1989) as amended by Com. (91) 174 (OJ C176 of 8 July 1991).

[43] Although adopted under Article 100a rather than Article 235.

[44] Directive 94/47/EEC, OJ L 280/83, 29 Oct. 1994, Recital 1.

a contract if they do not speak the local language or are unfamiliar with the local law . . .'[45]

This theme is repeated in the Directive itself, where the Recitals make reference to the fact that lack of awareness of the rules governing contracts for the sale of goods and services may deter consumers from entering into transactions in other Member States.[46]

These thought processes could, if applied in relation to land law, also lead the Union to propose approximation measures for, or common forms of ownership of, real property. Although real property investment does already take place across borders in the Union, it is nevertheless recognized that the differential in 'terms of trade' between different states operates as a disincentive.[47] There is a marked variation in standard lease terms between Member States.[48] There are also considerable variations in the environment of property investment: land-use planning rules, transaction costs, taxation on purchases, sales, and income,[49] and so on. On most counts, the UK commerical property market is perceived to be an attractive investment—transaction costs are relatively low and the commercial lease structure provides a relatively long-term secure income flow. Since the late 1980s the amount of money invested by Continental Europeans in the London property market has steadily increased.[50] With the increasing international interest in the UK property market, new forms of investment are being created which provide an easy access route to indirect investment in property via property derivatives. In turn, Britons are more commonly buying property abroad as a second or retirement home, in particular in France,[51] Spain,[52] and Portugal. Large construction groups have followed this outward investment, taking on major developments in these countries. Given these types of movements, and the psychological importance of land to political and social order, it is possible to see the attraction of some form of 'Euro-title'

---

[45] Commission consultation, Supplement 1/84, Bulletin of the European Communities.

[46] Directive on Unfair Terms in Consumer Contracts, 93/13/EEC, OJ L95/29, 21 Apr. 1993, Recital 5.

[47] See Morell and McNamara, 'International Property Investment: A UK Institutional Perspective' [1996] Property Rev. 70; McIntosh, 'Institutional Investment in Europe' (1995) 05 EG 152.

[48] See Bright and Gilbert, *Landlord and Tenant Law: The Nature of Tenancies* (Oxford: Oxford University Press, 1995), 67 and references therein.

[49] In the case of Value Added Tax, the EC has sought to harmonize the taxation base and to adopt a uniform approach to the letting of property: see Sixth Directive on the harmonization of the laws relating to turnover taxes, 77/388/EEC, OJ L145/1, 13 June 1977.

[50] See table in McIntosh, 'Institutional Investment in Europe', 154.

[51] In 1991 it was said that about 200,000 British people owned second homes in France, and that the figure could double by the end of the century (Thomas, *Buying Property in France*, (London: Law Society's Gazette, 1991), Introduction).

[52] In 1989 there were more than one million foreign owners of dwellings in Spain (Conference Report, Law Society Gazette, 1 Nov. 1989, p. 12).

as a grand design of European institutions. It could, for example, be argued that a company seeking to establish a base in more than one Member State will be able to operate more easily if there were a common form of ownership of real property. This would also be true of, for example, German banks or funds investing in UK commercial property, or of property developers operating in a number of Member States. The notion of 'estates' developed in English law is hard to comprehend to persons from a civil law background who are used to more direct ownership of land.

These various factors could lead to moves for a 'Euro-title' as has taken place in the field of trade marks and is under discussion for companies. There is, however, a vital difference between the creation of trade marks and companies and the creation of interests in land. Trade marks and companies are new interests, not interests created or carved out of any pre-existing entity. All land (or an estate in land) is already owned, and, in order to create a Union Land Interest, there would, of necessity, be interference with the existing forms of property ownership. This, as discussed above, is prohibited by Article 222 of the Treaty.

Although it is unlikely that the Union will (even if it can) act to create some kind of 'Euro-title' in immoveable property, there are many other areas in which the Union is already acting which have a direct impact upon land use.

Environmental Policy and Land

The Community has been actively concerned with environmental issues since the early 1970s when the first community action programme on the environment was prepared. Although the Treaty did not expressly set out Community competence in the field of environmental protection, European Community initiatives were manifold and the ECJ affirmed environmental protection as one of the 'Community's essential objectives'.[53] The legal basis for action was strengthened by the Single European Act, with Article 130r setting out the environmental objectives of the Union as being to preserve, protect, and improve the quality of the environment, to contribute towards protecting human health, and to ensure prudent and rational utilization of natural resources. Environmental regulation can now, therefore, emerge from a variety of different provisions: Articles 130r–t empower the Community to introduce measures directly concerned with environmental protection, Articles 100 and 100a can be used when environmental issues impact upon the establishment of an internal market, and other Treaty provisions can be used where pursuance of other Community objectives raise environmental matters, as with measures

[53] Case 240/83, *Procureur de la République* v. *Association de Defense des Bruleurs d'Huiles Susagées* [1985] ECR 531.

promoting agricultural policy under Article 43. European directives are a major force behind much domestic legislative action on the environment which affects land. Following the Environmental Assessment Directive,[54] environmental impact assessments have to be conducted whenever a project is likely to have significant effects on the environment. Preparation of these can represent a major additional requirement in the planning process of development projects. Environmental measures seeking to reduce pollution of the elements will also affect land use. There is control over the discharge of dangerous substances affecting groundwater,[55] on environmentally dangerous activities,[56] and a directive has recently been adopted on integrated pollution prevention and control which will affect industrial users of land where the use is likely to pollute air, water, or land.[57] The framework Directive on Waste[58] set out the Community policy on waste management emphasizing the polluter-pays principle and the use of recycling as a method of control. There is, additionally, a proposed directive on landfill.[59]

Consumer Protection Policy

The terms upon which an interest in land is acquired are perceived to be an area within which the Union is competent to act. It impacts upon the four freedoms in that persons should be able to invest freely in immoveable property throughout the Member States. The Timeshare Directive[60] provides evidence that the Union is concerned about consumer-protection issues arising from transactions related to land. The Directive is designed to ensure that contracts for the purchase of the right to use property on a timeshare basis contain certain minimal elements of protection, including the right to a written document covering prescribed issues and giving the purchaser a cooling-off period. The Recitals to the Directive make clear that these transactions are perceived to impact upon the four freedoms:

Recital 4: Whereas the purchase of a right to utilize one or several immovable properties on a time-share basis is very largely of a transfrontier nature by reason of the geographical location of supply and demand in most cases, and hence has an impact on the free movement of persons, services and capital . . .

[54] The Environmental Impact Directive 85/337/EEC OJ L175/40, 6 July 1985, implemented in England and Wales by the Town and Country Planning (Assessment of Environmental Effects) Regulations 1988, SI 1988/1199 (since amended).

[55] See Directive on Groundwater, 80/68/EEC OJ L20/43, 26 Jan. 1980.

[56] Convention on Civil Liability for Damage Resulting from Activities Dangerous to the Environment (concluded at Lugano on 21 June 1993).

[57] See Directive 96/61/EEC, OJ L257/26, 10 Oct. 1996.

[58] 75/442/EEC, OJ L194/39, 25 July 1975; amended by Directive 91/156/EEC OJ L78/32, 26 Mar. 1991.

[59] OJ C156, 24 May 1997.   [60] Directive 94/47/EEC, OJ L 280/83, 29 Oct. 1994.

Recital 6: Whereas the application of the rules of ordinary law in some Member States and of specific legislation, albeit with different rules, in others creates disparities which might hamper the orderly development of this sector of economic activity; whereas this situation is thus prejudicial to the proper functioning of the internal market . . .

The Unfair Terms Directive[61] shows a similar concern with consumer protection. This applies to contracts for the sale of goods or supply of services, and, whilst there may be some room for debate over whether or not it applies to contracts relating to land, there is little doubt that it applies to mortgage transactions and strong arguments that it applies to interests in land more generally.[62]

Agricultural Policy and Land

The common agricultural policy is one of the central activities of the Community. Article 3(c) lists as one of the Community's activities a common policy in the sphere of agriculture and fisheries, and again Article 38(1) states the 'common market shall extend to agriculture and trade in agricultural products'. Although one of the stated objectives of the common agricultural policy is to increase agricultural production,[63] there has been concern about overproduction since the 1950s.[64] Community structural policies designed to control production levels through diversification of land use and set-aside have had a considerable impact upon land use in the UK. These Community policies have led to various domestic measures which provide incentives to reduce the overall amount of actively farmed agricultural land. These incentives take the form of grant aid available either to farmers wishing to diversify into alternative ancillary land uses, such as the farm diversification scheme,[65] or to farmers adopting set-aside policies which involve the removal of arable land from agricultural production.[66] The recent reform to agricultural tenancy law also encourages use of land for mixed agricultural and non-agricultural enterprises in line with

---

[61] Directive 93/13/EEC, OJ L95/29, 21 Apr. 1993.

[62] See Bright and Bright, 'Unfair Terms in Land Contracts: Copy Out or Cop Out?'.

[63] Article 39(1)(a).

[64] Organization for European Economic Cooperation, *Agricultural Policies in Europe and North America: Price and Income Policies* (Paris: 1957), 420–3; Commission of the European Economic Community, *First General Report on the Activities of the Community* (Luxembourg: 1958), 70.

[65] Farm and Conservation Grant Regulations 1991, SI 1991/1630 (since amended).

[66] Council Regulation (EEC) No. 1094/1988, OJ L106/28, 27 Apr. 1988, Commission Regulation (EEC) No. 1272/1988; Council Regulation (EEC) No. 1765/92, OJ L181/12, 1 July 1992. Implemented through the Set Aside Regulations 1988, SI 1988/1352 (and later amendments); Arable Areas Payments Regulations 1995, SI 1995/1738 (and later amendments).

Community diversification policies.[67] There is also a stream of measures designed to encourage environmentally sensitive farming, which require Member States to introduce a range of aids for environmentally sensitive farming[68] that will promote farming practices compatible with the protection of the environment and natural resources or landscape and countryside requirements. In this country, these measures are promoted by the ability (*inter alia*) to designate certain areas as 'Environmentally Sensitive Areas'[69] or as 'Nitrate Sensitive Areas'.[70] Areas so designated will be subject to a management agreement to advance conservation of the environment and there will be a grant made to the occupier of the land.

Housing Policy

It is unlikely that a European housing policy will emerge even though the four freedoms do impact upon national housing law and policies.[71] Despite various Resolutions of the European Parliament calling for action in particular areas,[72] the Community seems disinclined to take any initiatives in this area, at least for the time being:

The European Economic Community does not include the issue of housing within its competences. Moreover, because of their different histories, cultures and institutions, the various European countries do not have the same approach to, or perception of, the problems of exclusion in housing.[73]

Further it can be argued that housing policy is an area in which the principle of subsidiarity should apply, leaving the determination of policy as a matter for Member States.[74]

---

[67] The Agricultural Tenancies Act 1995; see Bright, 'Tenant Farming: For the Good of the Nation?' [1995] Conveyancer 445.

[68] See Council Regulation (EEC) No. 797/85, Council Regulation (EEC) No. 2328/91 OJ L218/1, 6 Aug. 1991, Council Regulation 2078/92, OJ L15/85, 30 July 1992.

[69] See Agriculture Act 1986, s. 18.

[70] See Nitrate Sensitive Areas Regulations 1994, SI 1994/1729; Nitrate Sensitive Areas (Amendment) Regulations 1995, SI 1995/1708; Nitrate Sensitive Areas (Amendment) (No. 2) Regulations 1995, SI 1995/2095.

[71] See n. 27 and accompanying text.

[72] Such as the Resolution on the Rehousing of Families from the Place de la Reunion, Paris, and on the Right to Decent Housing, 12 July 1990, calling for a Community policy on housing and the residential environment, referred to in McCrone and Stephens, *Housing Policy in Britain and Europe* (London: UCL Press, 1995), 180.

[73] Official Communiqué from the meeting of European Housing Ministers, CEC 1992:110, referred to in McCrone and Stephens, *Housing Policy in Britain and Europe*, 181.

[74] Argued in McCrone and Stephens, *Housing Policy in Britain and Europe*, 180–4.

EUROPEANIZATION OF LAND LAW

There is undoubtedly an increasing 'Europeanization' of English law as legislative measures, judicial decisions, and academic work are influenced by ideas from Continental legal systems. The impact to date has been greatest in the law of obligations, but ever closer links between political, legislative, judicial, and academic institutions will no doubt accelerate the pace of change and cross-fertilization of ideas. As lawmakers have to respond to new legal challenges, English property law will be touched by ideas and solutions developed in other legal systems.[75] Some evidence for this is seen in cases such as *Hunter* v. *Canary Wharf*,[76] in which Lords Goff and Cooke draw an analogy with German law in deciding whether the presence of a building causing interference with television signals constitutes an actionable nuisance. On the legislative front, the introduction into the domestic laws of Member States of competition laws akin to those of the European Community will undoubtedly have an impact. The process of convergence and harmonization has only just commenced. Of course, as other federal or confederal systems such as the USA and Canada demonstrate, the process has limits. There is scope for different approaches, just as there is for learning from other systems.

CONCLUSION

Land lawyers need to be aware not just of English law but also of the normative hierarchies within which it exists, which have their own legal and policy imperatives. They cannot assume that Brussels, Luxembourg, and Strasbourg are simply places on a tour of Europe. Opportunities exist to draw on the European system to aid the development of land law. Even when such developments are not sought, encroachments will in any event take place. It may be that issues of title will remain primarily for the nations of the Union—other issues will present themselves.

---

[75] On the development of a 'common law' of Europe, see De Witte and Forder (eds.), *The Common Law of Europe and the Future of Legal Education* (Deventer, Netherlands: Kluwer, 1992); Markesinis, *The Gradual Convergence* (Oxford: Oxford University Press, 1994). For a comparative discussion of property rights, see Rudden, 'Economic Theory versus Property Law: The *Numerus Clausus* Problem', in Eekelaar and Bell (eds.), *Oxford Essays in Jurisprudence* (3rd ser.; Oxford: Oxford University Press, 1987).

[76] [1997] 2 WLR 684.

15

OCCUPYING 'CHEEK BY JOWL': PROPERTY ISSUES ARISING FROM COMMUNAL LIVING

David Clarke

This chapter is concerned with the legal challenges which arise from multi-occupancy, usually of a large single building,[1] by a number of occupiers, all of whom regard themselves as having a long-term stake in the property.[2] Necessarily, such occupants share facilities and have some community of interest in the way the building is maintained and run. By virtue of that long-term interest in the property, they cannot walk away from any communal problems which may arise.[3] If the basis of the occupier's property interest is leasehold, there will be a freeholder—and perhaps intermediate leaseholders—who do not occupy yet have an investment interest in the same property. The focus of this chapter is on the legal difficulties which face these residential occupiers—but some comparisons with business occupants of such property will highlight the significant differences in the concerns of those who choose or are forced to make their homes in flats or apartments. The chapter is not concerned with the wider general problems of proximate living. So, although the anti-social behaviour of neighbours can create all sorts of noise pollution and nuisance, these are not peculiar to multi-occupancy with shared facilities. It is rather the particular concerns and legal problems arising from the interrelated proprietary interests, usually within a single building, that will be discussed.[4]

LIVING UNDER THE SAME ROOF

'Communal living' conjures up a number of different images and most are not the concern of this chapter. Very few of us choose to live—or work—

---

[1] There may be a series of buildings but the key will be a sharing of facilities essential to the enjoyment of the property which, in other circumstances, are the sole preserve of a single property-owner.

[2] A long-term stake may often arise from the investment of capital; it can equally arise, particularly in commercial situations, from the assumption of continuing obligations.

[3] As a person renting a flat on a periodic or short fixed-term basis can do.

[4] Though it is suggested that finding the best arrangement of the various property interests also provides a better framework for the resolution of antisocial behaviour.

quite alone. In Western societies, the nuclear family has, until recently at least, been a central feature of society and the desire of each newly wed couple was to secure a roof over their heads.[5] The aim for many was a separate roof for the family, even if in a terraced or semi-detached house, on a piece of land they could call their own. But land is a scarce resource and for many the prospect of affording a plot for a single dwelling close enough to the workplace in ever larger cities is increasingly remote. The alternative is to share a roof.

Community life in the most radical sense—where each individual puts aside all self-interest and all property is enjoyed in common—has not been a successful model in Western societies,[6] outside religious communities at least.[7] Such relationships rarely raise issues which relate to the *land* communally occupied, title to which is likely to be vested in some sort of corporate body in which the residents of the community either have no proprietary rights or at best have limited interests arising under a trust.[8] A more obvious scenario where land law issues ought to exist is the renting of space[9] for a periodic or short term in a single building such as a block of flats, creating a much more involuntary community united only by a desire for living accommodation in that particular building. It is often the least affluent in society who find they have no choice but to find a home in such a way. Public housing is frequently provided in this manner. In the UK, the council flat of the 1960s is giving way to the housing association apartment of the 1990s. Now that new residential lettings can be granted at open market rents, private sector landlords are returning to rent out large buildings for such weekly or monthly payments. A community of occupiers is thereby created within that building or block of flats. Certainly, the resulting relationship between property-owner and resident is one which is the concern of land law. Such a relationship may be cast in a proprietary fash-

[5] Illustrated by the Abbey National's continuing logo of an umbrella over a couple in the shape of a roof.

[6] Western legal systems are having to come to terms with indigenous communal and shared property rights. Recognition may arise through judicial decision, as in Australia (*Mabo v. Queensland (No. 2)* (1992) 175 CLR 1, which recognized native communal rights to land) or by a re-evaluation of property rights of native peoples as a group giving rise to government compensation (as in New Zealand, where substantial claims based on the 1840 Treaty of Waitangi have been met—e.g. the settlement of the claims of the Ngai Tahu Maori tribe to much of South Island of New Zealand announced on 23 Sept. 1997).

[7] For a detailed historical evidence and analysis of shared and communal land regimes, see Ellickson, 'Property in Land', 102 Yale LJ 1315 (1993).

[8] *Lakeside Colony of Hutterite Brethren* v. *Hofer* (1992) 97 DLR (4th) 17 is a Canadian example of the courts having to rule on the expulsion of members of a religious community where, since all property was held in common, expulsion meant the loss of homes on colony land.

[9] The amount of space may vary. In very crowded cities, such as Hong Kong or in Japan, the space rented may only be sufficient for a single individual to recline.

ion as a lease[10] or as a contractual licence only.[11] However, the community relationships (between each resident tenant of space as opposed to the landlord–tenant relationship) are only peripherally the concerns of land law.[12] Even where issues such as easements covering rights of access or service pipes or conduits are raised, they are likely to be raised between landowner and tenant and not between adjoining occupiers.[13] The central point is that not only has the tenant paying a market rent no contractual or proprietary relationship with the other occupiers, but such a person also has no permanence or financial 'stake'[14] in that part of the property occupied. Even when the regime of the Rent Acts was fully in force, the 'twin pillars' of that legislation—security of tenure and fair rents—were essentially tools of public law housing policy. The statutory tenancy that arose after the contractual tenancy was terminated may have been a valuable right, but it was essentially personal,[15] giving nothing more than a status of irremoveability,[16] and it did not impact directly upon other residential occupiers. In all such cases, the landowner retains management control of the building as a whole. Complaints arising from the problems of communal living by renting occupiers are naturally directed against the owner of the building with that management control[17] or to public authorities. Legal remedies directly against other occupiers are unlikely to involve land law or property issues.[18] Similarly, the investment or capital value of the property communally occupied is wholly vested in that overall landowner. The tenant or occupier has no capital value in the property, which can be transferred to a third party.[19]

[10] But such leases are invariably unassignable, so it could be argued that, as between landowner and tenant at least, the issues are essentially contractual rather than proprietary.

[11] *Street* v. *Mountford* [1985] AC 509. The Housing Act 1988 which permitted property-owners to grant assured shorthold tenancies which gave no security of tenure soon led to a rapid decline in the incidence of residential licences.

[12] If they exist at all. Living in proximity does not necessarily result in communication or social intercourse with neighbours.

[13] *Liverpool City Council* v. *Irwin* [1977] AC 319, where appalling conditions in a block of flats led to a largely unsuccessful action against the local-authority landlord for breach of implied covenants when the problems were the result of actions by hooligans and other residents.

[14] Lord Denning in *Marchant* v. *Charters* [1977] 3 All ER 918 at 922 propounded the now discredited test of whether an occupier had a stake in a room to distinguish a lease from a licence. The real difference in a financial stake is between those tenants paying a market rent so that their lease has no or little capital value, even assuming it can be assigned, and those who pay a low rent and buy the lease for a substantial premium to be recouped, hopefully at a profit, when the long lease is assigned to a purchaser.

[15] See Megarry, *The Rent Acts* (11th edn., London: Stevens, 1988), 251–7.

[16] *Keeves* v. *Dean* [1924] 1 KB 685 at 686, per Lush J.

[17] As in *Liverpool City Council* v. *Irwin* [1977] AC 319.

[18] Certainly not beyond the landlord–tenant relationship.

[19] It is very common for residential leases at a market rent to have an absolute covenant against assignment. A statutory tenant with Rent Act protection will have a right of

The communal occupation with which this chapter is concerned is different. It occurs whenever a person seeks to purchase a proprietary interest of significant value in part of the building which is realizable by sale or assignment and which gives an exclusive right to occupy a part only of that building.[20] Typically, in return for a long lease at a low rent, a substantial upfront payment or premium will be paid to a developer or property-owner. The new occupier is normally styled 'leaseholder'[21] rather than 'tenant', for, though the basic legal relationship may be the same as a tenant paying a market rent, the expectations are very different. The new resident has not only secured a home under a shared roof but has invested capital in part of the property by means of the price paid when the flat was purchased.[22] Such a leaseholder expects the investment to be permanent and recouped by a sale of the property interest at any time of his choosing. However, the value of that property interest will be reduced if the legal arrangements with other occupiers are inadequate and by the rights of a freeholder who retains an interest in the building as a whole if those rights are adverse to the leaseholder. The leaseholders will have a collective self-interest in issues of repair, maintenance, and management of the buildings as a whole, and a degree of united and coherent action is often appropriate. However much a resident improves the accommodation or keeps the interior of the apartment well decorated, its value will be determined largely by the efficacy of the arrangements which are in place with the other persons who have a proprietary interest in the same building to secure efficient maintenance and management.[23] Further, if (as is usual in England) the property interest is a lease, the length of the term of the lease and the nature of the covenants also impact upon the value of the leaseholder's interest. The freeholder, with title to the whole building, retains an investment interest—and the concerns of such a person, often a property company, are radically different and often diametrically opposed to those of the residential occupiers.

Not dissimilar problems face commercial occupiers sharing facilities with other entrepreneurs in a single building or complex. Such situations occur frequently in office blocks, where there is a communal interest in repair and services, or in modern business parks, which have shared access and joint

continued occupation, but any potential monetary value of such a right can be released only by cooperation with the landlord.

[20] Though usually one building in England, it may be a complex of buildings.

[21] 'Leaseholder' will be the term used in the rest of this chapter to denote a person who has paid a premium for a long lease of an apartment at a low rent.

[22] Technically, the price paid for a lease is known as a premium.

[23] A tenant under a short lease at market rent or having a periodic tenancy will also have an interest in the way the whole building is managed but will have no interest of capital value which is affected adversely by bad management. Such a tenant will also have no responsibility for management.

benefits from landscaping and security services. In England, the vehicle for such arrangements is again the lease. The key difference is that, unlike long residential leases, commercial leases will usually be at a full open market rent,[24] though longer terms at a ground rent are not uncommon.[25] The freehold will be held as an investment[26] by a property company or pension fund. It is in the interests of such a freeholder to have what is known as a 'clear lease' so that the income in the form of rent comes clear of the cost of repairs, maintenance, and insurance of the building as a whole.[27] These costs are recovered by means of a service charge recouped in full proportionately from the occupiers.[28] Once again, there is a situation where the rights, responsibilities, and concerns of the occupiers are primarily channelled through the landlord–tenant relationship in the lease.[29] The law has little impact on the relationship between the various commercial occupiers.[30]

A final proprietary interest can be added to the equation—namely, the security interest usually of a lease of an individual flat or possibly of the freehold reversion as a whole. Many leaseholders will purchase the lease, as with any form of property, with the aid of a loan secured by a mortgage. Business leases may have some capital value and be offered as security. It is the reconciliation of all these diverse property interests into a framework which provides protection for each which is the topic of this chapter.

Sadly, English law has so far conspicuously failed to address the issues of principle arising from multiplicity of property interests in one building. Thus, no provision has been made in English Law for any form of freehold

[24] This means that a commercial tenant will, unlike a long leaseholder, have a lease of little or no capital value when granted. Changes in rental values achieved in the open market result in such leases gaining temporary capital value on assignment (until the next rent review) when rents are rising. In a time of falling commercial rents, such leases, in contrast, become 'overrented', have negative capital value, and a tenant can usually only escape from the lease by paying to surrender the lease to the landlord or paying a 'reverse premium' on assignment of the lease to another incoming tenant. But such 'capital element', if any, is usually of little significance when compared to the amount of rent paid.

[25] The ground rent reflects only the value of the undeveloped site. The original leaseholder will often have paid for the cost of the buildings erected. The term of the lease, typically 125 years, will be calculated to cover the anticipated life of the building. It is likely to be very rare to have a group of tenants with ground rents sharing facilities in the way that is the concern of this chapter.

[26] The open-market rent, which will be subject to regular reviews, will provide the principal return on the capital investment.

[27] Such leases are known as 'FRI' leases—full repairing and insurance leases.

[28] Though the commercial tenants in such leases end up paying for the cost of the repairs and services, the management control is invariably retained by the freeholder.

[29] This can be illustrated by the exceptionally large amount of litigation between commercial landlords and tenants about the terms of the lease which define their commercial relationship.

[30] There is no contractual relationship between such occupiers.

ownership of a unit within a building subject to multi-occupancy. The
resulting reliance on leasehold tenure has meant that there must be a landlord or freeholder having title to the building as a whole, whether or not
the division of interest implicit in any lease is appropriate to the situation.
If there is a landlord–freeholder, the result is a person with an interest in the
property but who does not occupy it. The interest is one of investment and
management dissimilar and opposed to that of an occupier. Such a division
is perhaps a fair reflection in commercial leases granted at a market rent.
The tenant pays the going rate on a periodical basis for the value of the right
to occupy. Such a commercial tenant often does not wish to have capital
vested in the property. The desirability of this inevitable division of interests in the case of the provision of homes has not been addressed. Instead, a
series of statutes applying to residential occupiers with long leases have only
tackled the worse abuses on a case-by-case basis as they have arisen. Such
remedies have often been badly drafted and have left the basic problems
unaddressed.

FLYING FREEHOLDS, LONG LEASEHOLDS, AND CONVEYANCING CONTRIVANCES

The common law has always been ill equipped to cater for situations which
call for a variety of property interests under the same roof. The ancient concept of the owner of land owning everything above the surface to the heavens and below to the very depths[31] is a principle introduced in the first
pages of the basic texts.[32] In times when there was less population pressure
on land and engineering techniques limited the practical height of buildings, the concept may have substantially accorded with the reality. Vertical
division of freehold property was the norm and horizontal division was to
be avoided. The 'flying freehold' might be permitted in theory,[33] inadver-
tently created[34] or even tolerated as a local eccentricity,[35] but pressure on

[31] *Cuius est solum eius est usque ad coelum et ad inferos* ('he who owns the land owns everything reaching up to the very heavens and down to the depths of the earth').

[32] e.g. Gray, *Elements of Land Law* (2nd edn., London: Butterworths, 1993), 6.

[33] From Coke ('A man may have an inheritance in an upper chamber though the lower
buildings and soil be in another', Co. Litt. 48b) to the Law of Property Act 1925 (where the
definition of land expressly permits horizontal division, s. 205(1)(ix)) there has never been
any doubt about the theoretical validity of freehold flats.

[34] For what was effectively a claim to a subterranean flying freehold, see *Grisby* v. *Melville*
[1973] 3 All ER 455, arising out of a division of property which failed to take account of a
cellar. See also (1950) 14 Conv. (NS) 350 (Tolson).

[35] The flying freeholds in Lincoln's Inn have existed for centuries. Thus, in 1787,
Ashhurst J could remark 'We know that in London different people have several freeholds
over the same spot . . . that is the case in the Inns of Court' (*Doe d. Freeland* v. *Burt* (1757)
1TR 701, 99 ER 1330 at 1331).

land was generally met by building right up to the edge of the plot owned and not by building taller and dividing horizontally. The law could cope with the consequent legal issue of proximity provided there was vertical division. The principles of easements (which of course require two 'tenements' in proximity and usually side by side)[36] could be developed—for example, into complex rules on the ownership and repair of the party walls created between adjoining properties[37] and into rights of light across one piece of land for the benefit of the other. As plots for building in cities became smaller, the tall thin building and the terraced house became the norm, sometimes as elegant Regency or Georgian properties, elsewhere to degenerate into slums for another generation to remove.

The common law was, however, unable adequately to cope with the demands of horizontal division of property. In a simple example of a property on three floors with each floor consisting of a flat or apartment with freehold title, the person with title to the middle flat has only a freehold of a block of airspace. The market value of such a title is dependent upon the support provided by the lower flat and the protection from the weather provided by the flat above. It is, therefore, essential that the freeholders of these flats are under an obligation to support, on the one hand, and maintain the roof, on the other.[38] Indeed, there must be mutual enforceability of repairing obligations, with the middle flat-owner paying a fair proportion of the benefit by contributing to repair and maintenance. Such mutual enforceability is prevented by the common law principle that the burden of a freehold covenant does not run with the land. A subsequent owner cannot be forced to pay by virtue alone of title to the property.[39]

The unsuitability of English law to cope with the issues of a shared roof are illustrated by *Rhone* v. *Stephens*.[40] The roof of a property known as Walford House also covered part of the adjoining property, Walford Cottage. Once in common ownership, the two dwellings had been sold off separately in 1960. At the time of the sale, the position of the roof had been recognized and the vendor, retaining Walford House, had covenanted, on

[36] Gray, *Elements of Land Law*, 1044, 1060.

[37] See now Party Walls etc. Act 1996, which extends the provisions of the London Buildings Acts to the rest of England and Wales and came into force on 1 July 1997.

[38] The law is capable of implying rights of support—see *Dalton* v. *Angus* (1881) 6 App. Cas. 740 at 792 (Lord Selborne LC); *Caledonian Railway Co.* v. *Sprot* (1856) 2 Macq. at 450; but not capable of ensuring that there is an obligation to maintain and repair that support.

[39] For a discussion of implied rights of support in the case of freehold flats see Bodkin, 'Rights of Support for Buildings and Flats' (1962) 26 Conveyancer (NS) 210 and esp. 211–13. Implied rights of support would seem to depend on the building being complete before the division into separate freehold flats, because the general rule is that the natural right of support avails only when land is in its natural state (*Latimer* v. *Official Co-operative Society* (1885) 16 LR Ir. 305 at 308); and see Gray, *Elements of Land Law*, 1057.

[40] [1994] 2 AC 310.

behalf of himself and his successors in title, to maintain the roof in wind and
watertight condition to the reasonable satisfaction of the purchasers of the
cottage and their successors in title. Without a knowledge of legal limitations, this seems to be an eminently reasonable provision. The roof was primarily that of the house, but the cottage would suffer if it was not kept in
repair. Unfortunately, the conveyancer of Walford Cottage had forgotten
what is 'imparted at an elementary stage to every student of the law of real
property'[41] that a covenant requiring expenditure or positive action can be
enforced directly only against the person making the promise. The House
of Lords upheld that rule on the basis that enforcement of a promise to act
or to expend money can arise only in contract by virtue of the personal
obligation entered into.[42] While restrictive covenants became an accepted
feature of property law[43] (since they were seen as treating the land subject
to a defined restriction which any purchaser could take into account when
deciding whether to buy and how much to pay), the common law refused
to accept the next step of accepting a link between the current owner of
land and an obligation to expend money, the amount of which was necessarily uncertain.[44] As Farwell J put it: 'the land cannot expend money on
improving itself and there is no personal liability on the owner of land for
the time being because there is no contract on which he can be sued.'[45]

Perhaps significantly, the key limitations were laid down in nineteenth-
century cases which were not situations where there was any element of
interdependence when the positive obligation might have been viewed
more generously.[46] Indeed, the leading case of *Austerberry* v. *Oldham
Corporation*[47] was one where the owners of a property were seeking to
evade statutory liability as frontagers to the street to contribute to making
up the road. They sought to rely upon an old covenant to maintain by those

[41] *Rhone* v. *Stephens* at 321, *per* Lord Templeman.

[42] The distinction drawn by Lord Templeman—that to enforce a positive covenant is to
enforce a personal obligation while a restrictive covenant is justified because it only treats
land as subject to the restriction looks sound. Yet the law permits enforcement of similar
'personal' positive obligations by and against subsequent parties in leases and mortgages.

[43] *Tulk* v. *Moxhay* (1848) 2 Ph. 774, 41 ER 1143.

[44] It has been argued that the doctrine of *Tulk* v. *Moxhay*, as originally articulated, did not
limit enforceability only to restrictive covenants (see Bell, '*Tulk* v. *Moxhay Revisited*' [1981]
Conveyancer 55, and that the reasoning of the courts which later restricted the doctrine was
'unconvincing' (p. 60). North American commentators also argue that the distinction is
unjustified (see e.g. Ziff, *Principles of Property Law* (2nd edn., ed. Carswell, Scarborough,
Ontario: Thomson Professional Publishing, 1996), 361–2 and the authorities there cited).

[45] *Re Nisbett and Pott's Contract* [1905] 1 Ch. 391. However, it may be argued that there
is similarly no contract when the law chooses to enforce restrictive covenants.

[46] e.g. *Haywood* v. *Brunswick Permanent Benefit Building Society* (1881) 8 QBD 403, where
enforcement of the covenant to repair was sought not even by an adjoining owner of land
but by the owner of a rentcharge.

[47] (1885) 29 Ch. D. 750, approved in *Rhone* v. *Stephens*.

who had first constructed the road. By way of contrast, the Victorian cases which initially upheld the ability to enforce obligations to contribute money by the owner of a freehold, were dealing with situations where the contribution was vital to the use and capital value of that property—in one case, a covenant to maintain a sea wall by owners of lands below sea level[48] and in another a covenant to supply water from a well to houses.[49]

The inadequacy of the law has never been a bar to what is socially necessary and desirable. If the wish or need exists to have property arranged in flats or apartments in buildings horizontally divided, then the means will be found. Indeed, conveyancing ingenuity has long been an excuse as an argument against change: 'There are ways and means known to conveyancers by which it could be done with comparative ease.'[50] Indeed, the list is well known to students from basic texts and was set out in the 1965 *Report* of the Committee on Positive Covenants affecting Land.[51] Some of the devices there listed have no relevance to those needing to find a way of mutual enforcement in communal-living situations,[52] while others have never commanded the confidence of the profession or, more significantly, lenders on the security of the property interests.[53]

SOLUTIONS IN OTHER JURISDICTIONS

The problem of finding an acceptable device to regulate relationships in communal-living situations is one that has had to be faced by all common law jurisdictions. The answer found has varied, partly because of differences in statutory changes to the common law and partly, no doubt, because of different social settings in which the communal living is to operate. Once adopted and established, the device is honed and accepted, at least by the conveyancers involved. In most cases the devices are found wanting and inadequate, leading to reform and statutory solutions being introduced or proposed.

[48] *Morland* v. *Cook* (1868) LR 6 Eq. 252.

[49] *Cooke* v. *Chilcott* (1876) 3 Ch. D. 694.

[50] Lindley LJ in *Austerberry* v. *Oldham Corporation* at 783.

[51] Cmd. 2719 (London: HMSO, 1965), para. 8. See also Burn, *Cheshire & Burn's Modern Law of Real Property* (15th edn., London: Butterworths, 1994), 612–13, and Pritchard, 'Making Positive Covenants Run' (1973) 37 Conveyancer (NS) 194.

[52] Such as the idea of a chain of contractual indemnity covenants (because it inevitably breaks through death or disappearance of one of the parties in the end), or the very limited remedies of the anomalous easement of fencing or the use of statutory powers.

[53] The creation of a rentcharge on an estate of freehold land, expressly preserved by the Rentcharges Act 1977, was the preferred solution suggested in *Austerberry* (*per* Lindley LJ at 783) and utilized in *Morland* v. *Cook*. But despite more recent analysis of its efficacy (Bright, 'Rentcharges and the Enforcement of Positive Covenants' [1988] Conveyancer 99), there seems to be little enthusiasm in practice.

In Scotland, advantage was taken of the survival of the feudal system to permit the enforcement of positive obligations. A vendor of property could sell part of land being developed by subinfeudation and thereby impose what became recognized as a 'real burden'.[54] Once so recognized, it became possible to create such positive real burdens on any conveyance of part of land, thus permitting enforcement of such positive obligations by successive owners of the reserved land against successive owners of the conveyed land. Thus 'a system that had been devised for the orderly Government of Medieval Europe became, rather unexpectedly, a means of orderly urbanisation in Victorian Scotland'.[55] English law could not use such opportunities, as subinfeudation was prohibited as long ago as 1290.[56]

An alternative common law solution, used in very different situations in at least two jurisdictions, is the legal tenancy in common.[57] In Hong Kong, land is at a premium and housing costs are among the highest in the world. The vast majority of the people in what is, since 1 July 1997, a special administrative region of China make their homes in high-rise buildings. There is no freehold land,[58] and properties have title based on the original Crown Leases. There was, therefore, the familiar problem of how to give owners of flats[59] in high-rise blocks ownership rights in the whole building with the ability to enforce mutual repairing and other communal obligations. Instead of granting subleases, the solution found was and is to give an owner of a flat an equal undivided share as tenant in common in the head leasehold estate in the land. An exclusive right is given to possess the flat or unit. The unit owner shares co-ownership rights over the common parts with all the other 'owners'. A deed of mutual covenant is entered into by the co-owners. To overcome any problems about enforcement of those mutual covenants against those later owners who were no party to it, an Ordinance was passed by the government.[60]

One would have thought that, in New Zealand, communal living would be unnecessary with such a relatively small population and space for indi-

---

[54] *Tailors of Aberdeen* v. *Coutts* (1840) 1 Rob. 296.

[55] Reid, '700 Years at One Blow: The Abolition of Feudal Land Tenure in Scotland', in Jackson and Wilde (eds.), *The Reform of Property Law* (Aldershot: Dartmouth, 1997).

[56] *Quia Emptores*, still in force today and described by Megarry and Wade as 'one of the pillars of the law of real property' (*The Law of Real Property* (5th edn., London: Stevens, 1984), 30).

[57] Tenancy in common schemes also featured in New South Wales prior to the introduction of strata title (see Butt, *Land Law* (3rd edn., Sydney: LBC Information Services, 1996), 781–2.

[58] Except, it is commonly alleged, the site of the Anglican cathedral.

[59] Who will have often paid a very large price for the purchase of the flat.

[60] The Law of Property (Enforcement of Covenants) Ordinance 1956. For more details, see Sihombing and Wilkinson, *Hong Kong Conveyancing* (Hong Kong: Butterworths Asia, 1993), and Neild, *Hong Kong Land Law* (2nd edn., Hong Kong: Butterworths Asia, 1993), ch. 16, esp. 395–9.

vidual homes. Certainly, high-rise blocks of living accommodation are the exception rather than the rule. But, ironically, the very space available when the European settlers first came has created a very different form of communal living—and utilizes the same device of the legal co-ownership in common. The cities are laid out in 'sections', often of a minimum size, and development of each section requires a contribution by way of taxation for the benefit of the community.[61] Yet the size of the section, and the growth in the size of the communities, led to a demand for smaller homes, for dwellings with smaller gardens, and for residences closer to the city centres. The answer was to subdivide older sections, building two, three, or more homes on one section. To avoid the expense of fresh taxes arising on formal division of a section or to get round local rules requiring a minimum section size, the New Zealand conveyancers adopted a similar solution to that in Hong Kong, but in relation to freehold land rather than Crown leases. The freehold of the section is vested in all the owners as co-owners in common and all join in leasing the flats or homes on the section to each occupant, often for 999 years. The rights and obligations of the occupants between themselves are defined by the covenants in the leases. To ensure the scheme remains, it is invariably provided that the lease and the interest in common can be transferred only to the same person. The mutual enforceability of the necessary obligations arising from joint occupation of the site are thus secured.[62] In England, any such solution is prevented by the Law of Property Act 1925. Legal ownership in common can no longer exist and more than four co-owners cannot even hold on trust for themselves as owners in common because of the rule limiting title being held by more than four trustees.[63] In England and Wales, therefore, the device—for that is what it is when used for this purpose—used for communal living by persons each owning part has to be the long lease at low rent,[64] for the landlord–tenant relationship permits the enforcement of positive burdens against subsequent leaseholders.[65] The leasehold estate is evidenced and maintained by the rent, but the low or nominal amount usually payable and the long term granted show the real nature of the transaction as a purchase of a home.

[61] For example, for the provision of communal open spaces or 'reserves'.

[62] See Hinde, McMorland and Sim, *Introduction to Land Law* (2nd edn, Wellington, NZ: Butterworths, 1986).

[63] Law of Property Act 1925, s. 34(1), (2).

[64] In the Republic of Ireland, it is also usual to use long leases for flat sales. There, as in England and Wales, there is no statutory answer provided. See Lyall, *Land Law in Ireland* (Dublin: Oak Tree Press, 1994), 36–7.

[65] The Landlord and Tenant (Covenants) Act 1995, s. 3(1), now provides a straightforward statutory rule of enforceability for 'new leases', replacing the traditional basis where covenants are enforceable by 'privity of estate' (see Gray, *Elements of Land Law*, 845 ff.).

THE ENGLISH LONG LEASEHOLD FLAT

Any conveyancing practitioner in England and Wales is likely to come across old long leases at low rent; there is no doubt the device is of considerable antiquity.[66] Indeed, the wealth of the well-known London estates[67] derives from the long lease, often for a term of ninety-nine years, at a very low or nominal rent.[68] The premium payable for a lease for such a period of ninety-nine years, of a house or flat, is not very much different from the price which could be demanded for a freehold or 999-year lease. Yet within two or three generations the property reverts back to the freeholder,[69] who can then grant a fresh lease and take the market value of the same property for a second time. Though long leases of houses, and building leases of land, have been well known for some centuries, the widespread use of the long lease for flats, apartments, and maisonettes in one communal building with shared facilities is very much a creature of the twentieth century, and probably largely since 1945. There was a considerable expansion in home-ownership of houses after the war; for those who could not afford a house, or wished to live in city centres where land prices were high, the answer lay in the purchase of an apartment or flat in a building with others. The sale of such property freehold faced the legal problems already described, but the overriding reason for the use of the long lease was practical: 'Building societies have resolutely set their faces against lending on freehold flats'.[70] Thus the long-leasehold flat became the accepted device. But the exact form varies substantially and it is the interaction of these differences which creates both diversity and many of the problems in practice. The main variants are as follows:

---

[66] The author recently had occasion to advise on a title which commenced with a lease dated 1741 for 1,000 years at an annual rent of one shilling.

[67] Perhaps the best known is Grosvenor Estates, the holdings of the family of the Duke of Westminster. The land came into the family by marriage in 1677 and was developed by building leases. Building leases gave a double benefit. Not only did the descendants of the freeholder get the land back at the end of the lease, but it came back with the building erected on it. See South (ed.), *Leaseholds, The Case for Reform, Collected Papers* (London: Leasehold Enfranchisement Association, 1993).

[68] Not all are at nominal rents. Where the demand is high, as in the most desirable London residential areas, there may be leases for terms less than ninety-nine years at not insubstantial rents but for which a very considerable capital premium has also been paid.

[69] Or, rather, did do so until statute stepped in to give various forms of protection to the leaseholder (see below).

[70] George and George, *Sale of Flats* (5th edn., London: Sweet & Maxwell, 1984). The inability to enforce positive covenants in freehold land means there is no mechanism for securing repairs and management which are so vital to the value of the security.

1. The length of the lease will vary. The two standard periods commonly found are 999 and ninety-nine years.[71] Of course, there can be variants so that periods less than ninety-nine years are not uncommon for very expensive London apartments, but the key difference is that a 999-year lease, or similar period, is an indication that the freeholder or developer granting the lease is ignoring the theoretical right to possess the property at the end of the term.[72] Thus the value of the freehold interest can usually be calculated mathematically based on the amount of rent.[73] However, with a ninety-nine-year lease, the freeholder retains a genuine long-term interest and the reversion will have greater value than just the value of rent received. Such a period creates a lease which is, or very soon becomes, a 'declining asset'. Within twenty-five years of the grant, a purchaser will begin to discount the value of the lease; and, with fifty or even sixty years remaining on the lease, problems may begin to arise on sale, because a purchaser may find a lender considers the term remaining is no longer good security. Before the enactment of legislation giving rights to extend a lease or enfranchise, owners of such flats found they were forced to renegotiate the term of the lease, paying a fresh premium for the privilege.[74]

2. The nature of the freeholder will vary. Frequently with 999-year leases, and sometimes with shorter terms, the freehold reversion to the flat leases of the building as a whole will be transferred by the developer to a body controlled by the flat tenants.[75] This will often be a management company in which the tenants have a share. In other cases, often of the shorter terms, the freehold is sold off to an outsider such as a property company or retained as an investment.[76] In such a case, the interests of the

[71] The reason for these periods is often stated to go back to the time when solicitors were paid by the word so that 'nine hundred and ninety nine' was more remunerative than 'one thousand', but the author has never seen evidence to back this assertion.

[72] The hope of possession by forfeiture for breach of covenant may be an issue whatever the length of the term; see below, pp. 392–3.

[73] Known as 'years purchase'.

[74] Such renegotiation depended upon the freeholder being willing to negotiate; in any event, the freeholder could essentially dictate terms in such a situation. The problem is of vital concern to leaseholders. Thus, they claim that an 'exploitative' landlord may demand an unrealistically high premium to renew; or refuse to commit itself to renew; or deliberately not renew and claim dilapidations on expiry (see South (ed.), *Leaseholds, The Case For Reform, Collected Papers*, 4.

[75] A tenants' management company resolves two issues discussed below, pp. 393–4. Thus, management control is obtained—though the appropriateness of the arrangements put in place are vital. Similarly, there is no outsider able to forfeit the lease—though a majority of tenants may, through control of the freehold, threaten forfeiture against a recalcitrant fellow tenant.

[76] Even where leases are 999 years, there can be some value in the reversion if the leases are drawn to provide for an insurance rent and service charge controlled by the freeholder. Thus the author is aware of an estate of properties acquired when a builder disposed of all its reversions to leasehold property. The new freeholder was able to take the rental income

parties are quite different. A different management company may enter the equation, as party to the flat leases with management responsibilities but not this time controlled by the tenants. This sort of management company may have a head lease of the whole property, and thus be the tenants' immediate landlord, or have no legal estate in the land.

3. It goes without saying that the terms of the lease will be unique to each development. Flat leases drafted some decades earlier may now be seen to be deficient and fail to protect the flat-owner in terms of the covenants contained in the lease. In such a case, either the present parties must agree fresh leases or the flat-owners will find the value of their homes is lower because of the legal difficulties.

4. Differences of detail abound. The nature of the management company designed to hold the freehold on behalf of the flat tenants may be a company limited by shares or a company limited by guarantee. Neither is suited to the task.[77] Where there are only two flats or maisonettes in one building, there is a potential problem if the two occupiers cannot agree. Cross-leasing devices attempting to make one tenant the landlord of the other are sometimes found. Some developments are 'mixed', either part residential and part business occupancy, or, even if occupancy is entirely residential, some occupiers may have short-term leases at market rents or protected by the Rent Acts or Housing Acts while others have long leases at low rents and are effectively owners.

In all these diverse arrangements, the terms embodied in the lease to the first occupier are crucial and the determining factor. These terms fix the relationship between the flat-owner and whoever holds the freehold or is the immediate landlord. The opportunity is there for the developer to draft the lease and insist on the terms desired. The scope for later dispute is substantial. Certainly, long leaseholders may be at a disadvantage. Statutory invention has been considerable, piecemeal, and usually a response to particular needs or abuses as they arise rather than principled or even a comprehensive code.

Four themes or stages of statutory response in England and Wales can be discerned. These overlap and are certainly not consecutive historically. They are:

---

gross and employ a property-management firm as its agent. That reputable management firm was able to run the whole estate making a profit from insurance commissions and charges for arranging for the repair and management of each block of flats.

[77] Additionally, the cost of filing annual returns required of all companies can be out of all proportion in small blocks of flats. There is the risk that a moribund management company is struck off the Companies Register, for over 80,000 companies expire in this way every year.

1. Protection of the tenant's security of tenure at the end of the long lease, thus limiting the recovery of possession and the granting of fresh leases. Significant extra protection is now given to prevent recovery of possession by forfeiture of the lease before the term expires.[78] These steps restrict the freeholder's *possession rights* in the property.

2. Restriction and determination of the freeholder's power of management control of the building or block. Such measures enable the long leasehold owners to secure a variety of outcomes, giving information and audit rights, greater oversight, and the right to be consulted, through to the ability to take over decision-making powers. These measures cut down the ability of the freeholder to profit from and control *management rights* in the property.

3. A right to require the landlord to grant what is essentially a perpetual new lease at a nominal rent. This has the effect of terminating any long-term capital value of the freeholder and any intermediate leaseholder in the flat or apartment home. If a majority of the residents can agree to join together, they can go further and 'enfranchise'—that is, collectively buy out the freehold interest completely. In one or both of these ways, the *investment interest* of the landlord in the property can be terminated.

4. Finally, there are clear proposals, as yet unimplemented, for a new form of title for communal living in horizontally divided properties. Such schemes have been in place in other jurisdictions for some time, but at long last there seems a genuine prospect for change in England and Wales. If enacted, the *commonhold proposals* will end the need for the division of legal interest necessarily implied when the lease is used as the conveyancing mechanism.

RESTRICTING POSSESSION RIGHTS

The essential distinction between a freehold estate in land and a leasehold is the finite term of the latter.[79] It must end at a specified point in time. It can be argued that any person taking a lease of property as a home or business will know the date of expiry and should be prepared to leave on that date,[80] but for purchasers of flats and horizontally divided property there is no alternative to a lease. It is neither germane to the purpose of this chapter nor relevant to trace the rise and fall of the Rent Acts which applied to

---

[78] These measures to protect the security of tenure of tenants with long leases at low rents apply to tenants of houses as well as of flats and apartments.

[79] *Prudential Assurance Co. Ltd.* v. *London Residuary Body* [1992] 2 AC 386.

[80] Leaseholders certainly reject the argument that 'they knew what they were doing when they signed their leases' (see South (ed.), *Leaseholds, The Case for Reform, Collected Papers*, 112–14).

leases for terms less than twenty-one years and to houses and flats. What is apposite is that the existence of that legislation meant that, on expiry, owners of long leases were in a worse position than tenants at a rack rent and had to quit. Consequently, the Landlord and Tenant Act 1954, part I, extended Rent Act style protection to long tenancies on their termination.[81] The regime in the Housing Acts[82] gives much more limited protection,[83] and similarly a long residential tenancy at low rent granted after 1 March 1990 has protection only along the lines of that given to assured tenants on expiry of their leases.[84] Such restrictions on obtaining possession are not limited to long leases let alone those of flats, but are of general application.

However, another basic feature of a lease is that a freeholder may have the opportunity to obtain possession before expiry, by the use of forfeiture for breach of covenant. While still an important feature of commercial leases, forfeiture no longer applies to assured tenancies.[85] By way of contrast, there has been no similar legislative intervention for long residential leases, so forfeiture and re-entry for breach of covenant remain applicable. In the case of long leases of flats and apartments, the covenants by the leaseholder to contribute to repair and maintenance will necessarily be extensive and ultimately enforceable through forfeiture. Though the covenants may exist primarily for the joint benefit of all the occupiers,[86] they are made by each original tenant with the freeholder, and it is the freeholder[87] who has the power of enforcement. Unscrupulous freeholders may actively seek to create situations where forfeiture proceedings can be commenced. Using the powers of management granted by the lease, considerable sums may be expended on repairs and other works within the terms of the lease. No

[81] As recommended by the Leasehold Committee, *Final Report*, Cmd. 7982 (London: HMSO, 1950).

[82] Housing Acts 1988–96.

[83] See, generally, Arden and Partington, *Housing Law* (London: Sweet & Maxwell, 1994), and Evans and Smith, *Law of Landlord and Tenant* (5th edn., ed. Smith, London: Butterworths, 1997), ch. 18.

[84] Local Government and Housing Act 1989, sch. 10, Housing Act 1996, sch. 2A, para. 6.

[85] The regime of the Housing Act 1988 is designed to ensure that neither notice to quit nor forfeiture can operate. A landlord must commence court action and show one of the grounds for possession. This position is reinforced by criminal and potentially very severe civil penalties for harassment and eviction. See, Burnet, *Introduction to Housing Law* (London: Cavendish Publishing, 1996), 56–66, 167–77.

[86] The extent of the concern of the freeholder in repairs ought to be related to the impact on the value of the freehold proprietary interest. In the case of a series of flat leases at low rents with many years still to elapse on the leases, the value of the freehold is not related to the state of repair—but the possibility of forfeiting a flat lease for breach of covenant may add to the value.

[87] Or the intermediate leaseholder, if any.

attempt may be made to do the work economically.[88] These sums may then be sought, under the terms of the lease, by way of service charge.[89] If the leaseholders resist payment, a writ to forfeit for non-payment could be promptly issued. The Housing Act 1996 now restricts the right of a landlord to seek forfeiture of a residential tenancy on the grounds of non-payment of service charges,[90] but the right to forfeit for non-payment of rent[91] or breach of other covenants is not affected. Whenever forfeiture is achieved, the freeholder obtains a 'windfall' benefit, since the flat can be resold to a fresh purchaser paying a premium or market price for a new long lease. Though the 1996 Act has provided a safeguard where there are disputes over service charges, the ability to forfeit remains.[92] Providing for possession rights at termination of long leases or restricting the right to forfeit does not address the central issues. Should there be an alternative form of landholding for horizontally divided property other than a lease which allows arrangements between the occupiers directly without the controlling presence of a landlord? There is then no wasting asset, no interest which expires, and no forfeiture. If an alternative can be found, should residential long leases be permitted to continue?

CONTROLLING AND TRANSFERRING MANAGEMENT RIGHTS

There are two incontrovertible aspects to the management of a building containing a number of units sharing facilities. First, management is essential.[93] Secondly, there are bound to be disputes or differences of opinion if more than one decision-maker is involved. A third may be added: the occupiers are very likely to want to have a say in those decisions, especially if they have to pay the bills proportionately to their interests. Now in those jurisdictions where there is no need for a leasehold structure, management decisions are necessarily taken by the occupiers. If there is no one among

---

[88] A particular abuse was to have the work done, no doubt at a considerable profit, by an associated company controlled by the freeholder.

[89] The restrictions now placed on imposition of service charges are discussed below, p. 395.

[90] Housing Act 1996, s. 81.   [91] Provided no part relates to the cost of services.

[92] As where a flat-owner in 'negative equity' (owing more on the mortgage than the flat is worth) abandons the premises owing service charges. The freeholder can promptly seek to forfeit. The mortgagee of the flat can seek relief but only on payment of the rent and service charge arrears.

[93] For a particularly comprehensive analysis of the conveyancing choices to secure adequate management within the leasehold framework, see Cawthorn and Barraclough, *Sale and Management of Flats, Practice and Precedent* (2nd edn., ed. Barraclough, London: Butterworths, 1996).

their number able and willing to take on the management duties, then an agent can be appointed.[94] Such an agent will be employed by the residents and accountable to them. The possible difficulty in such a system is obtaining agreement—on, for example, such things as the colour scheme for the common parts. The leasehold system can be set up in a similar way where the freeholder is a corporate body with the residential tenants as the only shareholders. Through the medium of the corporate body, they too will have the management control.[95] By way of contrast, in many cases, particularly where there are ninety-nine-year leases, the freeholder's interest is held as an investment. The management control is often retained by the freeholder, if not directly then through the medium of a management company independent of the leaseholders. Such a system does have the merit of one person making the management decisions. Sadly, the landlord or his or her managing agent can easily exploit that control. First, the repairs and maintenance work may be undertaken by a company also controlled by the landlord. If, as is common, there is no regulation in the lease, one company can charge excessive fees to another company controlled by the same person and pass on these charges to the hapless occupiers. An alternative scenario is neglect—the freeholder or person charged by the lease fails to fulfil the repairing and maintenance obligations. Such has been the abuse that Parliament has had to step in with a growing number of provisions. These have been enacted piecemeal, often after extra-parliamentary pressure or Press campaigns highlighting the issues.

We have already noted how the levying of service charges might lead to a writ of forfeiture if disputed. There have been wider abuses, often stemming from the fact that the original leases would be drafted by the freeholder or developer and would often give very wide rights to levy and recover from the lessees all possible expenses—and sometimes there might be a generously drafted 'sweeping-up' clause. There are a number of concerns, including the interpretation of such clauses, overcharging, and charging for matters which are not recoverable under the lease. The courts have attempted, by processes of construction and implication of principles of reasonable recovery, to limit abuse.[96] These steps proved inadequate and there are now significant statutory controls. First, funds paid by way of service charge must be held on trust to pay for the matters specified, either in a single

---

[94] In jurisdictions where strata title and condominium are established, a body of professionals specializing in acting for the corporate persona of the tenants develops. See e.g., for New South Wales, Ilkin, *Strata Title and Community Title Management and the Law* (2nd edn., Sydney: Law Book Co., 1996), ch. 7, pp. 112–53.

[95] There are now a considerable number of tenant-controlled management companies, and literature has been produced to guide them. See Tabbish, *Resident Owned Flats: A Guide to Company Purchase and Management Control* (London: Sweet & Maxwell, 1994).

[96] See Evans and Smith, *Law of Landlord and Tenant*, 412–14 for a helpful summary.

fund or as two or more separate funds.[97] The trust is for the benefit of the contributing tenants for the time being. The trust safeguards against insolvency of the landlord and the service-charge payments being taken for creditors rather than for the expenses to be incurred. A second complaint was that work was often planned or carried out without consultation with the tenants. Tenants desire involvement in such diverse issues as consideration of the specifications for the work, obtaining and acceptance of quotes, and the colour schemes to be adopted. So, in 1985, rules requiring most tenants to be consulted were introduced, along with attempts to strengthen the principles of reasonableness applicable to claims for recovery.[98] Thus costs are recoverable only if reasonably incurred and two estimates must be obtained for certain qualifying works. What is significant for this chapter about this set of provisions in the 1985 Act is the piecemeal way they have been built up. Some matters pre-date 1985 and derive from the Housing Act 1980; and provisions had to be extended and modified in 1987.[99] Further protection has been added by the Housing Act 1996. Now a recognized tenants' association can appoint a surveyor to advise them[100] and such a surveyor has wide powers of inspection of documents and the premises.[101] More significantly, it was found that the costs were deterring tenants from challenging the reasonableness of service charges in the county court. The 1996 Act now gives an alternative right to apply to a leasehold valuation tribunal to determine a range of matters such as whether expenditure was reasonably incurred or works were done to a reasonable standard. An examination of the statutory complexity just on this issue alone[102] poses the question of whether a reactive response to the most pressing problems is really the effective answer—particularly if, after consultation, the landlord does not have to accept the views expressed. Statutory provision to give a say in insurance of the property and to require consultation on the appointment of managing agents has also been enacted.[103]

There is a further potential problem. The leases of the flats will be the prime regulator of the rights and duties of the parties. If they are deficient, they can be amended only with consent of all the occupiers and the landlord by drawing up new leases. Once again, statutory provision has had to be made to remedy the problems when agreement cannot be reached. Part IV of the Landlord and Tenant Act 1987 gives power to the county court to vary the provisions of a long residential lease where the lease fails to make satisfactory provision for various vital matters such as repair and maintenance of the flat, the building containing the flat, or the installations,

---

[97] Landlord and Tenant Act 1987, s. 42.
[98] Landlord and Tenant Act 1985, ss. 18–30.
[99] Landlord and Tenant Act 1987.   [100] Housing Act 1996, s. 84.
[101] Ibid., sch. 4.   [102] There are twenty sections and a schedule.
[103] Landlord and Tenant Act 1985, ss. 30A and 30B, added in 1987.

insurance, or the recovery or computation of the service charge. Such a power is inevitable if long leases are to remain the vehicle for the granting of proprietary interests simply because each lease is freshly prepared and only as good as the persons responsible for drafting it, perhaps many years ago. A better solution is a scheme where the basic provisions required for communal living are essentially the same for every development and can be modified if required to take account of social or other changes.

Management problems do not only arise from zealous landlords seeking to squeeze the maximum amount of income from their investment. If there is little to be gained from management except time and trouble, the vital repair, maintenance, and management of property can be neglected. So, again, statute has had to step in to provide some answer. A tenant has the right to apply to the court for the appointment of a manager if he can show a breach of an obligation to the tenant, that the breach is likely to continue, and that it is just and convenient to make an order.[104] Once again, it was found that this did not really work in practice. Landlords would assure the court about the future, orders would be denied, and the tenants often faced a bill for costs without any benefit. Once again, amendments have been pressed and enacted. Now, by virtue of the 1996 Act, the requirement that the breach be likely to continue has been removed and jurisdiction moved to the leasehold valuation tribunal, where the risk of costs is not so great.[105] The jurisdiction has been widened by allowing an order when unreasonable service charges have been proposed or made.

The logical final step has also been taken. A landlord who has been shown to have grossly neglected his or her repairing and related obligations may be subject to an application to acquire his or her interest.[106] Breaches of obligation must be shown and they must be likely to continue. Warnings and opportunities to put the failings right must be given. An alternative precondition is that an appointment of a manager order has been in force for a period recently reduced from three to two years.[107] Now such a step terminates the landlord's interest, but on the basis of poor management.

This hasty summary of complex provisions must beg the question of whether the leasehold vehicle should be abandoned as the mechanism for provision of homes on one building. A completely new system is an answer for new developments, but for existing leaseholders the next step is acceptance of the idea that they should be able to buy their landlord out.

---

[104] Landlord and Tenant Act 1987, part II.
[106] Landlord and Tenant Act 1987, part III.

[105] Housing Act 1996, s. 85–7.
[107] Housing Act 1996, s. 88.

TERMINATING THE INVESTMENT IN LONG
LEASEHOLD HOMES

Restricting the landlord's management control can only ever be partial while an investment interest is retained. While an investment interest continues, the landlord will have some legitimate interest in the way the building is repaired, maintained, and managed. If, however, the investment interest of the landlord is ended, then with the termination of that property interest the management control will inevitably be with the tenants and those who retain proprietary interests.[108]

An investment interest of a freeholder or head landlord will have all or some of the following aspects:

1. The right to receive the annual rent. The quantum of rent payable will have an impact on the value of that interest.
2. The right to possession at the end of the term.[109] The closer to the end of that term, the greater the impact on the value of the landlord's interest, which will appreciate as those of the occupying tenants decline in value.
3. The benefit of the covenants and other terms of the long leases of the flats. For example, the ability to take commission on insurance premiums or profit from the way the service charge is calculated has been a significant feature in the sale price achieved for some leasehold reversions.[110]
4. The value of any common parts, access ways, gardens, or other facilities which the landlord can use with the tenants. Additionally, the right may be reserved to grant other persons the right to use such facilities.
5. The value of any part of the building not let on long leases at low rents such as assured tenancies or business leases. When such flats fall vacant, there is the ability to grant a long lease at full market value.

The investment interest may be regarded as terminated once the freehold is conveyed to or otherwise controlled by or on behalf of the tenants. Sometimes, this is achieved by private negotiations which result in the transfer to a corporate body controlled by the tenants. There are two statutory mechanisms. The first is based on the idea that, if the landlord wants

[108] Lenders on the security of homes will continue to have a legitimate interest in the management of the building, as the state of repair and quality of management will impact on the security.

[109] Plus the hope value or *spes* of a possible forfeiture (see above).

[110] As discussed in the last section. The recent Lands Tribunal decision in *Maryland Estates Ltd* v. *63 Perham Road Ltd.* [1997] 35 EG 94 awarded an enfranchisement price which included the value of insurance premium commissions.

to sell, the tenants should have a right of first refusal. The second is where such a purchase is by way of exercise of a statutory right, even if the land-lord has no desire to sell, the acquisition being known as 'enfranchisement'.

In theory, the right of first refusal given by part I of the Landlord and Tenant Act 1987[111] ought to be uncontentious. There is a desire to sell, so why not let the tenants match the price offered elsewhere? In practice, it did not work out like that. The rushed legislation in 1987 was seriously defective,[112] and owners of freeholds or other head leasehold interests did not want the delay and expense of sending out the notices to tenants, espe-cially if the property to be sold was a portfolio of a number of leasehold reversions requiring a large number of separate notices. The result was that the 1987 Act was easily evaded and few tenants had the tenacity to perse-vere and secure the interest being sold. The legislation only succeeded in raising tenants' expectations but could not deliver the promised control of the head interest, while putting the legal process into disrepute. Yet again, the whole statutory system had to be subject to fundamental change.[113] Perhaps enfranchisement would provide the answer?

The principle of enfranchisement was introduced by the Leasehold Reform Act 1967, which applies only to houses, and initially only to those at a low rateable value.[114] The legislation was enacted after parliamentary pressure to end what was seen as a scandal. The reversions to long leases close to termination were being purchased for relatively nominal sums. The occupying leaseholders, many of whom had lived in these houses for many years, were then faced with demands that the repairing covenants be strictly enforced.[115] Many were being forced to leave their homes.[116] The ratio-nale behind the 1967 Act was the idea that the leaseholder had already paid for the house, by way of premium when the lease was purchased. The rent represented only the value of the site and it was inequitable that the current freeholder could benefit at the expense of the persons who had made their homes in these properties. The 1967 Act therefore gave the statutory right

[111] For a summary of the provisions, see Evans and Smith, *Law of Landlord and Tenant*, 406–10.

[112] It was rushed through Parliament before dissolution for the 1987 general election. The Act in its original form was judicially castigated as 'ill-drafted, complicated and con-fused' in *Denetower* v. *Toop* [1991] 1 WLR 945 at 952G.

[113] The amendments made by the Housing Act 1996 were so extensive that most of part I of the 1987 Act, now extending to thirty-five sections, is reprinted as a schedule to the 1996 Act.

[114] The leading authority on the 1967 Act is Hague, *Leasehold Enfranchisement* (2nd edn., London: Sweet & Maxwell, 1987).

[115] The 1954 Landlord and Tenant Act, part I, gave the right to continue to reside.

[116] Especially where the value of the house, even if freehold, was low and might be less than the cost of repairs. But the essential concern was that these people did not have the resources to meet even modest repairing demands and were being forced out of homes as a consequence.

to purchase the freehold according to a statutory formula.[117] Subsequently, the right was extended.[118] In the case of a single dwelling, enfranchisement was not difficult to achieve, however controversial it might be in principle. The freehold was conveyed to the tenant, the lease and freehold merged,[119] and the former tenant obtained a freehold in fee simple free of the lease. Enfranchisement cannot be achieved so easily in the case of a block of flats with a number of tenants. There can be no merger of estates and the freehold must continue.[120]

The right of a tenant of a long leasehold flat to terminate the investment interest of the landlord was achieved by the Leasehold Reform, Housing and Urban Development Act 1993. The history of this controversial and complex legislation has been traced elsewhere.[121] A tenant can now terminate that investment interest in one of two ways. First, by what is described as a 'right to a new lease', the Act provides[122] that a tenant of a flat can secure a new lease for ninety years, plus whatever remains of the current lease term, at a peppercorn rent.[123] Moreover, this is not a once and for all right. The right can be exercised again to extend for yet another ninety years—and so on. For a single premium,[124] the leaseholder buys out the rent and the right ever to take back the flat at the end of the term. The lease is essentially a perpetually renewable lease without rent—as close to a freehold as one can get. But any investment interest in the block of flats as a

[117] Contained in the Leasehold Reform Act 1967, s. 9. This original valuation basis, now contained in s. 9(1) and applicable to homes with the lowest rateable value, meant that the freeholder only received the value of the interest on the basis it was subject to the lease extended for fifty years.

[118] By the Housing Act 1974, adding s. 9(1A) and (1B) to the 1967 Act. The valuation basis in these sections, giving rights to homes with higher rateable values, is more generous to landlords. See *Norfolk* v. *Trinity College Cambridge* (1976) 32 P & CR 147 and Hill and Redman, *Law of Landlord and Tenant* (18th loose-leaf edn., London: Butterworths, 1988–98), division E, paras. 582–86.

[119] For the doctrine of merger, see Megarry and Wade, *Law of Real Property* (5th edn., London; Stevens, 1984), 685–6.

[120] The 1967 Act was so drafted as to ensure that, where there was horizontal division of property, the Act could not apply. That this was due to the 'inability of one freehold owner to enforce positive obligations against successors in title of the other' was recognized by Nourse LJ in *Duke of Westminster* v. *Birrane* [1995] QB 262.

[121] See Clarke and Shell, 'Revision and Amendment of Legislation by the House of Lords: A Case Study' [1994] PL 409.

[122] Leasehold Reform, Housing and Urban Development Act 1993, s. 39.

[123] s. 56. A peppercorn rent has been defined as a 'nominal rent not intended to be paid but stipulated for on the (erroneous) view that reservation of some rent is necessary to constitute a lease' (Woodfall, *Landlord and Tenant* (loose-leaf edn., London: Sweet & Maxwell/Stevens, 1994), 7.014).

[124] Technically, the leaseholder may have to pay again for any subsequent ninety years, but, since a peppercorn rent is now payable, the statutory formula is almost certainly going to result in either renewal for no premium at all or a very nominal sum.

whole remains. Moreover, the leaseholder who has exercised the right to a new lease still has a lease; there are still covenants and obligations to a landlord and a service charge to pay. Obtaining a new lease does not change the management position in any way—except perhaps to make it more likely that a freeholder will wish to transfer that control voluntarily.

Collective enfranchisement is the term given by the 1993 Act for the 'greater' right—namely, the ability to buy out the freehold in the whole block. The process is complex and daunting.[125] A specified minimum number of qualifying tenants must get together, agree on how to proceed, and put financing in place, and then commence the statutory procedure by an 'initial notice'. Once the process is under way, there are significant time constraints and penalties for delay.[126] The price the leaseholders have to pay, reflected in the statutory formula, covers not only the basic value of the landlord's reversion[127] but also at least half the cost of the 'marriage value'.[128] The prize for completing the course is that the tenants will have purchased the freehold of the whole block of flats. There will be no investment interest of an outsider and they will have the ability to grant fresh leases of the flats they own.[129]

The enactment of the 1993 Act was bitterly opposed. The enforced transfer of proprietary interests was as unacceptable to landlords and property interests in 1993 as in was in 1967,[130] perhaps more so because the benefits of the legislation were seen to accrue to many wealthy leaseholders.[131] Certainly, the principle that outside investment in homes should be terminated by purchase by the occupiers was not universally accepted. The legislation did not satisfy leaseholders either, who considered it too restrictive, too complex, and too expensive. While the presence of the statutory right has encouraged many transfers by private negotiation of freehold reversions, these have probably been largely where the investment interest is limited.[132] Certainly, the 1993 Act could be evaded by a determined land-

[125] The details can be found in Clarke, *Leasehold Enfranchisement—the New Law* (Bristol: Jordans, 1993), esp. 82 ff.

[126] Both financial, in terms of payment of both sides costs and procedural, as it may be necessary to wait a year to start again.

[127] Plus that of any intermediate leaseholders.

[128] Marriage value is the difference between the (lower) separate values of all the different leasehold and freehold interests in a property added together and the (higher) value of all those interests combined into one (see Clarke, *Leasehold Enfranchisement*, 248).

[129] The valuation of the marriage value in the price they pay assumes they obtain 999 years' leases at a nominal rent.

[130] During the passage of the Bill through the Commons, the description of the 1967 Act as a form of 'expropriation' was quoted and applied to the 1993 Bill see HC Deb. 218, 835.

[131] In the House of Lords debates, before a residence qualification was eventually conceded by the Minister, there was reference to absentee rich individuals who would profit at the expense of freeholders (HL Deb. 543, cc. 930–58).

[132] For example, where the tenants already have 999-year leases.

lord.[133] The worst abuses were put right in the Housing Act 1996.[134] Pressure for amending legislation to make it easier—and cheaper—to secure the freehold continues.[135]

A successful collective enfranchisement does not, however, end the problems that the occupiers face. They may need to consider the grant of fresh lease and will have to set up a management structure, perhaps with a new or revised management company. Not all the leaseholders may have participated in the collective enfranchisement.[136] Those non-participants will not have paid for a share in the value of the freehold and will find that fellow-leaseholders have been substituted as their landlord. What is still needed is a system which permits freehold ownership of horizontally divided property. Then, by definition, there is no outside investment. The freeholders will have the management control. There can be no forfeiture or fear of being evicted at the end of a lease term. Such a system is waiting to be enacted. It exists and operates successfully across common law jurisdictions. We call it commonhold.

PROVIDING A NEW SYSTEM:
STRATA TITLE AND COMMONHOLD

The common law has not served communal occupiers well. The refusal of the courts to permit the enforcement of positive covenants has led to a number of contrived solutions, which differ across the jurisdictions. None has proved entirely satisfactory. In England, piecemeal intervention has been necessary to the long leasehold system, putting restrictions on the landlord's possession and management rights and permitting the investment interest to be bought out. Overseas experience is that a better answer is to grant by statute what the common law permitted in theory but was never ready to allow to work in practice—namely, freehold ownership of horizontally divided property.

New South Wales led the way in reform.[137] As elsewhere, multi-storey

---

[133] The most notorious device was dividing the freehold reversion—often, ironically, creating flying freeholds—so that there was more than one freeholder.

[134] Housing Act 1996, s. 107, permitting a collective enfranchisement against multiple freeholders.

[135] The 1997 Labour Party manifesto contained just such a commitment, but it has not yet been activated.

[136] The minimum number to proceed is set out in s. 13(2) of the 1993 Act. The definition is untidy and complex (see Clarke, *Leasehold Enfranchisement*, 84), but essentially requires the notice to be given by two-thirds of the qualifying tenants as defined who together constitute over half the total number of tenants, and half of those proceeding must satisfy a residence condition.

[137] Ilkin, *Strata Title and Community Title Management and the Law*, and Butt, *Land Law*, ch. 21.

residential buildings and residential flats became an accepted form of privately owned accommodation after 1945. No less than three schemes found
favour with local conveyancers: leasehold, as in the UK, tenancy in common schemes similar to those described above for New Zealand,[138] and the
company title scheme where the freehold was held by a company. The
occupiers would have the only shares in the company and were given, not
a lease, but a right of occupation of the relevant part of the whole.[139] As
today in England, none of these gave both a separate land title and a sole
ownership. It was not the freehold prized and demanded by purchasers.
The answer was the Conveyancing (Strata Titles) Act 1961 (NSW), which
permitted subdivision into separate horizontal or strata titles with common-
property areas for the communal facilities. It was an immediate success sup-
planting the old schemes. Deficiencies of detail became apparent and the
Act was amended and consolidated into the Strata Titles Act 1973. The
concept was rapidly copied in other Australian jurisdictions,[140] in New
Zealand,[141] and in Singapore.[142] The condominium statutes in North
America are similar in structure.[143]

Though the details differ, the essentials of all such statutes are to provide
for the following:

1. A freehold or absolute registered title of the flat.
2. A specially designed corporate body managed by the occupiers to
   own and maintain common parts and communal facilities.
3. Provision of standard regulations so that there is a degree of uniformity and common practice but with the ability for change to suit the
   particular circumstances of the case.
4. Protection for mortgagees and other lenders on the security of the
   title of individual flats by permitting the lender to override the wishes
   of the flat-owner when changes to the regulations might prejudice the
   security.

---

[138] See above, pp. 386–7.

[139] Ilkin, *Strata Title and Community Title Management and the Law*, 5.

[140] See now Subdivision Act 1988 (Victoria), Strata Titles Act 1988 (South Australia),
Unit Titles Act 1970 (Australian Capital Territory), Unit Titles Act (Northern Territory),
and introduced in Tasmania by incorporation into Conveyancing and Law of Property Act
1884, part XIA. The most recent development is the Body Corporate and Community
Management Act 1997 (Qld), perhaps the most advanced form of group or community titles
legislation in Australia.

[141] Unit Titles Act 1972 (NZ).

[142] Land Titles Act Cap. 157 and Land Titles (Strata) Act Cap. 158.

[143] See Ziff, *Principles of Property Law*, 318–19, where the basic and contrasting approaches
of the Alberta (Condominium Properties Act 1980) and the Ontario (Condominium
Act 1990) statutes are set out. The British Columbia Condominium Act 1979 is another
example.

5. Minimum requirements for insurance of the whole, flats, and common parts, for reserve funds to spread the costs of repairs and cover future contingencies, and for a management council or committee to provide the necessary framework for equity between vendor and purchaser, for relationships between the occupiers for the time being, and for the vital confidence for banks and building societies.

In none of the jurisdictions where a statutory solution has been promulgated have the conveyancers persisted with the old solutions, and the widespread use suggests that they meet the needs of all parties. Yet, thirty-six years on, there is still no similar statute in England. There have been plenty of false dawns. Parliamentary Bills have been drafted and published[144] and a name offered—commonhold—designed to reflect the adaptation of the original idea for the home situation.[145] Election commitments in manifestos have not yet been fulfilled.[146]

The reasons for the lack of progress are diverse. For some time, attention was directed to a wider picture of reform of the basic rule to permit positive obligations in freehold land.[147] When it was suggested that a special scheme for flats on strata title lines would be more fruitful,[148] the whole issue was reinvestigated[149] (and the wider proposals not enacted either). Then the proposals came up against the pressure groups lobbying on behalf of existing, dissatisfied long leaseholders. They wanted change—but not just a change which only provided for new flat developments and left them trapped in inadequate leases. So the more contentious issue of enfranchisement was tackled first.[150] Any enthusiasm for commonhold was lost in the inter-party strife the issue generated.[151] The complexities of any common-

[144] The Commonhold draft Bill 1996, published by the Lord Chancellor's Department in July 1996, built on the earlier work which had culminated in *Commonhold—a consultation paper with draft Bill annexed*, Cm. 1345 (London: HMSO, 1990).

[145] The term 'commonhold' was put forward in Law Commission, *Commonhold: Freehold Flats and Freehold Ownership of Other Interdependent Buildings*, Report of a Working Group (the Aldridge Report) Cm. 179 (London: HMSO, 1987). See also Clarke, 'Commonhold, a Prospect of Promise' [1995] 58 MLR 486 esp. at 490–2.

[146] The manifesto commitment of the Conservative Party in 1992 was not implemented. The commitment was ambiguous—see the discussion in Clarke, 'Commonhold', 494.

[147] Committee on Positive Covenants affecting Land, *Report*, Cmnd. 2719 (1965); Law Commission, *Transfer of Land: The Law of Positive and Restrictive Covenants*, Law Com. No. 127 (1984). See also Wade, 'Covenants, a Broad and Reasonable View', [1972B] CLJ 157 esp. 157–62.

[148] Building Societies Association, *Leaseholds, Time for a Change*, (London: Building Societies Association, 1984).

[149] By the Alridge Committee (see n. 145).

[150] To ensure that the existing tenants had a way of obtaining control of the freehold.

[151] The opposition of the Conservative government's own backbenchers, in both the Commons and the Lords, left deep scars. Ironically, those very interests which strongly oppose the principle of enfranchisement are often to be counted among the enthusiasts for

hold legislation must not be forgotten either. Thus, to take one point of detail, there are genuine differences of opinion on whether a separate dispute mechanism to resolve differences between the occupiers is appropriate.[152] The necessity for some provision for what should happen if the building is destroyed and the commonhold wound up can easily end up with a wholesale adoption of existing insolvency provisions which could be argued to be far too detailed for this purpose.[153]

The latest Commonhold Bill[154] and the manifesto commitment of the government elected in 1997[155] does give cause to hope that there may be a new statutory basis for communal living in England in the new millennium. The 1996 Bill is shorter,[156] with more detail to be left to secondary legislation—which is more easy to change and improve in the light of experience. A relaxation of the limits for enfranchisement at the same time could see the new system being adopted by occupiers who have first secured the freehold of their blocks in this way and then have the opportunity to convert to commonhold.

CONCLUSION

The common law was never able to cope with the practical consequences of the theoretical acceptance it accorded to flying freeholds. Though nineteenth-century judges were prepared to accept restrictive covenants, they rejected the mutual enforceability of positive covenants long before there was a demand for purchase of flats and apartments with shared facilities. While leases have a significant and vital role in a variety of situations, for commercial leases, for open-market rented property, and the luxury flat, a lease is not an appropriate vehicle for those persons who wish to own their own home under a roof with others free of outside interference. The essential division of ownership between a landlord and a tenant has not proved a happy experience for many living in this way.

strata title or commonhold (see Grosvenor Estate, *Strata Title in England and Wales* (London: Grosvenor Estate, May 1987).

[152] See Clarke, 'Commonhold', 499, Kenny, 'Commonhold Title—Freehold Flats and Offices: Opportunity Knocks?' [1988] 12 EG 30, and College of Estate Management, 'Commonhold—Is the Cure Worse than the Complaint?', (Research Paper 90/03, Reading: College of Estate Management, 1990.

[153] The 1990 Commonhold Bill contained over fifty sections on winding-up alone.

[154] Published in July 1996 (see n. 144).

[155] There has been no indication so far, to the author's knowledge, of an intention by the Labour government, elected in 1997, to legislate. If parliamentary time can be found, the principle of the new system would appear to have the committed support of both major parties, the 1996 Bill having been prepared by the previous Conservative administration.

[156] Than its 1990 predecessor.

In *Rhone* v. *Stephens*, the judges rightly considered that any reform of the rules relating to positive covenants should be left to Parliament. The statutory schemes of strata title and condominium in other jurisdictions have been singularly successful and met the demand for a legal framework which permits a number of freehold or absolute owners each having an interest in a defined part of a building. There is no reason to suppose that commonhold would not be a similarly suitable answer for horizontally divided flats and apartments in England and Wales. Once this is made available, experience in other jurisdictions suggests it is the preferred legal vehicle and can also be adapted for use in a wide variety of mixed residential/business uses and in solely commercial situations. In the spirit of the age, the availability of commonhold alongside leasehold and freehold will allow a market choice.[157] Certainly, the need for statutory intervention to check the next set of abuses of long leases will end.

The law cannot legislate to ensure people can live contentedly together under the same roof. But it can and should provide a framework that makes that result more rather than less likely.

---

[157] Though it is likely that a Commonhold Bill will not permit an owner of a commonhold unit to grant a long lease of that unit, since such a step would recreate the long-term division of the interest which commonhold seeks to avoid.

16

LAND AND AGRICULTURAL PRODUCTION

Michael Cardwell

Despite years of encroachment for urban use, as at June 1996 agricultural land still covered some 76 per cent of the surface of the UK.[1] Furthermore, although the number of people working in agriculture continues to decline, the total remains in excess of half a million, approximately 2 per cent of the national workforce;[2] and to these must be added large numbers in the processing and other ancillary industries. The importance of agriculture may also be judged by the fact that (for the time being) it enjoys its own government department; and in terms of public expenditure the sums involved, already significant, have risen sharply. By way of illustration, for the 1995/6 financial year total agricultural expenditure was just over £2,900 million, of which £2,740.5 million was attributable to market regulation and other agricultural support measures under the Common Agricultural Policy. This total represented a rise of some £389 million in comparison with the previous year, notwithstanding the government's emphasis on financial stringency. Further, when the cost of the BSE crisis is brought into account, total expenditure for the 1996/7 financial year has been forecast to reach £4,413.9 million.[3]

Without doubt agriculture remains the predominant form of rural land use; but no longer may its central role be taken for granted. Following improvements in production techniques, farmwork cannot provide full employment in rural areas; and those same improvements have led to the creation of surpluses throughout the European Community and the consequent imposition of production controls. Against this background increased emphasis has been laid on diversification from traditional forms of agriculture; and the change in emphasis found full expression in the Government's White Paper issued in 1995, *Rural England—a Nation Committed to a Living*

---

[1] MAFF (Ministry of Agriculture, Fisheries and Food), *Agriculture in the United Kingdom 1996*, (London: HMSO, 1997), 6.

[2] For the provisional figures for the 1995 calendar year, see MAFF, *Agriculture in the United Kingdom 1995*, (London: HMSO, 1996), table 1.1. See also MAFF, *Agriculture in the United Kingdom 1996*, table 2.5.

[3] MAFF, *Agriculture in the United Kingdom 1996*, table 9.1.

Countryside.[4] Not least, a wide range of business activities was regarded as essential for the health of village communities.

At the same time increased efficiency in production has prompted concerns over the environment. The advocacy of sustainable methods of crop husbandry are a not unexpected response to these concerns; and much weight has been placed on the various schemes implemented under the Community's 'Agri-Environmental Regulation'.[5]

Accordingly, the overall impression is that of an agricultural industry no longer subject to the imperative of maximizing production and increasing the level of national self-sufficiency.[6] In this context three legal issues may be explored: first, the extent to which there remains a role for the tenanted sector; secondly, the control of food production (including consideration of alternative land uses); and, thirdly, the promotion of sustainable and environmentally sound land use.

A CONTINUING ROLE FOR THE TENANTED SECTOR?

In the nineteeth century agriculture in the UK was for the most part conducted by tenant farmers. Consistent with the economic and political power of landowners, such tenants enjoyed little statutory protection. Indeed, as late as 1908 some 88 per cent of agricultural land in Great Britain was rented or mainly rented.[7] However, by 1991 the tenanted sector accounted for only 36 per cent of agricultural land in England and Wales.[8] This decline has generally been attributed to the extensive statutory protection accorded to agricultural tenants, as consolidated just over a decade ago in the Agricultural Holdings Act 1986 ('the 1986 Act').[9] Such protection has received the highest judicial sanction, being justified as a matter of

[4] Department of the Environment and MAFF, Cm. 3016 (London: HMSO, 1995). For the equivalent documents for Scotland and Wales, see respectively Scottish Office, *Rural Scotland: People, Prosperity and Partnership*, Cm. 3041 (Edinburgh: HMSO, 1995) and Welsh Office, *A Working Countryside for Wales*, Cm. 3180 (London: HMSO, 1996). See also House of Commons Environment Committee, *Rural England: the Rural White Paper*, Third Report HC 163, Session 1995–6.

[5] Council Regulation (EEC) 2078/92, 1992, L215/85.

[6] See e.g. Britton (ed.), *Agriculture in Britain: Changing Pressures and Policies* (Wallingford, Oxon: CAB International, 1990).

[7] Committee of Inquiry into the Acquisition and Occupancy of Agricultural Land, *Report*, Cm. 7599 (London: HMSO, 1979), table 5.

[8] MAFF and Welsh Office Agriculture Department, *Agricultural Tenancy Law—Proposals for Reform: a Consultation Paper*, (1991), para. 2.

[9] There are many excellent works on the agricultural holdings legislation. See e.g. Densham and Evans, *Scammell and Densham's Law of Agricultural Holdings* (8th edn., London: Butterworths, 1997), and Muir Watt, *Agricultural Holdings* (13th edn., London: Sweet and Maxwell, 1987).

public interest.[10] Thus, it was stated to be a matter of vital importance 'both to the national economy and security, that the level of production and the efficiency of our farms should be maintained and improved'.[11] To achieve these aims it was also perceived to be of vital importance that tenants should be encouraged to farm in the long term, reinvesting their profits in their holdings. Accordingly, statute has long restricted the operation of notices to quit served by landlords. Further, there has long been close regulation of rent levels during the currency of a tenancy, together, *inter alia*, with statutory rights of compensation on termination.

While such measures had the effect of increasing protection for existing tenants, they also discouraged landlords from reletting land which became vacant. However, perhaps the greatest disincentive to reletting proved to be the introduction of rights of succession for tenants by the Agriculture (Miscellaneous Provisions) Act 1976. Up to two successions were permitted; and, although these were initially confined to succession on the death of the tenant, the Agricultural Holdings Act 1984 extended the provisions to cover succession on retirement. That having been said, the same 1984 Act also provided that, with certain exceptions, tenancies granted on or after 12 July 1984 did not carry with them any succession rights, whether on death or retirement.

This cut-off date of 12 July 1984 should arguably have reversed the decline in the tenanted sector; but all the evidence suggested that, when land became vacant, landowners still preferred either to enter into arrangements which fell completely outside the agricultural holdings legislation, such as share-farming or partnership agreements, or to structure tenancies in such a way that, while falling within the agricultural holdings legislation, they did not confer security of tenure. In the latter category empirical surveys detected heavy use of *Gladstone* v. *Bower*[12] agreements, fixed-term tenancies of more than one but less than two years.[13] Without doubt fear of conferring statutory protection was a major consideration for landlords; but arguably there were other considerations. Two examples may be given. First, landlords suffered significant tax disadvantages as against owner-occupiers. Not least, one of the criteria for full agricultural property relief under the Inheritance Tax legislation was that the landowner enjoy

---

[10] *Johnson* v. *Moreton* [1980] AC 37.

[11] Ibid., *per* Lord Salmon at 52. For discussion of the policy issues behind the agricultural holdings legislation, see e.g. Dawson, 'Public Policy, Security of Tenure and the Agricultural Holdings Acts' [1995] Web CLI 320–33.

[12] [1960] 2 QB 384.

[13] See e.g. Winter, Richardson, Short, and Watkins, *Agricultural Land Tenure in England and Wales* (London: Royal Institution of Chartered Surveyors, 1990); and the annual tenanted farms surveys prepared by the Central Association of Agricultural Valuers.

vacant possession or the right to obtain it within twelve months.[14] Secondly, many landowners were keen to participate directly in increasing levels of profitability. In particular, the rewards for farming in hand had been boosted by the widening range of Common Agricultural Policy subventions.

Against this background wholesale reforms were implemented by the Agricultural Tenancies Act 1995 ('the 1995 Act').[15] The encouragement of the letting of land was one of the three express objectives set out in the original Consultation Paper.[16] Moreover, another express objective, to deregulate and simplify, would seem to have like effect, with potential landlords no longer required to navigate the complexities of the 1986 Act. The final express objective, to provide an enduring framework which could accommodate change, will be considered below.

Following industry agreement, the 1995 Act came into force on 1 September 1995.[17] The vehicle for change is the farm business tenancy. To qualify as a farm business tenancy a tenancy must, *inter alia*, satisfy 'the business conditions' and either 'the agriculture condition' or 'the notice conditions'. The business conditions stipulate that there must have been commercial farming on all or part of the tenanted land since the beginning of the tenancy.[18] The agriculture condition is that the character of the tenancy is primarily or wholly agricultural, having regard to '(a) the terms of the tenancy, (b) the use of the land comprised in the tenancy, (c) the nature of any commercial activities carried on on that land, and (d) any other relevant circumstances'.[19] By contrast, provided that the parties exchange the requisite written notice, the notice conditions permit increased non-agricultural use over the course of the tenancy: it is necessary only for the character of the tenancy to be primarily or wholly agricultural at its beginning (having regard to the terms of the tenancy and any other relevant circumstances).[20]

If the farm business tenancy regime does apply, then freedom of contract

[14] The full rate of relief was raised to 100% by the Finance (No. 2) Act 1992, amending Inheritance Tax Act 1984, s. 116.

[15] For discussion of the reform process, see e.g. Sydenham and Mainwaring, *Farm Business Tenancies: Agricultural Tenancies Act 1995* (Bristol: Jordans, 1995), 3–10; and Gibbard and Ravenscroft, 'The Reform of Agricultural Holdings Law', in Jackson and Wilde (eds.), *The Reform of Property Law* (Aldershot: Dartmouth, 1997), 111–26.

[16] MAFF and Welsh Office Agriculture Department, *Agricultural Tenancy Law—Proposals for Reform: a Consultation Paper*, para. 4.

[17] Where a tenancy begins on or after that date the agricultural holdings legislation applies only in the exceptional circumstances set out in the 1995 Act, s. 4. These exceptional circumstances include succession tenancies under the 1986 Act.

[18] 1995 Act, s. 1(2).   [19] Ibid., s. 1(3).

[20] Ibid., ss. 1(4), (5). The detailed provisions require, *inter alia*, that the written notice be separate from any tenancy agreement (s. 1(6)).

is the hallmark of the landlord and tenant relationship. Indeed, such freedom of contract was perceived as the key to achieving not only deregulation and simplification but also the encouragement of the letting of land. Three examples may be given. First, and most significantly, the length of a farm business tenancy is for the most part a matter for agreement between the parties. The extensive restrictions on the operation of notices to quit as found under the agricultural holdings legislation are removed.

Thus, fixed-term tenancies for two years or less expire with effluxion of time. However, in the case of tenancies for more than two years, some positive action is required of the landlord. Rather than ending on the term date, they continue from year to year until terminated by the appropriate notice. Under the 1995 Act notice to terminate any tenancy from year to year must be in writing, take effect at the end of a year of the tenancy, and be given at least twelve but less than twenty-four months before it is to take effect. Accordingly, it recognizes the cycle of the agricultural year and the need for farmers to receive adequate warning of termination; but the length of tenure is so much more dependent upon the length of the term initially granted.[21]

Secondly, repairing obligations during the tenancy are now purely a matter for agreement between the parties: there is no fall-back position such as the 'model clauses' found under the agricultural holdings legislation.[22]

Thirdly, it has been the intention to introduce a more simple machinery for dealing with dispute resolution. Thus, the 1995 Act does not employ the Agricultural Land Tribunal procedure applicable under the 1986 Act. A different, but none the less statutory, procedure is imposed in the case of arbitrations on rent review, consent to improvements, and compensation for improvements; but otherwise the parties may agree an alternative dispute resolution mechanism. In the absence of agreement, there is the fall-back of arbitration, formerly under the Arbitration Acts 1950–79, and now under the Arbitration Act 1996.[23]

Notwithstanding this general emphasis on freedom of contract, the regulatory code imposed by the 1995 Act does extend beyond defining the farm business tenancy and the (albeit more limited) provisions governing termination and dispute resolution. In particular, the regulatory code covers rent review and compensation on termination. However, even with regard to rent review there is scope for agreement between the parties. They may agree in the instrument itself that there should be no rent review or that the rent is to be varied at a specified time or times during the tenancy. However, should

[21] 1995 Act, ss. 5–7. For commentary, see e.g. Sydenham and Mainwaring, *Farm Business Tenancies: Agricultural Tenancies Act 1995*, 99–102.

[22] The 'model clauses' are contained in the Agriculture (Maintenance, Repair and Insurance of Fixed Equipment) Regulations 1973 SI 1973/1473, as amended by the Agriculture (Maintenance, Repair and Insurance of Fixed Equipment) (Amendment) Regulations 1988 SI 1988/281.

[23] See, in particular, 1995 Act, ss. 28–30.

they adopt the latter alternative, the instrument must also provide that the rent is to be varied by or to a specified amount, or in accordance with a specified formula which must not be upwards only and which must not require or permit the exercise of any person's judgement or discretion.[24] In the absence of such agreement the statutory mechanism applies.

With regard to compensation on termination, the 1995 Act somewhat unusually adopts a more restrictive approach than earlier legislation. To the extent that improvements are covered by the 1995 Act, entitlement is governed by statute alone.[25] That having been said, there is a broader definition of 'tenant's improvement'. In particular, the definition includes 'any intangible advantage which—(i) is obtained for the holding by the tenant by his own effort or wholly or partly at his own expense, and (ii) becomes attached to the holding'.[26] As shall be seen, this wording is designed not only to catch such matters as milk quotas, but also to promote diversification, thereby achieving the third express objective of the 1995 Act.

It is difficult to divine the extent to which the 1995 Act may be said to encourage the letting of land and to deregulate and simplify. Considering first the encouragement of the letting of land, no clear pattern has yet emerged.[27] However, early signs are encouraging.[28] There is even some indication that land is being purchased for the purpose of letting on farm business tenancies.[29] However, data for the period immediately preceding the 1995 Act are likely to have been distorted by the prospect of such major reform;[30] and it is not easy to ascertain the extent to which increased lettings are attributable to the 1995 Act or to other factors. In particular, a vital consideration is amendment of the Inheritance Tax legislation so as to make available 100 per cent agricultural property relief for freehold land let on farm business tenancies.[31] That having been said, even after the enactment

---

[24] Ibid., s. 9.

[25] Ibid., s. 26. For guidance on entitlement under the 1986 Act, see the Agricultural Land Tribunal decision of *Barton* v. *The Lincolnshire Trust for Nature Conservation* (1997).

[26] Ibid., s. 15(b).

[27] On this aspect, generally, see Bright, 'Tenant Farming: for the Good of the Nation?' [1995] Conveyancer 445–52.

[28] See e.g. Central Association of Agricultural Valuers, *The Central Association of Agricultural Valuers Annual Tenanted Farms Survey 1996* (Coleford, Glos.: Central Association of Agricultural Valuers, 1997). See also Kerr, *New Farm Tenancies: New Farms and Land 1995–97* (London: Royal Institution of Chartered Surveyors, 1994), a survey predicting lettings within two years of the 1995 Act (but cf. Gibbard and Ravenscroft, 'The Reform of Agricultural Holdings Law', 111–26).

[29] See e.g. *The Central Association of Agricultural Valuers Annual Tenanted Farms Survey 1996*.

[30] See e.g. Bishop, 'Reforming Land Tenure: Farm Business Tenancies and the Rural Environment' [1996] Conveyancer 243–59.

[31] Finance Act 1995, s. 155. The other conditions set out in the Inheritance Tax Act 1984 must also be met. It may also be suggested that the purchase of land for letting on farm business tenancies is, in part at least, a function of rising rent levels.

of the 1995 Act and the amendment to the Inheritance Tax legislation there do remain incentives to enter into share-farming or partnership agreements. For example, such participatory arrangements still carry Capital Gains Tax, Income Tax, and Value Added Tax advantages; and the freehold-owner enjoys the benefit of close control of the land.

One aspect which must cause concern is that farm business tenancies would appear for the most part to be granted to established farmers. In particular, there is evidence that the majority of tenancies comprise only bare land, more suited to such established farmers seeking to spread their costs[32]—and arguably they receive further impetus as a result of the set-aside requirements under the Arable Area Payments Scheme. This is probably no more than a continuation of the trend found under the agricultural holdings legislation.[33]

However, it must represent a considerable disappointment in that an avowed purpose of the 1995 Act was to make available tenanted land for new entrants.[34] For the 1995 Act alone to reverse the trend may prove very difficult when high rent levels and high capital costs (including the costs of quotas) remain such a barrier to prospective farmers. Besides, landowners and lending institutions may be expected to continue their preference for applicants with proven experience.

Turning to the objective of deregulation and simplification, it cannot be denied that the 1995 Act imposes a significantly less extensive statutory code. The contrast is perhaps most marked in the case of the provisions governing termination. As indicated, in place of the complex measures restricting the operation of notices to quit under the agricultural holdings legislation, the 1995 Act specifies only two main forms of protection: first, fixed-term tenancies for more than two years do not end on the term date but continue from year to year unless determined by notice; and, secondly, in the case of tenancies from year to year the notice to quit must be in writing, take effect at the end of a year of the tenancy, and be given at least twelve months but less than twenty-four months before it is to take effect.

However, in other respects the law governing the termination of farm business tenancies may cause substantial difficulties for landlords. In particular, if a landlord wishes to terminate a farm business tenancy for breach of covenant, he is reliant upon the general law of forfeiture. There are no discrete and additional provisions as found under the 1986 Act. Thus, where farm business tenants commit irremediable breaches, their landlords may rue the fact that they have no specific sanction such as Case E in Schedule

---

[32] *The Central Association of Agricultural Valuers Annual Tenanted Farms Survey 1996.*

[33] For statistics under the agricultural holdings legislation, see Winter, Richardson, Short, and Watkins, *Agricultural Land Tenure in England and Wales*, 20–2.

[34] See e.g. the Minister of Agriculture, William Waldegrave, HC Deb. (6 Feb. 1995), 254, c. 23.

3 to the 1986 Act (confining a tenant to contesting the reason stated in the notice to quit).[35] Moreover, the general law of forfeiture has long been understood to give rise to uncertainties and delay, prompting the Law Commission to advocate wholesale reform.[36] Indeed, a landlord may be better advised to avoid the hazardous and lengthy process altogether. For example, if the tenancy is for a fixed term of two years or less, it may prove more swift and less expensive to permit the tenancy to expire by effluxion of time. It is even possible that forfeiture proceedings prove largely restricted to the termination of fixed-term tenancies with many years yet to expire.

Likewise, the fact that the 1995 Act eschews any statutory regulation of repairing obligations does not inevitably lead to a simpler regime. Without doubt there is now full deregulation in this respect; but even under the agricultural holdings legislation the parties were free to agree their own terms, with the 'model clauses' operating only as fall-back provisions. Further, those 'model clauses' precluded any risk of a lacuna in the repairing obligations, a lacuna which the court has shown itself reluctant to fill in the commercial context.[37]

By way of final example, dispute resolution may also prove an area where reform has not necessarily produced simplification. The Agricultural Land Tribunal procedure under the 1986 Act is definitely complex, and also subject to strict deadlines.[38] However, it at least has the merit of being compulsory across a wide range of disputes—and a similar procedure is applicable to arbitrations on the apportionment and prospective apportionment of milk quota. With regard to disputes under the 1995 Act, practitioners may need to be conversant with any agreed mechanism for alternative dispute resolution, arbitration under the Arbitration Act 1996 (replacing the Arbitration Acts 1950–79), and the modifications to that general arbitration procedure imposed by the 1995 Act.[39] Accordingly, the 1995 Act again

[35] Where landlords can rely on cases in Sch. 3 to the 1986 Act, the remedies available to tenants are curtailed (there being no opportunity to serve a counter-notice). See, generally, e.g. Densham and Evans, *Scammell and Densham's Law of Agricultural Holdings*, 176–214, and Muir Watt, *Agricultural Holdings*, 108–47.

[36] Law Commission, *Codification of the Law of Landlord and Tenant: Forfeiture of Tenancies*, Law Com. No. 142 (1985); and Law Commission, *Landlord and Tenant Law: Termination of Tenancies Bill*, Law Com. No. 221 (1994). The uncertainties are well illustrated by decisions where the court has somewhat surprisingly granted the tenant relief: see e.g. *Ropemakers Properties Ltd.* v. *Noonhaven Ltd.* [1989] 34 EG 39; and *Southern Depot Co. Ltd.* v. *British Railways Board* [1990] 33 EG 45.

[37] See e.g. *Demetriou* v. *Poolaction Ltd.* [1991] 25 EG 113; and *Crédit Suisse* v. *Beegas Nominees Ltd.* [1994] 4 All ER 803. Moreover, the default repairing obligations recommended by the Law Commission would not apply to farm business tenancies: *Landlord and Tenant: Responsibility for State and Condition of Property*, Law Com. No. 238 (1996), esp. para. 7.14.

[38] The detailed provisions are set out in the 1986 Act, sch. 11.

[39] As indicated, the 1995 Act imposes modifications with regard to arbitration on rent review, consent to improvements, and compensation for improvements.

enjoys the benefit of flexibility; but this flexibility is itself not without difficulties.

THE CONTROL OF FOOD PRODUCTION AND ALTERNATIVE LAND USES

Whether land is held under a tenancy or not, considerable changes have been effected by the implementation of production controls. While for the most part these controls are arms of economic policy within the European Community, they have also raised issues of property law.[40] In this context three aspects may be considered: first, the variety and scale of production controls; secondly, their effect on land use, including diversification from agriculture; and, thirdly, specific property issues raised by controls on food production.

The Variety and Scale of Production Controls

Production controls were a response to spiralling surpluses and, consequently, spiralling expenditure under the Common Agricultural Policy. The reasons for these surpluses were varied and complex, but certain key factors may be identified. First, in many sectors of the Common Agricultural Policy the Community was providing a high level of market support. Not least, there was widespread use of 'intervention' buying, the Community effectively purchasing surplus production at a fixed 'intervention price'. Secondly, farmers were well placed to make use of the intervention system by reason of significant improvements in productivity (many of these improvements flowing from technical developments). Thirdly, consumption within the Community was stagnating.

The effect of these factors may be illustrated from the dairy sector. In 1983 total milk supply within the Community was 110 million tonnes, but total demand was only 92.4 million tonnes.[41] Moreover, Council Regulation (EEC) 856/84 could recite that 'quantities of milk delivered are increasing at a rate such that disposal of surpluses is imposing financial burdens and market difficulties which are jeopardizing the very future of the common agricultural policy'.[42] In particular, heavy costs were being incurred to dispose of surplus production.

[40] For general works on the Common Agricultural Policy, see e.g. Usher, *Legal Aspects of Agriculture in the European Community* (Oxford: Oxford University Press, 1988); Gardner, *European Agriculture: Policies, Production and Trade* (London: Routledge, 1996); and Colman and Roberts, 'Economics of the CAP in Transition', in Artis and Lee (eds.), *The Economics of the European Union* (2nd edn., Oxford: Oxford University Press, 1997), 89–117.

[41] Court of Auditors, 'Special Report No. 2/87 on the Quota/Additional Levy System in the Milk Sector', OJ C266/1, 5 Oct. 1987, table 3.

[42] Preamble, Council Regulation (EEC) 856/84, OJ L90/10, 1 Apr. 1984.

Just as the reasons for the surpluses were varied and complex, so were the forms of production control. Indeed, this variety and complexity may be regarded as inevitable given that the controls were applied to different sectors of the Common Agricultural Policy at different dates.

Arguably the firmest response to surpluses has been the imposition of individual producer quotas. Thus, milk quotas were applied to the dairy sector as from 2 April 1984; and sheep and suckler cow quotas were introduced as part of the 1992 Common Agricultural Policy reforms.[43] However, while both may be categorized as individual producer quotas, they operate in a significantly different manner. An allocation of milk quota permits a farmer to produce milk or milk products without penalty up to the level of his individual quota. If the individual quota is exceeded, then there is a potential liability to levy on the excess production.[44] The rate of any levy payable is such as to render the excess production totally uneconomic. By contrast, sheep and suckler cow quotas do not penalize excess production as such. Under both the sheep and suckler cow regimes, producers have long received annual payments ('premiums') per sheep and suckler cow, the premiums being designed to support the incomes of producers; and it was to the number of premiums payable that individual producer quotas were applied, so limiting the support payable. The effect of sheep and suckler cow quotas is, however, similar to that of milk quotas: production in excess of the individual producer quota is rendered totally uneconomic.

Individual producer quotas have not been the only means of curbing surpluses. In particular, the cereal sector has been subjected to material constraints under the Arable Area Payments Scheme. Under this Scheme producers may receive compensatory payments for a wide range of qualifying crops on eligible land. However, for the vast majority of UK producers, the receipt of such payments is dependent upon taking a proportion of their eligible land out of production, the Community fixing annually the amount to be 'set aside'.[45]

---

[43] For general works on milk quotas, see e.g. Cardwell, *Milk Quotas: European Community and United Kingdom Law* (Oxford: Oxford University Press, 1996); and Trotman, *The Development of Milk Quotas in the UK* (London: Sweet & Maxwell, 1996). For a general work on sheep and suckler cow quotas, see Neville and Mordaunt, *A Guide to the Reformed Common Agricultural Policy* (London: Estates Gazette, 1993).

[44] Under the system as implemented in the UK, liability is dependent upon a number of factors. For example, where a producer makes wholesale deliveries to dairies (as opposed to selling directly for consumption), he will not pay levy unless, first, he exceeds his individual wholesale quota; secondly, the dairy to which he makes deliveries exceeds its purchaser quota; and, thirdly, the UK exceeds its national wholesale quota.

[45] For a general work on the cereal sector, see e.g. Neville and Mordaunt, *A Guide to the Reformed Common Agricultural Policy*.

The Effect of Production Controls on Land Use

Turning to the effect of production controls on land use, it is difficult to detect clear and rigid responses by farmers. None the less, certain responses may be suggested. First, there is some evidence that the imposition of individual producer quotas has led to extensification of production. For example, in the dairy sector producers have arguably moved towards the most economic means of filling their quota; and frequently this may lead to greater use of grass and less use of concentrates. A more concrete example is, however, provided by the detailed legislation governing suckler cow quotas. For the vast majority of UK producers the 1992 Common Agricultural Policy reforms made payment of suckler cow premium dependent upon compliance with stocking-density provisions. These stocking-density provisions have been tightened over the years and, as from 1996, there must not be more than two livestock units per forage hectare.[46] That having been said, for upland farmers at least, meeting this level of stocking density is unlikely to be problematic.

Secondly, the set-aside requirements under the Arable Area Payments Scheme provide perhaps the most visible manifestation of changes in land use. The environmental impact of taking land out of production will be considered later; but for the time being it may be noted that the overall effect has been less marked than anticipated. Not least, the set-aside rate has dropped away from its initial figure of 15 per cent; and, to the extent that land must be set aside, UK farmers have made good use of the exception which permits industrial, non-food use.[47]

A third response has been an increase in diversification from traditional agriculture. The scope for diversification has long been recognized by the UK government; and targeted financial incentives began to be made available in the 1980s. For example, the Farm Diversification Grant Scheme 1987 made available capital grants;[48] and the Farm Business Non-Capital Grant Scheme 1988 made available income grants.[49] Further, under the five-year, voluntary set-aside scheme (which pre-dated the Arable Area Payments Scheme), farmers could receive payment for converting land to non-agricultural use.[50]

However, the most comprehensive legislation for the promotion of alternative land uses is perceived to be the 1995 Act. As indicated, it was an express objective of the 1995 Act to enable the industry to respond to

---

[46] Council Regulation (EEC) 805/68, Art. 4g, JO L148/24, 28 June 1968, as amended by Council Regulation (EEC) 2066/92, OJ L215/49, 30 July 1992.

[47] For the detailed rules as first implemented, see Commission Regulation (EEC) 334/93, OJ L38/12, 16 Feb. 1993.

[48] SI 1987/1949 (as amended).   [49] SI 1988/1125 (as amended).

[50] Set-Aside Regulations 1988 SI 1988/1352 (as amended).

changes in policy and market conditions; and two provisions directed to achieving this end may be reiterated. First, the notice conditions permit increased non-agricultural use over the course of the tenancy, it being necessary only that the character of the tenancy be primarily or wholly agricultural at its beginning. Secondly, the definition of 'tenant's improvement' has been expanded beyond that contained in the 1986 Act so as to reward the adoption of alternative land uses. Not least, it expressly covers unimplemented planning permissions.[51] At the same time the 1995 Act contains a different measure of compensation for improvements from that applicable under the 1986 Act. Under the 1986 Act the measure of compensation for long-term improvements is the amount by which the improvement increases the value of the agricultural holding as a holding, having regard to its character and situation and the average requirements of tenants reasonably skilled in husbandry.[52] By contrast, under the 1995 Act the measure (in all cases but planning permissions) is simply the amount by which the improvement increases the value of the holding on termination as land comprised in a tenancy.[53] There is no longer any reference to the value of an *agricultural* holding.

In these ways the 1995 Act could be said to meet the objective of providing an enduring framework which can accommodate change. Above all, the notice conditions have introduced greater certainty where the tenant seeks to diversify from traditional agriculture.[54] Both landlord and tenant can be sure that, provided there is sufficient commercial farming to satisfy the business conditions,[55] the farm business tenancy regime will be applicable—even though agriculture ceases to be the primary form of land use.

That having been said, there are factors which suggest that the 1995 Act may fail to deliver substantially greater investment in non-agricultural enterprises. First, the courts had not in fact proved inimical to diversifying tenants under the agricultural holdings legislation. For example, in *Wetherall* v. *Smith* the Court of Appeal took the line that statutory protection would not be lost unless, during the two years preceding service of the notice to quit, agricultural use had been 'wholly or substantially abandoned'.[56] Moreover, in *Short* v. *Greeves* the tenant remained the tenant of an agricultural holding even though the trial judge had found that, on expansion of a

---

[51] ss. 18 and 21 address issues of especial relevance to planning permissions.

[52] 1986 Act, s. 66(1).   [53] 1995 Act, s. 20(1).

[54] On this aspect, see Rodgers, 'Reforming Land Tenure: Farm Business Tenancies and the Rural Economy' [1996] Conveyancer 164–85.

[55] The 1995 Act does not specify the extent of commercial farming necessary to constitute commercial farming of *part* of the land. Accordingly, this requirement could prove contentious.

[56] [1980] 2 All ER 530, *per* Sir David Cairns at 538.

garden centre, some 60 per cent of turnover was being derived from garden requisites and bought-in items.[57]

Secondly, the general effect of the 1995 Act is that tenants are subject to a regime which affords less security than either the agricultural holdings legislation or, indeed, the commercial code of the Landlord and Tenant Act 1954. This factor—and the large number of short-term farm business tenancies[58]—may outweigh the advantages of the specific measures which encourage alternative land uses.

Thirdly, it may be argued that the planning legislation was creating as great a barrier to diversification as the agricultural holdings legislation. By way of contrast with *Short* v. *Greeves*, sales of imported produce above a *de minimis* level appear to constitute a material change of use from agriculture, so requiring planning permission.[59] Moreover, under the agricultural holdings legislation the very grant of planning permission may prompt a landlord to serve notice to quit in reliance on either a contractual provision or Case B in Schedule 3 to the 1986 Act.[60]

These difficulties raised by the planning system have received widespread recognition; and, indeed, they were specifically addressed in the White Paper, *Rural England—a Nation Committed to a Living Countryside*. This included a commitment to publish a guide for local planning authorities to promote good practice in planning for rural diversification; a commitment to issue a consultation paper on the operation of a new rural business use class; and a commitment to set in motion further revision of Planning Policy Guidance note 7 on *The Countryside and the Rural Economy* (PPG 7), so as to allow, *inter alia*, greater discrimination in favour of the reuse of rural buildings for business rather than residential purposes. The first of these commitments was quickly carried into effect by publication of *Planning for Rural Diversification: a Good Practice Guide*;[61] and a revised PPG 7 was issued early in 1997. However, following consultation, the introduction of a rural business use class is not to be pursued.

---

[57] [1988] 08 EG 109. See also *Gold* v. *Jacques Amand Ltd.* (1992) 63 P & CR 1.

[58] See e.g. *The Central Association of Agricultural Valuers Annual Tenanted Farms Survey 1996*.

[59] See e.g. *Williams* v. *Minister of Housing and Local Government* (1967) 65 LGR 495; and *Allen* v. *Secretary of State for the Environment and Reigate and Banstead Borough Council* [1990] JPL 340.

[60] See e.g. *Fowler* v. *Secretary of State for the Environment and North Wiltshire District Council* [1993] JPL 365. As with Case E (*ante*), the only recourse for the tenant served with a notice under Case B is to contest the reason given in the notice.

[61] Department of the Environment (London: HMSO, 1995).

Specific Property Issues Raised by Controls on Food Production

Turning to specific property issues raised by controls on food production, two may be addressed: first, the extent to which production controls may legitimately restrict the use of agricultural land; and, secondly, the extent to which quota forms 'part of' or 'an interest in' land.

With regard to the first of these issues, it has already been seen that milk quotas were regarded as central to the survival of the Common Agricultural Policy. Moreover, the initial legislation also stated that their prompt introduction was a matter 'of overwhelming public interest'.[62] Against this background it is perhaps not surprising that challenges to the very principle of production control have met with little success.[63] Indeed, as long ago as 1980 the European Court of Justice could state that 'the laying down of quotas based on a reference period is a customary procedure in Community law and it is appropriate when it is necessary to check production in a particular sector'.[64] Farmers have contended that such measures infringe the right to property, a right guaranteed in the Community legal order. This argument was adopted by the applicant in the case of *Hauer* v. *Land Rheinland-Pfalz*, which concerned a prohibition on the planting of new vines.[65] The European Court emphasized that a prohibition of this kind could not be said to deprive the owner of property, since there was still freedom to dispose of it or to put it to other uses which were not prohibited. Rather, the measure operated as a restriction on the *use* of property. Having made this distinction, it was affirmed that restrictions on the use of property are valid to the extent that they are necessary for the protection of the general interest. Moreover, it was noted that in all Member States legislation gave concrete expression to the social function of the right to property. Accordingly, 'in all the Member States there is legislation on agriculture and forestry, the water supply, the protection of the environment and town and country planning, which imposes restrictions, sometimes appreciable, on the use of real property'.[66] On this basis it was impossible for the applicant to dispute the principle that the Community could restrict the exercise of the right to property in the context of a common organization of the market and for the purposes of a structural policy. It remained to ascertain whether the disputed provisions on the facts corresponded with objectives of general interest pursued by the Community or whether, with regard to the aim pursued, they gave rise to a 'disproportionate and intolerable interference with the rights of the owner, impinging upon the very substance of

---

[62] Preamble, Council Regulation (EEC) 857/84, OJ L90/13, 1 Apr. 1984.

[63] For a full discussion of the impact of Community law on agricultural operators, see e.g. Barents, *The Agricultural Law of the EC* (Deventer: Kluwer, 1994), 305–61.

[64] Case 138/79, *Roquette Frères* v. *Council* [1980] ECR 3333 at 3359.

[65] Case 44/79, [1979] ECR 3727.   [66] Ibid., at 3746–7.

the right to property'.[67] On the facts, they were held to be a proper limitation on the exercise of that right.

Although *Hauer* was specifically concerned with a prohibition on the planting of new vines, the issues were closely analogous to those raised by the imposition of quota regimes; and the judicial approach has rested on the same foundations. Thus, in the Irish case of *Lawlor* v. *Minister for Agriculture* the milk quota system was held valid in that it constituted no more than a delimitation of the exercise of certain rights of ownership, with a view to reconciling the exercise of ownership rights with the exigencies of the common good.[68] It did not attempt to abolish the right of private ownership or the general right to transfer, bequeath, or inherit property. For that reason no compensation was due. Accordingly, provided the requisite criteria are met, the imposition of production controls would seem to be a legitimate arm of Community policy.

Substantial difficulties have been created by the second issue, the extent to which quota forms 'part of' or 'an interest in' land. Resolution of this issue has long been recognized to give rise to important practical consequences, these being magnified by the high prices paid for both milk quotas and sheep and suckler cow quotas. For example, in the 1994/5 milk year permanent transfers of milk quota were concluded for sums in excess of 70 pence per litre. With such sums at stake, it has proved critical to determine, for example, whether or not quota follows the land on sale or on the grant or termination of a lease; and whether quota is a separate asset for tax purposes.

In this context the role of the implementing legislation cannot be overemphasized. However, it cannot always be expected to provide clear-cut answers. Not least, the degree of attachment to land may vary in order to meet differing Community priorities. That having been said, it would appear broadly that milk quota is 'linked' to the holding; and that sheep and suckler cow quotas remain a separate asset in the hands of the producer.

In the case of milk quota, it is provided that on the sale, lease, or transfer by inheritance of a holding, the corresponding quota or 'reference quantity'[69] is to be transferred to the producer who takes over the holding.[70] This is consistent with the general principle that land transactions are

---

[67] Case 44/79, [1979] ECR 3727 at 3747.

[68] [1990] 1 IR 356. For a similar view that the milk quota regime operates as a straightforward limitation on the use of real property, see the written observations of the Council in Case C–44/89, *Von Deetzen* v. *Hauptzollamt Oldenburg* [1991] ECR I-5119 at I-5129.

[69] The Community legislation consistently adopts the expression 'reference quantity' as opposed to 'quota'. However, the expression 'quota' is widely employed and, besides, is found in the UK legislation.

[70] For the current Community legislation, see Council Regulation (EEC) 3950/92, Art. 7, OJ L405/1, 31 Dec. 1992.

LAND AND AGRICULTURAL PRODUCTION

required to trigger transfers of milk quota, the purpose being to discourage speculation in quota as a free-standing asset.[71] Notwithstanding the numerous amendments to the milk quota legislation, the primacy of the general principle does continue, as articulated by both the European Court of Justice[72] and the UK national courts.[73] However, there have always been exceptions. For example, the initial legislation provided that, in return for compensation, producers could undertake to cease milk production definitively; and that their quota would be detached from the holding and added to the national reserve.[74] This derogation was justified on the basis that it promoted desirable restructuring of milk production. Further, there has been increasing scope to effect temporary transfers of quota for the currency of a milk year ('quota leasing') without any requirement for a land transaction;[75] and Council Regulation (EEC) 3950/92 now authorizes *inter alia* permanent transfers of quota without land (or vice versa) 'with the aim of improving the structure of milk production at the level of the holding or to allow for extensification of production'.[76]

The general principle, therefore, bends to meet specific policy requirements; but the price is some confusion as to the extent to which quota is 'part of' or 'an interest in' land. This confusion has been exacerbated by the UK practice of trading in quota through the medium of short-term leases. These short-term leases (which in England and Wales must be for a period of not less than ten months[77]) are apprehended to trigger a permanent transfer of quota; but in reality the land transaction is ancillary to the main purpose of transferring the quota.[78] Indeed, for Capital Gains Tax purposes at least, quota so transferred has been held to constitute a separate asset.[79]

By contrast, the position would seem to be somewhat clearer in the case of sheep and suckler cow quotas. When individual limits were placed on entitlement to premiums, the implementing legislation expressly referred to

[71] See e.g. the written observations of the Commission in Case 5/88, *Wachauf* v. *Bundesamt für Ernährung und Forstwirtschaft* [1989] ECR 2609 at 2618.

[72] See e.g. Case C–98/91, *Herbrink* v. *Minister van Landbouw, Natuurbeheer en Visserij* [1994] ECR I-223.

[73] See e.g. *Faulks* v. *Faulks* [1992] 15 EG 82; and *Davies* v. *H & R Ecroyd* [1996] 30 EG 97.

[74] Council Regulation (EEC) 857/84, Art. 4(1)(a), (2), OJ L90/13, 1 Apr. 1984. No such schemes are currently operating in the UK.

[75] For the current legislation see Council Regulation (EEC) 3950/92, Art. 6, OJ L405/1, 31 Dec. 1992; and Dairy Produce Quotas Regulations 1997 SI 1997/733, Reg. 13.

[76] Art. 8, OJ L405/1, 31 Dec. 1992. The UK has implemented only transfers of quota without land, not transfers of land without quota. For the current legislation, see Dairy Produce Quotas Regulations 1997 SI 1997/733, Reg. 11.

[77] Dairy Produce Quotas Regulations 1997 SI 1997/733, Reg. 7(5)(a)(ii).

[78] For analysis of this 'somewhat artificial short leasing device', see *Harries* v. *Barclays Bank plc*, unreported, High Court, 20 Dec. 1995.

[79] *Cottle* v. *Coldicott* [1995] SpC 40.

the producer-linked nature of the schemes, as opposed to any link with land.[80] The consequences for landlords were at once recognized. Whereas in the case of milk quotas any permanent transfer during the currency of a lease is subject to landlord's consent,[81] the legislation imposes no such restraint in the case of sheep and suckler cow quotas. Accordingly, there is nothing in principle to prevent a departing tenant from removing sheep or suckler cow quota from the holding. Particular difficulties are faced by landlords of upland farms where the scope for alternative forms of agriculture are limited. If they wish to take the farm in hand, they may need to acquire quota. If they prefer to relet, they may need to attract an incoming tenant with existing quota or the resources to acquire quota—in either case giving rise to injurious effect on rental income.[82] Against this background it was argued in *R. v. Minister of Agriculture, Fisheries and Food, ex p. Country Landowners Association* that Member States should be required to introduce a compensation mechanism for landowners.[83] The European Court rejected the claim: no such obligation was placed on Member States either by the regulations in question or by any general principle of Community law.[84]

THE PROMOTION OF SUSTAINABLE AND
ENVIRONMENTALLY SOUND LAND USE

Over recent years the promotion of environmental measures has been readily articulated. Such measures, highly acceptable in political terms, would seem to provide an alternative focus for an agricultural industry widely perceived as devoted to the maximizing of production. The calls for change have found concrete expression in a plethora of schemes; and emphasis may

[80] See Commission Regulation (EEC) 3567/92, Art. 13, OJ 1992, L362/41, 11 Dec. 1992 (in the case of sheep quotas); and Commission Regulation (EEC) 3886/92, Art. 39, OJ L391/20, 31 Dec. 1992 (in the case of suckler cow quotas).

[81] See Dairy Produce Quotas Regulations 1997 SI 1997/733, Regs. 7(2)(b) and 11(2)(b).

[82] On this account, *inter alia*, the House of Lords passed a Motion that the Sheep Annual Premium and Suckler Cow Premium Quotas Regulations 1993 SI 1993/1626 did not contain adequate measures to tackle the adverse economic effects which arise from the transferability of quotas away from particular holdings or to protect vulnerable livestock rearing areas and the communities that depend on them (HL Deb. (18 Oct. 1993), 549, cc. 445–94).

[83] Case C-38/94, [1995] ECR I-3875.

[84] At the same time the ECJ noted measures already taken by the UK which had the effect of cushioning the blow for landlords. Not least, where a producer permanently transfers quota separately from the holding, 15% of the quota is diverted without payment to the national reserve (15% being the maximum amount permitted under the Community legislation). For the UK legislation then in force, see Sheep Annual Premium and Suckler Cow Premium Quotas Regulations 1993 SI 1993/1626, Reg. 6(1). For the current UK legislation, see Sheep Annual Premium and Suckler Cow Premium Quotas Regulations 1997 SI 1997/2844, Reg. 5(1).

be laid on those implemented to comply with the 'Agri-Environmental Regulation'.[85] The effect of that Regulation may be seen, for example, in the creation of the Moorland Scheme and the Countryside Stewardship Scheme, and in extensions to the Environmentally Sensitive Areas Scheme. Indeed, over one million hectares are now covered by the twenty-two English Environmentally Sensitive Areas.[86] A further development of considerable importance is the introduction of Nitrate Vulnerable Zones under the Nitrates Directive.[87] Farmers within such zones are subject to *compulsory* restraints *without compensation*, which contrasts sharply with the earlier Nitrate Sensitive Areas Scheme, under which participation was voluntary and compensation payable.

At the same time environmental elements are being incorporated into quota schemes and the Arable Area Payments Scheme. A major advantage of these developments is that they are of such wide application. Whereas the schemes such as those implemented under the Agri-Environmental Regulation tend to focus on specific sites, the quota regimes and the Arable Area Payments Scheme are central to their respective sectors of UK agriculture.

By way of example, Community legislation states explicitly that environmental protection has become an important element under the various livestock regimes;[88] and, with this purpose in view, the UK has, *inter alia*, introduced penalties for overgrazing or the use of unsuitable supplementary feeding methods. Such penalties are potentially draconian, extending to the recovery of premiums.[89] With regard to the Arable Area Payments Scheme, the set-aside obligations have long been regarded as an opportunity to promote conservation. Indeed, Council Regulation (EEC) 1765/92 expressly recites that land set aside has to be cared for so as to meet certain minimum

---

[85] Council Regulation (EEC) 2078/92, OJ L215/85, 30 July 1992. On this aspect, generally, see e.g. Rodgers, 'Conservation and Land Use', in Lennon and Mackay (eds.), *Agricultural Law, Tax and Finance* (loose-leaf edn., London: Longmans, 1998); Reid, *Nature Conservation Law* (Edinburgh: W. Green/Sweet & Maxwell, 1994); and Whitby (ed.), *The European Environment and CAP Reform: Policies and Prospects for Conservation* (Wallingford: Oxon: CAB International, 1996).

[86] MAFF News Release 190/96.

[87] 91/676/EEC, OJ L375/1, 31 Dec. 1991. For the implementing legislation in England and Wales, see Protection of Water against Agricultural Nitrate Pollution (England and Wales) Regulations 1996 SI 1996/888.

[88] Council Regulation (EC) 233/94, OJ L30/9, 3 Feb. 1994 (in the case of the sheepmeat and goatmeat regime); and Council Regulation (EEC) 125/93, OJ L18/1, 27 Jan. 1993, and Council Regulation (EC) 3611/93, OJ L328/7, 29 Dec. 1993 (in the case of the beef and veal regime).

[89] See e.g. Sheep Annual Premium Regulations 1992 SI 1992/2677, as amended by Sheep Annual Premium (Amendment) Regulations 1994 SI 1994/2741.

environmental standards.[90] However, while the Scheme did from the start prohibit, *inter alia*, general use of fertilizers and pesticides on set-aside land,[91] the implementation of more specifically environmental programmes has taken some time to develop. An example of such developments is the recent express linkage between the Arable Area Payments Scheme and the Agri-Environmental Regulation, in that land entered into certain new programmes under the Agri-Environmental Regulation may count towards set-aside obligations.[92] This is justified on the basis that producers who take advantage of the amendment will still contribute to the reduction of surpluses. None the less, the more overtly environmental aspects remain for the most part confined to specific initiatives and options; and the legislature at both Community and national level has stopped short of imposing wide-ranging and strict cross-compliance.

The 1995 Act is also seen as a vehicle for the promotion of conservation. Although this objective was not expressly set out in the original Consultation Paper, it received considerable emphasis during passage of the Bill through the House of Lords.[93] In any event, there is no doubt that the earlier legislation as found in the Agriculture Act 1947 and the 1986 Act did not provide an ideal framework for tenants who wished to farm in a manner more beneficial to the environment. In particular, the rules of good husbandry as set out in the Agriculture Act 1947 required them to maintain arable land 'clean and in a good state of cultivation and fertility and in good condition'.[94] Failure to comply with these rules could lead to a claim for dilapidations on termination or, more drastically, could entitle the landlord to serve a notice to quit under one or more of the Cases in Schedule 3 to the 1986 Act. If the landlord were to obtain a certificate of bad husbandry, then he could serve notice under Case C; and prima facie it would seem there is a breach of the rules of good husbandry where the tenant cannot demonstrate active production.[95] Further, if the tenancy agreement

---

[90] Preamble, Council Regulation (EEC) 1765/92, OJ L181/12, 1 July 1992. For a full analysis of environmental considerations under the Arable Area Payments Scheme, see Rodgers, 'Environmental Gain, Set-Aside and the Implementation of EU Agricultural Reform in the United Kingdom', in Rodgers (ed.), *Nature Conservation and Countryside Law* (Cardiff: University of Wales Press, 1996), 111–37.

[91] Arable Area Payments Regulations 1994 SI 1994/947, sch. 2, part I, paras. 6–10, and part II, paras. 12–19.

[92] Council Regulation (EC) 1460/95, OJ L144/1, 28 June 1995, amending Council Regulation (EEC) 1765/92, OJ L181/12, 1 July 1992. See also the definition of 'set-aside land' in Arable Area Payments Regulations 1996 SI 1996/3142, s. 2(1).

[93] See e.g. HL Deb. (28 Nov. 1994), 559, c. 529. See also Sydenham and Mainwaring, *Farm Business Tenancies: Agricultural Tenancies Act 1995*, 5–7. For a full discussion of the extent to which the 1995 Act meets this objective, see Bishop, 'Reforming Land Tenure: Farm Business Tenancies and the Rural Environment'.

[94] s. 11.   [95] *Cambusmore Estate Trusteees* v. *Little* [1991] SLT (Land Ct) 33.

expressly provides that the tenant must comply with those rules, then the landlord could avail himself of Case D or, in more extreme circumstances, Case E (the former being applicable to remediable breach and the latter to irremediable breach).[96]

That having been said, in practice there is little evidence of landlords serving notices to quit on such grounds. Rather, it would seem that they have preferred to participate in the large sums receivable under the more lucrative environmental schemes, which have been held a 'relevant factor' in the assessment of the rent.[97]

Under the 1995 Act, as indicated, greater emphasis is placed upon freedom of contract; and the protection of the environment is no exception to this general rule. As a preliminary point, however, it may be highlighted that the 1995 Act retained the traditional definition of agriculture as found under the 1986 Act; and the rules of good husbandry have also survived (although, as shall be seen, not all their consequences). Accordingly, 'agriculture' still

includes horticulture, fruit growing, seed growing, dairy farming and livestock breeding and keeping, the use of land as grazing land, meadow land, osier land, market gardens and nursery grounds, and the use of land for woodlands where that use is ancillary to the farming of land for other agricultural purposes. . .[98]

While the definition is non-exhaustive, greater certainty might have been achieved by the express inclusion of, for example, land set aside. Indeed, such an amendment was advocated during the passage of the Bill through the House of Commons.[99]

Turning more specifically to environmental considerations, the incorporation of conservation clauses is left to agreement between the parties. While this was also the position under the 1986 Act, the emphasis on freedom of contract may encourage a more flexible approach and the dovetailing of agreements to suit the specific requirements of the tenanted

---

[96] Sch. 3 to the 1986 Act does, however, recognize environmental considerations by conferring a limited defence to notices to quit served under Cases C, D, and E. The defence applies where the tenancy agreement or any other agreement with the landlord indicates that its object is, *inter alia*, 'the conservation of flora or fauna' or 'the conservation or enhancement of the natural beauty or amenity of the countryside or the promotion of its enjoyment by the public'. If there is a provision to that effect, for the purposes of Case C the Agricultural Land Tribunal is to disregard any practice adopted by the tenant in accordance with it when assessing whether to grant a certificate of bad husbandry. Moreover, for the purposes of Cases D and E, the Agricultural Land Tribunal is to regard such a provision as not inconsistent with the responsibilities of the tenant to farm in accordance with the rules of good husbandry. That having been said, the efficacy of the defence is reduced by its dependence upon the incorporation of a conservation clause.

[97] *J. W. Childers Trustees* v. *Anker* [1996] 01 EG 102.

[98] 1986 Act, s. 96(1); and 1995 Act, s. 38(1). That having been said, there is a small amendment to the definition of 'livestock'.

[99] See e.g. HC Deb. (6 Feb. 1995), 254, c. 82.

land.[100] Further, the landlord cannot rely on the Cases set out in Schedule 3 to the 1986 Act; and, under the general law of forfeiture, it is not difficult to envisage a court granting relief where the tenant adopts non-traditional farming practices in accordance with a Community initiative.

None the less, there remains a danger that in the broader countryside the protection of the environment will be subordinated to the demands of commercial agriculture. In particular, the length of many farm business tenancies would not seem conducive to delivering an environmental dividend. Initial data have suggested that their average length is in the region of four years.[101] Although there has been a welcome increase in the number of tenancies for a period in excess of two years, this may in part be attributed to the fact that there is no longer such magic in the fixed term of more than one but less than two years, as required for *Gladstone* v. *Bower* agreements under the 1986 Act. In addition, there are firm indications that rent levels under the 1995 Act have been higher than those earlier pertaining under the 1986 Act; and there is a strong probability that tenants burdened with so high a rent will adopt farming practices calculated to maximize output in preference to any form of extensification.

CONCLUSION

Accordingly, notwithstanding its reduced status in the rural economy, agriculture continues to give rise to unique legal ramifications. The pressure to increase national self-sufficiency in food products may have diminished,[102] but the Common Agricultural Policy still confers on farmers many entrenched rights. At the same time, the level of expenditure is high by any standards—to the extent that payments under the Arable Area Payments Scheme have been instrumental in revitalizing the profitability of the arable sector. Further, such is the force of Community law that it can create new 'assets' in the form of quotas; and determine that milk quotas are 'linked' to the holding; but others (notably sheep and suckler cow quotas) are personal assets in the hands of the producer.

However, it is possible to detect changes in the direction of Community policy. Most notably, increased emphasis has been laid upon the protection of the environment. The number of schemes implemented under the Agri-Environmental Regulation has grown steadily; and there has also been a

[100] See e.g. Bishop, 'Reforming Land Tenure: Farm Business Tenancies and the Rural Environment'.

[101] See e.g. *The Central Association of Agricultural Valuers Annual Tenanted Farms Survey 1996*. As noted in the surveys, complete accuracy is difficult to achieve in view of such factors as periodic tenancies and break clauses.

[102] There are good grounds for arguing that the drive to increase national self-sufficiency has been replaced by a drive to increase Community self-sufficiency.

'greening' of the various livestock regimes and the Arable Area Payments Scheme. That having been said, in terms of expenditure the amount dedicated to specifically environmental schemes remains relatively low. For example, it has been seen that in the 1995/6 financial year the UK spent some £2,740.5 million on market regulation and other agricultural support measures under the Common Agricultural Policy. Yet, of that sum at best £117.5 million could be said to relate specifically to environmental initiatives.[103] In this light it might be argued that the simplest way to achieve an enhanced environmental dividend would be to impose stricter conditions on the receipt of subventions under the Arable Area Payments Scheme or the various livestock regimes. However, those measures are essentially economic and may not be the most appropriate vehicles for securing environmental benefits. Moreover, while their broad application is clearly of advantage, there is the concomitant disadvantage that it becomes difficult to focus on sites of particular importance.[104] Another significant factor is that such measures suffer frequent amendments to take account of changing economic imperatives; and, consequently, they may lack the permanence necessary for long-term gains.

At the same time it seems likely that agriculture within the European Community will become increasingly exposed to the forces of world competition. Conclusion of the Uruguay Round of the GATT Agreement may be regarded as an early step along this road. As a result there have been calls for wide-ranging reform, with emphasis on the need for a more market-oriented approach.[105] In the context of land tenure, the introduction of the more flexible farm business tenancies would already seem in line with such an approach. As indicated, there is evidence that large enterprises seeking to spread their costs have derived greatest benefit from the new regime; and it is such enterprises which would seem best placed to withstand the rigours of world market forces. However, the average length of farm business tenancies may not, as yet, meet fully the growing emphasis on diversification and the protection of the environment. Moreover, the demands of market forces may frequently clash with the demands of conservation. The response of large enterprises to increased competition may rather prove to be intensification of production.

[103] MAFF, *Agriculture in the United Kingdom 1996*, table 9.1. However, in addition £41.1m. was spent on support for conservation and other improvements under national initiatives; and £111.6m. on support for agriculture in special areas (in large part Hill Livestock Compensatory Allowances).

[104] For a full discussion of these aspects, see Rodgers, 'Environmental Gain, Set-Aside and the Implementation of EU Agricultural Reform in the United Kingdom'.

[105] See e.g. MAFF, *European Agriculture: The Case for Radical Reform—Conclusions of the Minister of Agriculture, Fisheries and Food's CAP Review Group* (London: HMSO, 1995). Less radical reform has, however, been advocated by the Europeen Commission in *Agenda 2000* COM(97) 2000.

17

REAL PROPERTY AND ITS REGULATION: THE COMMUNITY-RIGHTS RATIONALE FOR TOWN PLANNING

Denzil Millichap

Planning law in the UK could be said to reflect, implicitly or explicitly, a number of different rationales. Patrick McAuslan, for example, has suggested that planning law can be described as reflecting three different ideologies, of 'private property', 'public interest' and 'public participation'.[1] The first reflects the approach of the judiciary in the early years of state control, when they sought to limit the interventionist powers of public authorities by rediscovering natural justice principles. The natural justice in this case was that which enabled the property-owner to insist on appropriate procedural protections before the slums he owned (or was in the process of building) were pulled down. The second rationale, that of public interest, reflects the utilitarian basis of Victorian welfare legislation (but, as we shall see, may also be linked with the private-property approach). The third ideology reflects a more recent concern, which McAuslan identifies in policy, legislation, and case law. This is an ideology of ensuring that disadvantaged groups and individuals have a full say in decision-making procedures. According to McAuslan, by 'participating' actively in decision-making such subjects can more effectively protect their interests.

In the following I adopt a similar categorization: however (and here I part company with McAuslan), I suggest that, instead of 'participatory democracy', a more worthy basis for protecting the interests of community can be found in the richer concept of 'community rights'. The merits of this approach (first evident in case law relating to planning intervention in the 1920s) will be discussed, together with the way in which it has been eclipsed in the post-war era by the public interest rationale.

The following discusses these three rationales (private property, public interest, and community rights). The private-property rationale, used by the courts to protect private property, was borne out of an early Victorian concern to address the urban slums that had arisen as a result of rapid indus-

---

[1] McAuslan, *The Ideologies of Planning Law*, (Oxford: Pergamon Press, 1980). He discusses the three ideologies of planning law—private property, public interest, and public participation.

trialization. The community-rights rationale made a tentative appearance in the 1920s. It reflected the courts' acceptance at that time of the legitimacy of planning law's incursion on private-property rights: it then passed out of usage, being replaced by the rationale of public interest.

Unfortunately the various legal and non-legal sources where such rationales can be glimpsed do not always give a coherent and consistent expression to them. It is thus misleading to suggest that these three approaches, developing in a piecemeal fashion as they have over time and in different contexts, form coherent arguments justifying completely the decisions of those that rely on them. Indeed, as we shall see, there is frequently an overlap between them.

We begin with a brief discussion of the context in which the case for intervention in property rights was made.

PRIVATE PROPERTY UNDER ATTACK: THE 'SANITATION' CRUSADE

Public Health Act 1848

The process of industrialization and urbanization in the late eighteenth and nineteenth centuries created a range of problems familiar to us all. Overcrowded and unsanitary dwellings were the hallmarks of the new urban areas. These problems were not adequately addressed by established concepts of private law. The negative impacts of urbanizing development, largely due to speculative building for the residential sector, did not come before the courts. The initial response to this problem was to take the form of legislation dealing with sanitation issues. Such issues, brought to the attention of the expanding middle class by, amongst other things, outbreaks of cholera, were to attract the attention of the legislators in the early Victorian era. Sir Edwin Chadwick helped throw some light on the problems of city slums. As a result of his efforts, various commissions and committees looked at a range of issues related to the urban housing problem.[2] The 1848 Public Health Act was the first major attempt to deal with some of the physical problems that had been generated by such growth.

---

[2] The 1830 report of the Select Committee on Public Walks: this committee was appointed 'to consider the best means of securing Open Space in the Vicinity of populous Towns, as Public Walks and Places of Exercise calculated to promote the Health and Comfort of the Inhabitants'. A Select Committee Report on Health of Towns was produced in 1840; there followed a Select Committee Report on Intra-Mural Interments (1843), a Report on the Sanitary Condition of the Labouring Population (1842), a Report to the Poor Law Commission (1842), and two reports of the Royal Commission on the State of Large Towns (1844 and 1845).

The legislation of 1848 set out to achieve limited goals and conferred limited powers on state bodies. Its primary focus was the provision of proper sewerage and water supplies. It relied on local authorities adopting appropriate by-laws to enforce rudimentary controls relating to the construction of housing. The 1848 Public Health Act thus made inroads into the rights of property-owners, whose main interest was in making money from speculative housing development. The 'market' did not guarantee proper sanitary arrangements and appropriate space-standards for housing nor did it prevent housing being let to workers at high densities. The 1848 Public Health Act sought to remedy these deficiencies by setting out requirements for water supply, drains, and water closets. Construction of buildings that failed to conform could lead, if the Local Board of Health 'shall think fit',[3] to the execution of remedial works by the Board, whose expenses could then be recovered from the owner.

Such was the initial response to the problem of speculative housing development, which catered for all social classes. The legislation signalled that property and property rights were to become the focus of intervention. It is not surprising that this was to lead to arguments about the rationale underlying such intervention, and to counter-arguments (found, for example, in case law) that attempted to protect private property. In many cases, of course, the underlying rationales were not spelt out clearly, and there were contradictions both within and between various sources of official thinking, whether judge-made law or government policy. Nevertheless, even during the middle Victorian era, the principle that the Englishman's home was his castle was coming under attack by way of the public health legislation. An important weapon in that assault was the broad discretionary powers exercisable at the local level. However, this assault was to be rebuffed by the courts

The Victorian Courts Respond: Natural Justice Rediscovered

The rebuff came in *Cooper* v. *Wandsworth Board of Works*.[4] This involved a local act (the Metropolis Management Act 1855) which, in common with other items of local legislation during the Victorian era, addressed the problems posed by speculative housing by instituting a prior notice system. This meant that the property-owner had to give notice, in advance of construction, to the regulatory authority: this then allowed the regulator (the Local Board of Works) to oversee construction of the sewerage and drainage services for the building in question. In *Cooper* the requisite notice had not

---

[3] This phrase, significantly, retains a central role in the modern planning regime: see Town and Country Planning Act 1990, s. 70(2)—the power to impose conditions on the grant of planning permission.

[4] (1863) 14 CB (NS) 180.

been given. The Local Board followed the letter of the law and demolished the partially built structure. The builder brought a successful action for damages. He argued that the Local Board of Works was obliged to seek the views of the builder, despite the fact that the legislation required nothing of the sort.

Erle CJ said:

I think the board ought to have given notice to the plaintiff, and to have allowed him to be heard. . . . I can conceive a great many advantages which might arise in the way of public order, in the way of doing substantial justice, and in the way of fulfilling the purposes of the statute, by the restriction which we put upon them, that they should hear the party before they inflict upon him such a heavy loss.[5]

The main argument used by Erle CJ in justifying this judicial amendment was that it was 'required by a due consideration for the public interest'.[6]

The comments by Willes J suggest that property interests were the central issue: 'a tribunal which is by law invested with power to affect the property of one of Her Majesty's subjects, is bound to give such subject an opportunity of being heard before it proceeds: and that the rule is of universal application and founded on the plainest principles of justice. Now, is the board in the present case such a tribunal? I apprehend it clearly is . . .'.[7]

Protecting private-property rights by judicial interpolation of procedural safeguards was thus justified on a public-interest basis. Yet care is needed with the terminology and its usage. It should be noted that, for the Victorian judiciary, public interest could appear to mean protecting private-property rights against peremptory state interference. This may not seem unsurprising in an age where private-property interests still informed the legal culture of lawyers and the courts. Yet, in the face of plain legislation that had such a clear basis in the public interest of addressing the urban ills of early industrialization, such an approach is still remarkable from today's perspective.

The courts in the Victorian era, in responding to the first attempt to deal with various 'environmental injustices' that were not amenable to remedy under private-property law, established case law which continued to affect administrative procedures for many decades after. In protecting private-property rights, the courts have been criticized for committing an 'abuse of language'.[8] We may also, from a perspective where property rights are often constrained on public-interest grounds, question the nature of the public interest being protected in the *Cooper* case: we might now say that, in reality, the court was really adopting a private-property-rights rationale. However, it is not merely the courts that provided examples of such

---

[5] Ibid., at 188.   [6] Ibid.   [7] Ibid., at 190.
[8] Such a characterization is found in Wade and Forsyth, *Administrative Law* (Oxford: Clarendon Press, 1994), 502.

linguistic acrobatics. The malleability of concepts is something that will also be seen in policy language, devised by central government, that justifies intervention on public-interest grounds.

THE BACKGROUND TO INTERVENTION: POLITICAL, SOCIAL, AND ECONOMIC REFORM MOVEMENTS

Before turning to the public-interest rationale in planning law and policy, it is important to note some of the diverse influences which prompted intervention in the landowner's development of his land. The importance of these various influences is to be seen in particular legal principles and institutions that currently provide the framework for planning law and the procedures employed in the exercise of planning powers. Some of these influences are also important because of their long-term economic impacts on land, particularly in the rural areas. The responses of landowners, developers, and others to such changes were themselves to create new planning problems and solutions. Thus political issues such as free trade and the franchise had impacts on the nature of intervention. The legal and policy basis of modern planning control cannot be fully understood without understanding this background.

Art, Beauty, and the City

We have seen that the role of public regulation in addressing unsanitary housing in urban areas was established in the mid-Victorian era. However, some reformers concentrated on matters that went far beyond sanitation and related themes, such as the provision of public parks and open spaces. The Arts and Crafts Movement is a case in point: this was not, on the face of it, concerned much with legal intervention in property ownership. It can be said to be a reaction against the rapid industrialization and its consequent impacts for both the physical and the spiritual life of ordinary people. The Arts and Crafts Movement encouraged issues to be seen from the viewpoint of the craftsman, the small neighbourhood, and the community.[9] The supporters of this movement harked back to a (mythical) past of the craftsman, where Art and Craft were fused in both the working and the domestic environment. In practice its influence on the development of town planning was most obviously felt by way of its impact on architectural ideas. The

---

[9] A good example is found in the life and work of Charles Ashbee—architect, designer, founding father of the School and Guild of Handicraft, and a town planner who worked in the UK and also in Jerusalem. See e.g. Crawford, *C. R. Ashbee* (New Haven, Conn.: Yale University Press, 1985).

movement thus influenced those involved in matters of urban design, an issue closely allied to town planning.

There was also a similar school of thought that emphasized the small-scale and local character of traditional towns and cities. A notable example of such concerns being of direct relevance to planning was the City Beautiful Movement. Its genesis is often associated with the Austrian architect Camillo Sitte and his work in Vienna. Sitte, who was allied to the Arts and Crafts Movement in Europe, exemplifies this exchange of ideas from different reform movements, many of which had impacts on early ideas of planning. The intermarriage of ideas from continental Europe, the UK (and the USA) was to be seen, for example, in the first edition—in December 1896—of the Chicago-based architectural magazine, *House Beautiful*. This included illustrations by Ashbee and other architects influenced by Sitte and others.[10] Such concerns may seem far removed from property law principles, but, as we shall see, they were to have an important impact on the legal criteria that came to be applied by the legislature, the courts, and public bodies. (The importance of the 'city beautiful' and related concepts was thus to find expression in the important statutory term—'amenity'—which was, and still remains, a key element in the statutory planning system in the UK. The importance of this term is discussed below.)

'Land Societies', Political Reform, and Free Trade

There was also a more radical tradition, in which arguments over political and legal rights intertwined. For some, the answer to the problems of urban squalor lay in radical proposals to alter the basis of landownership. Here, the 'land question' was taken as the real issue that needed to be addressed. This was, of course, a political issue with a considerable pedigree. For example, after the Civil War, there flourished early radical movements, such as the Diggers, which linked political and economic rights in the cause of land reform. In the Victorian era such issues remained very much alive. In many cases the issues of land and the franchise were intertwined. Thus 'land societies' were formed in the early Victorian era to promote landownership, not only for the purpose of enabling homes to be built but also to secure the franchise for home-owners. So, instead of housing built for the masses by speculative builders, the land societies encouraged self-build housing that did not create the unsanitary conditions associated with the normal form of housing development in the urban areas. Wholesale land reform was not to take place. However, despite this, the land societies did have a long-term

---

[10] Ibid., 407. See also Elworthy and Holder, *Environmental Protection: Text and Materials* (London: Butterworths, 1997), ch. 3, for a discussion of the various influences leading to the public health legislation of the nineteenth century and the planning legislation of the twentieth.

and indirect influence on the development of planning control. The reason
for this was that the 1832 Reform Act had given the franchise to '40 shilling
freeholders'. (This economic threshold was pitched squarely at the middle
classes and did not include the urban masses who lived in the speculative
housing built in the exploding conurbations of Victorian Britain.) Both
political parties saw land societies as a means of increasing their electoral
support among the middle classes and so land societies were promoted by
both parties: the aim was to gain the votes of those who had been helped
to acquire housing which would then give them the franchise. This link
between landownership, the franchise, and political support was exploited
by others. Thus Cobden used the link between landownership and the franchise to increase support for the anti-Corn Law League. The League's aims
were achieved with the repeal of the Corn Laws: so the legislation that had
subsidized the farming industry was swept away, and this allowed competi-
tioin from the New World to affect the UK's rural economy. This liberalization of trade was, until the reintroduction of subsidies after the Second
World War, to help push many rural areas into long-term economic
decline. This had various impacts on such areas by reducing land values. It
helped the expansion of urban areas and facilitated the growth of housing
on the urban fringe. Indirectly, the free trade movement's success in removing subsidies from the farmer was, therefore, to help lay the basis for a
radical vision for a new form of community—the 'social city' of Ebenezer
Howard.[11] The broad currents of social, political, and economic change
that created the climate for Howard's ideas were thus related to electoral
reform and the continuing activity of those advocating land reform. The
visionary call by Howard for integrating both town and country (the former with its overcrowding and the latter with its stagnant economy and
depopulated areas) was to be a major influence in the development of the
planning movement—and in particular the new-town legislation. In the
background, however, can be seen more fundamental and long-term factors that come to a head in Victorian Britain.

Addressing the social, political, and economic consequences of rapid
industrialization was something which concerned certain philanthropic
industrialists and landowners. They made their contribution (to improving
working and living conditions) by establishing model communities.
Notable examples of early 'private' town planning include Bournville, Port
Sunlight, Saltaire, and then (through Howard's direct involvement)
Letchworth. This enlightened approach, however, was not one which

[11] For a fuller account of Howard's 'garden-city' thinking and the degree to which it was
reflected in statutory provisions and policy initiatives such as those relating to London's
green belt, etc., see Millichap, 'Green Belt Policy and Law: A Study in Transitions', in
Herbert-Young (ed.), *Law, Policy and Development in The Rural Environment* (Cardiff:
University of Wales Press, forthcoming).

informed the practice of the average landowner on the urban fringe. He was keen to benefit from rapid urban expansion and the demand for more land. For such landowners the long-term costs in terms of health, urban services, and the efficient utilization of land were irrelevant factors. Such 'externalities' were irrelevant to the economic equations of landowners and developers. Intervention which threatened economic loss (by forcing owners to internalize some of those costs) was not going to be suffered lightly: the sanitation case law was evidence of that (as noted above).[12]

Bleak Housing

Other, less radical, approaches sought to address the overcrowded and unsanitary conditions in urban areas. Paternalistic Toryism, of the sort evident in the work of Lord Shaftesbury, also played a role in the development of planning and, indirectly, planning law. Lord Shaftesbury helped to form the Artizans', Labourers' and General Dwellings Company (Limited) in 1867. The Company built houses to rent. Its first venture was the Shaftesbury Park Estate in Battersea, which was opened in 1874. The importance for the future development of regulatory controls lay in the regular monotony of the street plan that dominated the design of this estate. It comprised long straight roads, small front gardens, and gothic and tudor decorative detail. Such monotony in the street plan was to be evident in the 'by-law' housing built for the working classes under the regulatory controls imposed by the public-health legislation. Paternalistic Toryism also had its impact on middle-class housing: the Noel Park Estate (Wood Green) was started by the Company's architect (Rowland Plumbe) in 1883 and was also to follow simple geometric patterns. It favoured a grid pattern, following the precepts of a former army officer T. J. Maslen. He, some forty years earlier, had proposed streets 'as long and as straight as possible'.[13] As a simple pattern book for other speculative builders who did not want to employ an architect, such models served to meet the standards imposed by public-health legislation (particularly those imposed under the codified public-health legislation in the 1875 Public Health Act) in a cost-effective way.

[12] The notion of 'externalities' has been imported into discussions of regulatory law from the discipline of welfare economics: see, e.g. Coase, 'The Problem of Social Cost', 3 Journal of Law and Economics 1 (1960). The term has now recently appeared in a House of Lords decision on the proper use of regulatory powers under the planning legislation—see the discussion below, under the heading 'Community Rediscovered?'.

[13] See Edwards, *The Design of Suburbia* (London: Pembridge, 1981), 53–4, for an account of Maslen (and the by-law housing style that later developed as an expression of his rather regimented approach to urban housing design). The purpose of straight streets was, in Maslen's view, to ensure that inhabitants would 'act openly and honestly in the sight of all': the narrow alleys, courts, and culs-de-sac of towns and cities had been seen as a source of crime, ill health, and other evils by many of those investigating the urban conditions of the time.

This rather functional (one might say, economically prudent) response to the sanitary conditions of urban housing in fact created a reaction. The bleak housing that was to be the hallmark of the public-health legislation fell short of the ideals of those more radical groups, such as the Arts and Crafts Movement. The sanitation crusade may have won its victory, but the crusading spirit demanded more. Attention now turned to the regulation of private development in order to promote amenity (and not only for public-health reasons). Landowners were soon to be required to meet aesthetic criteria as well as sanitary standards. The Arts and Crafts tradition thus combined with the unintended consequences of Tory paternalism further to erode the sanctity of property rights. By the end of the nineteenth century, then, these different movements and influences were having an impact on ideas about how the private-property-owner's control over the built environment should be regulated. Those movements critical of the rather limited response produced by the sanitation legislation were, in particular, to be important in the development of the modern planning legislation and its emergence from the narrow sanitation-based approach of the Victorian public-health legislation. Their influence is symbolized in the language used in the first planning legislation, the 1909 Act: a key term is 'amenity'.

'AMENITY'—A BROADER ATTACK ON LANDHOLDERS' RIGHTS

Community Rights and Landowners Duties

The bleak adequacy of by-law housing prompted the Housing and Town Planning Act 1909. This Act introduced new concepts into the legal vocabulary, such as 'planning'. Another was 'amenity': yet both of these terms were left undefined by the legislation. However, the general aim of the legislation was clear: intervention in private development was to address not only sanitation but also beauty. The arts and crafts/city beautiful aims underlying the legislation can also be discerned in the rhetoric employed by John Burns MP (President of the Local Government Board). In commending the new regime to Parliament he talked of its purpose as being to produce 'the house healthy, the home beautiful, the town pleasant, city distinguished and the suburb salubrious'.[14] The 1909 Act was clearly aimed at making good the aesthetic deficit of the public-health approach. The new communities that would be regulated by this legislation would be both sanitary *and* pleasing to the eye. The landowner would have to forgo even more of his speculative profits in order to ensure that the community had

---

[14] HC Deb., 188, cc. 949.

its interests protected. Such economic impacts were not going to be suffered lightly.

One landowner took up the challenge by seeking compensation for limitations imposed under the 1909 Act affecting his proposed development in Ruislip. In the case of *Re Ellis and the Ruislip–Northwood Urban Council*, one of the issues for the Court of Appeal to examine was the breadth of the powers granted to authorities under the 1909 Act.[15] The planning scheme in question had imposed a building line on some frontages preventing the owners from building too near the street. The authority argued that this was based on amenity and so qualified under the statute as a use of statutory powers for which no compensation would be payable.

Scrutton LJ had this to say:

In my view the express provisions of the Act of Parliament, when fairly construed, require me to give them a meaning which excludes Mr. Ellis's claim to compensation because he is not allowed to build right up to the edge of his land in a narrow street. I can quite understand that Parliament may have taken a view that a landowner in a community has duties as well as rights, and cannot claim compensation for refraining from using his land where they think that it is his duty so to refrain.[16]

For a senior member of the Bench (even though he was in the minority as regards the narrow matter of construction which the Court had to consider) to acknowledge that landowners owed duties to the community is striking. Parliament could legislate to that effect and at least one prominent judge was clearly able to accept that the rationale of private property could not justify judicial rewriting of primary legislation. The legislation had imposed duties on landowners and they could not evade them by asking the courts to intervene.

This approach also implicitly recognized that the necessary correlative of the duties of landowners is that the community has 'rights' against landowners. We might therefore rephrase the notion, expressed by Scrutton LJ, of property owner duties as 'community rights'. The case indicates that the judiciary was coming to accept that intervention, in private property, on the basis of a community-rights doctrine, was a basic element of the planning regime. The comment by Scrutton LJ, to the effect that 'Parliament appears to have sacrificed the individual to the welfare of the area . . .', reflects a utilitarian line of thinking.[17] The starting point is the community, not the

[15] [1920] 1 KB 343. The claim arose out of an agreement between the owner and the local authority—which was designed to settle a dispute that had lasted some years over different plans for development of the land. An arbitration clause was included in the agreement and it was the arbitrator's ruling that was challenged in the courts.

[16] Ibid., at 372.

[17] Ibid., at 370. The discipline of welfare economics (see n. 12) has its philosophical basis in the works of the utilitarians—such as Bentham. Returning to the jurisprudential roots of

individual: when this is acknowledged by a senior member of the Bench, then the implications deserve examination. This recognition of the importance of the community marks a dramatic shift in judicial perspective, which until then had been dominated by that of private property when interpreting planning legislation. The welfare of the community, not the profit of the landowner, was now the primary issue in construing the planning legislation. Private property had to bow to community rights, and community (at least for Scrutton LJ) now took centre stage when the courts were asked to construe the planning legislation.

However, this did not of itself provide a ready made list of these community rights. *Re Ellis* itself is not particularly eloquent on this point: it merely shifts the perspective from landowner to community. At the most basic we might say that such rights were to be expressed in the content of the legislation's planning schemes. These established general dimensional limits, building lines, and so on, for new residential schemes: so in one sense the precise content of community rights in any particular case was to be determined by the planning scheme, not the judges. The local authority determined (under central government supervision) the content of these schemes. The definitive source of community rights could thus, at this stage, be said to be the planning schemes themselves, not the judiciary. For the landowner this was probably not too much of an imposition: at least the planning schemes provided landowners with clear guidance (in the form of simple dimensional standards) as to what was and was not acceptable.

Natural Justice Eclipsed?

The *Cooper* case, discussed above, had relied on concepts of natural justice in order to protect private property. The strong dissenting judgment by Scrutton LJ in *Re Ellis* appears to mark a sea change in judicial attitudes to regulation. It might be thought that his approach was something out of the ordinary. However, he was not alone. Both Parliament and the courts had already circumscribed the natural justice case law that had been spawned by *Cooper*. Parliament had introduced a 'hearing' requirement into the statutory scheme dealing with unsanitary premises: this meant that the legislation was no longer silent on the right to be heard, so that, arguably, there was no longer a gap to be filled by judicial interpolation. The success of this move was clear from a case that was decided shortly before *Re Ellis*. In *Local Government Board* v. *Arlidge*,[18] the House of Lords found that the adminis-

---

planning will necessarily mean addressing that basic issue that has to be confronted by utilitarianism—its treatment of the individual and his rights—when outvoted by the majority. It also bears on notions of property rights. For a discussion of the influence of utilitarianism on planning, see McAuslan, *Ideologies*.

[18] [1915] AC 120.

trative appeal system (also set out in the 1909 Act) for making closure orders (covering property unfit for human habitation) was such as to put the case on a different footing from that of *Cooper*. The legislation now expressly provided the landowner with his right to be heard. The appeal had to be made to the Local Government Board—the body at central government level charged with oversight of the various regimes in the 1909 Act.

In *Arlidge* there had been a public inquiry: the legislative code providing for hearings had been triggered. However, the owner still objected to the appeal decision which went against him. His objection was founded on natural justice arguments, which went up to the House of Lords. Clearly, there was an important issue here: did the legislative scheme achieve its objective of keeping the courts at bay or would they require even more than just a hearing? The appellant thought so and argued that the courts should still intervene to make good the deficit in natural justice. In particular it was pointed out that the officer at central government level (in the Local Government Board) who actually dealt with the appeal decision was not the inspector holding the inquiry and taking the evidence: this, argued the owner, conflicted with the principles of natural justice—the *audi alteram partem* principle. The appellant had not been allowed to put his case directly to the decision-maker. The appellant also objected to the non-disclosure of the inspector's report, on the basis that this was contrary to natural justice. He argued that such non-disclosure meant that he could not know the full extent of the case that he had to meet, nor whether the inspector had made any material errors. Such failings were clearly apt to justify intervention by the courts, he argued, in a way similar to the *Cooper* case.

The House of Lords, however, declined to intervene, holding that the statutory scheme would not be supplemented by natural justice requirements imposed by the courts. It was won over (partly) by the fact that the decision in question was made by a government department. In dismissing the appeal, Lord Shaw clearly had in mind problems for the judiciary if it sought to rewrite legislation when the discretionary powers under scrutiny were those vested in an organ of central government. He said,

The words 'natural justice' occur in arguments and sometimes in judicial pronouncements in such cases. My Lords, when a central administrative board deals with an appeal from a local authority it must do its best to act justly and to reach just ends by just means. If a statute prescribes the means it must employ them. If it is left without express guidance it must still act honestly and by honest means. In regard to these, certain ways and methods of judicial procedure may very likely be imitated: and lawyer-like methods may find especial favour from lawyers. But that the judiciary should presume to impose its own methods on administrative or executive officers is a usurpation.[19]

---

[19] Ibid., at 138.

Lord Shaw thus characterized the process as one involving administrative (rather than judicial) issues. This meant that the natural justice principles applied so enthusiastically in *Cooper* were not to be applied when the statute had prescribed an appeal process of this sort. Natural justice and its role in protecting private property rights thus had their limits. Indeed, *Arlidge* is seen by leading commentators as an abrupt break with the *Cooper* line of case law. In terms of its approach to what is now called the principle of fairness, it has been characterized as 'a turning-point, in which the law failed to keep abreast of the standard of fairness which public opinion demanded.'[20] From the viewpoint of the public-sector decision-maker the judgment is clearly an important one. It supported action to tackle the urban slums and unsanitary conditions of Victorian speculative housing. Lord Justice Scrutton was, therefore, not alone in taking the courts into a new era: when he gave voice to a rationale that has the seeds of an approach which stresses the importance of community rights he was supporting Parliamentary action by way of welfare legislation. Both judges accepted that public authorities should be supported in their efforts to deal with the problems partly caused by the private-property rationale. Lord Justice Scrutton may have been in the minority on the technical issue before him, but his general characterization of the impact of planning was clearly in line with the new approach being taken by the judiciary towards a regulatory regime that did provide some modest form of hearing for the property-owner. The legalistic approach to protecting property rights was yielding to a utilitarian-based support for the community rights. Such an approach was ceding power to the decision-maker entrusted with statutory powers that affected property-owners. In the light of this the prospects for the new planning schemes did not look quite so black: Lord Justice Scrutton's views even hint at the courts playing a role in protecting community rights against attacks from private-property interests.

Local Government—Rules and Discretion

Although the judges were important actors in the development of planning law, the role of local government during this period should not be forgotten. In the nineteenth century, local government promoted local Acts through Parliament to give them powers to deal with the legacy of speculative domestic building that was quickly erected for the urban masses. Manchester is a good example of such local activity. The Manchester Corporation Waterworks and Improvements Act 1867, s. 41, created a procedure to declare as 'not fit for human habitation' any building in Manchester Corporation's jurisdiction; the Manchester Improvement Act

---

[20] Wade and Forsyth, *Administrative Law*, 504.

1871 provided for an appeal process in relation to such procedures. The efforts of local governments were boosted in the 1875 Public Health Act, which codified and regularized the various regimes and established a more coherent system for addressing such issues.

However, the role of the local authority was not diminished by this national legislation. Local authority by-laws continued to be an important vehicle for the implementation of this statutory regime. This use of local legislation continued well into the next century and formed the basis of planning control from the 1909 Act until the Town and Country Planning Act 1947. The planning schemes of the pre-1947 planning system were, effectively, no more than a refined version of the public-health by-laws: their legislative origins were signalled in the procedures leading to their adoption. They had to be laid before Parliament before becoming fully effective. They were vetted by the Local Government Board, which used model clauses as part of the process. Their legislative basis was made clear in section 54(5) of the 1909 Act: this provided that a town planning scheme, when approved by the Local Government Board, was to have the force of an Act of Parliament.

Three characteristics of the 1909 regime need to be emphasized. First, it entailed the use of interventionist powers directly backed by special legislation. Secondly, those powers were subject to central government control and supervision. The former was to protect regulatory intervention against judicial assault and the latter was to ensure consistency in the use of such powers across the country. Thirdly, these powers resulted in a set of prescriptive and well-defined limitations: they comprised relatively simple criteria (the central government models helped in this) covering heights, set-back from property lines, and so on. Property rights were affected, but the impact could be easily determined as they provided little room for interpretation by the regulatory authorities. (The straight streets and grid patterns popularized by Tory paternalism also offered a readily calculable basis for determining the extra costs imposed by regulatory intervention on speculative housing development.) Of these three elements, the first and second are evident in the regulation of development till this day. Simple prescriptive standards (the third element) are, nowadays, however, less evident. Simple rules mechanically applied have been replaced by broad discretionary powers.

Central Government's Shield against Judicial Intervention

Arlidge and *Re Ellis* suggested that procedural provisions to protect the interests of property owners were to offer a good defence against judicial rewriting of planning legislation. However, it was protection bought at a price. The self-reliant local authorities, who had done much on their own account in the closing years of the Victorian era to establish a strong local tradition of intervention, were now beginning to be tied to central government by a non-judicial appeal system. This was to complement the confirmatory procedures already in place as regards the making of by-laws, the mechanism employed for the sanitation regulation of the public-health legislation. The planning schemes introduced by the 1909 Act still followed the by-law model of the public-health regime.[21] So the legislative protection afforded by the hearing procedure further tied local government to the models and policy guidance of central government. The new planning powers, as they were amended and proliferated over the years, were thus to involve an element of centralized control that is still evident in the current system. The courts were no longer the primary check on local authority decision-making: central government was to extend its control over such activity by a range of confirmatory, appellatory, and supervisory powers. Model clauses for planning schemes were issued, which had the incidental merit of helping to prevent judicial intervention on the basis of manifest unreasonableness.

According to the classic statement, in *Kruse* v. *Johnson* by Lord Russell CJ, the basis for striking down such rules was limited: 'If . . . they involved such oppressive or gratuitous interference with the rights of those subject to them as could find no justification in the minds of reasonable men, the Court might well say, "Parliament never intended to give authority to make such rules; they are unreasonable and ultra vires." '[22]

Model clauses ensured both that arguments based on manifest unreasonableness would be hard to sustain, and helped to simplify the procedure of gaining central government approval: a proposed clause was easier to vet if there was already a model setting the standard. Models also allowed a consistency in approach throughout the country, though allowing for local flexibility if a good case could be made to the central government body. Clauses following such models would generally be less innovative than pro-

---

[21] All by-laws were tied closely to central government models and a confirmatory procedure: Public Health Act 1985, s. 184, provided that by-laws had to be confirmed by the Local Government Board; a similar confirmatory role is still exercised by the Secretary of State under Local Government Act 1972, s. 236.

[22] [1898] 2 QB 91, per Lord Russell CJ at 99–100. The 'unreasonableness' criterion was later taken up by the courts in the *Wednesbury* case: *Associated Provincial Picture Houses Ltd.* v. *Wednesbury Corporation*, [1947] 2 All ER 680. This has become the classic exposition of the 'manifest unreasonableness' standard by which the courts can strike down discretionary decisions. The term 'Wednesbury unreasonable' is thus frequently found in the case law: an example is the judgment of Lord Hoffman in the *Tesco* case—see text to n. 38. The planning law equivalent of the *Wednesbury* test is to be found in case law on planning conditions—*Newbury District Council* v. *Secretary of State for the Environment* [1980] 1 All ER 731 (also discussed by Lord Hoffman in the *Tesco* case).

visions drafted afresh by local authorities: less room, therefore, for judicial attack on manifest unreasonableness grounds.

Guidance from central government on the operation of the powers was a concomitant of such model clauses. In some cases this could take the form of generalized statements regarding the purpose of the legislative provisions or the appropriate use of the powers in general. An example of this is to be found (in the early planning system) in a Ministry of Health pamphlet of 1932.[23] This stated, in paragraph 1, that the objective of the town planning scheme was:

to provide that development, if and when it takes place, shall be in accordance with a plan which has been prepared in the interests of the community as a whole, industrial and commercial as well as residential, land owners as well as tenants, and thus help to secure for the future, so far as reasonable foresight can do so, the welfare and prosperity of the district and its inhabitants.

Policy guidance and model provisions provided central government with the tools to control the precise manner in which local government used a range of broad powers.[24] The role of such guidance in the planning regime cannot be overemphasized: the day-to-day importance of the policy framework imposed by central government makes such guidance even more important, for practical purposes, than the case law (even though that is not insignificant). (An example of central government enforcing its preferences as to policy issues is to be found in the *Tesco* case—discussed below.) The two-tier system, with central government controlling the local tier through various political, financial, and legal mechanisms, which has become the dominant feature of the administration of planning, was thus foreshadowed in the early part of this century. The shield protecting local government against judicial intervention was thus to be a tool of control in the hands of central government. However, such protections did not make the courts redundant. Local and central government were both to face, in the post-war era, legal challenges to their increasingly discretionary powers. Before turning to that topic, however, it is important to note how concepts of private law were viewed by another important group—the policy-makers who were to lay the basis for post-war planning.

---

[23] Ministry of Health, *Town Planning in England and Wales* (London: HMSO, 1932).

[24] The complexity of such guidance has increased dramatically over the years. The 1932 advice comprised 23 pages A5 pages. Current planning advice comprises numerous circulars, 24 Planning Policy Guidance Notes, 15 Minerals Policy Guidance Notes, and 13 Regional Planning Guidance Notes. Giving voice to community rights is a much more wordy affair than it was in the 1920s.

TENURE, PLANNING, AND LAND REFORM

The Crown Reversionary Interest Proposal

Further assaults on the private-property rationale were to be seen in the policy arena after the Second World War. The physical devastation of many cities created an opportunity for redevelopment, which were seized by a number of key policy-makers. Three special committees (Scott, Barlow, and Uthwatt) are particularly noted for their contribution to the broader issues of economic planning, land policy, and land-use planning. The resulting reports are generally credited with providing the conceptual basis for the land-use regime instituted by the 1947 legislation. For our purposes there is a particularly interesting discussion surrounding the use of the exist-ing schema of property rights as a framework for achieving radical land tenure reform. Uthwatt developed the notion of the 'Crown reversionary interest', which amounted, in effect, to a proposal for the nationalization of the development potential of land.

The Uthwatt Report had the following to say about this strategy:

348. The proposal submitted to us for the unification of the reversion to land is as follows:
That all land in Great Britain be forthwith converted into leasehold interests held by the present proprietors as lessees of the State at a peppercorn rent for such a uni-form term of years as may reasonably, without payment of compensation, be regarded as equitable, and subject to such conditions enforceable by re-entry as may from time to time be applicable under planning schemes.
349. The immediate result of the adoption of the scheme would be that the State as landlord would enforce town planning restrictions in the same way as is com-mon under the long leasehold system in England and Wales. If the covenant is bro-ken, the State should be given a power of re-entry. But that power of re-entry, just as in the case of a private landlord, would be subject to the jurisdiction of the Court to give relief. The practice of the Court in freely giving relief is settled and well known.
This method of securing compliance with town planning restrictions would have the effect of impressing upon landowners that landholding involves duties as well as rights.[25]

After noting that this proposal did not have the full support of all members of the committee the report stated that those members who did not object to this proposal 'hold it to be the task of this generation to take stock of the possible needs and views of succeeding generations with respect to National Planning. They wish to start time running in favour of succeeding genera-tions.'[26]

[25] Expert Committee on Compensation and Betterment, *Final Report*, Cmd. 6386 (London: HMSO, 1942), paras. 348–351.
[26] Ibid.

The excerpted material shows a continuing concern for the 'community', even to the extent of looking at the 'future' community and its 'needs'. Land nationalization was back on the agenda. It might even be said to be a pre-echo of the sustainable-development theme, where environmental impacts on a global scale are the concern of policy-makers. As policy initiatives across the full range of government activity are affected by global issues such as climate change, there have been indications (in planning policy) of reference to the global and temporal (i.e. inter-generational) dimensions of community.[27]

This implicit recognition that the needs of different communities (most particularly the present community versus the future community) may be in conflict points to the strength of the community-rights rationale: it actively prompts analysis of such difficult issues. All this emphasizes that there is a radical agenda underlying the community-rights rationale as it takes the community as the starting point, not the landowner. The Uthwatt Report's discussion of the 'Crown reversionary interest' was an opportunity to build upon the community rights message and community-first perspective in *Re Ellis*. It emphasized again that landowners owed duties to the community, including communities of the future.[28] Yet, the post-war era saw another perspective displacing that of the community. The perspective shifted yet again—this time to the decision-maker. This is the perspective promoted by the public-interest rationale. Yet this move to a public-interest justification should have been cause for some concern: we have already come across such an argument. It was used in the *Cooper* case to justify the private-property rationale—the rationale that takes the landowner's perspective. Looking back beyond the immediate post-war period to the Victorian natural justice renaissance we can thus see a potential problem with public-interest language: that problem is its malleability (a feature evident in the use made of such language in the *Cooper* case). The following examines in more detail the plastic nature of this particular conception.

THE PUBLIC–INTEREST RATIONALE

Public Interest and Planning Policy

Case law and policy in the early years of planning suggest that 'community rights' had some claim to be a key principle underlying the regime: the

[27] See Millichap, 'Sustainability: A Long-Established Concern of Planning' [1993] JPL 1084, for a discussion of 'community rights', 'amenity', and their relevance to the implementation of sustainable development principles.

[28] See Lichfield, 'Land Nationalisation', in Hall (ed.), *Land Values* (London: UCL Press, 1965) for a discussion of the Uthwatt proposals and related proposals.

community-rights rationale seemed to justify the new system and establish a counterweight to the competing rationale which had championed private-property rights. However, even in the early stages of the post-1909 planning regime there were signs of an attachment to the public-interest rationale. For example, a 1932 Ministry of Health pamphlet refers to the public interest in the following terms, (in the context of administrative delay in planning decisions): 'A lengthy interval between the passing of the resolution to plan and the formulation of definite proposals places owners in a position of uncertainty and of unwillingness to incur the risks of development, and this may be detrimental, not only to them, but to the public interest.'[29]

This language suggests that the public interest is advanced by securing timely (economic) development. This early reference to public interest does not, therefore, seem that far removed from the private-property rationale which was also protective of the property-owner and his economic interests. Although the focus is on the broader economic interests of an area, it is clear that public-interest arguments do not necessarily treat economic issues, and private interests, as irrelevant.

Current planning policy, Planning Policy Guidance Note 1 (PPG1), shows yet another dimension to the phrase.[30] Paragraph 64 of PPG1 stresses the importance of looking not at individual economic interests but at the 'public interest'. This version of the public-interest rationale is thus more of a reminder to local authorities not to use the planning system to favour one commercial enterprise over another. Advice on 'propriety' in decision-making thus now takes up four paragraphs in the guidance, with one paragraph discussing 'private interests'.[31] Paragraph 60 starts with the phrase 'The members of the local planning authority are elected to represent the interests of the whole community in planning matters.' This seems to be the perspective championed by community rights. However, the policy does not follow this line. It references one of the main authorities on the scope of the planning system—*Stringer* v. *Minister of Housing and Local Government*.[32] The guidance goes on to say that 'the public interest . . . may require that the interests of individual occupiers should be considered. The protection of individual interests is one aspect, and an important one, of the public interest as a whole. (*Stringer* v. *MHLG* 1971.) It can be difficult to

---

[29] Ministry of Health, *Town Planning in England and Wales*, para. 38.

[30] Department of the Environment, *Planning Policy Guidance Note 1: General Policy and Principles* (London: HMSO, 1997).

[31] The guidance in PPG1 references the report by Audrey Lees, *Enquiry into the Planning System in North Cornwall District* (London: HMSO, 1993), which investigated a number of substantiated complaints about grants of permission that conflicted with policy clearly set out in the statutory development plan.

[32] [1971] 1 All ER 65.

distinguish between public and private interests, but this may be necessary on occasion.'

This rather unhelpful advice almost takes us back to *Cooper* and the perspective of the private-property owner. In paragraph 39, instead of a 'warning' we have some rather generalized purposive statements about the planning system:

The town and country planning system regulates the development and use of land in the public interest. The planning system, and the preparation of the development plans in particular, is the most effective way of striking the right balance between the demand for development and the protection of the environment. Thus it has a key role to play in contributing to the Government's strategy for sustainable development by helping to provide for necessary development in locations which do not compromise the ability of future generations to meet their needs.

This suggests that the public interest also involves striking the right balance between development and conservation. The reference to sustainable development implies that development must be both 'necessary' and also located in areas which do not sterilize or destroy important resources.

The policy-makers seem to have a rather confused idea of what the public-interest criterion means. PPG1 is thus unclear about the parameters that define the role of this particular concept. Is the overriding principle one of forcing property-owners to respect the aims of 'sustainable development' (and so protect the interests of future generations) or does the present-day constituency that elected the local authority members have the right to demand that its needs be satisfied—no matter what this means for future generations?[33]

Public Interest and the Planning Case Law

There is also some lack of clarity in the case law. One of the leading cases from the post-war era sums up the general approach of the courts to the seemingly unfettered discretion given to authorities when exercising their powers to impose planning conditions. In *Pyx Granite Co. Ltd.* v. *Minister of Housing and Local Government*, Lord Denning stated:

Although the planning authorities are given very wide powers to impose 'such conditions as they think fit,' nevertheless the law says that those conditions, to be valid, must fairly and reasonably relate to the permitted development. The planning authority are not at liberty to use their powers for an ulterior object, however desirable that object may seem to them to be in the public interest.[34]

---

[33] Confusion over the meaning of the phrase was identified over thirty-five years ago in the social sciences literature (Sorauf, 'The Conceptual Muddle', in Friedrich (ed.), *The Public Interest* (New York: Atherton Press, 1962), 183–90; Schubert, in 'Is there a Public Interest Theory?', ibid. 162–76).

[34] [1958] 1 QB 554 at 572.

We see here a reference to 'public interest', with the court acknowledging that planning conditions must fulfil planning aims and not pursue other goals. (This naturally leaves open the interesting question as to the scope of 'planning'.) Other references to the public interest are also found in litigation over the use of development control powers. Shortly after *Pyx Granite*, for example, the case of *Buxton* v. *Minister of Housing* suggested some judicial hesitation between a public-interest model (whatever that might mean in practice) and the older community-rights approach. In the *Buxton* case, the notion of the 'public's rights' was used in terms similar to the community-rights approach. As the court noted:

Before the town and country planning legislation any landowner was free to develop his land as he liked, provided he did not infringe the common law. No adjoining owner had any right which he could enforce in the courts in respect of such development unless he could show that it constituted a nuisance or trespass or the like. The scheme of the town and country planning legislation, in my judgment, is to restrict development for the benefit of the public at large and not to confer new rights on any individual members of the public, whether they live close to or far from the proposed development. The legislature made the local planning authority, under the general supervision of the Minister, custodians of the public's rights.[35]

The last sentence brings the two-tier system, the public and the concept of custodianship, into the picture. This approach seems to be closer to the community-rights perspective. Even though it emphasizes the role of the decision-maker, that role is clearly seen as having very special parameters. We might even discern something akin to a 'trusteeship' obligation being imposed on the 'custodian'. This is not something which has a significant role in the various statements regarding the public-interest rationale. By contrast, community rights appear to have a richer (and more coherent) content, focusing more rigorously on the decision-maker and his obligations in the decision-making process.

   The transitional case of *Buxton* suggests that community rights, in treating the decision-maker as a custodian/guardian of community rights, require that he act 'in utmost good faith', to use a term from trust law, in reaching his decision. This is a fundamental difference between public interest and community rights. The former has no intrinsic concern with the decision-making process as such: there is nothing in the phrase that serves to define parameters to constrain and guide the decision-maker. That is not so with community rights, where the phrase itself leads naturally to questions such as 'which community?' and 'whose rights?' Community rights, by asking such questions, impose on the decision-maker an obligation to address these issues: the community perspective is the starting point,

---

[35] [1960] 3 All ER 408 at 411.

but it is paired with a demanding set of standards applied to the decision-maker. If the courts were to take up this set of complementary perspectives, we would then see them requiring that proper account is taken of the various communities and their various rights. Community rights are thus given their dues if the decision-maker fulfils his guardianship duties. For all practical purposes the perspective is that of the decision-maker *qua* guardian: it is a more focused public-interest conception, one which stresses the duties of the decision-maker to the wider community.

This guardianship perspective of the community-rights rationale also provides the basis for differentiating it from McAuslan's 'participatory democracy' ideology. McAuslan advocates this ideology as it would lead to 'more open government, more searching debates on major policy issues, decisions bringing about positive discrimination in the allocation of resources in favour of deprived persons and groups in the community, and an institutional framework which allows those groups power, subject to appropriate safeguards, to determine their own future.'[36] The community-rights rationale, as briefly sketched here, shares the emphasis on openness and searching debate: these are some of the concrete elements in the decision-making process that guardianship requires of the decision-maker.

However, future and global communities cannot exercise their rights to be involved in decision-making in the way that McAuslan advocates. An approach based on participatory democracy does not seem to cater for those communities that are disenfranchised by time and space. In contrast, community rights, because they concentrate on the decision-maker and his duties towards such communities, enable those communities (even if only indirectly) to be represented in the decision-making process. Community rights are a better basis for ensuring that such communities are given their dues. Participatory democracy fails such communities as it appears to be rooted in the political processes that serve the present and local community—benefiting those who have the physical and legal competence to engage in the relevant processes. So the community-rights rationale attempts to counteract the 'tyranny of the (present) majority', to adapt a well-known phrase of de Tocqueville. It meets this challenge by shifting attention to the decision-maker and requiring, by way of legal rather than political mechanisms, that this guardian meet his obligations to define, express, and adjudicate on the various rights and interests in a transparent and accountable manner. This rationale, because it explicitly addresses the challenges for decision-making posed by a diverse (spatially and temporally) community, has a much broader perspective (spatially and temporally) than that of the public-participation ideology. It forces the decision-maker to address in explicit terms those factors that are implicit in describing,

[36] See McAuslan, *Ideologies*, 272.

analysing, and weighing the impacts (and risks) affecting the relevant communities. Yet the decision as to which community will be required to forgo
benefits (or endure disbenefits) is still one for the decision-maker and not
the court. The community rights rationale does not give decision-making
power to the courts: but in insisting on this rationale the court can justifiably require that the political issues involved in taking community rights
seriously should be addressed openly. With public-interest language such
issues are kept below the surface and the courts cannot easily insist on transparency. The political mechanism of the ballot box is left to perform the
supervisory task: yet this is precisely the mechanism which totally ignores
the rights of the future and global community. Public interest (as the term
is used today) may support the power of the decision-maker against the
property-rights attack of landholders: however, it does not subject the
decision-maker to the critical gaze of the community in whose interests he
is supposedly acting.

Despite all this, however, the orthodoxy of public interest has come to
dominate planning thought in the post-war era. This is largely due to the
policy guidance (now found in PPG1) which, effectively, determines the
mind-set of planners and even planning lawyers when engaged in their
respective tasks. One reason for the policy guidance taking on board this
rationale in preference to that first suggested by *Re Ellis* is that its rather general and unspecific terms mean that it can perform a number of roles.
Although (and particularly for the idealist reformers) planning for the
benefit of the community (and its various components) was the positive
clarion call, the day-to-day administration of planning required some more
mundane guidance. Another reason for public interest being dominant is
that it enabled those in control of planning to wrest the new system away
from lawyers and the courts: whereas lawyers talk of 'private-property
rights'—the *Cooper* case and related case law testify to the potency of this
approach—the planners and administrators were concerned with broader
issues of public welfare. Those concerned with 'rights' and their protection
thus clash with those concerned with 'public welfare' and its furtherance.[37]
The most obvious way in which the courts could therefore avoid conflict
with the executive was to adopt a legal analysis which supported interven-

---

[37] McAuslan (ibid.) provides a cogent discussion of the way in which the public-interest
ideology (of the administrators and planners) overcame the private-property ideology of the
courts and lawyers. My threefold categorization showing how the courts/policy-makers
have responded to regulatory controls covers similar ground: the rediscovery of natural
justice thus served to protect private property—showing the judges adopting the private-
property ideology; the prevailing rationale for planning is that of public interest—a rationale
that clearly equates with McAuslan's 'public-interest' ideology. However, the community
rights rationale differs significantly from McAuslan's ideology 'participatory democracy'—as
the text here indicates. McAuslan makes no reference to *Re Ellis*.

tion. 'Public interest' was the obvious tag, being already found in case law and having a degree of malleability that would allow it to serve as the justification for the use of broad interventionist powers.

COMMUNITY REDISCOVERED? EXTERNALITIES AND JUDICIAL EXPLORATION OF PLANNING'S RATIONALE

The Tesco Case

A view of property rights that starts with the community and the onerous burden placed on the decision-maker is one which has its basis in Victorian welfare legislation and the utilitarian justification for intervention. Welfare economics is another strand in this community-based perspective. Since the primary attribute of real property is (in modern times) its economic role, then an economic perspective on community rights would involve discussing the economic mechanism involved in planning control. An economic perspective on the planning system would stress that the decision-making process, triggered by a planning application, is the means by which the private sector can be forced to bear the costs of impacts that would otherwise be ignored. In this way the externalities are internalized—by way of planning conditions, and so on. This means that development (and, normally, the antecedent economic decisions made by vendors and purchasers) will reflect such factors (and the costs) in development schemes: so instead of the private sector (landowner, developer, etc.) ignoring those factors, the economic costs reflecting such issues are internalized. Consequently, the costs of tackling, *ex post facto*, the externalities are avoided.

It is, therefore, interesting to note that this description (from welfare economics) of the role of planning has only recently found expression in the House of Lords case of *Tesco Stores Ltd.* v. *Secretary of State for the Environment*.[38] In this case we can see an interesting attempt to look at the planning regime from a historical basis. The case involved two contentious issues that have been ever-present aspects of planning action: the relationship between

---

[38] [1995] 2 All ER 637. The case involved two rival applications for a superstore in Oxford. One applicant (Tesco) offered, as part of its development proposals, to make the local authority a payment of £6.6 million to construct a road some distance from the site. It was accepted that the new road would serve traffic needs largely unrelated to those generated by the superstore. The local authority, however, supported this development proposal because, *inter alia*, the payment would help meet a shortfall in the roads budget. The Secretary of State (dealing with both planning applications by way of his powers to 'call in' applications) decided that, in line with his policy advice on planning gain, he should not give any weight to the road element in the Tesco development proposals. The rival scheme was given permission and Tesco challenged the decision arguing that, as a matter of law, the Secretary of State had erred in taking this approach.

central and local government and the range of the externalities that can be addressed by the decision-maker. These two issues came together in a planning permission for a retail development, which was predicated on the developer assuming responsibility for an item of public expenditure—a classic planning gain issue, with the local authority taking a different policy line on the weight to be given to planning gain offers from that set out in government guidance.[39] The comments made by Lord Hoffman show how the courts may have started to look more deeply into the social, economic, historical, and political basis of planning in order to attempt a more sophisticated analysis of the role of the decision-maker.[40]

The Hoffman description of the background to planning and planning decisions, though welcome in terms of its historical, economic, and political awareness, has a number of flaws. For our purposes the most pertinent one is a continued adherence to a rationale of planning (the public-interest theory) that cedes the decision-making process almost totally to the public authority. This is evident in his discussion of law and policy on such issues in the USA. He notes that openness and 'economic transparency' are important aspects of decision-making in the USA and that the US courts also get involved in carrying out a sophisticated analysis on economic issues such as double taxation, and so on. However, Lord Hoffman then bluntly reasserts the quite different approach adopted by the English courts: 'My Lords, no English court would countenance having the merits of a planning decision judicially examined in this way. The result may be some lack of transparency, but that is a price which the English planning system, based on central and local political responsibility, has been willing to pay for its relative freedom from judicial interference.'[41]

The UK courts do not, therefore, see transparency as an issue of principal importance when addressing the broad discretionary powers of planning authorities. The Hoffman analysis may encompass externalities but the process by which these are internalized (by means of planning permissions) is subject to very little scrutiny to ensure that full account is taken of community rights. There is nothing about the importance of the decision-maker meeting onerous standards of guardianship. Local authorities are not to be subject to close scrutiny (appropriate to those in the position of

[39] For planning gain generally, see e.g. Loughlin, 'Planning Gain: Law, Policy and Practice' [1981] 1 OJLS 61, and Jowell, 'Bargaining in Development Control', [1977] JPL 414.

[40] McAuslan, *Ideologies*, 648–61.

[41] Ibid. 659. Lord Hoffman refers to two articles looking at the US experience: Purdue, Healey, and Ennis, 'Planning Gain and the Grant of Planning Permission: Is the United States' Test of the 'Rational Nexus' the Appropriate Solution?' [1992] JPL 1012, and Callies and Grant, 'Paying for Growth and Planning Gain: An Anglo-American Comparison of Development Conditions, Impact Fees and Development Agreements' (1991) 23 The Urban Lawyer 221.

trustee) by the courts. Although this is a plausible reading of much of the history of planning law and its underlying policies, it overlooks some relevant aspects of that history, especially the dissenting voice of Scrutton LJ in *Re Ellis*. If that fuller perspective had been adopted, Hoffman might have accorded more weight to transparency and accountability in the decision-making process. By limiting his survey to the post-war law, Lord Hoffman necessarily restricts his discussion to a system that is informed by a public-interest rationale.

CONCLUSION—FROM COMMUNITY RIGHTS TO ENVIRONMENTAL JUSTICE

The earliest attempts at addressing the problems arising from unregulated development of large-scale speculative housing met with judicial rediscovery of natural justice: this was justice for property-owners. A clear dissenting message came from the Court of Appeal in 1920, proclaiming that landowners now had duties as well as rights. Such community-rights language continued to echo (largely in policy language) down the years: it held out the promise of a more sophisticated approach, one which set the parameters for a more demanding standard of decision-making by those operating the planning system. However, a more generalized notion based on the opaque public-interest rationale has taken root. Its failings become ever more apparent as the planning regime is required to encompass broader horizons, such as sustainable development. In meeting the demands of future generations and communities, the need for a richer and more rigorous rationale will become more evident. The need for a rationale that actively examines the role played by the decision-maker in fully addressing the legitimate demands of various communities (differentiated along spatial and temporal lines) will become more urgent.

Rediscovering community rights would prompt decision-makers to address fully the trustee status conferred upon them by the planning legislation and highlighted by issues such as sustainable development. Decision-makers would have to make explicit their approach to describing and protecting the interests of the future and global community. These and other elements of the community can legitimately demand equitable treatment in the decision-making process. Fairness was, after all, a key issue for property-owners in the nineteenth century and continues to be a fundamental issue in administrative law today. We should remember that the courts responded to the concerns of those property-owners by rediscovering natural justice. In the late twentieth century they should respond to the concerns of the community by rediscovering more recent case law—case law that hints at a rationale based on community and doing justice on a broader front (one that encompasses the future and global dimensions of community). This will entail a significant step in our legal system's accommodation of a broader conception of property rights, a conception that already accepts that the planning system can supply the criteria for judging when the use of land is actionable on the grounds of nuisance.[42] Planning standards and processes, if informed by the community-rights rationale, could then perhaps also interact with, and modify, the private law principles relating to real property. This would result in a notion of real property that integrates landowners duties and community rights. Not only planning decisions but also the framework governing the application of principles of private-property law could thereby respond to the challenges facing property-owners and regulatory bodies. Such an evolution in the principles governing public- and private-sector decisions would thus help provide a principled basis for delimiting property rights (and duties). Such a scheme would enable both private and public law to encompass fully a range of planning and environmental issues taking the perspective of the community as a starting point. What we might then see—to adopt, with modification, the phraseology of Willes J in the *Cooper* case—are criteria 'of universal application . . . founded on the plainest principles of environmental justice'.[43]

[42] 'Control of building height is such a common feature of modern town planning regimes that it would be inadequate to say that at the present day owners of the soil generally enjoy their rights *usque ad coelum et ad infernos*. Although the primary responsibility for enforcement falls on the administering authorities, I see no reason why neighbours prejudicially affected should not be able to sue in nuisance if a building does exceed height, bulk or location restrictions. For then the developer is not making either a lawful or a reasonable use of landowning rights. This is to treat planning measures not as creating rights of action for breach of statutory duty but as denoting a standard of what is acceptable in the community' (*Hunter* v. *Canary Wharf Ltd.* [1997] 2 All ER 427, *per* Lord Cooke at 466).

[43] See text to n. 7.

PART FIVE
DOCTRINAL ISSUES IN LAND LAW

18

BEFORE WE BEGIN: FIVE KEYS TO LAND LAW

Peter Birks

Land Law is a complex subject. It is not in the end a very difficult one. It is less unstable than other areas of the law. Yet it is hard to get into. The purpose of this chapter is to make access easier. It is impossible to improve access to a completely unknown quantity. The first section, therefore, asks what kind of category we are trying to understand.

WHAT KIND OF CATEGORY?

The name 'land law' suggests a simple contextual category: all the law about land. The law does use many such categories, ordered only by the alphabet: all the law about aviation, banks, commerce, dogs, education, and so on. They take as their subject some aspect of life, just as a non-lawyer would identify it. But in this case things are not quite so straightforward. By the end of this section we will have formulated a more complex proposition: land law, as generally understood, is a contextual subset of a legal-conceptual category.

The Socio-Historical Context

It will help to start with some background. The role of land, and hence of land law, has changed dramatically since the Industrial Revolution and the rise of the limited liability company. The paragraphs which follow sketch in that change and two others.

The Managed Fund

For institutions and individuals with serious wealth, land has lost its central role. The managed fund has displaced the rolling acres. Land used to be the pre-eminent form of wealth. Landed property was the focus of dynastic ambition. Land opened the door to high social status and political power. A landed family had by that fact alone a stake in governmental power. Keeping land in the family mattered. That has changed. Land, important as it is, has lost its pride of place. For the mega-wealthy, land has become just one species of investment, just as agriculture has become just one more industry. Pension funds and wealthy institutions hold mixed portfolios. They hold some land, some works of art, and many shares in many companies. Rich individuals do the same. The dynastic urge has been translated, with one eye constantly on the tax man, into trust funds and private companies.[1]

The image of land tied into one family is therefore out of date. Among the technicalities of land law we shall briefly encounter the phenomenon of 'overreaching' which enables interests to be detached from the land and attached instead to the money obtained by selling it. Lawyers and legislators have encouraged the use of that mechanism and others scarcely distinguishable from it. Such mechanisms vividly illustrate the shift towards treating land as just another tradeable asset. The policy is to keep the land itself as easily tradeable as possible.

A pale reflection of dynastic ambition is the natural anxiety on the part of those who have the necessary resources to meet the family's needs for accommodation. That can be done through out-and-out gifts, though without achieving any layering to reflect the needs of different generations. Statute has recently made it easier to achieve that layering through the use of a trust of land.[2] Without a survey of the intentions of the very rich, it is impossible to say whether that limited facility will encourage in a minor key a recrudescence of the dynastic urge to tie up land. Even if it does, it will not be on a scale to challenge the hegemony of the managed fund.

The Fragility of the Environment

The notion of land as scarce and fragile is relatively new. The Industrial Revolution created a few black spots. Blake's dark, satanic mills were terrible to behold, but local. It is only relatively recently that we have realized that our transport systems, our power stations, our industrial processes, and our intensive agricultural methods have the potential utterly to destroy this green and pleasant land. The private law of nuisance, the historic role of which was to control annoying activities as between one neighbour and another, cannot sufficiently express the social interest in the safety of this scarce resource.[3] Protection of the environment means more social control

---

[1] On the basic structure of funds, see Lawson and Rudden, *The Law of Property* (2nd edn., Oxford: Oxford University Press, 1982), 38–9, 105–13.

[2] This facility has been hidden in the actual practice of what are called 'trusts for sale', but the new Trusts of Land and Appointment of Trustees Act 1996 has brought the matter out into the open, allowing beneficiaries in certain circumstances to have a right of occupation.

[3] For a superb account of the tort of nuisance battling with the Industrial Revolution, see Simpson, *Leading Cases in the Common Law* (Oxford: Oxford University Press, 1995), 163, on *Tipping* v. *St. Helen's Smelting Company* (1865) 4 B & S 608, 616; 122 ER 588, 591. The law of tort will not prevent obstruction of the flow of television waves (*Hunter* v. *Canary Wharf plc* [1997] 2 All ER 426) any more than deliberate interruption of water percolating through the ground (*Bradford Corporation* v. *Pickles* [1895] AC 587).

of land use. There will have to be more planning control, more conservation legislation, more anti-pollution legislation. The tradition of freedom reacts against this heavy public control, but there is no other way. The energy available to defend our freedom will be best directed, not against social control, but towards ensuring that we have an ethos, and a legal system, which keeps the necessary bureaucracy humane, incorruptible, and transparent.

Public-Sector Housing

Local government is nowadays a powerful force in the provision of housing, adding a public law dimension new to land law as it has been historically determined. During the Thatcher era the public sector experienced an upheaval, partly from shortage of money, partly from being opened to the private market through the right-to-buy legislation.[4] That legislation was driven by the vision of a property-owning democracy in which citizens would have both the independence and the responsibility of people of substance. Sadly some bad effects followed. The public-sector housing stock was diminished, and a fall in the price of houses left many buyers financially overcommitted. Many repossessions followed. It is too early to say whether the advent of a new Labour government will revivify the sector and replenish the supply of public housing. The public sector ultimately rests on concepts identical to those of the private sector, overlaid by principles of public law and a mass of highly technical legislation. It is in every way a part of land law, but, because of the mass of detail, it has become a specialism. As a lawyer you have at some stage to decide whether to make yourself an expert in that field. The same is largely true of the statutory regime controlling the relations of landlord and tenant in the private sector.[5]

The Core of Land Law

A target has a centre. Taking land law as a simple contextual category, we can identify at least five topics, all of which have already figured in the discussion. Four of these must on reflection be located in the second or third circles, just outside the bull's-eye at which we are aiming. They matter, but they do not relieve us of the intellectual necessity of mastering the core. Two belong largely in public law. One of these comprises the social control essential if the environment is to be protected. The other is the housing law which applies to local government tenancies. Within private law, a third unit lies in the law of civil wrongs and deals with the duties imposed

[4] Housing Act 1980, followed by the Housing Act 1985.

[5] Entry to this specialism and its relation to the public sector is now made easier by Bright and Gilbert, *Landlord and Tenant Law: The Nature of Tenancies* (Oxford: Oxford University Press, 1995).

by the law for regulating the behaviour of neighbours towards each other, especially through the torts of nuisance and trespass to land. Fourthly, there is the structuring of mega-wealth, the mission of the old Lincoln's Inn conveyancers. That is breaking away, not specifically land law any longer but wealth management. Its principal vehicle is the trust, often enough offshore, in which land becomes just one kind of asset in a rolling fund. Fifthly and last of all, there is the unit at the very centre of the target. When lawyers speak of land law, it is usually to this core that they refer.

Every business needs premises, every factory needs a site. For most of us as private individuals our home is the centre of our lives. Functionally, this core of land law has the task of providing the structure within which people and businesses can safely acquire and exploit land for daily use, to live and to work. To discharge that function, it has to have its own conceptual apparatus. The proper content of this fifth unit thus becomes the nature, creation, and protection of interests in land. Those interests and their implications are the conceptual apparatus of our land law.

The word 'interests' is slightly evasive. The law recognizes different kinds of rights, among them property rights.[6] By 'interest' we mean 'property right'. The category of all property rights (or, in other words and more simply, 'the law of property') is a legal-conceptual category. It differs from, say, the law of dogs in that its subject is a legal concept, the concept of a proprietary right. The core of land law is the subset formed when the conceptual category of 'property right' is confined to one context: the law relating to property rights in land. To focus on that core is neither to downgrade the importance of the units in the next circles nor to forget that in real life all the units which we have identified, and others, cohere together.

Land law in this core sense is, therefore, a contextual subset of a legal-conceptual category. There is a recurrent problem. Property rights in land have roots a millennium deep in a pre-commercial society in which land and wealth were virtually synonymous. The structuring of landed wealth, and the power that went with it, was then land law's principal mission. The subject of land law—the law, that is, of the recognized proprietary interests in land—is therefore intellectually entangled in a history not always obviously relevant to its contemporary function.

THE FIVE KEYS

The five keys have one-word tags: Time, Space, Reality, Duality, and Formality. There is a pervasive theme which has its own label: Facilitation. This might be said to be the string on which the five keys hang. There is

---

[6] For a discussion of 'reality', see text at n. 26.

also a complication. All five keys have to be turned together. Exposition is easiest when each point has a natural priority. Here there is no natural priority, and no expository device to achieve what King Arthur intended when he seated his knights at a round table.

Facilitation

Some areas of law are primarily concerned to inhibit undesirable conduct. This is most obviously true of the law relating to wrongs, whether criminal or civil. Even there, behind the inhibition, lies a facilitative goal—namely, to allow civilized life to be conducted free from the fear of harm. The wrong of nuisance facilitates the enjoyment of land, but primarily by inhibiting unreasonable interference. By contrast, other areas are primarily facilitative. The law of contract, for example, helps people do something which by and large they want to be able to do—namely, to make reliable agreements.

Like contract, land law is primarily facilitative. Each of the five keys, though some more obviously than others, can be seen as facilitating the achievement of goals which people routinely want to achieve. It helps very much to keep in mind what landowners and would-be landowners are likely to want. What sort of property rights will they want to grant or to acquire? However, the theme of facilitation can never free itself from the counter-theme of inhibition. Blackbirds have strong territorial ambitions. They fight like hell for territory. For the weaker, death is the only alternative to flight. Any ageing blackbird will tell you that the main threat to his territoriality is simply the territoriality of others. Human territoriality encounters all sorts of conflicts, between one generation and another, between one neighbour and another, and between individuals and the community as a whole. Such conflicts create a tension between facilitation and inhibition. And in that tension most of the difficulties of land law arise.

A landowner may be willing to pay a large sum for a permanent proprietary right to prevent building on the neighbouring land. The first instinct is to facilitate, but there are arguments the other way. Should he be able to sterilize the economic use of that land? In fact the law does allow such a right to be created. Restrictive covenants, as property rights, are a relatively new invention.[7] But there are millions of restrictive covenants, against building or, say, against erecting more than one house, or against using premises for the purposes of trade or commerce. But this kind of thing has to be kept under control. Suppose that the landowner is very rich and wants to buy such a right over one field after another, to the foothills of a distant mountain. He wants to preserve the view from his house, for ever. The law draws a line. Sterilization of that kind has to be prevented. The law has to

---

[7] Their root lies in the attempt to keep Leicester Square 'in an open state, uncovered with any buildings, in neat and ornamental order' (*Tulk* v. *Moxhay* (1848) 2 Ph. 774; 41 ER 1143).

facilitate, but it also has to inhibit, in order to achieve a reconciliation between conflicting interests. And that is why the law of restrictive covenants is intricate.

TIME

Although bits do occasionally wash away or slip into the sea, land is in general permanent. For most human purposes we have to regard it as lasting for ever. There is a powerful urge to deal in slices of time. It is not confined to land. The institution of the trust makes it relatively easy to turn all kinds of wealth into an enduring fund, and that facility in turn excites and to a degree gratifies the urge to deal in slices of time. However, it is the natural permanence of land which makes slices of time a dominant feature of land law.

Two Motivations

Why do people want to deal in slices of time? It is an urge which has been fed from at least two sources. One is essentially commercial, the other not.

The commercial motivation

Commercial motivation means, in plain words, the desire to get money out of land. There are all sorts of ways of getting money out of land. For instance, one can farm the land and sell the produce. The most extreme method of all is to sell one's whole interest in the land. That means selling the whole slice of time over which one has control. The largest interest in land—the greatest slice of time—is 'for ever'. In everyday conversation I tend to say 'my house' or 'the house I own'. In all probability, what I actually have in my house is 'for ever', a slice of time measured by the length of time the land will last. There is no harm in calling that ownership. That is what in effect it is. But in the technical language of the law that huge slice of time measured by the life of the land itself is called a fee simple.[8] The fee simple in the land on which my house stands is worth about £200,000. I could mortgage it or sell it. But there is another possibility. I could keep 'for ever' and deal instead in a shorter slice of time.

The commercial motivation for dealing in lesser slices of time is to realize in money some of the value of the land without giving up one's whole interest. The lease is the proprietary interest which most obviously facilitates this. I might let my land for a fixed number of years, say for ten years. If I go for that option, I have further choices. I could take a single capital sum, or I might prefer a flow of income in the form of an annual rent, or a

---

[8] The term is cautiously explored in connection with the history of this interest at n. 11.

mixture of both, say £20,000 now and £5,000 per annum by way of rent. Whichever I choose, the fee simple remains mine, though occluded by the lease. When the ten years have passed, the shadow occluding my interest will vanish, and my fee simple will once again be unencumbered. The reversion has value even during the ten years during which I am out of possession. If I choose to, I can sell it even while the ten years are running.

The family motivation

The primary non-commercial motivation for dealing in slices of time is concern for one's family. In obsolescent aristocratic terms this might be restated as a dynastic motivation. The idea of benefiting the different generations of one's family is perfectly natural. The desire to keep land permanently in the family or part of the family has been a routine temptation. The link between the ownership of land and social hierarchy having been largely broken, the dynastic urge to keep a specific piece of land locked into one family has weakened. The law now does everything it can to ensure that land is freely alienable and that any future interests granted to descendants are detached from the land and transferred to the fund represented by the money for which it is sold. Since the great reforms of 1925, anyone wanting to deal in slices of time other than leases, and less than for ever, has had to do it in equity, behind the curtain of a trust.[9] In other words, in front of the curtain there are now only two slices of time known to the law, 'for ever' and the lease for whatever time is agreed. All other slices of time once recognized directly by the common law have been abolished. Despite these changes, a proper understanding of land law cannot be achieved without knowing something of how the battle over time was fought.

The Evolution of the Doctrine of Estates

In ordinary language the sentence 'Mr Smith has an estate in Suffolk' suggests a goodish patch of Constable landscape of which Mr Smith is the owner. But in land law an estate is a slice of time. The doctrine of estates is the learning which tells you what slices of time the law allows or has allowed a landowner to deal in. A 'life estate' was a recognized estate at common law.

The life estate and the estate for another's life

Suppose that my great-grandfather, AHB, had a life estate in a farm in Suffolk. That means, in effect, that he was entitled to the benefits associated with ownership, but only for his life. Suppose he then sold and conveyed his estate to his brother, BHB, for £2,000. BHB would have been well

---

[9] Law of Property Act 1925, s. 1.

advised to insure AHB's life, for *nemo dat quod non habet* (nobody gives what he does not have). AHB could not transfer more than he had, and all that he had was a slice of time measured by his own life. By AHB's conveyance, BHB therefore acquired in the land a slice of time measured by AHB's life. The language of the common law was originally French. An estate measured by another person's life was always known as an estate *pur autre vie* (pronounced as though it were English).

Carried to extremes, the dynastic temptation might have led to an infinite series of life estates: to *A*, my eldest son, for life, then to *A*'s eldest son for life, then to the eldest son of *A*'s eldest son, and so on. The effect would have been to give each successive son only the slice of time measured by the thread of his life. He could deal in that slice, but no buyer would ever get, or pay for, more than an estate *pur autre vie*. But this is a clear case for inhibition. Some of the bad effects of such an arrangement are instantly appreciable. Nobody would ever have a marketable slice of time. No money could be raised to invest in the land. It is in nobody's interest to produce an impoverished class of landowners. If such arrangements prevailed, the value of the land would be locked up and sterilized.

An enormous amount of legal energy has gone into restraining the urge to tie up land for long periods and, on the other side, into pushing against those restraints. The most obvious outcome of that particular battle between facilitation and inhibition was ultimately the rule against perpetuities, the effect of which is to destroy all future interests which do not vest within a certain time.[10] However, there were much earlier manifestations of the same policy against tying land up for the future. They were responsible for the evolution of the principal estates known to the common law.

The fee simple

The history of the fee simple[11] is bound up with the interpretation of grants 'to *A* and his heirs'. Under such a grant it might be thought that *A* would

---

[10] The old rule fiercely destroyed any future interest which could conceivably vest beyond a period defined by lives in being at the date of the gift plus twenty-one years. A modern liberalization kills off only those which actually do fail to vest within either that period or, if the grantor elects for the clarity of a fixed period, within eighty years (Perpetuities and Accumulation Act 1964).

[11] The word 'simple' is straightforward enough in this. It signifies something like 'unqualified' or 'nothing more nor less': nothing more nor less than the fee. But 'fee' is difficult. It is the same word as the 'feu' in 'feudal' and as 'fief'. You will also encounter 'enfeoffment' (a formal conveyance) and 'feoffee' (a person enfeoffed). The medieval Latin is 'feodum'. The underlying meaning of all these is elusive. It may not be far from the lay sense of 'property' or 'belongings'. The modern German for 'cattle' is 'Vieh' and it is supposed that an old Frankish predecessor was 'fehu-od' (cattle-property). The link between 'cattle' and 'property' and 'money' is present in classical Latin in the word 'pecunia'. Even the element of reward may not be absent. In the feudal system the fee simple was the belonging

not be able to defeat the interest of his heir, his heir's heir, and so on. Would not A be able to sell only the slice of time measured by his own life? The early common law took the contrary view. It interpreted the words 'and his heirs' as merely fixing the length of the slice of time vested in A. That is to say, A took, and could dispose of, an estate in the land measured by the survival on earth of his heirs. No heir took anything by the grant. Whether A's immediate heir ever got anything therefore depended entirely on whether A chose to let him have it. A grant 'to A and his heirs' was thus construed as giving A the 'for-ever' interest called the fee simple. In the technical language of the common law the words 'and his heirs' became words of limitation, not words of purchase. That is, they were words which defined the length of the interest at A's disposal.

Suppose that A had received a grant of land 'to A and his heirs'. If a life tenant could sell only an estate measured by his own life and thus confer an estate *pur autre vie*, logic would seem to suggest that A could sell only the slice of time measured by the survival on this earth of his own heirs. That logic was not applied. A would sell to 'B and his heirs', and B would take the slice of time measured by the survival of his own, B's, heirs. Formally, that appears to break the rule *nemo dat quod non habet*. In substance it does not, simply because 'and his heirs' was, so to speak, double Dutch for 'for ever'.

This transition may be explained by the fact that, though it can at any one time be impossible to find the heir to a given person, yet, so long as there is no restriction to lineal descendants so that collaterals can also be taken into account, the difficulty of finding an heir is no proof that there is actually no heir at all. Be that as it may be, the estate conferred on A by a grant 'to A and his heirs' was construed as nothing other than the slice of time measured by the survival of the land itself or, in other words, for ever. If A sold and conveyed the land 'to B and his heirs', the law refused to say that B took only that slice of time measured by the survival of A's heirs. There would have been no point. The reality was that A had 'for ever' in the land, and that is what he conveyed to B.

The emergence of the fee simple as the 'for-ever' interest thus demonstrates a double act of interpretation in favour of full and free alienability. First, the words 'and his heirs' were understood as not creating a string of life estates. Secondly, a conveyance by one who had received a grant in those terms did not follow the logic of the estate *pur autre vie*: the recipient did not obtain an estate defined by the survival of another person's heirs.[12]

which you got in return for the services undertaken to your lord. But it is necessary to tread cautiously. We know what a fee simple is we do not know what precise shade of meaning 'fee' originally had. Onions is agnostic (Onions, *The Oxford Dictionary of English Etymology* (Oxford: Oxford University Press, 1985), s.v. 'fee').

[12] The rule in *Shelley's Case* (1579) 1 Co. Rep. 88b, 76 ER 199, which has earlier roots, is part of this same story: 'When by the same instrument in which a life estate is given, the

Just as ownership of a car is the interest which gives control of the whole life of the car, so, except that the language is different, a fee simple in land is the interest which gives control of the whole life of the land. It is in effect ownership of the land. The reason why even now we have to say 'in effect' will become apparent when we later encounter tenure. In one word it is because in a spectral sense only the Crown owns the land.

The fee tail

A grantor might cut down the class of heirs referred to in his grant. Suppose that the grant said 'to A and the heirs of his body' or 'to A and the heirs of his body begotten on his wife B'. Would such words serve to tie the land into the family of the grantee? Once again the law construed the grant as conferring a slice of time on A, giving the heirs nothing beyond the hope of inheriting. But here the slice of time was cut down. *Talliatum* in Latin, and *taillé* in French, mean 'cut down'. These cut-down fees thus acquired the name 'fee tail' or just 'entail'. This slice of time was more precarious. The slice of time which A acquired was measured by the survival on earth of lineal heirs, heirs descending from him or, in the case of the narrower grant, heirs descending from the union of A and B. Here there was a real possibility that the estate would terminate. A might have no issue. Or, further down the line, war, disease, and infertility might wipe out all his lineal descendants. The grantor holding the fee simple who made a grant 'to A and the heirs of his body' thus had something left: he retained a reversion or had a remainder to dispose of. The grantee, A, had no more to give than that slice of time measured by the survival of his lineal heirs.

Here the logic of the estate *pur autre vie* did operate. A buyer buying from a tenant in tail would get only what was called a base fee, a period of time measured by the survival of the lineal heirs of the original grantee in tail or, more precarious still, a special class of those lineal heirs. That was not a very attractive prospect. To that extent the grantor in tail had succeeded in tying the land to the family of the grantee. He had ensured that the land could not be attractively sold. However, there were further moves in the game of chess. The ingenuity of conveyancers soon brought it about that, in violation of the principle *nemo dat*, a tenant in tail could sell a fee simple. Ways were found to bar entails. The barring of the entail destroyed the reversion or remainder and thus made it possible to sell and convey a full fee simple. (A modern parallel can be found in the statutory regime for the 'enfranchisement' of leaseholds, under which a person who holds a very long lease

remainder is limited to the heirs or heirs of the body of the tenant for life, whether immediately or subject to other estates, the life estate and the remainder shall unite, and the intended tenant for life shall be entitled to a fee simple or fee tail, but so as not to prejudice any intervening interests.' For all the background, Simpson, *Leading Cases in the Common Law*, see 13–44.

can destroy the reversion by converting his interest into a fee simple.[13])
Even that was not the last move in the game, for by settlement and resettlement the dynast's lawyers could still keep land pretty closely tied into a
family.[14]

We have now introduced the all-important theme that land law facilitates
dealing in slices of time. At the same time it remains vigilant against the sterilization of wealth which too liberal a facilitation would lead to.
Landowners have to be allowed to deal in slices of time. They must not be
allowed too much control of the future. When the law is talking technically, an 'estate' is a slice of time. We have introduced estates recognized by
the common law, the fee simple, the fee tail (and base fee), the life estate
(and the estate *pur autre vie*); also the lease, an estate which lasts for a fixed
time, long or short. The common law, in the narrow sense in which it is
contrasted with equity, has since 1925 recognized only two estates, the fee
simple and the lease. That does not mean that all dealing in slices of time
shorter than 'for ever' has to be done through leases. It means only that,
within what is permitted by the rule against perpetuities, all other manipulation of slices of time has to be done in equity, behind the curtain of a trust.
We will return to that below. In the modern law an owner can, subject to
the rule against perpetuities, carve up slices of time behind a trust. But the
old game of chess is over. Even if he does create successive interests in land
behind a trust, it is likely that those interests will very easily be transferred
from the land to its value. The beneficiaries will then take their interests in
a fund.

SPACE

Mention of a piece of land by name—as, for example, Lord's Cricket
Ground or Wembley Stadium—brings to mind an image of the surface of
the land. But the surface is merely a cross-section of a space which, in a flat-
earthish sort of way, we still think of as stretching infinitely up and down.
Modern cosmology requires modification of the image of that space, but
some of the mind's worst problems in comprehending its true shape have
been overtaken by much humbler science. First balloons and then aero-
planes necessitated a rethink. The tube in which estates subsist has had to
be cut off in order to deprive the surface-owner of exclusive control of the

---

[13] By a deed of enlargement a leasehold tenant with 200 years still to run can, other conditions being met, give himself a fee simple. Other Acts permit, not a unilateral enlargement,
but a compulsory transfer of the fee simple: Leasehold Reform Act 1967, Landlord and
Tenant Act 1987, Leasehold Reform, Housing and Urban Development Act 1993.

[14] To catch a flavour of the old land law, read Professor Sir Guenter Treitel's account of
the role of settlements of land in the plots of *Pride and Prejudice, Persuasion,* and *Sense and
Sensibility* (Treitel, 'Jane Austen and the Law' (1984) 100 LQR 549).

upper air.[15] Subject to such controls as the law imposes in the interests of the community as a whole or the neighbours in particular, the owner of the fee simple is free to use or not to use the space. Those who have lesser slices of time are in a similar position, except that they have to accept restrictions inherent in their shorter interests.

Flying Freeholds

Suppose the owner of the fee simple wants to split the space horizontally. Let it be that he wants to sell the airspace between the altitudes of 50 and 60 metres, perhaps because that slice of air is occupied by the top floors of a skyscraper. There is no theoretical objection. But it has proved impossible in English law to cope with the secondary problems of interdependence. Scots law manages it well enough, probably because, as Dr Johnson already observed, tall buildings have long been a feature of the Scottish urban landscape and flat-dwelling has been correspondingly common even among the well off. Interdependence supposes the need for a regime of positive and negative duties regulating the relations between vertical neighbours. English law can establish such a regime in relation to leasehold, but seemingly not in relation to freehold. However, there is a demand for flying freeholds, and proposals to facilitate the achievement of that goal lie on the table.[16]

Single Strands of the Economic Potential

Within the defined space the law has to meet a demand for another kind of splitting, not literally of space, but of individual strands of the economic potential inherent in the space. Property rights consisting in fractions of potential enjoyment are grouped by the law as easements, restrictive covenants, or profits. But it is not necessary at this level to enter into those distinctions. It is sufficient to know that a landowner can get money out of the land, not only by selling fractions of time, but by dealing in strands of enjoyment. A neighbour may be willing to pay for a right of way over the land. Another may be interested in creating a binding obligation never to build on or trade from the land. An angling club may be interested in the right to take fish. A road-building company may be willing to pay a high price to extract the gravel from a gravel bed or to take stone from a quarry.

---

[15] *Pickering* v. *Rudd* (1815) 4 Camp. 219; *Lord Bernstein of Leigh* v. *Skyviews and General Ltd.* [1978] QB 479. Quite where the tube is cut is difficult to say, but above the level of economic exploitation. The swinging jib of a giant crane can trespass (*Anchor Brewhouse* v. *Berkley House* (1987) BLR 82).

[16] Law Commission, *Commonhold: Freehold Flats and Freehold Ownership of Other Interdependent Buildings, Report of a Working Group* (the Aldridge Committee) Cm. 179 (London: HSMO, 1987).

A case in 1978, *Re Brocklehurst*,[17] contains a wonderful example. The eccentric owner of some 4,000 acres struck up a friendship in his late eighties with the proprietor of a local garage. After his death his relatives discovered to their horror a transaction which they sought in vain to have set aside. Lord Denning MR described it like this:

It was a transaction by which he severed the shooting rights from the estate and gave them to a garage proprietor for 99 years. He gave him the whole of the shooting rights. Not only over the Roaches and the Gun Moor. But also over the park land and farms, and even the gardens and lawns of the Hall, right up to the windows. He gave them to the garage proprietor with full right to assign or sublet those rights at whatever profit he could make . . . It was a disastrous transaction for anyone who was to inherit the estate . . . The value would be reduced by £90,000. It might make the house virtually unsaleable.[18]

The relatives' failure vividly illustrates the law's willingness to facilitate dealing in particular strands of the potential of the space. Mr Brocklehurst had validly transferred a ninety-nine-year right to shoot the game on the land. The next section will investigate more closely two modes in which this kind of thing can be done. It can be done by creating personal or proprietary rights. Mr Brocklehurst created a proprietary right, and it is with rights of that kind that land law is peculiarly concerned.

Anticipating the next section, it is essential to underline one crucial point. As those who inherited from Mr Brocklehurst knew, property rights bind the land itself. Because of this characteristic, they have the potential to sterilize the wealth which inheres in that land. They are the product of an exploitation of that wealth, but, once in being, they to one degree or another sterilize other uses of the land. This means that the law has to inhibit a free for all in the creation of such proprietary interests. In one leading case the plaintiff claimed to have an exclusive right to put pleasure boats on a stretch of canal. The defendant was a rival in the same business. It was held that that right could not exist as a proprietary right.[19] Pollock CB insisted that new forms of proprietary right 'cannot be created at the will and pleasure of the owner of property', and Martin B thought that to concede the plaintiff's demand 'would lead to the creation of an infinite variety of interests in land'.[20]

The necessary control is usually a matter, not of identifying particular content, but of laying down more abstract conditions. An unusually simple example is the general principle (to which occasional exceptions have been allowed) that none of these fractional rights can compel the doing of positive acts: you cannot have a proprietary right compelling neighbouring land

---

[17] [1978] Ch. 14.   [18] [1978] Ch. 14, 26.
[19] *Hill* v. *Tupper* (1863) 1 H & C 121, 159 ER 51.
[20] 1 H & C 121, 127, 128; 159 ER 51, 53.

to see to your ploughing, dig your ditches, and so on. There can be an easement to run drains through a neighbours' land or lead water over that land,
but it cannot impose a duty on the neighbour to maintain the drains or
channels.[21] Much of the difficulty of this area derives from the elusiveness
of the requirements to which these fractional proprietary rights have to
conform.[22]

REALITY

In the technical language of the law 'real' never denotes the opposite of 'illusory' or 'fake'. It is usually an anglicization of the adjective from *res*, which is
Latin for 'thing.' Hence, 'real' always indicates that something has some
quality of or relation to a thing. If a creditor, about to lend money, asks for
real security, he means that he wants to be able to turn against a thing for the
purpose of obtaining what is due to him. That contrasts with personal security. A guarantee will allow the creditor an extra recourse, against the person
of guarantor. We could talk about 'thing-security' and 'person-security'. We
do not. We distinguish instead between real and personal security.

A lawyer cannot be frightened of technical meanings. It helps, however,
if each word pressed into technical service has just one technical meaning.
Here there is more than one. The law uses 'real' to mean 'in some significant way thing-related', but the nature of the relation is not always the
same. Very importantly, there is a difference between the 'reality' which is
indicated in the contrast between real and personal property and the 'reality' indicated in the contrast between real and personal rights. Though the
distinction between real and personal property is ancient and venerable, it
is nowadays far less important than the distinction between real and personal rights.

Realty and Personalty

There is an almost perfect match between the category of real property and
land. If a lay person hears 'real property', or 'real estate', or 'realty', what
will come to mind will be an image of land. For most lawyers the effect will
be the same. Some lawyers may just manage to remind themselves that they

[21] *Duke of Westminster* v. *Guild* [1985] QB 688, 702–3. The owner of such an easement
may enter to maintain the drains and channels himself.

[22] Essential as a foundation for thinking about this is the comparative and economic study
by Bernard Rudden, showing that it is difficult to enlist the support of law and economics
for a strict *numerus clausus* (finite number) of real rights in land, whence either the economists' reasoning must be deficient or the lawyers' conviction that a *numerus clausus* is essential is hysterical (Rudden, 'Economic Theory versus Property Law: The *Numerus Clausus*
Problem' in Eekelaar and Bell, (eds.), *Oxford Essays in Jurisprudence* (3rd ser., Oxford: Oxford
University Press, 1987), 239–63).

should be thinking more abstractly, not of the land itself, but of interests in land. 'Personal property' or 'personalty' similarly evoke cars, cows, televisions, crockery, pictures, money, and a host of other moveable things. In fact the correlation is not quite perfect. A lease of land, however long, is technically personalty, and some moveable things are heirlooms and fall within the category of realty. The right to call a parson to the freehold in a church, called an advowson, was always realty.

In what sense is realty 'thing-related' and in what sense are personal things like cars not 'thing-related'? Our law settled on a remedial scheme which in general refused specific recovery and preferred instead what the Romans called *condemnatio pecuniaria* (condemnation in money). Condemnation in money means that, whatever the nature of the claim, the successful plaintiff ends up with a money judgment. Even if the plaintiff is in essence saying 'That cow, Buttercup, which you have, is mine!', the system which takes this remedial option gives him no right actually to get the cow back. A judgment in money can be called 'personal', because it gives the victorious plaintiff no right in or to any particular thing but merely a right that a person, the defeated defendant, pay the sum in question, a right backed by the law's machinery for executing judgments. There are good reasons in favour of this preference for personal remedies in money, and classical Roman law made no exceptions.[23]

English law did make some exceptions. In some actions you could recover the thing itself. Those actions came to be called 'real actions', 'real' meaning 'thing-related' in the simple sense that the person claiming would recover the very thing claimed. The subject matter of 'real actions' then became 'real property' or 'realty', the especial thing-relatedness of such assets being their specific recoverability: if it came to litigation, you would get back the thing itself.[24] It is almost a perfect truth that the category of specific recoverability extended no further than land. Hence the near-perfect correlation between realty and land.

---

[23] Exceptions were made in the post-classical period. It is important to underline, anticipating the next meaning of 'real', that the Roman *vindicatio* was an unequivocal assertion of a proprietary right: 'That thing is mine!' Yet it gave rise to a personal money judgment. The judge had a discretion to allow (not to order) specific surrender of the *res* but he could condemn only for its value. This perfectly illustrates that specific recoverability is not a necessary quality of a proprietary claim. See further Lawson (ed.), *Buckland and McNair's Roman Law and Common Law* (2nd edn., Oxford: Oxford University Press, 1952), 412–13, also 76–7. See also Maitland's comment quoted in the next note.

[24] Maitland, *The Forms of Action at Common Law*, ed. Chaytor and Whittaker (Cambridge: Cambridge University Press, 1965 repr. from 1909), 74–5. Notice especially, 'This remark [of Bracton, at fo. 102b] which made the reality or personality of the action depend not on the nature of the right asserted by the plaintiff but on the result of the judgment, has had results which as I think are much to be regretted' (p. 74).

Why was the lease of land left out? In the first generation of common law actions there was no action for specifically realizing that kind of slice of time in land. In other words, there was no real action for a leaseholder. It was not until the sixteenth century that the leaseholder was finally equipped with what was in effect a real action.[25] But by that time the categories had set. Legal language might then have coined the contradictory-sounding phrase 'real personalty' to express the nature of the lease, meaning personalty which could be specifically recovered. It did not. It did the next best thing. It took to calling leases 'chattels real'. 'Chattel' is a word for any item of moveable property,[26] and, by extension, for any item of personalty, and 'real' means 'thing-related' in this sense of 'specifically recoverable.'

Real Rights and Personal Rights

We move now to the kind of 'reality' or 'thing-relatedness' which matters in the modern law. The key proposition is that land law is, centrally, the law of real rights in land. The slice of time which we call a lease, or, less commonly, a 'term of years', is for historical reasons personalty or personal property, but it is indisputably a real right in land and as such central to land law. A fee simple is similarly a real right in land, the greatest of all.

People's wealth—their 'property' in the widest sense of that slippery word—consists in rights of two kinds, real rights and personal rights. It is important to say at once that there are different ways of expressing this distinction. 'Real' and 'personal' here anglicize the Latin labels *in rem* and *in personam*. Many people prefer to use the Latin labels. The Latin tells us that a right *in rem* is a right in or against a thing, while a right *in personam* is a right in or against a person.

One can change to different language. A right *in personam* can be called an obligation. A right *in personam* and an obligation are one and the same thing, but looked at from different ends. I have an overdraft. I owe my bank £1,000. The bank has a right *in personam*, the person here being me. I have an obligation to pay. The relationship can be named from either end, and in practice we usually name it from the liability end. Hence we very frequently speak, not of the law of personal rights or of rights *in personam*, but of obligations. As for rights *in rem*, if we drop both the Latin and the latinate English, they usually become 'property rights' or 'proprietary rights'.

---

[25] The roots of this development lie in the fifteenth century, but it appears to have been secured in 1525. A detailed account is to be found in Baker, 'Spelman's Reports', vol. 2 (1977) 94 Selden Society 180.

[26] 'Chattel' is related to 'cattle' and both are derived, as is 'capital', from the Latin *'caput'* which means 'head' and, by transference, things important or essential. The exact relation between 'cattle' and 'chattel' is probably not the most obvious—namely, that cattle were centrally important items of moveable property (Onions (ed.), *The Oxford Dictionary of English Etymology*, s.v. 'chattel').

We sometimes use 'property' loosely to mean 'wealth'. In that loose sense 'property' wobbles . Sometimes 'my property' evokes and is intended to evoke specific things, such as cars and clothes and cottages. Sometimes, and rather more technically, 'my property' denotes mere rights vested in me, such as a fee simple, a lease, ownership, or the obligations of my debtors. Whichever the focus, the loose notion of property as wealth is too broad to be useful in analysis. To think clearly the law has to draw a bright line between two classes of right, both of which can fall within the loose notion of wealth.

The bright line distinguishes between property and obligations. When that line is drawn, property clearly has a narrower and much more technical sense. Within wealth, taken as including all assets, the law of obligations is the law of rights *in personam* and the law of property is the law of rights *in rem*. Hence a 'property right' or 'proprietary right' is a real right, is a right *rem*. The law of property is the law of all known real rights, and land law is the law of real rights in land.

What is the difference? The practical difference bears on this question. Against whom can the right be demanded? 'Demandability' is intelligible but not really English. But another word for 'to demand' is 'to exact', which gives us 'exigible' and 'exigibility'. A right *in rem* is a right the exigibility of which is defined by the location of a thing. The exigibility of a right *in personam* is defined by the location of the person. Where I have a right *in personam* the notional chain in my hand is tied round that person's neck. Where I have a right *in rem*, the notional chain in my hand is tied around a thing. Between me and the car which I own there is such a chain.[27]

Most of the landowner's ambitions in respect of space and time can be met to some extent by the law of contract. It is important to see that this is true. The facility offered by the law of contract is indeed often used. But it is equally important to see why the contractual answer does not go far to satisfying the fundamental needs. It is an unsatisfactory solution because contracts by nature create only personal rights. Most of the landowner's legitimate desires can be achieved only if the law allows them to be given effect *in rem*—that is, as proprietary rights. We can show this by two examples, one from the exploitation of space, one from the exploitation of time.

[27] We must notice Hohfeld's brilliant but flawed attempt to eliminate the notion of a right *in rem*. He thought they were illusions, simply ways of representing rights *in personam* available against a multitude of persons (Hohfeld, *Fundamental Legal Conceptions*, ed. Cook (New Haven, Conn.: Yale University Press, 1964), 68–94 (reprinting an article originally published in (1917) 26 Yale LJ 710)). Harris shows that the Hohfeldian redescription is worse than cumbersome (Harris, *Property and Justice* (Oxford: Oxford University Press, 1996), 119–38. See also Penner, 'The "Bundle of Rights" Picture of Property' (1996) 43 UCLA Law Rev. 711 at 726–31, some parts of which are now incorporated in Penner, *The Idea of Property in Law* (Oxford: Oxford University Press, 1997), ch. 4–6.

Let us suppose that I am in a position to offer my neighbour access to his land along the edge of my wood. If it could only be done by a contract, giving a personal right, I could not get much for it. My neighbour would know that I might sell my land a month later and he would be left at best with a right against me. The new owner could tell him my contractual obligations were nothing to do with anyone but me. For a purely personal right against me obliging me to let him use my land for access to his, my neighbour might indeed pay a small sum, perhaps £100 per annum. He would not pay the £10,000 which I am interested in getting. People do make such purely contractual arrangements, but they do not meet the real need. The law recognizes the need for a right of way *in rem*. An easement of way is a proprietary interest. For the grant of an easement of way I may well be able to get the £10,000. My land will, of course, later sell for less. My neighbour will have a right in the land itself, exigible against all comers and therefore, and especially, against my successors in title. The invisible chain in his hand will be attached at the other end to the land itself.

And, in fact, the law goes further. It puts the benefit of the easement, not in his hand, but, so to speak, in the hand of his land. The effect is that the easement will run with the land at both ends of the invisible chain by which we are representing the right. When he sells on to someone else, the new owner of his land will get the easement by virtue of his acquisition of the land. And when I sell on, the 'real' quality of the right which I have conceded will mean that my buyer will take subject to the burden of the easement. It is important to emphasize that the real quality of a right has no logical implications for the behaviour of the benefit of the right. Even many personal rights can be alienated and often are. If you owe me £100, I can sell and assign my right *in personam* to someone else, perhaps a professional debt collector. And there is nothing contradictory in the notion of an inalienable right *in rem*.[28] It is no part of the logic of real rights that they must be alienable, much less run, at the benefit end, with the land which benefits. That is something extra, which some real rights have and some do not.

Time can also be exploited through contract. People do make contracts to allow other people to use their land for this or that purpose for a given time. Just as Hertz and Avis exploit the temporal dimension of ownership of cars through the contract of hire, so it is possible to make what are essentially contracts of hire of land. In the early common law, the lease was no different from a contract of hire. But the lease was later given effect *in*

---

[28] In Roman law the usufruct (functionally equivalent to the life estate in English law) was inalienable, as also its more restricted cousins, but all were unequivocally rights *in rem* (Nicholas, *An Introduction to Roman Law* (3rd edn., Oxford: Oxford University Press, 1962), 144–5).

rem.[29] If I grant you a lease of my land for twenty-one years and then sell and convey my fee simple, the purchaser from me will take subject to your lease. The reason is that your slice of time is a proprietary interest, an interest *in rem*, exigible against the land itself and hence against my successors in title.

A pressure point

Because proprietary rights are invisible threats to strangers, and also because they have the potential to sterilize the economic value of land, the law keeps them, as we have seen, under strict control.[30] They are recognized under conditions as to content and mode of creation. There is no free for all. However, there is always pressure on the closed list. Not infrequently, people are surprised and disappointed to find that they are exposed to the weakness of purely personal rights. Sometimes they have been manœuvred into that position by a combination of strong market forces and legal ingenuity working for the other side. There is a strong market in accommodation, especially in student accommodation. A great deal of ingenuity has gone into the business of renting out houses for accommodation without actually granting a lease, usually by calling it a mere licence.

The same sort of thing can happen without any exercise of ingenuity. Suppose an employer makes an arrangement with a widow of an employee that she can stay on in a cottage for as long she wants to. The employer later sells the fee simple. The new owner insists on vacant possession. Either the old lady can be shown to have a recognized right *in rem* or she is in terrible trouble.[31] Some of the most difficult areas of land law are produced in this area of pressure on the privileged list of rights *in rem*. The pressure is to add to the list or, failing that, to obtain some limited fraction of the protection accorded to full proprietary rights. Sometimes something on those lines can be achieved by ingeniously enlisting all possible help from the combined forces of the law of contract and the law of wrongs. The modern history of the licence, once merely a personal permission to use land falling short of a lease of that land, provides the best example. In essence it reruns the old story which turned the lease into an estate in land. Only, in the case of the licence, the story is still working itself out.[32]

---

[29] This is not quite the same story as that which is given above, text to n. 25 above. The real action came later than the right *in rem* (Simpson, *A History of the Land Law* (2nd edn., Oxford: Oxford University Press, 1986; repr. 1996), 74–5).

[30] Text from n. 18.

[31] The example is based on *Binions* v. *Evans* [1972] Ch. 359, in which different judges found different ways to save the widow from disaster.

[32] *Ashburn Anstalt* v. *Arnold* [1989] Ch. 1 might be said to have drawn a line short of full proprietary recognition, offering instead the combined assistance of contract and wrongs (here equitable wrongs), but that is the matrix from which new proprietary interests have grown before, not only the lease but also restrictive covenants, in *Tulk* v. *Moxhay* (1848) 2 Ph. 774, 41 ER 1143, on which see text to n. 7.

DUALITY

There is duality where a proposition is true in one conceptual dimension but is falsified or heavily modified in another. Our land law is shot through by instances. There is one of ubiquitous and fundamental importance—namely, the duality between law and equity. There is another, now of fading significance, which emanates from tenure. A third consists in the difference between beneficial interests and security interests. A fourth, perhaps inessential at the point of access to the subject, turns on the relativity of title.

Law and Equity

Proprietary rights in land can be legal or equitable. The mind can cope with the proposition that English law is different from Scots law. It is more difficult to accept the existence within English law itself of two legal systems with different answers to many questions. Yet for centuries that was the position. The courts of common law administered common law, and the court of chancery administered its own law, called equity. And on many issues the court of chancery took a position different from that of the courts of common law. The institutional duality was abolished more than a century ago. Modern courts administer both law and equity, and the conflicts' rule laid down by statute is that, where law and equity differ, equity prevails.[33] The conceptual duality continues. In some areas it has weakened and will weaken further.[34] But, wherever the law of trusts has a role to play, the duality is here to stay. Where there is a trust, the law says A is owner but equity disagrees and prefers B. Or we might put it the other way about: wherever equity thinks B should be owner, even though the common law takes a different view, there is a trust. A, the owner at common law, becomes a trustee for B.

The law of trusts was equity's principal creation, and trusts have become the distinctive feature of the Anglo-American law of property. Land law being essentially the law of property interests in land, it follows that the law of trusts is one of its dominant features. Wherever there is a trust, the proposition that someone is entitled in fee simple at law remains true but is in substance heavily qualified by the equitable entitlement outstanding in another person. The legal estate is thus reduced to a bare right. Trusts arise, most obviously, by the decision of the owner of a legal estate to convey that estate to trustees on trust, as to the interests which he specifies, for his chosen beneficiaries. But express trusts are only one kind of trust. The law itself, or more accurately equity, will often raise an equitable interest in someone

[33] Supreme Court of Judicature Act 1873, s. 25 (11).
[34] Birks, 'Equity in the Modern Law: An Exercise in Taxonomy' (1996) U. Western Australia LR 1.

other than the owner of the legal estate. That is to say, trusts often arise by operation of law. Sometimes this is done subject to proof of contrary intent, so that the prima facie trust can be displaced by evidence that no trust was intended. In many cases, however, the trust arises irrespective of intent, simply because facts have happened which in the eye of equity require the legal owner to hold for someone else or partly for someone else.

It is a disputed matter whether these two kinds of non-express trust ought to be clearly distinguished. The currently dominant view is the traditional one which draws a bright line between what are called resulting trusts and what are called constructive trusts.[35] In the small class of cases where equity raises a prima facie trust subject to contrary intent, it is an observable fact that it does so with a view to carrying back a beneficial interest to the person from whom the legal estate was transferred, in substance cancelling out the effect of the transfer. This feature gives these trusts their name. 'Resulting' has nothing to do with outcomes or consequences, as might be inferred from the modern sense of 'result'. It is a latinate word from *resalire,* meaning 'to jump back'. In these trusts the equitable interest jumps back to the person from whom it came. The other category of non-express trusts, in which intent does not even have a negative role, are called constructive trusts. The name is here related to the word 'construe' in the sense of 'interpret' or 'infer'. Such trusts arise merely by the interpretation of law or as an inference of law.

The reasons why equity raises non-express trusts are diverse. Nor have they ever been systematically ordered. The uncertainty which surrounds them makes them a fertile source of litigation. It may be right to say that they arise in response to the creation of legitimate expectations, whether by contract or in other ways, to wrongs, and to unjust enrichments. But it would be unsafe not to add a fourth category of miscellaneous other events. There is one huge body of case law in which all these themes can be detected, often not disentangled one from another. It arises from a combination of great social changes and the tendency of house prices to inflate. There are many versions of the story. A sketch will capture the essence of the matter.

Two people live together. As for almost all of us, their home is the biggest purchase of their lives, usually involving mortgage finance. But it happens, notwithstanding the joint nature of the venture, that the legal estate is taken in the name of only one of them. Later, perhaps after a quarrel or a death, that person with the paper title insists that the other has or had no interest at all. At common law that is right. Has equity raised an interest under a resulting or constructive trust? If not, the partner with the legal estate will run off with everything. Many have been sacrificed on the altar of this kind

[35] *Westdeutsche Landesbank Girozentrale* v. *Islington LBC* [1996] AC 669, especially the speech of Lord Browne-Wilkinson.

of litigation. Even if we do not know quite how it should best be explained, we do now know that on most versions of the story equity does indeed raise a trust, compelling the partner with the legal estate to acknowledge the other's beneficial interest.[36]

In general law is no less flexible than equity but in the land law this is not so, partly because of the special demands of legal certainty in this area and partly because common law has in many respects been set hard by statute. The example just given serves to illustrate equity's flexibility. Through its use of non-express trusts it can escape formal requirements for the creation of proprietary interests. Common law interests in land have to be conveyed formally. The spouses and *de facto* spouses who benefit from the particular intervention of equity just described have neither deed nor registration nor even writing to rely on. We will return to this theme when we deal with formality in the next section. Equity was always inclined against formality.

Another aspect of equity's flexibility relates to the content of the real rights which it is willing to recognize. In the days when landowners were still seriously interested in reaching forwards to create future interests in land, a principal attraction of creating an express trust and doing the job in equity was that common law could offer only a limited number of building blocks—namely, the particular estates which it then recognized. They could not be modified and there could be no gaps between them. Equitable estates could be made to shift and spring. That is, in reaching into the future the settlor could stipulate that an equitable estate should terminate prematurely in a certain event and shift to another person, or he could deliberately create a gap in the succession of interests, so that the next in line would spring up after an interval. The notion of a short list of immutable slices of time is alien to equity. That remains true today, and all the more obviously in that common law estates have been cut down to two. However, when it comes to fractional rights to single strands of enjoyment, it is necessary to be more cautious. The control of such rights, to curb sterilization, would be utterly subverted if equity had a free hand. Hence, in relation to such rights equity's creativity must be regarded as spent, save as to the manner in which they can be created. In that department, equity's traditional preference for substance over form still has some room for manoeuvre.[37]

---

[36] Among many such cases: *Eves* v. *Eves* [1975] 1 WLR 1338; *Pascoe* v. *Turner* [1979] 1 WLR 431; *Grant* v. *Edwards* [1986] Ch. 638; *Lloyds Bank plc* v. *Rosset* [1991] AC 107. A warning against making universal assumptions: *Burns* v. *Burns* [1984] Ch. 317. For a notable attempt to sort the ideas out, see Gardner, 'Rethinking Family Property' (1993) 109 LQR 263.

[37] For a brilliant but difficult account of this, see Moriarty, 'Licences and Land Law: Legal Principles and Public Policies' (1984) 100 LQR 376, noting esp. 397. It will be seen that the matter is complicated by the fact that, under closer examination, the line between simple division of enjoyment through time and fractional interests tends to dissolve.

Equity's flexibility is bought at a certain cost. Legal certainty, which does not necessarily mean morbid rigidity, is undermined by excessive fluidity. Modern equity is in some areas excessively fluid. A different cost is that equitable interests are more vulnerable than legal interests. If a person acquires the legal estate, he may take free of equitable interests. This happens only where the purchaser of the legal estate gives value, is in good faith, and has no notice of the equitable interest. The fact that the defence of *bona fide* purchase has this effect of protecting certain strangers, allowing them to take clear of the adverse equitable interests, sounds dangerous enough to deter deliberate recourse to trusts. The danger should not be exaggerated. The conditions of the defence were made difficult to satisfy. Moreover, mandatory conveyancing practices were designed with the same end in view, though they obviously cannot help to save such equitable interests as arise without a conveyance under a non-express trust.

We have noticed that the demand for tying up land has dwindled. The seriously wealthy, whether institutional or individual, make trusts in order to establish a managed fund of wealth, not of land. Parallel with that change in what is actually wanted, a long series of statutory interventions has brought it about that the interests of the beneficiaries in trusts of land can easily be overreached, so as to be exigible only against the money received for the land. In practice the land may indeed be retained, especially if it bears a house in which the principal beneficiaries want to live.[38] But the truth is that land held on trust can now almost always be sold and the interests of the beneficiaries transferred to the money. This is the point of contact between land law and the managed fund of wealth.

As we leave the particular duality which consists in the difference between legal and equitable rights, it is worth bringing to mind a really difficult problem: could we dispense with this conceptual duality? If, ditching the history, we forced ourselves to think in a single conceptual dimension, what would equitable interests then be? The answer might be that they would merely be 'weak' proprietary rights or 'flexible' proprietary rights. However, neither their weakness nor their flexibility should be exaggerated. In practice the habit of duality makes it unnecessary finally to master this intellectual challenge. It saves us from having to ask what an equitable right really is.

Tenure

Tenure was once co-equal in importance with estates. After the Conquest all land was vested in the king. The king made grants to tenants in chief in return for military and other services. The tenants in chief subinfeudated to

---

[38] On the instigation of the Law Commission, a limited facility has been overtly introduced by statute to allow continuing occupation by beneficiaries (Trusts of Land and Appointment of Trustees Act 1996, esp. s. 12).

others, and so on, creating the characteristic feudal pyramid. Tenure was the service by which one held one's estate. Different tenures carried different incidents. In 1290 Edward I forbade further subinfeudation of freeholds. Alienation thenceforth could only be by substitution.[39] An alienor had to step out of the pyramid and put the buyer into his place.

We need not follow out the rest of the story. We are interested only in the vestiges of tenure which survive in the modern law. There are only two points which matter. The most obvious is that all land is still technically held of the Crown, so that, in the tenurial dimension, it remains technically true that only the Crown owns the land. Every fee simple is held of the Crown by a notional tenure involving no services at all. The other is the duality between freehold and leasehold. To explain that, it is necessary to go back to the days of subinfeudation and the feudal pyramid.

When one subinfeudated, adding another level to the pyramid, one retained one's fee simple. It remained true that one was tenant in fee simple of the land in question. But the dimension of tenure heavily qualified that proposition, because, below one's own fee simple, there was another, held by whatever services had been reserved. In essence the fee simple at the higher level had been turned into a lordship entitled to the services now owed by the land and, very importantly, to the incidents of that tenure, which could be valuable. That duality is past history in every respect except one.

It is still true that when a tenant in fee simple grants a lease, what we see is technically a subinfeudation. Suppose that the lease is for ninety-nine years. In substance that is a grant of a fraction of the slice of time (for ever) which is the fee simple. But conceptually it is not. The tenant in fee simple, holding of the Crown, retains his fee simple. He grants a dependent estate, the lease for ninety-nine years. In effect he becomes a lord, as in the old days. He becomes a landlord. He still owns the fee simple. In the tenurial dimension, that proposition is heavily qualified. Beneath his fee simple, there is another estate, the ninety-nine-year lease. Perhaps he will have reserved a ground rent. That is the service by which the lease is held. This gives us the difference between freehold and leasehold. The fee simple is freehold, held by a freehold tenure of the Crown. The lease is leasehold, held of the freeholder by leasehold tenure. The tenurial duality allows the two to coexist.

Beneficial interests and security interests

This can be dealt with very shortly, though security is an immensely important subject. The vast majority of purchases of land are made at least in part with borrowed money, secured on the land which is acquired or on other

---

[39] Simpson, *A History of the Land Law*, 54–6.

land. This is common knowledge. Getting a mortgage is a crucial stage in acquiring a house; and when one starts losing heavily in a game of Monopoly one has to mortgage Oxford Street and Regent Street to the bank, to keep going. The word 'mortgage' covers a variety of differently structured securities. Nowadays the commonest kind is unequivocal, for the mortgagee acquires a right which can only be security interest, 'a charge by way of legal mortgage'. But it is possible for the same estate to be either a beneficial or a security interest. Historically, the lender-mortgagee took the fee simple. But the proposition that he was tenant in fee simple was heavily qualified by the fact that he held that estate as a security interest, not as a beneficial interest. His fee simple was held subject to the borrower's right to redeem. Since 1925 mortgagors no longer transfer the fee simple. But a lease can still be granted by way of security. A long lease taken as security is a security interest, not a beneficial interest. It is taken subject to the borrower's right to redeem. The right to redeem is strenuously protected by equity. Hence 'equity of redemption' or simply 'equity'. When house prices collapse, buyers find themselves with 'negative equity'. The difference between what they borrowed on the security of the house and what they can get by selling is a negative quantity.

Relativity of title

The interest one holds has to be distinguished from the title by which one holds it. Suppose you are unlucky enough to take a conveyance of a fee simple from someone who is merely a squatter. You go into possession of the land. *Nemo dat quod non habet*. The maxim suggests that you have nothing. You took a conveyance from someone who had nothing to give. However, you do have something. The reason lies in relativity of title. The law will protect a good title against a bad one, and a bad one against a worse one. You have a fee simple, but you have it by a very short rope. And it might have been yet shorter. This story started with a conveyance. It need not have done so. You might have been the squatter. By the shortest string of all, even a squatter has a fee simple which can in theory be assigned, mortgaged, and so on.

Let us suppose that, somewhere in the southern hemisphere, an absent person holds the fee simple in this land by a very good title. She holds it by a very long rope. Before she went away she was in possession of the land, and in a box in her lawyer's office she has the deeds which trace its descent through deaths, gifts, and sales over a couple of hundred years. She has a fee simple by a good title. You have one by a lousy title. If she finds out what has happened, she can blow you away. But she is in danger. There is a time within which she must put things right. It is possible to acquire an invincible title by what is called adverse possession. After twelve years you will have a better title than she. Developers sometimes have problems of this kind. They set out to buy up all interests in the site. In respect of, say, 2 per cent of the land, they can find nobody to deal with. They go ahead anyway. The buyer of the house on the stolen land will get a discount and, instead of a good title, will take a fee on a very short rope backed, for the period of adverse possession, by an insurance policy maintained at the developers' expense, against the risk of the appearance of someone with a better title.

FORMALITY

Formal requirements oblige people to do things in particular ways, usually ways which put them to some slight extra trouble. It might be, for example, that the law would treat a promise as binding only if you made it meekly kneeling upon your knees. In practice writing and registration are the formalities usually insisted upon. There can be lighter and heavier versions of both.

Land law insists on formality above all at two crucial points in the acquisition of real rights, contract and conveyance. If a landowner decides to make a gift, there will be no contract. Suppose she wants to give her daughter the fee simple in a strip of woodland. She will move straight to the conveyance, for centuries done by deed.[40] The conveyance confers the real right. The sacrosanct formal requirement of a deed is now being made to give way to public registration and, more precisely, to computerized entries on the register. Direct gifts of land, other than by will, are not all that common. Another kind of gratuitous transfer is a conveyance to trustees upon trusts declared by the settlor. The declaration of a trust of land, which accompanies the conveyance, has to be evidenced in writing.

Generally speaking a conveyance follows a contract, usually a contract of sale. Contracts to convey interests in land are void unless they are made in writing.[41] The usual sequence is, first, an informal agreement 'subject to contract'; secondly, the formal contract made in writing, by which the parties for the first time become bound to make, and take, the conveyance; thirdly, the conveyance, which confers the right. In England there is usually a deplorable delay between the first and second stages, though in Scotland the lawyers manage to move from stage one to stage two in two or three days.

This delay means that parties are forced to rely on each other long before there is any legal tie. The unscrupulous can then exploit the fact that there is no sanction for withdrawal during this long first stage. The result is

---

[40] Once sealed in wax, a deed is now no more than a signed and witnessed writing which declares itself to be a deed (Law of Property (Miscellaneous Provisions) Act 1989, s. 1).

[41] This requirement has been stiffened, and equitable intervention on the basis of part performance crippled, by Law of Property (Miscellaneous Provisions) Act 1989, s. 2.

gazumping and gazundering. A gazumper is a seller who suddenly says that he will withdraw unless the buyer pays more. A gazunderer is a buyer who threatens to pull out unless the seller will take less. These practices are unknown in Scotland. They are not a by-product of formality. They are a by-product of the practice of the professionals who run the housing market and in particular of their practice in not executing the formal contract at the point at which all contracts are normally finalized—namely, the moment from which the parties need to be able to rely on one another.

What does formality facilitate? What ends does it serve? Even though it lies outside the land law, it is convenient to answer by reference to the best-known formality of all. Everyone knows that a last will has to be made in writing and signed before witnesses. It is no use just scribbling it on the back of an envelope or whispering it to one's best friend. There are huge advantages in this formal requirement. It helps the person making the will think hard about the job to be done. Later, it goes a long way towards eliminating doubt and argument at a juncture in human affairs at which strife is all too near the surface. All hell would break out if a deceased's last will were a matter of proving by general evidence, and in the absence of the only person who could really know, what the last wishes really were. The formal will settles the matter.

It is much the same in land law. There is an extra reason too. It derives from the invisibility of real rights. Just as one cannot see a fee simple, so one cannot see an easement or a restrictive covenant. A neighbour's right to pass over a field does not reveal itself in a pink line, nor will even an infra-red camera disclose his right to restrict or forbid building. If one is buying a fee simple from a company, and a firm of solicitors is in daily occupation of the premises doing the business of soliciting, one might reasonably infer that the firm holds a lease. But still a lease is not visible, nor a pyramid of sub-leases. Real rights have to be made apparent through documents. Acquiring land would otherwise be a nightmare unless the law made really massive erosions of the principle of *nemo dat*. In relation to land, massive erosions of that principle are wholly unacceptable. Some such erosion does indeed have to be tolerated. We have already seen that the price of equity's recognition of real rights created without formality is just such an erosion, the defence of *bona fide* purchase for value without notice. Moreover, the protection of the system of registration involves some inevitable sacrifice of unregistered interests.

There is an inescapable tension. Formality breeds hard cases. What of the person who did not know or was badly advised? She did the job but not in the precise way in which the law required it to be done. In such cases there is a terrific clash between two simple principles. One is that you cannot have your cake and eat it. You cannot take the advantages of formality and at the same time let off all those who do things in their own informal way.

The other is that pain should not be inflicted except in case of pressing necessity. It is not so easy to send someone away empty-handed who would have taken a fortune if only the right piece of paper had been used. Wherever there are formal requirements, there will be litigation in which these two principles meet head to head.

Whether the rigour of the one will yield ground to the merciful other will depend on several factors, most obviously on the value attached to the formality in question, also on the scale of the exception likely to be created by a concession. If the formality is thought to be really valuable (like the formal requirements of wills), concessions are unlikely to be made, unless perhaps it can be shown that the facts in question will recur infrequently or for some other reason pose no substantial threat to the policy of certainty through formality.[42] One crucially important factor is whether the interests of any third party are involved, in such a way as to be threatened if effect is given to the informal transaction. And has that third party given value? The defence of *bona fide* purchaser for value without notice, which we have already met, illustrates the respect due to the interests of a stranger who has given value. And, where the sanctity and efficacy of a register are at stake, that stranger is likely to prevail even without proof of good faith.[43]

Suppose that you have dealt informally with me, in circumstances in which a decent argument can be made that, but for failure to satisfy formal requirements, you would have an interest in my house. If it is just a matter between you and me, with no stranger involved, it may be possible for you to make some headway. It will be more difficult if I have already sold my legal fee simple in the house to some stranger. You will have a much harder time against that stranger who has given value. Suppose the law untouched by the requirement of registration. Your informally created equitable interest, even if you succeed in establishing that you acquired one, will be vulnerable to the defence of *bona fide* purchase without notice. If we add back the requirement of registration, that still fiercer hurdle stands in your way. It is highly unlikely that you will have registered your interest, which in the absence of special circumstances will be void against the buyer from me.

Some interests override the register. They bind even without registration. This represents the attempt of the legislator to anticipate the most

[42] Secret and half-secret trusts have been allowed to nibble at testamentary formality. Nevertheless, 'there is at least a strong argument that in neither of them does the balance of advantage lie in suspending the rules [as to formality] . . .' (Gardner, *An Introduction to the Law of Trusts* (Oxford: Oxford University Press, 1990), 86.

[43] *Midland Bank Trust Co Ltd.* v. *Green* [1981] AC 513. But the House of Lords did not deny that positive proof of fraud would disable the third party from relying on register. This famous litigation contains a warning for lawyers. The destruction of an interest for want of registration will often entail a liability for professional negligence (*Midland Bank Trust Co. Ltd* v. *Hett, Stubbs and Kemp* [1979] Ch. 384). Others may also incur other tortious liabilities (*Midland Bank Trust Co. Ltd.* v. *Green (No. 3)* [1982] Ch. 529).

obvious instances of the problem endemic in formality. One category of overriding interest is the interest of a person in actual occupation.[44] In *Hodgson* v. *Marks*[45] an elderly lady conveyed her house to her lodger in a thoroughly ill-advised attempt to protect him from her nephew. The nephew was hostile to the lodger's influence. She had no real intent that the lodger should have the substance of ownership of the house. But, so far as the formal requirements of the law were concerned, she had reserved no interest for herself. The lodger sold and conveyed the land to a third party. The old lady found herself in danger of losing her house. It was not so very difficult to find that on these facts she had obtained an equitable interest under a non-express trust. But she had, of course, not registered that equitable interest. The purchaser from the lodger maintained that he was not bound by it. She was saved by the fact that she had been in actual occupation at the time of the sale. The underlying idea is that a buyer can see to his own protection from adverse interests held by those in occupation. Questions can be put. However, the interest of a person in occupation overrides the register simply because its owner is in occupation. It is not necessary to prove that the buyer was at fault in failing to make reasonable enquiries: 'If there is actual occupation, and the occupier has rights, the purchaser takes subject to them. If not, he does not. No further element is material.'[46]

CONCLUSION

The purpose has been to introduce five aspects of land law, with a view to making access to it easier. It was said at the beginning that none of the five has any natural priority. This conclusion summarizes in slightly different order.

(1) It is the business of land law to say what property rights can exist in land. A property right is a real right, a right *in rem*. It has special characteristics, which distinguish it from a personal right, a right *in personam*. It is not exigible solely against the person against whom it arose.

(2) English law has an inheritance of duality. There are dualities implicit in tenure, in the difference between security interests and beneficial interests, and in the relativity of title. But above all there is the duality between law and equity. The real rights which land law recognizes can be legal or equitable. In a historically unitary system, equitable rights might be called 'weak' proprietary rights. Equitable proprietary rights are more vulnerable than legal rights. That is the price of equity's more relaxed attitude to 'reality'.

---

[44] Land Registration Act 1925, s. 70(1)(g).   [45] [1971] Ch. 892.

[46] *Williams and Glyn's Bank Ltd.* v. *Boland* [1981] AC 487 at 504 (Lord Wilberforce).

(3) The value of legal certainty, which the equitable jurisdiction seems on occasion to undermine, is in general reinforced by insistence on the rigour of formality, especially as against strangers who have given value. Formality has meant writing in one form or another, but nowadays it means above all the public registration of real rights in land. The legislator, in providing that some interests override the register, has attempted to foresee the cases in which, even against strangers, the destruction of unregistered interests would give rise to screams of pain.

(4) The surface of a piece of land is a cross-section of a space. Every space has the potential for multiple uses. The law goes some way towards allowing those uses to be split up and dealt with strand by strand. Proprietary facilitation of that goal has to be kept within limits. The sometimes obscure nature of those limits is a stumbling block.

(5) Time and slices of time have been the dominant theme. Land law continues to facilitate dealing in slices of time, most obviously through the lease. But the rise of the managed fund of wealth has brought it about that the long fight over tying up the land itself is no longer fought. The law has seen to it that, behind a trust, such future interests can in general be detached from the land to become interests in a fund. A residual facility remains to meet the accommodation needs of the family through a trust of land. The days have gone when land law's principal mission was to structure wealth and power. Institutions and individuals alike, if they have wealth worth planning, managing, and tying up, prefer trust funds with mixed portfolios.

19

INFORMALLY CREATED INTERESTS IN LAND

Graham Battersby

The purpose of this chapter is to consider the extent to which, and the mechanisms by which, English law allows for the informal creation of interests in land. By 'interests in land' is meant those rights in or over land which are capable of binding third parties, as distinct from personal rights which, even if capable of being assigned to somebody else, are incapable of being asserted against third parties.[1] Since third parties—for example, subsequent purchasers or mortgagees—may thus take subject to existing interests in land, the law needs to provide a system (a conveyancing system) whereby those interests can be discovered and their contents ascertained.

To this end, the law requires that, subject to exceptions to be discussed, interests in land shall be created by various kinds of documents in writing. Thus, the conveyance or creation of a legal estate in land must be in the form of a deed.[2] Any other interest in land can be created or disposed of only by a signed document in writing.[3] A declaration of trust respecting land or any interest in land must be manifested and proved by a document in writing signed by the person able to declare the trust.[4] Further, some transactions in land, especially sales and the grant of long leases, will be carried out in two stages, the contract stage and the completion stage. Completion, the transfer of the legal estate, will require a deed, but there are also formal requirements for the contract, that it be in writing in a document embodying all the terms of the contract and signed by both parties.[5] A valid contract, if specifically enforceable, will itself create an equitable interest. Furthermore, where a transaction fails to comply with the requisite formalities for the transfer or creation of a legal estate (for example, the grant of a twenty-one-year lease, where a deed is necessary, but the document is not valid as a deed because the parties' signatures are not witnessed),

---

[1] *National Provincial Bank Ltd.* v. *Ainsworth* [1965] AC 1175; *Ashburn Anstalt* v. *Arnold* [1989] Ch. 1.

[2] Law of Property Act 1925, s. 52(1). The requirements for the execution of a deed by an individual are contained in the Law of Property (Miscellaneous Provisions) Act 1989, s. 1. The present requirements for the execution of a deed by a corporation are not very satisfactory and are being examined by the Law Commission: see their Consultation Paper No. 143 (1996).

[3] Law of Property Act 1925, s. 53(1)(a).   [4] Ibid., s. 53(1)(b).

[5] Law of Property (Miscellaneous Provisions) Act 1989, s. 2.

equity will treat the document as a valid contract provided that the transaction is supported by consideration and the document satisfies the contract formalities. Hence, there exist in equity analogues of all the estates and interests which can exist at law: equitable leases,[6] equitable mortgages,[7] equitable easements, and so on.

For the sake of completeness, mention should also be made of dispositions of land on death. A will must be in writing and signed by the testator in the presence of two witnesses present at the same time, who must then sign the will in the presence of the testator.[8] Whether land passes to a beneficiary under a will or on intestacy, the personal representative of the deceased, empowered by a formal grant of probate or administration, must transfer the legal estate by an assent in writing.[9]

The law also requires that the interest to be transferred or created shall be defined with reasonable certainty. So, for example, the creation of a lease for a fixed term requires that the date of commencement shall be specified in advance, and the date of termination shall be ascertained by the time that the term of the lease commences.[10] Another example is the rule that the grant of any right purporting to be an easement must be defined with reasonable certainty; this is one reason why the right to a view has never been recognized as an easement.[11]

The effect of these formal requirements is to serve the conveyancing system and to ease the task of a purchaser of land. The documents will form the paper title to the land and the purchaser, by perusing the documents, will be able to discover the interests which bind the land. Equitable interests which are not discoverable through the documents, or by making other reasonable inspections and inquiries, would, on pre-1926 principles, be defeated by a purchaser of the legal estate, relying on the plea of equity's darling.[12]

That point brings us to the third aspect of formality, the need for interests in land to be registered in order to bind a subsequent purchaser. The

---

[6] *Walsh* v. *Lonsdale* (1882) 21 Ch. D. 9.

[7] An equitable mortgage of a legal estate depends upon a specifically enforceable contract that must comply with Law of Property (Miscellaneous Provisions) Act 1989, s. 2 (*United Bank of Kuwait plc* v. *Sahib* [1997] Ch. 107).

[8] Wills Act 1837, s. 9. Land may also pass on death under a *donatio mortis causa*, which, remarkably, avoids the formalities both for a gift *inter vivos* and for a will (*Sen* v. *Headley* [1991] Ch. 425). After that decision it would surely be strange for the courts to insist on written evidence of a half-secret trust of land: (cf. *Re Baillie* (1886) 2 TLR 660).

[9] Administration of Estates Act 1925, s. 36(4).

[10] As to the commencement date, see *Harvey* v. *Pratt* [1965] 1 WLR 1025. As to the termination date, see *Lace* v. *Chantler* [1944] KB 368; *Prudential Assurance Co. Ltd.* v. *London Residuary Body* [1992] 2 AC 386.

[11] *William Aldred's Case* (1610) 9 Co. Rep. 57b at 58b; *Harris* v. *De Pinna* (1886) 33 Ch. D. 238 at 262, *per* Bowen LJ; *Campbell* v. *Paddington Corporation* [1911] 1 KB 869 at 875 f.

[12] See Law of Property Act 1925, s. 199(2).

1925 legislation recognized that the system of conveyancing by title deeds (the 'old system') was likely to continue for some time before being overtaken by the 'new system' of registered conveyancing. The legislature decided to try to improve on the vagaries of the classical doctrine of notice (the duty to make reasonable inquiries) by creating a system for the registration of incumbrances, the land charges system. Certain interests in land, principally post-1925 equitable interests, are required to be registered; registration constitutes actual notice to a purchaser[13] and failure to register will make the interest void against a purchaser as defined in the Land Charges Act 1972.[14]

The legislature in 1925 also provided for full-scale registration of title, which finally became compulsory in all parts of England and Wales on 1 December 1990.[15] The essential feature of the land registration system is that all interests in the land must be entered on the register (the mirror principle), with exceptions provided for overriding interests[16] and through the possibility of rectification of the register.[17]

So, looking at the situation in a broad brush way, provided that an intended interest in land is defined with sufficient certainty, there are two further hurdles which face its recognition as an informally created interest. The first is whether the interest can be created at all without a written document. The second is whether the interest, when created, needs to be entered on a register in order to bind a purchaser. How does English law answer these questions?

It is essential to distinguish two different kinds of informally created interests. The first category derives from the desire of the law to legitimate long-standing situations by ultimately treating as lawful what began in an unlawful way; under this head falls the law relating to the acquisition of title by adverse possession and the acquisition of easements and profits by prescription. The second category comprises those situations where the law allows arrangements respecting land to create proprietary interests without compliance with the normal requirements of writing and registration. It is essential to keep these two categories distinct, because the policy issues affecting the two categories are different. The fundamental justification for the first category is that long user, which will often be accompanied by acquiescence and inertia on the part of the servient owner, generates a

[13] Ibid., s. 198(1).

[14] The provisions for the protection of a purchaser are complicated. The various parts of the Act contain six definitions of purchaser.

[15] Land Registration, England and Wales: The Registration of Title Order 1989 (SI 1989/1347). The ultimate goal, when all land in England and Wales has a registered title, will be greatly accelerated by the new triggers for first registration contained in Land Registration Act 1997, s. 1.

[16] Principally defined in Land Registration Act 1925, s. 70.

[17] Land Registration Act 1925, s. 82.

moral claim which the law should recognize. The second category rests fundamentally on the notion that persons who have been led to believe that they will have an interest in another person's land, and who have relied on that belief, have a legitimate expectation that their belief will be fulfilled; it is right, therefore, that the law should waive its usual requirements for documentation. The problems relating to compliance with the registration requirements also differ between these two categories.[18]

LEGITIMATING THE ORIGINALLY UNLAWFUL

Adverse Possession

The law of adverse possession is based on the fundamental proposition that actions for the recovery of tangible property—land and goods—are founded on possession, not ownership: a person in possession of the property, even if acquired wrongfully, will succeed against any later possessor, but will fail against any prior possessor up to and including the true owner and against someone claiming through a prior possessor. The principal reason for this rule is to avoid a free for all; if factual possession were not so protected, anyone could take the property from the wrongful possessor, and the physically strong would always succeed against the weak.[19] The fundamental concept here is relative title. So, to take two simple examples, if A, the fee simple owner, is dispossessed by a trespasser, B, B immediately acquires a title to the fee simple. Of course, A may bring an action for possession against B, and, if the action is commenced within the period provided by the Limitation Act 1980, the action will be successful. However, B's possession gives him a title to the fee simple which behaves in accordance with all the normal rules: for example, subject to the usual formalities, it may be transferred *inter vivos* or on death.[20] The position is the same in relation to goods. If, as in *Parker* v. *British Airways Board*,[21] A finds a gold bracelet on B's land, A will have a better title than B unless B can show prior

---

[18] This chapter will not consider the creation of short-term leases under Law of Property Act 1925, s. 54(2), nor implied grant and reservation as methods of creating easements and profits.

[19] See *Parker* v. *British Airways Board* [1982] QB 1004 at 1009, *per* Donaldson LJ.

[20] *Asher* v. *Whitlock* (1865) LR 1 QB 1; *Perry* v. *Clissold* [1907] AC 73; *Wheeler* v. *Baldwin* (1934) 52 CLR 609; *Allen* v. *Roughley* (1955) 94 CLR 98. B's fee simple is a legal estate within Law of Property Act 1925, s. 1(1); the fact that it can be defeated by A reflects the quality of the title, not the nature of the estate. See Goode, *Commercial Law* (2nd edn., Harmondsworth: Penguin Books, 1995), 35, n. 37: 'Most law students, asked what interest a trespasser has in land which he occupies *animo domini*, are incredulous at the statement that he acquires a relative title to a fee simple absolute in possession—but that is the law.'

[21] [1982] QB 1004.

possession by proving a manifest intention to exercise a high degree of control over the land and anything that may be found upon it. A's title will prevail over any later possessor—for example, a jeweller to whom the bracelet is taken for valuation[22]—but will be defeated by any prior possessor up to and including the true owner.[23] The concept which is established, therefore, is that a person with possession, whether of land or goods, has a title, which may be relatively weak or relatively strong, to the absolute legal interest in the property concerned.

That is the position at common law, onto which are engrafted the provisions of the Limitation Act 1980.[24] The structure of the Act may be summarized as follows. A person wrongfully dispossessed of tangible property has only a limited time in which to bring an action for the recovery of the property: that period, reckoned from the date when the cause of action accrues, is six years in the case of goods[25] and twelve years in the case of land.[26] In both cases, when the limitation period expires the title of the person dispossessed is extinguished.[27] As against a person with a future interest, the limitation period expires six years after that interest vests in possession, or twelve years after the accrual of the cause of action, whichever is the later.[28]

It is most important to realize that the effect of these provisions is to extinguish the title of the person dispossessed, which, therefore, ceases to exist; there is no statutory transfer (or parliamentary conveyance) of the title of the dispossessed owner to the successful claimant. So, where adverse possession is against a lessee, the effect of the limitation period is to extinguish the lease, not to transfer it to the successful claimant, who therefore does

---

[22] *Armory* v. *Delamirie* (1722) 1 Stra. 505.

[23] Even a person claiming to be the true owner may have to rely on undisturbed prior possession in order to establish ownership: see e.g. *Moffatt* v. *Kazana* [1969] 2 QB 152, where ownership of money was established, on the balance of probabilities, by relatively slight acts of possession. Similarly, proof of title to unregistered land rests on a good root of title which is at least fifteen years old: Law of Property Act 1969, s. 23. That period is relatively short in the history of a piece of land; it does not show indefeasible ownership, only a good marketable title which, subject to any contrary agreement, the purchaser is bound to accept. Even in the case of registered land an absolute freehold title is not indefeasible, since it is subject to the possibility of rectification under Land Registration Act 1925, s. 82. See also n. 30.

[24] General justifications for a principle of limitation are set out in the Law Reform Committee's 21st Report, *Final Report on Limitations of Actions*, Cm. 6923 (London: HMSO, 1977), para. 1.7. For further conveyancing justifications relating to the recovery of land, see Goodman, 'Adverse Possession of Land—Morality and Motive' (1970) 33 MLR 281; Dockray, 'Why Do We Need Adverse Possession?' [1985] Conveyancer 272.

[25] Limitation Act 1980, ss. 2, 3. [26] Ibid., s. 15(1). [27] Ibid., ss. 3(2),17.

[28] Ibid. s. 15(2), sch. 1, para. 4. Adverse possession of trust property by a stranger does not bar the trustee's title until all the beneficiaries have been barred (ibid., s. 18(2), (3), (4)).

not become liable on the covenants in the lease—for example, to pay rent.[29]

The above account relates to unregistered land, but the system of registered title seeks to apply the same principles. Section 75(1) of the Land Registration Act 1925 provides that 'The Limitation Acts shall apply to registered land in the same manner and to the same extent as those Acts apply to land not registered . . .'.[30] That principle is then carried into effect by section 70(1)(f), which provides that 'rights acquired or in the course of being acquired under the Limitation Acts' shall be an overriding interest. However, the proposition that the original owner's estate is extinguished, not transferred, is difficult to apply to registered land. If, for example, the original owner is registered as proprietor of the freehold estate, and the limitation period is completed against him, the registration will continue until the squatter applies to have his title registered; if the application is successful, the original registered title will be closed and a new title will be opened in favour of the squatter. However, until that point arrives, section 75(1) provides that the original registered title 'shall not be extinguished but shall be deemed to be held by the proprietor for the time being in trust for the [squatter] . . .'. That statutory trust seems to bring about a parliamentary conveyance (not of the legal estate but of the beneficial interest), a result strenuously denied in the equivalent situation in unregistered land.

Such authority as there is shows the courts' reluctance to give literal effect to the statutory trust;[31] rather they stress the need to keep the regis-

---

[29] *Tichborne* v. *Weir* (1892) 67 LT 735; *Taylor* v. *Twinberrow* [1930] 2 KB 16; *Tickner* v. *Buzzacott* [1965] Ch. 426.

[30] Torrens systems of land registration adopted in Australasia, Canada, and elsewhere, have tended to emphasize the indefeasibility of the registered title. Where indefeasibility is the first priority, acquisition of title by adverse possession (and acquisition of easements and profits by prescription) will be regarded as incompatible with the system and will therefore be abolished. See, for example, the position in New Zealand as summarized by Howard and Hill, 'The Informal Creation of Interests in Land' (1995) 15 LS 356 at 373. Indefeasibility of title has never been the approach of the English system, which recognizes classes of title less than absolute (good leasehold, possessory and qualified), gives effect to wide categories of overriding interests, and provides that even the absolute title of a registered proprietor in possession is subject to the possibility of rectification under Land Registration Act 1925, s. 82(3). Smith (*Property Law* (London: Longman, 1996), 65 n. 72), points out that New South Wales originally abolished adverse possession, but reintroduced it in 1990. See Woodman and Butt, 'Possessory Title and the Torrens System in New South Wales' (1980) 54 ALJ 79, cited by Smith. See also Ruoff and Roper, *The Law and Practice of Registered Conveyancing* (6th edn., London: Sweet & Maxwell, 1991), para. 2-04; Jackson, 'Security of Title in Registered Land' (1978) 94 LQR 239.

[31] See Cooke, 'Adverse Possession—Problems of Title in Registered Land' (1994) 14 LS 1, showing that a literal application of the statutory trust will lead to anomalous and unacceptable consequences.

tered land position in line with that in unregistered land. In *Fairweather* v. *St Marylebone Property Co. Ltd.*,[32] Lord Radcliffe said:

I am not at all satisfied that section 75(1) does create a trust interest in the squatter of the kind that one would expect from the words used . . . The trust of the dispossessed owner's title under subsection (1) must somehow be reconciled with the provision under subsection (2) for the squatter to apply to register his own title, which would presumably be his independent possessory title acquired by adverse possession.[33]

The particular facts of the *Fairweather* case have caused great difficulties both to the courts and to academic commentators, and they show the difficulty of reconciling the position in unregistered and registered land. In *Fairweather* a tenant had been dispossessed by a squatter for the limitation period, which expired in 1932. The lease was for ninety-nine years from 1893 and was therefore still running at the date when the limitation period expired against the tenant. At that stage the limitation period would not expire against the freeholder until six years after the lease terminated. The tenant then, in 1959, surrendered the lease to the freeholder, who sought possession against the squatter. The House of Lords, by a majority of 4 to 1, held in favour of the freeholder. The result seems correct. The effect of adverse possession is merely between the squatter and the tenant; it does not vest the lease in the squatter and has no effect either in favour of or against the freeholder.[34] It follows that, as between the freeholder and the tenant, the lease still exists and may be surrendered. The contrary argument of Lord Morris,[35] based on the *nemo dat* rule, must therefore fail.

However, there are great problems in translating that result into the registered land scheme. First, the statutory trust is in danger of vesting the lease in the squatter, which would completely reverse the unregistered land position. Secondly, if the squatter applies for a registered title, the registered system may have to face the possibility of two registered fees simple, one vested in the original freeholder and the other vested in the squatter.[36] Can those problems be solved?[37] The Land Registry has found an appropriate

---

[32] [1963] AC 510. See also *Jessamine Investment Co.* v. *Schwarz* [1978] QB 264.

[33] [1963] AC 510 at 542.

[34] *Tichborne* v. *Weir* (1892) 67 LT 735; *Taylor* v. *Twinberrow* [1930] 2 KB 16; *Tickner* v. *Buzzacott* [1965] Ch. 426.

[35] Supported by Wade, 'Landlord, Tenant and Squatter' (1962) 78 LQR 541.

[36] Smith (*Property Law*, 75, n. 165) refers to 'the spectre of two registered fees simple.'

[37] The registered land position arose directly in *Spectrum Investment Co.* v. *Holmes* [1981] 1 WLR 221, but there the Registry had pre-empted the position by registering the squatter as proprietor of a possessory *leasehold* title and closing the title of the dispossessed tenant. It was held, correctly, that the original tenant no longer had a lease which could be surrendered, a result which is the complete converse of the position in unregistered land. That result, however, shows that the Registry was wrong in registering the squatter as proprietor of the lease.

solution by granting the squatter a qualified title, which excepts from the registered title the claims of any reversionary owner, in particular those arising on the determination of the lease.[38] However, apparently the practice of the Registry is then to close the original title, after notice to the registered proprietor of that title;[39] this is supposedly on the basis that to allow both titles to remain open would run contrary to the philosophy of registered title.[40] That seems questionable. Since, as we have seen, 'the Limitation Acts . . . apply to registered land in the same manner and to the same extent as those Acts apply to land not registered', the register ought to reflect so far as it can the unregistered land position. The fact is that, under the general law, both the freeholder and the squatter have a legal estate, and both can deal with that legal estate. The owner of each estate has a title which is limited to the extent of the other. It is, therefore, suggested that the unregistered land position should be reflected on the register. Both titles should be left open (if that is contrary to the philosophy of registration, so be it); the squatter's title should be qualified by excepting the rights of any reversionary owner, and the freeholder's title should be qualified by excepting the rights of the squatter acquired against the erstwhile tenant.[41]

   This solution certainly seems to reflect more faithfully the unregistered land position. The existence of two registered freehold titles may seem startling, but on reflection that is not so, because each is qualified by reference to the other and therefore they are not in conflict. Since the registered land system adopts the concept of relative title, and, since the concept of relative title acknowledges that there may be more than one title to the same property, it seems to follow inevitably that there may be two registered titles. Provided that each reflects the existence of the other, no harm is done, and the purchaser of either is made aware of the position. In any event, it seems to be the only method by which the registered land position can be kept fully consistent with the position in unregistered land, as section 75(1) of the Land Registration Act 1925 requires. However, this logical and consistent position can be maintained only by, in effect, ignoring the statutory trust imposed by section 75(1). That trust has proved to be a completely inappropriate device, and it should be abolished at the earliest opportunity. Such a proposal could emerge from the Law Commission's present re-examination of the registered title system.

---

[38] See Cooke, (1994) 14 LS 1, 11. The award of a possessory title would not have the desired effect, because that title would be capable of being automatically upgraded under Land Registration Act 1925, s. 77.

[39] See Cooke, (1994) 14 LS 1, 11.   [40] Ibid., and see n. 36.

[41] If it be objected that the Chief Land Registrar has no power to downgrade an absolute title to a qualified title, the answer is that the squatter's rights have now become an overriding interest affecting that title under Land Registration Act 1925, s. 70(1)(f), and therefore the register can be rectified under s. 82(1) or s. 82(3).

Prescription

It is ancient, and in many ways, archaic law that easements and profits[42] may be acquired by long user or prescription. Here again the law is clothing with legality what began unlawfully, and recognizing the moral claim that long user generates, especially when coupled with acquiescence and inertia on the part of the servient owner. This chapter need not consider the substantive law. It is ancient in origin and was last revised by the Prescription Act 1832, a statute which is almost universally regarded as poorly drafted and poorly thought out. The Law Reform Committee in 1966 unanimously proposed radical reform.[43] It is extraordinary, and unacceptable, that some thirty years have now passed without any legislative action. However, there is a more fundamental point: should the idea of prescription be retained (and reformed) or should it be abolished? The arguments are evenly balanced and the Law Reform Committee was completely split on the issue in 1966. By a majority of 8 to 6 the Committee recommended the total abolition of prescription, whereas the minority favoured its retention for easements, but not profits,[44] based on a twelve-year period of user.

Obviously, it is unlikely that rights acquired by prescription will be entered on the register. In the case of unregistered land, they are not registrable because they take effect as legal interests. In the case of registered land, it would not be rational to require them to be protected on the register, and section 70(1)(a) of the Land Registration Act 1925 rightly provides for them to be overriding interests. An argument that should not be accepted is that the whole idea of prescription is incompatible with the land registration system (the mirror principle) and should therefore be abolished. To accept that argument would be to allow the tail to wag the dog.[45] If, in principle, the idea of prescription is right, then the registration system must cope with it. It does so at present by providing that the rights acquired by prescription (and for that matter by implication) are overriding interests.

[42] In much the same way, public rights of way can be created by uninterrupted use over a period of twenty years (Highways Act 1980, s. 31(1)).

[43] Law Reform Committee, *Acquisition of Easements and Profits by Prescription*, 14th Report, Cm. 3100 (London: HMSO, 1966).

[44] The Committee set out not very convincing reasons for the distinction in para.98 of the Report. The Committee recommended special provision for rights of support and shelter: paras. 84–96.

[45] That was one of the (subsidiary) arguments deployed by the majority of the Law Reform Committee. Yet, when the same (though differently constituted) Committee considered the law on adverse possession in 1977, there was no suggestion that the whole concept was inconsistent with the land registration system. Rather, the emphasis was on amending provisions in the Land Registration Act 1925 so as to make the registered land position more consistent with that in unregistered land. See the Committee's *Final Report on Limitation of Actions*, Cm. 6923, paras. 3.71–3.79.

No convincing argument has yet been presented for changing that position.[46]

INFORMAL ARRANGEMENTS

There are two methods by which the law allows informal arrangements respecting land to create proprietary interests. The first is by informally created trusts under section 53(2) of the Law of Property Act 1925. The second method is by proprietary estoppel.

An Informal Trust

Section 53(2) of the Law of Property Act 1925 provides that a trust relating to land may arise informally if it is an implied, resulting, or constructive trust. That provision allows for the wide-scale creation of informal interests, since the legislature has left it to the courts to decide exactly when an informal trust shall arise, and the justification in a particular case (or category of case) for allowing the normal formalities to be waived. Section 53(2) has been widely exploited as a mechanism for the creation of informal interests, especially in the context of the matrimonial or family home. For at least 200 years[47] courts of equity have held that, where land is vested in one person, but some other person, typically a wife or cohabiting partner, has contributed to the acquisition of that land, equity will presume, in the absence of contrary evidence, that the parties intended that they should have interests in the property proportionate to their respective contributions. Equity will give effect to their intention by imposing a trust on the legal owner.[48] Over the years two main problems have concerned the courts: (1) what is to be regarded as a contribution? and (2) how is a contribution, and the interest to which it gives rise, to be quantified? After many vicissitudes,[49] and no doubt with some further shifts to come, the law is now authoritatively stated in the speech of Lord Bridge in *Lloyds Bank plc* v. *Rosset*.[50] There are two categories. The first is where there is an agree-

---

[46] It is accepted by the Law Commission in *Property Law: Third Report on Land Registration*, Law Com. No. 158, paras. 2.26 *et seq.* (1987). Cf. Howard and Hill, (1995) 15 LS 356, 372–5.

[47] *Dyer* v. *Dyer* (1788) 2 Cox 92.

[48] This will now be a trust of land under Trusts of Land and Appointment of Trustees Act 1996, s. 1.

[49] The history is briefly recounted in the author's commentary on *Midland Bank* v. *Cooke* [1995] 4 All ER 562: Battersby, 'How Not to Judge the Quantum (and Priority) of a Share in the Family Home' (1996) 8 C & FLQ 261.

[50] [1991] AC 107. The approach of the English courts, now culminating in *Rosset*, is far removed from the way the law has been shaped in other common law jurisdictions,

ment, arrangement, or understanding, based on express discussions between the partners, that the property is to be shared beneficially. The partner relying on the agreement must then show that she has acted to her detriment or significantly altered her position in reliance on the agreement, arrangement, or understanding. The effect will be to give rise to a constructive trust or proprietary estoppel. The second category is where there is no such agreement, arrangement, or understanding. Everything then depends on the conduct of the partners. Direct contributions to the purchase price, whether by contribution to the original deposit or later payments towards the mortgage, will readily found the inference of a common intention and thus give rise to an interest by contribution.[51] Indirect contributions, it would seem, cannot fall within the second category, only the first. The latter proposition does not seem in line with previous authorities, which were prepared, in some circumstances, to play down the distinction between a direct and an indirect contribution.

Suppose a household in which both husband and wife have paid employment and each has a separate bank account. They systematically divide the household finances, so that the husband devotes his money to the acquisition and maintenance of the house, and the wife meets all the other household expenses. In such a case it ought to be possible to hold that the wife has made an indirect contribution by making it possible for her husband to devote his money to the house, such contribution falling within the second of the *Rosset* categories. Lords Reid and Pearson in *Gissing* v. *Gissing*[52] certainly took that view, as did Fox and May LJJ in *Burns* v. *Burns*.[53] It is surprising, therefore, that in *Ivin* v. *Blake*[54] the Court of Appeal, without any thorough review of the earlier authorities, held that the law was as stated by Lord Bridge in *Rosset*.[55] That is not an acceptable mode of judicial reasoning. The question of identifying indirect contributions is difficult, but it is arbitrary to treat indirect contributions as capable of falling only within the first of the *Rosset* categories.

It has been clear for some years now that anything other than a financial contribution, or a quite exceptional contribution in the form of work on

especially Australia and Canada: see the summary in Smith, *Property Law*, 154–5. Equally far removed is the suggestion of Gardner, 'Rethinking Family Property' (1993) 109 LQR 263, that the law should be based on unjust enrichment modified by a principle of communality.

[51] Lord Bridge thought that the result would be the imposition of a constructive trust, though it makes better sense to found the interest on an inference of a resulting trust (see *Re Densham (A Bankrupt)* [1975] 1 WLR 1519; *Drake* v. *Whipp* (1995) The Times, 19 Dec., *per* Gibson LJ).

[52] [1971] AC 886 at 896–7, *per* Lord Reid, at 903B, *per* Lord Pearson.

[53] [1984] Ch. 317, at 329B, *per* Fox LJ , at 344H, *per* May LJ.   [54] [1995] 1 FLR 70.

[55] Excessive reliance was placed on the decision of the Northern Ireland Court of Appeal in *McFarlane* v. *McFarlane* [1972] 1 NILR 59.

the property[56], will not count as a contribution at all. The pivotal case is
Burns v. *Burns*,[57] where the Court of Appeal, after the retirement of Lord
Denning MR, accepted for the first time the true logic of the decision of
the House of Lords in *Gissing* v. *Gissing*.[58] Mr and Mrs Burns were not married but lived together for nearly twenty years in a house bought entirely
with money provided by Mr Burns and vested in his sole name. There were
two children of the relationship. Mrs Burns devoted herself to looking after
the children and the house, but made no financial contribution to the
acquisition of the house. When eventually the relationship broke down it
was held that she was not entitled to any interest in the house. The result is
legally correct but wholly unacceptable. If the parties had been married and
then divorced, Mrs Burns could have applied for an order under section 24
of the Matrimonial Causes Act 1973, and there can be little doubt that, in
view of the history of their relationship and her non-financial contributions
to the welfare of the household, she would have been awarded a substantial property or financial settlement. It cannot be right that the absence of a
formal marriage should make such a huge difference.

Then there is the problem of quantifying an interest arising by contribution. This question was considered in *Midland Bank plc* v. *Cooke*.[59] On the
basis of her financial contribution, Mrs Cooke's share amounted to 6.47 per
cent, and there was no agreement between Mr and Mrs Cooke that she
should have any larger share. Yet the Court of Appeal held that, once a
direct contribution was established, the court must review the whole history of the marriage in order to determine what would be an equitable
share; in the result, Mrs Cooke was awarded a 50 per cent share. It might
be more realistic to regard the court as exercising a discretionary jurisdiction to vary the property rights of the parties. That might be acceptable,
since it is analogous to the court's jurisdiction to make such an order as
ancillary to a decree of divorce, judicial separation, or nullity of marriage.[60]
An order made under the discretionary jurisdiction cannot bind a third
party such as a mortgagee, and it is significant therefore that, when *Cooke*
reached the Court of Appeal, the mortgagee was no longer claiming priority over Mrs Cooke's share. The decision would certainly be objectionable

---

[56] See e.g. *Eves* v. *Eves* [1975] 1 WLR 1338. The renovation work done by Mrs Rosset
was not enough.

[57] [1984] Ch. 317. See also *Midland Bank plc* v. *Dobson and Dobson* [1986] 1 FLR 171.

[58] [1971] AC 886.   [59] [1995] 4 All ER 562.

[60] Matrimonial Causes Act 1973, s. 24. However, the decision in *Midland Bank plc* v.
Cooke points an odd contrast with *Burns* v. *Burns*. Mrs Cooke had made a small contribution in money, and therefore her other contributions to the family welfare could be taken
into account in order to quantify her share as 50%. Mrs Burns had made no financial
contribution, and her other contributions did not count at all; she was therefore entitled to
nothing.

where the mortgagee had priority, since the extent of that priority would be wholly unpredictable.

Overall, the law as to gaining an interest by contribution remains uncertain and unsatisfactory. That benefits no one but lawyers. It is, therefore, good news that the Law Commission has embarked on a study of the property rights of all home-sharers.[61] The project is in its early stages, but the first indications are that the Property and Trust Law Team at the Law Commission would favour a much tighter formulation of property law— that is, the circumstances in which an interest can be created by contribution, but coupled with an adjustive regime which would allow the court to vary the property rights of those who had shared a home. Such an approach deserves a broad welcome. The adjustive regime would clearly allow the court to achieve a just result in a case like *Burns* v. *Burns*.[62] For more than twenty years an unmarried cohabitant has been able to claim against the estate of the deceased partner, although still not exactly on the same basis as a surviving spouse;[63] there cannot be any good reason for treating the position as different where the unmarried relationship has simply broken down.[64] Moreover, where the unmarried relationship has lasted for a significant period of time, or has resulted in children of the family, there seems every reason to treat it as equivalent to marriage.[65] However, it seems inevitable, whatever the outcome of the Law Commission's study, that the law will continue to recognize interests created under an informal trust. The conveyancing system must, therefore, cope with them. In the case of unregistered land they are (rightly) exempt from registration under the Land Charges Act 1972,[66] but that has the uncomfortable result for a purchaser that they are subject to the doctrine of notice. In order to protect the beneficiary's interest, the courts seem inclined to pitch the purchaser's duty

[61] See Law Commission, *Twenty-Ninth Annual Report 1994*, Law Com. No. 232 (1994), para. 2.78. The study was welcomed by Waite LJ in *Midland Bank plc* v. *Cooke* [1995] 4 All ER 562 at 564j, and by Peter Gibson LJ in *Drake* v. *Whipp* (1995) The Times, 19 Dec.

[62] [1984] Ch. 317.

[63] Inheritance (Provision for Family and Dependants) Act 1975, as amended by Law Reform (Succession) Act 1995, s. 2. Two years' cohabitation is required.

[64] Charles Harpum, now the Law Commissioner in charge of the home-sharers' project, made that point many years ago in 'Adjusting Property Rights between Unmarried Cohabitees' (1982) 2 OJLS 277 at 287.

[65] Cf. Australian legislation: De Facto Relationships Act 1984 (New South Wales), s. 20; Property Law Amendment Act 1987 (Victoria), s. 285. It is arguable that any legal distinction between married and unmarried couples is contrary to Articles 8 and 14 of the European Convention for the Protection of Human Rights and Fundamental Freedoms, Cm. 86969 (1953). Such an issue will become justiciable in domestic courts when the government's Human Rights Bill is enacted. Cf. *Miron* v. *Trudel* [1995] 2 SCR 418, a decision of the Supreme Court of Canada on the Canadian Charter of Rights and Freedoms.

[66] See s. 2(4)(b)(ii), as amended by the Trusts of Land and Appointment of Trustees Act 1996, sch. 2, para. 12.

of inspection and inquiry at a very high level.[67] In registered land such interests are minor interests requiring protection on the register, but, if accompanied by actual occupation, as they usually will be, they become overriding interests.[68] In both registered and unregistered land such interests can be overreached by a disposition of the legal estate by two trustees.[69] This conveyancing framework seems satisfactory.

In summary, the conclusion has to be that the law relating to the acquisition and quantification of these informal interests by contribution is unsatisfactory and urgently in need of reform; on the other hand, the formality and registration provisions operate satisfactorily enough.[70]

Proprietary Estoppel

This is the second method by which informal arrangements are recognized as capable of creating proprietary interests. This doctrine is entirely the creation of the courts of equity and is not subject to any statutory regulation.

The doctrine covers many different situations, but its essence is that, if one person, *A*, represents by his words or conduct to another person, *B*, that *B* has or will have some interest in *A*'s land, and if *B* acts in reliance on the understanding that *A* has thus created, an equity arises in favour of *B*, and a court of equity will decide how, in the absence of agreement, that

---

[67] See *Kingsnorth Finance Co. Ltd.* v. *Tizard* [1986] 1 WLR 783, in effect disapproving *Caunce* v. *Caunce* [1969] 1 WLR 286.

[68] Land Registration Act 1925, s. 70(1)(g); *Williams & Glyn's Bank Ltd.* v. *Boland* [1981] AC 487. Compare the grotesquely unfair result in *Lloyds Bank plc* v. *Carrick* [1996] 4 All ER 630, where Mrs Carrick's equitable interest in unregistered land arose from an informal but enforceable contract made in 1982. She was in occupation of the land when the plaintiff bank acquired its legal mortgage, but she had failed, lacking legal advice, to register a class C(iv) land charge. The bank made no inquiries of Mrs Carrick. The Court of Appeal held the contract void for non-registration and the bank succeeded in its claim for possession. The Court recognized (1) that the result would have been different if the title had been registered, because Mrs Carrick would have had an overriding interest under Land Registration Act 1925, s. 70(1)(g), and (2), ironically, that Mrs Carrick's informal contract would not now be enforceable, because of Law of Property (Miscellaneous Provisions) Act 1989, s. 2, and her interest would then arise by way of an informal trust or proprietary estoppel, in either case not requiring registration.

[69] *City of London Building Society* v. *Flegg* [1988] AC 54. The beneficiary can also easily lose priority to a mortgage in which the beneficiary acquiesces: *Bristol & West Building Society* v. *Henning* [1985] 1 WLR 778; *Paddington Building Society* v. *Mendelsohn* (1989) 40 P&CR 244; *Abbey National Building Society* v. *Cann* [1991] 1 AC 56; *Equity & Law Home Loans Ltd.* v. *Prestidge* [1992] 1 WLR 137; *Castle Phillips Finance* v. *Piddington* [1995] 1 FLR 783. In view of these authorities the decision in *Woolwich Building Society* v. *Dickman* [1996] 3 All ER 204, seems incomprehensible and must be wrong.

[70] Nevertheless, there are aspects of the formality provisions in s. 53, especially s. 53(1)(c), which are not satisfactory, and it is welcome news that the Law Commission has also embarked on a study of those provisions.

equity will be satisfied. The ultimate decision is therefore highly discretionary but may result in the creation of a proprietary interest.[71] The substantive law is now well developed through numerous decisions in the English courts and in other Commonwealth jurisdictions.[72]

Two important questions remain subject to debate. The first is whether proprietary estoppel is capable of creating proprietary rights which the general law would not recognize as having proprietary effect. In particular, the question is whether estoppel licences can bind third parties.

Over a period of some thirty years the Denning Court of Appeal developed the idea that a contractual licence to occupy created an equitable interest.[73] At the time, this was a major contribution to the law of informal arrangements creating interests in land. If, for example, parents allowed their daughter and son-in-law to occupy the parents' house rent free but paying the mortgage instalments, the result would be a contractual licence for an indefinite period of time on terms determined by the court, and an equitable interest would be created.[74] That line of authority was brought to an abrupt end by *Ashburn Anstalt* v. *Arnold*,[75] where the Court of Appeal delivered an elaborately reasoned (albeit strictly obiter) decision which destroyed the idea that a contractual licence could create a proprietary interest.[76] The reasoning relied on by the Court of Appeal was that the notion of a contractual licence as a proprietary interest was contrary to previous binding authority.[77] Another good reason would have been that these forms of family contractual licence were too imprecise to be capable of constituting proprietary interests: their duration and contents would have been wholly incapable of ascertainment by subsequent purchasers or mortgagees, and the conveyancing system would therefore have been subverted.[78]

---

[71] See e.g. *Crabb* v. *Arun District Council* [1976] Ch. 179, where an easement (right of way) arose, and *Pascoe* v. *Turner* [1979] 1 WLR 431, where transfer of the fee simple was ordered.

[72] There is a full and excellent account in Gray, *Elements of Land Law* (2nd edn., London: Butterworths, 1993), ch. 11.

[73] The starting point was *Errington* v. *Errington and Woods* [1952] 1 KB 290, and the line of authority culminated in *Re Sharpe (A Bankrupt)* [1980] 1 WLR 219.

[74] The example is based on *Hardwick* v. *Johnson* [1978] 1 WLR 683.   [75] [1989] Ch. 1.

[76] Although strictly obiter, the decision has been accepted and followed: see *IDC Group Ltd.* v. *Clark* [1992] 1 EGLR 187, 65 P & CR 179; *Canadian Imperial Bank of Commerce* v. *Bello* (1992) 64 P & CR 48; *Camden LBC* v. *Shortlife Community Housing Ltd.* (1992) 90 LGR 358; *Nationwide Anglia Building Society* v. *Ahmed and Balakrishnan* (1995) 70 P & CR 381.

[77] Particularly *King* v. *David Allen and Sons (Billposting) Ltd.* [1916] 2 AC 54, and *Clore* v. *Theatrical Properties Ltd.* [1936] 3 All ER 483.

[78] In *Hardwick* v. *Johnson* [1978] 1 WLR 683 at 688H, Lord Denning MR referred to a family arrangement as 'an equitable licence of which the court has to spell out the terms'. Later at 689F he said: 'It is unnecessary to decide today in what circumstances the mother could revoke the licence. No doubt circumstances might arise in which it could be done.' It would be wholly unsatisfactory to regard such a vague arrangement as capable of binding third parties.

However, the Court of Appeal also held that, in exceptional situations, a particular purchaser might so conduct himself that it would be unconscionable for him to claim to take free from a licence—for example, if a purchaser agreed to take subject to a licence and in consequence paid a lower price. In such circumstances, a constructive trust will be imposed on the purchaser, and the licence will then bind him.[79]

In cases of proprietary estoppel it is quite common for the original relationship between the parties to be that of licensor and licensee. Typically, the owner of the land informally allows some other person, perhaps a cohabitant or a member of the owner's family, to go into occupation. When subsequently the original licence is overtaken by circumstances giving rise to an estoppel, it sometimes happens that the court, in deciding how the equity shall be satisfied, uses language suggesting the creation of a further licence. The question then is whether such an estoppel licence is proprietary, and so is capable of binding third parties who subsequently acquire an interest in the land, when its contractual counterpart is non-proprietary.

Two Court of Appeal decisions will illustrate the point. The first is *Inwards* v. *Baker*.[80] The defendant's father in 1931 encouraged the son to build a bungalow on the father's land. The defendant built the bungalow at his own expense and lived there with his family. No interest in the land was ever formally granted to the defendant. The father died in 1951, and under his will the land vested in trustees holding for persons other than the defendant. In 1963 the trustees commenced these possession proceedings against the defendant. The Court of Appeal rightly held that this was a case of proprietary estoppel and dismissed the action. The court stated that the defendant's equity 'can be satisfied by holding that the defendant can remain there as long as he desires as his home'.[81] That certainly sounds like the language of a licence,[82] and the Court of Appeal could be forgiven for assuming at that time, long before *Ashburn Anstalt* v. *Arnold*,[83] that the licence had proprietary effect.

The second example is *Matharu* v. *Matharu*,[84] a decision of the Court of Appeal in 1994, when *Ashburn Anstalt* v. *Arnold* had dramatically changed the landscape. *Matharu* concerned an extended Bangladeshi family. The

---

[79] *Binions* v. *Evans* [1972] Ch. 359, was explained as a case where it was proper to impose a constructive trust. It is a moot point whether the purchaser's successors would also be bound. Arguably, the constructive trust is here being used in remedial fashion to impose personal liability on the purchaser whose conscience is affected.

[80] [1965] 2 QB 29.

[81] Ibid., at 37G, *per* Lord Denning MR; Danckwerts and Salmon LJJ agreed.

[82] However, in *Dodsworth* v. *Dodsworth* (1973) 228 EG 1115, it was interpreted as creating a life interest and therefore invoking the Settled Land Act 1925.

[83] [1989] Ch. 1.   [84] [1994] 2 FLR 597.

plaintiff was the registered proprietor of a house occupied by his widowed daughter-in-law and the five children of her marriage to the plaintiff's son, Raghbir. They had lived in that house since 1981, but the plaintiff now wished to occupy the house himself, and he commenced possession proceedings in 1992. The plaintiff argued that she could take advantage of an estoppel created between the plaintiff and Raghbir. The plaintiff had allowed Raghbir and his wife and family to live in the house, and Raghbir had then, with the knowledge of his father, made considerable improvements to the house at his own expense. The Court of Appeal accepted the estoppel argument; an equity had arisen in favour of the defendant and the court had to decide how that equity should be satisfied. It was held that the defendant was entitled to a licence to remain in the house for her lifetime or such shorter period as she should decide, subject to various obligations mainly concerned with the upkeep of the house.

These two decisions, therefore, appear to create licences. The question then is whether the licences so created can bind third parties who subsequently acquire an interest in the land. The fact that the licences are created by a court order can surely give them no greater effect than if they were created by the parties themselves. Proprietary estoppel is, in this respect, merely a mechanism for the informal creation of rights over the land which the parties themselves have failed to create. If, therefore, the court in a particular case wishes the remedy to be the creation of a proprietary interest, it should choose from the available menu of conventionally recognized proprietary interests, fashioning an order which will either itself create the desired interest or direct one or other of the parties to create the interest.[85] Thus, in *Pascoe* v. *Turner*,[86] where the decision was that the plaintiff should vest his fee simple in the defendant, the effect of the court's order is that the plaintiff must execute a deed conveying the fee simple to the defendant. If it were registered land, the defendant would then, of course, need to apply to become the registered proprietor. Once the court's order has been implemented by execution of the appropriate document and compliance with any registration requirement, the interest, according to its nature, will then automatically bind third parties.

If, on the other hand, the right created or ordered by the court is non-proprietary under the general law, such as a licence or monetary compensation, the result is that it cannot bind third parties, except in the rare

---

[85] Since 1996, with the coming into force of the Trusts of Land and Appointment of Trustees Act 1996, s. 2, the creation of a life interest may, in appropriate cases, be regarded as more attractive than formerly, since it will take effect under a simple trust of land, rather than under the complicated structure of the Settled Land Act 1925 (Trusts of Land and Appointment of Trustees Act 1996, s. 2). Cf., under the old law, *Ungarian* v. *Lesnoff* [1990] Ch. 206, and *Costello* v. *Costello* (1994) 27 HLR 12.

[86] [1979] 1 WLR 431.

circumstances where a constructive trust is imposed on a particular purchaser.

This distinction seems obvious and compelling. If it is not observed, the law will become irrational and incoherent. One consequence would be to inhibit the settlement of disputes without litigation; if a court order has greater proprietary power than the parties' agreement, there will be some circumstances where a court order will be necessitated. That result does not serve any public interest.[87]

The second debated question concerns the status of the estoppel before the court awards a remedy (or the parties settle the matter by agreement). Suppose that the land changes hands while the estoppel is still at that inchoate stage; can the court grant a remedy against the third party? In principle, the answer is not straightforward, because, at the inchoate stage, it is uncertain whether the court will ultimately award a proprietary interest (it might award a non-proprietary right[88] or, indeed, no right at all).[89]

Distinguished commentators, notably Lord Browne-Wilkinson (extra-judicially)[90] and Professor David Hayton,[91] have argued that the estoppel does not bind third parties. However, the cases are against them. Let us again consider *Inwards* v. *Baker*,[92] for example. There the land changed hands some thirteen years before the court's decision, but the court made an order against the third parties (the trustees of the father's will). Similarly, there have been decisions that the inchoate equity binds a trustee in bankruptcy,[93] a donee,[94] and a purchaser with notice.[95] The matter therefore seems settled by authority. But how does it stand in principle?

---

[87] In *Matharu* v. *Matharu* [1994] 2 FLR 597, the licence created by the Court of Appeal was subject to various terms, including a provision that the freeholder should be responsible for structural repair of the house. Under the general law that provision would not bind the freeholder's successors in title: *Rhone* v. *Stephens* [1994] 2 AC 310. Would the court's order overcome this limitation under the general law?

[88] See e.g. *Dodsworth* v. *Dodsworth* (1973) 228 EG 1115, and *Baker* v. *Baker and Baker* (1993) 25 HLR 408, where monetary compensation was awarded.

[89] See Ferguson, 'Constructive Trusts—A Note of Caution' (1993) 109 LQR 109 at 114; Baughen, 'Estoppels Over Land and Third Parties: An Open Question' (1994) 14 LS 147; Glover and Todd, 'Occupation for Life: Satisfying the Equity' [1995] Web JCLI; Milne, 'Proprietary Estoppel, Purchasers and Mortgagees: An Alternative Approach' [1997] Web JCLI.

[90] Browne-Wilkinson, 'Constructive Trusts and Unjust Enrichment' (Presidential Address to the Holdsworth Club, 1990–1) (1996) 10 Trust Law International 9.

[91] Hayton, 'Equitable Rights of Cohabitees' [1990] Conveyancer 370; 'Constructive Trusts of Homes—A Bold Approach' (1993) 109 LQR 485; Underhill and Hayton, *Law of Trusts and Trustees* (15th edn., London: Butterworths, 1995), 385 *et seq.*

[92] [1965] 2 QB 29.

[93] *Re Sharpe (A Bankrupt)* [1980] 1 WLR 219 (part of the reasoning is based on proprietary estoppel).

[94] *Voyce* v. *Voyce* (1991) 62 P & CR 290.

[95] *Duke of Beaufort* v. *Patrick* (1853) 17 Beav. 60; *Hopgood* v. *Brown* [1955] 1 WLR 213;

If we look, yet again, at the facts of *Inwards* v. *Baker*,[96] that decision surely reached a just result. By the time the proceedings were brought, the defendant and his family had lived for some thirty-two years in the bungalow which he had built on his father's land. He could not rely on adverse possession because his occupation had at all times been licensed, but the beneficiaries under the father's will must have known perfectly well about the bungalow in which the son and his family had lived for so many years. It is true that they could not know for sure what kind of right over the land the son had; it might be proprietary or non-proprietary, but they surely knew that he had a right of some kind. It would have been manifestly unjust to allow them to take free from that right, whatever it turned out to be. The argument from that case, therefore, is that it is right in principle for an inchoate estoppel to be recognized as proprietary and therefore bind third parties. There is an analogy with the law relating to a pending land action— that is, an action in which the plaintiff claims an interest in the land.[97] Just as the plaintiff in a pending land action may not be successful in claiming to be entitled to an interest in the land, so an estoppel claimant may not be successful in claiming a proprietary right (or any right at all) against the defendant's land, but a purchaser with notice of the claim should take subject to any proprietary interest which results from that claim.[98] It may be that in unregistered land the claim should be classed as a mere equity, rather than as an equitable interest, since it is a step along the way to the establishment of a full proprietary interest; it would not be registrable under the Land Charges Act 1972 and would be defeated by a purchaser for value of any interest in the land affected taking in good faith and without notice. In registered land the claim would be a minor interest, requiring protection on the register, but, if coupled with actual occupation, would become an overriding interest.

CONCLUSION

This chapter has shown that there are significant exceptions to the law's normal requirements of formality for transactions in land. The chapter has

E. R. *Ives Investment Ltd.* v. *High* [1967] 2 QB 379; *Lee-Parker* v. *Izzet (No. 2)* [1972] 1 WLR 775; *Lloyds Bank plc* v. *Carrick* [1996] 4 All ER 630.

[96] [1965] 2 QB 29.

[97] See the definition of pending land action in Land Charges Act 1972, s. 17(1).

[98] If an action has been commenced based on the estoppel and claiming a proprietary interest, that would itself constitute a pending land action which, in the case of unregistered land, would be registrable under Land Charges Act 1972, s. 5: see *Haslemere Estates Ltd.* v. *Baker* [1982] 1 WLR 1109 at 1119–20, *per* Megarry V-C. In the case of registered land the pending land action would be a minor interest, but would become an overriding interest if the plaintiff were in actual occupation of the land affected.

accepted that there are good reasons for the exceptions in the four situations discussed. The principal concern has been to examine how satisfactory in operation is the current state of the law. Criticisms have been made in relation to all four situations. In relation to adverse possession as it affects registered land, prescription, and informal trusts, there is an urgent need for legislative reform, and there are good reasons for hoping that the Law Commission will make proposals before too long. In the case of proprietary estoppel, it seems likely that the law will continue to be judge-made; when a suitable case arises, the courts should review the law, and in particular should reverse their present assumption that licences arising by estoppel are proprietary.

20

TAKING FORMALITIES SERIOUSLY

Patricia Critchley

> In the case of last wills, a set of formalities are prescribed, and of course
> on pain of nullity, by a statute commonly and not inappositely termed
> the *Statute of Frauds*. . . . three points in relation to this statute are
> beyond dispute: the mischievousness of it, the uselessness of it, and the
> corruption in which it was begotten and has been preserved.[1]

> . . . there are positive goals to be achieved by utilization of such for-
> malities in the wealth transmission process. It is our attitude towards
> those formalities which, in the end, creates the burdensome tension
> between private ownership and restrictions upon disposition.[2]

Difficult though it may be to believe, the above quotations are actually discussing the same legal rule. This rule (now found in section 9 of the Wills
Act 1837) stipulates that wills must be written, signed, and witnessed—
hardly the sort of requirement one might expect to provoke vehement disagreement. Somewhat surprisingly, however, such conflicts of opinion as to
the significance of formality requirements are relatively commonplace. The
purpose of this short discussion is to investigate in more detail the legal phenomenon of formality, with the aim of distilling from the various competing viewpoints a basic set of principles which could be used as a tool to
assess, analyse, and criticize decision-making about formality.

BUT WHAT *IS* 'FORMALITY'?

Before proceeding any further, we should define our terms. Formality is a
phenomenon not confined to legal discussions; for example, we talk quite
naturally of business correspondence being 'formal', or of a social occasion
being 'informal'. This cultural, or lay, understanding of the concept of formality may be at odds with the legal perception of formality: thus, a lawyer

---

[1] Bentham, *Rationale of Judicial Evidence*, ii (London: Garland Publishing, 1978; facsimile
of 1827 edition, published by Hunt and Clarke under the title *Rationale of Judicial Evidence,
Specially Applied to English Practice*), 553–4.

[2] Nelson and Starck, 'Formalities and Formalism: A Critical Look at the Execution of
Wills', 6 Pepperdine L. Rev. 331 at 356–7 (1979).

may tell his client that a simple contract requires no 'formality', but the client, faced with a document littered with seemingly arcane terminology ('hereinafter'; 'parties of the first part'), might well disagree. This means that, for the purposes of our discussion, we must begin by finding a *legal* definition of formality.

One good starting point might be the common legal distinction between matters of 'substance' and 'form'. This suggests a definition of formality as something which is external or *added* to the transaction, rather than a constituent, substantive part of it. In legal usage, formality is generally also seen as a *requirement*, rather than a mere habit or convention, so it would be helpful for our definition to express the notion that formality is something mandatory. Further, it is typical (though not essential), where a legal formality is imposed, to have some sort of *sanction* for breach of the rule: some legal disbenefit, or some failure to obtain a legal benefit. The sanction is frequently the invalidation of a non-complying transaction,[3] but there are other possibilities: for example, there might be procedural disadvantages (limiting the type of evidence which may be used to prove the transaction in legal proceedings);[4] or the transaction might be valid as regards the original parties to it, but invalid against third parties.[5] Whatever the sanction is, it would clearly also be useful to have a definition which would cover a formality rule with a sanction attached. Putting all of this together, then, we reach the following definition: 'in law, a formality is a requirement that matters of substance must be put into a particular form (in order to have a specified legal effect).'

To give an example: if a landlord wishes to grant a legal lease of land for a fixed term of five years, this must satisfy two sets of legal requirements in order to be fully valid. First, there are the substantive requirements: thus, there must be granted a right of exclusive possession, for a certain term.[6] Secondly, there is the formality rule: section 52 of the Law of Property Act 1925 says that 'all conveyances of land or of any interest therein are void for the purpose of conveying or creating a legal estate [which includes a lease] unless made by deed'. The substantive elements are therefore insufficient: they must be cast into a particular form (a deed) in order to have the specified legal effect (the creation of a legal lease).

Requirements such as those in section 52 are easily recognized as 'formalities' falling within the scope of the proposed definition. However, land law contains other rules which would also qualify. For example, most of the Land Registration Act 1925 is concerned with formality, on the above definition, since dealings with registered land must usually be entered on the

---

[3] e.g. Law of Property Act 1925, s. 53(1)(c).

[4] e.g. ibid., s. 53(1)(b).   [5] e.g. Land Charges Act 1972, s. 4(6).

[6] *Street* v. *Mountford* [1985] AC 809; *Prudential Assurance Co. Ltd.* v. *London Residuary Body* [1992] 2 AC 386.

register in order to achieve (full) legal validity.[7] And it is necessary also to look outside land law to the wider area of property law, since there are rules of form which apply irrespective of the type of property involved, such as the requirements for *testamentary* dispositions.[8]

THE IMPORTANCE OF FORMALITY FOR LAND LAW

But, in that case, why discuss formality in a collection of essays specifically on *land* law? Requirements of form are obviously a general legal phenomenon, rather than one peculiar to the law of real property. This objection is valid, but it does not take account of the fact that formality rules seem to proliferate in the area of property law, and in particular in the law of real property. Textbooks on the law of contract, for example, devote relatively little space to the question of formality precisely because contract law has relatively few important requirements of form;[9] indeed, some of the most significant contractual formalities are those relating to contracts concerning land.[10] In contrast, land law is hedged about at almost every turn by formality requirements. To transfer a freehold property by way of sale from one person to another at its simplest usually requires at least two formalities: first, a written contract of sale signed by both parties,[11] and, secondly, a deed of conveyance.[12] A more complex transaction multiplies the formalities: for instance, if the purchaser is to hold as trustee for himself and another, this should properly be put into writing, if the trust is to be enforceable.[13] To cap it all, if title to the land is registered, the transaction must be entered on the register to be fully valid.[14] Given the number of formality rules which affect land law transactions, then, the questions of whether formality is useful or useless, and of when (if at all) it should be required, are of particular relevance to land lawyers.

---

[7] e.g. Land Registration Act 1925, s. 19 (but cf. s. 70(1)).

[8] e.g. Wills Act 1837, s. 9.

[9] See Treitel, *The Law of Contract* (9th edn., London: Sweet & Maxwell, 1995), ch. 5, esp. 162–3.

[10] e.g. Law of Property (Miscellaneous Provisions) Act 1989, s. 2, which requires contracts for the sale or disposition of an interest in land to be made in signed writing.

[11] See n. 10. It is possible, though not particularly common, to omit the stage of contract and to proceed immediately to conveyance.

[12] Law of Property Act 1925, s. 52.   [13] Ibid., s. 53(1)(b).

[14] Land Registration Act 1925, s. 19.

MAKING DECISIONS ABOUT FORMALITY

Legal rules may be created for a variety of reasons. Some parts of the law may have their origins largely in a particular (party) political objective: for example, an unpopular tax may be abolished to retain public support for the government of the day. However, formality rules do not seem especially contentious, politically speaking. If anything, they appear peculiarly technical: true 'lawyers' law'. It therefore seems somewhat implausible that formality rules are created solely for political reasons, although some have argued this: for example, Bentham insists that formality rules are designed by lawyers to keep themselves in fees.[15] None the less, if our aim in this discussion is to develop a critique of decision-making about formality, a motivation of self-interest such as Bentham suggests would seem to be too easy a target for criticism; and, if the decision-making process itself is indefensible, this will distract attention away from the question of whether the decisions taken under it are defensible.

'Benefits', 'Detriments', and the Importance of Context

We therefore need to start by identifying a prima facie justifiable decision-making process. Perhaps the most obvious choice is a process under which formality rules are imposed on the basis that they are, on balance, a good thing: that their beneficial consequences outweigh their detrimental ones. However, this raises a fresh problem in its turn: how do we know what counts as a 'benefit' or a 'detriment'? The difficulty is that the classification of consequences into benefits and detriments will depend upon the value system which governs the context of the discussion; and even legal discussions of the benefits and detriments of formality (say, in legal writings) will not be free of this value dependence, because legal views on this issue will not have developed in some neutral 'vacuum'. Instead, they are likely to have been influenced by the principles and values (political, social, jurisprudential, economic) which inform and underpin the legal system of which the rules are a part.

Some examples may help to illustrate the problem. Imagine that there is a formality provision, one consequence of which is the protection of individual property rights. A legal system operating in a communist or socialist context would probably deem this a 'detriment' of the provision, since these value systems are (very crudely speaking) seeking to move away from

[15] Bentham, *Rationale of Judicial Evidence*, ii. 462 n., 478–81, 554. See also the detailed analysis of the professional/political influences on modern land law rules in Anderson, *Lawyers and the Making of English Land Law 1832–1940* (Oxford: Oxford University Press, 1992), and Offer, 'The Origins of the Law of Property Acts 1910–25' (1977) 40 MLR 505.

individual property ownership and towards collective or public ownership. Under a libertarian or *laissez-faire* system, it is also possible, though less certain, that this consequence would be seen as 'detrimental'. To some extent, the final decision would turn on the answer to a further question: are these property rights to be protected against the heedless action or perversity of the individual himself (in which case the formality rule is paternalistic and so disapproved of by classical libertarian thinking), or is the protection against harm and depredation by others?[16] None the less, an individualistic system based upon *laissez-faire* (or on some principle of autonomy[17]) would still be more likely to welcome this consequence unreservedly as a 'benefit' than would one which looked to the collective welfare of society (such as classical utilitarianism[18]). Yet another system, based upon particular moral, ethical, or theological views (for example, an Islamic or Christian state), might again require further information before deciding: thus, is the protection of individual rights intended to guard against theft or the exploitation of a weaker party by a stronger (in which case it might be seen as beneficial); or does it, conversely, tend to encourage individual greed and covetousness (a 'detrimental' outcome)?

The fact that 'benefits' and 'detriments' are so dependent upon context and value judgements has two significant implications for our discussion. First, there is the fact that any observations which can be made concerning the role of formality in one legal system cannot safely be transferred wholesale into another legal system. The examples given above clearly illustrate this difficulty. We will, therefore, confine our discussion to the English legal system.

Secondly, there is the fact that, even within one legal system, there may be conflicting principles. Legal systems are rarely wholly self-consistent and coherent. In particular, whether a formality rule is seen as 'beneficial' may well depend upon the standpoint from which the question is viewed. For example, formality rules may be seen as undesirable by those subject to them because of the additional legal costs they frequently generate.[19] On the other hand, it may be argued that the fees paid in such transactions will effectively subsidize other socially important but less profitable work (such as legal-aid cases), thus providing a benefit to the community overall by ensuring that all types of legal problems are catered for by practitioners.[20] Such different viewpoints mean that, even if we limit our study to our own legal system, we may find that none of the conclusions which we reach

---

[16] See Mill, *On Liberty* (London: J. W. Parker & Son, 1859).
[17] See Raz, *The Morality of Freedom* (Oxford: Oxford University Press, 1986), esp. ch. 14.
[18] See Lyons, *Forms and Limits of Utilitarianism* (Oxford: Oxford University Press, 1967).
[19] See p. 520.
[20] See comments by Bogan, 'To Fix or Not to Fix?', (1995) 139 SJ 892.

can be wholly unqualified, because few legal systems are likely to be that simple.

However, these problems need not make the whole project a non-starter. Provided that we bear this twofold difficulty in mind, we should be able to formulate tenable, although not conclusive, propositions about decision-making on formality in the English legal system, relying upon what reasonably appears to be the most widely accepted viewpoint on any issue.

The Problem of Weighting

Once we have identified our main benefits and detriments—which we will do below—we run up against a further difficulty. How do we weigh benefits and detriments against each other so as to arrive at a particular decision in a particular context? This is a rather difficult question to answer. Many value systems or schools of thought do not overtly address this question; but some do: the best example is perhaps utilitarianism, which explicitly takes as its aim (in the simplest form) 'the greatest happiness of the greatest number'. However, this only gives us a principle, or theory, as to how we should perform the balancing exercise. How *in practice* does one go about weighing 'happiness'?

One solution, proposed by law and economics theorists, is to use a common currency which will make this comparison possible: money.[21] 'Happiness' is converted into 'value', which is measured by consumer willingness to pay for the factor in question. So, if A (a factory-owner) values the right to create noise and pollution at £100,000, and B (the sole neighbouring landowner and resident) values the right to be free from noise and pollution at only £75,000, then happiness is maximized by recognizing A's right, rather than B's. Again, however, this does not really solve our problem, because the standard of 'willingness to pay' requires empirical data which it is impracticable, if not impossible, to assemble. The examples commonly used by law and economics theorists are situations involving individuals: a court-case scenario, with one plaintiff, one defendant, whose willingness to pay can (fairly easily) be discovered. But there are other considerations even for a judge adjudicating on an individual case: for example, is the decision likely to provoke additional litigation, with social costs in terms of the detriment to the administration of justice? When we turn to look at the position of the legislature, which must decide upon a particular provision in the abstract, so to speak, the empirical approach seems unworkable: it is not feasible to discover and collate the 'willingness to pay' of all those who might potentially be affected by the proposed rule.

[21] For an overview of law and economics theories and their development, see Minda, *Postmodern Legal Movements: Law and Jurisprudence at Century's End* (New York: New York University Press, 1995), ch. 5.

So does this problem of weighting mean we have reached an impasse? Perhaps, but only in so far as we might wish our analysis to provide us with the 'right answer' to every possible question of formality. If our aim is more modest—in effect, to identify a checklist of factors which should be taken into consideration when decisions are being taken about formality, rather in the style of much recent legislation[22]—then the inability to reach a conclusive answer is not problematic. Our analysis will still be able to do two things. First, it will provide an additional dimension to any consideration of formality; and secondly, it will enable us to identify decisions which are badly wrong: for example, where formality is imposed even though it can have no possible benefits and may have significant detriments. This is akin to the supervisory jurisdiction of the High Court in judicial review, under which the court refuses to overturn a decision purely on its merits, but will intervene in cases where something has gone seriously awry. Our analysis may therefore provide a *Wednesbury* test for decisions on formality.[23]

BENEFITS OF FORMALITY

Now it is time to consider the individual benefits and detriments of formality. Starting with the plus side of the equation, the following discussion will identify the principal advantages of formality which are commonly accepted as such in the English legal system.[24] As we have already noticed, whether the consequences of imposing a formality rule are seen as beneficial or detrimental may depend upon whose position is being considered. For this reason, the analysis which follows is divided into different positions, or 'viewpoints'.

The Viewpoint of the Parties to the Transaction

One important benefit of formality is that it *warns* parties who are entering into a transaction that their actions may have legal effects. By forcing the parties to stop and think, formality helps guard against rash or ill-considered

[22] See e.g. Children Act 1989, s. 1(3); Trusts of Land and Appointment of Trustees Act 1996, s. 15(1).

[23] The name is taken from *Associated Provincial Picture Houses Ltd.* v. *Wednesbury Corporation* [1948] 1 KB 223, in which Lord Greene MR first formulated the relevant propositions of law. There are various versions of the test (see Fordham, *Judicial Review Handbook* (2nd edn., Chichester: John Wiley & Sons Ltd., 1997), 587–90); a fairly representative example is the formulation given in *Council of Civil Service Unions* v. *Minister for the Civil Service* [1985] AC 374, *per* Lord Diplock at 410G: 'a decision which is so outrageous in its defiance of logic or of accepted moral standards that no sensible person who had applied his mind to the question to be decided could have arrived at it.'

[24] For a contrary view, see Baron, 'Gifts, Bargains and Form' 64 Ind. LJ 155 (1989).

decisions, which might be regretted later on.[25] More generally, it helps to ensure that the parties do not enter a transaction which, unbeknownst to them, has an effect in law. The best formalities for this purpose are those which are required for the transaction to be legally valid (for example, the formalities prescribed for a conveyance of land),[26] since the parties will be warned that their actions may have legal effects *before* the transaction is binding upon them. They therefore have the opportunity to investigate what the consequences of their actions will be (for example, by obtaining legal advice), and so can make a fully informed decision as to whether or not they wish to proceed with the transaction. A formality which has some other sanction is less useful in this respect.

Another benefit of formality is that it *protects* against outside pressures, such as undue influence or duress. By making it more difficult to enter a transaction, formality makes it correspondingly more difficult to pressurize someone into it. It is easier to say 'I give you my house' than it is to sit down, make out a deed to that effect, sign it, get it witnessed, and then dispatch it to the Land Registry. In the latter case, the influence or duress must at the very least be sustained over a longer period; and, since the formality requires the presence of a (disinterested) third party, as a witness, there is a greater risk of such influence being detected, which may discourage those exercising it. Similarly, fraud or misrepresentation is hindered by the presence of formality requirements. Although to some extent this protective role has been taken over by substantive doctrines of undue influence, misrepresentation, and the like,[27] formality requirements have a distinct advantage over such doctrines, in that they help to *prevent* the victim of pressure from entering an unwanted transaction, rather than allowing him to *escape* from it. Undoing a transaction vitiated by external influences generally requires the victim to take some positive action. This is not always possible: for example, what if the fraud is not discovered?

In particular, formalities may produce a beneficial protective effect where they require or lead to the involvement of legal professionals. The existence of a formality requirement may often lead the parties to obtain legal advice, in which case the lawyers involved should be able to detect and prevent the application of external pressure (hence the general position that the provision of independent legal advice will usually be a defence to claims of undue influence, misrepresentation, or suchlike).[28] Alternatively, the formality may have to be fulfilled by a legal professional, as is the case with notarial

[25] Mechem, 'The Requirement of Delivery in Gifts of Chattels and of Choses in Action Evidenced by Commercial Instruments', 21 Ill. L. Rev. 341 at 348–9 (1926–7).

[26] Law of Property Act 1925, s. 52.

[27] Gulliver and Tilson, 'Classification of Gratuitous Transfers', 51 Yale LJ 1 at 9–13 (1941).

[28] See *Barclays Bank plc* v. *O'Brien* [1994] 1 AC 180 at 196F–197B.

wills under civil law systems, or with the swearing of affidavit evidence before a commissioner for oaths.

A third benefit of formality to the parties is that it helps to *clarify* the terms of the transaction.[29] For example, if the formality requires signed writing to transfer an interest in land, the very act of reducing the agreement to writing will help to highlight gaps or uncertainties in its terms. What is the nature of the interest? How long is it to last? What consideration (if any) is to be given for it, and when? These are all matters which it is better to resolve at the outset. The parties may consult a legal adviser, especially if the formality has any degree of complexity, and such a person should be trained to spot potential sources of dispute and to make provision for them.

Formality can also *educate* the parties as to the precise legal effects of their transaction.[30] For example, under ground 3, schedule 2, of the Housing Act 1988, notices must be provided to tenants taking short fixed-term tenancies, warning the tenant of the limited security of tenure afforded by the tenancy agreement. Similarly, consumer credit agreements must be made in a prescribed form which sets out the basic legal rights and obligations of each party in straightforward language.[31] The Law Commission has recommended that mortgages of residential property should follow the same pattern.[32] This educative effect of formality is slightly different from the previous advantage discussed, since the prescribed form will tell the parties what effects their transaction will *actually* have, taking into consideration all relevant rules of law and statutory rules.[33] This is not necessarily the same as the effects which the parties *intended* to create by the terms of their transaction. A mortgage agreement might state that the mortgagee owes no duty to the mortgagor to keep the mortgaged property in repair if he takes possession of it. However, under the Law Commission proposals, the intended exclusion of the duty of repair would be ineffective, and the prescribed form would say so. Finally, the presence of formality may again lead the parties to obtain legal advice, which will also assist in educating them as to their precise rights and obligations.

The next, and perhaps most obvious, advantage of formality is the *evidence* which it secures. Quite apart from any evidentiary benefit to third parties (which we will consider below), the parties to the transaction may themselves need evidence of the existence or terms of the transaction, to

---

[29] Perillo, 'The Statute of Frauds in the Light of Functions and Dysfunctions of Form', 43 Fordham L. Rev. 39 at 56–8 (1974).

[30] Ibid. 60–2.   [31] Consumer Credit Act 1974, ss. 60–1.

[32] Law Commission, *Transfer of Land: Land Mortgages*, Law Com. No. 204, (London: HMSO, 1991), paras. 5.9–5.11.

[33] See Bentham, *Rationale of Judicial Evidence*, ii. 482–7, outlining a scheme of 'contract papers' specific to every common type of contract, which would contain 'an indication . . . of so much of the law, as concerns the species of contract, to the expression of which, the paper is adapted'.

forestall or settle disputes at some future point, when memories have become unreliable.[34] This is important for transactions involving property rights, since they tend to be of longer duration than purely personal rights (such as those arising under contract); and it is particularly important for transactions relating to *land*, because one of the notable features of real (as compared with personal) property is its sheer durability.[35] The most effective type of formality for this purpose is one requiring some permanent record—writing, registering, and the like—which in fact all current English land law formalities prescribe. However, even a requirement that a transaction be completed in front of witnesses is better in this respect than total informality, since it increases the stock of (impartial) oral evidence and thus the chance that the transaction can be reconstructed accurately.

A final advantage of formality for the parties has been described as *channelling*.[36] This term, coined by Fuller, is intended to describe how the parties may be able to use formality as a legal tool in order to ensure that their transaction has legal effect. The formality 'channels' their intention towards a particular legal goal. For example, the seal formerly had a good channelling effect in English law, because it was generally sufficient to give legal validity to the document to which it was attached. Land law formalities are less useful in this respect, since there are a number of possible substantive reasons why a land law transaction may fail, even if the formalities are properly completed. Because of this, land law formalities have only a negative channelling effect: if you do not comply with them, you can generally be sure that your transaction will *not* be effective.[37] A slightly different type of channelling effect permits the parties to indicate by the outward form of their transaction the specific category of legal transaction which they intend to enter.[38] This is particularly useful with regard to documents such as negotiable instruments (for example promissory notes), which are treated as an equivalent to money and so must be readily identifiable without detailed investigation of their substance.[39]

The Viewpoint of Third Parties

Third parties have a different set of priorities when it comes to formalities. The main benefit which such rules can bring here is *publicity*: ensuring that

[34] Austin, 'Fragments—On Contracts' in *Lectures on Jurisprudence*, ii (5th edn., London: John Murray, 1885), 907.

[35] Lawson and Rudden, *The Law of Property* (2nd edn., Oxford: Oxford University Press, 1982), 22–5.

[36] Fuller, 'Consideration and Form', 41 Colum L. Rev. 799 at 801 ff. (1941).

[37] Ibid. 802.

[38] Perillo, 'The Statute of Frauds', 50–2; Fuller, 'Consideration and Form', 801.

[39] Chafee, 'Acceleration Provisions in Time Paper', 32 Harv. L. Rev. 747 at 750–2 (1919).

other parties know of the existence and terms of a transaction which might (adversely) affect them.[40] Although this appears similar to the evidentiary benefits of formality which we have just discussed, both advantages will not necessarily be provided by the same formality. For example, a requirement of writing will have all the evidentiary benefits described above as far as the parties to the transaction are concerned, but the necessary writing *could* be created and then kept hidden from third parties. What is needed is some formality which insists upon disclosure of the transaction—such as the system of title registration, which is intended to provide a 'mirror' of title, open to public inspection.[41]

In addition, formalities can *protect* third parties when publicity is not forthcoming.[42] When a transaction adversely affecting land is not registered, and therefore there is the risk that third parties will have no means of finding out about it, it is usual to find a rule to the effect that the transaction is ineffective against the third party, at least as a purchaser for value.[43] Here both the sanction for non-compliance and the actual requirements of the formality are tailored so as to benefit third parties.

The Viewpoint of the Courts

The chief benefit of formality to the courts is that of *evidence*. If a judge is requested to adjudicate upon an alleged transaction, she will need evidence of its existence and terms even more than the original parties, because she will not have been involved in the events leading up to the transaction.[44] Note, too, that formalities can have a secondary evidentiary function for the courts, because of the other beneficial effects which they tend to produce. For example, one advantage of formality is that it makes parties stop and think before entering transactions. If they then go ahead and comply with the formality, this is good, though not *conclusive*, evidence that they genuinely intended to enter that transaction.[45] This secondary evidence is particularly significant in the case of a will, where the most important party will not be around to give evidence,[46] but it is also useful in *inter vivos* transactions. If a mortgagor claims that he never knew the extent of the

---

[40] Perillo, 'The Statute of Frauds', 59–60.

[41] See *Abbey National Building Society* v. *Cann* [1991] 1 AC 56, *per* Lord Oliver at 78C; although note that the existence of (for example) overriding interests means that the register does not reflect the state of the title 100% accurately.

[42] See Youdan, 'Formalities for Trusts of Land and the Doctrine in *Rochefoucauld* v. *Boustead*' (1984) 43 CLJ 306 at 312–14 (discussing protection as a motivating force behind the enactment of the Statute of Frauds 1677).

[43] See e.g. Land Registration Act 1925, s. 20(1), and Land Charges Act 1972, s. 4.

[44] Gulliver and Tilson, 'Classification of Gratuitous Transfers', 3.

[45] Ibid. 3–4. The channelling effect of formality is also useful in this respect.

[46] Ibid. 6.

mortgagee's rights, the fact that he signed a document which set out those rights in plain English on its front cover is good evidence against his claim.

The Viewpoint of the State

The assertion that formality rules are of interest outside the legal system may seem surprising, but formality has some important benefits for the executive government. One of the most significant of these is its *fiscal* role, where the formality requirement is used as an aid to the imposition of a tax upon the transaction.[47] For example, stamp duty is a tax on instruments, rather than transactions. However, it is primarily worthwhile having stamp duty because of the numerous formality rules which require transactions in valuable assets—such as land—to be made by written instrument. In the area of property law, the factor of tax has had a discernible influence upon (for example) the interpretation of section 53(1)(c) of the Law of Property Act 1925, where most of the reported cases concern oral transactions in equitable interests deliberately left informal so as to avoid liability to taxation.[48]

Another advantage of formality requirements in the eyes of the state is that they may facilitate the *collation of important data*. For example, the land registration system assists in the gathering of information on current trends in the property market, which is useful in gauging the state of the economy.[49]

The Possibility of 'Natural' Formality

So far we have been talking about the benefits of imposing a formality rule where people would otherwise act informally. However, it is possible that a particular factual context may develop its own 'natural' formalities, enforced by custom or internal sanctions rather than by law, which produce some or all of the benefits which might otherwise be secured by a legal formality rule.[50] For example, there is no legal rule stating that commercial contracts must be in writing; yet there is a flourishing social practice

---

[47] Gény, *Science et technique en droit privé positif*, iii (Paris: Librairie de la Société du Recueil Sirey, 1921), 115; Bentham, *Rationale of Judicial Evidence*, ii. 455–6.

[48] See e.g. *Grey* v. *Inland Revenue Commissioners* [1960] AC 1; *Oughtred* v. *Inland Revenue Commissioners* [1960] AC 206; but cf. *Vandervell* v. *Inland Revenue Commissioners* [1967] 2 AC 291.

[49] The Land Registry produces a regular Residential Property Price Report (now accessible over the Internet (http://www.open.gov.uk/landreg/rpprind.htm)), which contains details of property prices and volume of sales analysed according to different variables (for example, type of property, location within the UK) and shows how those prices have increased or decreased as against the same period in the previous year.

[50] Fuller, 'Consideration and Form', 805.

whereby such contracts are written.[51] If we were then to impose a legal formality requirement to this effect, it would achieve little which the existing social practice did not; but it could create significant additional detriments (for example, the failure of any transactions which happened not to comply fully with the formality). There is, therefore, nothing to be gained—and potentially much to be lost—by imposing a legal formality rule. Of course, the social practice would need to be very widespread before the benefits of formality would be reduced like this, but it could (theoretically) happen.

DETRIMENTS OF FORMALITY

Given the apparent usefulness of formalities, as shown above, why have they provoked the sort of vilification which appears in the opening quotation? Here we must turn to the debit side of the balance sheet. A formality rule may have a number of disadvantages, stemming either from the mere fact that some formality is required, or from the particular requirements of the rule or the factual context to which it applies.[52]

Before we consider these in detail, it is necessary to make one important cautionary remark. It seems self-evident that *any* legal rule (at least, if accompanied by sanctions) is likely to have some disadvantageous consequences, so it is wholly unrealistic to expect a formality rule to have no detriments. The question of detriment must, therefore, be one of degree. However, this is, of course, true also of benefits: why did we not emphasize the relative nature of the question there? The difference is that detriment is especially difficult to deal with because of its emotive nature. Although outside observers may believe the legal community to be desensitized to the hardship caused by legal rules, the reality may well be that lawyers are (for this very reason) sensitive about appearing to condone such detrimental effects. There is, therefore, a risk that judges will accept arguments of detriment in cases where the evidence does not in fact support that conclusion. This is compounded by the fact that judges see individual cases, in which actual detriment looms large, and the benefits of formality seem abstract and theoretical by comparison.[53] The need for a sufficient degree of detriment to counterbalance the identified benefits of formality must therefore be emphasized.

With this caveat in mind, we can now turn to the detriments themselves. These are of two broad types.

[51] See Elias, *Explaining Constructive Trusts* (Oxford: Oxford University Press, 1990), 106.
[52] Bentham, *Rationale of Judicial Evidence*, ii. 447–8.
[53] Flour, 'Quelques remarques sur l'évolution du formalisme' in *Le Droit privé français au milieu du XXe siècle: Études offertes à Georges Ripert*, i (Paris: Librairie Générale de Droit et de Jurisprudence, 1950), 112–13.

The Costs of Compliance

The root of this first detriment can be found in the definition of formality itself.[54] Formality is something which is *added* to the basic requirements of the law in relation to a particular transaction. It therefore creates a separate obstacle which must be surmounted if we are to enter the transaction. If we manage to get over this obstacle, we will have been put to extra trouble and cost: for example, the delay needed to find a witness, or the fees charged by the Land Registry for registering a transaction.[55] Although this additional cost is a problem created by all formality rules, it may vary in severity according to the type of formality required and/or the factual context to which the rule is applied. To give a simple example, a rule which requires registration has a specific cost: the cost of setting up (if necessary) and running the register.[56] This would not be generated by a formality rule requiring mere writing. Alternatively, a formality rule which has acceptable costs in one factual context may prove to be particularly unsuitable for (and so costly within) a different context. One example might be the stock market, which depends upon speed for its efficacy. If every transaction had to satisfy section 52 of the Law of Property Act 1925, even technological advances such as faxing would probably be insufficient to make the formality requirement efficient and workable.[57] To deal with this problem, it might be necessary either to make an exception for stock-market transactions, or to select a less burdensome formality as the general rule. Another example might be where the costs of compliance were so high that a particular section of the population was financially unable to enter a particular type of transaction: a problem which might require some special dispensation for that group.

The Failure of Informal Transactions

Where the formality rule has a sanction attached to it, there is a second disadvantage, from the point of view of the parties, at least: the failure of informal transactions. Apart from the fact that a formality provision which is not

[54] See p. 508.

[55] Of course, if there is no sanction attached to the rule, it is perfectly possible for those who wish to avoid the costs of compliance to refuse to comply; which is arguably why formality rules typically *do* have legal sanctions for non-compliance.

[56] Such costs may fall on various parties: thus, the cost of running the register falls in the first instance upon the government, but may be redistributed (*a*) through taxation, to the public as a whole, and (*b*) through registration fees, to users of the register.

[57] Although note that such institutions may develop 'natural' formalities (social practices producing many of the same benefits as a formality rule) (see pp. 518–19).

complied with seems unlikely to achieve significant benefits,[58] this failure may, in itself, be a sufficient detriment to counterbalance the benefits of formality. Whether this is so will depend upon factors such as the extent of the 'failure' (is the transaction wholly invalid, or is there merely the loss of some peripheral advantage?), the probable proportion of transactions of the relevant type which will fail, and the adverse consequences of the failure (for example, are these particularly severe for a specific group of individuals?).

Even if the detriment to the parties is insufficient in itself, the failure of informal transactions may also be detrimental to society as a whole (at least if such failure is likely to occur in a significant number of cases). To explain this requires a little digression into the various reasons which may underlie the failure to comply with formality.

The basic underlying cause of much non-compliance is that formality requirements generally require deliberate, positive action—writing, signature, attestation—which is unlikely to occur accidentally (by chance) or coincidentally (as a mere by-product of other transactions). Therefore the transaction to which the formality requirement relates must also be one which is intentionally or deliberately undertaken by the party to whom the formality provision is directed.[59] This means that, if the individuals required to comply with the formality

1. do not know of (or do not understand) the formality; or
2. do not know that the formality applies;[60] or
3. do not wish to comply with the formality, or do not wish to bring about the particular consequences of complying with the formality;

there is likely to be non-compliance. In case 1 or 2 the parties will not take the deliberate action required owing to ignorance; in case 3 they will deliberately fail to do so. There are two additional reasons for failure which are less directly related to the deliberateness of formality:

4. where the failure to comply is due to carelessness (for example, a bungled attempt at compliance);[61] and
5. where it is impossible or impracticable[62] for the parties to comply with the formality.

[58] The mere knowledge of the existence of a formality requirement *may* have a limited warning benefit, even though the formality is not complied with. However, this benefit may be considered minimal.

[59] See Gény, *Science et technique*, 105–6.

[60] This is distinct from case 1, in that the party may know there is a formality requirement applying to transactions of type x, but he may not realize that his transaction is of that type.

[61] This is distinct from case 1, which would cover only careful but misguided attempts at compliance.

[62] In some cases it will be literally impossible to comply with the formality requirement. More often, circumstances mean that compliance is sufficiently difficult to justify less strict

Thus, our heading of 'failure of informal transactions' in fact embraces five scenarios, not all of which will necessarily be detrimental for the same reasons. So what are the detriments of formality which concern us here? These are twofold.

Unfairness or Injustice

A commonly heard complaint is that requiring formality works injustice in cases where there is non-compliance. Now, it does not seem particularly unjust to penalize non-compliance arising through lack of care (case 4). However, according to Bentham, the penalizing of non-compliance with formalities which is due to ignorance of the formality requirements (case 1) causes injustice. Thus, 'unless things be so ordered that every one shall know what formalities are required, every law or rule of law imposing, on pain of nullity, the necessity of complying with any such formality, is a breach of faith on the part of the ruling power'.[63] This argument seems equally applicable to case 2 (ignorance of applicability of formality requirements). But there is a snag: proving such ignorance in every individual case is likely to be extremely difficult;[64] and, given the general ignorance of legal requirements in modern society, such a criterion would require informality in any case not involving a legal professional or legally advised parties. In addition, an individual's ignorance of the law has rarely, in other contexts, been seen as sufficient to excuse his non-compliance with it: why should formality be different? We need to isolate those cases in which the ignorance is, in effect, justifiable.

One good way of doing this is to ask whether it is unreasonable to expect the parties to *acquire* the necessary knowledge—for example, by taking legal advice. This criterion was used by the Law Commission in its *Third Report on Land Registration* to determine which rights should be 'overriding interests' in the land registration system: thus, 'interests should be overriding where protection against purchasers is needed, yet it is . . . *not reasonable to expect* . . . any entry on the register'.[65] Good examples are the rights of occupiers and of tenants under short leases, which are currently overriding interests under (respectively) sections 70(1)(g) and (k) of the Land

---

(or no) requirements. What counts as 'sufficiently difficult' is, like (for example) 'reasonableness', a legal construct. The situation mentioned at p. 520, in which the costs of compliance are beyond the means of the parties, may be an example of impracticability.

[63] Bentham, *Rationale of Judicial Evidence*, ii. 476.

[64] It would be difficult to *assume* of any person other than a legal professional (and perhaps not even of such a person, if he did not specialize in the relevant field?) that he knew of the requirement in question.

[65] Law Commission, *Property Law: Third Report on Land Registration*, Law Com. No. 158 (London: HMSO, 1987), paras. 2.6, 2.40, 2.64 (emphasis added).

Registration Act 1925. The Law Commission, when it reviewed these provisions, suggested that such rights should continue to be protected without the formality of registration because they often arose informally and without legal advice, so that the possessors of such rights would (reasonably and justifiably) be unaware of the need for registration. The same reasoning may underlie the exemption of short leases from section 52 of the Law of Property Act 1925.[66]

Another example of this sort of justifiable ignorance relates to the family home, and in particular, the informal trusts found under the line of authority based upon the House of Lords' decision in *Gissing* v. *Gissing*.[67] Strictly speaking, trusts of land should be evidenced in writing;[68] but this requirement may be unreasonable in the context of a marital or quasi-marital relationship. While the relationship is still going strong, the parties will probably never even consider the question of property rights. The couple in *Midland Bank plc* v. *Cooke* are typical here. In cross-examination, the husband was asked:

Q. Do you now have any recollection of discussing . . . with your wife the precise arrangements in relation to the house?
A. Not really, No. We were just happy, I suppose, you know [sic].[69]

Indeed, we do not generally *expect* couples to act in this way. In the words of Lord Hodson in *Pettitt* v. *Pettitt*, 'the conception of a normal married couple spending the long winter evenings hammering out agreements about their possessions appears grotesque'.[70] Instead of clear express arrangements, then, the type of conduct which has been held to give rise to a trust in this context includes the making of financial contributions,[71] or the carrying-out of work on the property[72] (in conjunction with some 'imprecise' agreement or understanding).[73] Now, most couples or families do not think in terms of property rights when they pay gas bills or even mortgage instalments, let alone when they redecorate or renovate. Their concern is with the 'use' value of the property, rather than with its 'investment' value; with the house as a means of shelter and amenity, rather than as a means of accumulating wealth. The investment view tends to emerge only in two limited contexts: where the property is used as security for one

---

[66] See Law of Property Act 1925, ss. 52(2), 54(2); but cf. *Long* v. *Tower Hamlets London Borough Council* [1996] 3 WLR 317.

[67] [1971] AC 886. [68] Law of Property Act 1925, s. 53(1)(b).

[69] [1995] 4 All ER 562 at 568b–c.

[70] See [1970] AC 777 at 810F; and note also Lord Morris at 799H ('it would be unnatural if at the time of acquisition there was always precise statement or understanding as to where ownership rested').

[71] e.g. *Hazell* v. *Hazell* [1972] 1 WLR 301; *Walker* v. *Hall* [1984] FLR 126.

[72] e.g. *Eves* v. *Eves* [1975] 1 WLR 1338.

[73] See *Lloyds Bank plc* v. *Rosset* [1991] 1 AC 107, *per* Lord Bridge at 132F.

or both parties' business ventures, and where questions of inter-generational (usually testamentary) dispositions arise, generally towards the end of life. In those rare cases where the investment view is uppermost, it is more likely that parties will seek legal advice and so it may be justifiable to expect them to comply with the formality. But in the general run of cases it seems unreasonable (and thus unjust), given the type of relationship with which we are dealing, to expect these 'settlors' to know that their actions are in fact producing what the law considers to be a trust, or that this trust must be placed upon a formal footing.

Parties in this situation may also fail to comply with formality because of a common misunderstanding of the law: there are widespread beliefs that separate property becomes jointly owned by spouses once they are married,[74] and that there is a special legal status known as 'common-law marriage' which affects (inter alia) the property rights of cohabiting partners.[75] The parties will therefore (quite reasonably) not take legal advice because they honestly believe that they know the relevant law.[76] In such a situation, their ignorance of the need for formality again appears justifiable, and consequently it seems unjust to require compliance with formality.

But what if the parties in such a family relationship do think about questions of entitlement, and do know of the need to make their own arrangements, but fail to comply with the formality requirement none the less? Surely in this case—which is the situation envisaged in case 3 above—it is not unjust to penalize the parties for non-compliance? This may often be true in case 3 scenarios; indeed, if the decision not to comply with formality is motivated by the desire to avoid the specific consequences of compliance, then the parties are unlikely even to view the failure of the transaction as a penalty.

However, it is possible to think of some exceptions;[77] and in particular in the family relationship, there may be strong emotional factors which cause the partners to refrain from formalizing their arrangements even though they wish them to be legally valid. As a general rule, such partners will tend to act in mutual trust and cooperation, rather than at arm's length,

[74] See e.g. Law Commission, Family Law: Matrimonial Property, Law Com. No. 175 (London: HMSO, 1988), para. 1.5; and note statements in cases such as Hammond v. Mitchell [1991] 1 WLR 1127, 1131E ('when we are married it will be half yours anyway').

[75] Rignell v. Andrews [1991] FCR 65; Oliver, 'Why Do People Live Together?' [1982] JSWL 209 at 215–16.

[76] However, it may be argued, against this, that, if the formality provision is strictly enforced, most 'misunderstandings' will be cleared up: eventually people will become aware of the (true) legal requirements.

[77] For example, if the requirement offended deeply held religious or other convictions (although this may be problematic in some instances: should anarchists be excused from compliance with legal rules if they do not believe that such rules should exist?).

effectively relying upon a sense of security which is induced by the emotional relationship but extended to cover property matters.[78] There may be emotional pressure from the other party against formalizing property relations: Lord Browne-Wilkinson in *Barclays Bank plc* v. *O'Brien* pointed out in a similar context that 'the sexual and emotional ties between the parties provide a ready weapon for undue influence: a wife's true wishes can easily be overborne because of her fear of destroying or damaging the wider relationship between her and her husband if she opposes his wishes'.[79] Or the emotional pressure may be self-induced: a party may feel that asking for a formal agreement would suggest a lack of commitment to the relationship on his own part, or (almost superstitiously, perhaps) that talking about separate rights to the property will in some way contribute to a breakdown of the relationship. For all these reasons, it may again be argued to be unjust to penalize non-compliance with formality in such cases, even though the non-compliance is, in effect, deliberate.

Finally, it also seems unjust to require someone to do what is impossible (case 5), as well as being potentially damaging to the reputation (and consequently to the effectiveness) of the legal system. To cite Bentham again: 'Every law requiring a man, under a penalty, to do that which is not in his power . . . is an act of tyranny. Pure suffering, suffering without benefit, pure evil, is the fruit of it.'[80]

Often impossibility in a particular type of case can be identified, and an exception made for that situation, in advance: for example, section 11 of the Wills Act 1837, which allows sailors and military personnel on active service to make informal wills, may be connected with the risk that such persons will find themselves suddenly near to death and without the time or materials to make a formal will.[81] Or the courts may be left to make such general exceptions in the process of statutory interpretation. A good example, again from the area of wills, is the interpretation of the requirement of 'signed' writing in section 9 of the Wills Act 1837 as including signature by mark (so as to permit the making of wills by those testators unable to sign their names in the usual manner, owing to illiteracy or illness).[82]

Alternatively, and less commonly, cases of impossibility may be dealt with in a more *ad hoc* manner, where an unusual occurrence within a class of cases where compliance is usually possible renders it impossible on a

---

[78] Gardner, 'Rethinking Family Property' (1993) 109 LQR 263 at 279–82, 286 ff; *Midland Bank plc* v. *Cooke* [1995] 4 All ER 562 at 575a–d.

[79] [1994] 1 AC 180 at 190H–191A.

[80] Bentham, *Rationale of Judicial Evidence*, ii. 474.

[81] See *In the goods of Hiscock* [1901] P 78, *per* Sir F H Jeune P at 80, stating this as the underlying rationale for the exemption; and note (for example) *Re Jones (deceased)* [1981] Fam. 7 (soldier fatally wounded by a terrorist attack making oral will before death).

[82] *Baker* v. *Dening* (1838) 8 Ad. & E 94; *In the goods of Chalcraft (deceased)* [1948] p. 222.

particular occasion. Illustrations of this are harder to find;[83] perhaps the nearest example is the decision in *Re Rose*,[84] in which the Court of Appeal decided that where the only (formal) steps which remained to be completed in a transfer of shares were those of a third party, a constructive trust of the shares would be imposed—thus saving the transaction from invalidity—pending completion of those steps.

Damage to Other Legal Policy Aims

Alternatively, the failure of informal transactions may hinder the achievement of legal aims other than that of achieving fairness or justice. Here, it does not matter what causes the failure. For example, imagine a transaction which can be effected wholly involuntarily. The parties, being ignorant of the legal transaction, would logically also be ignorant of the applicability of the formality requirements—case 2—and therefore would not comply with them. However, the legal doctrine or rule which says that the transaction takes place in such a situation must have been established for a purpose. The failure of the transaction will therefore be detrimental, not only to the parties concerned, but also to the specific purpose underlying the legal rule.

An example might be the 'automatic' resulting trust which arises upon the failure of a trust to exhaust the beneficial interest in property.[85] Since this arises as a 'default' provision by operation of law where the settlor has failed to make more definite arrangements, it would be self-defeating to require that it be made subject to a formality requirement which the settlor would have to fulfil by deliberate action; and the failure of the resulting trust would be detrimental, because the point of such a trust (it may be argued) is that it fills in such (undesirable) gaps.[86] This may explain why such trusts are exempted from the formality requirement applicable to trusts of land in general.[87] The same sort of argument might apply if the parties did know of the existence of the formality and the transaction, but the formalities were so complex and difficult to understand that errors were legion (case 1).

Again, formality may be detrimental to the achievement of policy aims in a case 3 situation, where the parties wish to avoid certain specific consequences of the transaction to which formality is attached. Thus, it might be

[83] Bentham's examples of this type of impossibility (see Bentham, *Rationale of Judicial Evidence*, ii. 488 n.) are arguably a little far-fetched.

[84] [1952] Ch. 499. Although compliance here was not literally impossible, it *was* impossible as regards the party seeking the aid of the court.

[85] See *Re Vandervell's Trusts (No. 2)* [1974] Ch. 269 at 289G–H and 294G–H.

[86] See *Vandervell* v. *Inland Revenue Commissioners* [1967] 2 AC 291 *per* Lord Wilberforce at 329B–C and *Re Vandervell's Trusts (No. 2)* [1974] Ch. 269 *per* Lord Denning MR at 320C–D.

[87] See Law of Property Act 1925, ss. 53(1)(b), (2).

thought to be inadvisable to introduce strict formal requirements for short leases or periodic tenancies, since it is more than probable that landlords seeking to defeat the statutory protection granted to lessees by housing legislation would deliberately ensure that there was failure to comply with such requirements, in order to ensure that there was no lease.[88] The aim of the legislature (to protect tenants, who are often the weaker party in terms of bargaining power) would thus be defeated. Similar arguments may be made in relation to situations within cases 4 and 5.

CONCLUSION:
THE UTILITY OF FORMALITY-CENTRED ANALYSIS

In a very real sense, the above analysis is merely a starting point for consideration of formality rules and decisions made about them. It provides us with a tool for criticizing such decisions, the routine use of which can be most illuminating, since it prompts us to investigate the underlying substantive reasons for legal rules and doctrines which we often take for granted. Obviously, if a major problem comes to light as a result of this process, the significance of the analysis will be self-evident; but it may be equally useful if it leads us to understand exactly why formality has *properly* been applied or forgone in a particular case.

For example, much effort has been spent in trying to decide whether certain trusts (secret trusts, trusts based on *Gissing* v. *Gissing*,[89] and so on) are properly to be classified as 'constructive trusts' and thus as within the exemption from formality created by section 53(2) of the Law of Property Act 1925. Our analysis could add an extra dimension to this debate by prompting (and answering) the following three questions. First, looking at those trusts which have already been recognized as 'constructive' trusts within section 53(2), what detriment(s) of formality do they display which might explain their exemption from formality? Secondly, do secret trusts or *Gissing* trusts share these characteristic(s)? If so, then we have a reason based upon the formality provision itself for suggesting that secret trusts or *Gissing* trusts should be classed as 'constructive' trusts: a useful adjunct to the existing debate, which has concentrated primarily upon the substantive law, independently of the formality provision. Thirdly, if the answer to our second question is negative, are there other detrimental feature(s) of secret trusts or *Gissing* trusts which would suggest that they ought none the less to be exempted from formality? If we can answer this question in the affirmative, then we can use our answer to confirm case law which bestows such

[88] Note, for example, the machinations of the landlord in *Street* v. *Mountford* [1985] AC 809.
[89] [1971] AC 886.

an exemption, or to support arguments in favour of the creation of a new statutory exemption.

Primarily, then, the above analysis is an academic tool, although it could equally be of use to judges or law reform bodies. Its purpose is to get rid of the notion that there is such a thing as a 'mere' formality: to deepen and sophisticate current discussion about formality, with the ultimate aim of stimulating reasoned and self-consistent suggestions for enhancing the utility of formal rules. It is only when we can pinpoint the proper usage of formality that we can possibly see how to employ it as a precise and bene-ficial legal device, instead of the damaging and ineffectual blunt instrument which it may sometimes appear to be.

21

OF ESTATES AND INTERESTS: A TALE OF OWNERSHIP AND PROPERTY RIGHTS

Susan Bright

> It is probable that many of those who open this book have heard of a distinction made in law between real and personal property. They are perhaps aware that the law of real property has to do with ownership of land; and it is very unlikely that they have formed no opinions on the subject of the laws of property. Popular notions of law often contain an element of truth; but they are rarely exact. The student of real property law will, therefore, do well to begin by considering the exact meaning of one or two terms, with the common use of which he is doubtless familiar.[1]

A basic distinction lies at the heart of the 1925 property legislation. Section 1 of the Law of Property Act 1925 expresses this in terms of 'estates' and 'interests' in land, expressions which are defined in technical language and which immediately assume a mystical quality. Underlying this distinction is, however, a simple idea: that estates are to do with ownership of land and interests are to do with having rights over the land of another.[2]

The aim of this chapter is to explore these ideas further. If estates are really to do with ownership, what does ownership itself mean? Is there some essential difference between 'owning' and 'having rights over'? These thoughts are followed through in the first part of this chapter.

The second part of this chapter addresses another distinction important to land law: the distinction between rights which are capable of being enforced against all future owners of the land (proprietary interests), and rights which are enforceable only against the present owner (non-proprietary interests). Only rights falling within recognized categories—such as easements, profits, and restrictive freehold covenants—are given

My thanks to various people who have commented on earlier versions of this chapter, especially Professor J. Harris, and Dr J. Penner

[1] *Williams on Real Property* (23rd edn., London: Sweet & Maxwell, 1920), 1.

[2] This is not to deny that 'in England there is no law of ownership, but only a law of possession' (Burn, *Cheshire and Burn's Modern Law of Real Property* (15th edn., London: Butterworths, 1994), 26), adopted by Lord Hoffman in *Hunter* v. *Canary Wharf Ltd.* [1997] 2 WLR 684 at 706). Possession is to do with proving title; 'ownership' captures the essence of what it means to have a title to land. See also Harris, 'Ownership of Land in English Law', in MacCormick and Birks, *The Legal Mind* (Oxford: Oxford University Press, 1986).

proprietary status, and the courts have been unwilling to expand these categories into new areas. Why is it that particular rights have proprietary status but not others? All too often attempts to explain this collapse into a circularity of definition: they are property rights because they are enforceable against third parties, they are enforceable against third parties because they have proprietary features.[3] Is there some common theme to these rights after all?

MYTHS ABOUT OWNERSHIP OF LAND

One of the great contributions that English land law is said to have made to the legal theory of ownership is the separation of the land itself from the 'estate in the land'. It is not the land that is owned, but an estate. The doctrine of estates focuses on the quantum of time for which land is held[4] but not explicitly on the nature of ownership. Nevertheless, the very notion of 'land for a time' implies that estates are to do with ownership. An estate owner is able to make the claim 'the land is mine'; an interest-holder is not. What does this claim mean?

Before exploring the concept of estate ownership, it is helpful to discuss some myths about ownership. First is the myth that ownership confers absolute powers. Blackstone, writing in the heyday of liberalism, portrayed property as giving 'sole and despotic dominion over the external things of the world, in total exclusion of the right of any other individual in the universe'.[5] The picture is of the owner pointing both literally and metaphorically to the boundary of his property and stating that no one, individual or government, can cross this line without permission; within the boundary the owner is Ruler, free to do with the land whatever he wishes. Property thus becomes a powerful concept. It represents autonomy, control, and freedom from interference. The owner is free to act in any way, in total disregard of the moral and social claims that those outside the property may have.

This is an image full of rhetoric, but it is a false image.[6] Even the holder of a fee simple estate, undoubtedly an owner, and the fullest ownership

[3] See Gray, 'Property in Thin Air', [1991] CLJ 252 at 293 for a condemnation of this 'radical and obscurantist nonsense'.

[4] In *Walsingham's Case* (1573) 2 Plowden 547 at 555 it was said that 'An estate in the land is a time in the land, or land for a time'.

[5] *Bl. Comm.*, ii. 2.

[6] The mythical rhetoric of property is discussed by Gordon, 'Paradoxical Property', in Brewer and Staves (eds.), *Early Modern Conceptions of Property* (London: Routledge, 1995), 108.; also Nedelsky, American Constitutionalism and the Paradox of Private Property', in Elster and Slagstad, (eds.), *Constitutionalism and Democracy* (Cambridge: Cambridge University Press, 1993).

known to English land law, is not such a Ruler. His freedom to use the land is wide but not absolute. All sorts of limitations are placed upon land use, some specific to the particular land (for example, restrictive covenants and easements) and some general to all land (such as planning laws, tort laws, and environmental laws). The idea of the owner having unrestrained freedom to use, and abuse, the land is a myth; it is not this that can be used to define what ownership is, at least not ownership of land.

If user powers are not absolute, does ownership not at least involve the claim 'it is mine and no one can take it from me'? It is a feature of landownership that, if another wrongfully takes possession of the land, the true owner is entitled to recover possession of the land itself.[7] This could be used as the distinguishing feature between ownership and lesser interests; it is a characteristic shared by owners of the two types of legal estate (the freehold and the leasehold) and not enjoyed by holders of other interests in land. The holder of a right of way over Redacre cannot recover possession of the land from another, for possession was never his in the first place; he can claim a right to non-interference with the exercise of the right of way against the owner of Redacre, and against all others, but cannot claim the land itself. In contrast, both the freeholder and leaseholder of Redacre can recover the land if it is 'taken' by someone else. Nevertheless, this cannot form the basis of a conceptual distinction. It would mean that 'ownership' is an entirely different conception in the case of chattels, where specific recovery is not available. Suppose land law were changed in two ways: every trespass was criminal; but, as against an intruder, there was no civil right to recover the land itself, only damages. It would be ridiculous to suggest that there would then be no ownership of land; it is just that the form of protecting the ownership would have changed.

Nor does the claim 'it cannot be taken from me' provide a bulwark against state intervention. Most legal systems accept that land can be compulsorily acquired in the public interest for transport routes, slum clearance, and so on. Even when the 'right to property' is given constitutional protection, the aim of the protection is to ensure not that there can be no taking of property but that any such taking is justified in the public interest and adequately compensated.[8]

[7] *Williams on Real Property*, explained ownership on this basis: 'ownership chiefly imports the right of exclusive enjoyment of some thing. The owner in possession of a thing has the right to exclude all others from the possession or enjoyment of it; and if he be wrongfully deprived of what he owns, he has the right to recover possession of it from any person. This right to maintain or recover possession of a thing as against all others may, we think, be said to be the essential part of ownership' (p. 2), and 'a tenant for years has long enjoyed a true property in his holding; for he has the right to maintain or recover possession of his land during the term against all others, including his landlord' (p. 553, footnotes omitted).

[8] The American constitution states in Article 5 that 'No person shall . . . be deprived of life, liberty, or property, without due process of law; nor shall private property be taken for

A further claim associated with ownership is the right to exclude others from the property, following the image of owner as Ruler. It is expressed in the owner's claim 'keep off, this is my land and you have no right to come onto it'. This right of exclusion has a strong foundation in English law. It is used as the point of divide between leases (estates) and licences (non-estate, and not even proprietary). The right to exclude is still upheld as an essential right of landowners.[9] Even owners of what Gray labels 'quasi-public' property have a right to exclude particular individuals on a selective basis, for any (or no) reason, notwithstanding that the public generally is invited onto the property.[10]

This right to exclude comes close to the essence of what ownership is about, but even this right need not be absloute in order for there to be ownership. Although such is not English law at present,[11] it is quite possible to imagine laws requiring that owners allow the public to have access to certain kinds of lands such as woodlands,[12] countryside,[13] and shopping malls, for the purposes of recreation, walking, or shopping.[14] Public rights of access would not, however, destroy ownership. It is still meaningful to describe the fee simple owner of the woodland as 'owner' even if he no longer has a right to exclude all comers.

public use without just compensation.' Article 1 of the First Protocol to the European Convention for the Protection of Human Rights includes the right that: 'Every natural or legal person is entitled to the peaceful enjoyment of his possessions. No one shall be deprived of his possessions except in the public interest and subject to the conditions provided for by law and by the general principles of international law.'

[9] In *Hunter* v. *Canary Wharf Ltd.* [1997] 2 WLR 684 at 706 Lord Hoffman describes exclusive possession as the bedrock of English land law. See also *R.* v. *Secretary of State for Wales, ex p. Emery* [1996] 4 All ER 1 at 19.

[10] In *CIN Properties Ltd.* v. *Rawlins and Others* [1995] 2 EGLR 130 the owner of a shopping centre mall was granted injunctions excluding certain youths who had allegedly been making a nuisance of themselves.

[11] But see 'Access to the Open Countryside in England and Wales' (London: Department of the Environment, 1998).

[12] In Germany there is a right to wander freely in all woodland, whether in public or private ownership.

[13] As proposed in the Countryside Bill issued for consultation in Dec. 1995, providing for public access on foot to 'open country'.

[14] Gray argues that there may be 'moral limits' on the right to exclude, especially with 'quasi-public' property to which there should be free access (Gray, 'Property in Thin Air', 286–92). The idea is developed further in Gray, 'Equitable Property', (1994) 47(2) CLP 157, esp. at 172–81. Already there may be no general right to exclude where land is owned by 'quasi-public' bodies (see *British Airports Authority* v. *Ashton* [1983] 1 WLR 1079). Some US states have held owners unable to exclude members of the public from access to shopping centres (*Pruneyard Shopping Center* v. *Robins* 100 S. Ct. 2035 (1980)) and gaming casinos (*Uston* v. *Resorts International Inc.* (1982) NJ 445 A 2d 370); contrast *Prinz* v. *Great Bay Casino Corp.*, Lexis, 28 Apr. 1983, *Harrison* v. *Carswell* (1975) 62 DLR (3d) 68.

An alternative way of describing ownership that is popular in US jurisprudence is to explain ownership as a 'bundle of rights'.[15] An owner of property possesses an infinite variety of rights in relation to the property, typically including 'the right (liberty) of using as one wishes, the right to exclude others, the power of alienating and an immunity from expropriation'.[16] There are, however, various difficulties with this analysis as a conceptual tool. Although it is true that at any given moment in time an owner of property does possess a bundle of rights in relation to the property, this can also be true of relationships to property less than ownership. If I borrow a pen, I have a right to use the pen but it does not make it mine. The question is whether within this bundle of rights there are any which are perceived to be essential to ownership and that distinguish ownership from other relationships. This has not, however, been the focus of the 'bundle-of-rights' analysis. Most of the US jurisprudence has been in the context of the 'Takings Clause', with courts having to determine if a particular interference with property consitutes a 'taking of property'.[17] Rather than seeking to define the core of ownership, the approach has been more expansive, painting the picture of the owner having a large bundle of rights, so that taking any stick from this bundle is viewed as a taking of property. As a result, the bundle-of-rights approach provides at best a snapshot descriptive account of the rights, privileges, powers, and immunities that an owner has at any one point in time; it cannot provide a normative account of the concept of ownership itself.[18]

Although none of these approaches provides a watertight definition of ownership, each provides us with a glimpse of what is important within ownership: the owner has extensive user rights over the property, albeit not

---

[15] Underkuffler-Freund explores 'bundle-of-rights' theories in 'Takings and the Nature of Property', (1996) 9 Can. J. L. and Juris. 161, esp. at 169–71. For criticism, see Penner, 'The "Bundle of Rights" Picture of Property' (1996) 43 UCLA L. Rev. 711.

[16] Cf. Mosk J (dissenting) in *Moore* v. *Regents of the University of California* (1990) 793 P. 2d 479: 'the concept of property is often said to refer to a "bundle of rights" that may be exercised with respect to that object—principally the rights to possess the property, to use the property, to exclude others from the property, and to dispose of the property by sale or by gift'. Underkuffler-Freund argues that, in US takings law, these rights are not given equal weighting—rights to exclude and devise are near absolute but other rights have lesser protection (see 'Takings and the Nature of Property', at 186).

[17] See Article 5 of the American Constitution, above, n. 8. One exception is *Moore* v. *The Regents of the University of California* 793 P. 2d 479 (1990) where the Supreme Court of California used the bundle-of-rights approach to decide if Moore had property in his removed spleen.

[18] Cf. Penner, 'The "Bundle of Rights" Picture of Property', 754–5. Penner is critical of property being fractionated into individual rights as if there are some independent individual rights which must coexist before there can be property. Such individuation of property rights serves as 'momentary functional descriptions' but should not be raised to the status of conceptual truths about the nature of property.

absolute; ownership claims are jealously protected by law; and owners are able to exercise control over who is able to make use of the land.

OWNERSHIP AS AN OPEN-ENDED CONCEPT

It is these notions that Harris captures in his book on Property and Justice[19] when he describes a property institution as dependent upon both trespassory rules and an ownership spectrum. The trespassory rules are the rules that protect ownership, the rules that prevent others (non-owners) from making use of the property. Ownership itself is a set of open-ended use privileges and open-ended powers to control the use made by others of the property. Rather than attempt to identify any core essential rights that an owner has, what is special about ownership is the very 'open-endedness' of the use privileges and control powers. It is simply not possible to list all the potential uses which the owner may make of the property—she can live on it, use it for growing crops, climb trees on it, and so on. And not only can the owner make personal use of the property; she can also allow others to use the property in a variety of ways.[20]

OWNERSHIP AND USE PRIVILEGES

It is the open-endedness of the use privileges that ownership brings that sets estates apart from other interests in land. In fact, many interests in land do not confer use privileges at all. Non-estate rights in relation to land fall basically into four categories: rights to use the land of another (easements, licences, profits), rights to control the use of another's land (covenants), rights of security (mortgages), and rights to purchase land (estate contracts, options). It is only the first category that confer use privileges in any real sense. Covenants give no use privileges over the land. Rights to purchase are rights to acquire an ownership interest but are not ownership interests themselves. Mortgages and charges give only limited use privileges, the right to possess and ultimately to sell,[21] but can in no way be said to confer 'open-ended use privileges'. Most interests in land are therefore quite unlike ownership claims.

---

[19] Harris, *Property and Justice* (Oxford: Oxford University Press, 1996).

[20] Penner and Gray also acknowledge that any definition of property must accommodate the social use made of property and the ability of the owner to license the use made by others of the property (see Penner, 'The "Bundle of Rights" Picture of Property', 744–5; Gray, 'Property in Thin Air', esp. 268, 294).

[21] Exercise of these is strictly regulated in the case of residential mortgages (see Administration of Justice Act 1970, s. 36).

It is only in the first category (easements and so on) that the whole point of the right is to give use privileges over land and it is the width of the use privileges that helps to determine on which side of the divide the right falls: ownership or non-ownership. This is vividly illustrated in cases which explore the divide between easements (mere interests) and full ownership. It is of the essence of a fee simple that the owner is able to use the land for *any* purpose (subject to general laws, and any covenants affecting the land) rather than only for a particular defined purpose. If land is granted for a limited purpose, this smacks of an easement, not ownership. In *Deterding* v. *United States*[22] land was 'conveyed' for the purpose of widening and straightening the Sacramento River and for incidental works. The deed also gave the grantor the right to use the land for purposes which did not interfere with the purposes of the deed. The issue later arose as to whether the grantor still owned the gas on the land, and the answer turned on whether the deed constituted a conveyance of the land coupled with a reservation of rights, or the simple grant of an easement. Notwithstanding the fact that the language of conveyance/transfer had been used, Madden J preferred the view that there had been the grant of an easement. The grant had been for a limited purpose only and the grantor was able to make a wider use of the land than the grantee:

Since the purpose of entering on the land to change the course of the stream, is much more in the nature of a jus in re aliena than the right, for example, which the grantor was clearly intended to have, to occupy and cultivate the land, we think the conventional pattern of legal interests is better followed by treating the grantee's particular interest as the easement, and the grantor's retained interest as the corporeal and residuary interest in the land.[23]

Conversely, the purported grant of an easement may be interpreted as a transfer of ownership if it is so wide as to give the grantee unlimited use of the land. In *Reilly* v. *Booth*[24] the purchaser of stables was simultaneously granted 'exclusive use' of a gateway leading to the street. The grantee fixed various signs and lights to the gateway, and the Court of Appeal took the view that he was quite entitled to and could in fact use the gateway for any lawful purpose. The Court did not have to determine the actual nature of

[22] 69 F. Supp. 214 (1947) (Court of Claims).

[23] *Deterding* v. *United States* 69 F. Supp. 214 (1947) at 216. See also *Lynch* v. *Cypert* 302 SW 2d 284 (Supreme Court of Arkansas), where the plaintiff was seeking to argue that a conveyance of land to be used 'for depot grounds' was an easement and not a full conveyance. There was little to support this contention on the facts and the claim was built around the limited purpose for which the land was to be used. The court, however, thought that the width of permitted use militated against this construction, contrasting a right of way which 'brings to mind the thought of an easement' (p. 285) and a depot site which suggests 'a more extensive use of the land' (p. 285).

[24] (1890) 44 Ch. D. 12.

the grantee's interest itself, but it is quite clear that it inclined to the view that the grantee had not merely an easement but full ownership. Lopes LJ said: '[the] exclusive or unrestricted use of a piece of land . . . beyond all question passes the property or ownership in that land, and there is no easement known to law which gives exclusive and unrestricted use of a piece of land.'[25]

Although the generalized legal concepts of 'estates' and 'interests' are distinguishable by the open-ended use privileges conferred by estate ownership, it can be misleading in particular cases to describe an estate owner as having open-ended use privileges. The fee simple owner of a house may be required by freehold or leasehold covenants, and by planning laws, to use the house for residential purposes only. Further, if the home has been enfranchised, there may be an estate management scheme that places restrictions on how the property is to be managed, even to the point of controlling the external decor of the property. In the case of listed buildings, there may be strict controls on making alterations to the property that stem from conservation laws. Leasehold owners will often face even greater restrictions, being prevented from keeping pets and being told where to put the rubbish bins.

Furthermore, the actual permitted use that an estate owner can make of land may not be dissimilar to the permitted use that a non-estate holder can make of the land. Compare the weekly tenant of a flat with a licensee. Both have the right to live in the flat and may be subject to similar restrictions (no washing hanging out of the window, no right to decorate, and so on), but one is an estate owner and the other does not even have a proprietary interest in the land.

What can be said, however, is that, stepping back from the particular case, it is true of estates in land that the owner has open-ended use privileges. There are no natural limits on the use privileges that stem from the estate itself; the limits are lines drawn from outside that concept, from public laws and from private agreement. To say that X has a fee simple of Blackacre tells us that X has wide use privileges, reduced only by the constraints of the general law and any restrictions specific to Blackacre. For interests in land it is completely different. It is the lines drawn that are used to tell us what sort of interest we have and what sort of use privileges are being created. To say that Y has a licence or an easement tells us nothing of what Y is permitted to do; we need to know also that it is a licence or easement to cross Blackacre. The use privileges need to be defined in the case of non-estate interests in land, and they are then limited, not open-ended.

---

[25] *Reilly* v. *Booth* (1890) 44 Ch. D. 12 at 26. Luther gives an excellent analysis of some of the difficult easement cases involving user excluding the owner (Luther, 'Easements and Exclusive Possession' (1996) 16 LS 51).

OWNERSHIP AND CONTROL POWERS

There is another difference between estates and interests in land. Estate ownership carries with it the power to 'control', to say who is able and who is not able to use the land.[26] There are two aspects to control. Control over access gives the ability to say who can come onto the land and who cannot. Alienation powers give the ability to create interests in others—licences, leases, and, ultimately, transfer.

Alienation Powers

Alienation powers are not unique to ownership-type claims. It is true that freehold and leasehold owners have powers to transfer their entire interest in the property and powers to create new interests in relation to the land, but alienation powers also exist for other, non-ownership, interests.[27] A mortgagee is, for example, able to create lesser interests (sub-mortgages) and to assign the mortgage itself. Alienation powers indicate that something is owned—a transferable right—but this right need not itself relate to the ownership of land.

Control over Access

Powers to control access can be either permissive or exclusionary. Permissive access powers give the power to allow persons onto the land. Exclusionary powers give the right to prevent all other persons from having access to the land. Whilst non-estate owners may have permissive access powers, they do not have the right to exclude all others from the land. A licensee may allow visitors onto the land (as with the licensee of a flat), but he does not have the right to exclude everyone else.[28] The licensee cannot exclude the licensor, whereas the tenant can exclude the landlord. In *Street*

[26] Most theoretical models of property regard these control powers as important to ownership. See Harris, *Property and Justice*; Penner, 'The "Bundle of Rights" Picture of Property', 742 ff.

[27] A leaseholder's powers may be curtailed by the leasehold contract. This does not take the powers away from the leaseholder but will render the lease liable to be forfeited if there is an alienation which breaches the contractual provisions.

[28] Harris treats licensees as owners, seemingly attaching importance to the permissive access control powers rather than the right to exclude as the defining feature of ownership (see Harris, *Property and Justice*, 21–2, 73–4). It may be that what Harris describes would in fact be a lease under English law, not a licence: Harris's licensee can do with the dwelling what she pleases, including permitting others to use it, so long as it is not damaged or destroyed, but she cannot substitute anyone else as 'licensee'.

v. *Mountford*[29] Lord Templeman remarked that the 'tenant possessing exclusive possession is able to exercise the rights of an owner of land, which is in the real sense his land albeit temporarily and subject to certain restrictions'. Some non-estate interests give no control powers. An easement holder can prevent her right from being interfered with but apart from that she has no say over who is allowed onto the land. This right to exclude, and the territorial control inherent to it, distinguishes estates from interests, ownership from non-ownership. There is, however, one caveat. Earlier it was suggested that even the right to exclude need not be absolute in order for there to be ownership. There may, for example, be rights of access conferred on the general public to enter particular types of lands, such as woodland. In this case it is not, however, the estate itself that imposes the restriction but something external to the estate itself (government regulation). The crucial point of distinction is that ownership of an estate gives the right to exclude all others from the land, a right that may be limited by external regulation or private agreement, whereas other interests in land give no rights of exclusion.

NON-OWNERSHIP PROPERTY RIGHTS

Estates in land are a form of ownership that would be recognized as such by most theoretical models of property. Most property theories cannot, however, account for the fact that in land law even non-ownership interests are also categorized as a form of property.[30] These rights, such as easements and covenants, do not give open-ended use privileges or the right to exclude but are none the less property rights.

When land lawyers describe a non-ownership interest as a 'property right', what is meant is that the right can be enforced not only against the person who granted it (as with a 'personal right') but also against any successor in title to the burdened (servient) land (subject to complying with formalities and registration requirements). The comparison sometimes drawn is between property rights as 'rights in rem' in contrast to 'rights in personam', but this is apt to mislead. Rights in rem are generally taken to refer to rights 'enforceable against the world'. The defining feature of property rights, however, is not that they are enforceable against 'persons generally' but that they are enforceable against the successor in title to the

---

[29] [1985] AC 809 at 816.

[30] The distinction made by Hill is between ownership and encumbrances (Hill, 'Intention and the Creation of Proprietary Rights: Are Leases Different?' (1996) 16 LS 200). An encumbrance is defined as 'a right or bundle of rights relating to property which is less than ownership, which Y can enjoy over X's property and which restricts or encumbers X's ownership' (p. 202).

burdened (servient) land. This right of property 'does not actually bind everybody: the only person actually bound is the person in whose hands the property currently is'.[31] Some of these rights might *also* give claims 'against the world'; the holder of an easement of way can prevent the landowner *and all other persons* from interfering with the right of way. But what tells us whether these rights are property is whether the same package of 'rights, privileges, etc.' that the right-holder possesses can continue to be enforced when there is a new owner of the burdened land.

The other point to note is that, in classifying rights as 'property' rights, the emphasis is upon the transmission of the *burden*.[32] With contract law in general, the benefit is freely assignable whereas the burden is not; it is thus the passing of the burden which marks out property rights as something different from simple contractual rights.

In order to qualify as a property right, the right must fall within one of the closed group of rights recognized as such: easements, profits, covenants, mortgages, and other rights historically accepted as property rights. Not all rights enjoyed over the land of another are accorded this status. Indeed there is a limited list of what qualifies as a property right.

The central question is why it is that certain rights have been accorded proprietary status and not others. The answer, in part, lies in history and the incremental development of the common law and equity. But surely there might be some more principled explanation of why lines are drawn where they are?

The problem with this type of enquiry is that there is little to guide. Case-law and land law texts tend to accept existing boundaries and work within them rather than seek to explain them. Nevertheless, if we start from first principles and build up, it is possible to develop principles that can be used to guide whether or not rights should be accepted as property rights.

The enquiry must start at the point at which property rights depart from other rights, the passing of the burden to a third party. Given that a property right will bind a third party who has had no direct or personal involvement with the grantee then:

(1) if the right-holder's interests can be adequately protected without the right being made to bind a third party, it should not be a property right;

(2) in order to be a property right it must be the type of right which is suitable for binding such an independent third party; and

[31] Bell, *The Modern Law of Personal Property in England and Ireland* (London: Butterworths, 1989), 9.

[32] Hill describes this quality as durability; 'transmissibility' being used for passing the benefit (Hill, 'Intention and the creation of proprietary rights: are leases different?').

(3) in the interests of certainty and transactional fairness, a third party should be able to acquire ownership of the land with knowledge of the burdens that the land is subject to. This concern is reflected in the rules on registration and will not be focused upon here save where it touches upon the more general principles discussed below.

Taking these ideas it is possible to identify the features that property rights must possess.

PROTECTING THE RIGHT-HOLDER'S INTERESTS

Proprietary Intent

Before exploring the essential qualities of property rights, it should be noted that, if the parties intend the right to be personal and not to benefit or burden others, then rights which might otherwise qualify as property rights may remain personal only.[33]

Uniqueness

In order to justify the burden being imposed upon a third party, there must be no other way of adequately protecting the interests of the right-holder. Common to all property rights is that their function is to provide a specific 'enjoyment' content in relation to the land; the particular mode of enjoyment is crucial to the right. If a monetary award would be just as good as a right enforceable against the land, there is no need to admit the interest into the category of property rights.[34] This was the premiss underlying the trust for sale: the interests of the beneficiaries were viewed as being eminently substitutable. So long as the purpose of the trust was perceived to be the provision of an income stream, beneficiaries were adequately protected if the capital proceeds of sale were substituted for the land itself. This model came under increasing pressure as the pattern of home ownership changed and the basic premiss was seen to be misconceived; it was no longer true (if ever it was) that the beneficiaries were adequately protected by having a general form of protection rather than specific protection against the land.[35]

Property rights in land are unique, not substitutable.

---

[33] See ibid. 203–6 for illustrations. Leases are the exception, as parties cannot direct that a lease be non-proprietary.

[34] See Rudden, 'Things as Thing and Things as Wealth' (1994) 14 OJLS 81.

[35] Hence the changes introduced by, and the abandonment of the implied trust for sale in, the Trusts of Land and Appointment of Trustees Act 1996.

SUITABILITY AS A PROPERTY RIGHT

Practical Enforcement

Uniqueness of the right is not all that is required for rights to be proprietary. It must also be possible and practical to give specific protection of the right. This is generally not a problem when the right is enforceable by injunction or an order for specific performance. A restrictive covenant can be protected by an injunction restraining the prohibited behaviour; estate contracts and options can be protected by orders for specific performance; the mortgage is protected by attaching as a charge to the estate in the land.

Rights giving use privileges are less straightforward. Some user rights involve only restricted use of the land for a specified purpose, as with a right of way, and can be enforced by a simple injunction not to interfere with physical access. But other user rights can involve much more extensive shared use of the land, as with a house-sharing arrangement. To make the right work a considerable degree of mutual cooperation and personal interaction must exist between the sharers. These types of rights are difficult to enforce. The greater the level of cooperation and mutual trust that is required between the right-holder and the landowner, the less suitable the right is for acceptance as a property right.

These concerns feature in the case law. In *Thompson* v. *Park*[36] the Court of Appeal declined to enforce a sharing arrangement between two schoolmasters, Goddard LJ commenting that 'the court cannot specifically enforce an agreement for two people to live peaceably under the same roof'. Similarly, in *Hounslow LBC* v. *Twickenham Garden Developments*,[37] Megarry J accepted that there may be good reasons for distinguishing between exclusive licence arrangements and sharing ones:[38] 'If the courts sought to enforce a licence to share, a multitude of practical problems would arise which would be absent if the licence was for exclusive occupation'. These problems are magnified if it is sought to enforce the rights against a stranger. There would, therefore, be good sense in stating as a general principle that all rights requiring active cooperation and mutual trust and confidence between the right-holder and the landowner cannot be property rights. If ownership of the land is transferred, causing a breach of the right, the remedy lies against the grantor, not against the third party. This could explain the exclusion of many licence arrangements from the realm of property.

This might also explain why rights imposing positive burdens have not been accepted as property rights. Courts have traditionally been reluctant

---

[36] [1944] KB 408 at 409.   [37] [1971] Ch. 233 at 250.

[38] Better expressed as a distinction between licences requiring high levels of mutual cooperation and other licences.

to order specific performance of positive obligations, especially if they require 'constant supervision'.[39] If specific performance is not the normal remedy for breach of positive obligations, then it could explain why positive covenants are not permitted to run with the land,[40] and why so many ways around this rule have developed.[41] Perhaps the advantage that many devices have is that they provide a more effective means of enforcement of positive covenants than would specific performance of the positive obligation *per se*. For example, positive obligations can be attached to an 'estate rentcharge' within section 2 of the Rentcharges Act 1977 and are enforceable by the rent-owner having a power of entry in the event of breach.[42]

Not 'Personality Dependent'

A further principle governing property rights is that it must be possible for *any* third party to step into the shoes of the servient landowner and for the same privilege of use or right of control to be enjoyed as before. Not only must the privilege or right be technically the same but it must also bear the same meaning, to the right-holder and to the third party, as it did with the previous owner. Unlike the previous principle, which was to do with the practicability of enforcement, this principle concentrates on the 'meaning' or the 'function' of the right. This follows through an idea discussed by Penner.[43] Property is *thing*-related. Rights to things are protected by rights enforceable against persons and not directly against the thing itself. A right to light is protected by being able to obtain an injunction preventing a person from building on the servient land. Where the identity of the persons is important to the relationship, so that a change in identity of the persons fundamentally alters the nature of the relationship, the relationship is outside the realm of property. Penner describes this as a 'personality-rich' relationship. Although Penner's discussion does not relate to land, the approach can be used to show us something very important about property rights. If the substitution of a new person into the relationship fundamentally affects the nature of that relationship, the right cannot be a property right.

For some rights the identity of the parties is unimportant. A right of way across land remains the same whether it is *B*'s land or *C*'s land that it is exer-

---

[39] Although in some areas there may be greater willingness to order specific performance (*Jeune* v. *Queens Cross Properties Ltd.* [1974] 1 Ch. 97), the House of Lords has recently set its face against specific performance as a general remedy (*Co-operative Insurance Society Ltd.* v. *Argyll Stores (Holdings) Ltd.* [1997] 2 WLR 898).

[40] *Rhone* v. *Stephens* [1994] 2 All ER 65.

[41] For a list, see Burn, *Maudsley & Burn's Land Law Cases and Materials* (6th edn., London: Butterworths, 1992), 828–30.

[42] Law of Property Act 1925, s. 121. See further Bright, 'Rentcharges and the Enforcement of Positive Covenants' [1988] Conveyancer 99.

[43] Penner, 'The "Bundle of Rights" Picture of Property' 802–3.

cised over. It does not matter what the servient land is used for by B or C so long as they do not interfere with the right of way. For other rights, however, the identity of the owner and the intended use of the burdened land is more significant. A licence to sell a designer brand of clothes in a major department store would be fundamentally altered if the store were bought by a supermarket chain. A licence to share a house with the owner will be fundamentally different if there is a new owner (as well as being practically difficult to enforce). Even a licence to advertise on the wall of a cinema may be fundamentally altered if, to take an extreme example, the licence was to advertise tobacco products and the premises are bought to be used as a health clinic. The truth is that many licences depend upon a 'personality-rich relationship' which will not remain the same once the ownership of the 'thing' changes hands. There will be some exceptions, of licences that could perfectly well be exercised against the new owner,[44] but land law has to be built upon a system involving some level of predictability and so it may be that the law has been right all along to shut licences out of property because they depend upon a 'personality-rich relationship'.

The idea that property rights must not be dependent upon a 'personality-rich relationship' could also explain the distinction drawn in relation to freehold and leasehold covenants between those that 'touch and concern the land' (capable of running with the land/estate) and 'personal covenants' (which do not pass). Indeed, rather than use the unsatisfactory formula of 'touch and concern' which has always been hard to tie down, it would be better to focus on the true concern: is this a covenant which principally relates to the property or does it depend in some manner upon the identity of the landlord or tenant?[45]

IDENTIFIABILITY AND THIRD PARTIES

It follows from much of what has already been said that, if a specific burden is to be imposed upon a third party, it is only fair that the third party has an opportunity to learn of the extent of the burden before acquiring the

[44] Maybe these should be reclassified. A licence to cross land is not substantively different from an easement. The difference turns on other rules: the need for a dominant tenement (discussed below), formalities, and the duration of the interest.

[45] This test would have led to more satisfactory outcomes in *Caerns Motor Services Ltd.* v. *Texaco Ltd.* [1994] 1 WLR 1249 (the importance of the identity of the landlord to the tenant should have meant that the tie covenant did not pass to the new landlord), and in *Hua Chiao Commercial Bank Ltd.* v. *Chiaphua Industries Ltd.* [1987] AC 99 (the obligation to repay the rent deposit was not personality dependant and should have bound the new landlord). The Landlord and Tenant (Covenants) Act 1995 abandons the formal distinction based on 'touch and concern'; for new leases all covenants will run and covenants which are not intended to run with the lease must be expressed to be personal (s. 3(6)(a)).

ownership of the burdened land. Although in part this principle is to do with the conveyancing process itself and rules on priorities, it does also tell us something about the nature of property rights. In *National Provincial Bank Ltd* v. *Ainsworth*[46] Lord Wilberforce referred to the fact that an interest in land must be 'definable, identifiable by third parties, capable in its nature of assumption by third parties, and have some degree of permanence or stability'. These criteria have been lost sight of in some of the discussions of estoppel claims. As Battersby has pointed out, it is crucial to distinguish an estoppel claim (the inchoate right) from a crystallized right which originated in an estoppel-based claim.[47] The estoppel claimant will be arguing that she has acted to her detriment in reliance upon some assurance made by, or encouragement received from, the owner of the land that she will have some interest in the land and that it would be inequitable then to deny her this interest. Prior to crystallization (the time when the court declares what type of remedy is to be given—proprietary, compensatory, or other (or none)), the claimant has just that, a claim. There are no 'rights' but simply an assertion that she has been 'hard done by', treated unfairly, and is deserving of some remedy. The only 'right' that the claimant has at this stage is a privilege of access (the owner's behaviour has made it clear that the claimant is a licensee and not a trespasser). Further, in advance of the court action, it is impossible to predict accurately whether the claim will succeed and, if so, what will be done to remedy the injustice. Such a vague and discretionary claim cannot possibly form the basis of a property right as it is impossible for the successor to the land to know what it is he is taking the land subject to. The remedy of the claimant lies in a personal action against the representor, not in property law.[48]

Lord Wilberforce also referred to the fact that interests in land must demonstrate 'permanence and stability'. It cannot be that by this he meant that only perpetual rights can be property; easements are clearly within the class of property rights and yet can be granted for a fixed term. The context of the *Ainsworth* case shows in what sense the 'deserted wife's equity' failed to qualify: her right to occupy would depend on the whole matrimonial circumstances (including their conduct and whether the husband could provide alternative accommodation); she may have to leave immediately or after a period or if there was a change in circumstances. A property right must not then be evanescent. Further, as mentioned earlier, property rights must be intended to endure through different ownerships; an interest that is intended to be personal cannot be property.

---

[46] [1965] AC 1175 at 1248.

[47] Battersby, 'Contractual and Estoppel Licences as Proprietary Interests in Land' [1991] Conveyancer 36.

[48] The status of estoppel claims to land remains highly controversial in both case law and literature.

THE NEED FOR DOMINANT LAND

Some rights which satisfy all of the above criteria are still not accepted as property rights. Neither easements nor covenants can be property rights unless there is dominant land which benefits.[49]

This is not peculiar to English law. Rudden refers to the fact that most legal systems operate a closed group of property rights, and burdens will run only if other land is benefited thereby.[50] The reason for this is not clear. In *London & Blenheim Estates Ltd.* v. *Ladbroke Retail Parks Ltd.*[51] Peter Gibson LJ saw it as an outworking of the policy 'against encumbering land with burdens of uncertain extent'; but, if the easement is clearly defined, then surely there is no uncertainty.[52] He also refers to the 'reluctance of the law to recognise new forms of burden on property conferring more than contractual rights'. Rudden has explored the possible reasons for this reluctance and finds no wholly satisfactory explanation.[53] At the end of the day, the most convincing reason for there being a closed group is a perception that, if too many rights are allowed to burden land, land will become sterile. The more burdens on land, the less attractive it will be to purchasers. A balance has to be struck. Requiring there to be dominant land which benefits is one way of doing this, as is limiting the category of property rights.

PROPERTY RIGHTS THAT BREAK THE MOULD

There may be sound policy reasons to allow rights to be property that do not fit the criteria outlined earlier. This is the case with the spouse's statutory right of occupation under the matrimonial homes legislation (now the Family Law Act 1996), which is treated as a property right even though it does not meet the usual conditions for proprietary status. In this instance, however, Parliament has determined that the social interest in providing secure accommodation for the spouse in the matrimonial home justifies this special treatment. Given that the right can be exercised against a third party

[49] Inconsistently, profits can exist in gross.

[50] Rudden, 'Economic Theory versus Property Law: The *Numerus Clausus* Problem', in Eekelaar and Bell (eds.), *Oxford Essays in Jurisprudence* (3rd ser., Oxford: Oxford University Press, 1987), 257. Another common feature is that rights which impose a positive obligation (a 'duty to') upon the servient owner are not recognized as property rights (p. 242).

[51] [1994] 1 WLR 31 at 37.

[52] In *Hunter* v. *Canary Wharf Ltd.* [1997] 2 WLR 684 at 727 Lord Hope suggested that easements are limited to recognized categories because they restrict an owner's freedom. When the easement is created by 'express agreement' rather than by prescription concerns over such restrictions are lesser.

[53] Rudden, 'Economic Theory versus Property Law'. See also Sturley, 'Easements in Gross' (1980) 96 LQR 557.

only if it is registered, this does not cause any particular unfairness to the third party.

CONCLUDING REMARKS

The system of estates set out in the 1925 property legislation has proven remarkably adaptable given the social and economic changes throughout the remainder of the century. The very fact that estates have been defined in terms of 'time' rather than ownership content has meant that the package of rights that ownership confers can change without straining the conceptual structure of land law. An estate owner can claim no particular sacred and inviolable rights. Rather, she has a fluid package of rights, for a time, which is liable to be varied in order to guard and serve the interests of the wider community.

The malleability of the estate is to be contrasted with the rigidity of other, non-estate, interests in land. The inheritance of a closed group of property rights has led to a blinkered development of the law and an absence of vigorous critical debate about the essential qualities of property. Lord Brougham LC warned in *Keppell* v. *Bailey*[54] that 'incidents of a novel kind' should not be 'attached to property, at the fancy or caprice of any owner'. The response was to bolt the door on the existing categories. It is about time that the door was opened and new rights admitted on a more principled basis.

[54] (1834) 2 My. & K. 517 at 535.

BIBLIOGRAPHY

Abraham, 'Are Rights the Right Thing? Individual Rights, Communitarian Purposes and Crockpot Revolutions', 25 Conn. L. Rev. 947 (1993).

African National Congress, 'Restitution of Land Rights Policy' (n.d.).

—— A Draft Bill of Rights for a New South Africa (Cape Town: Center for Development Studies, University of Western Cape, 1990).

Aldridge Committee, Commonhold: Freehold Flats and Freehold Ownership of Other Interdependent Buildings, Report of a Working Group (the Aldridge Report), Cm. 179 (London: HMSO, 1987); see also under Law Commission.

Alexander, 'The Dead Hand and the Law of Trusts in the Nineteenth Century', 37 Stan. L. Rev. 1189 (1985).

—— 'Freedom, Coercion, and the Law of Servitudes', 73 Cornell L. Rev. 883 (1988).

—— 'Conditions of "Voice": Passivity, Disappointment, and Democracy in Homeowner Associations', in Barton and Silverman (eds.), Common Interest Communities: Private Governments and the Public Interest (Berkeley and Los Angeles: University of California Institute of Government Press, 1994).

—— 'Ten Years of Takings', 46 J. of Legal Educ. 586 (1996).

—— 'Commodification, Housing, and Democracy', in van Maanen and van der Walt (eds.), Property at the Threshold of the 21st Century (Antwerp: Maklu Press, 1996).

— 'Civic Property', 6 Social and Legal Studies 217 (1997).

Anaya, Indigenous Peoples in International Law (Oxford: Oxford University Press, 1996).

Anderson, 'Land Law Texts and the Explanation of 1925' (1984) 37 CLP 63.

—— 'The Proper Narrow Scope of Equitable Conversion in Land Law' (1984) 100 LQR 86.

—— Lawyers and the Making of English Land Law 1832–1940 (Oxford: Oxford University Press, 1992).

Andrews (ed.), Citizenship (London: Lawrence & Wishart, 1991).

Anon. (1843) 1 Law Times 189.

Applebome, After Hugo, A Storm over Beach Development, New York Times, 24 Sept. 1989, at 1.

Arblaster, The Rise and Decline of Western Liberalism (Oxford: Blackwell, 1984).

Arden and Hunter, Homelessness and Allocations (London: Legal Action Group, 1997).

—— and Partington, Housing Law (London: Sweet & Maxwell, 1994).

Ashcraft, 'Lockean Ideas, Poverty and the Development of Liberal Political Theory', in Brewer and Staves (eds.), Early Modern Conceptions of Property (London: Routledge, 1995).

Austin, 'Fragments—On Contracts', in Lectures on Jurisprudence, ii (5th edn., London: John Murray, 1885).

Australian Law Reform Commission Report, Matrimonial Property, Report No. 39 (Canberra: AGPS, 1987).

Baker, 'Spelman's Reports', vol. 2 (1977) 94 Selden Society 180.

Baker, 'Property and its Relation to Constitutionally Protected Liberty', 134 U. Pa. L. Rev. 741 (1986).

Balchin, *Housing Policy: An Introduction* (London: Routledge, 1995).

Ball, 'Constitution, Courts, Indian Tribes', American Bar Foundation Research J. 1 (1987).

Banks, *The Endeavour Journals of Joseph Banks, 1769–1771*, ed. Beaglehole (Sydney: Angus & Robertson, 1962).

Barbalet, *Citizenship; Rights, Struggle and Class Inequality* (Buckingham: Open University Press, 1988).

Barents, *The Agricultural Law of the EC* (Deventer: Kluwer, 1994).

Baron, 'Gifts, Bargains and Form', 64 Ind. LJ 155 (1989).

Barron, *Not Worth the Paper . . .?* (Women's Aid Federation England, 1990).

Barron and Scott, 'The Citizen's Charter Programme' (1992) 55 MLR 526.

Barton, '*Animus and possessio nomine alieno*', in Birks (ed.), *New Perspectives in the Roman Law of Property* (Oxford: Oxford University Press, 1989).

Basch, *In the Eyes of the Law: Women, Marriage, and Property in Nineteenth-Century New York* (Ithaca, NY: Cornell University Press, 1982).

Battersby, 'Contractual and Estoppel Licences as Proprietary Interests in Land' [1991] Conveyancer 36.

—— 'How Not to Judge the Quantum (and Priority) of a Share in the Family Home' (1996) 8 C & FLQ 261.

Baughen, 'Estoppels Over Land and Third Parties: An Open Question' (1994) 14 LS 147.

Beerman and Singer, 'Baseline Questions in Legal Reasoning: The Example of Property in Jobs', 23 Georgia L. Rev. 911 (1989).

Bell, '*Tulk* v. *Moxhay Revisited*' [1981] Conveyancer 55.

Bell, *The Modern Law of Personal Property in England and Ireland* (London: Butterworths, 1989).

Bellamy and Greenaway, 'The New Right Conception of Citizenship and the Citizen's Charter' (1995) 30 Government and Opposition 469.

Bentham, *An Introduction to the Principles of Morals and Legislation*, ed. Harrison (Oxford: Oxford University Press, 1948).

—— *Rationale of Judicial Evidence*, ii (London: Garland Publishing, 1827; facsimile of 1827 edition, published by Hunt and Clarke, London, under the title *Rationale of Judicial Evidence, Specially Applied to English Practice*).

Bevan, Kemp, and Rhodes, *Private Landlords and Housing Benefit* (York: University of York, 1995).

Bhabha, *The Location of Culture* (London: Routledge, 1994).

Binney, Harkell, and Nixon, *Leaving Violent Men* (Women's Aid Federation England, 1981).

Bird, *Domestic Violence: The New Law* (Bristol: Family Law, 1996).

Birks, 'The Roman Law Concept of Dominium and the Idea of Absolute Ownership' [1985] Acta Juridica 1.

—— 'Equity in the Modern Law: An Exercise in Taxonomy' (1996) U. Western Australia LR 1.

Bishop, 'Reforming Land Tenure: Farm Business Tenancies and the Rural Environment' [1996] Conveyancer 243.

Blackburn (ed.), *Rights of Citizenship* (London: Mansell, 1993).

Blackstone, *Commentaries on the Laws of England* (4 vols., 1st edn., Oxford: Oxford University Press, 1765–9; repr. Chicago: University of Chicago Press, 1979).

Bodkin, 'Rights of Support for Buildings and Flats' (1962) 26 Conveyancer (NS) 210.

Bogan, 'To Fix or Not to Fix?' (1995) 139 SJ 892.

Bolingbroke, *Some Reflections on the Political State of the Nation*, cited in Langford, *Public Life and the Propertied Englishman, 1689–1798* (Oxford: Oxford University Press, 1991).

Booth, Darke, and Yeandle (eds.), *Changing Places: Women's Lives in the City* (London: Paul Chapman, 1996).

Bottomley, 'Self and Subjectivities: Languages of Claim in Property Law', in Bottomley and Conaghan (eds.), *Feminist Theory and Legal Strategy* (Oxford: Blackwell, 1993).

—— 'Figures in a Landscape: Feminist Perspectives on Law, Land and Landscape', in Bottomley (ed.), *Feminist Perspectives on the Foundational Subjects of Law* (London: Cavendish Publishing, 1996).

Bottomley (ed.), *Feminist Perspectives on the Foundational Subjects of Law* (London: Cavendish Publishing, 1996).

Bracton, *De legibus et consuetudinibus angliae*, *c.*1225 (4 vols., ed. Woodbine, trans. Thorne, Cambridge, Mass.: Belknap Press, 1977).

Bradbrook, MacCallum, and Moore, *Australian Real Property Law* (Sydney: Law Book Company Ltd., 1991).

Braidotti, *Nomadic Subjects* (New York: Columbia University Press, 1994).

Bramley, 'Explaining the Incidence of Statutory Homelessness in England' (1993) 8 Housing Studies 128.

Bridge, 'Former Tenants, Future Liabilities and the Privity of Contract Principle: The Landlord and Tenant (Covenants) Act 1995' [1996] CLJ 313.

Bright, 'Rentcharges and the Enforcement of Positive Covenants' [1988] Conveyancer 99.

—— 'Tenant Farming: For the Good of the Nation?' [1995] Conveyancer 445.

Bright and Bright, 'Unfair Terms in Land Contracts: Copy Out or Cop Out?' (1995) 111 LQR 655.

—— and Gilbert, *Landlord and Tenant Law: The Nature of Tenancies* (Oxford: Oxford University Press, 1995).

Britton (ed.), *Agriculture in Britain: Changing Pressures and Policies* (Wallingford: Oxon.: CAB International, 1990).

Browne-Wilkinson, 'Constructive Trusts and Unjust Enrichment' (Presidential Address to the Holdsworth Club, 1990–1) (1996) 10 Trust Law International 9.

Buckland, *Elementary Principles of the Roman Private Law* (Cambridge: Cambridge University Press, 1912).

—— 'Interpolations in the Digest', 33 Yale LJ 343 (1923–4).

—— 'The Conception of Servitudes in Roman Law' (1928) 44 LQR 426.

—— 'The Protection of Servitudes in Roman Law' (1930) 46 LQR 447.

—— *The Main Institutions of Roman Private Law* (Cambridge: Cambridge University Press, 1931).

—— *A Textbook of Roman Law from Augustus to Justinian* (3rd edn., ed. Stein, Cambridge: Cambridge University Press, 1963).

Buckland, and McNair, *Roman Law and Common Law* (2nd edn. by Lawson, Cambridge: Cambridge University Press, 1952).

Building Societies Association, *Leaseholds: Time for a Change* (London: Building Societies Association, 1984).

Bull, *Housing Consequences of Relationship Breakdown* (London: HMSO, 1993).

Bulmer and Rees, *Citizenship Today* (London: UCL Press, 1996).

Burn, *Cheshire & Burn's Modern Law of Real Property* (14th edn., London: Butterworths, 1988).

—— *Maudsley & Burn's Land Law Cases and Materials* (6th edn., London: Butterworths, 1992).

—— *Cheshire & Burn's Modern Law of Real Property* (15th edn., London: Butterworths, 1994).

Burnet, *Introduction to Housing Law* (London: Cavendish Publishing, 1996).

Butt, *Land Law* (3rd edn., Sydney: LBC Information Services, 1996).

Cabinet Office, *The Citizen's Charter* (London: HMSO, 1991).

Cairns, 'Craig, Cujas, and the Definition of *feodum*: Is a Feu a Usufruct?', in Birks (ed.), *New Perspectives in the Roman Law of Property* (Oxford: Oxford University Press, 1989).

Caldwell, 'Rights of Ownership or Rights of Use?—The Need for a New Conceptual Basis for Land Use Policy', 15 William and Mary L. Rev. 759 (1973–4).

Cane, *An Introduction to Administrative Law* (Oxford: Oxford University Press, 1996).

Cannadine, *The Decline and Fall of the British Aristocracy* (London: Yale University Press, 1990).

Cardwell, *Milk Quotas: European Community and United Kingdom Law* (Oxford: Oxford University Press, 1996).

Carey, *Private Renting in England 1993/4* (London: HMSO, 1995).

Carlen, 'The Governance of Homelessness: Legality, Lore and Lexicon in the Agency-Maintenance of Youth Homelessness' (1994) 41 Critical Social Policy 18.

—— *Jigsaw: A Political Criminology of Youth Homelessness* (Buckingham: Open University Press, 1996).

Carlen and Wardhaugh, *Shropshire Single Homeless Survey* (Keele: Shropshire Probation and University of Keele, 1992).

Carroll, *The Concept of Land Reform* (New York: FAO, 1955).

Castles, *An Australian Legal History* (Sydney: Law Book Company Ltd., 1982).

Cawthorn and Barraclough, *Sale and Management of Flats, Practice and Precedent* (2nd edn., ed. Barraclough (London: Butterworths, 1996).

Central Association of Agricultural Valuers, *The Central Association of Agricultural Valuers Annual Tenanted Farms Survey 1995* (Coleford, Glos: Central Association of Agricultural Valuers, 1996).

—— *The Central Association of Agricultural Valuers Annual Tenanted Farms Survey 1996* (Coleford, Glos: Central Association of Agricultural Valuers, 1997).

Central Housing Advisory Committee, *Council Housing Purposes, Procedures and Priorities* (London: HMSO, 1969).

Chafee, 'Acceleration Provisions in Time Paper', 32 Harv. L. Rev. 747 (1919).

Chesterman, 'Family Settlements on Trust: Landowners and the Rising Bourgeoisie', in Rubin and Sugarman (eds.), *Law, Economy and Society, 1750–1914: Essays in the History of English Law* (Abingdon: Professional Books, 1984).

Ching-Liang Low, *White Skins Black Masks: Representation and Colonialism* (London: Routledge, 1996).

Chonchol, *El Desarrollo de America y la Reforma Agraria* (Madison, Wisc.: Land Tenure Center, University of Wisconsin, n.d.).

Chused, 'Married Women's Property Law: 1800–1850', 71 Georgetown LJ 1359 (1983).

Citizen's Charter (London: HMSO, 1991).

Clanchy, *From Memory to Written Record* (2nd edn., Oxford: Blackwell, 1993).

Clarke, *Leasehold Enfranchisement—the New Law* (Bristol: Jordans, 1993).

—— 'Commonhold, a Prospect of Promise' (1995) 58 MLR 486.

—— and Shell, 'Revision and Amendment of Legislation by the House of Lords: A Case Study' [1994] PL 409.

Coase, 'The Problem of Social Cost', 3 Journal of Law and Economics 1 (1960).

Cohen, 'Property and Sovereignty', in Macpherson (ed.), *Property: Mainstream and Critical Positions* (Toronto: University of Toronto Press, 1978).

Cohen and Arato, *Civil Society and Political Theory* (Cambridge, Mass.: MIT Press, 1995).

Coke, *The First Part of the Institutes of the Laws of England* (11th edn., London, 1719).

Cole and Furbey, *The Eclipse of Council Housing* (London: Routledge, 1994).

Coleman, *Foundations of Social Theory* (Cambridge, Mass: Belknap Press, 1990).

College of Estate Management, 'Commonhold—Is the Cure Worse than the Complaint?' (Research Paper 90/03, Reading: College of Estate Management, 1990).

Colman and Roberts, 'Economics of the CAP in Transition', in Artis and Lee (eds.), *The Economics of the European Union* (2nd edn., Oxford: Oxford University Press, 1997).

Commission of the European Economic Community, *First General Report on the Activities of the Community* (Luxembourg, 1958).

Committee of Inquiry into the Acquisition and Occupancy of Agricultural Land, *Report*, Cm. 7599 (London: HMSO, 1979).

Committee on Positive Covenants Affecting Land, *Report*, Cmd. 2719 (London: HMSO, 1965).

Cooke, 'Adverse Possession—Problems of Title in Registered Land' (1994) 14 LS 1.

Cooper, 'Fiduciary Government: Decentring Property and Taxpayers' Interests' (1997) Social and Legal Issues 234.

Coppel and O'Neill, 'The European Court of Justice: Taking Rights Seriously?' (1992) CML Rev. 669.

Cornish and Clark, *Law and Society in England 1750–1950* (London: Sweet & Maxwell, 1989).

Council of Mortgage Lenders, *Avoiding Possession: Arrears Management in Practice* (London: Council of Mortgage Lenders, 1992).

—— *Statement of Practice* (London: Council of Mortgage Lenders, 1995).

Court of Auditors, 'Special Report No. 2/87 on the Quota/Additional Levy System in the Milk Sector', OJ (1987), C266/1.

Cowan, 'A public dimension of a private problem' [1992] Conveyancer 288.

—— 'Accommodating Community Care' (1995) 22 Journal of Law and Society 212.

—— *Homelessness: The (In-)Appropriate Applicant* (Aldershot: Dartmouth, 1997).

—— 'Doing the Government's Work' (1997) 60 MLR 276.

—— (ed.), *The Housing Act 1996: A Practical Guide* (Bristol: Jordans, 1996).

—— & Fionda, 'Back to Basics: The Government's Homelessness Proposals' (1994) 57 MLR 610.

Cranston, *Legal Foundations of the Welfare State* (London: Weidenfeld & Nicolson, 1985).

Crawford, *C. R. Ashbee* (New Haven, Conn.: Yale University Press, 1985).

Cretney, 'The Politics of Law Reform: A View from the Inside' (1985) 48 MLR 493.

— 'The Law Commission: True Dawns and False Dawns' (1996) 59 MLR 631.

—— and Masson, *Principles of Family Law* (6th edn., London: Sweet & Maxwell, 1997).

Crook, 'Private Rented Housing and the Impact of Deregulation', in Birchall (ed.), *Housing Policies in the 1990s* (London: Routledge, 1992).

—— and Kemp, 'The Revival of Private Rented Housing in Britain' (1996) 11 Housing Studies 51.

—— Hughes, and Kemp, *The Supply of Privately Rented Homes* (York: Joseph Rowntree Foundation, 1995).

Dahrendorf, 'The Changing Quality of Citizenship', in Van Steenbergen (ed.), *The Condition of Citizenship* (London: Sage, 1994).

—— 'Citizenship and Beyond: The Social Dynamics', in Turner and Hamilton (eds.), *Citizenship, Critical Concepts Volume I/II* (London: Routledge, 1994).

—— 'Citizenship and Social Class', in Bulmer and Rees (eds.), *Citizenship Today* (London: UCL Press, 1996).

Daly, *Homeless* (London: Routledge, 1996).

Davenport and Hunt (eds.), *The Right to the Land* (Cape Town: David Philip, 1974).

Davey, 'Privity of Contract and Leases-Reform at Last' (1996) 59 MLR 78.

Davies, 'The First 150 Years', in Berndt and Berndt (eds.), *Aborigines of the West* (Nedlands: UWA Press, 1980).

Davies, 'Feminist Appropriations: Law, Property and Personality' (1994) 3 Social and Legal Studies 365.

Davis, 'Estoppel: An Adequate Substitute for Part Performance?' (1993) 13 OJLS 99.

Dawson, 'Public Policy, Security of Tenure and the Agricultural Holdings Acts' [1995] Web Journal of Current Legal Issues 320.

Deech, 'A tide in the Affairs of Women' (1972) 122 New Law Journal 742.

—— 'Williams and Glyn's and Family Law' [1980] New Law Journal 896.

Demsetz, 'Toward a Theory of Property Rights' 57 Amer. Econ. Rev. (Papers & Proceedings) 347 (1967).

Densham and Evans, *Scammell and Densham's Law of Agricultural Holdings* (8th edn., London: Butterworths, 1997).

Denzin, *The Research Act: A Theoretical Introduction to Sociological Methods* (London: McGraw-Hill, 1978).

Department of the Environment, *Housing: The Government's Proposals*, Cmnd. 214 (London: HMSO, 1987).

—— *Access to Local Authority and Housing Association Tenancies* (London: DoE, 1994).

—— *Planning for Rural Diversification: A Good Practice Guide* (London: HMSO, 1995).

—— *Rough Sleepers Initiative: Future Plans* (London: DoE, 1995).

—— *Planning Policy Guidance Note 1: General Policy and Principles* (London: HMSO, 1997).

—— and MAFF *Rural England—a Nation Committed to a Living Countryside*, Cm. 3016 (London: HMSO, 1995).

Department of Trade and Industry, *The Unfair Terms in Consumer Contracts Regulations 1994. Guidance Notes* (London: DTI, 1995).

De Sousa Santos, *Towards a New Common Sense: Law, Science and Politics in the Paradigmatic Transition* (London: Routledge, 1995).

Dewar, 'Give and Take in the Family Home' [1993] Family Law 231.

De Witte and Forder (eds.), *The Common Law of Europe and the Future of Legal Education* (Deventer, Netherlands: Kluwer, 1992).

Diamond, 'The Law Commission and Government Departments', in Zellick (ed.), *The Law Commission and Law Reform* (London: Sweet & Maxwell, 1988).

Dickerson, *Canada's First Nations: A History of Founding Peoples from the Earliest Times* (Norman: University of Oklahoma Press, 1994).

Diderot, 'Citoyen', in Turner and Hamilton (eds.), *Citizenship, Critical Concepts Volume I* (London: Routledge, 1994).

The Digest of Justinian, ed. Mommsen and Krueger, ed. and trans. Watson (4 vols., Philadelphia: University of Pennsylvanis Press, 1985).

Diosdi, *Ownership in Ancient and Preclassical Roman Law* (Budapest: Akadimiai Kiads, 1970).

Dockray, 'Why Do We Need Adverse Possession?' [1985] Conveyancer 272.

Donahue, 'The Future of the Concept of Property Predicted from its Past', in Pennock and Chapman (eds.), *Nomos XXII: Property* (New York: New York University Press, 1980).

Dorner (ed.), *Land Reform in Latin America*, (Madison, Wis.: Land Tenure Center, University of Wisconsin, 1971).

—— and Thiesenhusen, 'Selected Land Reforms in East and Southeast Asia: Their Origins and Impacts' (1990) 4(1) Asian-Pacific Economic Literature 65.

Douzinas and Warrington, *Justice Miscarried: Ethics, Aesthetics and the Law* (Brighton: Harvester Wheatsheaf, 1994).

du Plessis and Corder, *Understanding South Africa's Transitional Bill of Rights* (Cape Town: Juta, 1994).

Dukeminier and Krier, *Property* (3rd edn., Boston: Little, Brown & Co., 1993).

Dummett, 'Immigration and Nationality', in McCrudden and Chambers (eds.), *Individual Rights and the Law* (Oxford: Oxford University Press, 1995).

Durkheim, *Professional Ethics and Civic Morals*, trans. Brookfield, 1957, repr. in Lukes and Scull (eds.), *Durkheim and the Law* (Oxford: Robertson, 1983).

Eagleton, *Heathcliffe and the Great Hunger* (London: Verso, 1995).

Edwards, *The Design of Suburbia* (London: Pembridge, 1981).

Eekelaar, *Family Law and Social Policy* (London: Weidenfeld & Nicolson, 1978).

—— *Regulating Divorce* (Oxford: Oxford University Press, 1991).

—— 'The Family Law Bill: The Politics of Family Law' [1996] Family Law 45.

—— 'Family Justice: Ideal or Illusion?' (1995) 48 CLP 191.

Elias, *Explaining Constructive Trusts* (Oxford: Oxford University Press, 1990).

Ellickson, 'Property in Land' 102 Yale LJ 1315 (1993).

Elster, 'Introduction', in Elster (ed.), *Rational Choice* (New York: Cambridge University Press, 1986).

Elworthy and Holder, *Environmental Protection: Text and Materials* (London: Butterworths, 1987).

Epstein, 'Covenants and Constitutions', 73 Cornell L. Rev. 906 (1988).

—— 'Notice and Freedom of Contract in the Law of Servitudes', 55 So. Calif. L. Rev. 1353 (1982).

Ermisch, *Household Formation and Housing Tenure Decisions of Young People* (Colchester: University of Essex, 1997).

Evans and Smith, *Law of Landlord and Tenant* (5th edn., ed. Smith, London: Butterworths, 1997).

Evans-Jones and MacCormack, '*Iusta causa traditionis*', in Birks (ed.), *New Perspectives in the Roman Law of Property* (Oxford: Oxford University Press, 1989).

Expert Committee on Compensation and Betterment, *Final Report*, Cmd. 6386 (London: HMSO, 1942).

Feenstra, '*Dominium* and *ius in re aliena*: The Origins of a Civil Law Distinction', in Birks (ed.), *New Perspectives in the Roman Law of Property* (Oxford: Oxford University Press, 1989).

Fehlberg, *Sexually Transmitted Debt: Surety Experience and English Law* (Oxford: Oxford University Press, 1997).

Ferguson, 'Constructive Trusts—A Note of Caution' (1993) 109 LQR 109.

Flour, 'Quelques remarques sur l'évolution du formalisme', in *Le Droit privé français au milieu du xxe siècle: Études offertes à Georges Ripert*, i (Paris: Librairie Générale de Droit et de Jurisprudence, 1950).

Ford, *Which Way Out?* (London: Shelter, 1995).

—— and Wilcox, *Reducing Mortgage Arrears and Possessions: An Evaluation of the Initiatives* (York: Joseph Rowntree Foundation, 1992).

—— Kempson, and Wilson, *Mortgage Arrears and Possessions: Perspectives from Borrowers, Lenders and the Courts* (London: HMSO, 1995).

Fordham, *Judicial Review Handbook* (2nd edn., Chichester: John Wiley & Sons Ltd., 1997).

Forrest and Murie, *Right to Buy? Issues of Need, Equity and Polarisation in the Sale of Council Houses* (Bristol: SAUS, 1984).

—— —— *Selling the Welfare State* (London: Routledge, 1991).

Foster, *No New Homes* (London: Shelter, 1990).

—— *Mortgage Rescue: What Does It Add Up To?* (London: Shelter, 1992).

Fraenkel, *La Signature: Genèse d'un signe* (Paris: Gallimard, 1992).

Frazer and Lacey, *The Politics of Community* (Brighton: Harvester Wheatsheaf, 1993).

Frei and Trivelli, 'Mensaje del ejecutivo al Congreso proponiendo la aprobacion del proyecto de ley de reforma agraria', in Vodavonic, *Ley de reforma agraria* (Santiago: Editorial Nascimento, 1967), trans. Hazleton.

Freyfogle, 'Context and Accommodation in Modern Property Law', 41 Stan. L. Rev. 1529 (1988–9).

—— 'The Construction of Ownership', U. Ill. L. Rev. 173 (1996).

—— 'Water Rights and the Common Wealth', 26 Environmental Law 33 (1996).

Friden, 'Recent Developments in EEC Intellectual Property Law: The Distinction between Existence and Exercise Revisited' (1989) 26 CML Rev. 193.

Fuller, 'Consideration and Form', 41 Colum. L. Rev. 799 (1941).

Gaius, *Institutiones Iuris Civilis, The Institutes of Gaius*, ed. and trans. de Zulueta (Oxford: Oxford University Press, 1946).

Galbraith, *A History of Economics: The Past as the Present* (Harmondsworth: Penguin, 1989).

Gale, *Law of Easements* (1st edn., London: Sweet & Maxwell, 1839).

Gardner, *An Introduction to the Law of Trusts* (Oxford: Oxford University Press, 1990).

—— 'Rethinking Family Property' (1993) 109 LQR 263.

Gardner, *European Agriculture: Policies, Production and Trade* (London: Routledge, 1996).

Gatens, *Feminism and Philosophy: Perspectives on Difference and Equality* (Cambridge: Polity Press, 1991).

Gény, *Science et technique en droit privé positif*, iii (Paris: Librairie de la Société du Recueil Sirey, 1921).

George and George, *Sale of Flats* (5th edn., London: Sweet & Maxwell, 1984).

Getzler, 'Theories of Property and Economic Development' (1996) 26 J. of Interdisciplinary History 639.

—— 'Judges and Hunters: Law and Economic Conflict in the English Countryside 1800–60', in Brooks and Lobban (eds.), *Communities and Courts in Britain 1150–1900* (London: Hambledon Press, 1997).

Gibbard and Ravenscroft, 'The Reform of Agricultural Holdings Law', in Jackson and Wilde (eds.), *The Reform of Property Law* (Aldershot: Dartmouth, 1997).

Gibson, 'The Law Commission', 39 CLP 57.

Gilroy, 'Bringing Tenants into Decision Making', in Cowan (ed.), *Housing: Participation and Exclusion* (Aldershot: Dartmouth, forthcoming).

—— and Woods (eds.), *Housing Women* (London: Routledge, 1994).

Ginsburg, 'Racism and Housing: Concepts and Reality', in Braham, Rattansi, and Skellington (eds.), *Racism and Antiracism* (London: Sage, 1992).

Glendon, 'Is there a Future for Separate Property?' (1980) 14 Family Law Quarterly 315.

—— *The Transformation of Family Law: State, Law and the Family in the United States and Western Europe* (Chicago: University of Chicago Press, 1989).

Glover and Todd, 'Occupation for Life: Satisfying the Equity' [1995] Web Journal of Current Legal Issues.

—— —— 'The myth of common intention' (1996) 16 LS 325.

Goff and Jones, *The Law of Restitution* (4th edn., London: Sweet & Maxwell, 1993).

Gombrich, *Gombrich on The Renaissance*, ii (3rd edn., London: Phaidon, 1984).

Goode, *Commercial Law* (2nd edn., Harmondsworth: Penguin Books, 1995).

Goodman, 'Adverse Possession of Land—Morality and Motive' (1970) 33 MLR 281.

Goodrich, *Languages of Law* (London: Weidenfeld & Nicolson, 1990).

Gordon, 'The Importance of the *iusta causa* of *traditio*', in Birks (ed.), *New Perspectives in the Roman Law of Property* (Oxford: Oxford University Press, 1989).

Gordon, 'Paradoxical Property', in Brewer and Staves (eds.), *Early Modern Conceptions of Property* (London: Routledge, 1995).

Goss, 'Can Children be Tenants of their Homes?' (1996) May Childright 5.

Gray, *Elements of Land Law* (1st edn., London: Butterworths, 1987; 2nd edn., 1993).

—— 'Property in Thin Air' [1991] CLJ 252.

—— 'The Ambivalence of Property', in Prins (ed.), *Threats without Enemies* (London: Earthscan Publications, 1993).

—— 'Equitable Property' (1994) 47(2) CLP 157.

—— 'Property in Common Law Systems', in van Maanen and van der Walt (eds.), *Property Law on the Threshold of the 21st Century* (Antwerp: MAKLU, 1996).

Green and Hansbro, *Housing in England 1993/4* (London: HMSO, 1995).

Greve, Page, and Greve, *Homelessness in London* (Edinburgh: Scottish Academic Press, 1971).

Grewal, *Home and Harem: Nation, Gender, Empire, and the Cultures of Travel* (London: Leicester University Press, 1996).

Grosvenor Estate, *Strata Title in England and Wales* (London: Grosvener Estate, May 1987).

Gulliver and Tilson, 'Classification of Gratuitous Transfers', 51 Yale LJ 1 (1941).

Gutto, *Property and Land Reform: Constitutional and Jurisprudential Perspectives*, (Durban: Butterworths, 1995).

Habakkuk, *Marriage, Debt and the Estates System: English Landownership 1650–1950* (Oxford: Oxford University Press, 1994).

Habermas, *Between Facts and Norms: Contributions to a Discourse Theory of Law and Democracy* (Cambridge, Mass.: MIT Press, 1996).

Hague, *Leasehold Enfranchisement* (2nd edn., London: Sweet & Maxwell, 1987).

Hague, Malos, and Dear, *Multi-Agency Work and Domestic Violence* (Bristol: Policy Press, 1996).

Haraway, 'Shifting the Subject', in Bhavnani and Phoenix (eds.), *Shifting Identities, Shifting Racisms: A Feminist and Psychology Reader* (London: Sage, 1994).

Hardin, 'The Tragedy of the Commons', 162 Science 1243 (1968).

Hardy and Ward, *Arcadia for All: The Legacy of a Makeshift Landscape* (London: Mansell, 1984).

Hargreaves, 'Terminology and Title in Ejectment' (1940) 56 LQR 376.

Harpum, 'Adjusting Property Rights between Unmarried Cohabitees' (1982) 2 OJLS 277.

—— 'Overreaching, Trustees' Powers and the Reform of the 1925 Legislation' [1990] CLJ 277.

Harris, 'Ownership of Land in English Law', in MacCormick and Birks (eds.), *The Legal Mind* (Oxford: Oxford University Press, 1986).

—— 'Legal Doctrine and Interests in Land', in Eekelaar and Bell (eds.), *Oxford Essays in Jurisprudence* (3rd ser., Oxford: Oxford University Press, 1987).

—— *Property and Justice* (Oxford: Oxford University Press, 1996).

Hawes, *Homelessness and Older People* (Bristol: Policy Press, 1997).

Hayton, 'Equitable Rights of Cohabitees' [1990] Conveyancer 370.

—— 'Constructive Trusts of Homes—A Bold Approach' (1993) 109 LQR 485.

Heater, *Citizenship: The Civic Ideal in World History, Politics and Education* (New York: Longman, 1990).

Held (ed.), *Property, Profits and Economic Justice* (Belmont: Wadsworth Publishing Company, 1980).

Helmholz, 'Continental Law and Common Law: Historical Strangers or Companions?' [1990] Duke LJ 1207.

Hill, *The World Turned Upside Down: Radical Ideas during the English Revolution* (London: Martin Temple Smith, 1972).

Hill, 'Intention and the Creation of Proprietary Rights: Are Leases Different?' (1996) 16 LS 200.

Hill and Redman, *Law of Landlord and Tenant* (18th loose-leaf edn., London: Butterworths, 1988–98).

Hinde, McMorland, and Sim, *Introduction to Land Law* (2nd edn., Wellington, NZ: Butterworths, 1986).

HM Land Registry, *Annual Report 1988–1989* (London: HMSO, 1989).

Hogg, 'The Mortgage Charge of the Land Transfer Acts' (1907) 59 LQR 68.

Hohfeld, *Fundamental Legal Conceptions,* ed. Cook (New Haven, Conn.: Yale University Press, 1964).

Holmes, *Augustan England* (London: George, Allen & Unwin, 1982).

Honoré, *Gaius* (Oxford: Oxford University Press, 1962).

—— 'Property, Title and Redistribution', in Held (ed.), *Property, Profits and Economic Justice* (Belmont: Wadsworth Publishing Company, 1980).

Hopkins, 'The Trusts of Land and Appointment of Trustees Act 1996' [1996] Conveyancer 411.

—— 'Overreaching and the Trusts of Land and Appointment of Trustees Act 1996' [1997] Conveyancer 81.

Howard and Hill, 'The Informal Creation of Interests in Land' (1995) 15 LS 356.

Howell, 'The Doctrine of Notice: An Historical Perspective' (University of Manchester Faculty of Law Working Paper No. 19; 1996).

Hughes, '*The Law of Contracts Relating to Real Property*' (1845–6) 6 Law Times 289.

—— 'The Law of Contracts Relating to Real Property' (1846) 7 Law Times 246.

Hughes and Lowe, *Social Housing Law and Policy* (London: Butterworths, 1995).

Hunter and Miles, 'The Unsettling of Settled Law on "Settled Accommodation" ' (1997) 19 Journal of Social Welfare and Family Law 267.

Ibbetson and Lewis (eds.), *The Roman Law Tradition* (Cambridge: Cambridge University Press, 1994).

Ilkin, *Strata Title and Community Title Management and the Law* (2nd edn., Sydney: Law Book Co., 1996).

Institute of Housing, *One Parent Families: Are they Jumping the Housing Queue?* (Coventry: IoH, 1994).

Jackson, 'Security of Title in Registered Land' (1978) 94 LQR 239.

Jowell, 'Bargaining in Development Control' [1977] JPL 414.

John, *Politics and the Law in Late Nineteenth-Century Germany: The Origins of the Civil Code* (Oxford: Oxford University Press, 1989).

—— 'The Peculiarities of the German State: Bourgeois Law and Society in the Imperial Era' (1989) 119 Past and Present 105.

Jolowicz, 'Political Implications of Roman Law' (1947) 22 Tulane L. Rev. 62.

—— 'Some English Civilians' (1949) 2 CLP 139.

—— and Nicholas, *Historical Introduction to the Study of Roman Law* (3rd edn. by Nicholas, Cambridge: Cambridge University Press, 1972).

Justinian's Institutes, ed. Krueger, ed. and trans. Birks and McLeod (London: Duckworth, 1987).

Kagan, 'The Nature of Servitudes and the Association of Usufruct with Them' (1947) 22 Tulane LR 94.

Kahn-Freund, 'Matrimonial Property and Equality before the Law: Some Sceptical Reflections' (1971) 4 Human Rights Journal 493.

Karn, 'Remodelling a HAT: The Implementation of the Housing Action Trust Legislation 1987–92', in Malpass and Means (eds.), *Implementing Housing Policy* (Buckingham: Open University Press, 1993).

Karst, *Latin American Legal Institutions: Problems for Comparative Study* (Berkeley and Los Angeles: University of California Press, 1966).

Kelman, *A Guide to Critical Legal Studies* (Cambridge, Mass.: Harvard University Press, 1987).

Kemeny, *The Myth of Home Ownership* (London: Routledge & Kegan Paul, 1981).

Kemp, 'The Ghost of Rachman', in Grant (ed.), *Built to Last* (London: Roof, 1992).

Kemp and Rhodes, *Private Landlords in Scotland* (Edinburgh: Scottish Homes, 1994).

Kennedy, 'Cost-Benefit Analysis of Entitlement Problems: A Critique', 33 Stan. L. Rev. 387 (1981).

—— 'Distributive and Paternalist Motives in Contract and Tort Law, with Special Reference to Compulsory Terms and Unequal Bargaining Power', 41 Maryland L. Rev. 463 (1982).

—— 'Neither the Market nor the State: Housing Privatization Issues', in Alexander and Skapska (eds.), *A Fourth Way? Privatization, Property, and the Emergence of New Market Economies* (New York: Routledge, 1994).

—— and Michelman, 'Are Private Property and Contract Efficient?', 8 Hofstra L. Rev. 711 (1980).

—— and Specht, 'Limited Equity Housing Cooperatives as a Mode of Privatization', in Alexander and Skapska (eds.), *A Fourth Way? Privatization, Property, and the Emergence of New Market Economies* (New York: Routledge, 1994).

Kenny, 'Commonhold Title—Freehold Flats and Offices: Opportunity Knocks?' [1988] 12 EG 30.

Kercher, *An Unruly Child* (St Leonards, NSW: Allen & Unwin, 1995).

—— *Debt, Seduction and Other Disasters* (Sydney: Federation Press, 1996).

Kerr, *New Farm Tenancies: New Farms and Land 1995–97* (London: Royal Institution of Chartered Surveyors, 1994).

King, *Land Reform: A World Survey* (Boulder, Colo.: Westview Press, 1977).

Kirby, 'Re: Mapping Subjectivity: Cartographic Vision and the Limits of Politics', in Duncan (ed.), *Body Space: Destabilizing Geographies of Gender and Sexuality* (London: Routledge, 1996).

Kirk, *Portrait of a Profession* (London: Oyez Publishing, 1976).

Klein, 'Property and Politics in the Early Eighteenth Century Whig Moralists: The Case of *The Spectator*', in Brewer and Staves (eds.), *Early Modern Conceptions of Property* (London: Routledge, 1995).

Kleyn and Boraine, *The Law of Property* (3rd edn., Durban: Butterworths, 1987).

Kommers, *The Constitutional Jurisprudence of the Federal Republic of Germany* (Durham, NC: Duke University Press).

Kozol, *Penury in the Land of Plenty* (Community Care, Sept. 1988), quoted in Lister, *The Exclusive Society* (London: Child Poverty Action Group, 1990).

Larson, *The Rise of Professionalism* (Berkeley and Los Angeles: University of California Press, 1977).

Latour, 'Visualization and Cognition. Thinking with Hands and Eyes' (1986) 6 Knowledge and Society 1.

Law Commission: see separate entry.

Law Reform Committee, *Acquisition of Easements and Profits by Prescription*, 14th Report, Cm. 3100 (London: HMSO, 1966).

—— *Final Report on Limitations of Actions*, 21st Report, Cm. 6923 (London: HMSO, 1977).

Lawson, *The Rational Strength of the English Law* (London: Oxford University Press, 1951).

—— 'Geoffrey Chevalier Cheshire' (1979) 65 Proceedings of the British Academy 611.

—— (ed.), *Buckland and McNair's Roman Law and Common Law* (2nd edn., Oxford: Oxford University Press, 1952).

Lawson and Rudden, *The Law of Property* (2nd edn., Oxford: Oxford University Press, 1982).

Leasehold Committee, *Final Report*, Cmd. 7982 (London: HMSO, 1950).

Leca, 'Individualism and Citizenship', in Turner and Hamilton (eds.), *Citizenship, Critical Concepts Volume II* (London: Routledge, 1994).

Lee, *An Introduction to Roman–Dutch Law* (5th edn., Oxford: Oxford University Press, 1953).

Lees, *Enquiry into the Planning System in North Cornwall District* (London: HMSO, 1993).

Lewis, 'Markets, Regulation and Citizenship: A Constitutional Analysis', in Brownsword (ed.), *Law and the Public Interest* (Stuttgart: Franz Steiner, 1993).

—— *Choice and the Legal Order* (London: Butterworths, 1996).

—— and Birkinshaw, *When Citizens Complain* (Buckingham: Open University Press, 1993).

—— Seneveritane, and Cracknell, *Complaints Procedures in Local Government* (Sheffield: University of Sheffield, 1987).

Lichfield, 'Land Nationalization', in Hall (ed.), *Land Values* (London: UCL Press, 1965).

Lidstone, 'Rationing Housing to the Homeless Applicant' (1994) 9 Housing Studies 459.

—— 'Women and Homelessness', in Booth, Darke, and Yeandle (eds.), *Changing Places: Women's Lives in the City* (London: Paul Chapman, 1996).

Lim and Green, *Cases and Materials in Land Law* (2nd edn., London: Pitmans Publishing, 1995).

Lines, *Taming the Great Southern Land: A History of the Conquest of Nature in Australia* (Sydney: Allen & Unwin, 1991).

Lister, *The Exclusive Society* (London: Child Poverty Action Group, 1990).

Lloyd, *The Man of Reason: 'Male' and 'Female' in Western Philosophy* (London: Methuen, 1984).

Locke, *The Second Treatise of Government*, ed. Peardon (Indianapolis: Bobs-Merrill Educational Publishing, 1952).

Loney, 'A War on Poverty or on the Poor?', in Walker and Walker (eds.), *The Growing Divide: A Social Audit 1979–1987* (London: Child Poverty Action Group, 1989).

Lord Chancellor's Department, *Commonhold, a consultation paper with draft Bill attached*, Cm. 1345 (London: HMSO, 1990).

Loughlin, 'Planning Gain: Law, Policy and Practice' [1981] 1 OJLS 61.

—— *Local Government in the Modern State* (London: Sweet & Maxwell, 1986).

—— *Legality and Locality* (Oxford: Oxford University Press, 1996).

Loveland, 'Legal Rights and Political Realities: Governmental Responses to Homelessness in Britain' (1991) 18 Law and Social Inquiry 249.

—— 'Square Pegs, Round Holes: The 'Right' to Council Housing in the Post-War Era' (1992) 19 Journal of Law and Society 339.

—— 'Administrative Law, Administrative Processes and the Housing of Homeless Persons: A View from the Sharp End' (1992) Journal of Social Welfare Law 4.

—— 'Cathy Sod Off! The End of the Homelessness Legislation' (1994) 16 Journal of Social Welfare and Family Law 367.

—— 'Irrelevant Considerations?', in Richardson and Genn (eds.), *Administrative Law and Government Action* (Oxford: Oxford University Press, 1994).

—— *Housing Homeless Persons* (Oxford: Oxford University Press, 1995).

—— *Constitutional Law: A Critical Introduction* (London: Butterworths, 1996).

Low, 'A Tale of Two Citizenships: Henry Jones, T. H. Marshall and Conceptions of Citizenship in Twentieth-Century Britain', in *Contemporary Political Studies* (London: Political Studies Association, 1997).

Luke and Sculls (eds.), *Durkheim and the Law* (Oxford: Martin Robertson, 1983).

Luther, 'Easements and Exclusive Possession' (1996) 16 LS 51.

Lyall, *Land Law in Ireland* (Dublin: Oak Tree Press, 1994).

Lyons, *Forms and Limits of Utilitarianism* (Oxford: Oxford University Press, 1967).

McAuslan, *The Ideologies of Planning Law* (Oxford: Pergamon Press, 1980).

McCluskey, *Acting in Isolation* (London: Campaign for the Homeless and Rootless, 1994).

McCrone and Stephens, *Housing Policy in Britain and Europe* (London: UCL Press, 1995).

McDowell, 'Spatializing Feminism: Geographic Perspectives', in Duncan (ed.), *Body Space: Destabilizing Geographies of Gender and Sexuality* (London: Routledge, 1996).

McIntosh, 'Institutional Investment in Europe' (1995) 05 EG 152.

MacKenzie and Phillips, *A Practical Introduction to Land Law* (6th edn., London: Blackstones, 1996).

Macpherson (ed.), *Property: Mainstream and Critical Positions* (Toronto: University of Toronto Press, 1978).

MAFF, *European Agriculture: The Case for Radical Reform—Conclusions of the Minister of Agriculture, Fisheries and Food's CAP Review Group* (London: HMSO, 1995).

—— *Agriculture in the United Kingdom 1995* (London: HMSO, 1996).

—— *Agriculture in the United Kingdom 1996* (London: HMSO, 1997).

—— and Welsh Office Agriculture Department, *Agricultural Tenancy Law—Proposals for Reform: A Consultation Paper* (1991).

Maitland, *The Forms of Action at Common Law,* ed. Chaytor and Whittaker (Cambridge: Cambridge University Press, 1965; repr. from 1909).

Maitland-Walker, 'Ice-Cream Wars: An Honourable Peace or the Beginning of a Greater Conflict?' (1995) 8 ECLR 451.

Malos and Hague, *Domestic Violence and Housing* (Women's Aid Federation England, and Bristol: School of Applied Social Studies, University of Bristol, 1993).

Malpass, 'Housing and Young People', in Malpass (ed.), *The Housing Crisis* (London: Routledge, 1986).

—— and Murie, *Housing Policy and Practice* (Basingstoke: Macmillan, 1994).

Mandelson, 'Labour's Next Steps: Tackling Social Exclusion', unpublished lecture (14 August 1997).

Markesinis, *The Gradual Convergence* (Oxford: Oxford University Press, 1994).

Marshall, *Citizenship and Social Class and Other Essays* (Cambridge: Cambridge University Press, 1950).

—— *Sociology at the Crossroads and Other Essays* (London: Heinemann, 1963).

—— *Class, Citizenship and Social Development* (London: Greenwood Press, 1964).

Marx, *On the Jewish Question*, in *Karl Marx: Early Writings*, ed. Bottomore (New York: McGraw Hill, 1964).

Massumi, *A User's Guide to Capitalism and Schizophrenia: Deviations from Deleuze and Guattari* (Cambridge, Mass.: MIT Press, 1993).

Matthews, 'If it ain't broke, don't fix it' (1996) 10 TLI 97.

Means and Smith, *Community Care: Policy and Practice* (Basingstoke: Macmillan, 1994).

Mechem, 'The Requirement of Delivery in Gifts of Chattels and of Choses in Action Evidenced by Commercial Instruments', 21 Ill. L. Rev. 341 (1926–7).

Megarry, *The Rent Acts* (11th edn., London: Stevens, 1988).

Megarry and Wade, *The Law of Real Property* (5th edn., London: Stevens, 1984).

Mercer, *Welcome to the Jungle: New Positions in Black Cultural Studies* (London: Routledge, 1994).

Michelman, 'Ethics, Economics, and the Law of Property', in Pennock and Chapman (eds.), *Nomos XXIV: Ethics, Economics, and the Law* (New York: New York University Press, 1982).

Miles, 'Eminent Practitioners: The New Visage of Country Attorneys c.1750–1800', in Rubin and Sugarman (eds.), *Law, Economy and Society, 1750–1914: Essays in the History of English Law* (Abingdon: Professional Books, 1984).

Mill, *On Liberty* (London: J. W. Parker & Son, 1859).

Miller, 'Time to End the Two-Tier Tenancies' (1997) Sept.–Oct. ROOf 12.

—— 'Green Belt Policy and Law: A Study in Transitions', in Herbert-Young (ed.), *Law, Policy and Development in the Rural Environment* (Cardiff: University of Wales Press, forthcoming).

Milne, 'Proprietary Estoppel, Purchasers and Mortgagees: An Alternative Approach' [1997] Web Journal of Current Legal Issues.

Milsom, *The Legal Framework of English Feudalism* (Cambridge: Cambridge University Press, 1976).

Milsom, *Historical Foundations of the Common Law* (2nd edn., London: Butterworths, 1981).

Minda, *Postmodern Legal Movements: Law and Jurisprudence at Century's End* (New York: New York University Press, 1995).

Ministry in the Office of the President, The Rural Development Strategy of the Government of National Unity, Oct. 1995, in *Government Gazette*, No. 16679, 3 Nov. 1995 (South Africa).

Ministry of Health, *Town Planning in England and Wales* (London: HMSO, 1932).

Minutes of Evidence, Cape Native Laws Commission, Cape Town, 1883.

Moffat, 'Trusts Law: A Song Without End?' (1992) 55 MLR 123.

Moffat (with Bean and Dewar), *Trusts Law: Text and Materials* (2nd edn., London: Butterworths, 1994).

Morell and McNamara, 'International Property Investment: A UK Institutional Perspective' [1996] Property Rev. 70.

Moriarty, 'Licences and Land Law: Legal Principles and Public Policies' (1984) 100 LQR 376.

Moroney and Harris, *Relationship Breakdown and Housing: A Practical Guide* (London: Shelter, 1997).

Muir Watt, *Agricultural Holdings* (13th edn., London: Sweet & Maxwell, 1987).

Mullen, Scott, Fitzpatrick, and Goodlad, *Tenancy Rights and Repossession Rates: In Theory and Practice* (Edinburgh: Scottish Homes, 1996).

Mullins, Niner, and Riseborough, 'Large-Scale Voluntary Transfers', in Malpass and Means (eds.), *Implementing Housing Policy* (Buckingham: Open University Press, 1993).

Murphy, 'After Boland: Law Com. No. 115' (1983) 46 MLR 330.

—— 'The Oldest Social Science? The Epistemic Properties of the Common Law Tradition' (1991) 54 MLR 182.

—— 'Domestic Violence: The New Law' (1996) 59 MLR 845.

—— and Clark, *The Family Home* (London: Sweet & Maxwell, 1983).

—— and Rawlings, 'The Matrimonial Homes (Co-Ownership) Bill: The Right Way Forward?' [1980] Family Law 136.

Murray, *Underclass: The Crisis Deepens* (London, Institute for Economic Affairs, 1994).

National Association of Citizens Advice Bureaux, *Dispossessed* (London: NACAB, 1993).

Nedelsky, *Private Property and the Limits of American Constitutionalism: The Madisonian Framework and its Legacy* (Chicago: University of Chicago Press, 1990).

—— 'American Constitutionalism and the Paradox of Private Property', in Elster and Slagstad (eds.), *Constitutionalism and Democracy,* (Cambridge: Cambridge University Press, 1993).

Neild, *Hong Kong Land Law* (2nd edn., Hong Kong: Butterworths Asia, 1993).

Nelson and Starck, 'Formalities and Formalism: A Critical Look at the Execution of Wills', 6 Pepperdine L. Rev. 331 (1979).

Neville and Mordaunt, *A Guide to the Reformed Common Agricultural Policy* (London: Estates Gazette, 1993).

Newton, 'At the Whim of the Sovereign: Aboriginal Title Reconsidered', 31 Hastings LJ 1215 (1980).

Nicholas, *An Introduction to Roman Law* (3rd edn., Oxford: Oxford University Press, 1962).

Nixon, Smith, Wishart, and Hunter, *Housing Cases in County Courts* (London: The Policy Press, 1996).

Oakley, 'The Trusts of Land and Appointment of Trustees Act 1996' [1996] Conveyancer 401.

O'Donovan, 'A New Settlement between the Sexes? Constitutional Law and the Citizenship of Women', in Bottomley (ed.), *Feminist Perspectives on the Foundational Subjects of Law* (London: Cavendish Publishing, 1996).

Offer, 'The Origins of the Law of Property Acts 1910–25' (1977) 40 MLR 505.

—— *Property and Politics, 1870–1914: Land Ownership, Law, Ideology and Urban Development in England* (Cambridge: Cambridge University Press, 1981).

—— 'Farm Tenure and Land Values in England, *c.*1750–1850' (1991) Economic History Review 1.

—— 'Lawyers and Land Law Revisited' (1994) 14 OJLS 269.

Ogus, 'Economics and Law Reform: Thirty Years of Law Commission Endeavour' (1995) 111 LQR 407.

O'Hagan, 'Quantifying Interests under Resulting Trusts' (1997) 60 MLR 420.

Oliart, *El legalismo como ideologia politica en las leyes de reforma agraria latinoamericana*, trans. Ocran (Bogota, 1970).

Oliver, 'Why Do People Live Together?' [1982] JSWL 209.

—— *Government in the United Kingdom* (Buckingham: Open University Press, 1991).

Onions, *The Oxford Dictionary of English Etymology* (Oxford: Oxford University Press, 1985).

Organization for European Economic Cooperation, *Agricultural Policies in Europe and North America: Price and Income Policies* (Paris: 1957).

Parkinson, *Tradition and Change in Australian Law* (Sydney: Law Book Company Ltd., 1994).

Partington, 'Citizenship and Housing', in Blackburn (ed.), *Rights of Citizenship* (London: Mansell, 1993).

Partridge, 'Enclosures, Clearances and the Diggers', in Girardet (ed.), *Land for the People* (London: Crescent Books, 1976).

Pascall, *Social Policy: A New Feminist Analysis* (London: Routledge, 1997).

Pateman, *The Disorder of Women* (Cambridge: Polity Press, 1989).

Pearce and Wilcox, *Home-Ownership, Taxation and the Economy* (York: Joseph Rowntree Foundation, 1991).

Peart, 'Towards a Concept of Family Property in New Zealand' (1996) 10 International Journal of Law, Policy and the Family 105.

Penner, 'The "Bundle of Rights" Picture of Property', 43 UCLA L. Rev. 711 (1996).

—— *The Idea of Property in Law* (Oxford: Oxford University Press, 1997).

Perillo, 'The Statute of Frauds in the Light of Functions and Dysfunctions of Form', 43 Fordham L. Rev. 39 (1974).

Perkin, *The Origins of Modern English Society 1780–1880* (London: Routledge & Kegan Paul, 1969).

—— 'Land Reform and Class Conflict in Victorian Britain', in Butt and Clark (eds.), *The Victorians and Social Protest* (Newton Abbott: David & Charles, 1973).

Perkin, *The Rise of Professional Society* (London: Routledge & Kegan Paul, 1989).

Pettit, 'Demise of Trusts for Sale and the Doctrine of Conversion?' (1997) 113 LQR 207.

Plant, *Modern Political Thought* (Oxford: Blackwell, 1991).

—— and Barry, *Citizenship and Rights in Thatcher's Britain: Two Views* (London: IEA Health and Welfare Unit, 1990).

Platsky and Walker, *The Surplus People: Forced Removals in South Africa* (Johannesburg: Ravan, 1985).

Pollock and Wright, *An Essay on Possession in the Common Law* (Oxford: Oxford University Press, 1888).

Posner, *Economic Analysis of Law* (4th edn., Boston: Little Brown, 1992).

Pottage, 'The Measure of Land' (1994) 57 MLR 361.

—— 'The Originality of Registration' (1995) 15 OJLS 371.

Powell, *Environmental Management in Australia: 1788–1914* (Melbourne: Oxford University Press, 1976).

Powell and Rohan, *Powell on Real Property* (rev. edn., New York: Matthew Bender, 1969–96).

Press Statement on the Extension of Security of Tenure Bill, Pretoria, 29 Jan. 1997.

Pritchard, 'Making Positive Covenants Run' (1973) 37 Conveyancer (NS) 194.

Prucha, *The Great Father* (Lincoln, Nebr.: University of Nebraska Press, 1984).

Putnam, *Making Democracy Work: Civic Traditions of Modern Italy* (Princeton: Princeton University Press, 1993).

—— 'Bowling Alone: America's Declining Social Capital' (1995), 6 J. of Democracy 65.

Radin, 'Property and Personhood', 34 Stan. L. Rev. 957 (1982).

—— 'The Liberal Conception of Property: Cross Currents in the Jurisprudence of Takings', 88 Col. L. Rev. 1667 (1988).

Randolph, 'The Re-Privatization of Housing Associations', in Malpass and Means (eds.), *Implementing Housing Policy* (Buckingham: Open University Press, 1993).

Raven, 'Defending Conduct and Property: The London Press and the Luxury Debate', in Brewer and Staves (eds.), *Early Modern Conceptions of Property* (London: Routledge, 1995).

Raz, *The Morality of Freedom* (Oxford: Oxford University Press, 1986).

Rehnquist Alters Restrictive Deed, New York Times, 16 Nov. 1986, s. 1, pt. 2, at p. 50.

Reich, 'The New Property', in Macpherson (ed.), *Property: Mainstream and Critical Positions* (Toronto: University of Toronto Press, 1978).

Reid, *Nature Conservation Law* (Edinburgh: W. Green/Sweet & Maxwell, 1994).

Reid, '700 Years at One Blow: The Abolition of Feudal Land Tenure in Scotland', in Jackson and Wilde (eds.), *The Reform of Property Law* (Aldershot: Dartmouth, 1997).

Richards, *The Imperial Archive—Knowledge and the Fantasy of Empire,* (London: Verso, 1993).

Robertson, 'Segregation Land Law: A Socio-Legal Analysis', in Corder (ed.), *Essays on Law and Social Practice in South Africa* (Cape Town: Juta, 1988).

—— 'Land and Rights in South Africa' (1990) 6 South African Journal on Human Rights 215.

Roche, *Rethinking Citizenship* (Cambridge: Polity Press, 1992).

Rodger, *Owners and Neighbours in Roman Law* (Oxford: Oxford University Press, 1972).

Rodgers, 'Environmental Gain, Set-Aside and the Implementation of EU Agricultural Reform in the United Kingdom', in Rodgers (ed.), *Nature Conservation and Countryside Law* (Cardiff: University of Wales Press, 1996).

—— 'Conservation and Land Use', in Lennon and Mackay (eds.), *Agricultural Law, Tax and Finance* (loose-leaf edn., London: Longmans, 1998).

—— 'Reforming Land Tenure: Farm Business Tenancies and the Rural Economy' [1996] Conveyancer 164.

Rose, 'Possession as the Origin of Property', 52 U. of Chicago L. Rev. 73 (1985).

—— 'The Comedy of the Commons: Custom, Commerce, and Inherently Public Property', 53 U. of Chicago L. Rev. 711 (1986).

Rose, *Feminism and Geography: The Limits of Geographical Knowledge* (Cambridge: Polity Press, 1993).

Roux, 'Property, Land as Property, and the Interim Constitution' (Cape Town: University of Cape Town, n.d.).

Rudden, 'The Terminology of Title' (1964) 80 LQR 63.

—— 'Economic Theory versus Property Law: The *Numerus Clausus* Problem', in Eekelaar and Bell (eds.), *Oxford Essays in Jurisprudence*, (3rd ser.; Oxford: Oxford University Press, 1987).

—— 'Things as Thing and Things as Wealth' (1994) 14 OJLS 81.

Ruoff and Roper, *The Law and Practice of Registered Conveyancing* (6th edn., London: Sweet & Maxwell, 1991).

Rutherford, *Criminal Policy and the Eliminative Ideal* (Southampton: University of Southampton, 1996).

Salmon, *Women and the Law of Property in Early America* (Chapel Hill, NC: University of North Carolina Press, 1986).

Samuel, 'Roman Law and Modern Capitalism' (1984) 4 LS 185.

Sanders, *The Institutes of Justinian* (London: John W. Parker, 1876).

Sandlands, 'The Real, The Simulacrum, and the Construction of "Gypsy" in Law' (1996) 23 JLS 383.

Saunders, 'Citizenship in a Liberal Society', in Turner (ed.), *Citizenship and Social Theory* (London: Sage, 1993).

Schubert, 'Is there a Public Interest Theory', in Friedrich (ed.), *The Public Interest* (New York: Atherton Press, 1962).

Schulz, *Principles of Roman Law* (Oxford: Oxford University Press, 1936).

—— *Classical Roman Law* (Oxford: Oxford University Press, 1951).

Scottish Law Commission, *Family Law Report on Matrimonial Property*, Scot. Law Com. No. 86 (Edinburgh: HMSO, 1984).

Scottish Office, *Rural Scotland: People, Prosperity and Partnership*, Cm. 3041 (Edinburgh: HMSO, 1995).

Searle, *The Construction of Social Reality* (London: Allen Lane, 1995).

Seebohm, *Report of the Committee on Local Authority and Allied Personal Social Services*, Cmnd. 3703 (London: HMSO, 1968).

Sewell, *A Letter to Lord Worsley on the Burdens Affecting Real Property, with Reasons in Favour of a General Registry of Title* (1846).

Shanley, *Feminism, Marriage and the Law in Victorian England* (Princeton: Princeton University Press, 1989).

Shick and Plotkin, *Torrens in the United States* (Lexington, Mass.: D. C. Heath & Co, 1978).

Short, *Imagined Country: Society, Culture and Environment* (London: Routledge, 1991).

Shurmer-Smith and Hannam, *Worlds of Desire, Realms of Power: A Cultural Geography* (London: Edward Arnold, 1994).

Siegel, 'The Modernization of Marital Status Law: Adjudicating Wives' Rights to Earnings, 1860–1930', 82 Georgetown LJ 2127 (1994).

—— 'Home as Work: The First Women's Rights Claims Concerning Wives' Household Labor, 1850–1880', 102 Yale LJ 1073 (1994).

Sihombing and Wilkinson, *Hong Kong Conveyancing* (Hong Kong: Butterworths Asia, 1993).

Simon, 'Social-Republican Property', 38 UCLA L. Rev. 1335 (1991).

—— 'Republicanism, Market Socialism, and the Third Way', in Alexander and Skapska (eds.), *A Fourth Way? Privatization, Property, and the Emergence of New Market Economies* (New York: Routledge, 1994).

Simpson, *Leading Cases in the Common Law* (Oxford: Oxford University Press, 1995).

—— *A History of the Land Law* (2nd edn., Oxford: Oxford University Press, 1986; repr. 1996).

Singer, 'The Reliance Interest in Property', 40 Stan. L. Rev. 611 (1988).

—— 'Property and Social Relations: From Title to Entitlement', in van Maanen and van der Walt (eds.), *Property Law on the Threshold of the 21st Century* (Antwerp: Maklu Press, 1996).

—— 'No Right to Exclude: Public Accommodations and Private Property', 90 Nw. U. L. Rev. 1283 (1996).

—— *Property Law: Rules, Policies, and Practices*, 2nd edn. (New York: Aspen Publishing, 1997).

—— and Beerman, 'The Social Origins of Property', 6 Canadian J. of Law and Jurisprudence 217 (1993).

Smith, *The Politics of 'Race' and Residence* (Cambridge: Polity Press, 1989).

Smith, *Rule by Records: Land Registration and Village Custom in Early British Panjab* (Delhi: Oxford University Press, 1996).

Smith, *Property Law* (London: Longman, 1996).

Social Trends (London: HMSO, 1997).

Sorauf, 'The Conceptual Muddle', in Friedrich (ed.), *The Public Interest* (New York: Atherton Press, 1962).

South (ed.), *Leaseholds, The Case for Reform, Collected Papers,* (London: Leasehold Enfranchisement Association, 1993).

South African Government, Department of Housing, White Paper on a New Housing Policy and Strategy for South Africa, in *Government Gazette*, No. 16178, 23 Dec. 1994.

—— Department of Land Affairs, Green Paper on South African Land Policy, Pretoria (Feb. 1996).

—— Department of Land Affairs, Executive Summary of the Extension of Security of Tenure Bill, Pretoria, 29 Jan. 1997.

—— White Paper on Land Reform, B-91, Cape Town (1991).

—— White Paper on Reconstruction and Development, Cape Town, 15 Nov. 1994, in *Government Gazette*, No. 16085, 23 Nov. 1994.

Spring, *The English Landed Estate* (Baltimore: Johns Hopkins University Press, 1963).

Stanley, 'Government Policies on Home Ownership in the 1980s', in *Home Ownership in the 1980s* (London: Shelter Housing Aid Centre, 1980).

Staves, *Married Women's Separate Property* (Cambridge, Mass.: Harvard University Press, 1990).

Stephenson (ed.), *Mabo: A Judicial Revolution* (Brisbane: University of Queensland Press, 1993).

Stewart, *Rethinking Housing Law* (London: Sweet & Maxwell, 1996).

Sturley, 'Easements in Gross' (1980) 96 LQR 557.

Sugden, *A Series of Letters to a Man of Property* (London, 1809).

Supperstone and O'Dempsey, *Immigration: The Law and Practice* (London: Longman, 1994).

Sutherland, *The Assize of Novel Disseisin* (Oxford: Oxford University Press, 1973).

Sydenham, *Trusts of Land: The New Law* (Bristol: Family Law, 1996).

—— and Mainwaring, *Farm Business Tenancies: Agricultural Tenancies Act 1995* (Bristol: Jordans, 1995).

Tabbish, *Resident Owned Flats: A Guide to Company Purchase and Management Control* (London: Sweet & Maxwell, 1994).

Temple Lang, 'Defining Legitimate Competition: Companies' Duties to Supply Competitors and Access to Essential Facilities' (1994) 18 Fordham International Law Journal 437.

Thatcher, *Let Our Children Grow Tall* (London: Centre for Policy Studies, 1977).

Thiesenhusen, 'Introduction: Searching for Agrarian Reform in Latin America', in Thiesenhusen (ed.), *Searching for Agrarian Reform in Latin America,* (Boston: Unwin Hyman, 1989).

—— (ed.), *Searching for Agrarian Reform in Latin America* (Boston: Unwin Hyman, 1989).

Thomas, *Institutes of Justinian: Text and Commentary* (Amsterdam: North-Holland, 1975).

—— *Textbook of Roman Law* (Amsterdam: North-Holland, 1976).

Thomas, *Buying Property in France* (London: Law Society Gazette, 1991).

Thome, 'The Process of Land Reform in Latin America', Wisconsin Law Review 9 (1968).

—— 'Agrarian Reform Legislation: Chile', in Dorner (ed.), *Land Reform in Latin America* (Madison, Wis.: Land Tenure Center, University of Wisconsin, 1971).

Thompson, *English Landed Society in the Nineteenth Century* (London: Routledge & Kegan Paul, 1963).

Thompson, 'The Role of Evidence in Part Performance' [1979] Conveyancer 402.

Thornton, 'Homelessness through Relationship Breakdown' (1988) 10 Journal of Social Welfare Law 67.

—— *The New Homeless* (London: SHAC, 1990).

Tolson, ' "Land" without Earth: Freehold Flats in English Law' (1950) 14 Conveyancer (NS) 350.

Tomas and Dittmar, 'The Experiences of Homeless Women: An Exploration of Housing Histories and the Meaning of Home' (1995) 10 Housing Studies 493.

Tomkins, 'Public Order Law and Visions of Englishness', in Bentley and Flynn (eds.), *Law and the Senses—Sensational Jurisprudence* (London: Pluto Press, 1996).

Topham, *The Law of Property Acts 1925: A Series of Lectures* (1926).

Torrance, 'Social Class and Bureaucratic Innovation 1780–1787' (1978) 78 Past and Present 56.

Treitel, 'Jane Austen and the Law' (1984) 100 LQR 549.

—— *The Law of Contract*, (9th edn., London: Sweet & Maxwell, 1995).

Trotman, *The Development of Milk Quotas in the UK* (London: Sweet & Maxwell, 1996).

Turner, 'Contemporary Problems in the Theory of Citizenship', in Turner (ed.), *Citizenship and Social Theory* (London: Sage, 1993).

Tyler, *Fisher and Lightwood's Law of Mortgage* (London: Butterworths, 1988).

Underhill and Hayton, *Law of Trusts and Trustees* (15th edn., London: Butterworths, 1995).

Underkuffler-Freund, 'Takings and the Nature of Property', 9 Can. J. L. and Juris. 161 (1996).

Usher, *Legal Aspects of Agriculture in the European Community* (Oxford: Oxford University Press, 1988).

van der Walt, 'Land Reform in South Africa Since 1990—an Overview' (1995) 10 SA Public Law 1.

Van Steenbergen, 'The Condition of Citizenship: An Introduction', in Van Steenbergen (ed.), *The Condition of Citizenship* (London: Sage, 1994).

Vattel, *Droit des gens ou principles de la loi naturelle appliqués aux affairs des nations et des souvrains*, ed. Chitty (1758; Philadelphia, T. & J. W. Johnson & Co., 1863).

Vincent-Jones and Harries, 'Tenant Participation in Contracting for Housing Management Services: A Case Study', in Cowan (ed.), *Housing: Participation and Exclusion* (Aldershot: Dartmouth, forthcoming).

Wade, 'Landlord, Tenant and Squatter' (1962) 78 LQR 541.

—— 'Covenants, a Broad and Reasonable View' [1972B] CLJ 157.

—— and Forsyth, *Administrative Law* (Oxford: Clarendon Press, 1994).

Wakefield, *A Letter from Sydney and Other Writings* (London: Dent, 1929).

Walter, 'The Landlord and Tenant (Covenants) Act 1995: A Legislative Folly' [1996] Conveyancer 432.

Walzer, *Spheres of Justice: A Defense of Pluralism and Equality* (New York: Basic Books, 1983).

Watchman and Robson, 'The Homeless Persons Obstacle Race' (1980) Journal of Social Welfare Law 1(pt. I), 65 (pt. II).

Watson, 'Acquisition of Possession and *uscapion per servos et filios*' (1967) 78 LQR 205.

Watson with Austerberry, *Housing and Homelessness: A Feminist Perspective* (London: Routledge, 1986).

Weir, 'Taking for Granted: The Ramifications of *Nemo Dat*' (Oxford: Oxford University Press, 1996).

Welsh Office, *A Working Countryside for Wales*, Cm. 3180 (London: HMSO, 1996).

Wendell Holmes, 'The Path of the Law', 10 Harv. L. Rev. 457 (1896–7).

West, 'Jurisprudence and Gender', 55 U. of Chicago L. Rev. 1 (1988).

Whitby (ed.), *The European Environment and CAP Reform: Policies and Prospects for Conservation* (Wallingford: Oxon.: CAB International, 1996).

White Paper on Reconstruction and Development, Cape Town (15 Nov. 1994), in *Government Gazette*, No. 16085 (23 Nov. 1994).

White Paper on Land Reform, B-91, Cape Town (1991).

Whitman, *The Legacy of Roman Law in the German Romantic Era: Historical Vision and Legal Change* (Princeton: Princeton University Press, 1990).

Wigley, 'Untitled: The Housing of Gender', in Colomina (ed.), *Sexuality and Space* (Princeton: Princeton, Architectural Press, 1992).

Wilcox, *Housing Finance Review 1993* (York: Joseph Rowntree Foundation, 1993).

Williams, *Principles of the Law of Real Property* (5th edn., London: Sweet, 1859).

Williams on Real Property (23rd edn., London: Sweet & Maxwell, 1920).

Williams, *Vendor and Purchaser* (3rd edn., London: Stevens, 1922).

Williams, 'Spirit-Murdering the Messenger: The Discourse of Fingerpointing as the Law's Response to Racism', 42 U. Miami L. Rev. 127 (1987–8).

—— 'On Being the Object of Property', 14 Signs: Journal of Women in Culture and Society 5 (1988).

Williams, *The American Indian in Western Legal Thought: The Discourses of Conquest* (New York: Oxford University Press, 1990).

Williams, *The Country and the City* (London: Hogarth Press, 1993).

Williams, 'Is Coverture Dead? Beyond a New Theory of Alimony', 82 Georgetown LJ 2227 (1994).

Williams (ed.), *Directions in Housing Policy* (London: Paul Chapman, 1997).

Wilson, *Outlines of a Plan for Adopting the Machinery of the Public Funds to the Transfer of Real Property* (1844).

Winokur, 'Choice, Consent, and Citizenship in Private Interest Communities', in Barton and Silverman (eds.), *Common Interest Communities: Private Governments and the Public Interest* (Berkeley and Los Angeles: University of California Institute of Government Press, 1994).

Winter, Richardson, Short, and Watkins, *Agricultural Land Tenure in England and Wales* (London: Royal Institution of Chartered Surveyors, 1990).

Wolstenholme, 'Simplification of Title to Land: An Outline of a Plan' (1862) 2 Papers Read Before the Juridical Society.

Woodfall, *Landlord and Tenant* (loose-leaf edn., London: Sweet & Maxwell/ Stevens, 1994).

Woodman and Butt, 'Possessory Title and the Torrens System in New South Wales' (1980) 54 ALJ 79.

Woods, 'Women and Housing', in Hallett (ed.), *Women and Social Policy* (Brighton: Harvester Wheatsheaf, 1996).

Woodward, 'Mobilising Opposition: The Campaign against Housing Action Trusts in Tower Hamlets' (1991) 6 Housing Studies 44.

Yakubu, *Land Law in Nigeria* (London: Macmillan, 1985).

Youdan, 'Formalities for Trusts of Land and the Doctrine in *Rochefoucauld* v. *Boustead*' (1984) 43 CLJ 306.

Zellick (ed.), *The Law Commission and Law Reform* (London: Sweet & Maxwell, 1988).
Ziff, *Principles of Property Law* (2nd edn., Scarborough, Ontario: Carswell, Thomson Professional Publishing, 1996).
Zweigert and Kötz, *Introduction to Comparative Law*, trans. Weir (2nd edn., Oxford: Oxford University Press, 1987).

LAW COMMISSION PUBLICATIONS

Working Papers and Consultation Papers (London: HMSO).

Provisional Proposals Relating to Obligations of Landlords and Tenants, Law Com. WP No. 8 (1967).
Provisional Proposals Relating to Termination of Tenancies, Law Com. WP No. 17 (1968).
The Law of Landlord and Tenant: Working Party's Provisional Proposals Relating to Covenants Restricting Dispositions, Parting with Possession, Change of User and Alterations, Law Com. WP No. 25 (1970).
Trusts of Land, Law Com. WP No. 94 (1985).
Commonhold: Freehold Flats and Freehold Ownership of Other Interdependent Buildings, Report of a Working Group, the Aldridge Report, Cm. 179 (1987).
The Law of Trusts: The Rules against Perpetuities and Excessive Accumulations, Law Com. CP No. 133 (1993).
The Execution of Deeds and Documents by or on behalf of Bodies Corporate, Law Com. CP No. 143 (1996).

Reports (London: HMSO).

First Programme of Law Reform, Law Com. No. 1 (1965).
First Annual Report 1965–1966, Law Com. No. 4 (1966).
Transfer of Land: Interim Report on Root of Title, Law Com. No. 9 (1967).
Landlord and Tenant: Report on the Landlord and Tenant Act 1954, Part II, Law Com. No. 17 (1969).
Transfer of Land: Report on Land Charges Affecting Unregistered Land, Law Com. No. 18 (1969).
Fifth Annual Report 1969–1970, Law Com. No. 36 (1970).
Transfer of Land: Report on Local Land Charges, Law Com. No. 62 (1974).
Ninth Annual Report 1973–1974, Law Com. No. 64 (1974).
Codification of the Law of Landlord and Tenant: Report on Obligations of Landlords and Tenants, Law Com. No. 67 (1975).
Transfer of Land: Report on Rentcharges, Law Com. No. 68 (1975).
Twelfth Annual Report 1976–1977, Law Com. No. 85 (1977).
Third Report on Family Property: The Matrimonial Home (Co-Ownership and Occupation Rights) and Household Goods, Law Com. No. 86 (1978).

Thirteenth Annual Report 1977–1978, Law Com. No. 92 (1978).

Property Law: The Implications of Williams & Glyn's Bank v. *Boland*, Law Com. No. 115 (1982).

Property Law: Land Registration, Law Com. No. 125 (1983).

Transfer of Land: The Law of Positive and Restrictive Covenants, Law Com. No. 127 (1984).

Nineteenth Annual Report 1983–1984, Law Com. No. 140 (1985).

Codification of the Law of Landlord and Tenant: Covenants Restricting Dispositions, Alterations and Change of User, Law Com. No. 141 (1985).

Codification of the Law of Landlord and Tenant: Forfeiture of Tenancies, Law Com. No. 142 (1985).

Property Law: Second Report on Land Registration, Law Com. No. 148 (1985).

Rights of Access to Neighbouring Land, Law Com. No. 151 (1985).

Property Law: Third Report on Land Registration, Law Com. No. 158 (1987).

Twenty-First Annual Report 1985–1986, Law Com. No. 159 (1987).[1]

Leasehold Conveyancing, Law Com. No. 161 (1987).

Landlord and Tenant: Reform of the Law, Law Com. No. 162 (1987).

Deeds and Escrows, Law Com. No. 163 (1987).

Transfer of Land: Formalities for Contracts for Sale etc. of Land, Law Com. No. 164 (1987).

Transfer of Land: The Rule in Bain v. *Fothergill*, Law Com. No. 166 (1987).

Review of Child Law: Guardianship and Custody, Law Com. No. 172 (1988).

Property Law: Fourth Report on Land Registration, Law Com. No. 173 (1988).

Landlord and Tenant Law: Privity of Contract and Estate, Law Com. No. 174 (1988).

Family Law: Matrimonial Property, Law Com. No. 175 (1988).

Landlord and Tenant: Compensation for Tenants' Improvements, Law Com. No. 178 (1989).

Transfer of Land: Trusts of Land, Law Com. No. 181 (1989).

Property Law: Title on Death, Law Com. No. 184 (1989).

Transfer of Land: Overreaching: Beneficiaries in Occupation, Law Com. No. 188 (1989).

Twenty-Fourth Annual Report 1989, Law Com. No. 190 (1990).

Landlord and Tenant: Distress for Rent, Law Com. No. 194 (1991).

Twenty-Fifth Annual Report, 1990, Law Com. No. 195 (1991).

Transfer of Land: Implied Covenants for Title, Law Com. No. 199 (1991).

Transfer of Land: Obsolete Restrictive Covenants, Law Com. No. 201 (1991).

Transfer of Land: Land Mortgages, Law Com. No. 204 (1991).

Domestic Violence and Occupation of the Family Home, Law Com. No. 207 (1992).

Landlord and Tenant: Business Tenancies—A Periodic Review of the Landlord and Tenant Act 1954 Part II, Law Com. No. 208 (1992).

Twenty-Seventh Annual Report 1992, Law Com. No. 210 (1993).

Landlord and Tenant Law: Termination of Tenancies Bill, Law Com. No. 221 (1994).

Twenty-Eighth Annual Report 1993, Law Com. No. 223 (1994).

Twenty-Ninth Annual Report 1994, Law Com. No. 232 (1995).

Sixth Programme of Law Reform, Law Com. No. 234 (1995).

[1] The Law Commission's Twenty-First to Twenty-Fourth Annual Reports also contain the four Reports of the Conveyancing Standing Committee.

Transfer of Land: Land Registration. First Report of A Joint Working Group on the Implementation of the Law Commission's Third and Fourth Reports on Land Registration, Law Com. No. 235 (1995).

Landlord and Tenant: Responsibility for State and Condition of Property, Law Com. No. 238 (1996).

Thirtieth Annual Report 1995, Law Com. No. 239 (1996).

INDEX